W9-DGB-542

BCOM¹¹

Business Communication

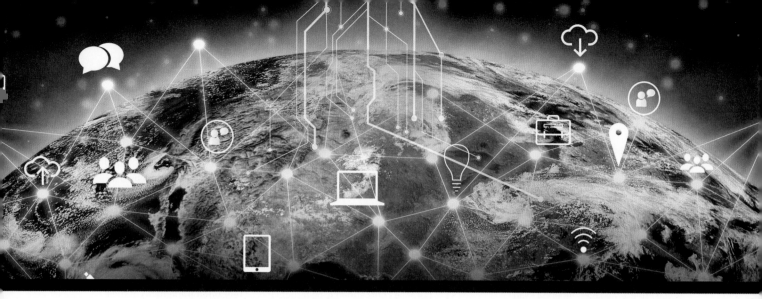

BCOM¹¹

Business Communication

Carol M. Lehman
Mississippi State University

Debbie D. DuFrene
Stephen F. Austin State University

Robyn Walker
University of Southern California

 Cengage

Australia • Brazil • Canada • Mexico • Singapore • United Kingdom • United States

BCOM, 11e
Lehman/DuFrene/Walker

SVP, Product: Erin Joyner

VP, Product: Thais Alencar

Portfolio Product Director: Joe Sabatino

Portfolio Product Manager: Heather Thompson

Product Assistant: Emily Klingberg

Learning Designer: Danae Kesel

Senior Content Manager: Allie Janneck

Digital Project Manager: Amanda Ryan

VP, Product Marketing: Jason Sakos

Director, Product Marketing: Danaë April

Product Marketing Manager: Tony Winslow

Content Acquisition Analyst: Erin McCullough

Production Service: Straive

Designer: Sara Greenwood

Cover Image Source: Apichet Chakreeyarut / Alamy Stock Photo

Last three editions, as applicable: © 2020, © 2018, © 2017

© 2024 Cengage Learning, Inc. ALL RIGHTS RESERVED.

No part of this work covered by the copyright herein may be reproduced or distributed in any form or by any means, except as permitted by U.S. copyright law, without the prior written permission of the copyright owner.

Unless otherwise noted, all content is Copyright © Cengage Learning, Inc.

Microsoft is a registered trademark of Microsoft Corporation in the U.S. and/or other countries.

The names of all products mentioned herein are used for identification purposes only and may be trademarks or registered trademarks of their respective owners. Cengage Learning disclaims any affiliation, association, connection with, sponsorship, or endorsement by such owners.

For product information and technology assistance, contact us at **Cengage Customer & Sales Support, 1-800-354-9706 or support.cengage.com.**

For permission to use material from this text or product, submit all requests online at **www.copyright.com.**

Library of Congress Control Number: 2022917094

ISBN: 978-0-357-90124-3

Cengage
200 Pier 4 Boulevard
Boston, MA 02210
USA

Cengage is a leading provider of customized learning solutions. Our employees reside in nearly 40 different countries and serve digital learners in 165 countries around the world. Find your local representative at **www.cengage.com.**

To learn more about Cengage platforms and services, register or access your online learning solution, or purchase materials for your course, visit **www.cengage.com.**

Printed in the United States of America
Print Number: 01   Print Year: 2023

Brief Contents

Contents

Part 3
Communication Through Voice, Electronic, and Written Messages 80

Part 4

Communication Through Reports and Business Presentations 150

9 Understanding the Report Process and Research Methods 150

10 Managing Data and Using Graphics 168

11 Organizing and Preparing Reports and Proposals 180

12 Designing and Delivering Business Presentations 198

Part 5
Communication for Employment 221

Melamory/Shutterstock

1 | Establishing a Framework for Business Communication

Learning Objectives

After studying this chapter, you will be able to ...

 1-1 Define communication and describe the value of communication in business.

1-2 Explain the communication process model and the ultimate objective of the communication process.

1-3 Discuss how information flows in an organization.

1-4 Explain how legal and ethical constraints, diversity challenges, changing technology, and team environment act as contextual forces that influence the process of business communication.

1-1 Value of Communication

We communicate to satisfy needs in both our work and private lives. Each of us wants to be heard, appreciated, and wanted. We also want to accomplish tasks and achieve goals. Generally, people communicate for three basic purposes: to inform, to persuade, and to entertain. However, in the professional workplace, some of these purposes have greater importance. Informing and persuading are common purposes of communication in the workplace; entertainment is less so. In addition, establishing and maintaining our credibility and positive relationships with others are also important purposes in an organizational setting.

What is communication? Communication is the process of exchanging and interpreting information and meaning between or among individuals through a system of symbols, signs, and behavior. In ideal situations, the goal is to reach mutual understanding. Studies indicate that managers typically spend 60 percent to 80 percent of their time involved in communication. In your career activities, you will communicate in a wide variety of ways, including:

- listening and contributing to decision making and problem solving while attending meetings;

- writing various types of messages to inform and persuade others about your ideas and the services and products your organization provides;

- presenting information and persuasive messages to large and small groups in face-to-face and virtual environments;

- explaining and clarifying management procedures and work assignments;

- coordinating the work of various employees, departments, and other work groups;

- evaluating and counseling employees and;

- promoting the company's products, services, and image using a variety of channels in various contexts.

1-2 The Communication Process

Effective business communication is essential to success in today's work environments. Recent surveys of executives demonstrate that abilities in writing and speaking are major determinants of career success in many fields.[1] Although essential to personal and professional success, effective business communication does not occur automatically. Your own experiences likely have taught you that a message is not interpreted correctly just because you transmitted it.

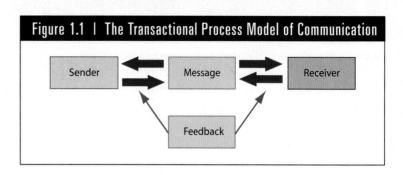

Figure 1.1 | The Transactional Process Model of Communication

Sender → Message → Receiver

Feedback

An effective communicator anticipates possible breakdowns in the communication process—the unlimited ways the message can be misunderstood. This mindset provides the concentration to plan and design the initial message effectively and to be prepared to intervene at the appropriate time to ensure that the message received is on target.

Consider the transactional process model of communication presented in Figure 1.1. These seemingly simple steps represent a very complex process.

Several communication process models exist. The transactional model is useful, though, because it illustrates the complexity of the communication process and reveals some of the challenges to effective communication that might emerge in a communication encounter.

According to the transactional process model, two parties involved in a communication encounter are potentially both communicating at the same time, particularly if the encounter is face-to-face. That's because in face-to-face communication situations, parties to the encounter are continuously interpreting each other's nonverbal signals. Some scholars say more than 90 percent of the information in a face-to-face encounter may be sent nonverbally. But even in a cellphone conversation, silences and tone of voice may be interpreted in various ways. Even a written message may provide information about the writer that they did not intend to convey.

Interruptions or distractions can create barriers to understanding.

In an ideal communication situation, one party would be able to encode their message in such a way that the receiving party would understand it exactly as intended. However, this goal can be challenging for a variety of reasons, or what are called **interferences** or *barriers* to effective communication. For example, differences in educational level, experience, culture, and other characteristics of the sender and the receiver increase the complexity of encoding and decoding a message; physical interferences in the channel, including noisy environments, interruptions, and uncomfortable surroundings, can occur; also, mental distractions, such as being preoccupied with other matters and developing a response rather than listening, create barriers to understanding.

Because of these barriers, and because both parties engaged in a communication encounter may be simultaneously sending information both orally and nonverbally, it can be very challenging to ensure that the information is received as intended. For this reason, it is particularly important to check for understanding rather than assume that it has taken place, particularly when communicating important messages to audiences that are less familiar to us.

You can surely compile a list of other barriers that affect your ability to communicate with friends, instructors, coworkers, supervisors, and others. By being aware of them, you can concentrate on removing these interferences.

1-3 Communicating Within Organizations

To be successful, organizations must create an environment that energizes and encourages employees to accomplish tasks by promoting genuine openness and effective communication.

Organizational communication is communication that occurs with an organizational context. Regardless of your career or level within an organization, your ability to communicate will affect not only the success of the organization but also your personal success and advancement within that organization.

interferences also called barriers; numerous factors that hinder the communication process

organizational communication the movement of information within the company structure

formal communication network a network of communication flow typified by the formal organizational chart; dictated by the technical, political, and economic environment of the organization

informal communication network a network of communication flow that continuously develops as people interact within the formal system to accommodate their social and psychological needs

1-3a Communication Flow in Organizations

Communication occurs in a variety of ways within an organization. Some communication flows are planned and structured, others are not. Some communication flows can be formally depicted, whereas some defy description.

Formal and Informal Communication Networks

Communication within an organization involves both formal and informal networks.

- **Formal communication network.** This channel is typified by the formal organizational chart, which is created by management to define individual and group relationships and to specify lines of responsibility. Essentially, the formal system is dictated by the managerial, technical, cultural, and structural environment of the organization. Within this system, people are required to behave and to communicate in certain ways simply to get work done.

- **Informal communication network.** This network, which is commonly called "the grapevine," continuously develops as people interact within the formal system to accommodate their social and psychological needs. Because the informal network undergoes continual changes and does not parallel the organizational chart, it cannot be depicted accurately by any graphic means.

The Formal Communication Network When employees rely almost entirely on the formal communication system as a guide to behavior, the system might be identified as a *bureaucracy*. Procedure manuals, job descriptions, organizational charts, and other written materials dictate the required behavior. Communication channels are followed strictly, and red tape is abundant. Procedures are generally followed exactly; terms such as *rules* and

The office grapevine carries informal messages.

iStock.com/MangoStar_Studio

policies serve as sufficient reasons for actions. Even the most formal organizations, however, cannot function long before an informal communication system emerges. As people operate within the organized system, they interact on a person-to-person basis and create an environment conducive to meeting their personal emotions, prejudices, likes, and dislikes.

In a workplace, employees are generally expected to satisfy a formal system of arriving at work on time, fulfilling their job duties, working well with others, and addressing their supervisor's requests. However, some employees may not openly accept these expectations and may arrive at work late and spend an undue amount of time visiting with colleagues. If these informal practices become more widely spread, the purposes of the group may move from a focus on completing tasks to that of socializing with others or speculating about organizational events or activities. Obviously, the informal system benefits people because it meets their needs, but it also may affect the overall communication of the group in important ways.

The Informal Communication Network As people talk casually during breaks, text one another, or chat online, the focus usually shifts from topic to topic. One of the usual topics is work—the company, supervisor, or fellow employees. Even though the formal system includes definite communication channels, the grapevine tends to develop and operate within all organizations. Consider these points related to the accuracy and value of grapevine communication:

- As a communication network, the grapevine has a reputation for being speedy but inaccurate. In the absence of alarms, the grapevine might be the most effective way to let occupants know that the building is on fire. It certainly beats sending an email.

- Although the grapevine often is thought of as a channel for inaccurate communication, it is no more or less accurate than other channels. Even formal communication can become inaccurate and filtered as it passes from level to level in the organizational hierarchy.

- The inaccuracy of the grapevine has more to do with the message input than with the output. For example, the grapevine is noted as a carrier of rumors, primarily because it carries informal messages. If the input is a rumor, and nothing more, the output obviously will be inaccurate. But the output might be an accurate description of the original rumor.

- In a business office, news about promotions, personnel changes, company policy changes, and annual salary adjustments often is communicated through the grapevine long before being conveyed through formal channels. The process works similarly in colleges, where information about instructors typically is not officially published but is known by students, often through word-of-mouth. How best to prepare for examinations, instructor attitudes on attendance and homework, and even faculty personnel changes are messages that travel over the grapevine.

- A misconception about the grapevine is that the message passes from person to person until it finally reaches a person who can't pass it on—the end of the line. Actually, the grapevine works as a network channel. Typically, one person tells two or three others, who each tell two or three others, who each tell two or three others, and so on. Thus, the message might spread to a huge number of people in a short time, especially now that the grapevine includes digital forms of communication, such as social networking sites.

- The grapevine has no single, consistent source. Messages might originate anywhere and follow various routes.

Due at least in part to widespread downsizing and corporate scandals during the last few years, employees in many organizations are demanding that they be better informed. Some companies have implemented new formal ways, such as newsletters and intranets, as well as informal ways, including blogs, wikis, Twitter, and other social networking platforms, for sharing information with their internal constituents. Company openness with employees about management decisions, process changes, and financial issues means conveying more information through the formal system rather than risking its miscommunication through informal channels. Online eyewear retailer Warby Parker, for example, grew from a small start-up to a 300-employee company in just three years. To keep the lines of communication open, the company has an "Ask Anything" segment of its weekly meetings, in which employees can ask anything. The Warby Parker Wiki enables employees to add notes from meetings, key lessons from the past or present, or team updates. The transparent company culture extends to each of its employees submitting weekly "happiness ratings" (on a 0 to 10 scale) and participating in quarterly, one-on-one, "360 reviews" in which brutal honesty is encouraged.[2]

An informal communication network will emerge from even the most carefully designed formal system. Managers who ignore this fact are attempting to manage blindfolded. Instead of denying or condemning the grapevine, the effective manager will learn to use the informal communication network. The grapevine, for example, can be useful in counteracting rumors and false information.

Directions of Communication Flow

The direction in which communication flows in an organization can be downward, upward, or horizontal, as shown in Figure 1.2. Because these three terms are used frequently in communication discussions, they deserve clarification. Although the concept of flow seems simple, direction has meaning for those participating in the organizational communication process.

Downward Communication The communication that flows from supervisor to employee, from policy makers to operating personnel, or from top to bottom on the organizational chart is called **downward communication**. A simple policy statement from the top of the organization might grow into a formal plan for operation at lower levels. Teaching people how to perform their specific tasks is an element of downward communication.

> **downward communication** a type of communication that flows from supervisor to employee, from policy makers to operating personnel, or from top to bottom on the organizational chart

Another element is orientation to a company's rules, practices, procedures, history, and goals. Employees learn about the quality of their job performance through downward communication.

Downward communication normally involves both written and spoken methods and makes use of the following assumptions:

Downward Communication

- People at high levels in the organization usually have greater knowledge of the organization's mission and goals than people at lower levels.
- Both spoken and written messages tend to become larger as they move downward through organizational levels. This expansion results from attempts to prevent distortion and is more noticeable in written messages.
- Spoken messages are subject to greater changes in meaning than written messages.

Figure 1.2 | Flow of Information Within an Organization

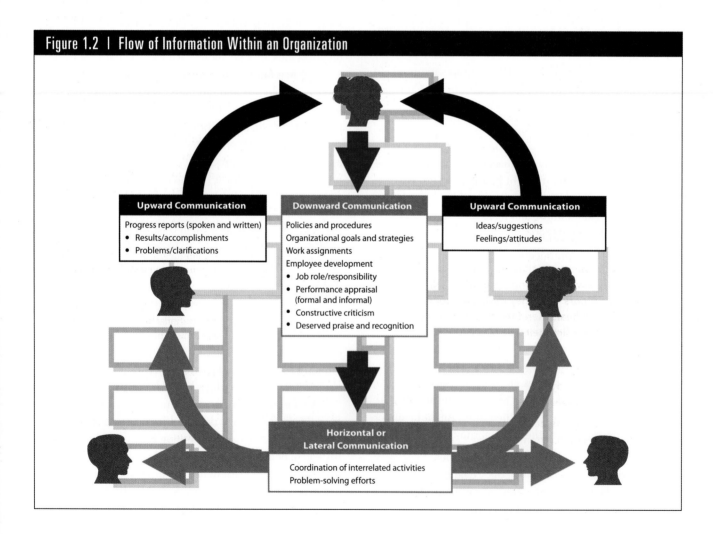

When a supervisor sends a message to a direct report employee who then asks a question or nods in agreement, the employee has given signs of feedback. Feedback can flow both downward and upward in organizational communication through traditional as well as informal channels.

Upward Communication The information that flows from the front lines of an organization to the top is **upward communication**. When management requests information from lower organizational levels, the resulting information becomes feedback to that request. Employees talk to supervisors about themselves, their fellow employees, their work and methods of doing it, customer needs and perceptions, and their own perceptions of the organization. These comments are commonly feedback in response to the downward flow transmitted in both spoken and written forms by group meetings, emails, procedures or operations manuals, company news releases, the company intranet, and the grapevine.

Although necessary and valuable, upward communication involves risks. The box on Upward Communication lists several important features to consider.

When effectively used, upward communication keeps management informed about the feelings of lower-level employees, taps the expertise of employees, helps management identify both difficult and potentially promotable employees, and paves the way for even more effective downward communication. Upward communication is key to keeping employees engaged and informed and is especially critical in tapping the power of younger employees who expect to collaborate rather than to be supervised.[3]

Upward Communication

▸ Upward communication is primarily feedback to the requests and actions of supervisors.

▸ Upward communication can be misleading because lower-level employees often tell their superiors what they think their superiors want to hear. Therefore, their messages might contradict their true observations and perceptions.

▸ Upward communication frequently involves risk to an employee and is dependent on their trust in the supervisor.

▸ Employees will reject superficial attempts by management to obtain feedback.

Horizontal Communication Interactions between organizational units on the same hierarchical level are called **horizontal or lateral communication**. These interactions reveal one of the major shortcomings of organizational charts—they do not recognize the role of horizontal communication when they depict authority relationships by placing one box higher than another and define role functions by placing titles in those boxes. Yet management should realize that horizontal communication is the primary means of achieving coordination in a functional organizational structure. Units coordinate their activities to accomplish task goals just as adjacent workers in a production line coordinate their activities. So, for horizontal communication to be maximally effective, the people in any system or organization should be available to one another.

Many companies realize that the traditional hierarchy organized around functional units is inadequate for competing in increasingly competitive global markets. They value work teams that integrate work-flow processes rather than specialists in a single function or product. Such work teams can break down communication barriers between isolated functional departments, and communication patterns take on varying forms to accommodate team activities.

1-3b Levels of Communication

Communication can involve sending messages to both large and small audiences. **Internal messages** are intended for recipients within the organization. **External messages** are directed to recipients outside the organization. When considering the intended audience, communication can be described as taking place on five levels: intrapersonal, interpersonal, group, organizational, and public. Exhibit 1.1 depicts the five audience levels. An effective communicator has a clearly defined purpose for each message and has selected strategies for targeting their intended audience.

> **upward communication** a type of communication that is generally a response to requests from supervisors
>
> **horizontal (or lateral) communication** interactions between organizational units on the same hierarchical level
>
> **internal messages** messages intended for recipients within the organization
>
> **external messages** messages directed to recipients outside the organization

Exhibit 1.1 | Levels of Communication

Communication Levels	Examples
Intrapersonal • Communication within oneself • Not considered by some to be true communication as it does not involve a separate sender and receiver	*Individual considers how others respond to their verbal and/or nonverbal communication*
Interpersonal • Communication between two people • Task goal is to accomplish work confronting them • Maintenance goal is to feel better about themselves and each other because of their interaction	*Supervisor and direct report two coworkers*
Group • Communication among more than two people • Goal of achieving greater output than individual efforts could produce	*Work group, project team, department meeting*
Organizational • Groups combined in such a way that large tasks may be accomplished • Goal of providing adequate structure for groups to achieve their purposes	*Company, organization*
Public • The organization reaching out to its public to achieve its goals • Goal of reaching many with the same message	*Media advertisement, website communication, annual report*

1-4 Contextual Forces Influencing Business Communication

All communication occurs within a **context**, which is the situation or setting. Context can influence the content, quality, and effectiveness of a communication event. The effective communicator will recognize the importance of context, identify the contextual elements that will influence communication, and adjust their messages in response. Four important contextual forces influence the communication process today and help determine and define the nature of the communication that should occur, as shown in Exhibit 1.2. These forces are legal and ethical constraints, diversity challenges, changing technology, and team environment.

context a situation or setting in which communication occurs

1-4a Legal and Ethical Constraints

Legal and ethical constraints act as contextual or environmental forces on communication because they set boundaries in which communication rightfully occurs. International, federal, state, and local laws affect the way that various business activities are conducted. For example, laws specify that certain information must be stated in messages that reply to credit applications and those dealing with the collection of outstanding debts. Furthermore, one's own ethical standards will often influence what a person is willing to say in

Exhibit 1.2 | Factors Influencing Business Communication

Legal and Ethical Constraints	Changing Technology	Diversity Challenges	Team Environment
• International Laws • Domestic Laws • Codes of Ethics • Stakeholder Interests • Ethical Frameworks • Personal Values	• Accuracy and Security Issues • Telecommunications • Software Applications • "High-Touch" Issues • Telecommuting • Databases	• Cultural Differences • Language Barriers • Gender • Education Levels • Age Factors • Nonverbal Differences	• Trust • Team Roles • Shared Goals and Expectations • Synergy • Group Reward • Distributed Leadership

a message. For example, a system of ethics built on honesty might require that the message provide full disclosure rather than a shrouding of the truth. Legal responsibilities, then, are the starting point for appropriate business communication. One's ethical belief system, or personal sense of right and wrong behavior, provides further boundaries for professional activity.

The press is full of examples of unethical conduct in business and political communities, but unethical behavior is not relegated to the papers—it has far-reaching consequences. Those affected by decisions, the **stakeholders**, can include people inside and outside the organization. Employees and stockholders are obvious losers when a company fails. Competitors in the same industry also suffer because their strategies are based on what they perceive about their competition. Beyond this, financial markets suffer due to the erosion of public confidence.

Business leaders, government officials, and citizens frequently express concern about the apparent erosion of ethical values in society. Even for those who want to do the right thing, matters of ethics are seldom clear-cut decisions of right versus wrong, and they often contain ambiguous elements. In addition, the pressure appears to be felt most strongly by lower-level managers, who are often recent business school graduates who are the least experienced at doing their jobs.

The Foundation for Legal and Ethical Behavior

Although ethics is a common point of discussion, many find defining ethics challenging. Most people immediately associate ethics with standards and rules of conduct, morals, right and wrong, values, and honesty. Dr. Albert Schweitzer defined *ethics* as "the name we give to our concern for good behavior. We feel an obligation to consider not only our own personal well-being but also that of others and human society as a whole."[4] In other words, **ethics** refers to the principles of right and wrong that guide you in making decisions that consider the impact of your actions on others as well as yourself.

Although the recorded accounts of legal and ethical misconduct would seem to indicate that businesses are dishonest and unscrupulous, keep in mind that millions of business transactions are made daily based on honesty and concern for others. Why should a business make ethical decisions? What difference will it make? Johan Karlström, former global chief executive officer of construction giant Skanska, gave a powerful reply to these questions:

> When you understand that profits and a strong values base go together, then you have a company that employees are so proud of. We want our team to feel that they're doing something that has a higher

meaning, that they feel like "I'm part of something bigger, part of a bigger puzzle driving society in a positive direction."[5]

Causes of Illegal and Unethical Behavior

Understanding the major causes of illegal and unethical behavior in the workplace will help you become sensitive to signals of escalating pressure to compromise your values. Unethical corporate behavior can have several causes:

- **Excessive emphasis on profits.** Business managers are often judged and paid on their ability to increase business profits. This emphasis on profits might send a message that the end justifies the means.

- **Misplaced corporate loyalty.** A misplaced sense of corporate loyalty might cause an employee to do what seems to be in the best interest of the company, even if the act is illegal or unethical.

- **Obsession with personal advancement.** Employees who wish to outperform their peers or are working for the next promotion might feel that they cannot afford to fail. They might do whatever it takes to achieve the objectives assigned to them.

- **Expectation of not getting caught.** Thinking that the end justifies the means, employees often believe illegal or unethical activity will never be discovered. Unfortunately, a great deal of improper behavior escapes detection in the business world. Believing no one will ever find out, employees are tempted to lie, steal, and perform other illegal acts.

- **Unethical tone set by top management.** If top managers are not perceived as highly ethical, lower-level managers might be less ethical as a result. Employees have little incentive to act legally and ethically if their superiors do not set an example and encourage and reward such behavior. The saying "The speed of the leader is the speed of the pack" illustrates the importance of leading by example.

- **Uncertainty about whether an action is wrong.** Many times, company personnel are placed in situations in which the line between right and wrong is not clearly defined. When caught in this gray area, the perplexed employee asks, "How far is too far?"

> **stakeholders** people inside and outside the organization who are affected by decisions
>
> **ethics** the principles of right and wrong that guide one in making decisions that consider the impact of one's actions on others as well as on the decision maker

- **Unwillingness to take a stand for what is right.** Often employees know what is right or wrong but are not willing to take the risk of challenging a wrong action. They might lack the confidence or skill needed to confront others with sensitive legal or ethical issues. They might remain silent and then justify their unwillingness to act.

Framework for Analyzing Ethical Dilemmas

Determining whether an action is ethical can be difficult. Learning to analyze a dilemma from both legal and ethical perspectives will help you find a solution that conforms to your own personal values. Figure 1.3 shows the four conclusions you might reach when considering the advisability of a particular behavior.

Dimension 1: Behavior That Is Illegal and Unethical When considering some actions, you will reach the conclusion that they are both illegal and unethical. The law specifically outlines the "black" area—those alternatives that are clearly wrong—and your employer will expect you to become an expert in the laws that affect your particular area. When you encounter an unfamiliar area, you must investigate any possible legal implications. Obviously, obeying the law is in the best interest of all concerned: you as an individual, your company, and society. Contractual agreements between two parties also offer guidance for legal decision making. Frequently, your own individual sense of right and wrong will also confirm that the illegal action is wrong for you personally. In such situations, decisions about appropriate behavior are obvious.

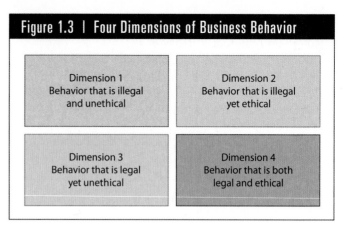

Figure 1.3 | Four Dimensions of Business Behavior

Dimension 1 Behavior that is illegal and unethical	Dimension 2 Behavior that is illegal yet ethical
Dimension 3 Behavior that is legal yet unethical	Dimension 4 Behavior that is both legal and ethical

Dimension 2: Behavior That Is Illegal Yet Ethical Occasionally, a businessperson will decide that even though a specific action is illegal, there is a justifiable reason to break the law. A case in point is a law passed in Vermont that makes it illegal for a pharmaceutical company to give any gift valued at more than $25 to doctors or their personnel.[6] Those supporting the law charge that the giving of freebies drives up medical costs by encouraging doctors to prescribe new, more expensive brand-name drugs. The law's opponents contend that the gifts do not influence doctors and are merely educational tools for new products. Although a pharmaceutical firm and its employees might see nothing wrong with providing gifts worth more than $25, they would be well advised to consider the penalty of $10,000 per violation before acting on their personal ethics. A better course of action would be to act within the law, possibly while lobbying for a change in the law.

Ethical Dilemmas ...

Identifying ethical issues in typical workplace situations can be difficult, and coworkers and superiors might apply pressure for seemingly logical reasons. To illustrate, examine each of the following workplace situations for a possible ethical dilemma:

- ▶ To achieve profit expectations, a stockbroker hides the financial risk of an investment product from potential clients.

- ▶ To prevent an adverse effect on stock prices, corporate officers deliberately withhold information concerning a possible corporate takeover.

- ▶ To protect the organization, management decides not to publicize a design flaw in an automobile that could lead to possible injury and even death to consumers, because the announcement might result in legal action.

- ▶ A supervisor takes advantage of their position and threatens an employee with dismissal if they do not acquiesce to their inappropriate requests and language use.

- ▶ Angry because of an unfavorable performance appraisal of a colleague, an employee leaks confidential information to the colleague that creates distrust among others in the department and results in a lawsuit.

Your fundamental morals and values provide the foundation for making ethical decisions. However, as the previous examples imply, even seemingly minor concessions in day-to-day decisions can gradually weaken an individual's ethical foundation.

Dimension 3: Behavior That Is Legal Yet Unethical

If you determine that a behavior is legal and complies with relevant contractual agreements and company policy, your next step is to consult your company's or profession's *code of ethics*. This written document summarizes the company's or profession's *standards of ethical conduct*. Some companies refer to this document as a *credo*. If the behavior does not violate the code of ethics, then put it to the test of your own personal integrity. You may at times reject a legal action because it does not "feel right." Most Americans were appalled to learn that the marketing of sub-prime loans packaged as reputable securities has been blamed for causing the "Great Recession." Although they might have acted legally, their profiting at the expense of company employees, stockholders, and the public hardly seemed ethical. You might be faced with situations in which you reject a behavior that is legal because you would not be proud to have your family and community know that you engaged in it.

Dimension 4: Behavior That Is Both Legal and Ethical

Decisions in this dimension are easy to make. Such actions comply with the law, company policies, and your professional and personal codes of ethics.

The Pagano Model offers a straightforward method for determining whether a proposed action is advisable.[7] For this system to work, you must answer the following six questions honestly:

1. Is the proposed action legal? (This is the core starting point.)
2. What are the benefits and costs to the people involved?
3. Would you want this action to be a universal standard, appropriate for everyone?
4. Does the action pass the light-of-day test? That is, if your action appeared on television or others learned about it, would you be proud?
5. Does the action pass the Golden Rule test? That is, would you want the same to happen to you?
6. Does the action pass the ventilation test? Ask the opinion of a wise friend with no investment in the outcome. Does this friend believe the action is ethical?

1-4b Diversity Challenges

Diversity in the workplace is another force influencing communication. Differences between the sender and the receiver in areas such as culture, age, gender, and education require sensitivity on the part of both parties so that the intended message is the one that is received.

Understanding how to communicate effectively with people from other cultures has become more integral to the work environment as many U.S. companies are increasingly conducting business with international companies or becoming multinational. Even *when* a person can communicate, it may differ in other countries. For example, France's administrative court recently ruled that tech workers' right to health and rest was not sufficiently protected by existing laws. What this means is that a tech worker in France can choose to not check their work email during their legally mandated rest period and not face retribution.[8] For Americans, who may not think of "unplugging," these cultural differences might require adjustments to their communication expectations.

When addressing cultural differences, successful communication must often span barriers of language and differing worldviews resulting from societal and religious beliefs and practices. When a person fails to consider these factors, communication suffers, and the result is often embarrassing and potentially costly. To be successful on an international scale, managers need to be aware of cultural differences and be willing to work to ensure that effective communication occurs despite these barriers.

Diversity challenges aren't limited to international communication situations, however. In 2022, 13 women sued the Black News Channel (BNC) for gender discrimination, accusing the Florida-based network of unequal pay for female employees and a workplace culture that forced them "to conform to sexist or misogynistic stereotypes about how women are supposed to behave."

The 13 plaintiffs allege that executives at the 2-year-old network disciplined or terminated female employees for being too vocal, pushy, and aggressive, creating a hostile work environment for women and paying them thousands of dollars less per year than their male counterparts.

Ashley Flete, a former anchor, said that a producer had been "berating" her about being "insufficiently feminine" through her earpiece while she was on the air. After filing a complaint with human resources, she said her contract was terminated 6 months into a 2-year contract.

Per the complaint, BNC claimed Flete was terminated because they no longer needed a morning show host, but she believed this action was in retaliation to her complaint.[9]

The potential barrier of language is obvious in international situations; however, successful communicators know that much more is involved when interacting across cultures, genders, ages, abilities, and other differences, regardless of national boundaries.

Communication Opportunities and Challenges in Diversity

As world markets continue to expand, U.S. employees at home and abroad will be doing business with more people from other countries. You might find yourself working abroad for a large American company, an international company with a plant in the United States, or a company with an ethnically diverse workforce. Regardless of the workplace, your **diversity skills**—that is, your ability to communicate effectively with people of all genders, ages, cultures, and underrepresented groups—will affect your success in today's culturally diverse global economy.

Workplace diversity can lead to misunderstandings and miscommunications, but it also poses opportunities to improve both workers and organizations. Employees must be prepared to communicate effectively with workers of different nationalities, genders, races, ages, abilities, and other characteristics.

Diversity skills to be developed include the following:

Cultivating Cultural Awareness and Belonging

Cultural awareness and belonging reinforce the primary goals of diversity skills to help each individual feel respected, valued, and treated fairly. This provides the foundation for a more inclusive work environment. It's important to create an individual sense of belonging to ultimately help strengthen each person's connection to their team and sense of purpose related to shared goals.

Cultural awareness and belonging aim to help people:

- Feel comfortable at work
- Connect with the people they work with
- Make meaningful contributions
- Understand their own unique strengths
- Respect colleagues
- Treat each other fairly

Confronting Bias Everyone has a unique cultural lens through which they see the world. Life experience and things we learn all shape our cultural lens. However, there may be some perceptions you have about the world you're unaware of. This is your unconscious bias.

It's important for you to evaluate your personal cultural lens and unconscious bias. Bias relies on making assumptions about specific groups of people without a basis. However, once you identify and understand your own unconscious bias, you can become more consciously inclusive.

Empathy is important to confront bias. Imagine what it's like to be a different

> **diversity skills** the ability to communicate effectively with people of all genders, ages, cultures, and underrepresented groups

person. This may be uncomfortable, but feeling uncomfortable or awkward is a good thing. This feeling can help you be more willing to learn and grow.

Mitigating Microaggressions A microaggression is a statement or action considered unintentionally, subtly, or indirectly discriminatory against a marginalized group or person. Microaggressions can be very common or subtle, and you may not even notice them. However, they can have a negative effect on the recipients, such as making them feel like an outsider. If you see or hear a microaggression, it's important to call it out and explain why someone should not do or say what they did.

Combating Stereotypes Stereotypes often stem from discriminatory practices. People stereotype one another based on their perceptions and previous experiences. People may stereotype others based on a variety of things, such as gender, age, or race. However, the United States Equal Employment Opportunity Commission prohibits most discriminatory practices in the workplace.

Diversity skills and training can help people respect and value one another more. Create opportunities for employees from different backgrounds or departments who may not usually work together to collaborate. Consider developing affinity groups to help like-minded and similar individuals to connect with each other.

Multicultural and Multiethnic Understanding

Multicultural and multiethnic understanding can help you better understand and appreciate diverse groups of people. This includes their life experiences, beliefs, and history. Greater cultural awareness and consideration can help foster a better community and develop a multicultural lens in your workplace. This helps strengthen the company's overall commitment to multiculturalism.[10]

Being a part of a diverse workforce will require you to communicate with *everyone* and to support colleagues in reaching their fullest potential and contributing to the company's goals. To lessen miscommunication, which inevitably occurs, increasing numbers of companies have undertaken *diversity initiatives* and are providing diversity training seminars to help workers understand and appreciate gender and age differences and the cultures of coworkers.

Culture and Communication

The way messages are decoded and encoded is not just a function of the experiences, beliefs, and assumptions of the person sending or receiving those messages but also is shaped by the society in which they live.

People learn patterns of behavior from their culture. The *culture* of a people is the product of their living experiences within their own society. Culture could be described as "the way of life" of a people and includes a vast array of behaviors and beliefs. These patterns affect how people perceive the world, what they value, and how they act. Differing patterns can also create barriers to communication.

Barriers to Intercultural Communication

Because cultures give different definitions of such basics of interaction as values and norms, people raised in two different cultures can clash in various ways.

- **Ethnocentrism.** Problems occur between people of different cultures primarily because people tend to assume that their own cultural norms are the right way to do things. They wrongly believe that the specific patterns of behavior desired in their own cultures are universally valued. This belief, known as **ethnocentrism**, is certainly natural, but learning about other cultures and developing sensitivity will help minimize ethnocentric reactions when dealing with other cultures.

- **Stereotypes.** We often form a mental picture of the main characteristics of another group, creating preformed ideas of what people in this group are like. These pictures, called **stereotypes**, influence the way we interact with members of the other group. When we observe a behavior that conforms to the stereotype, the validity of the preconceived notion is reinforced. We often view the other person as a representative of a class of people rather than as an individual. People of all cultures have stereotypes about other cultural groups they have encountered. These stereotypes can interfere with communication when people interact based on the imagined representative and not the real individual.

- **Interpretation of time.** The study of how a culture perceives time and its use is called **chronemics**. In the United States, we have a saying that "time is money." Canadians, like some northern Europeans who are also concerned about punctuality, make appointments, keep them, complete them, and waste no time in the process.

Although Americans and some Europeans believe "time is money," other cultures are less concerned about economy of time.

In some other cultures, time is the cheapest commodity and an inexhaustible resource; time represents a person's span on Earth, which is only part of eternity. To these cultures, engaging in long, casual conversations prior to serious discussions or negotiations is time well spent in establishing and nurturing relationships. On the other hand, the time-efficient American businessperson is likely to fret about wasting precious time.

- **Personal space requirements.** Space operates as a language just as time does. The study of cultural space requirements is known as **proxemics**. In all cultures, the distance between people functions in communication as "personal space" or "personal territory." In the United States, for example, for intimate conversations with close friends and relatives, individuals are willing to stay within about a foot and a half of each other; for casual conversations, up to 2 or 3 feet; for job interviews and personal business, 4 to 12 feet; and for public occasions, more than 12 feet. However, in many cultures outside the United States, closer personal contact is accepted, or greater distance might be the norm.

- **Nonverbal communication.** Nonverbal communication is not universal but, instead, is learned from one's culture. Even the most basic gestures have varying cultural meanings—the familiar North American symbol for "okay" means zero in France, money in Japan, and an expression of vulgarity in Brazil. Similarly, eye contact, posture, facial expressions, and use of space and time carry different meanings throughout the world.

- **Translation limitations.** Words in one language do not always have an equivalent meaning in other languages, and the concepts the words describe are often different as well. Translators can be helpful, but keep in mind that a translator is working with a second language and must listen to one language, mentally cast the words into another language, and then speak them. This process is difficult and opens the possibility that the translator will fall victim to one or more cultural barriers. Even if you cannot speak or write another language fluently, people from other cultures will appreciate simple efforts to learn a few common phrases.

---

ethnocentrism the assumption that one's own cultural norms are the right way to do things

stereotypes mental pictures that one group forms of the main characteristics of another group, creating preformed ideas of what people in this group are like

chronemics the study of how a culture perceives time and its use

proxemics the study of cultural space requirements

Developing Cultural Intelligence

One way to improve your ability to communicate with those from other cultures is to develop your *cultural intelligence*. Cultural intelligence can be defined as "a person's capability to adapt as they interact with others from different cultural regions."[11] There are three elements of cultural intelligence:

1. Cognitive knowledge: The possession of a wide-ranging information base about a variety of people and their cultural customs.

2. Motivation: Healthy self-efficacy, persistence, goals, value questioning, and integration.

3. Behavioral adaptability: The capacity to interact in a wide range of situations, environments, and diverse groups.

The global literacy competence (GLC) model offers a road map to begin the conceptualization of the stages of cultural intelligence development (refer to Figure 1.4 and Exhibit 1.3). The GLC assumes that ascending to a higher level of global functioning is not only possible but also required for excellence in a cross-cultural environment. To do so requires a commitment to personal growth, openness, and continuous learning about other cultures and customs.

Figure 1.4 | Global Leadership Competency Model

Adaptation
Internalization
Acceptance
Appreciation
Understanding
Awareness
Ignorance

Source: C. O. Chin, J. Gu, and S. Tubbs. (2001). Developing global leadership competencies. *Journal of Leadership Studies*, 7(4): 20–35.

Exhibit 1.3 | Levels of Global Communication Competence

Level	Description
Awareness	This is the novice stage; with exposure come vague impressions. They are brief sensations of which people are barely conscious. At this level, there is little or no sense-making but a dawning awareness of something different and possibly interesting, strange, frightening, or annoying.
Understanding	At this stage, individuals begin to exhibit some conscious effort to learn why people are the way they are and why people do what they do. They display interest in those who are different from themselves. Sanchez et al. (2000) refer to this as the "transition stage." This is a stage whereby the individual collects information through reading, observation, and real experiences as well as by asking questions to learn more about the new cultural phenomenon.
Appreciation	Individuals begin to take a "leap of faith" and experience a genuine tolerance of different points of view. Through understanding the basic differences as well as areas where one thinks, acts, and reacts similarly, a positive feeling toward the "new" cultural phenomenon begins to form. Individuals not only put up with the "new" culture but also display a genuine appreciation of and, in some cases, preference for certain aspects of the "new" culture.
Acceptance	In this stage, the possibility of interaction between cultures increases appreciably. People are more sophisticated both in terms of recognizing commonalities and in terms of effectively dealing with differences. At this stage, there is the willingness to acquire new patterns of behavior and attitudes. This is a departure from the ethnocentric notion that "my way is the best way and the only way."
Internalization	At this stage, the individual goes beyond making sense of information and actually embarks on a deliberate internalization process, with profound positive feelings for the once-unknown cultural phenomenon. At this stage, there is a clear sense of self-understanding leading to readiness to act and interact with the locals/nationals in a natural, appropriate, and culturally effective manner.
Adaptation	Cultural competence becomes a way of life. It is internalized, to the degree that it is out of one's consciousness, thus it becomes effortless and second nature. Individuals at this level display and possess (1) the capacity for gathering knowledge about different cultures, (2) drive or motivation, and (3) behavioral adaptability—the capacity to act effectively based upon their knowledge and motivation.

Source: C. O. Chin, J. Gu, and S. Tubbs. (2001). Developing global leadership competencies. *Journal of Leadership Studies*, 7(4): 20–35.

A related concept, "cultural competence," has various definitions but generally applies similar characteristics to organizations, agencies, or a set of professionals. Cultural competence requires that organizations have a defined set of values and principles, and demonstrate behaviors, attitudes, policies, and structures that enable them to work effectively across cultures. Like cultural intelligence, cultural competence is a developmental process that evolves over an extended period. Both individuals and organizations are at various levels of awareness, knowledge, and skills along the cultural competence continuum.

Cultural incompetence in the business community can damage an individual's self-esteem and career, but the unobservable psychological impact on the victims can go largely unnoticed until the threat of a class action suit brings them to light.

Five essential elements contribute to a system's, institution's, or agency's ability to become more culturally competent. These include:

1. Valuing diversity

2. Having the capacity for cultural self-assessment

3. Being conscious of the dynamics inherent when cultures interact

4. Having institutionalized cultural knowledge

5. Having developed adaptations to service delivery reflecting an understanding of cultural diversity.[12] These five elements should be manifested at every level of an organization, including policy making, administrative, and practice. Further, these elements should be reflected in the attitudes, structures, policies, and services of the organization.

It's critical in business to develop a cultural intelligence and cultural competence.

Rawpixel.com/Shutterstock

1-4c Changing Technology

Electronic tools create opportunities that range from new kinds of communications to improving the quality of the messages themselves. Electronic tools, such as the internet, intranets, data analytic tools, document production software, multimedia presentations, web publishing tools, social media, text messaging, and email, can help people in various ways, such as by (1) collecting and analyzing data, (2) shaping messages to be clearer and more effective, and (3) communicating quickly and efficiently with others in geographically dispersed locations.

Using various communication technologies, individuals can often work in their homes or other remote locations and send and receive work from the company office electronically. **Telecommuting** (also referred to as *teleworking*) offers various advantages, including reduced travel time and increased work flexibility. Laptops and smartphones provide computing power and connectivity for professionals wherever they are.

The COVID-19 pandemic has pushed companies and consumers to rapidly adopt new behaviors that are likely to stick well beyond the pandemic, including the greater adoption of telecommuting and e-commerce. A 2021 study conducted by the McKinsey Global Institute found that about 20 to 25 percent of the workforces in advanced economies could work from home between 3 and 5 days a week. This represents four to five times more remote work than before the pandemic and could prompt a large change in the geography of work, as individuals and companies shift out of large cities into suburbs and small cities. Some companies are shifting to flexible workspaces after positive experiences with remote work during the pandemic.

The study also found that many consumers discovered the convenience of e-commerce and other online activities during the pandemic. In 2020, the share of e-commerce grew at two to five times the rate before COVID-19. Roughly three-quarters of people using digital channels for the first time during the pandemic say they will continue using them when things return to "normal," according to McKinsey Consumer Pulse surveys conducted around the world.

telecommuting also called teleworking; working at home or other remote locations and sending and receiving work from the company office electronically

Other kinds of virtual transactions such as telemedicine, online banking, and streaming entertainment have also taken off. Online doctor consultations through Practo, a telehealth company in India, grew more than tenfold between April and November 2020. These virtual practices may decline somewhat as economies reopen but are likely to continue well above levels seen before the pandemic.[13]

These changes have spurred digital transformations in a matter of weeks rather than months or years. As nonessential workers shifted to working from home, 85 percent of respondents in another McKinsey survey said their businesses have somewhat or greatly accelerated the implementation of technologies that digitally enable employee interaction and collaboration, such as videoconferencing and filesharing. Roughly half of those surveyed reported increasing digitization of customer channels, for example, via e-commerce, mobile apps, or chatbots. Some 35 percent have further digitized their supply chains, for example, by connecting their suppliers with digital platforms in supply chain management.

Adoption of automation technologies—including robotics, autonomous vehicles, and artificial intelligence (AI)-driven software that can perform processing workflows—has also accelerated during the pandemic, although to a lesser extent than digitization. These trends reflect automation's ability to facilitate contactless interactions at a time of social distancing and heightened awareness of hygiene, as well as cost pressures that may arise from the economic slowdown caused by COVID-19. Another plus: robots don't get sick.

For example, during the pandemic, American Eagle Outfitters deployed robots to help it sort clothes in its warehouses to meet a surge of online orders, and IBM saw a surge in new customers in the second quarter of 2020 for its AI-driven Watson Assistant, a platform for deploying chatbots and other customer services.[14] Use of such technologies allows contactless customer interaction in a period when human contact is discouraged and builds resilience by limiting reliance on virus-susceptible employees. Providers of cloud services, such as Amazon and Alibaba, have announced plans to markedly step-up investment in cloud services, an indication that they expect increased demand related to changes in the workplace post-COVID.[15]

> **virtual team** three or more people who collaborate from different physical locations, perform interdependent tasks, have shared responsibility for the outcome of the work, and rely on some form of technology to communicate with one another

Other popular technological developments are being incorporated into the work world, including tools based on gaming. For example, "gamification" is being used to turn the, at times, tedious task of training into a fun and motivating opportunity. By giving employees goals to reach and levels to achieve, gamification of training programs can increase their interest in completing training assignments. "You could send people on scavenger hunts. You could tell people they have to go out into the organization to discover things and then report back on what they've learned," explains Bill Cushard, head of training at ServiceRocket. Gamification can give employees a goal to reach, an excuse to meet more of their colleagues, and a chance to learn about different areas of the organization.

Remote work may also put a dent in business travel as its extensive use of videoconferencing during the pandemic has ushered in a new acceptance of virtual meetings and other aspects of work. With today's technological advances, people can work together even when they are physically in different locations. A **virtual team** consists of three or more people who collaborate from different physical locations, perform interdependent tasks, have shared responsibility for the outcome of the work, and rely on some form of technology to communicate with one another. A phone line, fiber-optic cable, wireless signal, satellite signal, or other technology connects people who are communicating in a virtual team. Although technology seems to be a pervasive and revolutionary fact of life—in both our personal and our professional lives—communication researchers predict that technology will play an even larger role in how we collaborate with one another in the future. (Working in virtual teams is discussed more fully in the next section.)

Although many benefits are provided using technology in organizations, challenges or risks also must be recognized. Knowing how to "tunnel" through the vast amounts of irrelevant information available on the digital highway to find what you want can be overwhelming. The experience can also be expensive in terms of human time spent and charges incurred for online time. Locating information from electronic sources requires that you know the search procedures and methods for constructing an effective search strategy. There are also possible legal liabilities that can arise from improper use of technological resources.

Effective use of various communication technologies helps ensure timely, targeted messages and responses and helps build interpersonal relationships. This responsiveness leads to positive interactions with colleagues and strong customer commitment.

In addition to its many benefits, technology poses some challenges for the business communicator. For example, technology raises issues of ownership, as in the case of difficulties that arise in protecting the copyright of documents transmitted over the internet. Technology poses dilemmas over access, that is, who has the right to certain stored information pertaining to an individual or a company.

Technology threatens our individual privacy, our right to be left alone, free from surveillance or interference from other individuals or organizations. Common invasions of privacy caused by technology include:

- monitoring your internet use, infiltrating your information, and sending advertising based on your browsing history;

- monitoring the exact time employees spend on a specific task and between tasks and the exact number and length of breaks, and supervisors' or coworkers' reading of another employee's email and computer files; and

- spreading of spyware and various computer "bugs" through the internet.[16]

J.R. Bale/Alamy Stock Photo

1-4d Team Environment

As firms around the world face problems of decreasing productivity, faltering product quality, and worker dissatisfaction, work teams are seen as a way to help firms remain competitive globally. Decentralized decision making enables teams of people to communicate in a peer-to-peer fashion, rather than following traditional lines of authority; and new technologies give employees the ability to communicate easily and openly with one another and with those outside the firm.

Although worker involvement in the management process has long been the hallmark of Japanese business, many businesses in the United States and elsewhere are empowering self-directed work teams to accomplish various assignments.[17] The list of companies using self-directed work teams is diverse, including Hunt-Wesson, Federal Express, Kraft Foods, Inc., Hewlett-Packard, Southwest Airlines, Toyota, Motorola, General Electric, and Corning.

Work Team Defined

The terms *team*, *work team*, *group*, *work group*, *cross-functional team*, and *self-directed team* are often used interchangeably.[18] Whatever the title, a **team** is a small number of people with complementary skills who work together for a common purpose. Team members set their own goals, in

cooperation with management, and plan how to achieve those goals and how their work is to be accomplished. The central organizing element of a team is that it has a common purpose and measurable goals for which the team can be held accountable, independent of its individual members. Employees in a self-directed work team handle a wide array of functions and work with a minimum of direct supervision.[19]

Some major strengths of teams are as follows:[20] Teams make workers happier by causing them to feel that they are shaping their own jobs.

- Teams increase efficiency by eliminating layers of managers whose job was once to pass orders downward.

- Teams enable a company to draw on the skills and imagination of a whole workforce.

A key element in team success is the concept of **synergy**, defined as a situation in which the whole is greater than the sum of the parts. Teams provide a depth of expertise that is unavailable at the individual level. Teams open lines

> **team** a small number of people with complementary skills who work together for a common purpose
>
> **synergy** a situation in which the whole is greater than the sum of the parts

of communication that then lead to increased interaction among employees, and between employees and management. The result is that teams help companies reach their goals of delivering higher-quality products and services faster and with more cost-effectiveness.

Communication Differences in Work Teams

In the past, most businesses were operated in a hierarchical fashion, with most decisions made at the top and communication following a top-down/bottom-up pattern. Communication patterns are different in successful team environments as compared with traditional organizational structures:

- Trust building is the primary factor that changes the organization's communication patterns.

- Open meetings are an important method for enhancing communication, as they educate employees about the business while building bridges of understanding and trust.

- Shared leadership, which involves more direct and effective communication between management and its internal customers, is common.

- Listening, problem solving, conflict resolution, negotiation, and consensus become important factors in group communication.

- Information flows vertically up to management and down to workers, as well as horizontally among team members, other teams, and supervisors.

Communication is perhaps the single most important aspect of successful teamwork. Open lines of communication increase interaction between employees and management. All affected parties should be kept informed as projects progress (refer to Figure 1.5 for questions to ask to improve group communication).

The type of talk found within a group or organization can also affect the emotional well-being of members. Refer to Exhibit 1.4 for a description of the type of talk that can produce a defensive or supportive communication climate.

Maximizing Work Team Effectiveness

Grouping employees into a team structure does not mean that they will automatically function as a team. A group must go through a developmental process to begin to function as a team. Members need training in such areas as problem solving, goal setting, and conflict resolution. Teams must be encouraged to establish the "three Rs"—roles, rules, and relationships.[21]

The self-directed work team can become the basic organizational building block to best ensure success in dynamic global competition. Skills for successful participation in team environments are somewhat different from those necessary for success in old-style organizations. Today successful business communicators and team members must possess the ability to:

- give and take constructive criticism, actively listen, clearly impart one's views to others, and provide meaningful feedback;

Figure 1.5 | Group Interaction

To improve group communication, time needs to be set aside to assess the quality of interaction. Questions to pose about the group process might include the following:

Is the group dealing with conflict in a positive way?

What in the group process is going well?

What roles are members playing? For instance, is one person dominating while others contribute little or nothing?

What are our common goals?

What about the group process could be improved?

Rawpixel.com/Shutterstock

Exhibit 1.4 | Characteristics of Defensive and Supportive Communication Climates

Defensive	Supportive
1. Evaluation. To pass judgment on another.	1. Description. Nonjudgmental. To ask questions, present feelings, refrain from asking the other to change their behavior.
2. Control. To try to do something to another; to try to change behavior or attitudes of others.	2. Problem orientation. To convey a desire to collaborate in solving a mutual problem or defining it; to allow the other to set their goals.
3. Strategy. To manipulate another, to engage in multiple or ambiguous motivations.	3. Spontaneity. To express naturalness, free of deception; straightforwardness; uncomplicated motives.
4. Neutrality. To express a lack of concern for the other; the clinical, person-as-object-of-study attitude.	4. Empathy. To respect the other person and show it; to identify with their problems; to share their feelings.
5. Superiority. To communicate that you are superior in position, wealth, intelligence, and so on, to arouse feelings of inadequacy in others.	5. Equality. To be willing to enter into participative planning with mutual trust and respect; to attach little importance to differences of worth, status, and so on.
6. Certainty. To seem to know the answers and be dogmatic wanting to win an argument rather than solve a problem; seeing one's ideas as truths to be defended.	6. Provisionalism. To be willing to experiment with your own behavior; to investigate issues rather than taking sides; to solve problems, not debate.

Source: Jack Gibb. (1961). Defensive communication, *Journal of Communication*, 11: 141–48.

- break down emotional barriers, such as insecurity or condescension;

- promote team functioning by removing process barriers, such as rigid policies and procedures;

- understand the feelings and needs of coworkers so members feel comfortable stating their opinions and discussing the strengths and weaknesses of the team;

- overcome cultural barriers, such as stereotyped roles and responsibilities, that can separate workers from management and;[22]

- apply leadership skills in a dynamic group setting that results in team success. In dynamic team leadership, referred to as *distributed leadership*, the role of the leader can alternate among members, and more than one leadership style can be active at any given time.[23]

Although diversity is generally beneficial to group decision making, such differences—gender, cultural, and age, for example—can present challenges to team communication. Team members may need awareness training to assist them with dealing with the challenges presented by diversity as well as taking full advantage of its benefits.

Virtual Teams

The convergence of the last three developments—globalization and increased reliance on technology and teams—has resulted in the increased use of a special kind of team—the virtual team. A virtual team is defined as "a group of geographically, organizationally and/or time dispersed workers brought together by information and telecommunication technologies to accomplish one or more organizational tasks."[24] Members of virtual teams communicate electronically and may never meet face-to-face.

There are six key differences between the way face-to-face teams and virtual teams collaborate, although, as technology becomes more pervasive these differences also will moderate. Face-to-face team members typically communicate at the same time and in the same place and, because of this, there is less anonymity and, with it, less potential for deception. Part of this is because members have access to a wider range of nonverbal cues, while those in virtual teams tend to rely more on written messages.

Virtual teams can communicate under four conditions: (1) same time/same place, (2) same time/different place, (3) different time/same place, and (4) different time/different place.

An asynchronous message is a message that is not read, heard, or seen at the same time you send the message; there is a time delay between when you send and receive a message. Sending a text message to someone who is not monitoring Facebook or leaving a voice message for someone are examples of asynchronous messages. Synchronous messages are those that occur instantly and simultaneously—there is no time delay between when you send a message and the other person receives it. A live video conference is an example of a synchronous message.

The more synchronous our interaction, the more similar it is to face-to-face interactions. The more a technology resembles a face-to-face conversation, the more social presence there is. Social presence is the feeling we have when we act and think as if we're involved in an unmediated, face-to-face conversation. The key distinction among different forms of electronic messaging and the degree of social presence we experience is whether we feel we are in a synchronous interaction. When we send text messages back and forth or instant message with a group of people, we create a shared sense of social or psychological presence with our collaborators.

As with most technology-enabled developments, both advantages and disadvantages can result from virtual team use. Advantages include increased productivity, extended market opportunities, and improved knowledge transfer among employees across an organization.

Common disadvantages include reduced communication effectiveness caused by more limited access to various communication media, poor leadership, and incompetent team members. These disadvantages can be overcome through effective virtual team training, proper goal setting, team building, and successful coordination.

Ground Picture/Shutterstock

2 | Focusing on Interpersonal and Group Communication

Learning Objectives

After studying this chapter, you will be able to ...

2-1 Explain how theories about perception and self-awareness relate to business communication.

2-2 Describe the role of nonverbal messages in business communication settings.

2-3 Identify aspects of effective listening.

2-4 Identify factors affecting group and team communication.

2-5 Discuss aspects of effective meeting management.

2-1 Theories That Impact Communication

As discussed in the previous chapter, the COVID-19 pandemic has had a significant impact on the way that we work and do business. Of course, the potential for remote work depends on the mix of activities undertaken in each occupation and on their physical, spatial, and interpersonal context. For most workers, some activities during a typical day lend themselves to remote work, while the rest of their tasks require their on-site physical presence. According to a McKinsey Global Institute survey, 61 percent of the workforce in the United States can work no more than a few hours a week remotely or not at all.

For example, many physical or manual activities, as well as those that require use of fixed equipment, cannot be done remotely. These include providing care, operating machinery, using lab equipment, and processing customer transactions in stores. The ability to work remotely also depends on the need to use specialized equipment. According to the McKinsey survey, a chemical technician could work remotely only a quarter of the time because much of their work must be done in a lab housing the equipment they need. Among healthcare occupations, general practitioners who can use digital technologies to communicate with patients have a much greater potential for remote work than surgeons and X-ray technicians, who need advanced equipment and tools to do their work. Thus, among health professionals overall, the effective remote work potential is just 11 percent.

Additionally, employers have found during the pandemic that although some tasks can be done remotely in a crisis, they are much more effectively done in person. These activities include coaching, counseling, and providing advice and feedback; building customer and colleague relationships; bringing new employees into a company; negotiating and making critical decisions; teaching and training; and work that benefits from collaboration, such as innovation, problem-solving, and creativity. If onboarding were to be done remotely, for example, it would require significant rethinking of the activity to produce outcomes similar to those achieved in person.

This mixed pattern of remote and physical activities of each occupation helps explain the results of a recent McKinsey survey of 800 corporate executives around the world.[1] Across all sectors, 38 percent of respondents expect their remote employees to work two or more days a week away from the office after the pandemic, compared to 22 percent of respondents surveyed before the pandemic. But just 19 percent of respondents to the survey said they expected employees to work three or more days remotely. This suggests that executives anticipate operating their businesses with a hybrid model of some sort, with employees working remotely and from an office during the workweek.[2] JPMorgan has a plan for its 60,950 employees to work from home one or two weeks a month or two days a week, depending on the line of business.[3]

What this means for business communication is that although there is a need for high technical skills in the workplace, there remains a significantly higher need for interpersonal and group communication skills applied in face-to-face settings.

2-1a Perception

Hopefully, with the discussion of diversity and intercultural communication from the previous chapter, you are more aware that your perceptions of reality may differ from those around you. For example, if you have had an argument with a friend or family member, chances are it was based on different perceptions of a particular situation. Some would say that because of our experiences, beliefs, and values, it is impossible to comprehend what is really "out there" because everything is interpreted or filtered through our unique personal experiences and cultural beliefs. Because we all have different life experiences, value systems, worldviews, and beliefs, we may perceive reality differently. Even common barriers such as our mood and distractions such as noise, stress, and tiredness can affect what and how we perceive. These differences in perception can be enormous obstacles to effective communication, especially if we are not aware of them. These differences become even more important with the increased diversity of the workplace and the increased internationalization of business activities—that is, globalization.

The perceptual process reveals how differences in judgments of reality may occur. The first step in the process of perception is the receipt of information through our senses (refer to Figure 2.1). This sensory data is then selected and organized into a pattern from which we infer meaning. Selection is the way that we pay attention to sensory cues. It is often not a conscious process, and it is *selective*, which means that we generally pay attention only to some cues, not all of them. Obviously, then, selection can lead to misunderstanding if we are

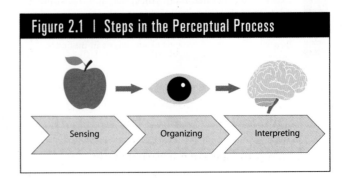

Figure 2.1 | Steps in the Perceptual Process

Sensing → Organizing → Interpreting

The old woman/young woman illusion.

communicating with someone who is paying attention to different cues than we are. You have probably had myriad conversations in which you asked your companion, "Did you see that?" and the response was, "No, I was paying attention to X." This is the process of selection at work.

Misunderstanding can also arise at the organization level of the perceptual process because we may fit the information into patterns that differ from the way that others see things. You have probably done exercises in class or elsewhere where you have been shown a diagram similar to the one in which some people see the face of a beautiful woman while others see the face of an older woman.

During the perceptual process, misunderstanding may occur based on the inferences we draw from the previously mentioned patterns. You have certainly had the unwinnable argument: "I think the movie was excellent because [fill in the blank here]," while your companion replied something like, "You've got to be kidding! That was the biggest disappointment of the century!" Because of differing values, experiences, and tastes, the inferences that we draw from stimuli may be unlike those of others and, if these inferences are not questioned, can create misunderstandings. These sorts of inferential errors are more likely in a world that is characterized by diversity of cultural backgrounds and demographic differences.

Because our opinions may often differ from others, it is not useful to try to ascertain who is right or wrong because it may simply depend on a matter of taste, values, beliefs, or personal preferences. We have all had experiences where our perceptions differ from others, a recognition that creates a problem for our more common sense understanding of the process of communication—the basic assumption that just because we communicated information, it was successfully received as we intended it and that meaning was shared.

Perceptual differences may lead to additional problems, such as those having to do with stereotyping, attribution, impression formation, and culture. **Stereotyping** is not necessarily a bad thing. On the one hand, it can be a label for a process of making sense out of what we perceive by categorizing or generalizing about it. On the other hand,

it can be an oversimplified way of labeling people unfairly with the intention of denigrating them in some way. This can be particularly problematic when dealing with people of other cultures. One type of stereotype that can be formed when interacting with people of other cultures is **projected cognitive similarity**, which is the tendency to assume others have the same norms and values as your own cultural group.[4] Research has shown that when an aggressive style of communication is exhibited in intercultural team decision making, people of East Asian cultures are less participatory, since this style contrasts with their own norms of politeness and modesty.[5] A second stereotype common to intercultural interactions is the **outgroup homogeneity effect**, which is the tendency to think members of other groups are all the same.[6] Although there are cultural tendencies, this belief denies the variation among individuals of any cultural group and can detract from the development of positive working relationships.

A second type of perceptual inference is called an **attribution**. When we form an attribution, we develop a "theory" for another's behavior. Attribution can also apply to how others see us. For example, if we are late to arrive at work, our boss may think we have a poor work ethic when we simply had a flat tire that delayed us that day. If we are not aware of these perceptual problems, then we can find ourselves in serious problems at work by discriminating against others, damaging relationships, and doing things that damage our own credibility or image.

A similar concept is **impression formation**. Basically, impression formation is the process of integrating a variety of observations about a person into a coherent impression of that person. Again, understanding this principle is important for the strategic communicator because we also attempt to manage the impression that others form of us. Today, for example, did you worry about your choice of clothing and how it might affect how others saw you? Did you worry about the state of your hair or whether you might have bad breath? Our ability to manage the impressions we make on others depends on our ability to see ourselves as others might see us.

> **stereotyping** a standardized mental picture that is held in common by members of a group and that represents an oversimplified opinion, prejudiced attitude, or uncritical judgment
>
> **projected cognitive similarity** the tendency to assume others have the same norms and values as your own cultural group
>
> **outgroup homogeneity effect** the tendency to think members of other groups are all the same
>
> **attribution** the assignment of meaning to other people's behavior
>
> **impression formation** the process of integrating a variety of observations about a person into a coherent impression of that person

Chronicle/Alamy

Perceptions may also differ by culture. The increased interdependence of people around the world and diversity in the workplace requires recognition of the contested perceptual nature of reality and our interpretation of it. It thus requires openness to others' views and opinions if we are to communicate effectively to reach anything approaching shared meaning. Unfortunately, the process of maturation may lead us to develop a sense that our identities are complete and fully formed. This process, and other psychological aspects, can lead to the perception by others that we have become a "closed system," unable to learn, change, and adapt to our often rapidly evolving social realities.

Understanding the role of perception in communication is critical for business communicators. Without this recognition, we may assume that others are perceiving reality just as we are, and if this assumption is in error, miscommunication is likely. Misunderstanding may be introduced during each of the steps in the perceptual process, and thus we may need to adjust our communication to lessen the occurrence of these problems. This adjustment relies on our ability to observe situations, analyze what is happening, and then make intentional choices about how best to manage the communication process. Finally, it is important to recognize that people make judgments about us based on our communication practices; this understanding gives us power to actively shape those perceptions. This ability must demonstrate respect for others, avoiding the use of negative interpersonal tactics and intentions, such as manipulation and deception.

2-1b Self-Awareness and Communication

A discussion of perception naturally leads to a look at self-concept and self-awareness. This is because how we perceive ourselves plays a critical role in communication. Our self-concept and awareness of it are important to effective business communicators for several reasons. First, to be effective, we must know ourselves, our strengths, and our weaknesses, so that we can leverage our strengths to better achieve our career goals and work on eliminating our weaknesses so that they don't become a stumbling block to that achievement. Second, our self-concept affects how we interact with others. These two reasons are interconnected. In the political climate of many business organizations, other people will be making observations and judgments about us regarding our strengths and weaknesses, and our ability to talk

self-concept how we think about ourselves and describe ourselves to others

self-fulfilling prophecy the idea that we see ourselves in ways that are consistent with how others see us

about both intelligently can help to enhance our credibility. In other words, today's complex business environment requires that we take steps to become more self-reflexive in our communicative actions. Leveraging our strengths and minimizing our weaknesses can also help to create productive work relationships that enable us to influence others and successfully navigate political terrains.

Self-concept is how we think about ourselves and describe ourselves to others. It is often the product of our experiences and, to some degree, the result of our interpretation of the messages that others send us. In other words, communication is foundational in the forming of our self-concept; people are the products of how others treat them and of the messages others send them. Dean Barnlund (1970) introduced the idea that individuals "construct" themselves—or their identities—through the relationships they have, wish to have, or perceive themselves as having. Barnlund developed the idea that "six persons" are involved in every two-person communication. These six persons emerge from the following:

1. How you view yourself.
2. How you view the other person.
3. How you believe the other person views you.
4. How the other person views themself.
5. How the other person views you.
6. How the other person believes you view them.

Barnlund's model emphasizes the relational nature of communication, the centrality of the self, and our perception of the self in communication. Perception is key in this process. From Barnlund's model comes the notion of the **self-fulfilling prophecy**, or the idea that you behave and see yourself in ways that are consistent with how others see you.[7] With this understanding, it should be obvious that, depending on our relationship and the situation, some people have differing expectations of us and will see us in ways that are different from how others see us. For example, friends and family may have an emotional attachment to us that makes us feel special, accomplished, and well loved. This emotional attachment is important for the development of self-esteem. However, those who do not have that strong emotional attachment—teachers, employers, new acquaintances, and strangers, among others—may see us in a different light, one in which they see our positive attributes as well as those areas that might be improved; in fact, they may focus on the negative, creating a perception that is very different from who we prefer to believe we are.

Depending on our experiences and relationships, our self-concept thus may be positive or negative, accurate or inaccurate. And how you view yourself can make a big difference in your ability to communicate and achieve your purposes.

For this reason, it is important to develop high levels of **self-awareness** or an understanding of the self, including your attitudes, values, beliefs, strengths, and weaknesses. Self-awareness is developed in two ways: by communicating with oneself and by communicating with others. Communication with ourselves is called **intrapersonal communication**, which includes "our perceptions, memories, experiences, feelings, interpretations, inferences, evaluations, attitudes, opinions, ideas, strategies, images, and states of consciousness."[8] According to Gardner and Krechevsky (1993), **intrapersonal intelligence** is the capacity to form an accurate model of oneself and to be able to use that model to operate effectively in life. Intrapersonal intelligence is developed by reflecting on our thoughts and actions to understand what motivates those thoughts and actions. Another word for this process is **reflexivity**.

Intrapersonal intelligence is a correlative ability to **interpersonal intelligence**.[9] Interpersonal intelligence is the ability to understand other people: what motivates them, how they work, and how to work cooperatively with them. Essentially, Gardner and Krechevsky claim that we must have self-awareness to understand others. For example, if our self-concept does not match the perception that others have of us, then we may misinterpret their responses to our messages. We may also misinterpret the way that our communication is interpreted by others. For example, we may believe that we are highly reliable; however, others may believe the opposite about us. This commonly happens in student teams in which a member is commonly late for meetings and with assignments but is able to rationalize that behavior in positive ways, whereas others begin to mistrust the person's reliability. Such contradictions in perception held by others can obviously negatively impact our ability to work with others. Furthermore, if we are unaware of these contradictions, then we are unable to change our communicative behaviors, both verbal and nonverbal, to better correspond with the message we want to send about ourselves. In addition, it is important that the messages we send through our actions correspond to those we send orally and in writing because people are more likely to believe the nonverbal communication cues. A third problem that may occur due to a lack of self-awareness is that we may not recognize differences in others; we may project our self-understanding onto them. This latter issue is a particular problem in diverse cultural settings and can negatively affect our ability to communicate as well as to demonstrate recognized leadership behaviors.

The second part of self-concept is **self-esteem**, or how we feel about ourselves and how well we like and value ourselves. Perception and communication are both affected by self-esteem. In the contemporary business world, high levels of self-awareness and self-esteem may help us be more open to the opinions and perspectives of others.

Without high levels of self-awareness and self-esteem, we may feel threatened when we meet others who are different from us, and that feeling may get in the way of our ability to be open to listening to and considering others' perspectives and opinions. A high level of self-esteem also is important because we must be willing to admit that perhaps we don't know everything; we always have opportunities to learn. According to Evered and Tannenbaum (1992), to engage in dialogue we must be able to take "the stance that there is something that I don't already know." We must be able to engage with others "with a mutual *openness* to learn," rather than becoming defensive or closed to other opinions.[10]

2-2 Nonverbal Communication

Managers use verbal and nonverbal messages to communicate ideas to employees. *Verbal* means "through the use of words," either written or spoken. *Nonverbal* means "without the use of words." Although major attention in communication studies is given to verbal messages, studies show that nonverbal elements can account for more than 90 percent of the total meaning of a message.[11] Nonverbal communication includes *metacommunication* and *kinesic messages*.

2-2a Metacommunication

A **metacommunication** is a message that, although *not* expressed in words, accompanies a message that *is* expressed in words. For example, "Don't be late for work" communicates caution, yet the sentence might imply (but not express in words) such additional ideas as "You are frequently late, and I'm warning you" or "I doubt your dependability." "Your solution is perfect" might also convey a metacommunication such as "You are efficient," or "I certainly like your work." Whether you are speaking or writing, you can be confident that those who receive your messages will be sensitive to the messages expressed in words and to the accompanying messages that are present but not expressed in words.

---

self-awareness an understanding of the self, including one's attitudes, values, beliefs, strengths, and weaknesses

intrapersonal communication one's perceptions, memories, experiences, feelings, interpretations, inferences, evaluations, attitudes, opinions, ideas, strategies, images, and states of consciousness

intrapersonal intelligence one's communication with oneself, including memories, experiences, feelings, ideas, and attitudes

reflexivity the capacity for reflection

interpersonal intelligence the ability to read, empathize, and understand others

self-esteem how we like and value ourselves and how we feel about ourselves

metacommunication a nonverbal message that, although not expressed in words, accompanies a message that is expressed in words

2-2b Kinesic Messages

People constantly send meanings through kinesic communication, which is an idea expressed through nonverbal behavior. In other words, receivers gain additional meaning from what they see and hear—the visual and the vocal:

- **Visual kinesic communication**—gestures, winks, smiles, frowns, sighs, attire, grooming, and all kinds of body movements.
- **Vocal kinesic communication**—intonation, projection, and resonance of the voice.

Following are some examples of kinesic messages and the meanings they can convey.

Action	Possible Kinesic Message
• A wink or light chuckle follows a statement.	• "Don't believe what I just said."
• A manager is habitually late for staff meetings and with email replies.	• "My time is more important than yours. You can wait for me."
• A group leader sits at a position other than at the head of the table.	• "I want to demonstrate my equality with other members."
• An employee wears clothing that reveals tattoos, which violates the company's dress code.	• "Rules are for other people; I can do what I want." Alternately, "I do not understand the expectations."
• A job applicant submits a résumé containing errors.	• "My language skills are deficient." Alternately, "I didn't care to do my best."

2-2c Other Nonverbal Messages

In addition to kinesics, proxemics, chronemics, and haptics are elements of nonverbal communication. **Proxemics**, or the study of human space, revolves around two concepts: territoriality and personal space. **Territoriality** refers to your need to establish and maintain certain spaces as your own. In a workplace environment, the walls of your cubicle or office often establish your territory. **Personal space** is the distance between you and others with which you feel comfortable. When someone invades your personal space, you often automatically move away from that person. However, personal space preferences can differ among people. For example, large people also usually prefer more space, as do men.

Similarly, personal space preferences differ by culture. People of the United States tend to need more space than those from Greece, Latin America, or the Middle East. The Japanese tend to prefer a greater distance in social situations than do people of the United States.

Cultural differences also extend to how people communicate through space in seating arrangements and the layout of offices. People in the United States, for example, prefer to converse face-to-face, while people in China prefer to sit side-by-side. This preference may allow them to avoid direct eye contact, which is the custom in that culture. In terms of the office environment, private offices have more status in the United States, while in Japan, only executives of the highest rank may have a private office, although it is just as likely that they have desks in large work areas. In the United States and Germany, the top floor of office buildings is generally occupied by top-level executives, while in France, high-ranking executives occupy the middle of an office area with subordinates located around them.

Chronemics, or values related to time, refers to the way that people organize and use time and the messages that are created because of our organization and use of time. Our use of time communicates several messages. Our urgency or casualness with the starting time of an event could be an indication of our personality, status, or culture. Highly structured, task-oriented people may arrive and leave on time, whereas relaxed, relation-oriented people may arrive and leave late. People with low status are expected to be on time, while those with higher status are granted more leeway in their arrival time. Being on time is more important in some cultures than others; for example, being on time is more important in North America than in South America, whereas people of Germany and Switzerland are even more time-conscious than people from the United States.

Another cultural issue to recognize is whether a country follows **polychronic time (P-time)** or **monochronic time (M-time)**. Countries that follow polychronic time work on several activities simultaneously. In these cultures, people are more important than schedules, so they don't mind interruptions and are accustomed to doing several things at once. People in polychronic cultures borrow and lend things and tend to build lifelong relationships. People from high-context cultures—those that pay attention to context of communication—tend to be polychronic, including Latin America, the Middle East, and Southern Europe.

---

visual kinesic communication gestures, winks, smiles, frowns, sighs, attire, grooming, and all kinds of body movements

vocal kinesic communication intonation, projection, and resonance of the voice

proxemics the branch of knowledge that deals with the amount of space that people feel it necessary to set between themselves and others

territoriality a term associated with nonverbal communication that refers to how people use space (territory) to communicate ownership or occupancy of areas and possessions

Countries that are monochronic in their time orientation include the United States, Germany, Switzerland, and England. In monochronic cultures, time is considered as something tangible, as reflected in such sayings as "wasting time" and "time is money." Time is seen as linear and manageable in such cultures. It is considered rude to do two things at once, such as answering the phone while someone is in your office or stopping to text someone while in a conversation. However, with the prevalence of cell phones, this consideration is rapidly changing. Monochronic people tend to respect private property, rarely borrow or lend, and are accustomed to short-term relationships.

Haptics, or touch, communicate a great deal. What is appropriate and people's tendency to touch differs by gender and culture. Studies indicate that women in the United States value touch more than men, women are touched more than men, men touch others more than women do, and men may use touch to indicate power or dominance.

People from different countries also handle touch differently. Sidney Jourard determined the rates of touch per hour among adults of various cultures. Adults in Puerto Rico touched 180 times per hour; those in Paris touched about 110 times an hour; those in Gainesville, Florida, touched 2 times per hour; and those in London touched once per hour.

In touch-oriented cultures, such as those of Italy, Spain, Portugal, and Greece, both males and females may walk arm-in-arm or hold hands. In Mexico, Eastern Europe, and the Arab world, embracing and kissing is common. However, in Hong Kong, initiating any physical contact in public should be avoided.

Some cultures also restrict where touching may occur on the body. In India and Thailand, it is offensive to touch the head because it is considered sacred. In Korea, young people do not touch the shoulders of elders.

Your clothing and other adornments, such as jewelry, hairstyle, cosmetics, shoes, glasses, tattoos, and body piercings, communicate to others your age, gender, status, role, socioeconomic class, group memberships, personality, and relation to the opposite sex. Such cues also indicate the historical period, the time of day, and the climate. Clothing and other artifacts also communicate your self-concept or the type of person you believe you are. Conforming to current styles has been correlated to a person's desire to be accepted and liked by others.

Individuals believe that clothing is important in forming first impressions. Clothing has been shown to affect others' impressions of our status and personality traits. For this reason, most advise that you should pay attention to dressing professionally in business situations because it can affect your credibility, attractiveness, and perceived ability

to fit within a professional culture. This rule can be particularly important when dealing with international audiences because they tend to make assumptions about another person's education level, status, and income based upon dress alone. Therefore, those who are interested in careers in international business should follow Molloy's rules for business dress: Clothing should be conservative, upper class, and traditional.

2-2d Understanding Nonverbal Messages

Nonverbal messages have characteristics that all communicators should consider.

- **Nonverbal messages cannot be avoided.** Both written and spoken words convey ideas in addition to the ideas contained in the words used. All actions—and even the lack of action—have meaning to those who observe them.

- **Nonverbal messages can have different meanings for different people.** If a team member smiles after making a statement, one member might conclude that the speaker was trying to be funny; another might conclude that the speaker was pleased about having made such a great contribution; and another might see the smile as indicating friendliness.

- **Nonverbal messages vary between and within cultures.** Not only do nonverbal messages have different meanings from culture to culture, but men and women from the same culture typically exhibit different body language. As a rule, U.S. men make less body contact with other men, than do women with other women. Acceptable male body language might include a handshake or a pat on the back, whereas women are afforded more flexibility in making body contact with each other.

- **Nonverbal messages can be intentional or unintentional.** "You are right about that" can be intended to mean "I agree with you" or "You are right on *this* issue, but you have been wrong on all others discussed."

---

personal space the physical space immediately surrounding someone, into which any encroachment feels threatening to or uncomfortable for them

polychronic time (P-time) a time orientation associated with polychronic cultures, which tend to value interpersonal relationships

monochronic time (M-time) a time orientation associated with monochronic cultures, which value schedules

haptics the use of the sense of touch

- **Nonverbal messages can contradict the accompanying verbal message and affect whether your message is understood or believed.** The adage "actions speak louder than words" reveals much about how people perceive messages. Picture a person who says, "I'm happy to be here," but looks at the floor, talks in a weak and halting voice, and clasps their hands timidly in front of their body. Because their verbal and nonverbal messages are contradictory, their audience might not trust their words. Similarly, consider the negative effect of a sloppy personal appearance by a job candidate.

- **Nonverbal messages can receive more attention than verbal messages.** If a supervisor repeatedly glances at their smartphone for text messages or rhythmically taps a pen while making a statement, the words might not register in the employee's mind. An error in basic grammar might receive more attention than the idea that is being transmitted.

- **Nonverbal messages provide clues about the sender's background, attitudes, and motives.** For example, excessive use of big words might suggest that a person reads widely or has an above-average education. It might also suggest a need for social recognition or insecurity about their social background.

- **Nonverbal messages are influenced by the circumstances surrounding the communication.** Assume that two men, Ganesh and Jacob, are friends at work. When they are together on the job, Ganesh sometimes puts his hand on Jacob's shoulder. To Jacob, the act could mean nothing more than "We are close friends." But suppose Ganesh is a member of a committee that subsequently denies a promotion for Jacob. Afterward, the same act could mean "We are still friends," but it could also cause resentment. Because of the circumstances, the same act could now mean something such as "Watch the hand that pats; it can also stab."

- **Nonverbal messages can be beneficial or harmful.** Words or actions can be accompanied by nonverbal messages that help or hurt the sender's purpose. Nonverbal communications can convey such messages as "I am competent and considerate of others," or they can convey the opposite. They cannot be eliminated, but you can make them work for you instead of against you by recognizing their value and becoming more aware of them.

---

casual listening listening for pleasure, recreation, amusement, and relaxation

2-3 Listening as a Communication Skill

Despite the fact that many professionals believe, incorrectly, that business communication is about presentation and not interaction, most employees spend a major part of their day listening to others. In fact, listening is our most used communication skill. In the corporate world, managers may devote more than 60 percent of their workday to listening to others.[12] Chief executives may spend as much as 75 percent of their communicating time listening.[13] Listening to supervisors, employees, customers, and colleagues commonly consumes more of employees' time than reading, writing, and speaking combined.

With smartphones, tablets, and 24/7 access to information, it is harder than ever to pay attention to something without a screen, let alone be an effective listener. But although people may be glued to their device of choice, listening is even more crucial to effective communication, and real knowledge. Learning happens not only by reading or researching; true learning comes from *sharing* ideas through conversation, which involves being fully engaged in listening, business, and life. Only then can ideas evolve, leaders lead, and teams flourish. Strategist Peter Senge emphasizes the value of developing "learning organizations" to deal with the rapid changes of a globalized world, and listening to others is a critical component of such an organization.[14]

Effective Listening Habits Pay Off in Several Ways

- ▶ Good listeners are liked by others because they satisfy the basic human needs of being heard and being wanted.

- ▶ People who listen well are able to separate fact from fiction, cope effectively with false persuasion, and avoid having others use them for personal gain.

- ▶ Effective listening leads to sensitivity and tolerance toward key individuals who are critical to the organization's success, such as employees, customers, and suppliers.

- ▶ Effective listeners are engaged and constantly learning—gaining knowledge and skills that lead to increased creativity, job performance, advancement, and satisfaction.

- ▶ Job satisfaction increases when people know what is going on, when they are heard, and when they participate in the mutual trust that develops from good communication.

Listening depends on your abilities to receive and decode both verbal and nonverbal messages. The best-devised messages and sophisticated communication systems will not work unless people on the receiving end of spoken messages actually listen.

2-3a Listening for a Specific Purpose

Individuals satisfy a variety of purposes through listening: (1) interacting socially, (2) receiving information, (3) solving problems, (4) sharing feelings with others, and (5) showing interest and resolving conflict. Listening is a more complex behavior than is typically acknowledged, with some suggesting more than two dozen different types. Each activity may call for a different style of listening or for a combination of styles.

- **Casual listening.** Listening for pleasure, recreation, amusement, and relaxation is casual listening. Some people listen to music all day long for relaxation and to mask unwanted sounds during daily routines, work periods, and daily commutes. Aspects of casual listening are as follows:

  - It provides relaxing breaks from more serious tasks and supports our emotional health.

  - It illustrates that people are selective listeners. You listen to what you want to hear. In a crowded room in which everyone seems to be talking, you can block out all the noise and engage in the conversation that you are having with someone.

  - It doesn't require much emotional or physical effort.

- **Listening for information.** Listening for information involves the search for data or material. In a lecture class, for example, the instructor usually has a strategy for guiding the class to desired goals. The instructor will probably stress several major points and use supporting evidence to prove or to reinforce them. When engaged in this type of listening, you could become so focused on recording every detail that you take copious notes with no organization. When listening for information:

  - Use an outlining process to help you capture main ideas and supporting sub-points in a logical way.

  - Watch the speaker as you listen to them, because most speakers exhibit a set of mannerisms composed of gestures and vocal inflections to indicate the degree of importance or seriousness that they attach to portions of their presentations.

- **Intensive listening.** When you listen to obtain information, solve problems, or persuade or dissuade (as in arguments), you are engaged in intensive listening. Intensive listening involves greater use of your analytical ability to proceed through problem-solving steps. When listening intensively:

  - Become a good summarizer.

  - Trace the development of the discussion, and then move from there to your own analysis.

- **Active listening.** Active listening requires that the listener fully concentrates, understands, responds, and then remembers what is being said. It is useful when receiving important instructions, resolving conflict, and providing or receiving critical feedback. When listening actively:

  - Observe the speaker's behavior and body language. Having the ability to interpret a person's body language lets the listener develop a more accurate understanding of the speaker's message.

  - Paraphrase the speaker's words. In doing so, the listener is not necessarily agreeing with the speaker—simply stating what was said to ensure understanding.

  - Ask questions as needed to ensure accurate understanding.

- **Empathetic listening.** *Empathy* occurs when a person attempts to share another's feelings or emotions. Counselors attempt to use empathetic listening in dealing with their clients, and good friends listen empathetically to each other. Empathy is a valuable trait developed by people skilled in interpersonal relations. When you take the time to listen to another, the courtesy is usually returned. When listening empathetically:

  - Avoid preoccupation with your own problems. Talking too much and giving strong nonverbal signals of disinterest destroy others' desire to talk.

  - Remember that total empathy can never be achieved simply because no two people are exactly alike. The more similar our experiences, however, the better the opportunity to put ourselves in the other person's shoes. Listening with empathy involves some genuine tact along with other good listening habits.

---

listening for information listening that involves the search for data or material

intensive listening listening to obtain information, solve problems, or persuade or dissuade

active listening requires that the listener fully concentrates, understands, responds, and then remembers what is being said

empathetic listening listening to others in an attempt to share their feelings or emotions

You might have to combine listening intensively, actively, and empathetically in some situations. Performance appraisal interviews, disciplinary conferences, and other sensitive discussions between supervisors and employees require listening intensively and actively to gain an accurate understanding of the message and background, as well as to understand feelings and preconceived points of view.

2-3b Bad Listening Habits

Most of us have developed bad listening habits in one or more of the following areas:

- **Faking attention.** Have you ever been introduced to someone only to realize 30 seconds later that you missed the name? We can look directly at a person, nod, smile, and *pretend* to be listening.

- **Allowing disruptions.** We welcome disruptions of almost any sort when we are engaged in somewhat difficult listening. The next time someone enters your classroom or meeting room, notice how almost everyone in the room turns away from the speaker, and the topic, to observe the latecomer.

- **Over listening.** When we attempt to record many details in writing or in memory, we can *over listen* and miss the speaker's major points.

- **Stereotyping.** We make spontaneous judgments about others based on such issues as appearances, mannerisms, dress, and speech delivery. If a speaker doesn't meet our standards in these areas, we simply turn off our listening and assume the speaker can't have much to say.

- **Dismissing subjects as uninteresting.** People tend to use disinterest as a rationale for not listening. Unfortunately, the decision is usually made before the topic is ever introduced. A good way to lose an instructor's respect when you have to miss class is to ask, "Are we going to do anything important in class today?"

- **Failing to observe nonverbal aids.** To listen effectively, you must observe the speaker. Facial expressions and body motions always accompany speech and contribute a lot to messages.

Many bad listening habits develop simply because the speed of spoken messages is far slower than our ability to receive and process them. Normal speaking speeds are between 100 and 150 words a minute. The human ear can actually distinguish words in speech in excess of 500 words a minute, and many people read at speeds well beyond 500 words a minute. Finally, our minds process thoughts at thousands of words per minute.

A second reason for poor listening habits is that it takes effort to listen, as opposed to simply hearing. We need to take steps to concentrate on what we are hearing to eliminate distractions, and to take notes, and engage in active listening techniques as described in the box "Suggestions for Effective Listening" in the next section.

2-4 Group Communication

Although much of your spoken communication in business will occur in one-to-one relationships, another frequent spoken-communication activity will likely occur when you participate in groups, committees, and teams.

2-4a Increasing Focus on Groups

In recent years, developments among U.S. businesses have shifted attention away from the employment of traditional organizational subunits as the only mechanisms for achieving organizational goals and toward the increased use of groups.

- **Flat organizational structures.** Many businesses today have downsized and eliminated layers of management. Companies implementing Total Quality Management programs are reorganizing to distribute the decision-making power throughout the organization. The trend is to eliminate functional or departmental boundaries. Instead, work is reorganized in cross-disciplinary teams that perform broad core processes (e.g., product development and sales generation) and not narrow tasks (e.g., forecasting market demand for a particular product).

In a flat organizational structure, communicating across the organization chart (among cross-disciplinary teams) becomes more important than communicating up and down in a top-heavy hierarchy. An individual can take on an expanded **role** as important tasks are assumed. This role can involve power and authority that surpass the individual's **status**, or formal position in the organizational chart. Much of the communication involves face-to-face meetings with team members rather than numerous, time-consuming "handoffs" as the product moves methodically from one department to another. Companies such as IKEA, the Swedish furniture manufacturer and retailer, are using flat organizational structures within stores to build an employee attitude of job involvement and ownership.

---

role tasks employees assume that can involve power and authority that surpass their formal position in the organizational chart

status one's formal position in the organizational chart

Monkey Business Images/Shutterstock

Although much research has been conducted in the area of group size, no optimal number of members has been identified. Groups of five to seven members are thought to be best for decision-making and problem-solving tasks. An odd number of members is often preferred because decisions are possible without tie votes.

positions at the top of organizations, and for esteem in their professions. Such competition is a healthy sign of the human desire to succeed, and in terms of economic behavior, competition is fundamental to the private enterprise system. At the same time, when excessive competition replaces the cooperation necessary for success, communication can be diminished, if not eliminated.

Just as you want to look good in the eyes of your coworkers and supervisors, units within organizations want to look good to one another. This attitude can cause behavior to take a competitive form, or a "win/lose" philosophy. When excessive competition has a negative influence on the performance of the organization, everyone loses.

Although competition is appropriate and desirable in many situations, many companies have taken steps through reward systems and open communication and information to reduce competition and increase cooperation. Cooperation is more likely when the competitors (individuals or groups within an organization)

- **Heightened focus on cooperation.** Competition has been a characteristic way of life in U.S. companies. Organizations and individuals compete for a greater share of scarce resources, for a limited number of

Suggestions for Effective Listening

You can enhance the effectiveness of your face-to-face listening by following these suggestions:

▶ **Minimize environmental and mental distractions. Take time to listen.** Move to a quiet area where you are not distracted by noise or other conversation. Avoid becoming so preoccupied with what you will say next that you fail to listen.

▶ **Get in touch with the speaker.** Maintain an open mind while attempting to understand the speaker's background, prejudices, and points of view. Listen for emotionally charged words and watch for body language, gestures, facial expressions, and eye movements as clues to the speaker's underlying feelings.

▶ **Use your knowledge of speakers to your advantage.** Some people seem to run on and on with details before making the point. With this kind of speaker, you must anticipate the major point but not pay much attention to details. Other speakers give conclusions first and perhaps omit support for them. In this case, you must ask questions to obtain further information.

▶ **Let the speaker know you are actively involved.** Show genuine interest by remaining physically and mentally involved. Provide nonverbal feedback by maintaining eye contact and smiling or nodding at statements with which you agree. Signal that you understand with such verbal messages as "I see," "go on," and "I agree."

▶ **Do not interrupt the speaker.** Try to understand the speaker's full meaning, and wait patiently for an indication of when you should enter the conversation.

▶ **Ask reflective questions that assess understanding.** Simply restate in your own words what you think the other person has said. This paraphrasing will reinforce what you have heard and allow the speaker to correct any misunderstanding or add clarification.

▶ **Use probing prompts to direct the speaker.** Use probing statements or questions to help the speaker define the issue more concretely and specifically.

▶ **Use lag time wisely.** Listening carefully should be your primary focus; however, you can think ahead at times as well. Making written or mental notes allows you to provide useful feedback when the opportunity arises. If you cannot take notes during the conversation, record important points as soon as possible so you can summarize the speaker's key points.

Exhibit 2.1 | Four Interpersonal Communication Styles

Aggressive	Verbally attacking someone else; being controlling, provoking, and maybe even physically intimidating or violent. *Example: "What is wrong with you? All you ever think about is yourself!"*
Passive-Aggressive	Retaliating in an indirect manner rather than expressing negative feelings, such as anger, directly. This type of behavior may cause confusion because the person on the receiving end may feel "stung" but can't be sure how or why. *Example: An employee who is angry about their low salary may make negative comments on Twitter about the company rather than discuss the issue with their supervisor.*
Passive	Withdrawing in an attempt to avoid confrontation. Passive people let others think for them, make decisions for them, and tell them what to do. *Example: Yolanda feels a colleague is treating her poorly. She feels resentful but doesn't express it because she believes her colleague will not listen to her concerns anyway. She is likely to feel down, perhaps even depressed, and avoids interacting with her colleague.*
Assertive	Knowing what you feel and what you want. This behavior involves expressing feelings and needs directly and honestly without violating the rights of others. Assertive people accept responsibility for their feelings and actions. *Example: "I was angry when you didn't show up for our meeting. I know that your time is as valuable to you as my time is to me. I would appreciate it if in the future you would call me if you know you can't make an appointment or if you are going to be late."*

understand and appreciate others' importance and functions. This cooperative spirit is characterized as a "win/win" philosophy. One person's success is not achieved at the expense or exclusion of another. Groups identify a solution that everyone finds satisfactory and is committed to achieving. Reaching this mutual understanding requires a high degree of trust and effective interpersonal skills, particularly empathetic and intensive listening skills, and the willingness to communicate long enough to agree on an action plan acceptable to everyone (refer to Exhibit 2.1 for a discussion of interpersonal styles).

2-4b Characteristics of Effective Groups

Groups form for synergistic effects. Through pooling their efforts, members can achieve more collectively than they could individually. At the same time, the social nature of groups contributes to the individual as well. Although communication in small groups leads to decisions that are generally superior to individual decisions, the group process can motivate members, improve thinking, and assist attitude changes.

As you consider the following factors of group communication, try to visualize your relationship to the groups to which you have belonged, such as in school, religious organizations, athletics, and social activities.

- **Common goals.** In effective groups, participants share a common goal, interest, or benefit. This focus on goals allows members to overcome individual differences of opinion and to negotiate acceptable solutions.

- **Role perception.** People who are invited to join groups have perceptions of how the group should operate and what it should achieve. In addition, each member has a self-concept that dictates how they will behave. Those known to be aggressive will attempt to be confrontational and forceful; those who like to be known as moderates will behave in moderate ways by settling arguments rather than initiating them. In successful groups, members play a variety of necessary roles and seek to eliminate nonproductive ones.

- **Longevity.** Groups formed for short-term tasks, such as arranging a dinner and program, will spend more time on the task than on maintenance. However, groups formed for long-term assignments, such as an accounting team auditing a major corporation, may devote much effort to maintenance goals. Maintenance includes division of duties, scheduling, recordkeeping, reporting, and assessing progress.

- **Size.** The smaller the group, the more its members have the opportunity to communicate with each other. Large groups often inhibit communication because the opportunity to speak and interact is limited. However, when broad input is desired, large groups can be good if steps are taken to ensure that there is effective communication. Interestingly, large groups generally divide into smaller groups for maintenance purposes, even when the large group is task-oriented.

- **Status.** Some group members will appear to have higher ranking than others. Consider a group in which the chief executive of an organization is a member. When the chief executive speaks, members agree. When members speak, they tend to direct their remarks to the one with high status—the chief executive. People are inclined to communicate with peers as their equals, but they tend to speak upward to their supervisor and downward to lower-level employees. In general, groups require balance in status and expertise.

- **Group norms.** A **norm** is a standard or average behavior. All groups possess norms. An instructor's behavior helps establish classroom norms. If some students are allowed to arrive late for class, others will begin to arrive late. If some are allowed to talk during lectures, the norm will be for students to talk. People conform to norms because conformity is easy, and nonconformity is difficult and uncomfortable. Conformity leads to acceptance by other group members and creates communication opportunities.

- **Leadership.** The performance of groups depends on several factors, but none is more important than leadership. Some hold the mistaken view that leaders are not necessary when an organization moves to a group concept. The role of leaders changes substantially, but they still have an important part to play. The ability of a group leader to work toward task goals, while contributing to the development of group and individual goals, is often critical to group success. Leadership activities may be shared among several participants, and leadership may also be rotated, formally or informally. As part of the group, the leader can affect the establishment of norms by determining who can speak and when, encouraging contribution, and providing motivation for effective group activity.[15]

2-4c Group Roles

Groups are made up of members who play a variety of roles, both positive and negative. Negative roles detract from the group's purposes and include those in the following list.

In healthy groups, members may fulfill multiple roles, which rotate as the need arises. Negative roles are extinguished as the group communicates openly about its goals, strategies, and expectations. The opinions and viewpoints of all members are encouraged and expected.

Negative Group Roles

- ▶ **Isolator**—one who is physically present but fails to participate
- ▶ **Dominator**—one who speaks too often and too long
- ▶ **Free rider**—one who does not do their fair share of the work
- ▶ **Detractor**—one who constantly criticizes and complains
- ▶ **Digresser**—one who deviates from the group's purpose
- ▶ **Airhead**—one who is never prepared
- ▶ **Socializer**—one who pursues only the social aspect of the group

A list of positive group roles can be found as follows:

Positive Group Roles

- ▶ **Facilitator (also known as *gatekeeper*)**—one who makes sure everyone gets to talk and be heard
- ▶ **Harmonizer**—one who keeps tensions low
- ▶ **Record keeper**—one who maintains records of events and activities and informs members
- ▶ **Reporter**—one who assumes responsibility for preparing materials for submission
- ▶ **Leader**—one who assumes a directive role

2-4d From Groups to Teams

Some use the terms *group* and *team* interchangeably; others distinguish between them. The major distinction between a group and a team is in members' attitudes and level of commitment. A team is typified by a clear identity and a high level of commitment on the part of members. A variety of strategies has been used for organizing workers into teams:

- A **task force** is generally given a single goal and a limited time to achieve it.

- A **quality assurance team**, or *quality circle*, focuses on product or service quality, and projects can be either short or long term.

norm a standard or average behavior

task force a team of workers that is generally given a single goal and a limited time to achieve it

quality assurance team a team that focuses on product or service quality; projects can be either short or long term

A growing body of research confirms that when people work together, smartly, it can unleash energy that boosts creativity, productivity, engagement, communication, and efficiency.

"Each individual has unique gifts, and talents and skills," says John J. Murphy, a specialist in business transformation and author of *Pulling Together: 10 Rules for High-Performance Teamwork*.[16] "When we bring them to the table and share them for a common purpose, it can give companies a real competitive advantage."

1. Great ideas don't come from lone geniuses.

   "Behind every genius is a team," says Murphy. "When people play off each other's skills and knowledge, they can create solutions that are practical and useful."

   That's why Murphy recommends the first thing you need to do is to ditch the too-pervasive idol mentality. "Tom Brady *is* all that, but remember: he doesn't win Super Bowls by himself."

2. Diverse perspectives help you come up with winning innovations.

   According to Frans Johansson, author of *The Medici Effect*, some of the most innovative ideas happen at "the intersection"—the place where ideas from different industries and cultures collide.[17]

   "Most people think success comes from surrounding yourself with others that are like you," says Johansson. "But true success and breakthrough innovation involves discomfort. Discomfort pushes you to grow. This is where difference of experience, opinion, and perspective come in. Diversity is a well-documented pathway to unlocking new opportunities, overcoming new challenges, and gaining new insights."

   A recent report from the consulting firm McKinsey & Company backs this up. It found teams made up of members from diverse backgrounds (gender, age, ethnicity, etc.) are more creative and perform better by up to 35 percent, compared to more homogeneous teams.[18] Instead of looking at an issue from your individual vantage point, you get a 360-degree picture, which can lead to an exponential increase in ideas.

   Research from Tufts University suggests that just being exposed to diversity can shift the way you think. A study on a diverse mock jury found that interacting with individuals who are different forces people to be more open minded and to expect that reaching consensus will take effort.[19]

3. Teamwork can make you happier.

   The Atlassian surveyed more than 1,000 team members across a range of industries and found that when honest feedback, mutual respect, and personal openness were encouraged, team members were 80 percent more likely to report higher emotional well-being.[20] Having happy employees is a worthwhile goal in itself, but the company benefits too. Research from the University of Warwick in England suggests happy employees are up to 20 percent more productive than unhappy employees.[21]

4. When you work in a team, you grow as an individual.

   "By sharing information and essentially cross-training each other, each individual member of the team can flourish," says Murphy. You might discover new concepts from colleagues with different experiences. You can also learn from someone else's mistakes, which helps you sidestep future errors.

   You might even learn something new about yourself, says Susan McDaniel, PhD, a psychologist at the University of Rochester Medical Center and one of the guest editors of "The Science of Teamwork."[22]

   "We all have blind spots about our behaviors and strengths that we may be unaware of, and feedback from a team member can expose them," she says. Recognizing these strengths and addressing the weaknesses can make you a better team member and even a better person. "Maybe working in a team you'll discover you could be a better listener. That's a skill you can grow in and then take home and use to improve your family interactions," McDaniel points out.

5. Sharing the workload eases burnout.

   A recent Gallup study of nearly 7,500 full-time employees found that 23 percent of employees feel burned out at work very often or always.[23] Another 44 percent say they sometimes feel this way. What helps? Sharing the load.

   Team members can provide emotional support to each other because they often understand the demands and stress of completing work even better than managers, says Ben Wigert, lead researcher for Gallup's workplace management practice.

6. **Dividing the work lets you grow your skills.**

   Changes in technology and increased globalization mean that organizations are facing problems so complex that a single individual simply can't possess all the necessary knowledge to solve them, says Wigert. When team members use their unique skills to shine in their own roles, it creates an environment based on mutual respect and cooperation that benefits the whole group, notes Murphy.

7. **Recognition from other team members can improve your productivity.**

   The 2014 TINYpulse Employee Engagement and Organizational Culture Report surveyed more than 200,000 employees.[24] Participants reported that having the respect of their peers was the number one reason they go the extra mile at work.

8. **Working in a team helps you take risks that pay off.**

   When you work alone, you might be hesitant to put your neck on the line. What if an idea you suggest falls flat? When you work on a team, you know you have the support of the entire group to fall back on in case of failure. That security typically allows teams to take the kind of risks that create "Eureka!" ideas.

   But here's one place where size does matter. The most disruptive ideas often come from small teams, suggests recent research in the journal *Nature*, possibly because larger teams argue more, which can get in the way of coming up with those big ideas.[25]

   Wharton Business School researchers also discovered that small is the secret to success: they found that two-person teams took 36 minutes to build a Lego figure while four-person teams took 52 minutes to finish—more than 44 percent longer.[26]

   There's no definitive ideal small team size, but consider following former Amazon CEO Jeff Bezos' 2 Pizza Rule: no matter how large your company gets, teams shouldn't be larger than what two pizzas can feed.[27]

9. **When you work in a team, you'll feel less stressed.**

   If your team has good energy—you encourage and inspire each other, and you have fun together—you'll feel less stressed, says Murphy. "Studies show that stress makes us stupid and leads us to make more mistakes," says Murphy.

10. **Good communication boosts your creativity.**

    When people with different perspectives come together in group brainstorms, innovative ideas can rise to the surface—with one caveat. Research shows this can only happen when communication within the team is open and collaborative, notes Wigert. The most creative solutions can only come up when there's a level of trust that lets team members ask "stupid" questions, propose out-there ideas, and receive constructive criticism.

Source: Middleton, T. (2021). The importance of teamwork (as proven by science). Retrieved January 20, 2022 from https://www.atlassian.com/blog/teamwork/the-importance-of-teamwork.

- A **cross-functional team** brings together employees from various departments to solve a variety of problems, such as productivity issues, contract estimations and planning, and multidepartment difficulties.

- A **product development team** concentrates on innovation and the development cycle of new products and is usually cross-functional in nature.

Whereas chain of command is still at work in formal organizational relationships and responsibilities, team structures unite people from varying portions of the organization. Work teams are typically given the authority to act on their conclusions, although the level of authority varies, depending on the organization and the purpose of the team. Typically, the group supervisor retains some responsibilities, some decisions are made completely by the team, and the rest are made jointly.

Merely placing workers into a group does not make them a functional team. A group must go through a developmental process to begin to function as a team. The four stages of team development include the following:

1. **Forming**—becoming acquainted with each other and the assigned task

> **cross-functional team** a team that brings together employees from various departments to solve a variety of problems
>
> **product development team** usually cross-functional in nature; a group of employees who concentrate on innovation and the development cycle of new products
>
> **forming** stage one of team development, in which team members become acquainted with each other and the assigned task

Exhibit 2.2 | Stages of Virtual Team Formation

Forming	Members begin to develop codes of virtual conduct, to review software and hardware requirements, and to raise and answer questions about how they will use technology to accomplish the group's goals. Some groups arrange a face-to-face meeting before going online, especially when members do not know each other, and the project or work is complex and requires a high degree of interaction.
Storming	Members must deal with the added complication imposed by the virtual environment. In addition to expressing opinions and debating substantive issues, the group may encounter technical problems and different levels in member expertise. For example, what should the group do if technical systems are not compatible or if some members are technically unskilled or apprehensive about using advanced technology? Virtual groups must solve technical problems if they hope to address task-related issues and move beyond this stage.
Norming	Virtual groups define members' roles, resolve conflicts, solve most technical problems, and accept the group's norms for interaction. They will be ready to focus on the task. They will also resolve issues related to differences in time, distance, technology, member cultures, and organizational environments.
Performing	Members engage in ongoing virtual interaction and encourage equal participation by all members. They have overcome or adjusted to technical roadblocks and have become comfortable with the virtual media used by the group.
Adjourning	A group may rely on virtual communication to blunt the separation anxiety that comes with the adjourning stage. If a group has matured and performed well, its members will be reluctant to give up relationships with colleagues. Even if a virtual group no longer operates in an official capacity, members may continue to use technological media to consult and interact with one another.

Source: I. N. Engleberg and D. R. Wynn. (2012). *Working in Groups: Communication Principles and Strategies*, 6th ed. Pearson.

2. **Storming**—dealing with conflicting personalities, goals, and ideas

3. **Norming**—developing strategies and activities that promote goal achievement

4. **Performing**—reaching the optimal performance level

5. **Adjourning**—concluding the project

For a variety of reasons, teams are often unable to advance through all four stages of development. Even long-term teams might never reach the optimal performing stage, settling instead for the acceptable performance of the norming stage. Studies indicate that virtual teams require additional attention to the planning and use of technology, as well as to members' attitudes and knowledge of such technology. Refer to Exhibit 2.2 for a discussion of the stages of virtual team formation.

Research into what makes workplace teams effective indicates that training is beneficial for participants in such areas as problem-solving, goal-setting, conflict resolution, risk-taking, active listening, and recognizing the interests and achievements of others. Participants need to be able to satisfy one another's basic needs for belonging, personal recognition, and support. Team members at the performing stage of team development exhibit the following behaviors:[28]

- **Commitment.** They are focused on the mission, values, goals, and expectations of the team and the organization.

- **Cooperation.** They have a shared sense of purpose, mutual gain, and teamwork.

- **Communication.** They know that information must flow smoothly between top management and workers. Team members are willing to face confrontation and unpleasantness when necessary.

- **Contribution.** All members share their different backgrounds, skills, and abilities with the team.

Teams have existed for hundreds of years throughout many countries and cultures. Teams are more flexible than larger organizational groupings because they can be assembled, deployed, refocused, and disbanded more quickly, usually in ways that enhance rather than disrupt more permanent structures and processes. Organizational changes are often necessary, however, because support must be in place for performance evaluation, recognition, communication, and training systems. Strategies for bringing about needed change might include arranging site visits to similar organizations that already have teams, bringing in a successful team to speak to the organization, and bringing in consultants to discuss the team development process.

storming stage two of team development, in which team members deal with conflicting personalities, goals, and ideas

norming stage three of team development, in which team members develop strategies and activities that promote goal achievement

performing stage four of team development, in which team members reach the optimal performance level

adjourning now widely accepted as stage five of team development, involves the conclusion of the project and team members going their separate ways, though they may continue to keep in touch

2-4e Decision Making

One of the biggest uses of groups or teams is decision making. Groups can be useful in making decisions because more people potentially bring more information to the task. In addition, groups tend to process the information they have more thoroughly through discussion. For effective decision making, groups should ensure that the process they use is a productive one. Although groups can be useful for decision making, they also face some challenges.

Groups tend to make better decisions if the pattern for doing so is explicitly identified so that the group can structure its discussion. Effective group decision making includes the following steps:

1. **Analyze the decision to be made by adequately assessing the present situation.** To analyze something is to break it down into its smaller components. Research suggests that how a group analyzes the information can dramatically affect the group's decision. Having too little evidence—or none—is one of the reasons groups sometimes fail to analyze the present situation accurately. Even if group members do have ample evidence, it may prove to be defective if they have not applied the proper tests to ensure the quality of the evidence. Whether the information a group has is good or bad, group members will tend to use the information if all members receive it, group members discuss it, and at least one group member champions the information. Just having information does not mean the group will use it well. Reasoning is the process of drawing conclusions from information. Flawed reasoning, like flawed data, can contribute to a bad decision.

2. **Seek input from each member.** One primary reason to work in groups and teams is the opportunity to tap the knowledge base of many people rather than just a few individuals. Research by John Oetzel documents what makes intuitive sense: Groups make better decisions when there is more equal participation in the discussion. Conversely, if several members dominate the conversation, decision quality suffers. Group members who believe they did not have an opportunity to voice their opinions and share information with others will not perceive the decision to have been reached fairly.

3. **Identify and clarify the goals of the decision.** After assessing the current situation, the group should identify its objectives. A group uncertain about its task will have difficulty making a quality decision. If its goal is clear, a group can begin to identify alternatives and then weight each as to its ability to meet that goal. A group that has not clearly spelled out what it hopes to accomplish by making a decision has no means of assessing the effectiveness of the decision.

4. **Identify multiple options.** The greater the number of alternatives a group generates, the greater the likelihood it will make a good decision. To identify good options, the group should review the information that it has gathered. Poor decision making occurs when groups pounce on the first or second option identified and fail to consider a wide range of possible options before making a decision.

5. **Review the pros and cons of the options identified.** A group must do more than identify alternatives; it should also assess the positive and negative implications of each alternative before making a decision. The pros and cons of each option should be based on the information the group has identified. A group that is so eager to make a decision that it does not take time to consider the pros and cons of its actions is setting itself up to make a bad decision. A critical error by ineffective groups is failing to consider the consequences of their decision before they make it.

6. **Select the best alternative.** The option selected should potentially have a maximum positive outcome with minimal negative consequences. A group is more likely to select the best alternative if it has carefully assessed the situation, considered group goals, identified several choices, and noted the positive and negative implications of each. Groups sometimes tend to make overly risky decisions, so it is important to critically analyze each option for possible negative implications.

A variety of methods can be used to make a final decision after the alternatives have been narrowed and weighed by the group. Knowing these methods can help the group select the best one for the situation.

- **Decision by Expert in Group:** One person in a group may seem to be the best informed about the issue, and members can turn to this person to make the choice. This expert may or may not be a group's designated leader. Deferring to an expert from within a group may be an efficient way to make a decision, but if there is not adequate discussion, the group may not be satisfied with the outcome.

- **Decision by Expert Outside Group:** A group may decide that none of its members has the credibility, knowledge, or wisdom to make a particular decision, and it may feel unable or unwilling to do so. Members can turn to someone outside the group who has authority to make a decision. Although an outside expert may

Exhibit 2.3 | Advantages and Disadvantages of Decision-Making Methods

Method	Advantages	Disadvantages
Decision by Expert: Group defers to the member who has the most expertise or experience or to someone outside the group with authority to make decisions	• Decision is made quickly • Uses the expertise of a knowledgeable source of information	• Group members may not be satisfied with the decision • The expert could be wrong
Averaging Individual Rankings or Ratings: Group members rank or rate possible outcomes, and the alternative with the highest ranking or best rating is selected	• Uses a democratic process that taps all group members' thinking • Useful when the group needs to assess where it stands on an issue	• The average ranking or rating may be an alternative that no group member supports • Group loses the opportunity for give-and-take discussion
Majority Rule: Decision is made by the majority of group members	• Often perceived as a fair way of making decisions • Can be an efficient way of making a decision	• Those who do not support the majority opinion may feel left out of the process • Group may lose cohesiveness
Decision by Consensus: Through discussion, group members reach a decision that all members can support	• Group members are more likely to be satisfied with the outcome • Group members are more likely to participate in implementing a decision that all members support	• Takes time • Takes skill

make a fine decision, a group that gives up its decision-making power to one person loses the advantages of the greater input and variety of approaches that come from being a group in the first place.

- **Averaging Individual Rankings or Ratings:** Group members can be asked to rank or rate possible alternatives. After the group averages the rankings or ratings, it selects the alternative with the highest average. This method of making decisions can be a useful way to start discussions and to see where the group stands on an issue. However, it is not the best way to make a final decision, because it does not take full advantage of the give-and-take of group discussion.

- **Majority Rule:** This is the most common method of group decision making because of its speed and efficiency. But there are several drawbacks. First, it can leave an unsatisfied minority. Second, a group that makes a decision on the basis of majority rule may sacrifice decision quality and group cohesiveness for efficiency.

- **Decision by Consensus:** Consensus occurs when all group members can support a course of action. This decision-making method is time-consuming and can be frustrating, but members are usually satisfied with

the decision. If group members must also implement the solution, this method works well. To reach a decision by consensus, group members must listen and respond to individual viewpoints and manage conflicts that arise. Consensus is facilitated when group members are able to remain focused on the goal, emphasize areas of agreement, and combine or eliminate alternatives identified by the group.

Exhibit 2.3 provides a summary of the different decision-making methods.

2-5 Meeting Management

Meetings are essential for communication in organizations. They present opportunities to acquire and disseminate valuable information, develop skills, and make favorable impressions on colleagues, supervisors, and direct reports. U.S. businesses spend more money on conducting meetings than any other country in the world, and they also spend more time in meetings than people of other countries.[29]

Workers frequently have negative attitudes toward meetings because they are perceived as a waste of time. Studies support this opinion, revealing that as much as one-third of the time spent in meetings is unproductive.

fizkes/Shutterstock

Face-to-face meetings continue to be a frequently used format in most organizations.

Negative attitudes toward meetings can be changed when meetings are conducted properly, giving attention to correct procedures and behavior. Successful meetings don't just happen; rather, they occur by design. Careful planning and attention to specific guidelines can help ensure the success of your meetings, whether they are conducted in a face-to-face format or electronically.

2-5a Face-to-Face Meetings

Face-to-face meetings offer distinct advantages and are appropriate in the following situations:[30]

- When you need the richest nonverbal cues, including body, voice, proximity, and touch

- When the issues are especially sensitive

- When the participants don't know one another

- When establishing group rapport and relationships is crucial

- When the participants can be in the same place at the same time

Face-to-face meetings can be enhanced with the use of various visual tools such as flip charts, handouts, and electronic slide decks. Although face-to-face meetings provide a rich nonverbal context and direct human contact, they also have certain limitations. In addition to the obvious logistical issues of schedules and distance, face-to-face meetings may be dominated by overly vocal, quick-to-speak, and high-status members.

2-5b Electronic Meetings

Electronic meetings allow companies to reduce travel budgets, save professional time, and minimize the environmental impact caused by travel. Electronic meetings are common for those working in virtual teams. A variety of technologies is available to facilitate electronic meetings. Participants may communicate with one another through telephones, computers, or video broadcast equipment using groupware or meeting management software applications, such as Zoom, a cloud-based video conferencing platform that can be used for video conferencing meetings, audio conferencing, webinars, meeting recordings, and live chat. According to research conducted by Owl Labs, Zoom is the most popular video conferencing solution for companies with 500 employees or fewer and the second-most popular solution for companies with more than 500 employees, after Skype for Business. According to Zoom's S-1 filing in early 2019, more than half of *Fortune* 500 companies are using Zoom.

Electronic meetings offer certain advantages. They facilitate geographically dispersed groups because they provide the choice of meeting at different places/same time, different places/different times, same place/same time, or same place/different times. Electronic meetings also speed up meeting follow-up activities because decisions and action items can be recorded electronically. Electronic meetings also have certain limitations:[31]

- They cannot replace face-to-face contact, especially when group efforts are just beginning and when groups are trying to build group values, trust, and emotional ties.

- They can make it harder to reach consensus, because more ideas are generated, and it might be harder to interpret the strength of other members' commitment to their proposals.

- The success of same-time meetings is dependent on all participants having excellent keyboarding skills to engage in rapid-fire, in-depth discussion. This limitation might be overcome as the use of voice input systems becomes more prevalent.

2-5c Suggestions for Effective Meetings

Whether you engage in face-to-face or electronic meetings, observing the following guidelines can help ensure that your meetings are productive:

- **Identify the purpose of the meeting.** Meetings typically have various purposes: to inform, to gather information, and to make decisions. Consider whether sending an email would be a better option as a channel choice. Be wary of meetings that have become "routine." Are you meeting simply because "it's time to have a meeting" or is there a need for a meeting for decision making or other key purposes?

Agenda for [name of group] **Meeting**
Prepared on [date agenda created]
By [*name of author of agenda*]

Attendees: [those invited to attend, often in alphabetical order]

Date and time of meeting:

Location of meeting:

Subject: [major issues to be discussed or purpose of meeting]

Agenda items:

1. Call to order

2. Routine business [procedural or administrative matters]   (10–15 minutes)
   (a) Approval of agenda for this meeting
   (b) Reading and approval of minutes of last meeting
   (c) Committee reports

3. Old business [unfinished matters from previous meeting]   (15–20 minutes)
   (a) Discussion of issue(s) carried over from previous meeting
   (b) Issue(s) arising from decision(s) made at previous meeting

4. New business   (20–25 minutes)
   (a) Most important issue
   (b) Next most important issue
   (c) Other issues in decreasing order of importance
   (d) Business from the floor not included on the agenda [only as
       time permits; otherwise, these issues should be addressed in the
       next meeting]

5. Adjournment

- **Limit meeting length and frequency.** Any meeting held for longer than an hour, or more frequently than once a month should be scrutinized. Ask yourself whether the meeting is necessary. Perhaps the purpose can be achieved in another way, such as email, instant messaging, or telephone.

- **Make satisfactory arrangements.** Select a date and time convenient for the majority of expected participants. For face-to-face meetings, plan the meeting site with consideration for appropriate seating for attendees, media equipment, temperature and lighting, and necessary supplies. For electronic meetings, check hardware and software and connectivity components.

- **Distribute the agenda well in advance.** The agenda is a meeting outline that includes important information: date, beginning and ending times, place, topics to be discussed, and responsibilities of those involved. Having the agenda prior to the meeting allows participants to know what is expected of them. A sample agenda template is provided in Model Document 2.1.

- **Encourage participation.** Although it is certainly easier for one person to make decisions, the quality of decision making is often improved by involving the team. Rational decision making may begin with **brainstorming**, that is, the generation of many ideas by team members. Brainstormed ideas can then be discussed and ranked, followed by some form of voting.

- **Maintain order.** An organized democratic process ensures that the will of the majority prevails; the minority is heard; and group goals are achieved as expeditiously as possible. Proper parliamentary procedure may be followed in formal meetings, as outlined in sources such as *Robert's Rules of Order* and *Jones' Parliamentary Procedure at a Glance*. For less formal

agenda a meeting outline that includes important information (e.g., date, beginning and ending times, place, topics to be discussed, and responsibilities of those involved)

brainstorming the generation of many ideas by team members

meetings, the use of parliamentary procedure may not be necessary to ensure effective contribution by attendees.

- **Manage conflict.** In an autocratic organization, conflict might be avoided because employees are conditioned to be submissive. Such an environment, however, leads to smoldering resentment. On the other hand, conflict is a normal part of any team effort and can lead to creative discussion and superior outcomes. Maintaining focus on issues and not personalities helps ensure that conflict is productive rather than destructive.

- **Seek consensus.** Although unanimous agreement on decisions is an optimal outcome, total agreement cannot always be achieved. **Consensus** represents the collective opinion of the group, or the informal rule that all team members can live with at least 70 percent of what is agreed upon.

- **Prepare thorough minutes.** Minutes provide a concise record of meeting actions, ensure the tracking and follow-up of issues from previous meetings, and assist in the implementation of previously reached decisions.

2-5d Additional Considerations for Electronic Meetings

In addition to these general rules for meetings, preparing for and holding virtual meetings include some extra considerations. First, it is important that participants are knowledgeable about the use of the meeting technology, therefore, training may be required. At the beginning of the meeting, individuals should introduce themselves, particularly if a meeting tool is being used that does not provide visual access to attendees. For clarity, questions and comments should be directed to specific individuals. It is also important that noise is reduced to ensure clear reception, so smartphones and pagers should be turned off, and side conversations should be avoided. For video-conferences, participants need to be aware of their nonverbal behaviors to avoid distracting or disconcerting practices, such as tapping a pen or reviewing text messages. Because you are on camera, it is important to maintain eye contact by looking at the camera. In addition, to these general considerations, users of videoconferencing tools such as Zoom, should:

- **Mute your microphone.** It's always best to mute your microphone when you're not actively speaking. Unexpected noises from a neighbor, child or pet can cause those speaking to lose their train of thoughts. The same goes for loud typing. Taking notes is great and shows engagement and interest. Just do so quietly, and be sure to look up from time to time so that it doesn't look like you've lost your attention.

- **Control background noise to the best of your ability.** When your microphone is on and you're actively speaking or waiting to respond, try to control the background as best as you can. Sometimes traffic outside or noisy neighbors can't be avoided. Do what you have the power to do to make background noise as little of a distraction as possible. If it's really bad, you might offer to reschedule.

- **Position the camera well.** Make sure your webcam is positioned at eye-level. It can be a distraction if you've got the camera angle coming in from too low or too high. Also, be sure you're completely in the picture. It indicates that you're actively listening and engaged.

- **Be an active listener.** A major part of video conferencing etiquette is making sure you're listening and understanding what's being said. It's not unusual to have a connection lag here and there. It's not rude to ask for clarification, but it can be rude if you're really not paying attention.

- **Avoid distractions.** Home in on your meeting with singular focus. Avoid distracting yourself or other meeting attendees with notifications, unless it's to signal you've lost connection or they are doing something horribly embarrassing and are unaware. Many computers come with a "Do Not Disturb" setting or another way to silence notifications, and these can be very helpful.

- **Avoid multitasking.** This is an often-overlooked rule. Research indicates that multitasking is counterproductive and can even reduce our IQ.[32] It's best to be mindful and give your full attention to one task at a time. Ultimately, you'll retain more from the meeting, and it will be a more valuable use of everyone's time.

- **Prepare materials in advance.** Make sure you have all windows, notes, and tabs where you need them to be ahead of time. This way, you're spending as little meeting time as possible switching between windows or searching for files. Also be sure all presentation materials are downloaded ahead of time.

- **Dress the part!** You may be working from home, but it's still worth it to make the effort to dress the part for business meetings. Dressing nicely for work can help you feel professional and confident, and it also shows those you're meeting with that you care about the meeting and yourself.

- **Do not eat or drink.** It can be off-putting for people

> **consensus** represents the collective opinion of the group, or the informal rule that all team members can live with at least 70 percent of what is agreed upon

Kate Kultsevych/Shutterstock

to see or hear you eat or drink. The one exception is water or coffee, especially if you've got a packed schedule. However, definitely try to be quieter if you choose to sip (not gulp) a beverage. This is a good time to mute your microphone.[33]

For those hosting Zoom meetings, it is important to take steps to avoid hijacking attempts or what has been called "Zoombombing." In September 2021, the FBI posted a warning about such hijacking attempts after it received reports of conferences being disrupted by pornographic and/or hate images and threatening language. The hijacking attempts can occur because users of the videoconferencing services are holding the meetings on public channels, which are then shared over the internet via URLs, making them accessible to anyone. In other cases, the hijackers can sometimes guess the right URL or meeting ID for a public Zoom session, giving them access to the feed. So, to stay safe, the FBI encouraged Zoom users, especially at schools, to make their videoconferencing sessions private.[34]

"In Zoom, there are two options to make a meeting private: require a meeting password or use the waiting room feature and control the admittance of guests," the agency said.[35] "Do not share a link to a teleconference or classroom on an unrestricted publicly available social media post. Provide the link directly to specific people."

In a statement, Zoom also said: "For those hosting large, public group meetings, we strongly encourage hosts to review their settings and confirm that only the host can share their screen." This will prevent unwanted hijackers from taking over the main video feed on a public session. "For those hosting private meetings, password protections are on by default, and we recommend that users keep those protections on to prevent uninvited users from joining."[36]

Meetings are an important management tool and are useful for idea exchange. They also provide opportunities for you, as a meeting participant, to enhance your credibility and communicate impressions of power, competence, and status. Knowing how to present yourself, and your ideas, and exhibiting knowledge about correct meeting management will assist you in your career advancement.

Roman Samborskyi/Shutterstock

3 | Planning and Decision Making

Learning Objectives

After studying this chapter, you will be able to ...

3-1 Consider the contextual forces that may affect whether, how, to whom, and when a message is sent.

3-2 Identify the purpose of the message and the appropriate channel and medium.

3-3 Develop clear perceptions of the audience to enhance the impact and persuasiveness of the message, improve goodwill, and establish and maintain the credibility of the communicator.

3-4 Apply tactics for adapting messages to the audience, including those for communicating ethically and responsibly.

3-5 Recognize the importance of organization when planning the first draft.

Figure 3.1 | Process for Planning and Preparing Spoken and Written Messages

Step 1	Step 2	Step 3	Step 4	Step 5	Step 6
Consider the applicable contextual forces.	Determine the purpose and select an appropriate channel and medium.	Envision the audience.	Adapt the message to the audience's needs and concerns.	Organize the message.	Prepare the first draft.

*You will focus on the planning process (Steps 1–5) in this chapter; you will learn to prepare the message in Chapter 4 (Step 6).

In a report titled "Writing: A Ticket to Work … or a Ticket Out," the National Commission on Writing reported that two-thirds of salaried employees in large companies have some writing responsibilities, and getting hired and promoted in many industries requires strong writing abilities. Although writing is important in most managerial-level jobs, the Commission also concluded that one-third of employees in corporate America write poorly. Knowing that effective communication is tied to the corporate bottom line and that many employees can't write well, businesses are investing $3.1 billion annually to train employees to write.[1] Remedies are needed to prevent confusion, waste, errors, lost productivity, and a damaged corporate image, which are all caused by employees, customers, and clients muddling their way through unreadable messages.

As a capable communicator, you can immediately add value to your organization and positively set yourself apart from your peers, who are struggling to articulate ideas in writing and in presentations. Communication that commands attention and can be understood easily is essential for survival during the information explosion that we are experiencing today. On the job, you will be expected to process volumes of available information and shape useful messages that respond to the needs of customers or clients, coworkers and supervisors, and other key business partners. Additionally, increased use of electronic communication (email, texts, instant messages, blogs, wikis, videoconferences, etc.) will require you to be technologically savvy and capable of adapting the rules of effective communication to the demands of emerging technology.

How can you learn to plan and prepare powerful business messages? The process of systematic analysis,

organizational culture a pattern of shared basic assumptions that the group has learned as it solved its problems with external adaptation and internal integration, and which has worked well enough to be taught to new members as the correct way to perceive, think, and feel in relation to these problems

outlined in Figure 3.1, will help you develop messages that save you and your organization valuable time and resources, and portray you as a capable, energetic professional. A thorough analysis of the audience and your specific communication assignment will empower you to create a first draft efficiently and to revise and proofread your message for accuracy, conciseness, and appropriate tone.

3-1 Step 1: Consider the Applicable Contextual Forces

Chapter 1 discussed four contextual forces that may affect whether, how, to whom, and when a message is sent. These were legal and ethical constraints, diversity challenges, changing technology, and team environment. In addition to these four forces, communication patterns within an organization are a contextual force that should also be considered when planning a message. The organizational culture as well as the four dimensions of context may influence how, whether, to whom, and when a message is sent. These two issues are discussed in the sections that follow.

3-1a Organizational Culture

Organizational culture can be variously defined depending on the theoretical assumptions of the definer. One perspective of culture is that it is "a pattern of shared basic assumptions that the group learned as it solved its problems of external adaptation and internal integration and that has worked well enough to be taught to new members as the correct way to perceive, think, and feel in relation to these problems."[2] This view assumes that culture exists outside of the participants and their communication patterns. Another perspective of organizational culture is that it is created and reproduced through the communication practices of its participants, with an expansive view of what constitutes communication: symbols; artifacts, such as company logos and accepted employee dress; and structural elements, such as office layout and design. Regardless of the perspective applied to defining the phenomenon, an organization's culture determines what it can and cannot do, and to the extent of individual members' socialization into that culture, it determines what they can and cannot do as well. This is true of actions, behaviors, communicative practices, and the use and inclusion of accepted artifacts.

In other words, organizational culture affects the type, amount, and quality of communication that is generally accepted within an organization (and vice versa in the latter definition of corporate culture). The culture of a business provides part of the *context* for interpreting the meaning of everyday organizational life, as well as determining what are considered appropriate messages, the proper or expected ways to convey them, and to whom.

For example, Adobe provides staff with opportunities to be innovative. They empower their staff to explore new ideas and provide permission to fail. Through the creation of its award-winning Kickbox program, Adobe invests in its employee's potential. Through the program, Adobe gives any staff member who requests it a red cardboard box filled with stationary, snacks, and $1,000 pre-paid credit card to explore their idea, no questions asked. The man behind the project, Vice President of Creativity, Mark Randall, describes the initiative as an investment in his people. Around 1,000 employees have taken on the challenge and 23 ideas have already been granted further investment. The Kickbox exemplifies Adobe's core value of innovation, providing opportunity for company development by fostering staff's creative potential.[3]

Compare these values with the type of culture that you might find in an investment banking firm in which competition, individualism, and the drive for profits and bonuses would be key elements, and it should be easy to see how culture might affect how communication occurs and what is expected and accepted within an organization in terms of behaviors.

Theorists have constructed a variety of models to try to capture the essence of corporate culture, a discussion of which goes beyond the scope of this text. But one simple model, based on the Competing Values Framework, distinguishes four culture types, which are summarized here to illustrate the differences that might emerge in corporate cultures:

1. **Clan culture (internal focus and flexible)**—A friendly workplace where leaders act like father figures.

2. **Adhocracy culture (external focus and flexible)**—A dynamic workplace with leaders who stimulate innovation.

3. **Market culture (external focus and controlled)**—A competitive workplace where leaders are hard drivers.

4. **Hierarchy culture (internal focus and controlled)**—A structured and formalized workplace where leaders act like coordinators or administrators.

Generally speaking, the culture of business can be characterized as typically having a bias toward action, a demand for confidence, and results orientation. The culture of business can be seen in everyday office interactions. Being knowledgeable about an organization's culture can help you gauge the type and quality of communication that takes place, as well as whether you are a good match with the organization. For example, does the organization have an open-door policy or are you expected to obey the hierarchical order of management when communicating concerns? Does the office have an open floor plan or do employees have private offices? Do people wear T-shirts and shorts or suits to work every day? The first situation in each of these cases signals that the culture is less formal in terms of its expectations and communication patterns, whereas the second situation may indicate a culture that is more formal in terms of its expectations regarding punctuality and communication choices and behaviors.

3-1b Dimensions of Context

In addition to the other elements of context discussed in previous chapters and sections, there are several dimensions to context, including the physical, social, chronological, and cultural. The *physical* context or setting can influence the content and quality of interaction. For example, if you were to ask your boss for a raise, the effect of the setting might dramatically affect your chances for success. How might the following settings affect the success of such an interaction, how it might take place, or whether it should take place: In the boss's office? At a company picnic? Over lunch at a restaurant? In your work area with others observing?

The *social context* refers to the nature of the relationship between the communicators, as well as who is present. In the same situation mentioned before, imagine how the relationship between your manager and yourself might affect your request for a raise, depending on the various scenarios that follow:

- You and the manager have been friends for several years, as opposed to a situation in which you and your manager have no personal relationship.

- You are the same age as your manager, or they are 15 years older (or younger) than you.

- You and the manager have gotten along well in the past, compared to a situation in which you and the manager have been involved in an ongoing personal conflict.

The *chronological context* refers to the ways time influences interactions. For example, how might the time of day affect the quality of an interaction? How might the communicator's personal preferences regarding time affect communication and its success? Is it a busy time of year for employees and managers? Has there just been a major layoff, downsizing, or profit loss? In this last case, you might want to put off your request for a raise until conditions improve.

The *cultural context* includes both the organizational culture as well as the cultural backgrounds of the people with whom you may be communicating. A person's cultural influences also can affect the kind and quality of communication that takes place, and they can help determine approaches that will be more effective. For example, young people have different expectations than seniors; Hispanic people have different expectations than Asian people; Californians have different expectations than people from the Midwest or East Coast; and men may communicate differently than women.

Environmental factors may also affect what should be communicated and how. For example, if the economy is doing poorly, then some messages may be inappropriate or have little chance for success. If you work in a highly litigious environment or one that is strongly regulated, then constraints may exist for what you can communicate and how. Larger social, political, or historical events may affect whether certain messages are appropriate or have a chance of success. As mentioned earlier, in an economic downturn, it may be difficult, depending on the industry, to be successful at negotiating a pay raise, because the employer may feel that employees should feel lucky to simply have a job during difficult times.

As this discussion shows, context is a complex, multidimensional force that should be considered when planning a message, and determines whether it should be sent, when it should be sent, to whom, and how.

3-2 Step 2: Determine the Purpose, and Select an Appropriate Channel and Medium

To speak or write effectively, you must think through what you are trying to say and understand it thoroughly before you begin. Ask yourself why you are preparing the message and what you hope to accomplish. Is the purpose to get information, to answer a question, to accept an offer, to deny a request, or to seek support for a product or idea? Condense the answers into a brief sentence that outlines the purpose for writing or the central idea of your message. You will use the central idea to organize your message to achieve the results you desire.

The major purpose of many business messages is to have the receiver understand logical information. Informative messages are used to convey the vast amounts of information needed to complete the day-to-day operations of the business: explain instructions to employees, announce meetings and procedures, acknowledge orders, accept contracts for services, and so forth. Some messages are intended to persuade: to influence or change the attitudes or actions of the receiver. These messages include promoting a product or service and seeking support for ideas and worthy causes presented to supervisors, employees, stockholders, customers or clients, and others. Additional purposes include establishing a good relationship with your audience, which is discussed later in this chapter, and establishing and maintaining your own credibility as a professional, both of which can help increase your persuasiveness. You will learn to prepare messages that are for each of these purposes later in this text. In addition to identifying the purposes of the message, it is also important to decide which channel and medium would be most effective and appropriate.

3-2a Selecting the Channel and Medium

Broadly speaking, four channels of communication exist: visual, written, oral, and nonverbal. However, these broad categories can be broken down further. For example, written communication can be disseminated using a variety of media or forms, including memos, letters, emails, instant or text messaging, press releases, company websites, blogs, blog applications, wikis, and reports. Oral communication can also use various media or forms such as face-to-face or interpersonal, telephone, voice messages, teleconferences and videoconferences, speeches, meetings, and podcasts. Typically, nonverbal communication supplements oral forms, but it shouldn't be underestimated because most communication in face-to-face situations is often nonverbal. Similarly, visual communication supplements both written and oral forms of communication in the form of slide presentations, diagrams, photographs, charts, tables, video, and artwork.

Channel choice might be influenced or informed by earlier steps in the planning process. For example, the contextual forces may affect how a message is sent. If the organization typically conveys most routine messages using email, for example, this may be the most obvious choice. The purpose of communication might affect channel choice as well. In a situation in which the purpose is primarily to establish a relationship or convey goodwill, a face-to-face meeting might be the best choice to achieve this goal. Audience analysis might yield information that indicates it prefers a particular medium of communication such as email or phone discussions.

Common channel choice considerations include the following:

- **Richness versus leanness.** Some channels of communication provide more information than others. Generally, the richest channels of communication provide nonverbal information in addition to that provided in written or oral form. For this reason, the richest channel of communication is face-to-face, or interpersonal. Face-to-face communication provides participants a rich source of information, including vocal cues, facial expressions, bodily movement, bodily appearance, the use of space, the use of time, touching, and clothing and other artifacts. In addition, face-to-face communication provides opportunities to facilitate feedback and establish a personal focus. These aspects also contribute to the richness of interpersonal communication as a channel of communication.

- **Need for interpretation.** Some channels of communication are more ambiguous, or leave more room for interpretation of the message being sent, than others. Nonverbal communication may be the most ambiguous channel of communication because it requires the audience to interpret the entirety of the message. Nonverbal communication is difficult to interpret for a variety of reasons, mainly because it is not generally considered a coded language. Because of this, one nonverbal code may communicate a variety of meanings. Similarly, nonverbal communication can be difficult to interpret because a variety of codes may communicate the same meaning. A third issue that may affect a person's ability to interpret nonverbal codes accurately is intentionality. Some nonverbal codes are sent intentionally and others unintentionally.

- **Speed of establishing contact.** Another important consideration, particularly in the business world, is the time it will take for a message to be delivered. For this reason, electronic forms of communication have become popular. Using the telephone, writing an email or text message, using blogs and blog applications or other social media such as Facebook or LinkedIn, posting to wikis, using Zoom, or using virtual team applications are nearly instantaneous channels of communication. In contrast, sending a written message or package by mail may take days.

- **Time required for feedback.** Just as we may need to contact someone immediately, we may also need a response from that person just as rapidly. The most rapid forms of communication, as explained previously, are generally electronic. However, depending on the person with whom you are communicating, their personality, and your relationship, communicating with a person via an electronic channel does not guarantee prompt feedback. In other words, corporate cultures and individual people may have preferences for specific communication channels or mediums and differing communication practices.

- **Cost.** Many channels of communication are relatively inexpensive for business users. Mail, email, text messages, telephones, wikis, blogs and blog applications, social media, and videoconferencing are generally considered inexpensive forms of communication. These tools have made it much less expensive for stakeholders, both inside and outside organizations, to communicate with each other, regardless of their location. Still, there are times when it may be appropriate to choose the greater expense of arranging a face-to-face meeting, such as when introducing members of a virtual team who will be working on an important project for some time or interviewing job applicants for key positions.

- **Amount of information conveyed.** The best channel for conveying large amounts of information is generally a written one. One reason is that most of us are generally poor listeners. Studies indicate that we retain only 10 percent or so of what we hear. Therefore, if you want people to have the opportunity to process and remember the information you have to deliver, particularly if the message is long or complex, then it is generally best delivered using a written channel rather than an oral one.

- **Need for a permanent record.** Businesspeople are often involved in situations where they must keep records of what occurred during various work activities throughout the day or week. These situations include the need to record what occurred at a department meeting, an employee's work history, the findings of an audit of a client's financial records, and an employee's travel expenses. Most legal documents, including contracts, use the written channel of communication for this reason: the need to maintain a record. Email messages and other electronic forums such as websites, social networking sites, and blogs, if stored and backed up properly, can also serve as a record.

- **Control over the message.** Written channels of communication also are often the best choice when you wish to maintain greater control of the message that you send. why? If information is presented orally and interpersonally, you have a greater chance of persons who disagree with you speaking out and potentially derailing or confusing the message. That is why many negative messages, such as informing a job applicant that they were not selected, are sent using a written channel of communication.

Exhibit 3.1 provides a summary of the proper use of differing media within an organizational context.

Medium	Best Uses	Medium	Best Uses
Exhibit 3.1 | Use of Communication Media			
Memo	• Simple, routine messages • Confirming policies • Distributing to a large, internal audience • Providing information when a response isn't required	Telephone	• Providing quick feedback or response • Sending confidential information • Discussing bad news • Confirming • Great for creating a personal connection • Easy to measure impact
Letter	• Communicating with an external audience • Conveying formality • Providing a written record • Writing a complaint • Communicating condolences or thanks	Voice mail	• Informing when feedback isn't needed • Confirming • Sending a simple message
Email	• Sending brief, impersonal, or routine messages • Can reach mass audiences fast • Cost effective and simple to use • A consistent and controlled message • Reaches the recipient directly • Providing a hard copy	Video conferencing	• Making a personal connection with a large audience • Economical and efficient • Training
Text or instant messaging	• Sending brief or routine messages • Quick and simple to use	Twitter	• Great for short bursts of information • Good for directing attention to other forms of communication, such as a website • Real-time tweets can make people, who are off-site, feel involved in site-based events • Good for generating a following • Quick, easy, and cheap • Attracts younger audiences
Web page	• Sharing information with large audiences in an economical fashion • Inspiring and motivating others • Demonstrating products or training • Allowing people to interact rather than receiving information passively	Facebook and other social networks	• Easy and inexpensive to do • Good way of directing readers' attentions to other forms of communication, such as a website • Good for gathering information about individuals • Good way to build a general profile • Allowing people to interact rather than receiving information passively
Oral presentation	• Introducing a persuasive message or following up on one when goodwill and credibility are especially important • Delivering bad news to a large audience when goodwill and credibility are especially important	LinkedIn and other professional networks	• Easy and cheap to do • Good way of directing the reader's attention to other forms of communication, such as a website • Good for gathering information about individuals • Good for providing additional benefits to prospects through peer-to-peer networking and posting career opportunities
Face-to-face	• Communicating confidential information • Negotiating • Promoting or firing an employee • Communicating personal warmth or care • Reading nonverbal communication cues	Team meetings	• Can make communication personal and relevant to the team involved • Opportunity for discussion, feedback, questioning, and ideas • Can help build understanding and involvement

3-3 Step 3: Envision the Audience

Perception is the part of the communication process that involves how we look at others and the world around us. Perception is a three-phase process of selecting, organizing, and interpreting information, objects, people, events, or situations (refer to Figure 3.2). It's a natural tendency to perceive situations from our own limited viewpoint. We use the context of the situation and our five senses to absorb and interpret the information bombarding us in unique ways.

Individual differences in perception account for the varied and sometimes conflicting reports given by eyewitnesses to the same accident. Our senses can be tricked when there is a difference in what we expect and what really is happening. For example, consider how your *perception* affects your ability to interpret an optical illusion accurately or completely.

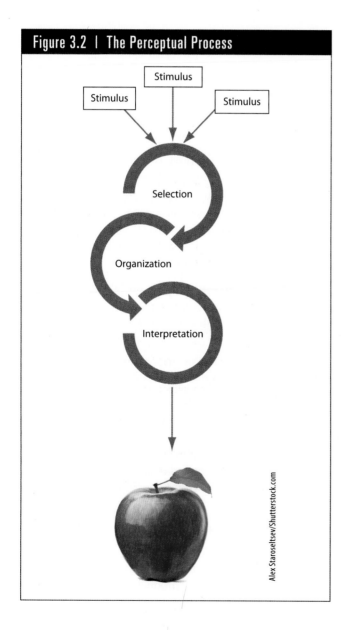

Figure 3.2 | The Perceptual Process

Alex Staroseltsev/Shutterstock.com

Perception of reality is also limited by previous experiences and our attitudes toward the sender of the message. We support ideas that are in line with our own and decide whether to focus on the positive or the negative aspects of a situation. We may simply refuse to hear a message that doesn't fit into our view of the world.

Much of the confusion in communication is caused by differences in the sender's and receiver's perceptions. For example, a manager's brief email requesting a status report on a task may come across as curt to the employees. Perceptions vary between individuals with similar backgrounds, and even more so when people from different cultures, generations, and genders communicate.

Overcoming perceptual barriers is difficult but essential if you are to craft messages that meet the needs and concerns of your audience. To help you envision the audience, first focus on relevant information you know about the receiver. The more familiar you are with the receiver, the easier this task will be. When communicating with an individual, you immediately recall a clear picture of the receiver: their physical appearance, background (education, occupation, religion, and culture), values, opinions, preferences, and so on. Most importantly, your knowledge of the receiver's reaction in similar, previous experiences will aid you in anticipating how this receiver is likely to react in the current situation. Consider the following audience characteristics:

- **Age.** A message answering an elementary-school student's request for information from your company would not be worded the same as a message answering a similar request from an adult.

- **Economic level.** A solicitation for a business donation for a charity project written to a small business owner would likely differ from one written to a representative of a major corporation.

- **Educational/occupational background.** The technical jargon and acronyms used in a financial proposal sent to bank loan officers may be inappropriate in a proposal sent to a group of private investors.

- **Needs and concerns of the audience.** Just as successful sales personnel begin by identifying the needs of the prospective buyer, an effective manager attempts to understand the receiver's frame of reference as a basis for organizing the message and developing the content.

- **Culture.** The vast cultural differences between people (e.g., language, expressions, customs, values, and religion) increase the complexity of the communication process as was discussed in Chapter 1 (refer to Exhibit 3.2). An email containing typical American expressions (e.g., "The estimate is in the ballpark," and

Exhibit 3.2 | Cultural Dimensions Identified by the Globe Studies

Uncertainty Avoidance	The extent to which a cultural group relies on established social norms, rituals, and procedures to avoid uncertainty.
Power Distance	The degree to which members of a cultural group expect and agree that power should be shared unequally.
Institutional Collectivism	The degree to which a cultural group encourages institutional or societal collective action. It is concerned with whether cultures identify with broader societal interests rather than with individual goals.
In-Group Collectivism	The degree to which people express pride, loyalty, and cohesiveness in their groups or families.
Gender Egalitarianism	The degree to which a cultural group minimizes gender role differences and promotes gender equality.
Assertiveness	The degree to which people in a culture are determined, assertive, confrontational, and aggressive in their social relationships.
Future Orientation	The extent to which people engage in future-oriented behaviors such as planning, investing, and delaying gratification.
Performance Orientation	The extent to which a cultural group encourages and rewards its members for improved performance and excellence.
Humane Orientation	The degree to which a culture encourages and rewards people for being fair, altruistic, generous, and caring to others.

Source: R. J. House, P. J. Hanges, M. Javidan, P. W. Dorfman, V. and Gupta (Eds.) (2004). *Culture, leadership, and organizations: The GLOBE study of 62 societies.* Thousand Oaks, CA: Sage Publications.

"Our new sales director really knows all the ropes.") would likely confuse a manager from a different culture. Differences in values influence communication styles and message patterns. For example, Japanese readers value the beauty and flow of words and prefer an indirect writing approach, unlike Americans who prefer clarity and conciseness.[4]

- **Rapport.** A sensitive message prepared for a longtime client may differ significantly from a message prepared for a newly acquired client. Emails discussing expectations for completing an assignment may be briefer and more direct when sent to an employee with whom you share a strong business relationship built on mutual trust. The rapport created by previous dealings with the recipient aids understanding in a current situation.

- **Expectations.** Because accountants, lawyers, and other professionals are expected to meet high standards, a message from one of them containing errors in grammar or spelling would likely cause a receiver to question the credibility of the source.

You may find that envisioning an audience you know well is often such an automatic action that you may not even recognize that you are doing it. On the other hand, envisioning those you do not know well requires additional effort. In these cases, simply assume an empathetic attitude toward the receiver to assist you in identifying their frame of reference (knowledge, feelings, and emotions). In other words, project mentally how you believe you would feel or react in a similar situation and use that information to communicate understanding back to the person.

Taking the time and effort to obtain a strong mental picture of your audience through firsthand knowledge or your empathetic attitude *before* you write will enhance your message in the following ways:

1. **Establishes the rapport and credibility needed to build long-lasting personal and business relationships.** Your audience will appreciate your attempt to connect and understand their feelings. A likely outcome is mutual trust, which can greatly improve communication and people's feelings about you, your ideas, and themselves.

2. **Permits you to address the audience's needs and concerns.** Such knowledge allows you to select relevant content and to communicate in a suitable style.

3. **Simplifies the task of organizing your message.** From your knowledge of yourself and from your experiences with others, you can reasonably predict the receivers' reactions to various types of messages. To illustrate, ask yourself these questions:

   ○ Would I react favorably to a message saying my request is being granted or that a new client is genuinely pleased with a job I'd just completed?

   ○ Would I experience a feeling of disappointment when I learn that my request has been refused or that my promised pay raise is being postponed?

   ○ Would I need compelling arguments to convince me to purchase a new product or support a new company policy?

Now, reread the questions as though you were the message recipient. Because you know *your* answers, you can predict *others'* answers with some degree of accuracy.

Consider the use (or lack) of empathy in the following workplace example:

Such predictions are possible because of commonality in human behavior.

Sample Message

A U.S. manager's instructions to a new male employee from an Asian culture named Liu Chen:

Mr. Chen,
We want to **move the ball forward** with the release of our latest product. We hope to **hit a home run** with our marketing plan; although, we anticipate that this will be **a marathon, not a sprint.** Do you understand?

Your commitment to identifying the needs and concerns of your audience before you communicate is invaluable in today's workplace. Organizations must focus on providing quality customer service and developing work environments supportive of talented, diverse workers. Alienating valuable customers and talented employees as a result of poor audience analysis is not an option in today's competitive environment.

Problem Analysis

- The use of expressions particular to the U.S. environment can confuse and intimidate.

- This open-ended question at the end disregards the importance of saving face to a person of Asian culture. Cultural influences may prevent an employee from asking questions that might indicate a lack of understanding.

- Misspelling the receiver's name and misinterpreting gender shows disrespect for the receiver.

- Omission of contact information reduces the writer's credibility and shows a lack of genuine concern for the sender's needs.

3-4 Step 4: Adapt the Message to the Audience's Needs and Concerns

After you have envisioned your audience, you are ready to adapt your message to fit the specific needs of your audience. Adaptations include focusing on the audience's point of view; communicating ethically and responsibly; building

and protecting goodwill; using simple, contemporary language; writing concisely; and projecting a positive, tactful tone.

3-4a Focus on the Audience's Point of View

Ideas are more interesting and appealing if they are expressed from the audience's viewpoint. Developing a "you attitude" rather than a "me attitude" involves thinking in terms of the other person's interests and trying to see a problem from the other's point of view. A letter, memo, email, or phone call reflecting a "you attitude" sends a direct signal of sincere concern for the receiver's needs and interest.

The use of the word *you* (appropriately used) conveys to receivers a feeling that messages are specifically for them. However, if the first-person pronoun *I* is used frequently, especially as the subject, the sender may impress others as being self-centered—always talking about oneself. Compare the following examples of sender-centered and receiver-centered statements:

How to Cultivate a "You Attitude"

To cultivate a "you attitude," concentrate on the following questions:

- **Does the message address the receiver's major needs and concerns?**

- **Would the receiver feel this message is receiver centered? Is the receiver kept clearly in the picture?**

- **Will the receiver perceive the ideas to be fair, logical, and ethical?**

- **Are ideas expressed clearly and concisely (to avoid lost time, money, and possible embarrassment caused when messages are misunderstood)?**

- **Does the message promote positive business relationships, even when the message is negative? For example, are** *please, thank you,* **and other courtesies used when appropriate?**

- **Are ideas stated tactfully and positively and in a manner that preserves the receiver's self-worth and cultivates future business?**

- **Is the message sent promptly and through the preferred channel to indicate courtesy?**

- **Does the message reflect the high standards of a business professional: accurate and appealing document design, quality printing, and absence of misspellings and grammatical errors?**

"I"—or Sender-Centered	**"You"—or Receiver-Centered**
• I wanted to inform you of an upcoming Zoom meeting. • We are changing policies regarding flex-time work.	• You are invited to a Zoom meeting. • You will find the new policy regarding flex-time work below.

Compliments (words of deserved praise) are another effective way of increasing an audience's receptiveness to ideas that follow. Give sincere compliments judiciously as they can do more harm than good if paid at the wrong time, in the wrong setting, in the presence of the wrong people, or for the wrong reasons. Likewise, avoid flattery (words of undeserved praise). Although the recipient may accept your flattery as a sincere compliment, it is more likely that the recipient will interpret your undeserved praise as an attempt to gain favor or special attention. Suspicion of your motive makes effective communication less likely.

3-4b Communicate Ethically and Responsibly

The familiar directive "With power comes responsibility" applies to your use of communication skills. Because business communication often affects the lives of many, you must accept responsibility for using it to uphold your own personal values and your company's standards of ethical conduct. Before speaking or writing, use the following guidelines to help you communicate ethically and responsibly.

Is the information stated as truthfully, honestly, and fairly as possible? Good communicators recognize that ensuring a free flow of essential information is in the interest of the public and the organization. Consumers nationwide who purchased Godiva chocolates between 2015 and 2021 were potentially eligible to claim up to $25 with proof of purchase thanks to a recent class action settlement. Plaintiffs in the class action lawsuit alleged the company violated the law through its representations that Godiva chocolates are made in Belgium when they are not.[5] Similarly, Living Essentials, the distributor of 5-Hour Energy, a high-selling energy drink, alleged that its energy drink shots were more effective than coffee and that doctors recommended it. Those claims were found to be deceptive, and the makers of 5-Hour Energy were ordered to pay $4.3 million in penalties and fees. The ruling was upheld in 2019 by the Washington Court of Appeals.[6] As these examples indicate, dishonesty can cost organizations money, as well as incur damage to their reputation.

At the personal level, honor, honesty, and credibility can help build strong, long-lasting relationships that contribute to the long-term success of your company. Sending complete, accurate, and timely information, regardless of whether it supports your interests, will help you build credibility.

Does the message embellish or exaggerate the facts? Legal guidelines related to advertising provide clear guidance for avoiding *fraud*, the misrepresentation of products or services; however, overzealous sales representatives or imaginative writers can use language skillfully to create less than accurate perceptions in the minds of receivers. As the previous examples illustrate, businesses have learned the hard way that overstating the capabilities of a product or service (promising more than can be delivered) is not good for business overall. For example, Quincy Bioscience agreed to resolve the claims that it misrepresented its Prevagen products as supporting brain health and helping with memory loss. Plaintiffs in the Prevagen brain health class action lawsuit claimed that Quincy Bioscience intentionally misrepresented their products as able to help with brain health and lessen memory loss. According to the class action lawsuit, the marketing and advertising representations on these products deceived consumers into thinking that their brain health and memory loss would be helped by taking the supplements. Quincy Bioscience did not admit any wrongdoing but agreed to resolve the claims against them in a settlement.[7]

Although surveys indicate many job seekers believe companies expect résumé padding, companies repeatedly report that this perception is not true. Whether you're telling a little white lie or a blatant fabrication, getting caught could amount to career sabotage—especially since today's technology and social media environments make it easier to get caught. And you will very likely get caught. Monster Career Expert and former corporate recruiter Vicki Salemi told Monster's virtual career panel, "We once had to fire someone because they lied on their résumé and then we found out *after* they were hired."[8] One example is the case of Mina Chang, who was hired as a senior administration official for the U.S. State Department in 2019. On November 12, 2019, NBC News reported that Chang had "embellished her résumé with misleading claims about her professional background" prior to joining the department. She claimed to be an alumna of Harvard Business School, which the school verified as correct, through the completion of a seven-week, non-degree certificate course. NBC News accused her of falsely claiming to be a former chief of staff of a nonprofit (NGO), to have had a role on a United Nations panel, and to have appeared on the front cover of *Time* magazine. The NBC News report also stated that she claimed to have spoken at both Democratic and Republican national conventions and that her résumé implied she had testified before Congress, all untrue.[9] A week after the report, Chang resigned.

Skill in communicating persuasively will be important throughout your profession. The techniques you will read about in this text, such as those related to writing a winning résumé and application message, will be helpful as you begin your career; however, these techniques should *not* be used if your motive is to exploit your audience.

- **Are the ideas expressed clearly and understandably?** If a message is to be seen as honest, you must be reasonably confident that the receiver can understand it. Ethical communicators select words that convey the exact meaning intended and that are within the reader's vocabulary.

- **Is your viewpoint supported with objective facts?** Are facts accurately documented to allow the reader to judge the credibility of the source and to give credit where credit is due? Can opinions be clearly distinguished from facts? Have you honestly evaluated any real or perceived conflict of interest that could prevent you from preparing an unbiased message?

- **Are ideas stated with tact and consideration that preserve the receiver's self-worth?** The metaphor "An arrow, once it is shot, cannot be recalled" describes the irrevocable damage caused by cruel or unkind words.[10] Ego-destroying criticism, excessive anger, sarcasm, hurtful nicknames, betrayed secrets, rumors, and malicious gossip pose serious ethical problems in the workplace because they can ruin reputations, humiliate, and damage a person's self-worth. Serious legal issues arise when negative statements are false, constituting defamation. Written defamatory remarks are referred to as **libel**, and similar spoken remarks are referred to as **slander**. If you choose to make negative statements about a person, be sure the facts in question are supported. Additionally, you'll hone your abilities to convey negative information and to handle sensitive situations in a constructive, timely manner rather than ignoring them until they are out of control. For considerate, fair, and civilized use of words, follow this simple rule: Communicate with and about others with the same kindness and fairness that you wish others to use when communicating with and about you.

- **Are graphics carefully designed to avoid distorting facts and relationships?** Communicating ethically involves reporting data as clearly and accurately as possible. Misleading graphics result either from the developers' deliberate attempt to confuse the audience or from their lack of expertise in constructing ethical graphics.

Step 5: Organize the Message

After you have identified the specific ways you must adapt the message to your particular audience, you are ready to organize your message. In a discussion on communication, the word *organize* means "the act of dividing a topic into parts and arranging them in an appropriate sequence." Before undertaking this process, you must be convinced that the message is the right message—that it is complete, accurate, fair, reasonable, ethical, and logical. If it doesn't meet these standards, it should not be sent. Good organization, writing, or speaking cannot be expected to compensate for a bad decision.

If you organize and write simultaneously, the task seems hopelessly complicated. Writing is much easier if questions about the organization of the message are answered first: What is the purpose of the message? What is the receiver's likely reaction? Should the message begin with the main point? Once these decisions have been made, you can concentrate on expressing ideas effectively.

3-5a Outline to Benefit the Sender and the Audience

When a topic is divided into parts, some parts will be recognized as central ideas and the others as minor ideas (details). The process of identifying these ideas and arranging them in the right sequence is known as **outlining**. Outlining *before* communicating complex messages provides numerous benefits:

- **Encourages accuracy and brevity.** Outlining reduces the chance of leaving out an essential idea or including an unessential idea.

- **Permits concentration on one phase at a time.** Having focused separately on (a) the ideas that need to be included, (b) the distinction between major and minor ideas, and (c) the sequence of ideas, total concentration can now be focused on the next challenge: expressing.

- **Saves time in structuring ideas.** With questions about which ideas to include and their proper sequence already answered, little time is lost in moving from one point to the next.

- **Provides a psychological lift.** The feeling of success gained in preparing the outline increases confidence

> **libel** written defamatory remarks
>
> **slander** spoken defamatory remarks
>
> **outlining** the process of identifying central ideas and details, and arranging them in the right sequence; this should be completed prior to writing

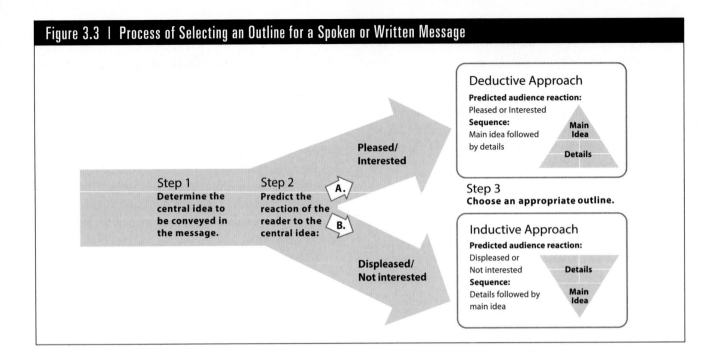

that the next step—writing or speaking—will be successful too.

- **Facilitates emphasis and de-emphasis.** Although each sentence makes its contribution to the message, some sentences need to stand out more vividly in the receiver's mind than others. An effective outline ensures that important points will appear in emphatic positions.

The preceding benefits derived from outlining are sender-oriented. Because a message has been well outlined, receivers benefit too:

- The message is more concise and accurate.
- Relationships between ideas are easier to distinguish and remember.
- Reactions to the message and its sender are more likely to be positive.

A receiver's reaction to a message is strongly influenced by the sequence in which ideas are presented. A beginning sentence or an ending sentence is in an emphatic position.

3-5b Sequence Ideas to Achieve Desired Goals

When planning your communication, you should strive for an outline that will serve you in much the same way that a blueprint serves a builder or an itinerary serves a traveler. Organizing your message first will ensure that your ideas are

> **deductive** a message in which the major idea precedes the details

presented clearly and logically, and all vital components are included. To facilitate your determination of an appropriate sequence for a business document or presentation, follow the three-step process illustrated in Figure 3.3. This process involves answering the following questions in this order:

1. **What is the central idea of the message?** Think about the *reason* you are writing or speaking—the first step in the communication process. What is your purpose? To extend a job offer, decline an invitation, or seek support for an innovative project? The purpose is the central idea of your message. You might think of it as a message condensed in one brief statement.

2. **What is the probable audience reaction to the message?** Ask, "If I were the one receiving the message I am preparing to send, what would *my* reaction be?" Because you would react with pleasure to good news and with displeasure to bad news, you can reasonably assume a receiver's reaction would be similar. By considering the anticipated audience reaction, you will build goodwill with the receiver. Almost every message will fit into one of four categories of anticipated audience reaction, as shown in Figure 3.3: pleasure, displeasure, interest but neither pleasure nor displeasure, or no interest.

3. **In view of the predicted audience reaction, should the central idea be listed first in the outline or should it be listed as one of the last items?** When a message begins with the major idea, the sequence of ideas is called **deductive** (refer to Model Document 3.1). When a message withholds

Dear Isabella Ruiz,

On behalf of Johnson Copiers, I extend our sincerest apologies for the bad experience you had with our sales associate, Bill. I understand that Bill made unprofessional remarks when you visited our storefront to inquire about a new copier. You came to us in search of information and instead were subjected to a pushy salesperson.

At Johnson Copiers, it's our goal to help you make an informed purchase decision without having to deal with aggressive sales tactics. Bill is a new employee that I've been training. I take full responsibility for his behavior. He has received a written reprimand and will be shadowing one of our senior sales associates until he has a better understanding of the Johnson Copiers' approach to customer service.

I'm grateful that you brought this issue to my attention, and I ask your forgiveness. We'd love to earn your business. I've included a voucher for 20 percent off your next purchase in our store as a thank you should you decide to give us a second chance. We hope to see you again soon!

Kind regards,

Suzy Lee, Sales Manager

---

the major idea until accompanying details and explanations have been presented, the sequence is called **inductive**.

Consider the audience to determine whether to use the inductive or deductive sequence. If an audience might be antagonized by the main idea in a deductive message, lead up to the main idea by making the message inductive. If a sender wants to encourage audience involvement (to generate some concern about where the details are leading), use the inductive approach. Inductive organization can be especially effective if the main idea confirms the conclusion that the audience has drawn from the preceding details—a cause is worthy of support, a job applicant should be interviewed, a product/service should be selected, and so on. As you learn in later chapters about writing letters, memos, and email messages, and about planning spoken communications, you will comprehend the benefits of using the appropriate outline for each receiver reaction:

Deductive Order (main idea first)	Inductive Order (details first)
• When the message *will* please the audience • When the message is *routine* (will not please nor displease)	• When the message will *displease* the audience • When the audience *might* not be *interested* (will need to be persuaded)

For determining the sequence of minor ideas that accompany the major idea, the following bases for idea sequence are common:

- **Time.** When writing a report or email message about a series of events or a process, paragraphs proceed from the first step through the last step.

- **Space.** If a report is about geographic areas, ideas

inductive a message in which the major idea follows the details

With successful inclusive marketing campaigns, marketers aim to break advertising norms by highlighting people or groups that might be under- or misrepresented, such as people of color, those who identify as LGBTQ+, those who affiliate with various religions, those who are disabled, or even people of certain ages and genders.

Procter & Gamble: The Talk

Source: Procter & Gamble

One example of a successful inclusive marketing story is that of Procter & Gamble (P&G), a company known for its ownership of a variety of cleaning and toiletry companies, including Tide, Dove, and Gillette. The corporation also creates initiatives to ensure inclusivity in its marketing and products.

Not only do some P&G ads include people from diverse backgrounds, but they also use their platform to tell stories that spread powerful messages about equality, tackle controversial issues, and discuss topics related to diversity and identity.

One example of P&G's inclusive commercials is a 2018 Emmy-winning ad called "The Talk." The commercial—which corresponded with P&G's "Black is Beautiful" and "Proud Sponsor of Moms" initiatives—depicts African American mothers in multiple decades as they have difficult conversations with their children about racism.[11]

At the beginning of the ad, a mother brushing her daughter's hair ominously says, "It's not a compliment." As you might wonder what she's referring to, you start to see scenes of other Black mothers talking to their children about racism and judgment that they'll face in life. For example, one mother tells her son, "There are some people who think you don't deserve the same privileges just because of what you look like. It's not fair. It's not."

The ad grows darker as you see mothers instructing their children of what to do when they are pulled over to avoid police brutality. At the climax of the ad, it's revealed that the daughter featured at the beginning was called, "Beautiful for a Black girl." Her mother tells her not to accept this compliment and concludes, "You are beautiful, period!" The ad ends with text in all caps stating, "LET'S ALL TALK ABOUT 'THE TALK'—SO WE CAN END THE NEED TO HAVE IT."

This commercial's goal is to expose the closed-door conversations that African American mothers need to have with their children to keep them safe and strong in the face of racism. By informing people of these conversations, P&G aims to create a discussion that might create change or end the need for mothers to feel they have to prepare their children for racism or judgment.

When it came to the commercial's goal of creating a discussion, "The Talk" was a success in that it was discussed by social media users, advocacy groups, and major news outlets.

Source: Bump. P. (n.d.). *Seven brands that got inclusive marketing right.* Retrieved January 2022 from https://blog.hubspot.com/marketing/inclusive-marketing-campaigns

can proceed from one area to the next until all areas have been discussed.

- **Familiarity.** If a topic is complicated, the presentation can begin with a known or easy-to-understand point and proceed to progressively more difficult points.

- **Importance.** In analytical reports in which major decision-making factors are presented, the factors can be presented in order of most important to least important, or vice versa.

- **Value.** If a presentation involves major factors with monetary values, paragraphs can proceed from those with greatest values to those with least values, or vice versa.

The same organizational patterns are recommended for written and spoken communication.

These patterns are applicable in email messages, blogs, letters, memos, and reports (refer to Model Document 3.2).

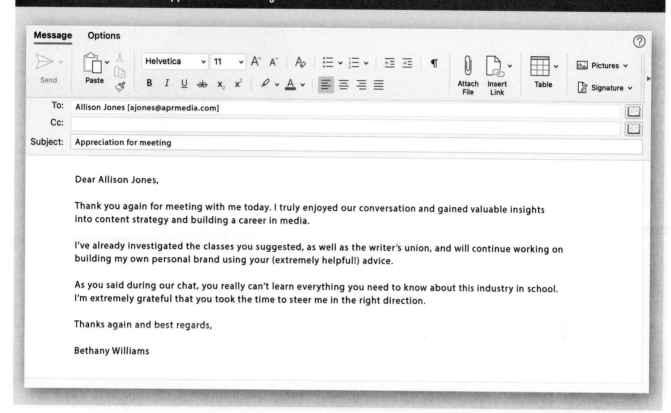

Message   Options

To: Allison Jones [ajones@aprmedia.com]

Cc:

Subject: Appreciation for meeting

Dear Allison Jones,

Thank you again for meeting with me today. I truly enjoyed our conversation and gained valuable insights into content strategy and building a career in media.

I've already investigated the classes you suggested, as well as the writer's union, and will continue working on building my own personal brand using your (extremely helpful!) advice.

As you said during our chat, you really can't learn everything you need to know about this industry in school. I'm extremely grateful that you took the time to steer me in the right direction.

Thanks again and best regards,

Bethany Williams

lightwavemedia/Shutterstock

4 | Preparing Written Messages

Learning Objectives

After studying this chapter, you will be able to ...

4-1 Understand the differences between academic and business writing.

4-2 Apply techniques for developing effective introductions, sentences, and unified and coherent paragraphs in business writing.

4-3 Prepare visually appealing documents that grab the reader's attention and increase comprehension.

4-4 Identify factors affecting readability, and revise messages to improve readability.

4-5 Revise and proofread a message for content, organization, style, and tone, as well as mechanics, format, and layout.

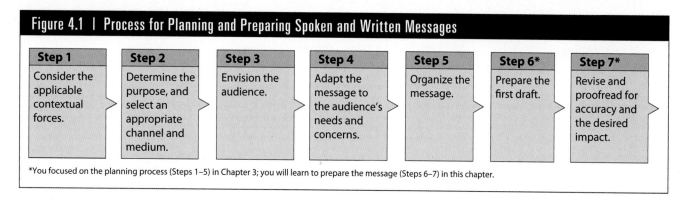

Figure 4.1 | Process for Planning and Preparing Spoken and Written Messages

Step 1	Step 2	Step 3	Step 4	Step 5	Step 6*	Step 7*
Consider the applicable contextual forces.	Determine the purpose, and select an appropriate channel and medium.	Envision the audience.	Adapt the message to the audience's needs and concerns.	Organize the message.	Prepare the first draft.	Revise and proofread for accuracy and the desired impact.

*You focused on the planning process (Steps 1–5) in Chapter 3; you will learn to prepare the message (Steps 6–7) in this chapter.

In Chapter 3, you learned about the importance of following a systematic process to develop business messages. The applications in Chapter 3 guided you in developing a clear, logical plan for your message that focused on the needs of the receiver (Steps 1–5). Effectively capturing your ideas for various business communication situations involves skillful use of language and careful attention to accuracy and readability issues—the remaining two steps in this important process are shown in Figure 4.1.

4-1 The Genre of Business Writing

Business writing is just one of several genres of writing. Obviously, it is different from fiction or poetry; it differs from academic or compositional writing in many ways and is more akin to technical writing. Therefore, learning to be a good business writer often requires unlearning some of the conventions of academic or compositional writing you may have acquired in your previous training.

To begin with, the context of business writing is very different from academic and compositional writing, including the elements of audience and purpose. Academic and compositional writing instruction is intended to teach students to write formally and correctly to an audience who loves writing and has the leisure time available to linger over it and appreciate its stylistic aspects. In an academic environment, the audience is often a teacher who may love literature and is paid to read and analyze writing for its finer qualities.

This is not the case for business audiences, many of whom do not like to read or write and don't have the time to linger over it. Most business audiences are not analyzing your writing for grammatical correctness and stylistic appeal, particularly in the case of routine messages. Instead, they are reading your messages to gather information they need to move forward in their job duties.

Another difference between business writing and academic or compositional writing is that, because of time pressures, business audiences are reading messages quickly. That means two things: Business writing should be complete yet concise, and it should be easy to skim. Therefore,

a business reader is likely never to ask you to write a four-page report on information that might easily be covered in two or three paragraphs. It also means that you need to learn to write in such a way as to provide sufficient "entry points" into your message to enable skimming.

The style and tone of business writing also differ from academic or compositional writing. Because compositional writing emphasizes the rules of English as used in the conservative environment of the academy, the style is often formal and the tone may be stilted due to the use of overly long sentences and multisyllabic words, both of which are more time-consuming to read—a "no-no" in a business context. In contrast, business writing tends to use less complex sentences, plain language, and a friendly, personable tone to cultivate positive relationships as an important strategic goal.

This latter issue becomes more critical in a growingly diverse, multicultural world in which business is global and often conducted using technological means. This means that messages are often shorter, more instantaneous, and may not be absolutely grammatically correct as English may not be the participants' first language. To address this change, researchers have developed approaches to English usage to better account for how businesspeople actually communicate in multicultural situations. For example, English for Specific Purposes (ESP) and Business English as Lingua Franca (BELF) look at how non-native English users communicate in a business setting. Research on BELF has shown that

- The grammatical rules and communication norms for BELF use are heavily influenced by the reason for its use (e.g., business, travel, etc.).

- BELF communication norms are more influenced by situational or functional circumstances than native-speaker norms.

- BELF users place a higher importance on using the language to achieve goals rather than being grammatically correct.

- BELF speakers will intersperse other, mutually-known languages when doing so will improve goal achievement.

Exhibit 4.1 | Differences Between Academic and Business Writing

Academic Writing	Business Writing
Writing is to be enjoyed by the reader; style is emphasized	Time is of the essence; writing should be concise and easy to read
Audience is well-educated, literary, and/or intellectually inclined	Audience is both specific and varied; often focused on practical task achievement
As the audience is often English teachers and students, mechanical and grammatical correctness is a common concern	Diverse audience, many are non-native English writers and speakers; clarity more important than grammatical correctness
Long paragraphs, long sentences, big words	Short paragraphs, short sentences, plain language
Purpose to inform and state a position; often not sensitive to broader context	Purposes to inform, persuade, convey goodwill, and establish or maintain credibility
Tone is formal; first- and second-person pronouns are avoided	Tone is personable; first- and second-person pronouns are common

In conclusion, it is important to remember that business writing is a different genre than academic writing, occurring in a different context with different audience expectations. Exhibit 4.1 illustrates the differences between academic and business writing.

4-2 Step 6: Prepare the First Draft

Once you have determined whether the message should be presented deductively (main idea first) or inductively (explanation and details first) and have planned the logical sequence of minor points, you are ready to begin composing the message.

Normally, writing rapidly (with intent to rewrite certain portions, if necessary) is better than slow, deliberate writing (with intent to avoid any need for rewriting portions). The latter approach can be frustrating and can reduce the quality of the finished work. Time is wasted in thinking of one way to express an idea, discarding it either before or after it is written, waiting for new inspiration, and rereading preceding sentences.

Concentrating on getting your ideas down as quickly as you can is an efficient approach to writing. During this process, remember that you are preparing a draft and not the final copy. If you are composing at the computer, you can quickly and easily revise your draft throughout the writing process. This seamless approach to writing allows you to continue to improve your working draft until the moment you are ready to submit the final copy. Numerous electronic writing tools are available, and technology will continue to enhance the writing process.

4-2a Select the Type of Introduction

Deductively organized messages will likely differ in the type of introduction used compared to an inductively organized message. Deductively organized messages typically start with a direct and straightforward introduction that immediately announces the purpose of the message from the audience's perspective and provides a brief overview of its contents or organization to aid in quickly grasping the overall scope of the message and its ordering.

For example, a message intended to respond to a reader's query for more information about a company's product offerings might begin as follows:

> In response to your request, you will find a summary of VizMeet's videoconferencing functionality. You will find an overview of each of the our plans' benefits as well as the needed hardware for each.

This introduction recognizes the reader's request for information and provides additional explanation of what they will find in the body of the message. This latter information orients the reader so they can quickly skim the document to find the specific information for which they are looking. It is important that the writer fulfills their promise to the reader to organize the information as announced.

For an inductively organized message, though, a buffer or goodwill opening might be used to soften the approach and the reader's reception.

For example, a message to a job applicant informing them that they were not selected might begin as follows:

> The Worldwide Restaurant Group wanted to let you know that we received your application for our position as Director of Marketing. Thank you for taking the time to send your résumé and cover letter, as we know how time-consuming this effort is.

This example illustrates the use of a short introductory paragraph to convey goodwill to the recipient for their interest in the company as well as to act as a buffer for the next paragraph, which delivers the bad news in a tactful way that they were not selected for the job opening.

4-2b Develop Coherent Paragraphs

Well-constructed sentences are combined into paragraphs that discuss a portion of the topic being covered. To write effective paragraphs, you must learn to (a) develop deductive or inductive paragraphs consistently, (b) link ideas to achieve coherence, (c) keep paragraphs unified, and (d) vary sentence and paragraph length.

Position the Topic Sentence Appropriately

Typically, paragraphs contain one sentence that identifies the portion of the topic being discussed and presents the central idea. That sentence is commonly called a **topic sentence**. For example, consider the operating instructions prepared for use of videoconferencing software. The overall topic is how to get satisfactory performance from the service. One portion of that topic is setup, another portion (paragraph) discusses operation, and so forth. Within each paragraph, one sentence serves a special function. Sentences that list the steps can appear as one paragraph, perhaps with steps numbered as follows:

To set up the system, take the following steps:

1. *Connect …*

2. *Go to menu settings to …*

In this illustration, the paragraphs are **deductive**; that is, the topic sentence *precedes* details. When topic sentences *follow* details, the paragraphs are **inductive**. As discussed previously, the receiver's likely reaction to the main idea (pleased, displeased, interested, or not interested) aids in selecting the appropriate sequence.

When the subject matter is complicated and the details are numerous, paragraphs sometimes begin with a main idea, follow with details, and end with a summarizing sentence. But the main idea might not be in the first sentence; the idea could need a preliminary statement. Receivers appreciate consistency in the placement of topic sentences. Once they catch on to the writer's or speaker's pattern, they know where to look for main ideas. It is important to remember, though, that most messages are deductive in organization because of the subject matter and because of the audience's needs. In other words, inductive organization is typically only used in bad news messages and persuasive messages written to resistant audiences. All other types of messages are typically deductive in organization.

This is because business audiences are typically pressed for time and deductively organized messages are easier to read if well crafted. Well-crafted deductive messages are easy to skim; the audience can quickly ascertain the purpose of the message, its contents, and its location in just a few seconds. This type of writing enables the audience to quickly grasp the message and immediately find the information they are seeking.

What this means is that most business readers do not read an entire document carefully but may jump to a specific section that contains information that is immediately needed, or is more important for their specific tasks. A good writer anticipates that the reader might skim a message and attempts to make this process easier for the reader.

To pass the "skim test," ensure that a deductively organized message has the following:

1. A clearly stated purpose in the introduction, as well as a brief overview of its contents

2. If it is a longer, more complex document, it uses clear headings to identify important subtopics

3. Uses topic sentences that clearly identify the subtopics listed in the introduction

These suggestions seldom apply to the first and last sentences of letters, memos, and email messages. Such sentences frequently appear as single-sentence paragraphs. But for reports and long paragraphs of letters, strive for paragraphs that are consistently deductive or inductive. Regardless of which is selected, topic sentences are clearly linked with details that precede or follow.

Link Ideas to Achieve Coherence

Careful writers use coherence techniques to keep receivers from experiencing abrupt changes in thought. Although the word **coherence** is used sometimes to mean "clarity" or "understandability," it is used throughout this text to mean "cohesion." If writing or speaking is coherent, the sentences stick together; each sentence is in some way linked to the preceding sentences. Avoid abrupt changes in thought, and link each sentence to a preceding sentence.

The following techniques for linking sentences are common:

1. **Repeat a word that was used in the preceding sentence.** The second sentence in the following example is an obvious continuation of the idea presented in the preceding sentence.

   … to take responsibility for the decision. This responsibility can be shared …

2. **Use a pronoun that represents a noun used in the preceding sentence.** Because "*it*" means "responsibility," the

---

topic sentence a sentence that identifies the portion of the topic being discussed and presents the central idea of the paragraph

deductive a paragraph in which the topic sentence precedes the details

inductive a paragraph in which the topic sentence follows the details

coherence cohesion, so that each sentence is linked to the preceding sentences in some way

second sentence below is linked directly with the first.

... to take this responsibility. It can be shared ...

3. **Use connecting words.** Examples include *however, therefore, yet, nevertheless, consequently, also,* and *in addition.* "*However*" implies "We're continuing with the same topic, just moving into a different phase." Remember, though, that good techniques can be overused. Unnecessary connectors are space consuming and distracting. Usually they can be spotted (and crossed out) in proofreading.

... to take this responsibility. However, few are willing to ...

Just as sentences within a paragraph must be linked together, paragraphs within a document must also be linked together. Unless a writer or speaker is careful, the move from one major topic to the next will seem abrupt. A good transition sentence can bridge the gap between the two topics by summing up the preceding topic and leading a receiver to expect the next topic:

Once the new accounting system is put into place, training employees in its operation is vital.

This sentence could serve as a transition between "Installation" and "Training" division headings. Because a transition sentence comes at the end of one segment and before the next, it emphasizes the central idea of the preceding segment and confirms the relationship of the two segments. Although transition sentences are helpful if properly used, they can be overused. For most reports, transition sentences before major headings are sufficient. Normally, transition sentences before subheadings are unnecessary.

Keep Paragraphs Unified

Receivers expect the first paragraph of a message to introduce a topic, additional paragraphs to discuss it, and a final paragraph to tie all of the paragraphs together. The middle paragraphs should be arranged in a systematic sequence, and the end must be linked easily to some word or idea presented in the beginning.

The effect of a message that is *not* unified is like that of an incomplete circle or a picture with one element obviously missing.

- A unified email message, letter, memo, or report covers its topic adequately but does not include extraneous material. The document should have a beginning sentence that is appropriate for the expected receiver's reaction, paragraphs that present the bulk of the message, and an ending sentence that is an appropriate closing for the message presented.

- A unified report or presentation begins with an introduction that identifies the topic, reveals the thesis, and previews upcoming points. The introduction often includes some background, sources of information, and the method for treating data. Between the beginning and the ending, a unified report should have paragraphs arranged in a systematic sequence. A summary or conclusion brings all major points together.

Vary Sentence and Paragraph Length

Sentences of short or average length are easy to read and preferred for clear communication. However, keeping *all* sentences short is undesirable because the message might sound monotonous, unrealistic, or elementary. A 2-word sentence is acceptable; so is a 60-word sentence—if it is clear. Just as sentences should vary in length, they should also vary in structure. Some complex or compound sentences should be included with simple sentences.

Variety is just as desirable in paragraph length as it is in sentence length. A paragraph can be from one line in length to a dozen lines or more. However, just as with sentence length, average paragraph length also should be kept short, as appropriate to the document type:

- Paragraphs in letters, memos, and email messages are typically shorter than paragraphs in business reports.

- First and last paragraphs are normally short (one to four lines), and other paragraphs are normally no longer than *six lines*. A short first paragraph is more inviting to read than a long first paragraph, and a short last paragraph enables a writer to emphasize parting thoughts.

- The space between paragraphs is a welcome resting spot. Long paragraphs are difficult to read and make a message appear uninviting. Paragraph length will vary depending on the complexity of the subject matter. However, as a general rule paragraphs should be no longer than *8 to 10 lines*. This length usually allows enough space to include a topic sentence and three or four supporting statements. If the topic cannot be discussed in this space, divide the topic into additional paragraphs.

To observe the effect that large sections of unbroken text can have on the overall appeal of a document, examine the memos in Figure 4.2. Without question, the memo with the short, easy-to-read paragraphs is more inviting than the memo with one bulky paragraph.

Although variety is a desirable quality, it should not be achieved at the expense of consistency. Using *I* in one part of a message and then, without explanation, switching to *we* is inadvisable. Using the past tense in one sentence and the present tense in another sentence creates variety at the expense of consistency—unless the shift is required

Old Message

To: All employees
From: Gina Park [gina.park@xyzco.com]
Subject: New employee policy

Everyone,

Dear Employees,

It has come to our attention that many employees are misusing the buffer of 15 minutes given to them for reporting to work. From the beginning of this company, we have been granting a time period of 15 minutes, that is from 10 am to 10:15 am, as buffer time for employees to report. However, almost all the employees are entering the office past 10:15 am. Hence, we are adding a new employee policy, wherein for every two days of late reporting, there will be one day's pay deducted. This policy is effective from today.

To date, we never had any policy regarding latecomers. But, this introduction has become the need of the hour as in recent months our productivity has been severely affected. We believe that the introduction of this new policy will enable us to maintain internal discipline – helping us to increase our client services. It will also enable us to retain more employees and provide good incentives.

We are looking forward to getting the cooperation of all the employees to make TechPro a better workplace.

New Message

To: All employees
From: Gina Park [gina.park@xyzco.com]
Subject: New employee policy

Dear Employees,

We are adding a new employee policy, wherein for every two days of late reporting, there will be one day's pay deducted. This policy is effective from today.

The change is due to the fact that many employees are misusing the buffer of 15 minutes given to them for reporting to work. From the beginning of this company, we have been granting a time period of 15 minutes, from 10 am to 10:15 am, as buffer time for employees to report. However, almost all the employees are entering the office past 10:15 am.

This policy change has become necessary because in recent months our productivity has been severely affected. We believe that the introduction of this new policy will enable us to maintain internal discipline—helping us to increase our client services. It will also enable us to retain more employees and provide good incentives.

We are looking forward to getting the cooperation of all the employees to make TechPro a better workplace.

to indicate actual changes in time. Unnecessary changes from active to passive voice and from third to first person are also discouraged.

4-2c Craft Powerful Sentences

Well-developed sentences help the receiver to understand the message clearly and to react favorably to the writer or speaker. In this section, you will learn how to predominantly use the active voice and to emphasize important points, which affect the clarity and goodwill of your message.

Rely on Active Voice

Business communicators normally use the active voice more heavily than the passive voice because the active voice conveys ideas more vividly. In sentences in which the subject is the *doer* of an action, the verbs are called *active*. In sentences in which the subject is the *receiver* of an action, the verbs are called *passive*. Review the differences in the impact of the **passive voice** and **active voice**:

The active sentence invites the receiver to see the sales reps as actively engaged in setting expectations, whereas the passive sentence draws attention to the reports. Using active voice makes the subject the actor, which places greater emphasis on their concerns.

Even when a passive sentence contains additional words to reveal the doer, the imagery is less distinct than it would be if the sentence were active: *Free refills of soft drinks are expected by our customer base and shouldn't be the focus of cutbacks. Free refills* gets the most attention because it is the subject. The sentence seems to let the audience know the *result* of the action before revealing the doer; therefore, the sentence is less emphatic.

Although active voice conveys ideas more vividly, passive voice is useful for the following purposes:

- Concealing the doer: "Shortages in inventory have been found," rather than employees are the cause of inventory shortages.

- Placing more emphasis on *what* was done and who or what it was *done* to than on *who*

Passive Voice	**Active Voice**
Reports are transferred electronically from remote locations to the corporate office.	Our sales reps transfer reports from remote locations to the corporate office.

passive voice   when the subject of a sentence is the receiver of an action

active voice   when the subject of a sentence is the doer of an action

did it: "The reports have been compiled by our sales representatives."

- Subordinating an unpleasant thought or avoiding finger-pointing: "The printer on the second floor is not working properly," rather than "Lucy apparently fouled up the printer on the second floor."

Emphasize Important Ideas

A landscape artist wants some features in a picture to stand out boldly and others to get little attention. A musician sounds some notes loudly and others softly. Likewise, a writer or speaker wants some ideas to be *emphasized* and others to be *de-emphasized*. Normally, pleasant and important ideas should be emphasized; unpleasant and insignificant ideas should be de-emphasized. Emphasis techniques include sentence structure, repetition, words that label, position, and space and format.

Sentence Structure

For emphasis, place an idea in a simple sentence. The simple sentence in the following example has one independent clause. Because no other idea competes with it for attention, this idea is emphasized.

A Simple Sentence Is More Emphatic	A Compound Sentence Is Less Emphatic
Travis accepted a position in marketing.	Travis accepted a position in marketing, but he would have preferred a job in finance.

For emphasis, place an idea in an independent clause; for de-emphasis, place an idea in a dependent clause. In the following compound sentence, the idea of finance work is in an independent clause. Because an independent clause makes sense if the rest of the sentence is omitted, an independent clause is more emphatic than a dependent clause. In the complex sentence, the idea of finance work is in a dependent clause. Compared with the independent clause that follows ("Travis accepted a position…"), the idea in the dependent clause is de-emphasized.

Compound Sentence Is More Emphatic	Complex Sentence Is Less Emphatic
Travis accepted a position in marketing, but he would have preferred a job in finance.	Although he would have preferred a job in finance, Travis accepted a position in marketing.

Repetition

To emphasize a word, let it appear more than once in a sentence. For example, a clever advertisement by Office-Max used the word *stuff* repeatedly to describe generically

several types of office supply needs ranging from paper clips to color copies, and then ended succinctly with "OfficeMax … for your office stuff." Likewise, in the following example, "successful" receives more emphasis when the word is repeated.

Less Emphatic	More Emphatic
The meeting was successful because …	The meeting was successful; the success was attributed to …

Words That Label

For emphasis or de-emphasis, use words that label ideas as significant or insignificant. Note the labeling words used in the following examples to emphasize or de-emphasize an idea:

> But most important of all …
> A less significant aspect was …

Position

To emphasize a word or an idea, position it first or last in a sentence, clause, paragraph, or presentation. Note the additional emphasis placed on the words "success" or "failure" (or its equivalent) in the examples in the right column, because these phrases appear early or late in their clauses.

Less Emphatic	More Emphatic
- Our efforts ensured the <u>success</u> of the project; without them, <u>failure</u> would have been the result.	- <u>Success</u> resulted from our efforts; <u>failure</u> would have resulted without them.
- The project was <u>successful</u> because of our efforts; without them, <u>failure</u> would have been the result.	- <u>Success</u> resulted; without our efforts, <u>failure</u> would have been the outcome.

In paragraphs, the first and last words are in particularly emphatic positions. An idea that deserves emphasis can be placed in either position, but an idea that does not deserve emphasis can be placed in the middle of a long paragraph. The word *I*, which is frequently overused in messages, is especially noticeable if it appears as the first word. *I* is more noticeable if it appears as the first word in *every* paragraph. Avoid using the word *However* as the first word in a paragraph if the preceding paragraph is neutral or positive. These words imply that the next idea will be negative. Unless the purpose is to place emphasis on negatives, such words as *denied*, *rejected*, and *disappointed* should not appear as the last words in a paragraph.

Likewise, the central idea of a written or spoken report appears in the introduction (the beginning) and the conclusion (the end). Good transition sentences synthesize ideas at the end of each major division.

Space and Format

The various divisions of a report or spoken presentation are not expected to be of equal length, but an extraordinary amount of space devoted to a topic attaches special significance to that topic. Similarly, a topic that receives an especially small amount of space is de-emphasized. The manner in which information is physically arranged affects the emphasis it receives and consequently the overall impact of the message.

4-2d Select the Appropriate Conclusion

Conclusions can serve a variety of purposes. First, they provide a positive sense of closure to the reader. In certain cases, they may emphasize an important topic or takeaway from a message. Finally, they might encourage the reader to act. These options are respectively called goodwill, summary, and call-to-action conclusions.

A goodwill conclusion is typically used for short routine messages or good news or thank you messages.

An example of a goodwill conclusion for a routine message reminding the recipient of an upcoming meeting might be as simple as "I look forward to seeing you tomorrow."

A summary conclusion is often used for more complex, informative messages. An example summary conclusion for a message outlining a change in travel expense filing might emphasize the following points:

The new method of filing your travel expenses should streamline the process by eliminating paperwork and by making expense processing quicker and more convenient. The result is that you will also receive your travel reimbursement in less time. Please remember the new process goes into effect next month. Any questions you might have should be directed to your human resources advisor.

Not only does this conclusion remind the reader of the key points of the body of the message in a more general way, it is also persuasive in that it reminds the reader of the benefits of the new process.

The third type of conclusion, a call to action, is often used in persuasive or sales messages. The call-to-action conclusion attempts to "seal the deal" by encouraging the reader to take the next step in the process. In today's time-pressured world, it is easy to avoid following up on a persuasive request, so a call-to-action should be easy to comply with to better ensure follow through.

An example of a call-to-action conclusion for ensuring the completion of a report by a deadline is as follows:

It is important that we meet deadline on this project so that the company can report completion to shareholders in the meeting two weeks

from today. Remember to please share your section of the report with the team by Tuesday at 1 p.m. by posting it in the team Dropbox.

Even for the most routine message, a conclusion should be provided to provide closure and convey goodwill to the reader. But conclusions can also be used to emphasize important points and better ensure that a specific action is taken. Because of the immediacy principle, the last part of a message is more likely to be remembered. The importance of a good conclusion should not be overlooked; therefore, savvy writers will take advantage of this final opportunity to make an impact on the reader.

4-3 Revise to Grab Your Audience's Attention

Professional writers often recognize that the real work of writing occurs during the revision process. It is this step, however, that is often overlooked or given short shrift by those who do not write for a living. Revising and proofreading effectively, therefore, require a change in mindset.

4-3a Cultivate a Frame of Mind for Effective Revising and Proofreading

The following suggestions will guide your efforts in developing business documents that achieve the purpose for which they were intended.

- **Attempt to see things from your audience's perspective rather than from your own.** Being empathetic with your audience isn't as simple as it seems, particularly when dealing with today's diverse workforce. Erase the mindset, "I know what I need to say and how I want to say it." Instead, ask, "How would

Revising and proofreading are critical steps in business writing.

Andrey_Popov/Shutterstock

my audience react to this message? Is this message worded so that my audience can easily understand it? Does it convey a tone that will build goodwill?"

- **Revise your documents until you cannot see any additional ways to improve them.** Resist the temptation to think of your first draft as your last draft. Instead, look for ways to improve, and be willing to incorporate valid suggestions once you have completed a draft. Experienced writers believe that there is no such thing as good writing, but there is such a thing as good rewriting. Author Dorothy Parker, who wrote for *Vanity Fair* and *Esquire*, once said, "I can't write five words but that I change seven."[1] Skilled speech writers might rewrite a script 15 to 20 times. Writers in public relations firms revise brochures and advertising copy until perhaps only a comma in the final draft is recognizable from the first draft. Even simple email messages require revision for clarity and mechanical errors, with extra passes needed depending on the number of recipients and the context of the message. Regardless of the message type, your careful revising will aid you in creating accurate, readable documents that produce results.

- **Be willing to allow others to make suggestions for improving your writing.** Because most of us consider our writing personal, we often feel reluctant to share it with others and can be easily offended if they suggest changes. This syndrome, called *writer's pride of ownership*, can prevent us from seeking needed assistance from experienced writers—a proven method of improving communication skills. On the job, especially in today's electronic workplace, your writing will be showcased to your supervisor, clients/customers, members of a collaborative writing team, and more. You have nothing to lose but much to gain by allowing others to critique your writing. This commitment is especially important considering the mistake hardest to detect is your own. However, you have the ultimate responsibility for your document; don't simply trust that someone else will catch and correct your errors.

The ability you've gained in following a systematic process for developing effective business messages will prove valuable as you direct your energies to developing effective messages as a member of a team. Refer to the "Check Your Communication" checklist on the Chapter 4 Review Card to review the guidelines for preparing and proofreading a rough draft.

The speed and convenience of today's electronic communication have caused many communicators to confuse informality with sloppiness. Sloppy messages contain misspellings, grammatical errors, unappealing and incorrect formats, and confusing content—all of which create a negative impression of the writer and the company, and affect the receiver's ability to understand the message. Some experts believe the increased use of email is leading to bosses becoming ruder. To combat against the harsh tone that often sets in when managers must respond to 300 to 500 emails weekly, Unilever is providing writing training and urging staff to think before they press the send button.[2]

As the sender, you are responsible for evaluating the effectiveness of each message you prepare. You must not use informality as an excuse to be sloppy. Instead, take one consultant's advice: "You can still be informal and not be sloppy. You can be informal and correct."[3] Take a good hard look at the messages you prepare. Commit to adjusting your message to the audience, designing appealing documents that are easily read, and following a systematic proofreading process to ensure error-free messages. This effort could save you from being embarrassed or jeopardizing your credibility.

4-3b Apply Visual Enhancements to Improve Readability

The vast amount of information created in today's competitive global market poses a challenge to you as a business writer. You must learn to create visually appealing documents that entice the audience to read rather than discard your message. Additionally, an effective design will enable you to highlight important information for maximum attention and to transition a receiver smoothly through sections of a long, complex document. These design techniques can be applied easily using word processing software. However, add visual enhancements only when they aid in comprehension. Overuse will cause your document to appear cluttered and will defeat your purpose of creating an appealing, easy-to-read document.

Enumerations

To emphasize units in a series, place a number, letter, or bullet before each element. Words preceded by numbers, bullets, or letters attract the receiver's special attention and are easier to locate when the page is reviewed.

Original	Highlighted
The department problems have been identified as tardiness, absenteeism, and low productivity.	The department problems have been identified as • tardiness, • absenteeism, • low productivity.

Enumerated or Bulleted Lists

Writers often want to save space; however, cluttered text is unappealing and difficult to read. *Chunking*—a desktop publishing term—is an answer to the problem. Chunking involves breaking down information into easily digestible pieces. It's the communication equivalent of Butterfinger BBs rather than the whole candy bar. The added white space divides the information into blocks, makes the page look more organized, and increases retention by 50 percent.[4]

Enumerated or bulleted lists can be used to chunk and add even greater visual impact to items in a series. Items appear on separate lines with numerals, letters, or various types of bullets (•, ◊, □, ✓, and so on) at the beginning. Multiple-line items often are separated by a blank line. This design creates more white space, which isolates the items from other text and demands attention. Bullets are typically preferred over numerals unless the sequence of the items in the series is critical (e.g., steps in a procedure that must be completed in the correct order). In the following excerpt from a long analytical report, the four supporting reasons for a conclusion are highlighted in a bulleted list:

Original	Highlighted
The Operations and Maintenance Department performs important plant tasks each day. The department moves employees within the St. Louis complex. The vans take employees from the gate to their work areas. Another function of the vans is to transport employees to storage areas to pick up supplies. Employees are also taken to areas such as the cafeteria and training rooms. In addition, the department delivers internal packages, tools, and inter-office mail.	The Operations and Maintenance Department performs the following five important plant tasks each day: • Moving employees within the St. Louis complex • Taking employees from the gate to their work areas • Transporting employees to storage areas to pick up supplies • Taking employees to areas such as the cafeteria and training rooms • Delivering internal packages, tools, and inter-office mail

Headings

Headings are signposts that direct the receiver from one section of the document to another. Studies have shown that readers find documents with headings easier to grasp and that they are more motivated to pay attention to the text, even in a short document such as a half-page warranty.[5] You'll find that organizing the content of various types of documents with logical, well-written headings will make the documents more readable and appealing. Follow these general guidelines for writing effective headings:

• Compose brief headings that make a connection with the receiver, giving clear cues as to the usefulness of the information (e.g., "How Do I Apply?"). Consider using questions rather than noun phrases to let readers know they are reading the information they need

(i.e., choose "Who Is Eligible to Apply?" rather than "Eligible Loan Participants").[6] Consider talking headings that reveal the conclusions reached in the following discussion, rather than general topic headings. For example, "Costs Are Prohibitive" is more emphatic than "Cost Factors."

• Strive for parallel structure of headings within a section. For example, mixing descriptive phrases with questions requires additional mental effort and distracts readers who expect parallel writing.

• Follow a hierarchy, with major headings receiving more attention than minor headings or paragraph headings. To draw more attention to a major heading, center it and use a heavier, larger typestyle or brighter text color.

Tables and Graphs

Tables and graphs are used to simplify and clarify information and to add variety to long sections of dense text. The clearly labeled rows and columns in a table organize large amounts of specific numeric data and facilitate analysis. Graphics such as pie, line, and bar charts visually depict relationships within the data. They provide quick estimates rather than specific information.

Lines and Borders

Horizontal and vertical lines can be added to partition text or to focus attention on a specific line or lines. For example, a thin line followed by a thick line effectively separates the identification and qualifications sections of a résumé. Placing a border around a paragraph or section of text sets that information apart and adding shading inside the box adds greater impact. For example, a pull-quote format might spotlight a testimonial from a satisfied customer in a sales letter, important dates to remember in a memorandum, or a section of a document that must be completed and returned.

Relevant Images

A variety of interesting shapes can be used to highlight information and add appeal. Examples include creating a rectangular call-out box highlighting a key idea, with an arrow pointing to a specific number in a table; surrounding a title with a shaded oval for added impact; and using built-in designs to illustrate a process, cycle, hierarchy, or other relationships. Clip art or photos can also be added to reinforce an idea and add visual appeal.

Battling to manage an avalanche of information, the recipients of your messages will appreciate your extra effort to create an easy-to-read, appealing document. These fundamental techniques will be invaluable as you enhance printed documents, such as letters, memos, reports, agendas, handouts, and minutes for meetings.

Step 7: Revise for Style and Tone

From using software designed to improve readability to selecting appropriate words and phrases, you can improve the style and tone of your messages by considering the following suggestions.

4-4a Improve Readability

Although sentences are arranged in a logical sequence and are written coherently, the receiver might find reading the sentences difficult. Several programs have been developed to measure the reading difficulty of your writing. Electronic tools aid you in making computations and identifying changes that will improve readability.

The grammar and style checker feature of leading word-processing software calculates readability measures to aid you in writing for quick and easy reading and listening. The Fog Index, a popular readability index developed by Robert Gunning, and the Flesch–Kincaid Grade Level calculator available in Microsoft Word consider the length of sentences and the difficulty of words, to produce the approximate grade level at which a person must read to understand the material. For example, a grade level of 10 indicates a person needs to be able to read at the tenth-grade level to understand the material. Fortunately, you don't have to calculate readability manually, but understanding the manual calculation of the Fog index will illustrate clearly how sentence length and difficulty of words affect readability calculations and will guide you in adapting messages.

Trying to write at the exact grade level of the receiver is not advised. You may not know the exact grade level, and even those who have earned advanced degrees appreciate writing they can read and understand quickly and easily. Also, writing a passage with a readability index appropriate for the audience does not guarantee the message will be understood. Despite simple language and short sentences, the message can be distorted by imprecise words, biased language, jargon, and translations that ignore cultural interpretations, to name just a few. The value of calculating a readability measure lies in the feedback you gain about the average length of sentences and the difficulty of the words. Revise and recalculate the readability index, and continue revising until you feel that the reading level is appropriate for the intended audience.

The grammar and style feature in word-processing programs also locates grammatical errors, including misspellings and common usage errors, such as the use of fragments, run-on sentences, subject–verb disagreement, passive voice, double words, and split infinitives. Because it can only guess at the structure of a sentence and then apply a rigid set of rules, a grammar and style checker, such as a spell checker, must be used cautiously. It is not a reliable substitute for a human editor who has an effective writing style and is familiar with the rules the software displays. Allow the software to flag misspellings and writing errors as you write; then, accept or reject the suggested changes based on your knowledge of effective writing, and use the readability measures to adjust your writing levels appropriately, as shown in Model Document 4.1.

> **clichés** overused expressions that can cause their users to be perceived as unoriginal, unimaginative, lazy, and perhaps even disrespectful

4-4b Eliminate Outdated Expressions

In addition to using software tools to approve readability, several additional steps can be taken to improve the style and tone of a written message. For example, using outdated expressions will give your message a dull, stuffy, unnatural tone. Instead, substitute fresh, original expressions that reflect today's language patterns.

Outdated Expressions	Improvement
• <u>As per your request</u>, the report has been submitted to the client.	• <u>As you requested</u>, the report has been submitted to the client.
• <u>Enclosed please find</u> a copy of my transcript.	• The <u>enclosed</u> transcript should answer your questions.
• <u>Very truly yours</u> (used as the complimentary close in a letter)	• Sincerely

4-4c Curb Clichés

Clichés, or overused expressions, are common in our everyday conversations and in business messages. These handy verbal shortcuts are convenient, quick, easy to use, and often include simple metaphors and analogies that effectively communicate the most basic idea or emotion or the most complex business concept. However, writers and speakers who routinely use stale clichés may be perceived as unoriginal, unimaginative, lazy, and perhaps even disrespectful. Less frequently used words capture the receiver's attention because they are original, fresh, and interesting.

Clichés present another serious problem. Consider the scenario of shoppers standing in line at a discount store with the cashier saying to each, "Thanks for shopping with us today. Please come again." Because the last shopper has heard the words several times already, they may not consider the statement genuine. The cashier has used an expression that can be stated without thinking

Step 1: Evaluate and respond to advice given for grammar and style errors detected.

Step 2: Use counts, averages, and readability indexes as guides for adjusting writing level appropriately.

Source: Microsoft Corporation

Source: Microsoft Corporation

Improving Your Writing With the Computer

Hone your computer skills to spend more time writing and less time formatting.

☑ Draft in a font style and size that can be easily read on-screen; postpone formatting until the revision is done.

☑ Use the *Find* and *Go To* commands to search and make changes.

☑ Learn time-saving keyboard shortcuts for frequently used commands such as *Copy* and *Cut*. Customize software so that you can access these commands easily.

☑ Use automatic numbering to arrange numerical or alphabetical lists and to ensure accuracy.

☑ Save time by using built-in styles such as cover pages, headers/footers, list and table formats, text boxes, and graphical effects.

☑ Save frequently used text such as a letterhead or your signature line so you can insert it with a single click.

☑ Use the *Citations and Bibliography* command to format references and the *Document Styles* feature to automatically generate a content page and index.

Use formatting features to create an organized and polished appearance.

☑ Add spacing between lines and paragraphs, and use crisp, open fonts such as Calibri for a contemporary look that is easy to read on-screen.

☑ Apply color-infused document themes and built-in styles to reflect a consistent brand identity.

Use proofing features to locate errors.

☑ Use the spell checker frequently as you draft and revise. Be aware that the spell checker will not identify miskeyings (*than* for *then*), commonly misused words, homophones (*principle, principal*), omitted words, missing or out-of-order enumerations, and content errors.

☑ Use grammar check to provide feedback on usage, reading level, comprehension factors, and other errors and weaknesses that cannot be detected electronically.

☑ Use a thesaurus only when you can recognize the precise meaning needed.

Cengage

and possibly without meaning. A worn expression can convey messages such as "You are not special," or "For you, I won't bother to think. The phrases I use in talking with others are surely good enough for you." Original expressions convey sincerity and build strong human relations.

Cliché	Improvement
• Pushed (or stretched) the envelope	• Took a risk or considered a new option
• Skin in the game	• Committed to the project
• Cover all the bases	• Get agreement/input from everyone
• At the end of the day	• Ultimately or finally
• Buy-in	• Agreement or commitment
• Raise the bar	• Elevate

4-4d Eliminate Profanity

Increasing tolerance of profanity is an issue of concern to society as a whole, and also for employers and employees as they communicate at work. You must consider the potential business liabilities and legal implications resulting from the use of profanity that may offend others or create a hostile work environment. Recognize that minimizing or eliminating profanity is another important way in which you must adapt your language for communicating effectively to foster human relations in a professional setting.

4-4e Use Simple, Informal Words

Business writers prefer simple, informal words that are readily understood and less distracting than more difficult, formal words. If a receiver questions the sender's motive for using formal words, the impact of the message may be diminished. Likewise, the impact would be diminished if the receiver questioned a sender's use of simple, informal words. This distraction is unlikely, however, if the message contains good ideas that are well organized and well supported. Under these conditions, simple words enable a receiver to understand the message clearly and quickly.

To illustrate, consider the unnecessary complexity of a notice that appeared on a corporate bulletin board: "Employees impacted by the strike are encouraged to utilize the hotline number to arrange for alternative transportation to work. Should you encounter difficulties in arranging for alternative transportation to work,

> **jargon** specialized terminology that professionals in some fields use when communicating with colleagues in the same field

please contact your immediate supervisor." A simple, easy-to-read revision would be, "If you can't get to work, call the hotline or your supervisor." For further illustration, note the added clarity of the following words:

Formal Words	Informal Words
• terminate	• end
• procure	• get
• remunerate	• pay
• corroborate	• support

Using words that have more than two or three syllables when they are appropriate is acceptable. However, you should avoid regular use of a long, infrequently used word when a simpler, more common word conveys the same idea. Professionals in some fields often use specialized terminology, referred to as **jargon**, when communicating with colleagues in the same field. In this case, the audience is likely to understand the words, and using the jargon saves time. However, when communicating with people outside the field, professionals should select simple, common words to convey messages. Using clear, jargon-free language that can be readily understood by non-native recipients and easily translated is especially important in international communication.

You should build your vocabulary so that you can use just the right word for expressing an idea and can understand what others have said. Just remember the purpose of business messages is not to advertise a knowledge of infrequently used words, but to transmit a clear and tactful message. For the informal communication practiced in business, use simple words instead of more complicated words that have the same meaning.

4-4f Communicate Concisely

Concise communication includes all relevant details in the fewest possible words. Abraham Lincoln's two-minute Gettysburg Address is a premier example of concise communication. Mark Twain alluded to the skill needed to write concisely when he said, "I would have written a shorter book if I had had time."

Some executives have reported that they read memos that are two paragraphs long but may only skim or discard longer ones. Yet it's clear that this survival technique can lead to a vital message being discarded or misread. Concise writing is essential for workers struggling to handle an avalanche of information, which is often read on the run on their smartphone. Concise messages save time and money for both the sender and the receiver, as the receiver's attention is directed toward the important details and is not distracted by excessive words and details.

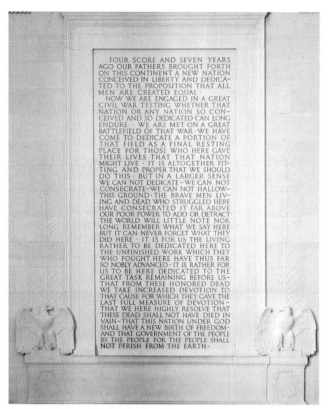

Abraham Lincoln's two-minute Gettysburg address is a classic example of concise communication.

Source: iStock.com/AS506

The following techniques will produce concise messages:

- **Eliminate redundancies.** A **redundancy** is a phrase in which one word unnecessarily repeats an idea contained in an accompanying word. "Absolutely necessary" and "negative misfortune" are redundant because both words have the same meaning; only "necessary" and "misfortune" are needed. A few of the many redundancies in business writing are shown in the following list. Be conscious of redundancies in your speech and writing patterns.

Redundancies to Avoid

Needless repetition:	advance forward, it goes without saying, best ever, cash money, important essentials, each and every, dollar amount, pick and choose, past experience
Unneeded modifiers:	new innovations, personal friend, actual experience, brief summary, complete stop, collaborate, disappear from sight, honest truth, trickle down, month of May, personal opinion, red in color, severe crisis, currently available
Repeated acronyms:	ATM machine, PIN number, SAT tests, SIC code

Redundancy is not to be confused with repetition used for emphasis. In a sentence or paragraph, you may need to use a certain word again. When repetition serves a specific purpose, it is not an error. Redundancy serves no purpose and *is* an error.

- **Use active voice to reduce the number of words.** Passive voice typically adds unnecessary words, such as prepositional phrases. Compare the sentence length in each of these examples:

Passive Voice	**Active Voice**
• Work schedules will be updated by department supervisors.	• Department supervisors will update work schedules.
• The project planning department will be transferred to the third floor next month by a moving company.	• Next month, movers will transfer the project planning department to the third floor.

- **Review the main purpose of your writing, and identify the relevant details needed for the receiver to understand and take necessary action.** More information is not necessarily better information. You may be so involved and, perhaps, so enthusiastic about your message that you believe the receiver needs to know everything that you know. Or perhaps, you just need to devote more time to audience analysis and empathy.

- **Eliminate clichés that are often wordy and not necessary to understand the message.** For example, "Thank you for your letter," "I am writing to," "May I take this opportunity," "It has come to my attention," and "We wish to inform you" only delay the major purpose of the message.

- **Do not restate ideas that are sufficiently implied.** Notice how the following sentences are improved when ideas are implied. The revised sentences are concise, yet the meaning is not affected.

Wordy	**Concise**
• John prepared Power-Point slides and practiced his presentation.	• John prepared for his presentation.
• The manager reviewed team reports and revised the project schedule.	• The manager revised the project schedule.

- **Shorten sentences by using suffixes or prefixes, making**

> **redundancy** a phrase in which one word unnecessarily repeats an idea contained in an accompanying word (e.g., "exactly identical")

changes in word form, or substituting precise words for phrases. In the following examples, the expressions in the right column provide useful techniques for saving space and being concise. However, the examples in the left column are not grammatically incorrect. Sometimes their use provides just the right emphasis.

Wordy	Concise
• She completed her work in <u>a competent manner.</u>	• She was a <u>competent worker.</u>
• His style of <u>writing</u> was quite <u>florid.</u>	• He had a <u>florid writing</u> style.
• He believes the new policy guidelines <u>to be of little value.</u>	• He believes the new policy guidelines are <u>valueless.</u>
• Sales staff <u>with high energy levels</u> ...	• <u>Energetic</u> sales staff ...
• ... arranged in <u>chronological order.</u>	• ... arranged <u>chronologically.</u>

- **Use a compound adjective.** By using the compound adjective, you can reduce the number of words required to express your ideas and, thus, save the reader a little time.

Wordy	Concise
• The corporation values employees <u>who speak well.</u>	• The corporation values <u>well-spoken</u> employees.
• <u>Karen Lewis, who is well liked by her colleagues,</u> will take ...	• <u>Well-liked Karen Lewis</u> will take ...
• The <u>intranet</u> will be down for <u>two days</u> for routine <u>upgrades</u> on July 23 and 24.	• The <u>two-day intranet upgrade</u> will occur on July 23 and 24.

4-4g Project a Positive, Tactful Tone

Being adept at communicating negative information will give you the confidence you need to handle sensitive situations in a constructive manner, resulting in a positive **tone**. The following suggestions reduce the sting of an unpleasant thought:

- **State ideas using positive language.** Rely mainly on positive words—words that speak of what can be done instead of what cannot be done, of the pleasant instead of the unpleasant. In each of the following pairs, both sentences are sufficiently clear, but

tone the way a statement sounds; it conveys the writer's or speaker's attitude toward the message and the receiver

the positive words in the improved sentences make the message more diplomatic and promote positive human relations.

Negative Tone	Positive Tone
• <u>You forgot</u> to fill in the last column of the annual budget report.	• Please fill in the last column of the annual budget report.
• We <u>cannot</u> complete your order without your email address.	• Please supply your email address so that we can complete your order.
• You <u>failed</u> to submit your expense report by the monthly deadline.	• Please submit your expense report by the next monthly deadline.

- **Avoid using second person when stating negative ideas.** Use second person for presenting pleasant ideas; use third person for presenting unpleasant ideas. Note the following examples:

Pleasant Idea (Second Person Preferred)	
• You delivered a compelling presentation.	• *The person will appreciate the emphasis placed on their excellent performance.*

Unpleasant Idea (Third Person Preferred)	
• The supply order was incorrectly filled out.	• *"You filled out the supply order incorrectly" directs undiplomatic attention to the person who made the error.*

- **Use passive voice to convey negative ideas.** Presenting an unpleasant thought emphatically (as active verbs do) makes human relations difficult. Compare the tone of the following negative thoughts written in active and passive voices:

Active Voice	Passive Voice (Preferred for Negative Ideas)
• Juanita did not complete the order form correctly.	• The order needed revision.
• Shelly missed the deadline for proposal submission by a week.	• The proposal was submitted a week after deadline.

- Positive words are normally preferred, but sometimes the addition of negative words can sharpen a contrast (and thus increase clarity):

> Please complete the online order form; phone and email requests will take longer to process. Original copies are to be submitted to the certification board; photocopies will not be accepted.

- Because the subject of each active sentence is the doer, the sentences are emphatic. As the idea is negative, Shelly probably would appreciate being taken out of the picture. The passive voice sentences place more emphasis on the job than on who failed to complete it. They retain the essential ideas, but the ideas seem less irritating. For negative ideas, use passive voice.

- **Use active voice to promote positive ideas.** Just as emphasis on negatives hinders human relations, emphasis on positives promotes human relations. Which sentence makes the positive idea more vivid?

Passive Voice	Active Voice (Preferred for Positive Ideas)
The proposal was submitted before the deadline.	Shelly submitted the proposal before the deadline.

Because "Shelly" is the subject of the active voice sentence, the receiver can easily envision the action. Shelly is recognized for meeting the deadline in this sentence. In the passive message, the fact that the deadline was met receives emphasis.

- **Use the subjunctive mood.** Sometimes the tone of a message can be improved by switching to the subjunctive mood. **Subjunctive sentences** speak of a wish, necessity, doubt, or condition contrary to fact, and use such conditional expressions as *I wish, as if, could, would,* and *might.* In the following examples, the sentence in the right column conveys a negative idea in a positive language, which is more diplomatic than negative language.

Negative Tone	Subjunctive Mood Conveys a Positive Tone
• I can't complete the report.	• When the information is made available, I can complete the report.
• I cannot attend the planning meeting.	• I could attend the planning meeting if the date were changed to next week.
• I don't believe his statements about the product's efficiency.	• I wish I could believe his statements about the product's efficiency.

Sentences in subjunctive mood often include a reason that makes the negative idea seem less objectionable and thus, improves the tone. Tone is important, but clarity is even more important. The revised sentence in each of the preceding pairs sufficiently *implies* the unpleasant idea without stating it directly. If for any reason a writer or speaker suspects the implication is not sufficiently strong, a direct statement in negative terms is preferable.

- **Include a pleasant statement in the same sentence.** A pleasant idea is included in the following examples to improve the tone:

Negative Tone	Positive Tone
• Your ability to meet deadlines is satisfactory.	• Although your ability to meet deadlines was satisfactory, your work to motivate your team was excellent.
• Increased health-care costs have decreased funds available for salary adjustments.	• Increased health-care costs have decreased funds available for salary adjustments, but we hope a shorter workweek will offset employee expectations.

4-4h Use Euphemisms Cautiously

A **euphemism** is a kind word substituted for one that may offend or suggest something unpleasant. For example, the idea of picking up neighborhood garbage does not sound especially inviting. Someone who does such work is often referred to as a *sanitation worker*. This term has a more pleasant connotation than *garbage collector*.

Choose the euphemistic terms rather than the negative terms shown in the following examples:

Negative Tone	Euphemistic Tone
• aged or elderly	• older persons
• dying	• fading away/near the end
• used or secondhand	• preowned
• prison	• correctional facility
• disabled or handicapped	• person with a disability
• patient management	• care coordination/supportive services

Generally, you can recognize such expressions for what they are—unpleasant ideas presented with a little sugarcoating. Knowing the sender was simply trying to be polite and positive, receivers are more likely to react favorably. You should avoid, however, euphemisms that

> **subjunctive sentences** sentences that speak of a wish, necessity, doubt, or condition contrary to fact, and employ such conditional expressions as *I wish, as if, could, would,* and *might*
>
> **euphemism** a kind word substituted for one that may offend or suggest something unpleasant

excessively sugarcoat or those that suggest subtle sarcasm. For example, to refer to a janitor as a *maintenance engineer* is to risk conveying a negative metacommunication, such as "This person does not hold a very respectable position, but I did the best I could to make it sound good." To the receiver (and to the janitor), just plain *janitor* would sound better.

You will also want to avoid doublespeak, also known as *doubletalk* or *corporate speak*. Such terms refer to euphemisms that deliberately mislead, hide, or evade the truth. This distortion of the truth is often found in military, political, and corporate language. A loss of credibility may result when a corporate leader says a department has a *negative cash flow* instead of saying the department is *spending more than it is allotted*. Another example would be a politician who talks of an *enhanced interrogation technique* rather than *torture*, or *collateral damage* or *friendly fire* rather than civilians killed accidentally by the military's own weapons. Companies use doublespeak when they make *workforce reductions* or offer workers a *career opportunity adjustment* or *voluntary termination*. One company called the permanent shutdown of a steel plant an *indefinite idling* in an attempt to avoid paying severance or pension benefits to the displaced workers.

Despite your training in writing, you may fall into the trap of mirroring the writing of people above you on the career ladder who prefer writing in doublespeak. They often choose doublespeak over clear, concise writing because of the misguided belief that doublespeak makes them sound informed and professional. Such vagueness protects them when they're unsure how their messages will be received and makes writing easy once they learn the code. Instead of falling into doublespeak, learn to develop clear, concise messages that clarify ideas and provide direction to recipients, regardless of their culture, while enhancing your credibility as an honest communicator. A CEO of a writing training company has another interesting angle on clear writing. They contend, "Articulation of thought is an element of intelligence, and you can increase your intelligence through writing." Working to articulate ideas clearly and logically through writing makes people smarter! That is a motivating reason for perfecting writing (and speaking) skills in our professional and personal lives.

> **doublespeak** also called doubletalk or corporate speak; euphemisms that deliberately mislead, hide, or evade the truth
>
> **goodwill** an attitude of kindness or friendliness that results in a good relationship
>
> **denotative meaning** the literal meaning of a word that most people assign to it
>
> **connotative meaning** the literal meaning of a word plus an extra message that reveals the speaker's or writer's qualitative judgment

4-4i Avoid Condescending or Demeaning Expressions

Condescending words seem to imply that the communicator is temporarily coming down from a level of superiority to join the receiver on a level of inferiority. Such words damage efforts to build and protect goodwill.

A demeaning expression (sometimes called a *dysphemism*) makes an idea seem negative or disrespectful. Avoid demeaning expressions because they divert attention from the real message to emotional issues that have little to do with the message. Many examples can be taken as contempt for an occupation or a specific job or position (*bean counters* for accountants, *ambulance chasers* for lawyers, *spin doctors* for politicians or public relations directors, and *shrinks* for psychiatrists). Like words that attack races or nationalities, words that ridicule occupations work against a communicator's purpose.

Many demeaning expressions are common across regions, ages, and perhaps even cultures. Some demeaning expressions belong to a particular company. For example, *turtles* was coined in one firm to mock first-year employees for their slow work pace. In 2020, the then-President Trump's rhetoric about the spread of COVID-19 was blamed for fueling a surge in harassment of Asian Americans. "Anti-Asian sentiment depicted in the tweets containing the term 'Chinese Virus' likely perpetuated racist attitudes and parallels the anti-Asian hate crimes that have occurred since," said Dr. Yulin Hswen, an assistant professor of epidemiology at University of California, San Francisco, and lead author of a study published on the issue. The study also found that the timing of the former president's tweet was significant. The first time he used "Chinese Virus" was March 16, 2020, and the following week saw an increase in anti-Asian hashtags and a rise in hate crimes.[7]

Effective communicators choose respectful expressions that build and protect goodwill.

4-4j Use Connotative Tone Cautiously

Human relations can suffer when connotative words are inadvertently or intentionally used instead of denotative words. The denotative meaning of a word is the literal meaning that most people assign to it. The connotative meaning is the literal meaning plus an extra message that reveals the speaker's or writer's qualitative judgment, as shown in this example:

Connotative Meaning with Negative Implication	Denotative Meaning (Preferred)
Please don't hassle the customer service representatives with too frequent questions.	Please don't question the customer service representatives too frequently.

The connotative meaning of *hassle* carries an additional message that the writer has a bias against asking questions. The connotation may needlessly introduce thoughts about whether asking questions is beneficial and may distract the receiver from paying sufficient attention to the statements that follow. Connotations, like metacommunications discussed in Chapter 2, involve messages that are implied. In the preceding example, the connotation seems to be more harmful than helpful.

At times, however, connotations can be helpful, as seen in the following examples:

Connotative Meaning with Positive Meaning (Preferred)	Denotative Meaning
• Our <u>corporate think tank</u> has developed an outstanding production process.	• <u>Research and Development</u> has developed an outstanding production process.
• Rita is a <u>real spark plug</u> when it comes to sales.	• Rita's <u>drive and enthusiasm</u> make her successful at sales.

In crafting business messages, rely mainly on denotative or connotative words that will be interpreted in a positive manner. To be sure that your connotative words are understood and will generate goodwill, consider your audience, the context, and the timing of the message.

- **Connotative words may be more easily misinterpreted than denotative words.** Because of differences in peoples' perceptions based on their life experiences, words that are perceived positively by one person may be perceived negatively by another. In some cases, receivers may simply not understand the connotative words. Damaged human relations occur when managers repeatedly convey connotative messages without considering whether employees can interpret the meanings as they are intended.

- **The appropriateness of connotations varies with the audience to which they are addressed and the context in which they appear.** For example, referring to a car as a *foreign job* or *sweet* might be received differently by teenagers than by senior citizens. Such expressions are less appropriate in a research report than in a blog or popular magazine.

4-4k Use Specific Language Appropriately

To help the receiver understand your message easily, select words that paint intense, colorful word pictures by using specific descriptions rather than generalities. Creating clear mental images adds energy and imagination to your message, thus increasing its overall impact.

General	Specific (Preferred)
• The <u>public outcry</u> was huge.	• <u>More than 3 million emails were received</u> from the public.
• Please get back to me soon about your proposal changes.	• Please supply me with the changes to the proposal by this Friday at noon.
• Sam is a great manager.	• Sara shines as a manager because of her <u>ability to stay on task and yet make people feel supported.</u>

Sometimes, using general statements can be useful in building and protecting goodwill. General words keep negative ideas from receiving more emphasis than they deserve. In addition, senders who don't have specific information, or for some reason don't want to divulge it, use general words.

General (Preferred)	Specific
• Three customers complained about their <u>service</u>.	• Three customers complained because their <u>food order was incomplete and the food was delivered cold.</u>
• I look forward to <u>working with you again</u>.	• I look forward to <u>working with you again because of your easygoing manner and attention to details.</u>

4-4l Use Bias-Free Language

Being responsive to individual differences requires you to make a conscious effort to use bias-free (nondiscriminatory) language. Using language that does not exclude, stereotype, or offend others permits them to focus on your message rather than to question your sensitivity. Goodwill can be damaged when biased statements are made related to gender, race or ethnicity, religion, age, or disability. The following guidelines will help you avoid bias:

1. **Avoid referring to men and women in stereotyped roles and occupations.** The use of *he* to refer to anyone in a group was once standard and accepted; however, this usage is considered insensitive and, to some, offensive. Therefore, do not use the pronoun *he* when referring to a person in a group that may include women or the pronoun *she* to refer to a group that may include men. Otherwise, you may unintentionally communicate an insensitive message that only women or only men can perform certain tasks

or serve in certain professions. Follow these four approaches to avoid gender bias:

Guideline	Gender-Biased	Improved
Avoid using a pronoun	• Each employee must complete his vacation request form.	• Employees must complete a vacation request form.
Repeat the noun	• Expect promptness from your guide. Ask him to …	• Expect promptness from your guide. Ask the guide to …
Use a plural noun	• Each employee should update and confirm his contact information.	• Employees should update and confirm their contact information.

2. **Use occupational titles that reflect genuine sensitivity to gender.** Note the gender-free titles that can be easily substituted to avoid bias:

Gender-Biased	Gender-Free
• Salesman	• Salesperson
• Chairman	• Chair

3. **Avoid designating an occupation by gender.** For example, omit "woman" in "A woman doctor has initiated this research." The doctor's profession, not the gender, is the point of the message. Similarly, avoid using the -ess ending to differentiate genders in an occupation:

Gender-Biased	Gender-Free
• Waiter or waitress	• Server
• Hostess	• Host

4. **Avoid using expressions that may be perceived to be gender-biased.** Avoid commonly used expressions in which "man" represents all humanity, such as "To go where no man has gone before," and stereotypical characteristics, such as "man hours," "man-made goods," and "work of four strong men." Note the improvements made in the following examples by eliminating the potentially offensive words.

Gender-Biased	Improved
• Our energy products will benefit all of mankind.	• Our energy products will benefit humanity.
• Laurence is the best man for the job.	• Laurence is the best person for the job.

5. **Avoid racial or ethnic bias.** Include racial or ethnic identification only when relevant, and avoid referring to these groups in stereotypical ways.

Racially or Ethnically Biased	Improved
• Please give your form to Sheila, the Asian woman.	• Please give the form to Sheila, the woman at that desk.
• The articulate African American engineer overseeing the product redesign plans suggested …	• The engineer overseeing the product redesign plans suggested …

6. **Avoid age bias.** Include age only when relevant, and avoid demeaning expressions related to age.

Age-Biased	Improved
George is the older gentleman who works downstairs.	George works downstairs in the office on the right.

7. **Avoid disability bias.** When communicating about people with disabilities, use people-first language. That is, refer to the person first and the disability second so that focus is appropriately placed on the person's ability rather than on the disability. Also avoid words with negative or judgmental connotations, such as *handicap*, *unfortunate*, *afflicted*, and *victim*. Consider these more sensitive revisions:

Insensitive	Sensitive (People-First)
• Blind employees receive …	• Employees with vision impairments receive …
• The elevator is for the exclusive use of handicapped employees and should not be used by normal employees.	• The elevator is for the exclusive use of employees with disabilities.

4-5 Proofread and Revise

Errors in writing and mechanics may seem isolated, but the truth is proofreading is important. You don't have to look far to see silly typos or obvious instances of writers relying only on the computer spell checker. The classifieds in a newspaper advertised "fully fascinated and spade damnation puppies." The advertisement was for fully vaccinated and spayed Dalmatian puppies. These errors clearly illustrate how spell check can fail, but goofs such as this one are not limited to newspapers.

In 2017, a typo in some debugging code caused a crippling server disruption for Amazon Web Services (AWS), costing its business customers an estimated $150 million. An AWS engineer was debugging an issue with the billing system for the company's popular cloud storage service S3 and accidentally mistyped a command. What followed was a several hours' long cloud outage that wreaked havoc across the internet and resulted in hundreds of millions of dollars in losses for AWS customers and others who rely on third-party services hosted by AWS.[8]

In 2019, Australia's latest A$50 note came with a big blunder hidden in the small print—a somewhat embarrassing typo. The Reserve Bank of Australia (RBA) spelled "responsibility" as "responsibilty" on millions of the new yellow notes. The RBA confirmed the typo and said the error would be fixed in future print runs. However, until that time, about 46 million of the notes bearing the typo were in use across the country. The bills were released late in 2018 and featured Edith Cowan, the first female member of an Australian parliament. It took more than six months for someone with a good magnifying glass to spot the typo.[9]

Each of these actual mistakes illustrates that inattention to proofreading can be potentially embarrassing and incredibly expensive.

Following systematic revision procedures will help you produce error-free documents that reflect positively on the company and you. Using the procedures that follow, you will see that effective proofreading must be done several times, each time for a specific purpose.

Follow these simple procedures to produce a finished product that is free of errors in content, organization, style, mechanics, format, and layout:

1. **Use the spell checker to locate simple keying errors and repeated words.** When the software cannot guess the correct spelling based on your incorrect attempt, you will need to consult a dictionary, other printed source, or online reference.

2. **Proofread the document onscreen, concentrating first on errors in content, organization, and style.** To locate errors, ask the following questions:

   ○ **Content.** Is the information complete? Have I included all the details the receiver needs to understand the message and to take necessary action? Is the information accurate? Have I checked the accuracy of any calculations, dates, names, addresses, and numbers? Have words been omitted?

   ○ **Organization.** Is the main idea presented appropriately, based on the receiver's likely reaction (deductive or inductive organization)? Are supporting ideas presented in a logical order? Does the document pass the "skim test"? Remember,

business audiences are often crunched for time, so it is imperative that the message is organized in such a way so as its meaning and content are immediately apparent. In other words, is the purpose and content of the message clearly communicated by the introduction, use of headings, and use of accurate topic sentences?

   ○ **Style.** Is the message clear? Will the receiver interpret the information correctly? Is the message concise and written at an appropriate level for the receiver? Does the message reflect a considerate, caring attitude and focus primarily on the receiver's needs? Does the message treat the receiver honestly and ethically?

3. **Proofread a second time, concentrating on mechanical errors.** You are searching for potentially damaging errors that the spell checker cannot detect. These problem areas are as follows:

   ○ **Grammar, capitalization, punctuation, number usage, and abbreviations.** Review the grammatical principles presented in the appendix if necessary.

   ○ **Word substitutions.** Check the proper use of words such as *your* and *you* and words that sound alike (*there*, *they're*, or *their*; *affect* or *effect*).

   ○ **Parts of the document other than the body.** Proofread the entire document. Errors often appear in the opening and closing sections of documents because writers typically begin proofreading at the first paragraph.

4. **Display the document in print preview mode, and edit for format and layout.** Follow these steps to be certain that the document adheres to appropriate business formats and is visually appealing:

   ○ Format according to a conventional format. Compare your document to the conventional business formats shown on your style and formatting cards, and make any revisions. Are all standard parts of the document included and presented in an acceptable format? Are all necessary special parts (e.g., attention line, enclosure, and so on) included? Does the message begin on the correct line? Should the right margin be justified or jagged?

   ○ Be sure numbered items are in the correct order. Inserting and deleting text might have changed the order of these items.

   ○ Evaluate the visual impact of the document. Could you increase the readability of long, uninterrupted blocks of text by using enumerated or indented lists, headings, or graphic or lined borders? Would adding images or varying print styles add visual appeal?

April 1, 2023

Louisa Fox, Marketing Manager
Exotica Hotel Group
2304 Pike Market Street
Seattle, ~~Washington~~ 90322   *WA*

Uses two-letter state abbreviation.

Dear Louisa ~~Fochs~~:   *x*

Corrects spelling of name.

The sales reps at Armstrong Inc. recently had a competition to see who among them had the longest scheduling email chain in their inbox. The winner? A junior sales rep who'd only been on the job for seven weeks. The winning email chain?

Twenty-three emails long.

Tells a story that reader finds compelling.

Twenty-three inbox-clogging emails, just to schedule a single meeting.

If that sounds absurd, consider that a study found it takes about eight emails, on average, to schedule a meeting. And with every back-and-forth exchange, leads have more time to drop off and grow cold. Worse, it can build frustration in the relationship.

Reads like a conversation.

<u>Since the sales reps' competition,</u> Armstrong's has ditched the old way of scheduling meetings. <u>All it took was a few hours to install our platform, and now their contacts can schedule meetings with the simple click of a button.</u> No back-and-forth emails, and no double-booking. Plus, with our handy automated notification system, they always have plenty of notice to prepare for important events.

Adds smooth transition to next paragraph.

Provides simple and concise instructions.

At ProTech, we help businesses like yours eliminate the pesky administrative tasks that drag down operations. And because we care about making sure our software works the way you want it; our services include personalized training modules designed for your staff's unique learning styles.

Cast in reader's viewpoint.

Interested in cutting down on waste and decluttering those inboxes? Request a demo today, and get a feel for how roomy your inbox can be.

Includes specific action ending.

Sincerely,

Tonya Chang
Engagement Director
Enclosure

Errors Undetectable by Spell Check:

- **Verify spelling of names.**
- **Correct proofreading grammatical error.**
- **Check correctness of word substitutions, such as "to" for "too" and "your" for "you."**

View web documents on several different browsers to ensure readability and appeal.

○ Be certain the document is signed or initialed (depending on the document). Ensure that email messages are addressed to the appropriate person or persons.

5. **Print a draft copy and proofread a third time if the document is nonroutine and complex.** Read from *right* to *left* to reduce your reading speed, allowing you to concentrate deliberately on each word. If a document is extremely important, you might consider reading the document aloud, spelling names and noting capitalization and punctuation, while another person verifies the copy.

6. **Print written documents on high-quality paper.** The message in Model Document 4.2 has been revised for (1) content, organization, and style; (2) mechanics; and (3) format and layout. Study the revisions made using the track-changes feature in word-processing software. The commentary makes it easy to see how revising this draft improved the document's quality.

To Recap:

▸ Use the spell checker to locate simple keying errors and repeated words.

▸ Proofread once, concentrating on errors in content, organization, and style.

▸ Proofread a second time, concentrating on mechanical errors.

▸ Edit for format and layout.

▸ Print a draft copy of the document.

▸ Proofread a third time if the document is nonroutine and complex.

▸ For documents to be delivered on paper, print on high-quality paper.

Master1305/Shutterstock

5 | Communicating Electronically

Learning Objectives

After studying this chapter, you will be able to ...

5-1 Understand the importance of safeguarding information communicated electronically.

5-2 Ensure that a technological communication channel is appropriate for your message.

5-3 Discuss the effective use of email, instant messaging, and text messaging in business communication.

5-4 Explain the principles of writing effectively for the web.

5-5 Discuss the effective use of voice and wireless technologies in business communication.

5-6 Use virtual collaboration tools to achieve your business communication goals.

5-1 Data Security

In the past several decades, computer technology has revolutionized the way that communication occurs in most organizations. Communication, using a variety of text-, audio-, and video-enabled tools, can be achieved almost instantaneously with others located around the globe. But with the many advantages of computer-mediated communication, a similar rise in the potential hazards associated with its use has occurred. Concerns about maintaining the privacy of, and information about, employees, partners, and customers, as well as corporate resources, have reached a critical point. According to the 2021 Annual Data Breach Report published by the Identify Theft Resource Center (ITRC), the overall number of data compromises (1,862) was up more than 68 percent compared to 2020 (1,108).[1] Out of the 1,862 compromises, 1,600 of those were cyberattacks.[2] A practice that is more difficult to judge in terms of its ethicality is that of data mining, which is used by many organizations on their social networking sites to learn more about customers for the enhancement of marketing techniques.

Organizations may be held liable for providing outside access to private information of their employees, customers, and other external groups. This information includes customers' credit card, bank account, and social security numbers, as well as employee details, such as health records, home addresses, email addresses, and login information. In 2021, crypto trading platform BitMart said a security breach allowed hackers to withdraw $150 million worth of cryptocurrency. Blockchain security company PeckShield said the losses were actually around $196 million, with about $100 million in various cryptocurrencies coming from Ethereum blockchain and $96 million coming from currencies on the Binance Smart Chain. NBC reported that the hackers behind the attack used 1inch and Tornado Cash to exchange the stolen coins for other cryptocurrencies and make it more difficult to be tracked. Hackers repeatedly attacked cryptocurrency and DeFi platforms in 2021. The week before the BitMart attack, cybercriminals stole about $120 million from DeFi platform Badger. Other thefts in 2021 included those of more than $600 million from Poly and $34 million from Cream Finance.[3]

In addition to protecting employee, supplier, distributor, and customer privacy, organizations are also concerned about protecting proprietary information about products, services, and business strategies.

Because of these concerns, many organizations have enacted policies to guide employees in the proper use of technology to safeguard information. These policies often address three data security risks: breaches of confidentiality, failing to offer choice in what information is shared, and reputational damage caused by data breaches. Often, everyone in the company is expected to ensure that data is collected, handled, and stored properly.

Such policies generally require that employees are properly trained in data use and storage, and how to keep data secure, making sure that data is not shared informally, that no information is shared with unauthorized individuals, and that no longer needed data is properly deleted or disposed of. It is very important to be well informed about an organization's data use policies and to follow policies to the letter to avoid breaches of data security.

Employee training should include but not be limited to:

- **Responsibility for Company Data.** Continually emphasize the critical nature of data security and the responsibility of each employee to protect company data. Employees have legal and regulatory obligations to respect and protect the privacy of information and its integrity and confidentiality.

- **Document Management and Notification Procedures.** Employees should be educated on the organization's data incident reporting procedure in the event an employee's computer becomes infected by a virus or is operating outside its norm (e.g., unexplained errors, running slowly, changes in desktop configurations, etc.). They should be trained to recognize a legitimate warning message or alert. In such cases, employees should immediately report the incident so the information technology team can be engaged to mitigate and investigate the threat.

- **Passwords.** Employees should be shown how to select strong passwords. Passwords should be cryptic so they cannot be easily guessed but also should be easily remembered so they do not need to be in writing. Company systems should be set to send out periodic automatic reminders to employees to change their passwords.

- **Unauthorized Software.** Employees should be aware that they are not allowed to install unlicensed software on any company computer. Unlicensed software downloads could make the organization susceptible to malicious software downloads that can attack and corrupt company data.

- **Internet Use.** Employees should be trained to avoid emailed or online links that are suspicious or from unknown sources. Such links can release malicious software, infect computers, and steal company data. The organization also should establish safe browsing rules and limits on employee internet usage in the workplace.

- **Email.** Responsible email usage is the best defense for preventing data theft. Employees should be aware of scams and not respond to email they do not recognize. Educate your employees to accept email that

- ○ Comes from someone they know.
- ○ Comes from someone they have received email from before.
- ○ Is something they were expecting.
- ○ Does not look odd with unusual spellings or characters.
- ○ Passes the organization's anti-virus program test.

- **Social Engineering and Phishing.** Employees should be trained to recognize common cybercrime and information security risks, including social engineering, online fraud, phishing, and web-browsing risks.

- **Social Media Policy.** Employees should be educated on social media and organizations should communicate, at a minimum, their policy and guidance on the use of a company email address to register, post, or receive social media.

- **Mobile Devices.** The organization should communicate its mobile device policy to employees for company-owned and personally owned devices used during the course of business.

- **Protecting Computer Resources.** Employees should be trained to safeguard computers from theft by locking them or keeping them in a secure place. Critical information should be backed up routinely, with backup copies being kept in a secure location. All employees should be responsible for accepting current virus protection software updates on company PCs.[4]

5-2 Appropriate Use of Technology

Technology offers numerous advantages, but a technological channel is not always the communication method of choice. Before sending a message, be certain the selected channel of communication is appropriate by considering the message's purpose, confidentiality issues, and human relations factors.

5-2a Determine the Purpose of the Message

If a message is straightforward and informative, chances are a technological option might be appropriate. Although the use of instantaneous and efficient communication methods is quite compelling, keep in mind that written communication, printed or online, cannot replace the personal interaction so essential in today's team-based work environments. Employees who are floors apart or in different offices or time zones benefit from email, messaging apps, and web

communications, but two people sitting side by side or on the same floor shouldn't have to communicate solely by electronic means.

A second question when selecting among communication options is whether a permanent record of the message is needed or if a more temporary form, such as a phone call or instant message, would suffice.

5-2b Determine Whether the Information Is Personal or Confidential

As a general guideline, keep personal correspondence off-line if you don't want it to come back and haunt you. The content of an email message could have embarrassing consequences since such documents often become a part of public records, and wireless communications might be unexpectedly intercepted. Your company technically "owns" your electronic communications and, thus, can monitor them to determine legitimate business use or potential abuse. Undeliverable email messages are delivered to an email administrator, and many networks routinely store backups of all email messages that pass through them.

Even deleted messages can be "resurrected" with little effort, as several public figures discovered when investigators retrieved archived email as evidence in court cases. For sensitive situations, a face-to-face encounter is often preferred.

5-2c Decide Whether Positive Human Relations Are Sacrificed

Be wary of using an electronic communication tool as an avoidance mechanism. Remember, too, that some people do not regularly check their email or voice mail, and some have unreliable systems that are slow or prone to losing messages. Some news will be received better in person than through an electronic format, which might be interpreted as cold and impersonal.

Additionally, some people, especially those of certain cultures, prefer a personal meeting, even if you perceive that an electronic exchange of information would be a more efficient use of everyone's time. Choose the communication channel carefully to fit both your purpose and the preference of the receiver.

5-3 Electronic Mail Communication

As you read in Chapter 1, the continuous evolution of technology has expanded communication options. Email, instant messaging, web communications, and voice and wireless technologies are important tools for accomplishing company goals. In fact, email remains the most common workplace communication tool.[5] The ability to use email communications effectively is essential for success in virtually every career.

5-3a Advantages of Email

Email offers numerous advantages. Its widespread availability, convenience, and ease of use have resulted in its skyrocketing popularity. The advantages of email are numerous:

- **It facilitates the fast, convenient flow of information among users at various locations and time zones.** Mail service is often too slow for communicating timely information, and calling someone can be inefficient and inconvenient to people in other time zones. For these reasons, email is especially effective when sending a single message to several recipients and when needing to communicate 24 hours a day, 365 days a year.

- **It increases efficiency.** Email reduces "phone tag" and unnecessary telephone interruptions caused when delivering messages that are unlikely to require a verbal response.

- **It makes retrieval easier.** Emails can be saved in folders and can thus be easily retrieved for review.

5-3b Guidelines for Preparing Email Messages

Following these guidelines will enable you to use email efficiently and effectively when communicating with both valued coworkers and outside parties (refer to Model Document 5.1):

- **Send to single or multiple addressees.** The same message can be sent to one or many recipients simultaneously. Routinely sending an email message to multiple recipients involves keying the email address of each recipient into a distribution list and selecting the distribution list as the recipient.

- **Provide a useful subject line.** A descriptive subject line assists the receiver's understanding of the message and is helpful for future reference to it. Additionally, a well-written subject line in an email message will help the receiver sort through an overloaded mailbox and read messages in priority order. When writing a subject line, think of the five Ws—Who, What, When, Where, and Why—to give you some clues for wording. For example, "Budget Committee Meeting on

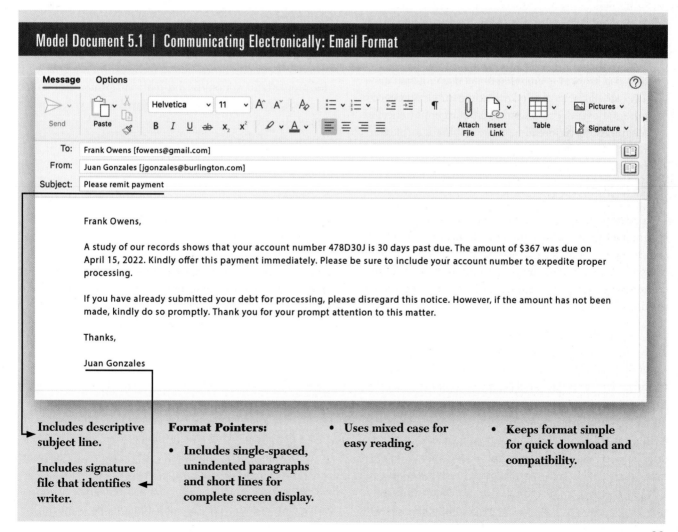

Model Document 5.1 | Communicating Electronically: Email Format

To: Frank Owens [fowens@gmail.com]
From: Juan Gonzales [jgonzales@burlington.com]
Subject: Please remit payment

Frank Owens,

A study of our records shows that your account number 478D30J is 30 days past due. The amount of $367 was due on April 15, 2022. Kindly offer this payment immediately. Please be sure to include your account number to expedite proper processing.

If you have already submitted your debt for processing, please disregard this notice. However, if the amount has not been made, kindly do so promptly. Thank you for your prompt attention to this matter.

Thanks,

Juan Gonzales

Includes descriptive subject line.

Includes signature file that identifies writer.

Format Pointers:

- Includes single-spaced, unindented paragraphs and short lines for complete screen display.

- Uses mixed case for easy reading.

- Keeps format simple for quick download and compatibility.

Thursday" is a more meaningful subject line than "Meeting."

- **Restate the subject in the body of the message.** The body of the message should be a complete thought and should not rely on the subject line for elaboration. A good opening sentence might be a repetition of most of the subject line. Even if the reader skipped the subject line, the message would still be clear, logical, and complete.

- **Focus on a single topic directed toward the receiver's needs.** An email message is generally limited to one idea rather than addressing several issues. If you address more than one topic in a single email message, chances are the recipient will forget to respond to all points discussed. Discussing one topic allows you to write a descriptive subject line, and the receiver can file the single subject message in a separate mailbox if desired. If you must send a lengthy email, preview the topics to be covered in the introduction, and then divide the message into logical sections for easy comprehension.

- **Sequence your ideas based on the anticipated reader reaction.** As you learned previously, ideas should be organized deductively when a message contains good news or neutral information. Inductive organization is recommended when the message contains bad news or is intended to persuade. Email messages should be organized according to the sequence of ideas, for example, time order, order of importance, or geography. As a general rule, present the information in the order that it is likely to be needed. For example, describe the nature and purpose of an upcoming meeting before giving the specifics (date, place, and time).

- **Make careful use of jargon, technical words, and shortened terms.** The use of jargon and technical terms is more common in email messages than in business letters. Such shortcuts save time with audiences who will understand the intent. In practicing empathy; however, consider whether the receiver will likely understand the terms used.

- **Use graphic highlighting to add emphasis.** Enumerated or bulleted lists, tables, graphs, pictures, or other images can be either integrated into the content of the email or attached as supporting material.

- **Revise your email before sending.** Even the average email requires at least one pass to ensure that the intended message is clear, concise, and error-free. The number of passes increases depending on the number of

netiquette the buzzword for proper behavior on the internet

people receiving the email and the complexity of the message. Revising for brevity and conciseness is a primary goal for messages that are often read on the run and on mobile devices. Keep to one screen, eliminate redundancies, and tighten wording. Avoid off-topic material that detracts from the email's single subject, as well as clever or amusing statements that are funny only to the writer.[6] Direct, concise messages sometimes sound impersonal and curt if not revised for goodwill. Question whether a phone call would be more appropriate for the message; a businesslike, yet conversational tone might sound less aggressive or demanding. Revise emails to achieve a similar tone.[7] Use the email spell checker and then proofread onscreen for content and grammatical errors.

5-3c Effective Use of Email

The email message in Model Document 5.2 illustrates guidelines for using professional email. The sender begins the email message by announcing the topic of computer system maintenance. The paragraphs that follow include details about the duration of the system downtime as well as how to contact the information technology group with questions.

Although email offers various advantages in speed and convenience, problems arise when it is managed inappropriately. Learning fundamental **netiquette**, the buzzword for proper behavior on the internet, will ensure your online success. The following guidelines will assist you in using email effectively:

- **Check email promptly.** Generally, a response to email is expected within 24 hours. Ignoring messages from coworkers can erode efforts to create an open, honest, and cooperative work environment. On the other hand, responding every second could indicate that you are paying more attention to your email than your job.

- **Do not contribute to email overload.** To avoid clogging the system with unnecessary messages, follow these simple guidelines:

  ◦ Be certain individuals need a copy of the email, and forward an email from another person only with the original writer's permission.

  ◦ Never address an email requesting general action to more than one person if you want to receive an individual response. Sharing responsibility will lead to no one taking responsibility.

  ◦ Avoid sending formatted documents. Messages with varying fonts, special print features (bold, italics, etc.), and images take longer to download, require more storage space, and could be unreadable on

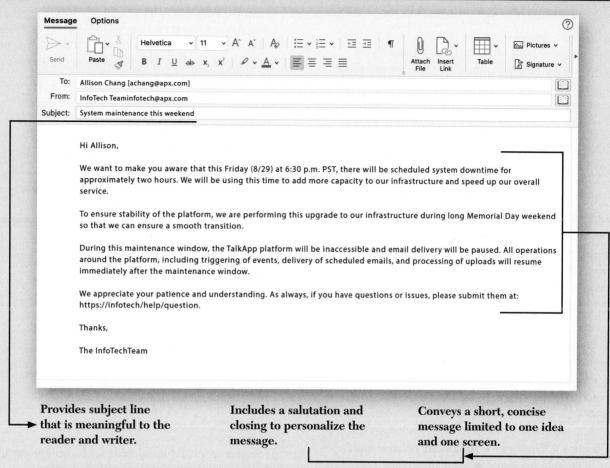

To: Allison Chang [achang@apx.com]
From: InfoTech Team infotech@apx.com
Subject: System maintenance this weekend

Hi Allison,

We want to make you aware that this Friday (8/29) at 6:30 p.m. PST, there will be scheduled system downtime for approximately two hours. We will be using this time to add more capacity to our infrastructure and speed up our overall service.

To ensure stability of the platform, we are performing this upgrade to our infrastructure during long Memorial Day weekend so that we can ensure a smooth transition.

During this maintenance window, the TalkApp platform will be inaccessible and email delivery will be paused. All operations around the platform, including triggering of events, delivery of scheduled emails, and processing of uploads will resume immediately after the maintenance window.

We appreciate your patience and understanding. As always, if you have questions or issues, please submit them at: https://infotech/help/question.

Thanks,

The InfoTechTeam

Provides subject line that is meaningful to the reader and writer.

Includes a salutation and closing to personalize the message.

Conveys a short, concise message limited to one idea and one screen.

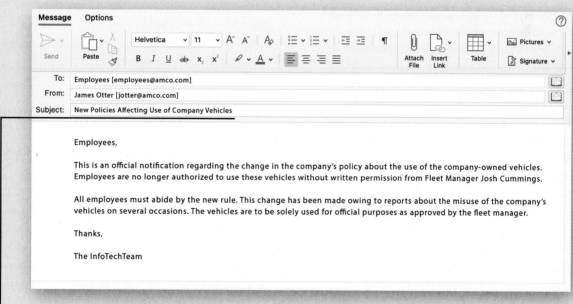

To: Employees [employees@amco.com]
From: James Otter [jotter@amco.com]
Subject: New Policies Affecting Use of Company Vehicles

Employees,

This is an official notification regarding the change in the company's policy about the use of the company-owned vehicles. Employees are no longer authorized to use these vehicles without written permission from Fleet Manager Josh Cummings.

All employees must abide by the new rule. This change has been made owing to reports about the misuse of the company's vehicles on several occasions. The vehicles are to be solely used for official purposes as approved by the fleet manager.

Thanks,

The InfoTechTeam

Provides subject line that is meaningful to the reader and the writer.

Format Pointer:

Composes short, concise message limited to one idea and one screen.

some computers. In addition, enhancing routine email messages does not support the goals of competitive organizations, and employees, clients, or customers might resent such frivolous use of time.

○ Edit the original message when you reply to email if the entire body of the original message is not needed for context. Instead, you can cut and paste pertinent sections that you believe will help the recipient understand your reply. You can also key brief comments in all caps below the original section.

○ Follow company policy for personal use of email. Obtain a private email account if you are job hunting or sending many private messages to friends and relatives.

- **Use email selectively.** Send short, direct messages for routine matters that need not be handled immediately (scheduling meetings, giving your supervisor quick updates, or addressing other uncomplicated issues).

- **Do not send messages when you are angry.** Email containing sensitive, highly emotional messages could be easily misinterpreted because of the absence of nonverbal communication (facial expressions, voice tone, and body language). Sending a *flame*, the online term used to describe a heated, sarcastic, sometimes abusive message or posting, might prompt a receiver to send a retaliatory response. Email messages written in anger and filled with emotion and sarcasm could result in embarrassment or even end up as evidence in litigation. Because of the potential damage to relationships and legal liability, read email messages carefully before sending them. Unless a response is urgent, store a heated message for an hour until you have cooled off and thought about the issue clearly and rationally. When you *must* respond immediately, you might acknowledge that your response is emotional and has not been thoroughly considered. Give this warning by using words such as "I need to vent my frustration for a few paragraphs" or "flame on—I'm writing in anger."[8]

- **Exercise caution against email viruses and hoaxes.** An ounce of prevention can avert the problems caused by deadly *viruses* that destroy data files or annoying messages that simply waste your time while they are executing. Install an *antivirus software program* that will scan your hard drive each time you start the computer or access

social networking sites websites that provide virtual communities in which people with shared interests can communicate

external devices, and keep backups of important files. Be suspicious of email messages that contain attachments if they are from people you don't know. Email text is usually safe to open, but the attachment could contain an executable file that can affect your computer's operations. **Social networking sites**, such as Facebook, are also common sources of viruses and spyware.

- Additionally, be wary of *computer hoaxes*—email messages that incite panic, typically related to risks of computer viruses or deadly threats that urge you to forward them to as many people as possible. Forwarding a hoax can be embarrassing and causes inefficiency by overloading email boxes and flooding computer security personnel with inquiries from alarmed recipients of your message. Investigate the possible hoax by visiting websites such as the following that post virus alerts and hoax information and provide tips for identifying a potential hoax:

○ PolitiFact: www.politifact.com

○ Snopes: www.snopes.com

○ Truth or Fiction: www.truthorfiction.com

If a bogus message is forwarded to you, reply to the person politely that the message is a hoax. This action allows you to help stop the spread of the malicious message and will educate one more person about the evils of hoaxes.

- **Develop an effective system for handling email.** Some simple organization will allow you to make better use of your email capability:

○ Set up separate accounts for receiving messages that require your direct attention.

○ Keep your email inbox clean by reading an email and acting immediately. Delete messages you are not using and those not likely to be considered relevant for legal purposes.

○ Move saved messages into a limited number of email folders for quick retrieval. The email search feature is also useful for identifying saved messages quickly. If you receive many messages, consider setting up your account to sort and prioritize messages, send form letters as replies to messages received with a particular subject line, automatically forward specified email, and sound an alarm when you receive a message from a particular person.

- **To Recap—Email Advantages**

○ Allows communication 24 hours a day, 365 days a year

- Reduces telephone interruptions by delivering messages that are unlikely to require a verbal response
- Saves companies the costs of long-distance telephone bills and postal mail-outs
- Reduces the need to print messages

- **To Recap—Effective Use of Email**

  - Check email promptly.
  - Do not contribute to email overload.
  - Use email selectively.
  - Do not send messages when you are angry.
  - Exercise caution against email viruses and hoaxes.
  - Develop an effective system for handling email.

5-3d Instant and Text Messaging

Texting and **instant messaging (IM)** have exploded in popularity over the last decade. As a result, many people now use the terms "text messaging" and "instant messaging" interchangeably, referring to both as "messaging." However, some key distinctions exist between the two.

Instant messengers allow you to send real-time messages through a software application. Facebook Messenger, WhatsApp, WeChat, and iMessage are examples of instant messaging apps that have steadily gained popularity over the years.

Instant messaging applications are often referred to as "over-the-top" (OTT) applications because they do not require a cellular network connection. However, to send and receive OTT messages, you need a device that connects to the internet, such as a smartphone, laptop, desktop, or tablet. Some instant messaging applications also allow users to make video and voice calls and share files.

Model Document 5.3 illustrates a sample IM conversation that occurred to arrange for last-minute project changes.

Many of the guidelines that apply to the use of email for business purposes also apply to instant messaging. With IM, however, spelling and grammar matter less when trading messages at high speed. IM users often use shorthand for common words and phrases. IM and telephone communication also share common challenges: being sure that the sender is who they claim to be and that the conversation is free from eavesdropping.

Some managers worry that employees will spend too much work time using IM to chat with buddies inside and outside the company. They also emphasize that IM is not the right tool for every business purpose.

> **instant messaging (IM)** a real-time email technology that blends email with conversation; sender and receiver who are online at the same time can type messages that both see immediately

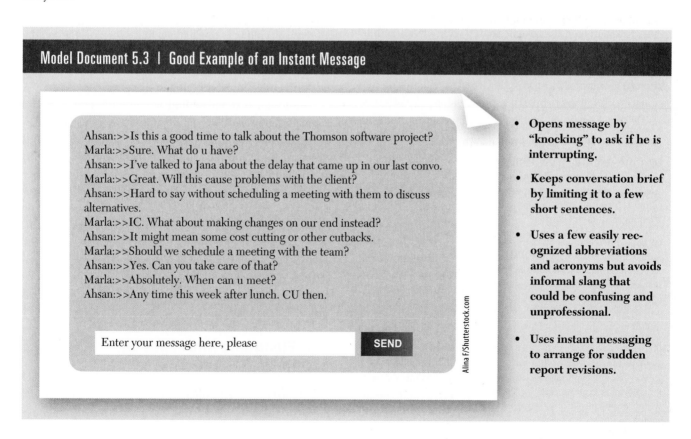

Model Document 5.3 | Good Example of an Instant Message

Ahsan:>>Is this a good time to talk about the Thomson software project?
Marla:>>Sure. What do u have?
Ahsan:>>I've talked to Jana about the delay that came up in our last convo.
Marla:>>Great. Will this cause problems with the client?
Ahsan:>>Hard to say without scheduling a meeting with them to discuss alternatives.
Marla:>>IC. What about making changes on our end instead?
Ahsan:>>It might mean some cost cutting or other cutbacks.
Marla:>>Should we schedule a meeting with the team?
Ahsan:>>Yes. Can you take care of that?
Marla:>>Absolutely. When can u meet?
Ahsan:>>Any time this week after lunch. CU then.

Enter your message here, please   SEND

Alina F/Shutterstock.com

- **Opens message by "knocking" to ask if he is interrupting.**

- **Keeps conversation brief by limiting it to a few short sentences.**

- **Uses a few easily recognized abbreviations and acronyms but avoids informal slang that could be confusing and unprofessional.**

- **Uses instant messaging to arrange for sudden report revisions.**

Employees should still rely on email when they need a record and use the telephone for a personal touch.

5-3e Text Messaging

Texting, or **text messaging**, is the process of sending short electronic messages between two or more mobile devices. Texting requires a cellular network to send messages.

Virtually every cell phone, regardless of whether it's a smartphone, is capable of sending and receiving text messages. More than 5 billion people own mobile devices, and more than half of those are smartphones. In addition, 88 percent of people use their phones primarily for texting, and approximately 41 million messages are sent out every minute.[9]

Both SMS (Short Messaging Service) and MMS (Multimedia Messaging Service) text messages fall under the texting umbrella. However, SMS and MMS do have a few slight differences.

Most SMS messaging platforms have a limit of 160 characters of text per message. In contrast, MMS messages enable you to add images, video, and other types of content to a text message.

An entire code book of acronyms and abbreviations has emerged, ranging from CWOT (complete waste of time) to DLTBBB (don't let the bed bugs bite). Use of emojis, memes, and GIFs also have become a staple in the 21st century. Entire conversations can be had without typing a single word, attitudes can be conveyed and understood in seconds, and emotions can be shared without vulnerability. An **emoji** is a small digital image or icon used to express an idea, emotion, etc. A **meme** is typically a photo or video, although sometimes it can be a block of text. When a meme resonates with many people, it's spread via social platforms like Twitter, Facebook, Instagram, texting, and more. The more a meme is spread, the greater the cultural influence it has. GIF is a computer file format for the compression and storage of visual digital information; it also refers to an image or video stored in this format.

While memes, GIFs, and emojis can be playful, they can also be misconstrued. "Your message might say 'this is fine' but then if you have a meme of a room on fire, the words probably have the exact opposite meaning," says Shana Simmons, general counsel at eDiscovery software company, Everlaw. "Employees come from many walks of life, and they bring a diverse array of viewpoints to the table so one person's idea of a joke is another person's offensive depiction or tone-deaf communication or politically unwelcome message."[10]

Training given to employees should cover more than just awareness about the words used in messages. It should also include a discussion about the use of emojis, GIFs, and memes. Not only will technology have to evolve to stay on top of digital messaging, but visual literacy will have to evolve, so organizations must ensure that such training is inclusive and nuanced, Simmons says.[11]

Texting is a viable alternative to phone calls for those with hearing impairments. Economic and cultural factors have also driven the advancement of text messaging in some parts of the world where voice conversations are more expensive than texting and short conversations are considered impolite. Some of the most avid users of text messaging are clustered in Southeast Asia. The Chinese language is particularly well suited to text messaging because in Mandarin the names of the numbers are also close to the sounds of certain words.[12] Japanese commuters use their cellphones to text silently, as talking on a phone on the train would be impolite. In the United States, teenagers have popularized texting and carry the habit into places of work. Both abroad and at home, text messaging can be used as an avoidance mechanism that preserves the feeling of communication without the burden of actual intimacy or substance. Like a wave or nod, they are meant to merely establish connection without getting specific.

Although text messaging is generally considered a social communication tool, it is finding more use for business. Text messages can be sent or retrieved in situations when a ringing phone would be inappropriate, such as during meetings. With research showing that many more text messages are opened than are email messages, advertisers are using text messages to send their marketing messages.[13] Refer to Figure 5.1, which compares the completeness and relative formality of an email message to the informal nature of the instant message and the abbreviated style of the text message. Each medium requires its own appropriate writing style to maximize effectiveness and social expectations.

5-3f Electronic Messages and the Law

U.S. courts have established the right of companies to monitor the electronic mail of an employee because they own the facilities and intend them to be used for

---

text messaging messages that can be sent from one cellphone to another, a cellphone to a computer, or computer to computer; a refinement of computer instant messaging

emoji any of various small images, symbols, or icons used in text fields in electronic communication (as in text messages, email, and social media) to express the emotional attitude of the writer, convey information succinctly, or communicate a message playfully without using words

meme an amusing or interesting item (such as a captioned picture or video) or genre of items that is spread widely online, especially through social media

Figure 5.1 | Levels of Formality Required by Various Technologies

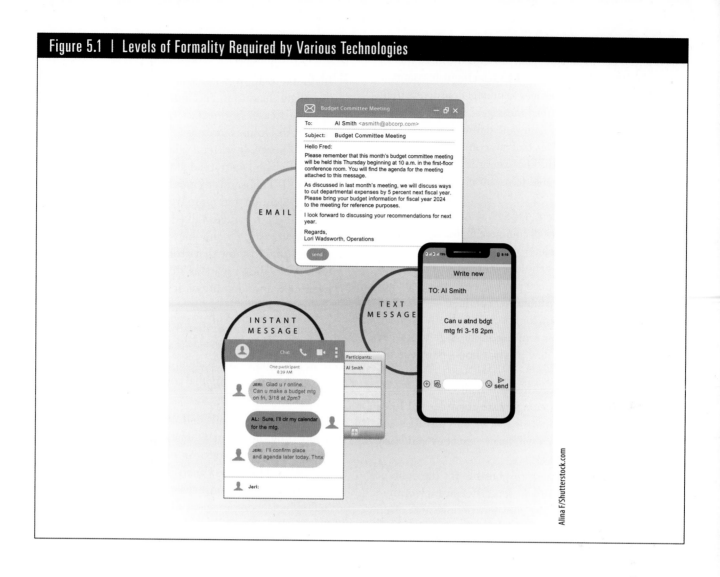

Alina F/Shutterstock.com

job-related communication only. On the other hand, employees typically expect that their email messages will be kept private. To protect themselves against liability imposed by the Electronic Communications Privacy Act (ECPA), employers simply provide a legitimate business reason for the monitoring (e.g., preventing computer crime, retrieving lost messages, and regulating employee morale) and obtain written consent to intercept email or at least notify employees. Employees who use the system after the notification may have given implied consent to the monitoring.[14]

The legal status of text messaging has been murkier. A 2008 court ruling made a distinction between electronic communications employers store on their servers and communication that is contracted out to third parties. Employers must have either a warrant or the employee's permission to view messages stored by someone other than the employer. Employers who intend to monitor electronic communications must be specific in their written employee policy statements that they intend to access text messages sent with company-issued devices.[15]

Text messaging has also become a common method of marketing to customers, and with this development, laws have been created to protect customers from unsolicited text messages and the collection of personal data. To uphold the privacy and protection of personal information, the Cellular Telecommunications Industry Association (CTIA) was formed to impose ethical text marketing practices. Other organizations and stakeholders, such as the Mobile Marketing Association (MMA), Federal Communications Commission (FCC), and Federal Trade Commission (FTC), also monitor, regulate, or enforce rules that apply to marketing.

Two laws in particular affect the type of text messaging that is allowed. The Telephone Consumer Protection Act (TCPA) is a product of the FCC. The TCPA is the primary anti-telemarketing law and leading regulator of SMS marketing. Under the TCPA, businesses may not send messages to consumers without their consent. Even if an individual provides their phone number or has a long-standing relationship with the business, the company cannot text the individual if they have not granted written consent. The CAN-SPAM (Controlling the Assault of Non-Solicited

Pornography and Marketing) Act works in conjunction with TCPA and is the main text spam law in the United States. Under the CAN-SPAM Act, the FCC can regulate commercial texts sent to wireless devices to protect consumers from unwanted mobile commercial messages. The act makes it illegal for businesses to send unwanted text messages to cell phone numbers and requires that any commercial message be easily identifiable by the receiver as an advertisement. Consumers must also be able to unsubscribe from receiving messages.

Despite its name, the CAN-SPAM Act doesn't apply just to bulk email. It covers all commercial messages, which the law defines as "any electronic mail message the primary purpose of which is the commercial advertisement or promotion of a commercial product or service," including email that promotes content on commercial websites. The law makes no exception for business-to-business email. That means all email—for example, a message to former customers announcing a new product line—must comply with the law.

Any company that uses text messaging to communicate with audiences must comply with the rules put forth by these regulators. Businesses that violate text message privacy and text spam laws will incur penalties and hefty fines.[16]

Remember that you are responsible for the content of any electronic message you send. Because electronic messages move so quickly between people and often become very informal and conversational, individuals might not realize (or might forget) their responsibility. If a person denies commitments made via an electronic message, someone involved can produce a copy of the message as verification.

Electronic communicators must abide by copyright laws. Be certain to give credit for quoted material, and seek permission to use copyrighted text or graphics from printed or electronic sources. Unless you inform the reader that editing has occurred, do not alter a message you are forwarding or reposting, and be sure to ask permission before forwarding it.

The development of law regarding electronic communication is lagging far behind technology; nevertheless, employers can expect changes in the laws as technology continues to develop. Electronic messages have often become the prosecutor's star witness, the corporate equivalent of DNA evidence, as it and other forms of electronic communication are subject to subpoena in litigation. Referring to this issue, former New York Attorney General Eliot Spitzer had this to say: "Never write when you can talk. Never talk when you can nod. And never put anything in an email [that you don't want on the front page of the newspaper]."[17] Several perils of "evidence" mail that companies must address are illustrated in these cases:

- Including inappropriate content in an email can humiliate, lead to indictment, or be used as evidence in a court case. In the 2021 trial of Theranos founder Elizabeth Holmes, dozens of text messages between her and her ex-boyfriend (and ex-business partner) Sunny Balwani were read aloud during Holmes' trial for fraud. Thousands of messages were released by the prosecution and more were obtained by CNBC. Some of the messages talked about problems with the blood testing technology, which were used by prosecutors to show that Holmes knew that the technology didn't work as advertised.[18] Holmes was eventually found guilty on four charges of defrauding investors.

- Failing to preserve, or destroying, email messages in violation of securities rules is a sure path to destruction. Deleting Enron scandal-related messages led to Arthur Andersen's criminal conviction and eventually to Enron's implosion.

Inability to locate emails and other relevant documents demanded by the courts is unacceptable and considered negligence by the courts. As part of a lawsuit that the American Civil Liberties Union (ACLU) of Minnesota filed in 2021 on behalf of journalists who said they had been assaulted by law enforcement officers while covering protests over the police killing of George Floyd, State Patrol troopers admitted to deleting text messages and emails shortly after responding to protests. "The purge was neither accidental, automated, nor routine," lawyers with the ACLU said in a court memo, adding that no one had been able to review the deleted communications to see if they might have been relevant to the case. "The absence of both contemporaneous communications and documentation makes it nearly impossible to track the State Patrol's behavior, apparently by design," the memo added.[19] Penalties for deleting electronic messages in similar cases have included monetary fines, assessment of court costs or attorney's fees, and dismissal of the case in favor of the opposing side.[20]

On the other hand, evidence mail can protect a company from lawsuits. A company being sued by a female employee because a male executive had allegedly sexually abused her retrieved a trail of emails with lurid attachments sent by the female employee to the male executive named in the case.[21]

To avoid the legal perils of electronic communications, employees must be taught not to write loose, potentially rude, and overly casual messages; to avoid carelessly deleting messages; and to take the time to identify and organize relevant messages for quick retrieval.

5-4 Web Page Communication and Social Media

Most organizations now have their own websites to accomplish a number of activities, such as updating employees and customers about organizational changes; selling products and services; advertising employment opportunities; and creating a first point of contact for customers through order entry, customer service systems, and online call centers. Although effective web page development is a highly specialized activity, understanding the process will be useful to any business communicator. Organizations can use the web not only to communicate with customers and clients but also to interact with business associates. Designing web pages that are accessible by the millions of people with permanent or temporary disabilities, including visual impairments, is good for business.[22] U.S. businesses also have legal requirements for online content to be available to everyone under equal opportunity and antidiscrimination laws. The number of U.S. lawsuits alleging that websites, apps, and digital videos were inaccessible to people with disabilities rose 64 percent in the first half of 2021 from a year earlier, according to a report by UsableNet Inc., a technology firm that offers accessibility-compliance technology and services.

A decision in a case involving Domino's Pizza LLC might encourage more lawsuits, accessibility advocates say. Guillermo Robles, who is blind, sued the pizza chain in 2016 after he was unable to order from its website using his screen-reader software. In June, federal Judge Jesus Bernal ruled that Domino's site violated the Americans with Disabilities Act and the Unruh Civil Rights Act, ordering the company to make its website accessible and pay $4,000 to Robles.[23]

The Americans with Disabilities Act (ADA), an effort to end discrimination based on differing abilities, requires organizations to provide "reasonable accommodations" to employees with disabilities. Although the ADA does not explicitly address online compliance, various courts around America have ruled that commercial websites are places of public accommodation and thus subject to ADA rules. Other cases have concluded that websites are bound by ADA regulations if there is a close "nexus" between the site and a physical location. Other courts have decided that the ADA as written simply does not offer any protections for online users.

Further complicating the issue, the United States recently appeared to be on the verge of adopting more comprehensive accessibility requirements. Federal regulations slated to go into effect in January 2018 would have held federal websites to the standards of Web Content Accessibility Guideline (WCAG) 2.0 Level AA, the set of guidelines that provide the basis for online accessibility rules for most of Europe and many other nations around the world. The Trump administration, however, withdrew this requirement as part of a general push toward deregulation. At time of publication, it was expected that the Biden administration would adopt rules based on the Web Content Accessibility Guideline. Regardless of how firm this standard may technically be, in practice, if organizations wish to avoid litigation and make their website accessible, the working standard for digital accessibility in is WCAG 2.1 A, AA in the United States (and Canada).

The WCAG website compliance standards involve four principles: perceivable, operable, understandable, and robust.

1. **Perceivable**—Information and user interface components must be presentable to users in ways they can perceive. This means that users must be able to perceive the information being presented (it can't be invisible to all of their senses). More specifically, websites must:

   ○ Provide text alternatives for non-text content.

   ○ Provide captions and other alternatives for multimedia.

   ○ Create content that can be presented in different ways, including by assistive technologies, without losing meaning.

   ○ Make it easier for users to see and hear content.

2. **Operable**—User interface components and navigation must be operable. This means that users must be able to operate the interface (the interface cannot require interaction that a user cannot perform). More specifically, this means that:

   ○ All functionalities must be available from a keyboard.

   ○ Users must be given enough time to read and use content.

   ○ Content may not be used that might cause seizures.

   ○ Users must be provided help to navigate and find content.

3. **Understandable**—Information and the operation of the user interface must be understandable. This means that users must be able to understand the information as well as the operation of the user interface (the content or operation cannot be beyond their understanding). Organizations should:

   ○ Make text readable and understandable.

   ○ Make content appear and operate in predictable ways.

   ○ Help users avoid and correct mistakes.

4. **Robust**—Content must be robust enough that it can be interpreted reliably by a wide variety of user agents, including assistive technologies. This means that users must be able to access the content as technologies advance (as technologies and user agents evolve, the content should remain accessible).[24]

The Web Content Accessibility Guidelines provided by the World Wide Web Consortiums (W3C) at www.w3.org are helpful resources for ensuring web accessibility. The same group has also developed Mobile Web Accessibility Guidelines for making websites usable from mobile devices.

5-4a Writing for a Website

Many of the same standard rules for writing apply, whether writing for the web or print. However, some important differences exist between readers of paper material and web users:[25]

- Web users do not want to read. They skim, browse, and hop from one highlighted area to another trying to zero in on the word or phrase that relates to their search.

- English-speaking readers typically start scanning at the top left side of the main content area. Their attention moves from top to bottom and from left to right. Given this pattern, placing frequently accessed items close to the top of the content area is important. Information should follow the pyramid style of writing that is common in newspaper writing: the main idea or conclusion is presented first, and subsequent sections and pages expand upon it.

- Users can more quickly scan items in columns rather than rows, especially if they are categorized, grouped, and have headings. You can have more lists on the web than in a typical print document.

- Users refer infrequently to directions. It is unlikely they will read little notes, sidebars, and help files, so directions must appear in simple, numbered steps.

- In recognition of these web user characteristics, writers should tailor their styles accordingly.

Effective web writing involves moving beyond the paper mode into the web mode of thinking. Understanding the distinctive expectations of web readers will allow you to structure your ideas effectively and efficiently.

Tip Sheet

The following tips will help you compose appropriate web content:[26]

Farknot Architect/Shutterstock

- ▶ Be brief. A good rule is to reduce the wording of any print document by 50 percent when you put it on the web.

- ▶ Keep it simple. Use short words that allow for fast reading by people of various educational backgrounds. Use mixed case because all caps are slower to read.

- ▶ Consider appropriate jargon. If all of your site users share a common professional language, use it. Otherwise, keep to concise yet effective word choices.

- ▶ Use eye-catching headlines. They catch interest, ask a question, present the unusual, or pose a conflict.

- ▶ Break longer documents into smaller chunks. Provide ways to easily move through the document and return to the beginning.

- ▶ Use attention-getting devices judiciously. Bolding, font changes, color, and graphics do attract attention but can be overdone, causing important ideas to be lost.

- ▶ Avoid placing critical information in graphic form only. Many users are averse to slow-loading graphics and skip over them.

5-4b Social Media

Web 2.0, which encourages online interaction, made it possible for people to participate on the web. Unlike web pages, which are not generally interactive, social media enables people to connect online and have a conversation. Web 2.0 technologies include blogs, wikis, video, and social networking sites that enable users to generate their own content.

More and more organizations are using social media tools to communicate with customers. Nearly 97 percent of all Fortune 500 enterprises use at least one social media platform to promote their initiatives and foster positive communication with stakeholders. Additionally, as of 2021, there were roughly 3.78 billion social media users all over the world, a 5 percent increase from 2020.[27] As with company websites, most employees are not responsible for posting to their organization's social media platforms, but as with web pages, employees should understand the process and expectations for doing so.

Writing for Weblogs

A **weblog**, or **blog**, is a type of online journal typically authored by an individual that does not allow visitors to change the original posted material but only to add comments. Some of the millions of blogs now populating the web are online scrapbooks for pasting links, information, and quotes. Some resemble personal diaries, often illustrated with digital snapshots. Others serve as digital soapboxes, providing a platform for airing opinions and commentary about the world at large or on a special topic of interest. Users (known as bloggers) add entries (referred to as posts) using a simple online form in their browsers, and the weblog publishing software takes care of formatting the page layout and creating archive pages.[28]

Blogs differ from websites in that blogs are dynamic, with rapidly changing content that does not require authorization to post. The creator of the message does not have to be familiar with special coding and uploads a message simply by clicking the "Publish" button.[29] Blogging allows average citizens to become publishers. Bloggers, however, should write each post with the realization that it is publicly available.

Blog formats have been adapted for business uses, including commercial publishing, marketing, and as a knowledge management tool. Blogs can store knowledge in searchable archives for future use. This function can be helpful, for example, for service teams as they search past communications to troubleshoot current problems. Many companies, such as Microsoft, Sun Microsystems, and General Motors, encourage blogging among employees.[30] Internal blogs can be established that are not published to anyone outside the company. They present similar legal issues to those surrounding email and instant messaging. One of the most important considerations is whether posts are truly anonymous. The potential for anonymous speech creates an atmosphere that can encourage irresponsible behavior, such as harassment, defamation, and gossip. To reduce this problem, IT professionals can configure internal blogs so that all users can be identified, at least by the company.[31]

Companies are increasingly recognizing the value of external blogs as well.

- 36 percent of Fortune 500 companies are using their blogs for thought leadership, product promotion, and engagement.

- Companies that blog receive 55 percent more traffic than companies that don't, and they have 434 percent more indexed pages compared to those that don't.

- Active company blogs have 97 percent more inbound links than websites without blogs.

- Active company blogs generate 67 percent more leads than websites without blogs.

- 81 percent of U.S. online consumers say that blogs are trusted sources of information and advice.

- 61 percent of U.S. online consumers have made a purchase based on recommendations from a blog.

- 68.5 percent of respondents say that a blog adds credibility to a website.[32]

An effective corporate blog begins with a clear goal, such as winning business or building customer loyalty, and then provides relevant, frequently updated information for the target audience to return to regularly. Like other effective web communications, blogs must be promoted creatively to attract avid readers.[33]

Writing Wikis

Although a traditional website's content is usually controlled by the sponsoring individual or agency, a wiki is a collaborative website that hosts the collective work of many authors. Similar to a blog in structure and logic, a wiki allows anyone to edit, delete, or modify content, even the work of previous authors. Although allowing everyday users to create and edit a website encourages cooperative use of electronic information, the content posted at such sites should not be considered authoritative. When wiki writing, avoid the

> **weblog (or blog)** a type of online journal, typically authored by an individual, that does not allow visitors to change the original material posted but only to add comments

Zapier is an online automation tool that connects your favorite apps, such as Gmail, Slack, MailChimp, and more than 1,000 others. Zapier allows you to connect two or more apps to automate repetitive tasks without coding or relying on developers to build the integration. It's easy enough to use that anyone can build their own app workflows with just a few clicks.

For example, maybe you get a lot of email attachments in your Gmail account and you want to save them to Dropbox. Every time you get an attachment, you could open up the email, click on the attachment, and then save it to Dropbox. Or you can have Zapier automate this for you, saving you time and effort. Other workflows that can be created include:

Michele Ursi/Shutterstock

▸ Automating your social media presence by sending new RSS items to Facebook as posts

▸ Keeping projects organized by copying new Trello cards into Evernote

▸ Staying in touch with prospects by adding form respondents from Typeform to your mailing list in MailChimp

▸ Making sure your team never misses a meeting by notifying a channel in Slack of upcoming Google Calendar events

---

first-person blogging style and conform to the tone and flow of the existing article. Wikis are not typically the place for personal opinion and analysis. Instead, present factual information in clear, concise, and neutral language.[34]

Many businesses make use of wikis to encourage free flow of ideas within the organization. Content in a wiki can be updated in real time without any real administrative effort or the need for deliberate distribution. Contributors simply visit and update a common website. Wikis facilitate the exchange of information within and between teams. They allow maintenance of a series of unique documents with evolving content. Placing a document in a wiki does not necessarily make it editable by everyone with access to the wiki. For example, the marketing department can make a PowerPoint slide deck available to the sales team or the company at large without letting them change or overwrite it. Most companies implement their wikis behind a firewall to limit participation to their internal user base.[35]

Social Networking

Social networking sites are for communities of people who share common interests or activities. Common social networking sites include Facebook, LinkedIn, Twitter, Instagram, Snapchat, TikTok, and YouTube. Early on, social networking sites were used largely for making personal connections, but more and more, companies are using them to interact with customers. For example, Sony's PlayStation, with a whopping 18.7 million followers, has become the most followed brand on Twitter. According to Unmetric, PlayStation has seen 376 percent growth in followers in the past 5 years alone, adding 12 million followers from 2014 to 2019.

One of the reasons for this is how active the brand is on the platform, continuously posting a mix of content to engage fans including new game trailers, gaming footage, and streaming events.

Another company taking advantage of social networking sites is Chipotle, which was one of the first brands to take a chance with TikTok. Most of its content involves the TikTok trend of challenges. Its first, #ChipotleLidFlip, generated more than 240 million views on the platform. Its second, #GuacDance, was even more successful with 430 million video starts in 6 days. By creating fun and unique content on TikTok, Chipotle has once again become relevant to younger consumers, succeeding in engaging them in this increasingly popular channel. Chipotle announced digital sales growth of 88 percent and revenue growth of 14.6 percent to $1.4 billion for the third quarter of 2019—a rise that has been partly put down to its renewed focus on social networking.[36]

Considerations for Social Media Use

As the use of social media platforms becomes more common in organizational settings, more companies are creating policies to ensure that employees use them responsibly. Harvard University, Intel Corp., and medical and religious organizations all have policies for use of social media. Typically, these policies address three broad areas: communicating honestly and ethically, protecting the corporation's proprietary information and employee privacy, and maintaining the employee's credibility and the organization's reputation.

- **Communicate honestly and ethically.** When using social media platforms, writers should be transparent about who they are, who they work for, their role, and whether they have a vested interest in an issue. Contributors should write about their area of expertise. For example, a marketing specialist should not contribute information about human resources practices.

- **Protect the company's proprietary and employees' private information.** This should be obvious. Sharing proprietary information can cost an organization thousands or millions of dollars. Sharing private employee information can expose the writer and the company to legal damages and may endanger or harm individuals if personal addresses or information that enables identity theft is publicized.

- **Protect yours as well as the company's reputation.** When communicating on social media sites, the writer should be concerned about projecting a professional persona for themselves as well as a reputable image of the company. Making negative statements about competitors, supervisors, colleagues, or company policies may expose the contributor to disciplinary measures or the company to legal threats or bad publicity.

5-5 Voice and Wireless Communication

Not so long ago, voice communication referred strictly to communication over phone lines, and using the telephone effectively is still an important skill in any profession. Although the traditional telephone still plays an important role in business activity, voice communication extends to voice mail systems and cellphone usage. Both voice and data can be transmitted now using wireless communication systems.

5-5a Voice Mail Communication

Voice mail technology allows flexibility in staying in touch without the aid of a computer and reduces phone tag. Just as email communication can be enhanced by adhering to some basic principles, voice mail communication can be more effective by following these recommended guidelines:[37]

- Update your greeting often to reflect your schedule and leave special announcements.

- Leave your email address, fax number, or mailing address on your greeting if this information might be helpful to your callers.

- Encourage callers to leave detailed messages. If you need certain standard information from callers, use your greeting to prompt them for it. Such information often eliminates the need to call back.

- Instruct callers on how to review their message or to be transferred to an operator.

- Check your voice mail regularly, and return all voice messages within 24 hours.

When leaving a message, you can improve your communication by following these tips:[38]

- Speak slowly and clearly, and repeat your name and phone number at the beginning and end of the message.

- Spell your name for the recipient, who might need the correct spelling.

- Leave a detailed message, not just your name and number, to avoid prolonged phone tag.

- Keep your message brief, typically 60 seconds or less.

- Ensure that your message will be understandable. Don't call from places with distracting background noise or an inadequate signal connection.

The sound of your voice makes a lasting impression on the many people who listen to your greeting or the messages you leave. To ensure that the impression you leave is a professional one, review your voice greeting before you save it. Rerecord to eliminate verbal viruses ("um," "uh," stumbles), flat or monotone voice, and garbled or rushed messages that are difficult to understand. Consider scripting the message to avoid long, rambling messages. As you are recording, stand, smile, and visualize the person receiving the message; you'll hear the added energy, enthusiasm, and warmth in your voice.[39]

Remember that the voice mail message you leave should be seen as permanent. In some systems the digital files are backed up and stored for possible retrieval by managers or other company personnel. A voice mail message can also be used as evidence in a lawsuit or other legal proceeding.[40]

5-5b Cellphone Communication

Cellphone use has significantly enhanced the ability to communicate when away from the office. It has also been shown to dramatically improve performance among salespersons by improving their outreach to clients.[41] Unfortunately, the increasing functionality and ease of use of cellphones have led to their misuse in many cases. To address this, some employers are developing policies for proper cellphone use. According to a recent poll, almost 7 out of 10 Americans say they observe poor cellphone etiquette at least once every day.[42] Cellphone abuse in the workplace causes annoyance and intrusion that leads to ineffectiveness and can endanger employee safety. Your attention to a few commonsense guidelines will help ensure that you are not seen as a discourteous cellphone user.[43]

- **Be aware of company cellphone policies and obey them.** Some companies do not allow cellphone use for personal reasons during work hours. Most companies have policies prohibiting the harassment of others, and today's smartphones make it easy to send thoughtless messages using various media instantaneously. Not only might these messages damage the sender, but they may also reflect poorly on the employer if posted to Twitter or some other public social medium.

- **Observe wireless-free quiet zones.** This obviously includes theaters, performances, and religious services, but can also include meetings, restaurants, hospitals, and other public places. Exercise judgment about silencing your ringer, switching to vibrate mode, or turning off your phone. To increase the effectiveness of meetings, cellphone policies in some businesses ask that employees leave their cellphones at their desks; vibrating mode is acceptable for an anticipated emergency. To encourage proper cellphone etiquette, one business requires managers to deposit a designated amount of money in a jar should their cellphones ring during a meeting; monies collected are donated to a charity.

- **Respect others in crowded places and be wary of publicizing company information.** Speak in low conversational tones, and consider the content of your conversation. You should use good judgment in determining when and where to discuss proprietary company information or client data. Divulging such information in public places might enable its abuse by others.

- **Think safety.** Some states and municipalities have banned the use of cellphones while driving. Others allow the use of hands-free devices only. Even if not illegal, cellphone usage increases the risk of an accident by distracting the driver. Some companies are implementing cellphone policies that prohibit operators of company-owned vehicles from using cellphones or other communication devices while driving to minimize risks to their employees, and liability resulting from accidents.

Cellphone users should remember that the technology is not secure. Perhaps you have overheard another party's phone conversation when using your cellphone. The radio frequencies that transmit the voice signals can be picked up by other equipment. For this reason, information that is confidential or sensitive should be shared using an alternate communication channel.

5-6 Collaborating in Virtual Teams

Working in virtual teams is becoming more and more pervasive in the workplace, particularly since the COVID-19 pandemic.

- 80 percent of global corporate remote work policies had shifted to virtual and mixed forms of virtual team collaboration during the early part of the coronavirus crisis.

- 64 percent of organizations say that the shift to virtual teamwork will likely be a permanent one because of COVID-19.

- 75 percent of virtual teams worldwide say that remote collaboration allowed them to be more effective in their jobs.

- 62 percent of employees worldwide say that they might think of resigning from a co-located organization to a company that offers remote work.[44]

Nattakorn_Maneerat/Shutterstock

Companies also are reaping a host of benefits by designing flexible workplace policies that formalize virtual teamwork. The benefits include better productivity, increased speed to market, reduced employee turnover, and overall operational success.

- In 2018, employers say that the top benefits of remote working are improved morale (57 percent), reduced employee turnover (52 percent), reduced absenteeism (50 percent), operational cost savings (50 percent), and reduced health insurance costs (31 percent).

- In 2019, the Society for Human Resource Management (SHRM) found that the biggest benefits to virtual teams include increased global perspectives (81 percent), diversity (72 percent), creativity (54 percent), access to talent anywhere (53 percent), cost-effectiveness (32 percent), and productivity (31 percent).

- The same SHRM study also noted that virtual teams are highly collaborative. In fact, 48 percent of human resource practitioners said that they have global teams that work closely and collaboratively daily.[45]

In the world of virtual working, communication is one of the hurdles that virtual teams face. Beyond this, teams face a host of other problems that emanate from language difficulties and working in different time zones. According to Culture Wizard's 2018 Virtual Teams Survey, the top challenges faced by virtual teams are time zone differences (88 percent), difficulty in communication (86 percent), managing conflict (86 percent), building relationships (86 percent), timelessness and responsiveness (80 percent), understanding different accents (80 percent), and lack of engagement from all members (76 percent). The same study found that for 84 percent of virtual workers, virtual communication is more difficult than face-to-face communication.[46]

Fortunately, communication and online collaboration software for virtual teams have made it possible for employees to connect and access company resources from any place. A 2018 study found that the most beneficial communication between virtual teammates were face-to-face meetings (93 percent), conference calls (93 percent), and video conferencing (84 percent). The study also found that 39 percent of virtual teams leveraged video technology for more than half of their meetings.[47] A 2019 SHRM report found that virtual teams bridge communication gaps with emails (98 percent), in-person meetings (91 percent), video conferencing (89 percent), phone calls (88 percent), instant messaging (50 percent), text (49 percent), and team collaboration hub (41 percent). A 2020 online survey involving more than 4.1 million organizations found that the top office productivity suite in the market is Microsoft Office 365, used by 48.6 percent of all virtual teams.[48]

5-6a Channels of Virtual Collaboration

Broadly speaking, all virtual communication is mediated by technology, but they differ because communication can be achieved through voice, text, video, or some combination of these.

Voice

The telephone conference call—one of the first uses of technology to support group and team meetings—involves a group of people agreeing to "meet" at a certain time by phone. One of the most popular tools used by virtual teams that enables voice communication is Slack, which accommodates chat, audio calls, and video calls as well as file sharing and screen sharing to improve online collaboration efforts. Other popular tools that provide voice communication are Jabber, Flock, Viper, and Workplace from Meta.

Many companies are taking advantage of voice-over-internet protocol (VoIP) to avoid the high costs of international calls. Using VoIP technology, users can make online phone calls and bring down the charges. Some of the best business phone systems also provide the ability to video call customers and employees. These systems include RingCentral, FreshCaller, JustCall, Ooma Office, Aircall, Cloud Talk, and Phone Burner. RingCentral, for example, provides cloud phone, messaging, online fax, and video conferencing. It provides international phone numbers to help businesses deepen customer relationships. While the feature works well for inbound customer communication, it can be used to simplify calls between teams situated in regional offices across the globe. These systems are particularly useful for virtual sales and customer support teams.

Text

Whether texting or emailing someone from your computer, using a social networking site such as Facebook, or sharing documents using Google docs or other document sharing software, you will likely use written text to send and receive collaborative messages.

Although email is the most common method of written communication in the workplace because of its effectiveness in dealing with routine business, it can be difficult for groups to make decisions using this mode of communication; although some research suggests that groups better analyze problems using email. One benefit of email is that it appears to minimize status differences that may be present if people meet face-to-face.

Virtual teams can also use web pages or wikis that can serve as an electronic bulletin board. Members can go to the web page for information and may be permitted to change or delete information. Each member has access to what others have gathered and shared. Group members can also add schedules onto the web page to help organize work.

Instant messaging provides real-time facilitation between the initiator and the recipient. Instant messaging promotes more regular communication and is one of the best ways to make superiors and colleagues more approachable. This is especially important when employees are still learning how to work remotely. Most importantly, instant messaging helps team managers to deliver more consistent support, advice, feedback, and praise to remote members. This way, it enables managers to reinforce team direction, objectives, and goals.

Popular instant messaging platforms include Flock, Viper, Slack, Jabber, and Workplace from Meta. For example, Flock is an all-in-one communication platform that unifies distributed teams of different sizes. It provides users with a wide range of functionality ranging from instant messaging to audio calls and video conferences. In addition, it comes with file-sharing options, search functionality, note-taking options, polling features, and other productivity tools.

Video

A video group or team conference occurs when three or more people are linked via the internet, using a camera that is connected or built into a computer, or via a satellite-linked TV. With the advent of mini-cameras, and affordable or free software, it has become increasingly easy for groups to hold video-conference meetings using programs, such as Zoom and Microsoft Teams. Somewhat surprising is that video conferences are more effective than face-to-face meetings when participants are involved in more structured discussion. This is because attendees prepare better for a video conference than for a face-to-face meeting, possibly because team members believe a video conference is more important than an ordinary meeting.

Electronic Meeting Systems

Electronic meeting systems (EMS) consist of computer software programs, which sometimes require special hardware, that help group members collaborate when not meeting face-to-face. Some EMS use only text, others combine text, PowerPoint, photos, and video. GoToMeeting is one popular software program that lets participants share what's on their personal computer with the entire group, including Power-Point slides, data summaries, and written reports. **Webinars** are seminars that are held via the internet, which could be as simple as voice messages combined with PowerPoint slides; some webinars use more sophisticated, interactive software.

EMS can be used by people who are sitting at computer keyboards in the same room at the same time, projecting what people type onto a large screen. Sometimes people

webinars seminars that are held using the internet for transmission

talk to each other directly, just as they would in any face-to-face meeting; at other times they can make contributions via their keyboards. Using EMS, group members can brainstorm ideas, vote, outline ideas, or expand on the ideas of others. EMS can also be used when people are not in the same room at the same time.

5-6b Virtual Team Collaboration Tools

Although the number of communication channels remains largely the same whether the communication occurs face-to-face or virtually, the methods for using these channels has become more and more complex as technology develops. This is particularly true for those working in virtual teams. That is, the challenges of effective teamwork become more and more complex as one looks at the variety of tasks involved, and the corresponding number of tools that are available to help achieve or complete those tasks. Hassan Osman, product management office (PMO) director at Cisco Systems, a major computer-networking equipment manufacturer, has divided virtual team management tools into ten categories:

- Collaboration: Tools that help you collaborate with your team through a central hub for sharing information.
- Project management: Tools that help you manage and plan your projects with your team through task assignments and scheduling.
- Document storing and file sharing: Tools that help you store and share your files securely among your team.
- Meeting (including video and audio conferencing): Tools that help you meet with your team through web conferencing and collaboration.
- High-end video conferencing: Tools that allow you to meet with your team through super high-definition or real size video conferencing.
- Instant messaging: Tools that allow you to chat in real time with your team members.
- Document co-creation: Tools that allow you to co-create and co-edit documents or visuals in real time with your team members.
- Social network: Tools that allow you to collaborate and interact with your team members through a social network.
- Scheduling: Tools that help you to schedule common meeting times with your team members.
- Team games: Virtual team games that help increase trust and enhance communication.

As Exhibit 5.1 indicates, virtual teams have many software options from which to select to better ensure effective communication and collaboration. As should be obvious, sufficient planning and testing is needed to select the appropriate tools for the appropriate tasks.

Exhibit 5.1 | List of Virtual Team Technology Tools*

Collaboration	Project Management	Document Storage/File Sharing	Meeting (Including Video and Audio Conferencing)	High-End Video-Conferencing	Instant Messaging	Document Co-Creation	Social Network	Scheduling	Team Games
• Slack • Webex Teams • Microsoft Teams • Redbooth • Huddle • Podio • Lighthouse • Blackboard • Collaborate • Zoho • Connect • eXo Platform	• Microsoft Project • Basecamp • ActiveCollab • Primavera • Smartsheet • Workfront • Wrike • Projecturf • Apollo • Teamwork • Redmine • Jira • Asana • Trello • ProofHub	• Dropbox • Google Drive • SharePoint • Box • Onehub • Zoho Docs	• Webex • Zoom • GoToMeeting • Google Hangouts • Adobe Connect • Skype • BlueJeans • Join Me • Anymeeting • GlobalMeet	• Cisco Telepresence • Polycom Telepresence • LifeSize	• Jabber • Grape • Rocket Chat • Skype • Mattermost	• Google Docs (part of Drive) • Prezi • Conceptboard • Scribblar • ONLYOFFICE • Xtensio	• Yammer • Chatter • Jive	• Calendly • Doodle • ScheduleOnce • TimeandDate • HubSpot Scheduling	• Prelude (a creative game that builds trust in virtual teams) • VirtuWall (a competitive game that helps break down silos) • Quiz-Breaker (an online icebreaker quiz game for remote teams) • Water Cooler Trivia (weekly office trivia questions using email or Slack)

*Some tools can belong to more than one category because of overlapping features and frequent tool updates.
Source: Osman, H. (2016). The ultimate list of virtual team tools. *The Couch Manager Blog*. Retrieved March 11, 2022 from https://www.thecouchmanager.com/the-ultimate-list-of-virtual-team-technology-tools/

Prostock-studio/Shutterstock

6 | Delivering Good- and Neutral-News Messages

Learning Objectives

After studying this chapter, you will be able to ...

6-1 Describe the deductive outline for good and neutral news and its adaptations for specific situations and international audiences.

6-2 Prepare messages that convey good news, including thank-you and appreciation messages.

6-3 Write messages presenting routine claims and requests, and favorable responses to them.

6-4 Write messages acknowledging customer orders, providing credit information, and extending credit.

6-5 Prepare procedural messages that ensure clear and consistent application.

6-1 Deductive Organizational Pattern

You read in Chapter 4 that you can organize business messages either *deductively* or *inductively* depending on your prediction of the audience's reaction to your main idea. Learning to organize business messages according to the appropriate outline will improve your chances of preparing a document that elicits the response or action you desire.

In this chapter, you will learn to compose messages that convey ideas that your audience will likely find either *pleasing* or *neutral*. Messages that convey pleasant information are referred to as **good-news messages**. Messages that are of interest to your audience but are not likely to generate an emotional reaction are referred to as **neutral-news messages**. The strategies discussed for structuring good- and neutral-news messages can generally be applied to North American audiences. Because message expectations and social conventions differ from culture to culture, the effective writer will adapt as necessary when writing for various audiences. People in organizations use a number of channels to communicate with internal and external audiences. When sending a message that is positive or neutral, you have numerous choices, as shown in Figure 6.1. Depending on the message, audience, and constraints of time and location, the best channel might be spoken or electronic. In addition to the electronic and verbal tools presented in Chapter 5 (email, instant messaging, web communications, and phone), companies also use written documents such as memorandums and letters to communicate information.

Many businesses have gone paperless or as close to it as possible. There are good reasons for doing so: it saves money and it helps reduce waste. Most paper communications in the workplace just get tossed in the trash or the recycling bin—not really a win for businesses trying to be more sustainable. Additionally, storing data digitally means that it's readily available—unlike the memo that may have ended up in a recycling bin.

Memos are still used in some offices, while others (like many startups) have never seen a printed memo since their founding. One of the main reasons memos still have a place in the office is because they get attention. They're formal, professional, and support more formatting styles. For messages that need to have a lasting impact, a physical memo cuts through the email noise and gets attention. It doesn't get lost in a cluttered inbox (though it can get lost in a cluttered desk.) Memos are also a good option for a news board, since they can be pinned up for everyone to see, unlike an email delivered straight to the inbox.

"It's true that we're no longer using memos as frequently as we once did," says communication coach and consultant Dan Oliverio, who sees the status of the once-mighty memorandum as now diluted under a tide of emails, texts, IMs, tweets, and Slacks. Oliverio defines the memo, in contrast to emails and

> **good-news messages** messages that convey pleasant information
>
> **neutral-news messages** messages that are of interest to the reader but are not likely to generate an emotional reaction

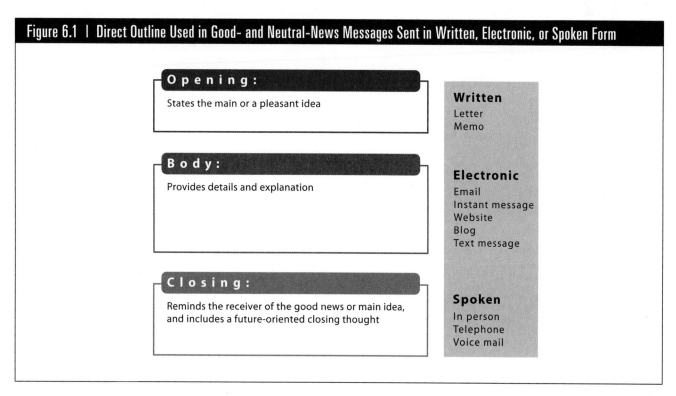

Figure 6.1 | Direct Outline Used in Good- and Neutral-News Messages Sent in Written, Electronic, or Spoken Form

Opening:
States the main or a pleasant idea

Body:
Provides details and explanation

Closing:
Reminds the receiver of the good news or main idea, and includes a future-oriented closing thought

Written
Letter
Memo

Electronic
Email
Instant message
Website
Blog
Text message

Spoken
In person
Telephone
Voice mail

letters, as communication that's always aimed at an internal audience, "usually longer, more detailed, and often standing independently as a reference document."[1]

"Nevertheless," argues Oliverio, "a company still needs a common set of facts, goals, and policies to be effective and coherent. Memos more than emails still fulfill that communication goal."[2]

Business memos still have a place in the office for the following purposes:

- **Policy changes.** When management changes a company policy that affects all employees in an organization, a business memo is an appropriate method to disseminate the information. The business memo provides the formality and authority a company-wide policy change requires. Managers and supervisors can post the business memo in an area visible to all employees.

- **Announcements.** A business memo is an appropriate type of communication to use when making company announcements such as an employee promotion. Companies also use the business memo to welcome new employees who will fill a vital role in the organization. The business memo documents the important announcement. Email can serve as the delivery method for a memo, but the memo should be written in a formal business format. Business memos can also announce a new product line for the company. Management can also send out a business memo to announce that the business hit a target or goal. Other company announcements may include holiday parties, new benefit programs, stock information, or the acquisition of a new client.

- **Action request.** Business memos are appropriate when management makes a request of all employees. For example, during an open enrollment period for health insurance, the human resource manager can use a business memo to inform and request that workers turn in policy changes by a specific date.

- **Reminders.** Employees and management can also distribute a business memo to remind workers about a task that workers must complete. A reminder memo can relate to office behavior, such as cleaning up the company breakroom.[3]

As with memos, printed-business letters are still used for many important, serious types of correspondence, including reference letters, employment verification, job offers, and more. Business letters

---

deductive (or direct) sequence when the message begins with the main idea followed by supporting details

---

are important as they serve as a formal method of communicating with audiences external to the organization, such as customers, clients, business partners, and suppliers, particularly in regard to legal matters.

Regardless of whether the audience is an internal or external one, communication should be carefully structured to achieve the desired purpose.

Good- or neutral-news messages follow a **deductive** or **direct sequence**—the message begins with the main idea. To present good news and neutral information deductively, begin with the major idea followed by supporting details, as depicted in Figure 6.1. In both outlines, the third point (closing thought) might be omitted without seriously impairing effectiveness; however, including it unifies the message and avoids abruptness.

The deductive pattern has several advantages:

- The first sentence is easy to write. After it is written, the details follow easily.

- The first sentence gets the attention it deserves in this emphatic position.

- Encountering good news in the first sentence puts your audience in a pleasant frame of mind, so it is more receptive to the details that follow.

- The arrangement might save your audience some time. Once it understands the important idea, it can move rapidly through the supporting details.

As you study sample deductive messages in this chapter, note the *poor example* notations that clearly mark the examples of ineffective writing. Detailed comments highlight important writing strategies that have been applied or violated. While gaining experience in developing effective messages, you will also learn to recognize standard business formats. Fully formatted messages are shown as printed documents (letters on company letterhead or paper memos) or as electronic formats (email messages or online input screens).

6-2 Good-News Messages

Messages delivering good news are organized using a direct approach, as illustrated in Figure 6.1. For example, you'll study examples of messages that convey positive news as well as thank-you and appreciation messages that generate goodwill.

6-2a Positive News

The memo sent to all employees in Model Document 6.1 begins directly with the main idea: record sales for the month. The discussion that follows includes thanks for

---

Interoffice Memorandum

To:	All Employees
From:	Gina Rodriquez, Sales Manager
Date:	December 5, 2023
Subject:	Record sales in November

We are very happy to inform you that our November sales reached $2 million, 30 percent more than the forecasted figure. This marks a huge improvement from last year and a sign that the business is moving in the right direction.

Starts with the main idea—announcement of record sales.

We would like to thank you all for your contribution and dedication. This would have not been possible without the combined effort of all of our staff.

In recognition of this remarkable achievement, the management has decided to award everyone a $500 bonus.

Provides additional good news.

Keep up the good work.

Regards,

Gina

---

everyone's hard work and the announcement of a monetary bonus for employees.

6-2b Thank-You and Appreciation Messages

Empathetic managers take advantage of occasions to write goodwill messages that build strong, lasting relationships with employees, clients, customers, and various other groups. People are usually not reluctant to say, "Thank you," "What a great performance," "You have certainly helped me," and so on. Despite good intentions, however, people don't often get around to sending thank-you and appreciation messages. Because of their rarity, written appreciation messages are especially meaningful—even treasured.

Thank-You Messages

After receiving a gift, being a guest, attending an interview, or benefiting in various other ways, a thoughtful person will take the time to send a written thank-you message. A simple handwritten note or email is sufficient for some social situations. However, when written from a professional office to respond to a business situation, the message might be printed on company letterhead. Your message should be written deductively and reflect your sincere feelings of gratitude.

Appreciation Messages

You will write appreciation messages to recognize, reward, and encourage the receiver; however, you will also gain satisfaction from commending a deserving person. Such positive thinking can be a favorable influence on your own attitude and performance. In appropriate situations, you might wish to address an appreciation message to an individual's supervisor and send a copy of the document to the individual to share the positive comments. In any case, an appreciation message should be sent to commend deserving people and not for possible self-gain.

To Express Thanks for a Gift

Thank you for the gift certificate to Bath Bubbles Boutique. You know how much I like to relax in a hot, aromatic bath after a stressful day at work! I was happy to fill in for you during the hiring meeting since our input is so important to our team. I hope your sister's wedding was a success.

To Extend Thanks for Information

Thank you for informing me of the recent job opening in Russell's marketing department. That information led to an interview with Ms. LeVal this morning, and that interaction made me feel confident that I could contribute effectively to her team's efforts. Please accept my invitation to lunch in appreciation for learning about this opportunity.

For full potential value, follow these guidelines for appreciation messages:

- **Send in a timely manner.** Sending an appreciation message within a few days of the circumstance will emphasize your genuineness. The receiver might question the sincerity of appreciation messages that are sent long overdue.

- **Avoid exaggerated language that is hardly believable.** You might believe the exaggerated statements to be true, but the recipient might find them unbelievable and insincere. Strong language with unsupported statements raises questions about your motive for the message.

- **Make specific comments about outstanding qualities or performance.** Compared to Model Document 6.2, the following message might lack the impact of one that contains more detail and is written with more care. Although the sender cared enough to say thank you, the message could have been given to any speaker, even if the sender had slept through the entire workshop. Similarly, a note merely closed with "sincerely" does not necessarily make the ideas seem sincere. Including specific remarks about understanding and applying the speaker's main points makes the message meaningful and sincere.

Original: Your workshop on using the new database software program was very much appreciated. I'm sure it will help staff tremendously. Thanks.

Model Document 6.2 | Good Example of an Appreciation Message

January 21, 2023

Carrie Lee

Regents Insurance Group

382 Ocean Avenue

Miami, FL 02391

Dear Carrie Lee,

Thank you for taking the time to talk with me today. I sincerely appreciate the time you spent reviewing my career goals and recommending strategies for achieving them. Your advice was very helpful and gave me a new perspective on available opportunities.

> **Extends appreciation for time spent in interview.**

I especially appreciate your offer to connect me to others in your network. I plan on following up with the contacts you emailed me right away. I will also use the online networking resources you recommended to further my job search.

> **Provides a specific example without exaggerating or using overly strong language or insincere statements.**

Any additional suggestions you may have would be welcome. I'll update you as my search progresses.

Again, thank you so much for your help. I greatly appreciate the assistance you have provided me.

> **Reiterates goodwill.**

Best Regards,

Susan Williams

> **Format Pointer:**
> Uses short lines, mixed case; omits special formatting, such as emoticons and email abbreviations, for improved readability.

Improved: Your workshop on the use of our new database software program has enabled staff to apply its broad array of features much more quickly.

One of the most important takeaways from the workshop was the emphasis you placed on creating and communicating clear procedures for work processes. Based upon your suggestions, our team created a draft of these guidelines during our first meeting. Thank you for the suggestions that have put my colleagues and me on the path to becoming a more effective virtual team.

The appreciation message in Model Document 6.2 conveys sincere appreciation for the positive results of a proposal. The net effects of this message are positive: The sender feels good for having passed on a deserved compliment, and the receiver is encouraged by the recipient's recognition of the value of his organization's work.

An apology is written much like an appreciation message. A sincere written apology is needed to preserve relationships when regrettable situations occur. Though difficult to prepare, a well-written apology will usually be received favorably.

6-3 Routine Claims

A **claim** is a request for an adjustment. When business communicators ask for something to which they think they are entitled (such as a refund, replacement, exchange, or payment for damages), the message is called a *claim message*.

6-3a Claim Message

Requests for adjustments can be divided into two groups: **routine claims** and **persuasive claims**. Persuasive claims, which are discussed in Chapter 8, assume that a request will be granted only after explanations and persuasive arguments have been presented. Routine claims (possibly because of guarantees, warranties, or other contractual conditions) assume that a request will be granted quickly and willingly without persuasion. Because you expect routine claims to be granted willingly, a forceful, accusatory tone is inappropriate.

When the claim is routine, the direct approach shown in Figure 6.1 is appropriate. Let's consider the situation referred to in Model Document 6.3. Surely, the cleaning company intended its services to be acceptable. Since they apparently were not, a refund can reasonably be expected, as shown in Model Document 6.3. Note, however, that the message in Model Document 6.3 is written inappropriately using an indirect approach—the details are presented before the main idea, and it ends abruptly.

6-3b Favorable Response to a Claim Message

Businesses *want* their customers to communicate when merchandise or service is not satisfactory. They want to learn of ways in which goods and services can be improved, and they want their customers to receive value for the money they spend. With considerable confidence, they can assume that writers of claim messages think their claims are valid. By responding fairly to legitimate requests in **adjustment messages**, businesses can gain a reputation for standing behind their goods and services. A loyal customer is likely to become even more loyal after a business has demonstrated its integrity.

Ordinarily, a response to a written message is also a written message. Sometimes people communicate to confirm ideas they have already discussed on the phone. When the response to a claim is favorable, present ideas in the direct sequence. Although the word *grant* is acceptable when talking about claims, its use in adjustment messages is discouraged. An expression such as "Your claim is being granted" unnecessarily implies that you are in a position of power.

Because the subject of an adjustment is related to the goods or services provided, the message can include a brief sales idea. With only a little extra space, the message can include resale or sales promotional material. **Resale** refers to a discussion of goods or services already bought. It reminds customers and clients that they made a good choice in selecting a company with which to do business or it reminds them of the good qualities of their purchase. **Sales promotional material** refers to statements made about related merchandise or service. For example, a message about a company's recently purchased office furniture might also mention available office equipment. Mentioning the office equipment is using sales promotional material. Subtle sales messages that are included in adjustments have a good chance of being read, whereas direct sales messages might not be read at all.

Consider the ineffective

> **claim** a request for an adjustment
>
> **routine claims** messages that assume that a claim will be granted quickly and willingly without persuasion
>
> **persuasive claims** messages that assume that a claim will be granted only after explanations and persuasive arguments have been presented
>
> **adjustment messages** messages that are fair responses by businesses to legitimate requests in claim messages by customers
>
> **resale** a discussion of goods or services already bought
>
> **sales promotional material** statements made about related merchandise or service

Dear Felipe Rodriguez,

<u>Our organization recently purchased 10 laptop computers from your company</u> for use by our customer service personnel. We have been very pleased with their performance. Unfortunately, one of the laptops is no longer functioning.

<u>This has created a problem for one of our most productive customer service team members</u>, Mario Cavetti, who is unable to resolve customer concerns without access to our intranet.

<u>You should receive the damaged laptop tomorrow via overnight freight.</u> Please replace or repair it and return it to us as soon as possible.

> **Introduction does not state the purpose of the message. Instead, it provides unneeded background.**

> **Paragraph provides more unnecessary background information.**

> **The routine request comes at the end of the message rather than at the beginning.**

Good Example of a Routine Claim

March 30, 2023

Ralph Hoffman
Squeaky Cleaners
P.O. Box 760
Spokane, WA 89043

Dear Ralph Hoffman,

This letter serves as a formal request for a refund of $99.99—the total paid to your company, Squeaky Cleaners, for office cleaning on March 3, 2023.

Your company advertises a "100 percent Satisfaction Guarantee" for customers, printed on the promotional postcard that was sent to my business. Unfortunately, I was dissatisfied with the quality of service. Your staff did not thoroughly clean my first-floor bathroom, and I found shoe marks on the breakroom floor after your team departed.

Please refund this balance to the credit card that was used to make the initial payment by April 1, 2023.

I look forward to a resolution of this matter. I can be reached at 555-980-7899 anytime.

Sincerely,

Julia Tompkins

> **Emphasizes the main idea (request for adjustment) by placing it in the first sentence.**

> **Provides an explanation.**

> **Ends on a positive note, reminding reader of immediate need.**

> **Format Pointers:**
> - **Composes a short, concise message that fits on one screen.**
> - **Includes a salutation and closing to personalize the message.**

response in Model Document 6.4 to a claim letter and the message it sends about the company's commitment. Now notice the explanation in the revision in Model Document 6.4. The good news appears in the first sentence. The details and closing sentence follow naturally and show a desire to correct the problem.

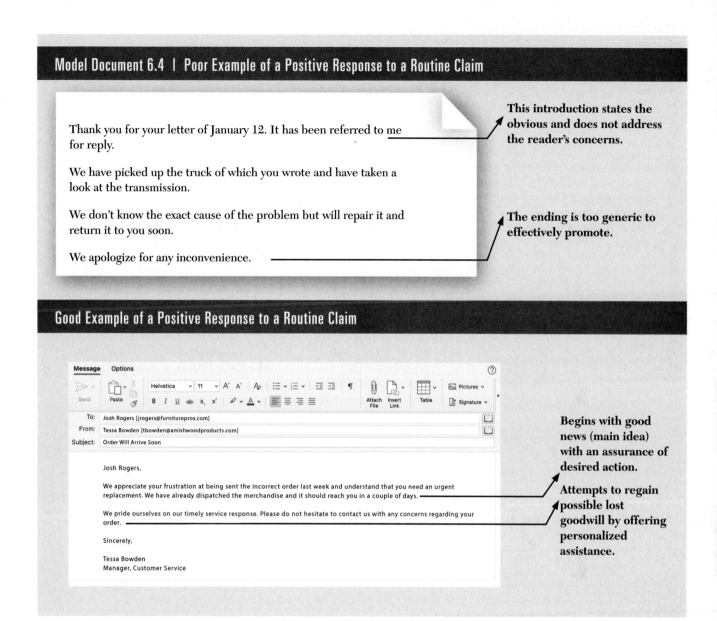

Thank you for your letter of January 12. It has been referred to me for reply.

We have picked up the truck of which you wrote and have taken a look at the transmission.

We don't know the exact cause of the problem but will repair it and return it to you soon.

We apologize for any inconvenience.

This introduction states the obvious and does not address the reader's concerns.

The ending is too generic to effectively promote.

Good Example of a Positive Response to a Routine Claim

To: Josh Rogers [jrogers@furniturepros.com]
From: Tessa Bowden [tbowden@amishwoodproducts.com]
Subject: Order Will Arrive Soon

Josh Rogers,

We appreciate your frustration at being sent the incorrect order last week and understand that you need an urgent replacement. We have already dispatched the merchandise and it should reach you in a couple of days.

We pride ourselves on our timely service response. Please do not hesitate to contact us with any concerns regarding your order.

Sincerely,

Tessa Bowden
Manager, Customer Service

Begins with good news (main idea) with an assurance of desired action.

Attempts to regain possible lost goodwill by offering personalized assistance.

6-3c Routine Requests

Like claims, requests are divided into two groups: **routine requests** and **persuasive requests**. Persuasive requests, which are discussed in Chapter 8, assume that action will be taken after persuasive arguments are presented. Routine requests and favorable responses to them follow the deductive sequence.

6-3d Requests for Information

Requests for information about people, prices, products, and services are common. Because these requests from customers and clients are door openers for future business, businesses accept them optimistically. At the same time, they arrive at an opinion about the sender based on the

quality of the message. Follow the points in the deductive outline for preparing effective requests that you are confident will be fulfilled.

The message in Model Document 6.5 does not follow an appropriate deductive outline for a routine request. The request is too vague and the sales manager receiving the message is not provided with enough useful information.

Note that the revision in Model Document 6.5 starts with a direct request for additional personnel. Then as much detail

routine requests messages that assume that a request will be granted quickly and willingly without persuasion

persuasive requests messages that assume that a requested action will be taken after persuasive arguments are presented

Subject: Need information

Our company is doing a periodic review of computer service providers to ensure that we are contracted with the company who provides the best quality service for the most competitive price. Based on a review of your website, it appears that your organization provides the type of service we need. Obviously, a website is a limited source of information, so I am uncertain as to whether your organization will be able to accommodate our needs.

Our organization has 500 networked desktops and 100 printers that need to be maintained and upgraded as needed. In addition, computer service personnel would be expected to provide technical support to our computer users. Does your company provide resources to support these needs?

I look forward to receiving your reply as quickly as possible.

- The subject line could be more informational.
- The introduction could more clearly state the purpose of the message.
- The writer's needs could be stated more clearly and systematically.
- The generic close fails to build goodwill or a sense of urgency.

Good Example of a Routine Request

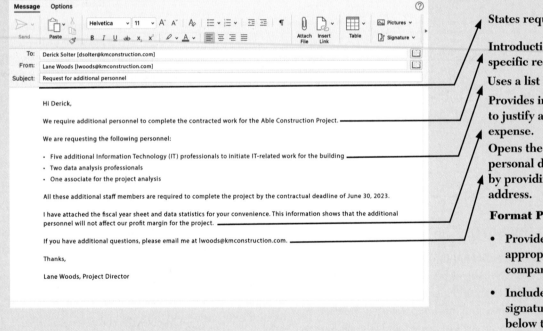

To: Derick Solter [dsolter@kmconstruction.com]
From: Lane Woods [lwoods@kmconstruction.com]
Subject: Request for additional personnel

Hi Derick,

We require additional personnel to complete the contracted work for the Able Construction Project.

We are requesting the following personnel:

- Five additional Information Technology (IT) professionals to initiate IT-related work for the building
- Two data analysis professionals
- One associate for the project analysis

All these additional staff members are required to complete the project by the contractual deadline of June 30, 2023.

I have attached the fiscal year sheet and data statistics for your convenience. This information shows that the additional personnel will not affect our profit margin for the project.

If you have additional questions, please email me at lwoods@kmconstruction.com.

Thanks,

Lane Woods, Project Director

- States request clearly.
- Introduction identifies specific request.
- Uses a list for emphasis.
- Provides information to justify additional expense.
- Opens the door for personal dialogue by providing email address.

Format Pointers:

- Provides a salutation appropriate for the company.
- Includes a complete signature block below the writer's name for complete reference.

as necessary is presented to enable the receiver to answer specifically. The email message is short, but because it conveys enough information and has a tone of politeness, it is effective.

6-3e Favorable Response to a Routine Request

The message in Model Document 6.6 responds favorably but with little enthusiasm to an online request for detailed information about a hotel and conference facility. With a little planning and consideration for the needs outlined in the request, the message in Model Document 6.6 on page 109 could have been written just as quickly. It provides detailed information about the facility and uses lists and headings to help the reader skim the message.

6-3f Positive Response to a Favor Request

Occasionally, as a business professional, you will be asked for special favors. You might receive invitations to speak at various civic or education events, spearhead fund-raising and other service projects, or offer your expertise in other ways. If you say "Yes," you might as well say it enthusiastically. Sending an unplanned, stereotyped acceptance suggests that the contribution will be similar.

If you find yourself responding to invitations frequently, you can draft a form message that you'll revise for each invitation you receive.

6-3g Form Messages for Routine Responses

Form messages are a fast and efficient way of transmitting frequently recurring messages to which the anticipated receiver reaction is likely to be favorable or neutral. Inputting the customer's name, address, and other variables (information that differs for each receiver) personalizes each message to meet the needs of its receiver. Companies might use form paragraphs that have been saved as template documents. When composing a document, select the appropriate paragraph according to your receiver's request. After assembling the selected files on the computer screen, input the particular information for the situation (e.g., name and address), and print a copy of the personalized message on letterhead to send to the receiver.

Form letters have earned a negative connotation because of their tendency to be impersonal. Many people simply refuse to read such letters for that reason. Personalizing a form letter can circumvent this problem.

Model Document 6.6 | Poor Example of a Positive Response to a Routine Request

RE: Information needed

Manuel Ortiz,

I read your request and hopefully my hurried response will provide you the information you need.

Atlantic City Resort and Spa can serve your needs with a 10,000-square foot conference center and accommodations for more than 700 guests. We also have three restaurants at the hotel as well as a coffee kiosk in the lobby. We are near shopping and restaurants located in the Boardwalk Plaza as well as local area attractions, such as the Atlantic City Aquarium, the Atlantic City casino complex, and nearby beaches.

We are happy you're considering Atlantic City and the Atlantic City Resort and Spa for your annual convention. Please contact either me or my staff to make the necessary reservations.

The subject line could be more informational.

The introduction could be more positive and speak more narrowly to the reader's concerns.

This discussion could provide the specific information requested.

The close could be more effective at building goodwill and demonstrating a sincere interest in meeting the organization's needs.

To: Lois Weyman [lweyman@namaa.org]

From: Dale Solter [dsolter@southerngardens.com]

Subject: Assistance Planning Exciting Convention in New Orleans!

Lois Weyman,

We'd like to extend our invitation to have your next NAMAA Writers Conference at our facility in New Orleans, Louisiana. As you know, New Orleans is rich in history and culture, and has always been home to many famous writers. We believe that your members will find our hotel and our city the perfect place to gather for inspiration and collaboration.

I've provided general information below about our hotel and conference facilities and offerings. Let's speak soon about plans to host your next great NAMAA Writers Conference here at the Southern Gardens Hotel & Conference Center in New Orleans.

General Description

We are ideally located on three private fenced acres at 1200 Gardenia Boulevard in New Orleans' famous Garden District. Our hotel has 164 rooms. If every room were filled to capacity, we could host more than 500 guests.

Our conference center consists of a suite of conference rooms that can be configured into seven small rooms, two very large ones, or any combination in between. The conference center also has four restrooms dedicated for its guests.

A lift device is available to assist guests into and out of the swimming pool and hot tub. Assisted hearing devices are available on request from the front desk. All signs, including room numbers, have Braille translations beneath the standard letters or numbers. The hotel offers complimentary shuttle service to and from the airport.

Taxis are easily available for transportation within the city. City buses stop only a short block from our site. And if you're looking for a romantic tour, horse-drawn carriage rides are also available.

Additional services include:

• Laundry, Ironing, or Clothing Repair. Our housekeeping staff will help you keep your clothes looking their best.
• High Speed Internet Wireless Connection. The internet is always available for your use anywhere on the hotel property.
• Concierge Service. Need to rent a car, find a tuxedo, or buy theatre tickets? Stop at our concierge desk in the front lobby and we'll assist you to fulfill any desire.
• 24-Hour Room Service. Got an urge for a milkshake at 3 a.m.? Just call the front desk and order any item from the Room Service menu conveniently located in your room.

Revises subject line after clicking "Reply" to communicate enthusiasm for providing exceptional personalized service.

Shows a sincere interest in the request and the person.

Tourist Destinations (continued...)

No visit to New Orleans would be complete without a tour of the French Quarter and the Garden District, both made famous in hundreds of books over the last two centuries. Other sites of particular interest to many writers are our notable cemeteries, which, due the high water table of the area, are populated with beautiful aboveground mausoleums, memorial statues, and crypts of all kinds. The Mississippi River also lures many visitors to its history-laden waters. All tours of Historical New Orleans can be reserved at the front desk of the hotel.

Conference Logistics Services

Our conference rooms can be configured to accommodate different sizes of groups. We can add or move partition walls as needed to create as many as seven small conference rooms or as few as two large ones. Rooms may be furnished with rows of folding chairs, long conference tables, dining tables, movable stages and lecterns, or any combination of these.

We need your conference room reservations 9 months before your start date, and a specific schedule of room setups 2 months before your start date. Each change to a conference room configuration takes approximately an hour.

Additional conference services include:

- **Hotel Room Reservations.** We will reserve a block of 100 hotel rooms for the use of your attendees. If these have not been reserved by your attendees 60 days in advance of the conference, we will release these rooms to other parties on request. Special accommodations such as wheelchair accessible rooms or assisted hearing or visual devices must be requested at least 60 days in advance.

- **Audio Visual Services.** Our subcontractors will provide audio visual setups and assistance during the conference. They require a schedule of services and a list of equipment 60 days before the event begins.

- **Catering Services.** Our catering partners can provide any food service you require, from elegant formal dinners to coffee and muffins or buffet snacks for a cocktail party. At the time of your conference reservation, they will contact you about your food and beverage needs.

Conference Center Rates

Entire Conference Center Facility: $450 per 2-hour block, or $1,500 per day. This includes initial room setup, and daily opening and cleaning costs, including restocking restroom supplies. All other facility services are separate. Refer to the Logistics page.

Individual Conference Rooms: Sizes and prices of conference rooms are variable. Contact our management for quotes on individual conference rooms.

Please call my direct line, (509) 569-7780, for more advice on organizing your exciting event in romantic New Orleans.

Sincerely,

Dale Solter, Sales Manager
Southern Gardens Hotel and Conference Center

Addresses the audience's concerns using an articulate, concise writing style.

Provides more useful information that communicates genuine interest in the person's need for information and expertise in the area of travel sales.

6-3h Routine Messages About Orders and Credit

Routine messages, such as customer order acknowledgments, are written deductively. Normally, credit information is requested and transmitted electronically from the national credit reporting agencies to companies requesting credit references. However, when companies choose to request information directly from other businesses, individual credit requests and responses must be written.

6-4 Acknowledging Customer Orders

When customers place orders for merchandise, they expect to get exactly what they ordered as quickly as possible. For an initial order and for an order that cannot be filled quickly and precisely, companies typically send an **acknowledgment message**, a document that indicates that an order has been received and is being processed. For companies using online ordering systems, these messages are generated automatically. However, if your organization provides services or goods through other means, acknowledgment messages may be provided through preprinted letters or an immediate email message that acknowledges the customer, assures quality service, and provides a detailed copy of the items included in the sales order as shown in Model Document 6.7.

Nonroutine orders, such as initial orders, custom orders, and delayed orders, require individualized acknowledgment messages. When well-written, these messages not only acknowledge the order but also create customer goodwill and encourage the customer to place additional orders.

6-4a Providing Credit Information

Replies to requests for credit information are usually simple—just fill in the blanks and return the document. If the request does not include a form, follow a deductive plan in writing the reply: the major idea first, followed by supporting details (refer to Model Document 6.7).

When providing credit information, you have an ethical and legal obligation to yourself, the credit applicant, and the business from which the credit information is requested. You must be able to document any statement you make to defend yourself against a defamation charge. Thus, good advice is to stick with facts; omit any opinions. "I'm sure they will pay promptly" is an opinion that should be omitted but include the documentable fact that "Their payments have always been prompt." Can you safely say a customer is a good

> **acknowledgment message**
> a document that indicates that an order has been received and is being processed

To Make a Form Letter More Personal?...

▶ **Add more variables to the standard text to tailor the message to the individual.**

▶ **Use personalized envelopes instead of mass-produced mailing labels.**

▶ **Be sure to spell names correctly.**

▶ **Produce a higher-quality document by using a good grade of paper and a high-quality printer.**

Pheelings media/Shutterstock

Tweeting the Customer Well

▶ **Email links, chat rooms, and bulletin boards on corporate websites foster dialogue that leads** to strong relationships. Today, an increasing number of businesspeople are participating in social exchange networking and blogging services, such as Twitter (www.twitter.com), to provide updates to customers.

▶ **"Tweet" postings must be brief; messages cannot exceed 280 characters.[4] Such forced brevity might be one reason for the service's popularity. If customers are invited to talk, companies must be prepared to respond with timely, effective—even if brief—messages.**

Travel man/Shutterstock

credit risk when all you know is that the customer had a good credit record when purchasing from you?

6-4b Extending Credit

A timely response is preferable for any business document, but it is especially important when communicating about credit. The Equal Credit Opportunity Act (ECOA) requires that a credit applicant be notified of the credit decision within 30 days of receipt of the request or application. The party granting the credit must also disclose the terms of the credit agreement, such as the address for sending or making payments, due dates for payments, and the interest rate charged.

When extending credit, follow these guidelines as you write deductively:

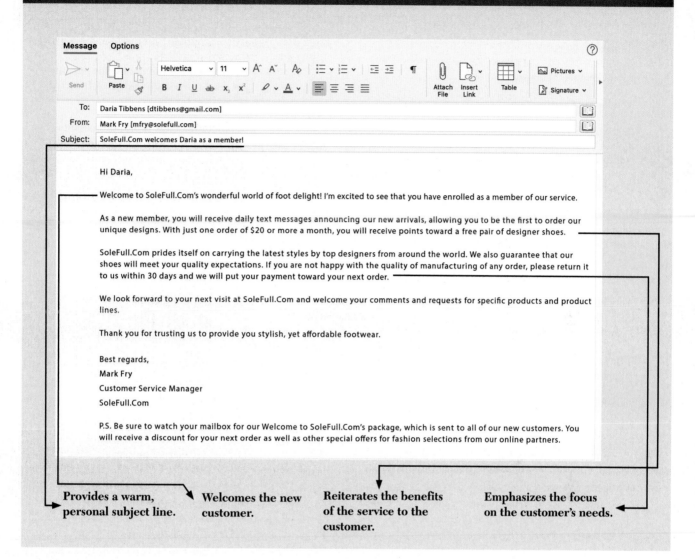

Message   **Options**

To: Daria Tibbens [dtibbens@gmail.com]
From: Mark Fry [mfry@solefull.com]
Subject: SoleFull.Com welcomes Daria as a member!

Hi Daria,

Welcome to SoleFull.Com's wonderful world of foot delight! I'm excited to see that you have enrolled as a member of our service.

As a new member, you will receive daily text messages announcing our new arrivals, allowing you to be the first to order our unique designs. With just one order of $20 or more a month, you will receive points toward a free pair of designer shoes.

SoleFull.Com prides itself on carrying the latest styles by top designers from around the world. We also guarantee that our shoes will meet your quality expectations. If you are not happy with the quality of manufacturing of any order, please return it to us within 30 days and we will put your payment toward your next order.

We look forward to your next visit at SoleFull.Com and welcome your comments and requests for specific products and product lines.

Thank you for trusting us to provide you stylish, yet affordable footwear.

Best regards,
Mark Fry
Customer Service Manager
SoleFull.Com

P.S. Be sure to watch your mailbox for our Welcome to SoleFull.Com's package, which is sent to all of our new customers. You will receive a discount for your next order as well as other special offers for fashion selections from our online partners.

Provides a warm, personal subject line.   **Welcomes the new customer.**   **Reiterates the benefits of the service to the customer.**   **Emphasizes the focus on the customer's needs.**

1. **Open by extending credit and acknowledging shipment of an order.** Because of its importance, the credit aspect is emphasized more than the acknowledgment of the order. In other cases (in which the order is for cash or the credit terms are already clearly understood), the primary purpose of writing might be to acknowledge an order.

2. **Indicate the basis for the decision to extend credit and explain the credit terms.** Indicating that you are extending credit on the basis of an applicant's prompt paying habits with present creditors might encourage this new customer to continue these habits with you.

3. **Present credit policies.** Explain policies (e.g., credit terms, authorized discounts, and payment dates). Include any legally required disclosure documents.

4. **Communicate a genuine desire to build a strong business relationship.** Include resale, sales promotional material, and comments that remind the customer of the benefits of doing business with you and encourage additional orders.

January 24, 2023

Jason Connors, Manager

Woodhouse Construction

4500 Main Street

Trenton, NJ 34409

Dear Jason Connors:

Although you're having trouble paying for excavation equipment rental, John Kerschbaum has assured us your cash flow problems will be alleviated once you complete the USA Bank building project. We think John's assessment is accurate. Therefore, we have decided to offer you a credit extension. This offer reflects the faith we have in Tri-County.

Woodhouse Construction has been a dependable and valued customer since 2019; therefore, we are offering our usual terms for payment: 3 percent/14 days/Net 30.

If these are acceptable, please call me at (209) 346-9078. You are a valued customer.

Sincerely,

Tom Perkins
Business Manager

Recognizes the dealer for earning credit privilege and gives the reason for the credit extension.

Includes sales promotion; assumes satisfaction with initial order and looks confidently for future business.

Includes credit terms and encourages taking advantage of discount.

Presents reseller with a reminder of product benefits and encourages future business.

Legal and Ethical Considerations:

- **Provides answer to request for credit within required time frame (30 days from receipt of request) and mentions terms of credit that will be provided, as required by law.**

- **Uses letter channel rather than email to communicate a contractual message.**

The letter in Model Document 6.8 was written to a retailer; however, the same principles apply when writing to a consumer. Each message should be addressed in terms of individual interests. Dealers are concerned about markup, marketability, and display; consumers are concerned about price, appearance, and durability. Individual consumers might require a more detailed explanation of credit terms.

Companies receive so many requests for credit that the costs of individualized letters are prohibitive; therefore, most favorable replies to credit requests are form letters. To personalize the letter, however, the writer should merge the customer's name, address, amount of the loan, and terms into the computer file containing the form letter information. Typically, form messages read something like this:

Although such form messages are effective for informing the customer that credit is being extended, they do little to build goodwill and promote future sales. Managers can personalize form messages so that recipients do not perceive them as canned responses.

6-5 Procedural Messages

Memos or email messages are the most frequently used methods for communicating standard operating procedures and other instructions, as well as changes related to personnel or the organization, and other internal matters for which a written record is needed.

Instructions to employees must be conveyed clearly and accurately to facilitate the day-to-day operations of the business and to prevent negative feelings that occur when mistakes are made and work must be redone. Managers must take special care in writing standard operating procedures to ensure that all employees complete the procedures accurately and consistently (refer to Model Document 6.9).

Interoffice Memorandum

To: PetroChem managers

From: Herb Allman, Hiring Manager

Subject: Employing Engineers without U.S. Citizenship

Because of the shortage of qualified engineers, managers have been requesting information about the process to hire employees from outside the country. To help you in that process, I am providing a step list for the procedure to apply for a U.S. work permit.

- Step #1—<u>Apply</u> for an immigration status that will enable the employee to work

  To get a Work Permit, employees need to have an immigration status that allows them to work in the US.

- Step #2—<u>Prepare</u> Form I-765E

  Qualified employees will use U. Citizenship and Immigration Services (USCIS) Form I-765, Application for Employment Authorization, to apply for a Work Permit. Form I-765 is pretty simple to complete. Applicants will fill in their name, contact information, and information about why they are eligible.

- Step #3—<u>Prepare</u> supporting documents

  Applicants need to submit six supporting documents with their Form I-765 to get a Work Permit:

  - A copy of their **passport photo page**
  - A copy of their **current U.S. visa** (if they are in the United States already)
  - A copy of their original **Form I-94 travel record** (front and back), or a printout of their electronic I-94, from their most recent entry into the United States
  - Copies of any of **previous work permits** (front and back)
  - Two 2-inch-by-2-inch **passport-style photos**
  - A copy of the "**receipt notice**" they received from the U.S. Government when you submitted their immigrant visa application

- Step #4—<u>Pay</u> the filing fee

  A charge of $410 fee is applied to process Form I-765. Applicants can pay the fee by money order, personal check, or cashier's check made out to the U.S. Department of Homeland Security.

- Step #5—<u>Submit</u> the Work Permit application

  Once applicants have completed their Form I-765, assembled their supporting documents, and paid the filing fee, it's time to submit the application for a Work Permit to USCIS. It is a good idea to include a cover letter with their paperwork so that the government knows precisely what they are receiving from the applicant.

Note: Applicants should make a complete copy of everything in your packet, including the checks, before sending it to USCIS.

Introduces the main idea.

Provides an enumerated step list to direct attention to each step and emphasize the need for a sequence.

Begins each item with an action verb to help employees visualize completing the procedure.

Once applicants have submitted their Work Permit application to USCIS, **the processing time is usually 5 to 7 months.** However, coronavirus and USCIS budget problems have caused significant application delays. USCIS will send a "Receipt Notice" when it receives paperwork. Applicants should receive this notice two to three weeks after you file. Once applicants receive this notice, they will be able to use the Receipt Number provided to track their application status on USCIS's website (https://www.uscis.gov/).

Dear [TITLE] [LAST NAME]

▸ Trueman's Electronics is pleased to extend credit privileges to you. Initially, you may purchase up to [CREDIT LIMIT] worth of merchandise. Our credit terms are [TERMS]. We welcome you as a credit customer at Trueman's Electronics and look forward to serving your needs for the latest electronics devices designed and manufactured by the world's top companies.

Before writing instructions, walk through each step to understand it and to locate potential trouble spots. Then attempt to determine how much employees already know about the process, and to anticipate any questions or problems. Then, as you write instructions that require more than a few simple steps, follow these guidelines:

1. **Begin each step with an action statement to create a vivid picture of the employee completing the task.** Using an action verb and the understood subject, *you,* is more vivid than a sentence written in the passive voice. For example, a loan officer attempting to learn new procedures for evaluating new venture loans can more easily understand "*identify* assets available to collateralize the loan" than "assets available to collateralize the loan should be identified."

2. **Itemize each step on a separate line to add emphasis and to simplify reading.** Number each step to indicate that the procedures should be completed in a particular order. If the order of steps is not important, use bullets rather than numbers.

3. **Consider preparing a flow chart depicting the procedures.** The cost and effort involved in creating a sophisticated flow chart might be merited for extremely important and complex procedures. For example, take a look at the flow chart in Figure 10.7, which demonstrates a flowchart of the customer service process.

4. **Complete the procedure by following your instructions step-by-step.** Correct any errors that you locate.

5. **Ask a colleague or employee to walk through the procedures.** This walk through will allow you to identify ambiguous statements, omissions of relevant information, and other sources of potential problems.

Consider the seemingly simple task of informing employees about safety training seminars. The safety manager might send a message "Sign up for a safety seminar ASAP." Incomplete verbal instructions (reported in haste) could lead to confusion about the training requirement and further questions. Instead, a message should include the schedule sent as an email attachment and be posted on the company intranet for easy reference.

fizkes/Shutterstock

7 | Delivering Bad-News Messages

Learning Objectives

After studying this chapter, you will be able to ...

7-1 Explain the steps and usages for specific situations of the inductive outline.

7-2 Employ strategies for developing the five components of a bad-news message.

7-3 Prepare messages refusing requests.

7-4 Prepare messages denying claims.

7-5 Write messages that handle problems with customers' orders and denying credit.

7-6 Prepare messages providing constructive criticism.

7-7 Write messages that communicate negative organizational news and messages responding to crises.

7-1 Choosing an Appropriate Channel and Organizational Pattern

An organization's ability to handle difficult situations with tact and empathy powerfully influences the perceptions of employees, local citizens, and the public at large. As a skilled communicator, you will attempt to deliver bad news in such a way that the recipient supports the decision and is willing to continue a positive relationship. To accomplish these goals, allow empathy for your audience to direct your choice of an appropriate channel and outline when presenting a logical discussion of the facts or an unpleasant idea. Use tactful and effective language to aid you in developing a clear, yet sensitive, message.

7-1a Channel Choice and Commitment to Tact

Personal delivery has been the preferred medium for delivering bad news because it signals the importance of the news and shows empathy for the recipient. Face-to-face delivery also provides the benefit of nonverbal communication and immediate feedback, which minimizes misinterpretation of these highly sensitive messages. Personal delivery, however, carries a level of discomfort and the potential for the escalation of emotion. A voice on the telephone triggers the same discomfort as a face-to-face meeting, and the increased difficulty of interpreting the intensity of nonverbal cues over the telephone only adds to the natural discomfort associated with delivering negative information.

You must be cautious when you deliver bad news electronically, whether by text messaging, email, or electronic postings. While you might feel more comfortable avoiding the discomfort of facing the recipient, the impersonal nature of the computer might lead to careless writing that is tactless, lacking in empathy, and, perhaps, may even be defamatory. Stay focused and follow the same communication strategies you would apply if you were speaking face-to-face or writing a more formal message. Regardless of the medium, your objective is to help your audience understand and accept your message, and this requires empathy and tact.

Tactlessness can have serious effects when your personal response fails to soothe negative feelings and ensure a harmonious relationship with a customer, client, or employee. You might find it difficult to show tact when you doubt the legitimacy of a request or simply don't have the time to prepare an effective bad-news message. When this conflict exists, you must remember that any message delivered on behalf of the company is a direct reflection on the company's image.

7-1b Use of the Inductive Approach to Build Goodwill

Just as good news is accompanied by details, bad news is accompanied by supporting reasons and explanations. If the bad news is presented in the first sentence, the reaction is likely to be negative: "They never gave me a fair chance," "That's unfair," "This just can't be." Having made a value judgment on reading the first sentence, receivers are naturally reluctant to change their minds before the last sentence—even though the intervening sentences present a valid basis for doing so. Once disappointed by the idea contained in the first sentence, receivers are tempted to concentrate on *refuting* (instead of *understanding*) supporting details.

From the communicator's point of view, details that support a refusal are very important. If the supporting details are understood and believed, the message might be readily accepted and good business relationships preserved. Because the reasons behind the bad news are so important, the communicator needs to organize the message in such a way as to emphasize the reasons.

The chances of getting your audience to understand the reasons are much better *before* the bad news is presented than *after* the bad news is presented. If the bad news precedes the reasons, the message might be discarded before this important portion is even read, or the disappointment experienced when reading the bad news might interfere with your audience's ability to comprehend or accept the supporting explanation.

The five-step outline shown in Figure 7.1 simplifies the process of organizing bad-news messages. These five steps are applied in messages illustrated in this chapter.

Although the outline has five points, a bad-news message may or may not have five paragraphs. More than one paragraph might be necessary for conveying supporting reasons. In the illustrations in this chapter, note that the first and final paragraphs are seldom longer than two sentences. In fact, one-sentence paragraphs at the message's beginning look inviting to read.

You might speculate that your audience will become impatient when a message is inductive. Concise, well-written explanations are not likely to make a reader impatient. They relate to the audience's problem, present information not already known, and help your audience understand. However, if a receiver becomes impatient while reading a well-written explanation, that impatience is less damaging to understanding than would be the anger or disgust that often results from encountering bad news in the first sentence.

Figure 7.1 | Inductive Outline Used in Bad-News Messages

Opening:

1. Begins with neutral idea that leads to refusal or bad news

Body:

2. Presents facts, analysis, and reasons for refusal or bad news

3. States bad news using positive tone and de-emphasis techniques

4. Includes counterproposal or "silver lining" idea when possible or appropriate

Closing:

5. Closes with ideas that shift focus away from refusal or bad news, and indicates continuing relationship with receiver

Written
Letter
Memo

Electronic
Email
Instant message
Website
Blog
Text message

Spoken
In person
Telephone
Voice mail

The Inductive Sequence of Ideas Has the Following Advantages:

▶ Sufficient identification of the subject of the message without first turning off the audience.

▶ Presentation of the reasons *before* the refusal, where they are more likely to be understood and will receive appropriate attention.

▶ Avoidance of a negative reaction. By the time the reasons are read, they seem sensible, and the refusal is foreseen. Because it is expected, the statement of refusal does not come as a shock.

▶ De-emphasis of the refusal by closing on a neutral or pleasant note. By showing a willingness to cooperate in some way, the sender conveys a desire to be helpful.

Placing a Refusal in the First Sentence Can Be Justified When One or More of the Following Circumstances Exist:

▶ The message is the second response to a repeated request.

▶ A very small, insignificant matter is involved.

▶ The request is obviously ridiculous, immoral, unethical, illegal, or dangerous.

▶ The sender's intent is to "shake" the receiver.

▶ The sender–recipient relationship is so close and longstanding that satisfactory human relations can be taken for granted.

▶ The sender *wants* to demonstrate authority.

7-1c Exceptions to the Inductive Approach

Normally, the writer's purpose is to convey a clear message and retain the recipient's goodwill; thus, the inductive outline is appropriate. In the rare circumstances in which a choice must be made between clarity and goodwill, clarity is the better choice. When the deductive approach will serve a communicator's purpose better, it should be used. For example, if you submit a clear and tactful refusal and your audience submits a second request, a deductive presentation might be justified in the second refusal. Apparently, the refusal needs the emphasis provided by a deductive outline.

In most situations, the preceding circumstances do not exist. When they do, a sender's goals might be accomplished by stating bad news in the first sentence.

7-2 Developing a Bad-News Message

Developing a bad-news message following the inductive outline is challenging. The following suggestions will aid you in writing the (1) introductory paragraph, (2) explanation, (3) bad-news statement, (4) counterproposal or "silver lining" idea, and (5) closing paragraph.

7-2a Writing the Introductory Paragraph

The introductory paragraph in the bad-news message should accomplish the following objectives: (1) provide a buffer to cushion the bad news that will follow, (2) let the audience know what the message is about without stating the obvious, and (3) serve as a transition into the discussion of reasons without revealing the bad news or leading the audience to expect good news. If these objectives can be accomplished in one sentence, then this sentence can be the first paragraph.

Here are several ideas that can be incorporated into an effective beginning paragraph:

- **Compliment.** A message denying a customer's request could begin by recognizing the customer's promptness in making payments.

- **Point of agreement.** A sentence that reveals agreement with a statement made in the message could get the message off to a positive discussion of other points.

- **Good news.** When a message contains a request that must be refused and another that is being answered favorably, beginning with the favorable answer can be effective.

- **Resale.** A claim refusal could begin with some favorable statement about the product.

- **Review.** Refusal of a current request could be introduced by referring to the initial transaction or by reviewing certain circumstances that preceded the transaction.

- **Gratitude.** In spite of the unjustified request, the audience might have done or said something for which you are grateful. An expression of gratitude could be used as a positive beginning.

7-2b Presenting the Facts, Analysis, and Reasons

The reasons section of the bad-news message is extremely important because people who are refused want to know why. If a message is based on a sound decision, and if it has been well written, recipients will understand and accept the reasons, and the forthcoming refusal statement, as valid.

Avoid the Following Weaknesses When Writing the Introductory Paragraph:

- **Empty acknowledgments of the obvious.** *"I am writing in response to your letter requesting … "* or *"Your message on the 14th has been given to me for reply"* wastes space and presents points of no value. Beginning with "I" signals the message might be writer-centered.

- **Tipping off the bad news too early.** *"Although the refund requested in your letter of May 1 cannot be approved …"* might cause an immediate emotional reaction resulting in the message being discarded or it might interfere with understanding the explanations that follow.

  The neutral statement, *"Your request for an adjustment has been considered. However, … "* does not reveal whether the answer is "Yes" or "No," but the use of "however" signals that the answer is "No" before the reasons are presented. Such a beginning has about the same effect as an outright "No."

- **Starting too positively so as to build false hopes.** Empathetic statements such as, *"I can understand how you felt when you were asked to pay an extra $54"* might lead the audience to expect good news. When a preceding statement has implied that an affirmative decision will follow, a negative decision is all the more disappointing.

To accomplish this goal, begin with a well-written first paragraph that transitions the reader smoothly into the reasons section. Then develop the reasons section following these guidelines:

- **Provide a smooth transition from the opening paragraph to the explanation.** The buffer should help set the stage for a logical movement into the discussion of the reasons.

- **Include a concise discussion of one or more reasons that are logical to the reader.** Read the section aloud to identify flaws in logic or the need for additional explanation.

- **Show audience benefit and/or consideration.** Emphasize how your audience will benefit from the decision. Avoid insincere, empty statements such as "To improve our service to you, …"

- **Avoid using "company policy" as the reason.** Disclose the reason behind the policy, which likely will include benefits to the reader. For example, a customer is more likely to understand and accept a 15 percent restocking fee if the policy is not presented as the "reason" for the refusal.

Your employment application package has been reviewed by Human Resources.	**Reveals the topic as a reply to a recipient's employment application.**
Human Resources personnel ...	**Uses "Human Resources personnel" to transition from the first to second paragraph.**
Following your request for permission to submit a proposal to continue subsidizing employees' access to exercise facilities, we reviewed recent records of attendance.	**Reveals the subject of the message as a reply to an employee's request.**
In the past two years, attendance ...	**Uses "recent" and "attendance" to tie the second paragraph to the first.**

The principles for developing the reasons section are illustrated in Model Document 7.1: a message written by a manager refusing a request.

7-2c Writing the Bad-News Statement

A paragraph that presents the reasoning behind a refusal at least partially conveys the refusal before it is stated directly or indirectly. Yet, one sentence needs to convey (directly or by implication) the conclusion to which the preceding details have been leading. A refusal (bad news) needs to be clear; however, you can subordinate the refusal so that the reasons get the deserved emphasis. The following techniques will help you achieve this goal.

- **Position the bad-news statement strategically.** Using the inductive outline positions the bad-news statement in a less important position—sandwiched between an opening buffer statement and a positive closing. Additionally, the refusal statement should be included in the same paragraph as the reasons, since placing it in a paragraph by itself would give too much emphasis to the bad news. When the preceding explanation is tactful and relevant, resentment over the bad news is minimized. Positioning the bad-news statement in the dependent clause of a complex sentence will also cushion the bad news. This technique places the bad news in a less visible, less emphatic position. In the sentence, *"Although the company's current financial condition prevents us from providing raises this year, we hope to make up for the freeze when conditions improve,"* the emphasis is directed toward a promise of raises at another time.

- **Use passive voice, general terms, and abstract nouns.** Review the *emphasis techniques* that you studied in Chapter 4 as you consider methods for presenting bad news with human relations in mind.

- **Use positive language to accentuate the positive.** Simply focus on the good instead of the bad, the pleasant instead of the unpleasant, or what can be done instead of what cannot be done. Compared with a

Model Document 7.1 | Developing the Components of a Bad-News Message

Thank you for your interest in new, emerging online technologies. The travel committee reviewed your request to attend the Technology Conference in Santa Ana, California in June. ——— **Reveals the subject of the message and transitions into reasons.**

The company increased its travel budget this year by $5,000. However, with the increase in requests we've received and because we are close to the end of a fiscal year, we have used all our travel funds for the year. ——— **Supports the refusal with logical reasoning.**

As much as we would like to fund your request, we just do not have the money to do so. Remember, though, if you have departmental funds available, you may use those. You may also want to check to see if any divisional monies are still available. ——— **States refusal positively and clearly using complex sentences and positive language.**

I do hope you will be able to attend the conference. Please contact me at mjohnson@techcorp.com if you need help finding another source of funding. ——— **Ends with a forward-looking message to enhance goodwill.**

negative idea presented in negative terms, a negative idea presented in positive terms is more likely to be accepted. When you are tempted to use the following terms, search instead for words or ideas that sound more positive:

Words That Evoke Negative Feelings

complaint	incompetent	misled	
regrettable	error	inexcusable	mistake
unfortunate	failure	lied	neglect wrong

Words That Evoke Positive Feelings

accurate	concise	enthusiasm	productive
approval	durable	generous	recommendation
assist	energetic	gratitude	respect

- **Imply the refusal when the audience can understand the message without a definite statement of the bad news.** By *implying* the "No" answer, the response has the following positive characteristics: (1) it uses positive language, (2) it conveys reasons or at least a positive attitude, and (3) it seems more respectful. For example, during the noon hour, one employee says to another, "Will you go with me to see this afternoon's baseball game?" "No, I won't," communicates a negative response, but it seems unnecessarily direct and harsh. The same message (invitation is rejected) can be clearly stated in an *indirect* way (by implication) by saying "I must get my work done," or even, "I'm a football fan." Note the positive tone of the following implied refusals:

Implied Refusal	Underlying Message
- I wish I could.	- Other responsibilities prohibit, but recipient would like to accept.
- Had you selected our newest calling plan, you could have reduced your monthly rates by 10 percent or more.	- States a condition under which the answer would have been "Yes" instead of "No." Note the use of the subjunctive words "had" and "could."
- By accepting the new terms, Southern Wood Products would have doubled its energy costs.	- States the obviously unacceptable results of complying with a request.

counterproposal in a bad-news message, an alternative to the action requested that follows the negative news and can assist in preserving future relationships with the audience

7-2d Offering a Counterproposal or "Silver Lining" Idea

Following negative news with an alternative action, referred to as a **counterproposal**, will assist in preserving a relationship with the reader. Because it states what you *can* do, including a counterproposal might eliminate the need to state the refusal directly. The counterproposal can follow a refusal stated in a tactful, sensitive manner. When Airbnb laid off 25 percent of its employees it also paid their health insurance costs for a year, on top of three months' salary.[1]

While the counterproposal might represent a tangible benefit, at times it is more intangible in nature. For example, in a letter that informs a job applicant that they were not selected to fill the position, the counterproposal might be an offer to reconsider the applicant's résumé when other appropriate positions become available. Any counterproposal must, of course, be reasonable. For example, when informing a customer of an inability to meet a promised delivery deadline, an unreasonable counterproposal would be to offer the merchandise at no charge. A reasonable counterproposal might be to include some additional items at no charge or to offer a discount certificate good for the customer's next order.

When no reasonable counterproposal is apparent, the sender might be able to offer a silver lining thought that turns the discussion back in the positive direction. For example, a statement to tenants announcing an increase in rent might be followed by a description of the improved lighting that will be installed in the parking lot of the apartment complex. When offering a counterproposal or silver lining statement, care must be taken to ensure that the idea does not seem superficial or minimize the recipient's situation.

7-2e Closing Positively

After presenting valid reasons and a tactful refusal, followed by a counterproposal or silver lining statement, a closing paragraph should demonstrate empathy without further reference to the bad news. A pleasant closing paragraph should end with an empathetic tone and achieve the following goals:

- **De-emphasize the unpleasant part of the message.** End on a positive note that takes the emphasis away from the bad news previously presented. A statement of refusal (or bad news) in the last sentence or paragraph would place too much emphasis on it. Preferably, *reasons* (instead of bad news) should remain uppermost in the audience's mind. Placing bad news last would make the ending seem cold and abrupt. When no reasonable counterproposal is apparent, the sender might be able to offer a bright side to a situation that turns the discussion back in the positive direction.

▶ **Trite statements that might seem shallow and superficial.** The well-worn statement "Thank you for your interest" is often used thoughtlessly. It might seem shallow and superficial. "When we can be of further help, please do not hesitate to call or write" is also well worn and negative. *Further help* might seem especially inappropriate to someone who has just read a denial.

▶ **Statements that could undermine the validity of your refusal.** The statement "We trust this explanation is satisfactory" or "We hope you will understand our position" could be taken as a confession of doubt about the validity of the decision. Use of *position* seems to heighten controversy; positions are expected to be defended. Saying "We are sorry to disappoint you" risks a negative reply: "If it made you feel so bad, why did you do it?" It can also be interpreted as an apology for the action taken. If a decision merits an apology, its validity might be questionable.

▶ **Statements that encourage future controversy.** Statements such as "If you have questions, please do not hesitate to let us know" could also be perceived as doubt and possibly communicate a willingness to change the decision. If the decision is firm, including this type of closing could result in your having to communicate the negative message a second time.

- **Add a unifying quality to the message.** Make your final sentence an *appropriate* closing that brings a unifying quality to the whole message. Repetition of a word or reference to some positive idea that appears earlier in the message serves this purpose well. Avoid restatement of the refusal or direct reference to it. This paragraph is usually shorter than the preceding explanatory paragraphs, often one or two sentences.

- **Include a positive, forward-looking idea.** This idea might include a reference to some pleasant aspect of the preceding discussion, or a future aspect of the business relationship, resale or sales promotion, or an offer to help in some way. Consider the following closures that apply these suggestions:

Reference to some pleasant aspect of the preceding discussion:

"Your decision to refinance your mortgage last year was a wise choice." Home mortgage and other provisions had been mentioned in the earlier part of a letter to a client who was refused a double-indemnity settlement.

Use of resale or sales promotional material:

"Selecting our new hybrid Breeze with its 50-miles-per-gallon fuel usage was a wise decision with today's gas prices." A reminder that the hybrid has superior gas mileage will assist in regaining goodwill after a customer's request for free repair has been refused.

An expression of willingness to assist in some other way:

Specifically, you might offer an alternative solution to the audience's problem, or useful information that could not be presented logically with the bad news. *"Our representative will show you some samples during next week's sales call."* The samples are being proposed as a possible solution to the reader's problem.

Note that the closing paragraph in Model Document 7.1 is a positive, forward-looking statement.

7-3 Refusing a Request

It's a good idea to use the inductive approach (reasons before refusal) for refusing requests for a favor, an action, or even a donation. Present clear, understandable reasons in a way that minimizes the audience's disappointment.

You can examine an agent's refusal to provide an organization with a speaker in Model Document 7.2. This *response* to prior correspondence uses the same principles of sequence and style that are recommended for messages that *initiate* communication about unpleasant topics. The same principles apply whether the communication is a spoken message, letter, memo, or email message.

Companies have learned that building employee relationships is just as important as developing customer goodwill. Refusing employees' requests requires sensitivity and complete, honest explanations, qualities that are not included in the bad email in Model Document 7.3.

The manager's hasty and vague response to a valued employee's request to enlarge the women's restrooms uses a direct, blunt approach. In the revision illustrated in Model Document 7.3, the manager takes the time to prepare a response with a detailed explanation supporting the refusal and a genuine respect for the employee.

March 21, 2023

Dr. Lea Miyaki

Anderson Corp.

375 Bayshore Drive

Rancho Cucamonga, CA 90731

Dear Dr. Lea Miyaki:

My sincere thanks for the thoughtful invitation to speak at your banquet next month. The event sounds like it will provide a much-earned opportunity for your employees to recognize their contribution to your organization's recent success.

My travel plans will take me away during that week, so I won't be able to be part of the program; otherwise, I would be pleased to accept your invitation. If you do not have another person in mind, you might consider inviting Gina Russo who recently returned from an assignment in China. I think you would find her insights very interesting.

In any case, I wish you a very successful evening. Thanks again for thinking of me.

Sincerely,

Jeremy Christiansen

Director of Human Resources

> **Introduces the subject without revealing whether the answer will be "Yes" or "No."**

> **Gives reasons that will seem logical to the reader.**

> **Subordinates the refusal by placing it in the dependent clause of a complex sentence. Provides an alternative.**

> **Conveys goodwill.**

Study the Techniques Used to Cushion This Bad-News Statement:

Although Richardson Contracting was selected as the building contractor, expertise with environmentally friendly construction techniques was considered a plus for S and S Builders.

▸ States what was done rather than what was not done.

▸ Includes a positive idea ("expertise with environmentally friendly construction techniques") to accentuate a positive aspect and cushion the bad news.

▸ Uses passive voice ("Richardson Contracting was selected") to depersonalize the message.

▸ Places the bad news in the dependent clause of a complex sentence ("although Richardson Contracting was selected"). The positive idea in the independent clause ("expertise with environmentally friendly construction techniques") will receive more attention.

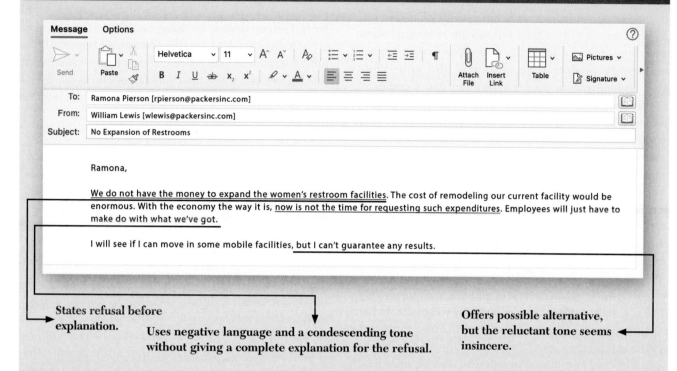

To: Ramona Pierson [rpierson@packersinc.com]
From: William Lewis [wlewis@packersinc.com]
Subject: No Expansion of Restrooms

Ramona,

We do not have the money to expand the women's restroom facilities. The cost of remodeling our current facility would be enormous. With the economy the way it is, now is not the time for requesting such expenditures. Employees will just have to make do with what we've got.

I will see if I can move in some mobile facilities, but I can't guarantee any results.

States refusal before explanation.

Uses negative language and a condescending tone without giving a complete explanation for the refusal.

Offers possible alternative, but the reluctant tone seems insincere.

Good Example of a Refusal to an Employee's Request

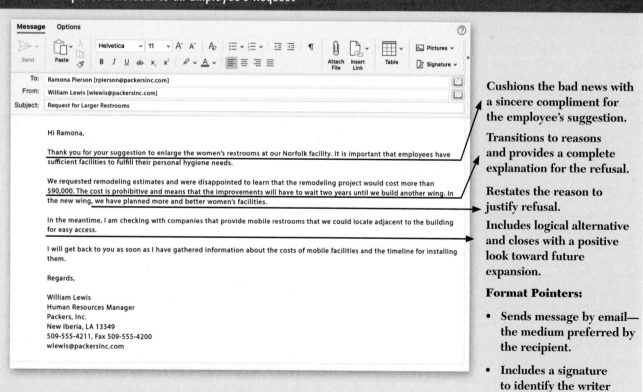

To: Ramona Pierson [rpierson@packersinc.com]
From: William Lewis [wlewis@packersinc.com]
Subject: Request for Larger Restrooms

Hi Ramona,

Thank you for your suggestion to enlarge the women's restrooms at our Norfolk facility. It is important that employees have sufficient facilities to fulfill their personal hygiene needs.

We requested remodeling estimates and were disappointed to learn that the remodeling project would cost more than $90,000. The cost is prohibitive and means that the improvements will have to wait two years until we build another wing. In the new wing, we have planned more and better women's facilities.

In the meantime, I am checking with companies that provide mobile restrooms that we could locate adjacent to the building for easy access.

I will get back to you as soon as I have gathered information about the costs of mobile facilities and the timeline for installing them.

Regards,

William Lewis
Human Resources Manager
Packers, Inc.
New Iberia, LA 13349
509-555-4211, Fax 509-555-4200
wlewis@packersinc.com

Cushions the bad news with a sincere compliment for the employee's suggestion.

Transitions to reasons and provides a complete explanation for the refusal.

Restates the reason to justify refusal.

Includes logical alternative and closes with a positive look toward future expansion.

Format Pointers:

- **Sends message by email—the medium preferred by the recipient.**

- **Includes a signature to identify the writer and provide contact information.**

7-4 Denying a Claim

Companies face the challenging task of refusing claims by customers while also maintaining goodwill and building customer loyalty. Claim refusals are necessary when a warranty does not apply, has expired, or a customer has misused the product. Companies must also write refusals when customers ask for something that a company simply can't do. For example, many retailers charge customers a $25–40 fee on returned checks. A retailer who receives a customer's request to waive the charge must refuse because the claim is inconsistent with the retailer's policies and objectives.

The inductive approach is helpful in communicating this disappointing news to customers. Presenting the explanation for the refusal first leads customers through the reasoning behind the decision and helps them *understand* the claim is unjustified by the time the refusal is presented. Tone is especially important when denying claims. Present the reasons objectively and positively without casting blame or judgment on the customer for the problem. Avoid lecturing a customer on the actions they should have taken to avoid the problem. Finally, close the message with resale or sales promotional material that indicates that you expect future business. Although disappointed with your decision, customers continue doing business with companies who make fair, objective decisions and communicate the reasons for those decisions in a positive, respectful manner.

Assume a camping equipment retailer received the following email from a customer:

> **New Message**
>
> To: Gala Foster [gfoster@northwoods.com]
>
> From: Jack Campbell [jcampbell@gmail.com]
>
> Subject: Refund request
>
> Please refund me the $179 I paid for a High Country backpack. The backpack was too small to carry the gear required for my recent trip down the Appalachian trail. I have attached a copy of the sales receipt for the merchandise, which was purchased last fall.

The company's return policy allows customers to return merchandise unless it was purchased during a sale. The return policy was posted during the sales event.

The customer's inquiry shows a lack of understanding of the return policy. Although a frustrated company representative might question why the customer can't read the return policy, the response must be more tactful than that illustrated in the New Message box. The example in Model Document 7.4 reveals the subject of the message in the first sentence and leads into a discussion of the reasons. Reasons for the refund denial, including benefits to the customer, precede the refusal. The tone is positive and respectful. The refusal statement uses several de-emphasis techniques to cushion its impact, and the final sentence turns the discussion away from the refusal with reference to future business with the customer.

7-5 Denying Credit

Once you have evaluated a request for credit and have decided "No" is the better answer, your primary writing challenge is to refuse credit so tactfully that you keep the business relationship on a cash basis. When requests for credit are accompanied with an order, your credit refusals might serve as order acknowledgments. Of course, every business message is directly or indirectly a sales message. Prospective customers will be disappointed when they cannot buy on a credit basis. However, if you keep them sold on your goods and services, they might prefer to buy from you on a cash basis instead of seeking credit privileges elsewhere.

Why Explain Credit Denial?

▶ Writers can show the fairness of the decision.

▶ Receivers are entitled to the truth.

▶ Receivers can learn to adjust bad habits.

When the credit investigation shows that applicants are poor credit risks, too many credit writers no longer regard them as possible customers. They write to them in a cold, matter-of-fact manner. They do not consider that such applicants might still be interested in doing business on a cash basis and might qualify for credit later.

In credit denials, as in other types of refusals, the major portion of the message should be an explanation for the denial. You cannot expect your audience to agree that your "No" answer is the right answer unless you give the reasons behind it.

Both writers and readers benefit from the explanation of the reasons behind the denial. For writers, the explanation helps to establish fair-mindedness; it shows that the decision was not arbitrary. For readers, the explanation not only presents the truth to which they are entitled, it also has guidance value. From it they learn to adjust habits and, as a result, qualify for credit purchases later.

You bought the backpack for which you are requesting a refund during our two-day Thanksgiving Blowout Sale. Signs posted during the sale said that we could offer no refunds or exchanges. Therefore, your refund request is denied.

Although we appreciate your business, I am sure you can appreciate that having to process returns and exchanges would greatly increase the price of the gear.

A more tactful explanation of the reason for the refusal might prepare the reader for an implied refusal at the end of the paragraph.

The conclusion does not build goodwill because it assumes what the recipient is feeling.

Good Example of a Claim Denial

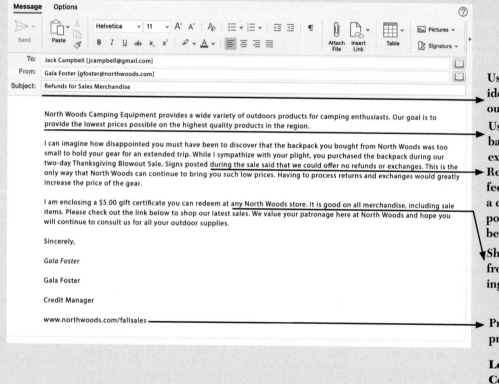

North Woods Camping Equipment provides a wide variety of outdoors products for camping enthusiasts. Our goal is to provide the lowest prices possible on the highest quality products in the region.

I can imagine how disappointed you must have been to discover that the backpack you bought from North Woods was too small to hold your gear for an extended trip. While I sympathize with your plight, you purchased the backpack during our two-day Thanksgiving Blowout Sale. Signs posted during the sale said that we could offer no refunds or exchanges. This is the only way that North Woods can continue to bring you such low prices. Having to process returns and exchanges would greatly increase the price of the gear.

I am enclosing a $5.00 gift certificate you can redeem at any North Woods store. It is good on all merchandise, including sale items. Please check out the link below to shop our latest sales. We value your patronage here at North Woods and hope you will continue to consult us for all your outdoor supplies.

Sincerely,

Gala Foster

Gala Foster

Credit Manager

www.northwoods.com/fallsales

Uses a subject line that identifies the subject without revealing the refusal.

Uses resale to cushion the bad news and leads into an explanation.

Recognizes the customer's feelings while presenting a clear explanation of the policy and the reasons behind it.

Shifts the emphasis away from the refusal by providing a gift certificate.

Provides link to latest promotions.

Legal and Ethical Consideration:

Avoids corrective language that might insult, belittle, or offend.

Because of the legal implications involved in denying credit, legal counsel should review your credit denial messages to ensure that they comply with laws related to fair credit practices. For example, the Equal Credit Opportunity Act (ECOA) requires that the credit applicant be notified of the credit decision within 30 calendar days following an application. Applicants who are denied credit must be informed of the reasons for the refusal. If the decision was based on information obtained from a consumer reporting agency (as opposed to financial statements or other information provided by the applicant), the credit denial must include the name, address, and telephone number of the agency. It must also remind applicants that the **Fair Credit Reporting Act** provides them the right to know the nature of the information in their credit file. In addition, credit denials must include a standard statement that the ECOA prohibits creditors from discriminating against credit applicants on the basis of a number of protected characteristics (race, color, religion, national origin, sex, marital status, and age).

To avoid litigation, some companies choose to omit the explanation from the credit denial letter and invite the applicant to call or come in to discuss the reasons. Alternately, they might suggest that the audience obtain further information from the credit reporting agency whose name, address, and telephone number are provided.

7-6 Delivering Constructive Criticism

A person who has had a bad experience as a result of another person's conduct might be reluctant to write or speak about that experience. However, because one person took the time to communicate, many could benefit. Although not always easy or pleasant, communicating about negatives can be thought of as a social responsibility. For example, a person who returns from a long stay at a major hotel might, upon returning home, write a letter or email message to the management commending certain employees. If the stay was not pleasant and weaknesses in hotel operation were detected, a tactful message pointing out the negatives would probably be appreciated. Future guests could benefit from the effort of that one person.

Before communicating about the problem, an individual should recognize the following risks: being stereotyped as a complainer, being associated with negative thoughts and perceived in negative terms, and appearing to challenge management's decisions concerning hotel operations.

Yet such risks might be worth taking because of the following benefits:

- The communicator gets a feeling of having exercised a responsibility.
- Management learns of changes that need to be made.
- The hotel staff about whom the message is written modifies techniques and is, thus, more successful.
- Other guests will have more enjoyable stays in the hotel.

When making the decision to communicate about negatives, the primary consideration is intent. If the intent is to hurt or to get even, the message should not be sent. Including false information would be *unethical* and *illegal*. To avoid litigation charges and to respond ethically, include only specific facts that you can verify and avoid evaluative words that present opinions about the person's character or ability. For example, instead of presenting facts, the message in Model Document 7.5 judges a cleaner assigned to work at a restaurant kitchen. Overall, the message is short, general, and negative. By comparison, the revision in Model Document 7.5 avoids potential legal and ethical problems by reframing the situation more positively. Not all criticisms can be reframed in this manner, but reframing negative messages is a solution to many potential bad-news situations.

Framing is a persuasive technique used to influence a receiver's perception of a situation. To "reframe" is to take a particular approach to a situation and redefine it. In the example provided in Model Document 7.5, the writer has decided to take a negative approach to solving a worker's performance. As discussed, certain legal and ethical risks can arise from this definition of the situation. These risks can be avoided by reframing the situation, not as one of criticism, but as an opportunity to provide constructive feedback. As Model Document 7.5 indicates, reframing the situation as one in which constructive feedback is provided reduces the need to discuss Richard Tanner's problems and enables the writer to focus on the positive attributes that he brings to the situation. In other words, the writer has redefined a potential negative situation into a more positive one.

Reframing negative situations is almost always a preferred method for dealing with bad news, unless doing so is deemed manipulative or deceptive.

7-7 Communicating Negative Organizational News

Being able to initiate messages that convey bad news about an organization is as important as responding "No" to messages from customers/clients and others outside

---

Fair Credit Reporting Act a federal law that provides consumers the right to know the nature of the information in their credit file and gives them other protections when they apply for and are denied credit

Richard Tanner, a junior cleaner at your company, is not working out well. He regularly arrives late for his shift and then spends most of his time talking on his cell phone. This makes his time at the restaurant even longer. He is often at the restaurant long after our bakers arrive to start their shifts in the kitchen.

This information should be placed in a second paragraph that describes specific behaviors to maintain neutrality.

Although Richard Tanner does a good job cleaning the kitchen, his lack of respect for others' time far outweighs his professional experience and expertise. I seriously hope Richard Tanner is able to take steps to correct the situation.

The close would be better at maintaining goodwill if it were more positive in tone and content.

Good Example of a Constructive Criticism

March 17, 2023

Connie Thompson

Spic and Span Cleaning

503 Westside Way

St. Louis, MO 60733

Dear Connie Thompson:

Your company has provided us with excellent cleaning services for the past five years. Your junior cleaner, Richard Tanner, who has been providing us services since February 25, 2020, has been ensuring that every nook and corner of our restaurant kitchen is as clean as new.

Acknowledges the positive aspects of the service provided.

Although Richard Tanner has been doing an excellent job at cleaning, there is one thing that I would like to bring to your attention: He has been reporting late for work. He is scheduled to arrive at 10 p.m. but has been arriving up to 30 minutes later. In addition, while he was working, he is on the phone much of the time, making his time in the restaurant even longer. He is still on the premises when our bakers arrive to begin their duties.

Provides good reasons for honoring the request.

I think it is important for staff to be punctual and professional along with delivering good performance. In case you need any more details, please get in touch with me. Please convey my thoughts to Richard Tanner confidentially so that he understands our appreciation for his excellent work.

Ends with a suggestion that makes honoring the request easier for the recipient.

Sincerely,

Ernesto Juarez

Manager

Legal and Ethical Consideration:

Avoids legal and ethical concerns by reframing a potential criticism as a direct request.

Format Pointer:

Uses letter channel rather than email to communicate a sensitive message.

the company. Employees and the public are seeking, and expecting, *honest* answers from management about situations adversely affecting the company—slumping profits, massive layoffs, bankruptcy, a variety of major changes in the organization, and negative publicity that affects the overall health of the business and retirement plans, to name a few.

Managers who can communicate negative information in a sensitive, honest, and timely way can calm fears and doubts and build positive employee and public relations. Effective managers recognize that employee morale, as well as public goodwill, is fragile—easily damaged and difficult to repair. If handled well, these bad-news messages related to the organization can be opportunities to treat employees, customers, and the general public with respect, thus building unity and trust.

Strong internal communication is a key to involving employees in corporate strategies and building an important sense of community. Transparency can have a positive effect on an organization's culture. According to a recent workplace survey, open, honest communication between corporate leaders and employees can lead to a more productive and ethical workplace. According to former Deloitte Chairperson Sharon Allen, motivating communication patterns are "increasingly critical to retaining talent and preserving the health of today's organizations."[2]

Obviously, business and competitive reasons prevent a company from always being completely transparent with its staff, but every attempt should be made to do so when possible. The best companies use a variety of communication tools that promote an open exchange of honest, candid communication and welcome input from employees. Newsletters, email updates, town hall or focus meetings, videoconferencing, phone calls, and discussion boards drive home relevant messages and allow employees to pose questions to management. This quality two-way communication involves employees in corporate strategies; employees who are aware of company goals and potential problems feel connected and accountable. Informed employees are also better prepared for bad news when it must be shared.

7-7a Breaking Bad News

Assuming this long-term commitment to keep employees informed, the following suggestions provide guidance in breaking bad news to employees and the public:[3]

- **Convey the bad news as soon as possible.** Timeliness will minimize damage caused by rumors and will give employees the concern and respect they deserve. Nestlé Purina and others in the pet food industry acted early and effectively to recall potentially deadly pet food tainted with wheat gluten from China and to assure pet owners that steps were in place to ensure healthy ingredients would be used in the future.[4]

- **Give a complete, rational explanation of the problem.** Be candid about what is happening, why, and its effect on employees, customers, and the public. Provide enough detail to establish your credibility and provide context so that your audience can understand the situation. Stressing positive aspects will provide needed balance and avoid sugarcoating or minimizing the severity of the news to the point that the message is misunderstood. Bridgestone, makers of Firestone tires, was criticized for botching its recovery efforts from claims of accidents being caused by faulty tires when it initially attempted to blame Ford for the problems instead of taking responsibility and seeking corrective actions.[5]

- **Show empathy.** There is really no good way to break bad news, such as the announcement of layoffs or closures, to employees. The economic downturn and job insecurity have resulted in increased stress for many employees, which raises the potential for workplace aggression. However, methods that reflect respect and proper timing reduce the likelihood of an emotional outburst.[6]

- **Respond to the feelings.** Allow people adequate time to react to the bad news. Listen attentively for understanding, and then address the concerns, issues, and potential problems presented.

- **Follow-up.** Let people know what will happen next— what is expected of employees or customers, and what the company will do and when. Plan to repeat your explanations and assurances that you are available to

There is really no good way to break bad news, such as the announcement of layoffs or closures, to employees, but methods that reflect respect and proper timing reduce the likelihood of emotional scenes in the workplace.

fizkes/Shutterstock

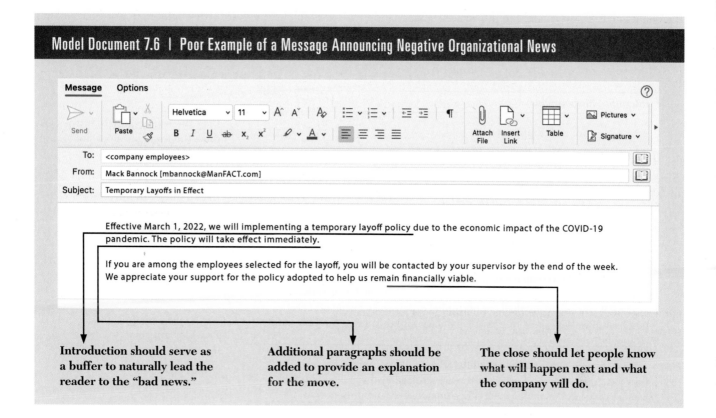

Model Document 7.6 | Poor Example of a Message Announcing Negative Organizational News

To: <company employees>
From: Mack Bannock [mbannock@ManFACT.com]
Subject: Temporary Layoffs in Effect

Effective March 1, 2022, we will implementing a temporary layoff policy due to the economic impact of the COVID-19 pandemic. The policy will take effect immediately.

If you are among the employees selected for the layoff, you will be contacted by your supervisor by the end of the week. We appreciate your support for the policy adopted to help us remain financially viable.

Introduction should serve as a buffer to naturally lead the reader to the "bad news."

Additional paragraphs should be added to provide an explanation for the move.

The close should let people know what will happen next and what the company will do.

respond to concerns in several communications that extend over a given time.

Consider the company president who emailed employees, informing them of a temporary layoff (Model Document 7.6). The president should not be surprised to learn that employees are fearful about the move, and some may perceive the company to be an enemy for sacrificing their financial stability for that of the company. In the revision (Model Document 7.7), the president anticipates the employees' natural resistance to this stunning announcement and crafts a more sensitive message.

A printed memo is a more effective channel for communicating this sensitive and official information, rather than the efficient, yet informal, email message. The revision indicates that the company's internal communications (newsletters and intranet) have been used to prepare the employees for this negative announcement. Thus, the official memo is no surprise, nor is the company's commitment to listen to the employees' concerns and provide up-to-date information as it develops.

7-7b Responding to Crisis Situations

Crises can occur in any organization, disrupting business activity and posing significant political, legal, financial, or governmental impacts. Crisis situations can result from various events, including accidents, weather-related disasters, equipment failures, procedural errors, and deliberate maliciousness. For example, in 2021, Colonial Pipeline was attacked by hackers causing a shutdown of delivery of fuel to the East Coast, resulting in shortages and long lines at the pump.[7] When crises such as this occur, the communication that is offered can either help ease situations or worsen them. Rather than waiting for a crisis to occur, an organization should examine its state of preparedness and have a carefully considered plan of action that includes the following steps:

- **Anticipate potential crises in terms of areas of vulnerability and what could happen.**

- **Establish emergency procedures, including an alternate command center and chain of command.** Ensure that more than one employee is media trained and able to respond appropriately if needed.

- **Identify who will need to be contacted, and plan for multiple means of disseminating information.** Cellphones and text messaging have proven themselves valuable when other contact means might not work, but keep in mind that telecommunication circuits can be overloaded in mass disaster situations, necessitating multiple means for sharing news.

Interoffice Memorandum

To: All Employees

From: Mack Bannock, President

Date: January 4, 2022

Subject: Proposed Plan for Managing the COVID-19 Pandemic and Its Effects

The spread of COVID-19 has affected not just the health of individuals but has affected the overall economy as well. Many companies have been significantly affected by economic setbacks due to the effects of COVID-19. The company is implementing policies to secure our financial stability. Although this is a difficult choice to make, effective next week, the company shall cut personnel expenses by laying off certain positions. We expect this layoff shall last until the end of the year, although that period may be lessened or extended.

All laid-off employees shall be eligible for unemployment benefits from your local unemployment office. If you are affected by this policy, please contact your local unemployment office immediately and present this letter as proof of your employment status and eligibility for applying for unemployment benefits. Once the company's finances start to stabilize, we shall recall all laid-off employees as warranted by business needs.

During this period, we will continue to provide periodic updates to affected employees. If you recently made changes to your home address, phone number, personal email address, or any other contact information, please inform Human Resources.

Your supervisor will communicate personally with you if you are affected by the temporary layoff. In the meantime, please visit the COVID-19 link on the company intranet to receive updated information on the situation. Let us continue to support one another until normal operations resume.

Uses the subject line to introduce the topic but does not reveal the bad news.

Uses a buffer to introduce a topic familiar to employees and leads into reasons.

Provides a reason for the bad news before announcing it.

Provides information about financial support options for affected employees.

Follows up by assuring continued exchange of timely information.

Ends with a positive appeal for unity.

Legal and Ethical Consideration:

Uses memo channel rather than email for conveying a sensitive message.

- **Ensure current contact information is available for employees, media, and other pertinent parties.**

- **Maintain an up-to-date fact sheet about the company, its products/services, locations, and operations.**

While crises can seldom be predicted, an organization can position itself to respond to them appropriately when they do occur by preparing for crises before they occur.

Adequate pre-crisis planning is necessary for a rapid, effective crisis response—the second stage of crisis management. A key task during crisis response is to identify the type of crisis to better develop communication messages. Three broad types of crises exist: victim, accident, and preventable crises.[8] In a victim crisis, the organization

Response in a Crisis

In responding to a crisis, the message conveyed is extremely important in reassuring employees and business partners, and in shaping public opinion. These guidelines can help ensure an effective message:

▶ Determine what your message is, and prepare a checklist of what it should contain before writing.

▶ Keep the message simple, and arrange it in logical sections.

▶ Include verbiage that demonstrates your concern, compassion, and control.

▶ Prepare separate messages for internal and external audiences, including the appropriate level of detail.

is viewed as a victim of the event. This type includes natural disasters, workplace violence, product tampering, and rumors. In an accident crisis, the event is considered unintentional or uncontrollable by the organization and includes accidents or harm from technical errors or equipment failure. In a preventable crisis, the event is considered purposeful and includes accidents or harm caused by human error as well as organizational misdeeds such as fraud.[9]

After identifying the type of crisis, you can select the appropriate components of an effective crisis message, as depicted in Exhibits 7.1 and 7.2.

Model Document 7.8 provides an example of an effective response to a critical situation. It includes the appropriate crisis communication components of showing concern, explaining corrective actions, providing instructions, and giving a brief justification.

During a crisis, the organization should monitor the situation carefully and provide quick and accurate communication to all stakeholders through all available communication channels. After the crisis has passed—the post-crisis stage of crisis management—the organization should carefully plan and create a consistent stream of messages to help repair any damage to its reputation sustained by the crisis.

Exhibit 7.1 | Components of Crisis Communication Responses

Concern	Express concern for all affected by the crisis.
Corrective Actions	Describe specific steps the organization is taking to correct the problem.
Instructions	Tell those affected what to do to stay informed and to protect themselves.
Excuse	Deny intent to harm or point out inability to control events.
Justification	Minimize the perceived damage of the crisis.
Compensation	Offer money or gifts to victims.
Apology	Take full responsibility for the crisis.

Sources: W. T. Coombs (2007). Protecting organization reputations during a crisis: The development and application of situational crisis communication theory. *Corporate Reputation Review* 10 (3), 163–176; W. T. Coombs (2004). Impact of past crisis on current crisis communications: Insights from situational crisis communication theory. *Journal of Business Communication* 41 (3), 265-289; W. T. Coombs & S. J. Holladay (2002). Helping crisis managers protect reputational assets: Initial tests of the situational crisis communication theory. *Management Communication Quarterly* 16 (2), 165–186.

Exhibit 7.2 | Types of Crises and Appropriate Message Components

Type of Crisis	Concern	Corrective Actions	Instructions	Excuse/Justification	Compensation/ Apology
Victim	X	X	X		
Accident	X	X	X	X	
Preventable	X	X	X	X	X

Sources: W. T. Coombs (2007). Protecting organization reputations during a crisis: The development and application of situational crisis communication theory. *Corporate Reputation Review* 10 (3), 163–176; W.T. Coombs (2004). Impact of past crisis on current crisis communications: Insights from situational crisis communication theory. *Journal of Business Communication* 41 (3), 265–289; W. T. Coombs & S.J. Holladay (2002). Helping crisis managers protect reputational assets: Initial tests of the situational crisis communication theory. *Management Communication Quarterly* 16 (2), 165–186.

The Lemon Tree Restaurant is saddened to report that 35 customers of our Miami, FL, location have fallen ill. Our thoughts are with every affected person and their loved ones, and our representatives are currently working on monitoring and compensating the affected individuals as we learn more.

Shows concern.

Although the cause of the illnesses has not yet been determined, The Lemon Tree is investigating all possible connections between these illnesses and our Miami restaurant. We are in constant contact with medical officials to explore all possible avenues. In the meantime, the Miami restaurant is temporarily closed for further review, and we are confident that after a thorough investigation, the Miami restaurant will reopen soon as a safe and healthy dining environment.

The Lemon Tree Restaurant chain places a strong focus on health and safety across all our locations. Each and every Lemon Tree employee nationwide will be tested on health code regulations to ensure that each Lemon Tree restaurant is a safe and healthy place for families to dine.

Explains corrective action.

The health of all customers and staff is of utmost importance to The Lemon Tree. The Lemon Tree will continue to update customers and staff on the progress made in our investigations and the health of our customers. If you have any further information or concerns, please contact us at lemontree@headquarters.com. You may also visit our website at www.lemontree.com to receive updates on the investigation.

Provides instructions.

fizkes/Shutterstock

8 | Delivering Persuasive Messages

Learning Objectives

After studying this chapter, you will be able to ...

8-1 Draft effective outlines and appeals for business messages that persuade.

8-2 Write effective sales messages.

8-3 Create effective persuasive requests (making a claim or asking for a favor or information) and persuasion within an organization.

8-1 Persuasion Strategies

Businesspeople regularly seek to persuade others. **Persuasion** is the ability to influence others to accept your point of view. It is not an attempt to trap someone into acting favorable to the communicator. Instead, it is an honest, organized presentation of information on which a person can choose to act. Professionals in all fields benefit from well-prepared communications that persuade others to accept their ideas or buy their products, services, or ideas.

How do you learn to persuade others through spoken and written communication? Have you ever made a persuasive request, written employment documents or an essay for college entry or a scholarship, or given a campaign speech? If so, you already have experience with this type of communication. While the persuasive concepts discussed in this chapter are directed primarily at written communication, they can also be applied in many spoken communication situations.

For persuasion to be effective, you must understand your product, service, or idea; know your audience; anticipate the arguments that might come from the audience; and have a rational and logical response to those arguments. Remember, persuasion need not be a hard sell; it can simply be a way of getting a client or your supervisor to say yes. Although much of this chapter concentrates on selling products and services, similar principles apply to selling an idea, your organization, and your own abilities.

8-1a Plan Before You Write

Success in writing is directly related to success in preliminary thinking. If the right questions have been asked and answered, the composing will be easier, and the message will be more persuasive. Specifically, you need information about (1) your product, service, or idea; (2) your audience; and (3) the desired action.

Know the Product, Service, or Idea

You cannot be satisfied with knowing the product, service, or idea in a general way; you need details. Get your information by (1) reading available literature; (2) using the product and watching others use it; (3) comparing the product, service, or idea with others; (4) conducting tests and experiments; and (5) soliciting reports from users.

Before you write, you need concrete answers to such questions as these:

- What will the product, service, or idea do for the reader(s)?

---

persuasion the ability of a sender to influence others to accept their point of view

---

- What are its superior features (e.g., design and workmanship or audience benefit)?
- How is the product or service different from its competition?
- How is the proposed idea superior to other viable alternatives?
- What is the cost to the receiver?

Similar questions must be answered about other viable alternatives or competing products. Of particular importance is the question, "What is the major difference?" People are inclined to choose an item (or alternative) that has some distinct advantage. For example, some people might choose a particular car model because of its style and available options; still others might choose the model because of its safety record.

Know the Audience

Who are the people to whom the persuasive message is directed? What are their wants and needs? Is a persuasive message to be written and addressed to an individual or to a group? If it is addressed to a group, what characteristics do the members have in common? What are their common goals, their occupational levels, and their educational status? To what extent have their needs and wants been satisfied? How might cultural differences affect your message?

Some people might respond favorably to appeals to physiological, security, and safety needs (to save time and money, to be comfortable, to be healthy, or to avoid danger). People with such needs would be impressed with a discussion of the benefits of convenience, durability, efficiency, or serviceability. Others might respond favorably to appeals to their social, ego, and self-actualizing needs (to be loved, entertained, remembered, popular, praised, appreciated, or respected). Consider the varying appeals used in a memo to employees and to supervisors seeking support of teleworking. The memo to employees would appeal to the need for greater flexibility and reduced stress. Appeals directed at supervisors would focus on increased productivity and morale, reduced costs for office space, and compliance with the Clean Air Act—a federal law requiring companies to reduce air pollution and traffic congestion.

Identify the Desired Action

What do you want the reader to do? Complete an online order and make a payment? Receive a demonstration version for trial? Return a card requesting a representative to call? Email for more information? Approve a request? Accept a significant change in service, style, and procedures? Whatever the desired action, you need to have a clear definition of it before composing your message.

8-1b Use the Inductive Approach

More than 100 years ago, Sherwin Cody summarized the persuasive process into four basic steps called **AIDA**, which stand for attention, interest, desire, and action.[1] The steps have been varied somewhat and have had different labels, but the fundamentals remain relatively unchanged. The persuasive approach illustrated in Figure 8.1 is inductive. The main idea, which is the request for action, appears in the *last* paragraph after presenting the details—convincing reasons for the audience to comply with the request.

Each step is essential, but the steps do not necessarily require equal amounts of space. Good persuasive messages do not require separate sentences and paragraphs for each phase of the outline. The message *could* gain the reader's attention and interest in the same sentence, and creating desire *could* require many paragraphs.

8-1c Apply Sound Writing Principles

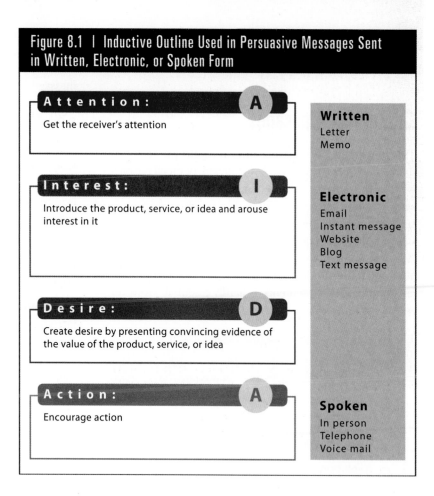

Figure 8.1 | Inductive Outline Used in Persuasive Messages Sent in Written, Electronic, or Spoken Form

Attention: **A**
Get the receiver's attention

Interest: **I**
Introduce the product, service, or idea and arouse interest in it

Desire: **D**
Create desire by presenting convincing evidence of the value of the product, service, or idea

Action: **A**
Encourage action

Written
Letter
Memo

Electronic
Email
Instant message
Website
Blog
Text message

Spoken
In person
Telephone
Voice mail

The principles of unity, coherence, and emphasis are just as important in persuasive messages as in other messages. In addition, the following principles seem to be especially helpful in preparing persuasive messages:

- **Keep paragraphs short.** The spaces between paragraphs show the dividing place between ideas, improve appearance, and provide convenient resting places for the eyes. Hold the first and last paragraph to three or fewer lines; a one-line paragraph (even a very short line) is acceptable. You can even use paragraphs less than one sentence long by putting four or five words on the first line and completing the sentence in a new paragraph. Be careful to include key attention-getting words that either introduce the product, service, or idea or lead to its introduction.

- **Use concrete nouns and active verbs.** Concrete nouns and active verbs help readers see the product, service, or idea and its benefits more vividly than abstract nouns and passive verbs.

- **Use specific language.** General words won't mean much unless they are well supported with specifics. Specific language is space consuming (saying that something is "great" requires fewer words than telling what makes it so); therefore, persuasive messages are usually longer than other messages. Still, persuasive messages need to be concise; they should say what needs to be said without wasting words.

- **Let readers have the spotlight.** If readers are made the subject of some of the sentences, if they can visualize themselves with the product in their hands, or if they can get the feel of using it for enjoyment or to solve problems, the chances of creating a desire are increased.

- **Stress a central selling point or appeal.** A thorough analysis ordinarily will reveal some feature that is unique or some benefit that is not provided by other viable alternatives—the **central selling point**. This point of difference can be developed into a theme that is woven throughout the entire message. Or, instead of using a point of difference as a central selling point, a writer could choose to stress a major satisfaction to be gained from

AIDA the four basic steps of the persuasive process, including gaining attention, generating interest, creating desire, and motivating action

central selling point the primary appeal on which a persuasive message focuses

using the item or doing as asked. A central selling point (theme) should be introduced early and reinforced throughout the remainder of the message.

8-2 Sales Messages

The four-point persuasive outline is appropriate for an *unsolicited sales message*—a letter, memo, or email message written to someone who has not requested it. A *solicited sales message* has been requested by a potential buyer or supporter; that is, the message is prepared to answer this interested person's questions.

A person requesting sales information has given some attention to the product, service, or idea already; therefore, an attention-getting sentence is hardly essential. However, such a sentence is needed when the audience is not known

---

Some Commonly Used Attention-Getting Devices Include:

▸ **A personal experience:** When a doctor gives you instructions, how often have you thought, "I wish you had time to explain" or "I wish I knew more about medical matters"?

▸ **A solution to a problem (outstanding feature/benefit):** Imagine creating a customized multi-media presentation that …

▸ **A startling announcement:** One in four auto accidents is the result of texting while driving.

▸ **A what-if opening:** What if I told you there is a savings plan that will enable you to retire three years earlier?

▸ **A question:** Why should you invest in a company that has lost money for six straight years?

▸ **A story:** Here's a typical day in the life of a manager who uses an iPad.

▸ **A proverb or quote from a famous person:** Vince Lombardi, one of the most successful coaches in the history of football, once said, "If winning isn't everything, why do they keep score?" At Winning Edge, we specialize in making you the winner you were born to be.

▸ **A split sentence:** Sandy beaches, turquoise water, and warm breezes … it's all awaiting you on your Mesa cruise.

▸ **An analogy:** Like a good neighbor, State Farm is there.

Other attention-getters include a gift, an offer, a bargain, or a comment on an enclosed product sample.

---

to have expressed an interest previously. The very first sentence, then, is deliberately designed to make a reader put aside other thoughts and concentrate on the rest of the message.

8-2a Gain Attention

Various techniques have been successful in convincing readers to consider an unsolicited sales message. Regardless of the technique used, the attention-getter should achieve several important objectives: introduce a relationship, focus on a central selling feature, and use an original approach.

Introduce a Relationship Between the Audience and the Product, Service, or Idea

Remaining sentences grow naturally from the beginning introductory sentence. If readers do not see the relationship between the first sentence and the sales appeal, they could react negatively to the whole message—they might think they have been tricked into reading it. For example, consider the following poor attention-getter:

> Would you like to be the chief executive officer of one of America's largest companies? As CEO of Graham Enterprises, you can launch new products, invest in developing countries, or arrange billion-dollar buyouts. Graham Enterprises is one of several companies at your command in the new computer software game developed by Creative Diversions Software.

The beginning sentence of the preceding ineffective example is emphatic because it is a short question. However, it suggests the message will be about obtaining a top management position, which it is not. All three sentences, when combined, suggest high pressure. The computer software game has relevant virtues, and one of them could have been emphasized by placing it in the first sentence.

8-2b Focus on a Central Selling Feature

Almost every product, service, or idea will, in some respects, be superior to its competition. If not, such factors as favorable price, fast delivery, or superior service can be used as the primary appeal. This central selling point must be emphasized, and one of the most effective ways to emphasize a point is by its position in the message. An outstanding feature mentioned in the middle of a message might go unnoticed, but it will stand out if mentioned in the first sentence. Note how the following opening sentence introduces the central selling feature and leads naturally into the sentences that follow:

> We disrupted the shaving industry in 2011 by delivering "Unbeatably Great Blades" at an awesome price, right to your door. We've been listening to our Members' needs

ever since, and now we have you covered from hair to toe with a growing list of top-shelf grooming products. We spend our days focused on helping you look, feel, and smell your best.

8-2c Use an Original Approach

To get the reader's attention and interest, you must offer something new and fresh. Thus, choose an anecdote likely unfamiliar to your audience or use a unique combination of words to describe how a product, service, or idea can solve the reader's problem:

> "I remember the first time I talked to one of my past clients, Matt. He was fresh out of a board meeting with his company's investors, and he was desperate. He'd just had to report that his company wasn't going to hit its second quarter sales goals. He hated feeling like he'd let them down and that their trust in him hadn't been warranted, but he didn't know what else to do. He'd hit a wall, and he was starting to think he'd be better off closing down for good than to keep burning himself and his team out chasing sales that weren't materializing.

> "I could hear in Matt's voice how upset he was, but I asked him to give it just one more chance. What Matt didn't know was that I've worked with plenty of entrepreneurs in his shoes before—and I knew that he didn't have a sales problem. He had a marketing problem. If I could just get him to start thinking about marketing in a new way, I knew that he too could enjoy the sales lift my past clients had experienced."

8-2d Generate Interest by Introducing the Product, Service, or Idea

A persuasive message is certainly off to a good start if the first sentences cause the reader to think, "Here's a solution to one of my problems," "Here's something I need," or "Here's something I want." You can lead the reader to such a thought by introducing the product, service, or idea in the very first sentence. If you do, you can succeed in both getting attention and creating interest in one sentence. An effective introduction of the product, service, or idea is cohesive and action centered, and continues to stress a central selling point.

Be Cohesive

If the attention-getter does not introduce the product, service, or idea, it should lead naturally into the introduction. In the following example, note the abrupt change in thought and the lack of connection between the attention-getter in the first sentence and the idea presented in the second sentence:

> Ninety percent of all mobile users open and read text messages within the first 30 minutes of receipt. SMS

provides a fantastic opportunity for businesses to be able to communicate with their audience in a way that is very natural and immediate—with vastly higher open rates than any other marketing channel (especially email).

- No word or phrase in the first sentence connects to the words of the second sentence, which creates an abrupt, confusing change in thought. In the following revision, the second sentence is tied to the first by the words *text messaging*. *Text messaging marketing* in the second sentence coincides with *text message marketing* in the third.

> Ninety percent of all mobile users open and read text messages within the first 30 minutes of receipt. It's no wonder why text message marketing is working so well for so many businesses.

> If your business relies on regular and fast communication with your audience, you should absolutely invest in text message marketing to help grow your business. With EZ Texting you can get started in as little as 5 minutes. You do not need any special knowledge or technology to begin connecting with your contacts.

Be Action-Oriented

To introduce your offering in an interesting way, you must place the product, service, or idea in your audience's hands and talk about using it or benefiting from accepting your idea. Your audience will get a clearer picture when reading about something happening than when reading a product description. Also, the picture becomes more vivid when the reader is in the spotlight. In a sense, you do not sell products, services, or ideas; instead, you sell the pleasure people derive from their use. Logically, then, you must focus more on that use than on the offering itself. If you put readers to work using your product, service, or idea to solve problems, they will be the subject of most of your sentences.

Some product description is necessary and natural. In the following example, the writer focuses on the product and creates an uninteresting, still picture:

> The Elise CR is a stripped-back racer that doesn't just deliver on the road. Eibach anti-roll bar and springs plus Bilstein sports dampers mean the Elise CR provides fingertip responsiveness on the racetrack, too.

In the revision, a person is the subject of the message and is enjoying the benefits of the sports car.

> Channel your inner Max Verstappen in this stripped-back racer worthy of the best Formula One tracks in the world. The Elise CR is an uncompromised sports machine that doesn't just deliver on the road. Eibach anti-roll bar and springs plus Bilstein sports dampers mean the Elise CR provides fingertip responsiveness on the racetrack, too. Handling is assisted further with the latest Lotus Dynamic Performance Management (DPM) system, and

selectable Sport setting, giving the driver ultimate power and control.[2]

Stress a Central Selling Point

If the attention-getter does not introduce a distinctive feature, it should lead to it. Note how the attention-getter in the following example introduces the distinctive selling feature, the need for lower prices, and how the following sentences keep the audience's eyes focused on that feature:

> Every idea starts with a problem and ours was simple: Glasses are too expensive.
>
> It turns out there's a simple explanation. The eyewear industry is dominated by a single company that has been able to keep prices artificially high while reaping huge profits from consumers who have no other options.
>
> Warby Parker was started to create an alternative. By circumventing traditional channels, designing glasses in-house, and engaging with customers directly, we're able to provide higher-quality, better-looking prescription eyewear at a fraction of the going price.

By stressing one main point, you do not limit the message to that point. For example, although lower prices is being stressed, other features are also mentioned.

8-2e Create Desire by Providing Convincing Evidence

After you have made an interesting introduction to your product, service, or idea, present enough supporting evidence to satisfy your audience's needs. Keep one or two main features uppermost in the reader's mind and include evidence that supports these features. For example, using fuel economy as an outstanding selling feature of hybrid cars, while presenting abundant evidence about performance, would be inconsistent.

Present and Interpret Factual Evidence

Few people will believe general statements without having supporting factual evidence. Saying a certain method is efficient is not enough. In the following example, the aspects of a sales letter included in the template are detailed in the questions provided. In the final sentence, the effectiveness of the template as a sales tool is highlighted through the use of a statistic.

> Let's face it, if you can't write a sales letter, you can't sell your products. It's a fact. That's why we're here to walk you through our proven template piece by piece, step by step so that you can emulate it to your hearts content.
>
> Where do you start in a sales letter? How do you create an attractive headline? How do you connect to your viewers in such a way that they can't take their eyes

of your site until they're purchased your product? We're about to answer all those questions and more.

> The great thing about this is you don't need to go on any extensive copywriting courses, you don't need to spend years practicing, and there's absolutely no need for you to be an expert or experienced writer. As long as you can write in English, this template works. In fact, our users have experienced a 50 percent increase in sales through the use of our template alone.

Presenting research evidence (hard facts and figures) to support your statements is another way to increase your chances of convincing your audience. Presenting results of a research study takes space but makes the message much more convincing than general remarks about superior durability and appearance.

Evidence must not only *be* authentic; it must *sound* authentic, too. Talking about pages treated with special protectants to slow aging and machine-sewn construction suggests the sender is well informed, which increases audience confidence. Facts and figures are even more impressive if they reflect comparative advantage, as illustrated in the following example:

> With thousands of new viruses created every day, relying on traditional security updates isn't enough anymore. Unlike the competition, exclusive McAfee Total Protection™ technology instantly analyzes and blocks new and emerging threats in milliseconds, so there's virtually no gap in your protection. McAfee is 99.9 percent effective in detecting malware, the best rating among competitors.[3]

Naturally, your audience will be less familiar with the product, service, or idea and its uses than you will be. Not only do you have an obligation to give information, you should interpret it if necessary and point out how the information will benefit the audience. Notice how the following example clearly interprets *why* an induction cooktop is superior to electric or gas cooktops. The interpretation makes the evidence understandable and thus convincing.

Cold Statement Without Interpretation	Specific, Interpreted Fact
Cooking with an induction cooktop is the latest in technology for a restaurant environment or for just the average household.	Induction cooking is an entirely new way of cooking. Forget about red-hot electric coils or open gas flames. An induction cooktop converts your cookware into the heating element by using a magnetic field to energize the atoms in the cookware. Your food cooks faster, using less energy, while providing you with instantaneous temperature control.

The previous example uses a valuable interpretative technique—the comparison. You can often make a point more convincing by comparing something unfamiliar with something familiar. Most people are familiar with electric coils and gas flames, so they can now visualize how the cookware becomes the heating element. A comparison can also be used to interpret prices. Advertisers frequently compare the cost of sponsoring a child in a third-world country to the price of a fast-food lunch. An insurance representative might write this sentence: *The monthly premium for $300,000 of term life insurance is $18, the cost of two movie tickets.*

Do not go overboard and bore or frustrate your audience with an abundance of facts or technical data. Never make your reader feel ignorant by trying to impress them with facts and figures they might not understand.

Be Objective

Use language people will believe. Specific, concrete language makes your message sound authentic. Excessive superlatives, exaggerations, flowery statements, unsupported claims, and incomplete comparisons all make your message sound like high-pressure sales talk. Just one such sentence can destroy confidence in the whole message. Examine the statements in the following paragraphs to see whether they give convincing evidence. Would they make a reader want to buy? Or do they merely remind the audience of someone's desire to sell?

This antibiotic is the best on the market today. It represents the very latest in biochemical research. Identifying the best-selling antibiotic requires gathering information about all antibiotics marketed and then choosing the one with superior characteristics. You know the sender is likely to have a bias in favor of the particular drug being sold. However, you do not know whether the sender actually spent time researching other antibiotics or whether they would know how to evaluate this information. You certainly do not know whether the sender knows enough about biochemical research to say truthfully what the very best and latest is.

Similarly, avoid preposterous statements (*Gardeners are turning handsprings in their excitement over our new weed killer!*) or subjective claims (*Stretch out on one of our memory foam mattresses. It's like floating on a gentle dream cloud on a warm, sunny afternoon. Ah, what soothing relaxation!*). Even though some people might be persuaded by such writing, many will see it as absurd.

Note the incomplete comparison in the following example: *SunBlock provides you better protection from the sun's dangerous ultraviolet rays.* Is SunBlock being compared with *all* other sunscreens, *most* other sunscreens, *one* unnamed brand, or others? Unless an additional sentence identifies the other elements in the comparison, you do not know. Too often, the writer of such a sentence hopes the reader will assume the comparison is with *all* others.

Written with such an intent, this incomplete comparison is *unethical*. Likewise, statements of certainty are often inaccurate or misleading.

Include Testimonials, Guarantees, and Enclosures

One way to convince prospective customers that they will like your product, service, or idea is to give them concrete evidence that other people like it. Tell what others have said (with permission, of course) about the usefulness of your offering. Guarantees and free trials convey both negative and positive connotations. By revealing willingness to refund money or exchange an unsatisfactory unit, a writer confesses a negative: the purchase could be regretted or refused. However, the positive connotations are stronger than the negatives: the seller has a definite plan for ensuring that buyers get value for money spent. In addition, the seller conveys willingness for the buyer to check a product, service, or idea personally and compare it with others. The seller also implies confidence that a free trial will result in a purchase and that the product will meet standards set in the guarantee. A long or complex guarantee can be included in an enclosure or attachment.

A message should persuade the audience to read an enclosure, attachment, or file link that includes more detailed information. Thus, refer to the added material late in the message after the major portion of the evidence has been given. An enclosure or link is best referred to in a sentence that is not a cliché ("Enclosed you will find," or "We have enclosed a brochure") and says something else:

> The enclosed annual report will help you understand the types of information provided to small- and medium-sized companies by Lincoln Business Data, Inc.

> Click here to view the huge assortment of clearance-priced items and other end-of-season specials.

Subordinate the Price

Logically, price should be introduced late in the message—after most of the advantages have been discussed. Use the following techniques to overcome people's natural resistance to price:

- **Introduce price only after creating a desire for the product, service, or idea and its virtues.** Let readers see the relationship of features and benefits to the price.

- **Use figures to illustrate that the price is reasonable or that the reader can save money.** Example: Purigard saves the average pool owner about $50 in chemicals each month; thus, the $200 unit pays for itself in a single swim season.

- **State price in terms of small units.** Thirty dollars a month seems like less than $360 a year.

- **Invite comparison of like products, services, or ideas with similar features.**
- **Consider mentioning price in a complex or compound sentence that relates or summarizes the virtues of the product, service, or idea.**
  Example: For just $139 a year, Amazon Prime brings you access to Instant Videos and Kindle Books as well as free two-day shipping on selected products.

8-2f Motivate Action

For proper clarity and emphasis, the last paragraph should be relatively short. Yet it must accomplish four important tasks: define the specific action wanted, present it as easy to take, encourage quick action, and ask confidently.

Make the Action Clear and Simple to Complete

Define the desired action in specific terms that are easy to complete. For example, you might ask the reader to complete an order blank and return it with payment, place a phone call, or order online. General instructions such as "Let us hear from you," "Take action on the matter," and "Make a response" are ineffective. Make action simple to encourage the audience to act immediately. Instead of asking readers to fill in their names and addresses on order forms or return cards and envelopes, do that work for them. Otherwise, they might see the task as difficult or time consuming and decide to procrastinate.

Restate the Reward for Taking Action (Central Selling Point)

The central selling point should be introduced early in the message, interwoven throughout the evidence section, and included in the last paragraph as an emphatic, final reminder of the reason for taking action.

Provide an Incentive for Quick Action

If the reader waits to act on your proposal, the persuasive evidence will be harder to remember, and the audience will be less likely to act. Therefore, you prefer the audience to act quickly. Referencing the central selling point (assuming it has been well received) helps stimulate action. Commonly used appeals for getting quick action are to encourage customers to buy while prices are in effect, while supplies last, when a rebate is being offered, when it is a particular holiday, or when they will receive benefits.

Ask Confidently for Action

If you have a good product, service, or idea and have presented evidence effectively, you have a right to feel confident. Demonstrate your confidence when requesting action: "To save time in organizing appointments and tasks, complete and return. . . . "Avoid statements suggesting lack of confidence, such as "If you want to save time in organizing appointments and tasks, complete and return . . .," "If you agree . . .," and "I hope you will . . . ."

Model Document 8.1 illustrates poor and good *unsolicited sales messages* for a service. Model Document 8.2 presents an unsolicited sales message promoting a product. The same principles apply when writing a *solicited sales message*, with one exception: because the solicited sales message is a response to a request for information, an attention-getter is not essential. Typically, sales messages are longer than messages that present routine information or convey good news. Specific details (essential in prompting action) require space.

More and more organizations are using email as a means to persuade existing and potential customers to buy their products. Although email marketing is a relatively new field, marketers are learning how to use email effectively with various audiences.

To gain the desired attention from customers, email messages must be carefully timed to arrive when they will gain the most attention. Over-messaging can be annoying, and under-messaging can cause the company to miss potential sales. The subject line is of utmost importance, as it must catch the attention of the reader and create a desire to learn more.

Observe How the Following Closing Paragraph Accomplishes the Four Important Tasks of an Effective Sales Message:

Simply dial 1-800-555-8341. Then input the five-digit number printed on the top right corner of the attached card. Your name and address will be entered automatically into our system—a speedy way to get your productivity software to you within five working days along with a bill for payment. When you order by August 12, you will also receive a free subscription to Time Resource Magazine. *TMC's new productivity software is as easy to use as it is to order!*

- ▶ Refers to the central selling point,
- ▶ Makes a specific action easy,
- ▶ Provides an incentive for quick action, and
- ▶ Asks confidently for action.

Dear Ju Chen:

I, Mathew Browning, marketing manager at Professional Food Supplies, would like to introduce my company to you. We are into supplying deli products, vegetables, fruits, and groceries along with an extensive range of goods for kitchen to hotels and restaurants.

We came to know that you are a new restaurant in town and because it is the initial stage, you have your staff employed to manage all the daily purchase for you. I would like to offer you our professional services which take complete care of your everyday needs so that you can focus on serving the best food to your guests. We promise to fulfill all your requirements with no compromises in quality that will not only save your time and energy but will also be cost-effective.

We have been in the industry from last 12 years, and we have been taking care of supplies of various restaurants and hotels in the city. You can email your everyday orders and your order will be delivered at your doorstep at the time of your choice with no extra charges. Our prices are competitive, and our quality is premium. We have a wonderful range of products that include dairy, fruits, vegetables, bakery, spices, pulses, grains, meat, etc., which are procured from different sources and different brands and are stored at our warehouse with proper care. Please find attached our catalogue and we would be happy to serve you. If you have any queries, please feel free to get in touch with me at (342) 555-8900 or email me at mathew@professionalfood.com.

Thank you for your time. Looking forward to work with you.

Introduction might better engage the reader by addressing their needs in a more personal way and being more reader focused.

The language is a bit vague in terms of concrete actions or results. This approach may damage the writer's credibility in the area of trust.

Sentence structure is also awkward

This paragraph adds little in terms of concrete actions or results.

Benefits to reader might more effectively be presented in a list format.

The close is too generic.

Good Example of a Sales Message Promoting a Service

March 31, 2023

Ivan Zhi, Sales Manager
Khan and Teller Consulting
1332 Fruitwood Avenue
St. Louis, MO 78801

Dear Ivan Zhi:

Are you sure that the marketing and advertising strategy for your hotel are fully optimized? Are you sure that your marketing team has the necessary training and background to implement everything needed to make that strategy work?

If you're not certain about the answers to these questions, it's time for you to consider enrolling your employees in a StarMaker Marketing and

Provides an opening intended to engage the reader in questions pertinent to their needs

(continued on next page)

Advertising course. The course is delivered online and can be finished in less than a week, but the impact it will have on the success of your hotel will be long-term.

We have attached a brief sample of the course materials in the hope that it will convince you to order the entire set. Please visit our website at www.starmaker.com to read customer reviews of our product that will show the usefulness and satisfaction they have gained from our course.

We will contact you soon to discuss our course and your sales personnel needs.

Sincerely,

Justine Young
Sales Manager
StarMaker Training.

Presents "everything-in-one-place" service as a solution to a problem and reinforces the central selling point.

States a specific action with a reward and makes the action easy.

Model Document 8.2 | Good Example of a Sales Message Promoting a Product

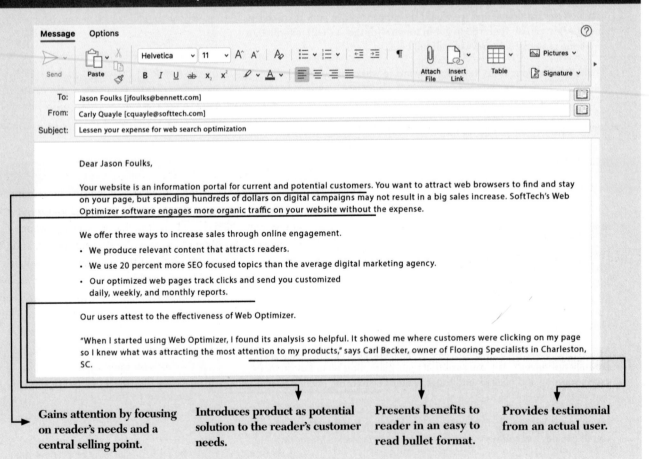

To: Jason Foulks [jfoulks@bennett.com]

From: Carly Quayle [cquayle@softtech.com]

Subject: Lessen your expense for web search optimization

Dear Jason Foulks,

Your website is an information portal for current and potential customers. You want to attract web browsers to find and stay on your page, but spending hundreds of dollars on digital campaigns may not result in a big sales increase. SoftTech's Web Optimizer software engages more organic traffic on your website without the expense.

We offer three ways to increase sales through online engagement.
- We produce relevant content that attracts readers.
- We use 20 percent more SEO focused topics than the average digital marketing agency.
- Our optimized web pages track clicks and send you customized daily, weekly, and monthly reports.

Our users attest to the effectiveness of Web Optimizer.

"When I started using Web Optimizer, I found its analysis so helpful. It showed me where customers were clicking on my page so I knew what was attracting the most attention to my products," says Carl Becker, owner of Flooring Specialists in Charleston, SC.

Gains attention by focusing on reader's needs and a central selling point.

Introduces product as potential solution to the reader's customer needs.

Presents benefits to reader in an easy to read bullet format.

Provides testimonial from an actual user.

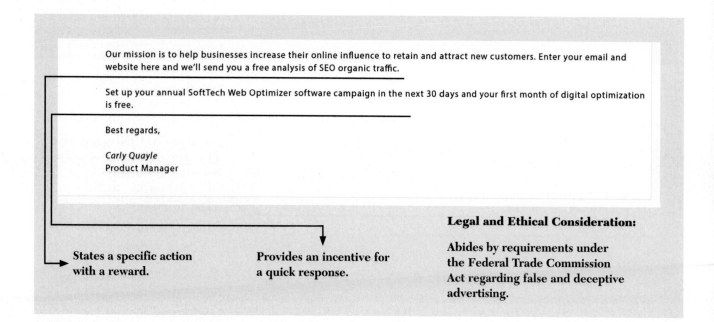

Our mission is to help businesses increase their online influence to retain and attract new customers. Enter your email and website here and we'll send you a free analysis of SEO organic traffic.

Set up your annual SoftTech Web Optimizer software campaign in the next 30 days and your first month of digital optimization is free.

Best regards,

Carly Quayle
Product Manager

States a specific action with a reward.

Provides an incentive for a quick response.

Legal and Ethical Consideration:

Abides by requirements under the Federal Trade Commission Act regarding false and deceptive advertising.

8-3 Persuasive Requests

The preceding discussion of sales messages assumed the product, service, or cause was sufficiently worthy to reward the audience for acting. The discussion of persuasive requests assumes requests are reasonable—that compliance is justified when the request is for an adjustment and that compliance will (in some way) be rewarded when the request is for a favor.

Common types of persuasive requests are claim requests and messages that ask for special favors and information. Although their purpose is to get favorable action, the messages invite action only after attempting to create a desire to take action and providing a logical argument to overcome any anticipated resistance.

8-3a Making a Claim

Claim messages are often routine because the basis for the claim is a guarantee or some other assurance that an adjustment will be made without need for persuasion. However, when an immediate remedy is doubtful, persuasion is necessary. In a typical large business, customer service representatives handle claims.

Often, any reasonable claim will be adjusted to the customer's satisfaction. Therefore, venting strong displeasure in the claim message will likely alienate the claims adjuster—the one person whose cooperation is needed. Remember, adjusters might have had little or nothing to do with the manufacture and sale of the product or direct delivery of the service. They did not create the need for the claim.

Companies should welcome claims. Only a small percentage of claims are from unethical individuals; the great bulk is from people who believe they have a legitimate complaint. Research indicates that only 4 percent of customers complain, so for every complaint received, many more customers have been satisfied. Complaints help companies identify problem areas and correct them. Another advantage that companies derive from the claim process is that when complaints are handled appropriately, complainers can become very loyal customers.[4] Therefore, the way a complaint is handled determines, to a large extent, the goodwill toward the company.

Like sales messages, persuasive claims should use an inductive sequence. Unlike routine claim messages, persuasive claims do not begin by asking for an adjustment.

The poor example shown in Model Document 8.3 could be improved by (1) writing inductively (to reduce the chance of a negative reaction in the first sentence), and (2) stressing an appeal throughout the message (to emphasize an incentive for taking favorable action). In a persuasive claim, an appeal serves the same purpose that a central selling feature does in a sales message. Both serve as a theme; both remind the reader of a benefit gained from doing as asked. Note the application of these techniques in the revision of this claim in Model Document 8.3.

Knowledge of effective claim writing should never be used as a means of taking advantage of someone. Hiding an unjustifiable claim under a cloak of untrue statements is difficult and strictly unethical. Adjusters typically are fair-minded people who will give the benefit of the doubt, but they will not satisfy an unhappy customer simply to avoid a problem.

On September 8, 2022, I visited the new office and discovered that your team is yet to complete the interior design work promised.

As you haven't informed me of any delays and, in fact, described the interior work as "proceeding nicely" on August 26, I find this completely unacceptable. Please return and complete the job to the agreed specifications by September 15 or pay damages for noncompletion as stipulated in section 5A of our contract.

> Introduction is too direct. May damage goodwill.

> The tone is too negative to be persuasive and fails to provide a clear and persuasive reason for the requested change.

> Close is too demanding to maintain goodwill.

Good Example of a Persuasive Claim

August 24, 2023

Denise Walters
Ultimate Design and Renovation, Inc.
221 27th Avenue
Boston, MA 19087

Dear Denise:

When Albrecht Financial Services negotiated with your firm to provide interior design and renovation services for our new office suite, we were impressed with your previous track record of success. Especially impressive was your ability to design and create elegant yet functional interiors quickly and at an attractive price point.

On September 8, 2022, I visited the new office and discovered that your team is yet to complete the interior design work promised. When I hired your company to refit the space on August 11, 2022, you signed a contract agreeing to have the shelving system fully installed and the new carpets at least part way finished by September 2. As far as I can tell, neither of these tasks have been started and only a small amount of plumbing work has been done on the bathrooms. I was hoping to move my staff into the refurbished office by the end of September, but I cannot see how this will be possible.

Please return and complete the job to the agreed specifications by September 15 or pay damages for noncompletion as stipulated in section 5A of our contract. I enclose a copy of our contract, which specifies the fine for noncompletion of services by the contracted date.

With Ultimate's reputation for timely completion of renovation projects, I am confident that the contracted services will be completed as agreed. I'd appreciate you calling me on 406-555-4461 to discuss this matter directly.

Sincerely,

Gillian London
Operations Manager

> Seeks attention by giving a sincere compliment that reveals the subject of the message.

> Continues central appeal—commitment to timely completion—while providing needed details.

> Presents request and reminds reader of contractual agreement.

> Connects the specific request with the firm's commitment to complete the project in a timely manner.

> **Legal and Ethical Consideration:**
>
> Uses letter rather than less formal email format to add formality to contractual agreement.

8-3b Asking a Favor

Occasionally, everyone must ask someone else for a special favor—an action for which there is little reward, time, or inclination. For example, suppose a professional association wants to host its annual fund-raiser dinner at an exclusive country club. The program chair of the association must write the club's general manager requesting permission to use the facility. Will a deductive message be successful?

When a deductive approach is used in a persuasive situation, chances of getting cooperation are minimal. For example, what might be a probable reaction to the following beginning sentence? *Please send me, without charge, your $450 interactive video training game on workplace safety.*

If the first sentence gets a negative reaction, a decision to refuse might be made instantly. Having thought "No," the reader might not read the rest of the message or might hold stubbornly to that decision in spite of a well-written persuasive argument following the opening sentence. Note that the letter in Model Document 8.4 asks the favor before presenting any benefit for doing so. The letter illustrated in Model Document 8.4 uses an inductive approach and applies the principles discussed earlier. As this message shows, if the preceding paragraphs adequately emphasize a reader's reward for complying, the final paragraph need not shout loudly for action.

8-3c Requesting Information

Requests for information are common in business. Information for research reports is frequently obtained by questionnaire, and the reliability of results is strongly influenced by the percentage of the return. If a message inviting respondents to complete a questionnaire is written carelessly, the number of responses might be insufficient.

The most serious weakness is asking for action too quickly and providing no incentive for action. Sometimes the reward for taking action is small and indirect, but the message needs to make these benefits evident.

8-3d Persuading Within an Organization

Many memos are of a routine nature and essential for the day-to-day operation of the business, for example, giving instructions for performing work assignments, scheduling meetings, and providing project progress reports. In many organizations, such matters are handled with email rather than paper memos. These routine messages, as well as messages conveying good news, are written deductively. However, some circumstances require that a supervisor write a persuasive message that motivates employees to accept a change in their jobs that might have a negative effect on the employees or generate resistance (e.g., a job transfer, a change in work procedures, or a software upgrade).

For example, imagine that Pub on the Green restaurant was faced with the challenge of communicating to its employees about a significant change in service and style, which included new uniforms. Rather than coercing or demanding that employees accept the change, a letter from the president could emphasize the reasons the changes were being made (benefits to guests, the company, and the employees) and the employee's important role in implementing the changes. Using a lighthearted, entertaining approach, the message could include (a) a visual model of the fresh, crisp, and professional look that the company expected with the uniform change and (b) helpful information on ways to achieve this look. The following excerpt shows how a "you" orientation, and "style flashes" could be interwoven into the letter:

- **Make sure your hair is neatly tied back.** Messy hair is a problem for guests—they don't want it getting it into their food. You might even get a better tip.

- **Don't wear a lot of bling.** Guests may think you don't need as large a tip.

- **Remember to smile.** Your smile is the first sign to guests that their Pub on the Green experience will be a memorable one. Your smile tells guests, "I'm glad you came!" But don't just take our word for it. A recent Bay College study found that smiling reflects an awareness of other people and their needs. That's probably why a "winning smile" is so charming!

The detailed language leaves no doubt in an employee's mind as to what management considers clean, crisp, and professional. However, by continually emphasizing the benefits employees gain from the change, management garners support for the high standards being imposed.

Similarly, employees must often make persuasive requests of their supervisors. For example, they might recommend a change in procedure, acquisition of equipment or software, or attendance at a professional development program. They might justify a promotion or job reclassification or recommendation for policy changes, and so on. Persuasive memos and email messages are longer than most routine messages because of the extra space needed for developing an appeal and providing convincing evidence.

When preparing to write the memo in Model Document 8.5, a manager recognizes that implementation costs could affect the president's reaction to their proposal to create an employee recreation room. Anticipating resistance, the manager writes inductively and builds a logical, compelling argument for their proposal.

I am writing to you today to ask if your pet supply store would be interested in making a donation to our animal shelter as we enter our busiest time of year.

You can reach me on my office phone at 319-555-4658 during the work-day or you can email me at aingalls@email.com. with your response.

Does not use an inductive approach to set a more positive tone. Fails to provide good reasons to comply with the request.

Close does little to build goodwill or encourage compliance.

Good Example of a Persuasive Request (Asking a Favor)

Viann Pope, Owner and Manager
South Shores Hardware
San Pedro, CA 84330
June 21, 2023

Dear Viann Pope:

As you likely know, spring and summer are the busiest time for animal rescues, as this is the time of year when feral and stray animals are likely to produce litters of kittens and puppies. At this time of year, WeCare Animal Rescue becomes inundated with animals in need of homes, many of them young and vulnerable. We have a large network of volunteers and fosters who help us care for the animals, however, this influx does require additional resources in the form of money, food and other supplies.

Describes the situation, which clarifies the need, setting the stage for the request that follows.

We would love to create a long-term partnership between our two organizations and would be happy to recognize you as one of our sponsors if you're interested. As part of the partnership, we are hoping that your business would be interested in providing us with financial support or with other resources you may have access to such as food, toys, bedding, and more.

Identifies the requested action and explains the benefits to the store.

By partnering with our organization, you will signal to your customers your concern for animal welfare in the community and strengthen your reputation as a community advocate. Please contact me at ltingen@gmail.com with your response to our request.

Connects a specific action to the rewards for taking the action.

Sincerely,

Lars Tingen

Lars Tingen

Deductive sequence (main idea first) works well for routine messages and good-news messages.

Inductive sequence (details first) works well if the reader needs to be persuaded.

Model Document 8.5 | Good Example of a Persuasive Message

Message	Options							⑦

To:	Jane Matusaka
From:	Ken Burnett
Subject:	Wellness Program

Date: June 4, 2023

During our monthly managers' meeting, HR Director Cathryn Willis noted a significant uptick in employee sick-day requests over the past year. A discussion followed about the cost of sick days to the company. As you recall, I offered to do some research on how other firms of our size have responded to this issue.

My research has found that on-site exercise programs have resulted in notable decreases in sick-pay requests. Obviously, we don't have space for such a program, but an alternative would be to provide an incentive for employees to exercise at the Buff workout facility located just a block from our offices.

In my research I found that a number of organizations offer employees incentives for their active involvement in exercise programs. These incentives include free movie tickets, dinners, coffee mugs, T-shirts, etc. I am proposing that we provide such incentives by using the savings we should achieve through decreased sick time. I have approached the management of Buff, and it is willing to offer our employees a discounted membership if we can guarantee a 50 percent sign-up rate.

With our goals of decreasing sick-leave requests, would you allow me to test the exercise incentive program in the sales department during May? Employees participating in the program would be asked to sign up for the program and to turn in a stamped card from Buff, indicating the number of times they have used the facility during the month. At the end of the pilot program, I will compile a report of the results, thereby allowing us to consider whether to expand the program to all departments.

Opens with a reference to a meeting discussion and company goal.

Presents a solution to the identified problem.

Builds interest by mentioning the benefits of the program.

Alludes to the benefits and closes with a specific action to be taken.

SFIO CRACHO/Shutterstock

9 | Understanding the Report Process and Research Methods

Learning Objectives

After studying this chapter, you will be able to ...

9-1 Identify the characteristics of a report and the various classifications of business reports.

9-2 Apply the steps in the problem-solving process for report writing.

9-3 Use appropriate printed, electronic, and primary sources of information.

9-4 Demonstrate the appropriate methods of collecting, organizing, and referencing information.

9-5 Explain techniques for the logical analysis and interpretation of data.

9-1 Characteristics of Reports

"Hi, Kate. This is Lewis in sales. Do you know whether the latest sales figures report is ready? My supervisor wants me to review it in preparation for next week's presentation."

"Hi, Lewis. Yes, I just finished a draft of the report yesterday. I will email it to you right now. If there are any changes, I will let you know."

This brief exchange illustrates a simple reporting task. A question has been posed, and the answer given (along with the supporting information) satisfies the reporting requirement. Although Kate may never have studied report preparation, she did an excellent job, so Lewis can prepare to report the sales figures. Kate's spoken report is a simple illustration of the four main characteristics of reports:

- **Reports typically travel upward in an organization because they usually are requested by a higher authority.** In most cases, people would not generate reports unless requested to do so.

- **Reports are logically organized.** In Kate's case, she answered Lewis's question first and then supported the answer with evidence to justify it. Through your study of message organization, you learned the difference between deductive and inductive organization. Kate's report was deductively organized. If Kate had given the supporting evidence first and followed with the answer that she would meet the deadline, the organization of her reply would have been inductive and would still have been logical.

- **Reports are objective.** Because reports contribute to decision making and problem solving, they should be as objective as possible. When nonobjective (subjective) material is included, the report writer should make that known.

- **Reports are generally prepared for a limited audience.** This characteristic is particularly true of reports traveling within an organization. This means that reports, like letters, memos, and emails, should be prepared with the receivers' needs in mind.

As more and more organizations use technology to generate data about their business operations, automated reporting has become more common. An automated report is a tool used by business professionals to create and share reports at a specific time interval without the need to update the information each time. These updates are usually made in real time with the help of automated reporting tools.

Automated reports completely eliminate traditional means of communicating data since they rely on business reporting software that uses cutting-edge business intelligence, technology, and smart features such as interactivity, a drag-and-drop interface, and predictive analytics, among others. These reports have the power to store all data and generate attractive dashboards that can tell a data narrative in a simple, visual way.

With many types of automatic reporting software, users just need to select a template, time frame, and frequency to generate reports. For example, a scheduled report containing the weekly website traffic can be set to automatically send out every Sunday at 10 p.m. so that the marketing department can use this report to analyze and discuss the traffic performance on Monday morning.

9-1a Types of Reports

Based on the four characteristics, a workable definition of a *report* is an orderly, objective message used to convey information from one organizational area to another or from one organization to another to assist in decision making or problem solving. Reports have been classified by management and by report-preparation authorities in numerous ways. The form, direction, functional use, and content of the report are used as bases for classification. However, a single report might fit several classifications. The following brief review of classification illustrates the scope of reporting and establishes a basis for studying reports.

- **Formal or informal reports.** The formal/informal classification is particularly helpful because it applies to all reports. A **formal report** is carefully structured; it is logically organized and objective, contains a lot of detail, and is written in a style that tends to eliminate such elements as personal pronouns. An **informal report** is usually a short message written in natural or personal language. An internal memo generally can be described as an informal report. All reports can be placed on a continuum of formality, as shown in Figure 9.1. The distinction between the degrees of formality of various reports is explained more fully in Chapter 11.

- **Short or long reports.** Reports can generally be classified as short or long. A one-page memo is obviously short, and a report of 20 pages is obviously long. What about in-between lengths? One important distinction generally holds true: as it becomes longer, a report takes on more characteristics of formal reports. Thus,

> **formal report** a carefully structured report that is logically organized and objective, contains a lot of detail, and is written in a style that tends to eliminate such elements as personal pronouns
>
> **informal report** usually a short message written in natural or personal language

Figure 9.1 | Report Formality Continuum

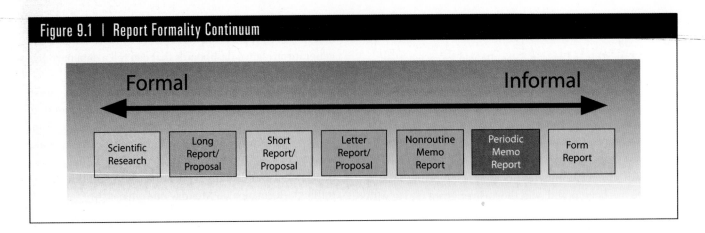

Figure 9.1 | Report Formality Continuum

Formal ← → Informal

| Scientific Research | Long Report/ Proposal | Short Report/ Proposal | Letter Report/ Proposal | Nonroutine Memo Report | Periodic Memo Report | Form Report |

the classifications of formal/informal and short/long are closely related.

- **Informational or analytical reports.** An **informational report** carries objective information from one area of an organization to another. An **analytical report** presents suggested solutions to problems. Company annual reports, monthly financial statements, reports of sales volume, and reports of employee or personnel absenteeism and turnover are informational reports. Reports on scientific research, real estate appraisal reports, and feasibility reports by consulting firms are analytical reports.

- **Vertical or lateral reports.** The vertical/lateral classification refers to the directions in which reports travel. Although most reports travel upward in organizations, many travel downward. Both represent vertical reports and are often referred to as *upward-directed* and *downward-directed* reports. The main function of **vertical reports** is to contribute to management *control*, as shown in Figure 9.2. **Lateral reports**, on the other hand, assist

Figure 9.2 | The General Upward Flow of Reports

Shareholders
Periodic Progress

Board of Directors
Policy Making

Executive Management
Decision Making

Operational and Staff Functions
Production   Finance   Distribution   Human Resources

in *coordination* in the organization. A report traveling between units on the same organizational level, such as between the production department and the finance department, is lateral.

- **Internal or external reports.** An **internal report**, such as a production or sales report, travels within an organization. An **external report**, such as a company's annual report to stockholders, is prepared for distribution outside an organization.

- **Periodic reports.** **Periodic reports** are issued on regularly scheduled dates. They are generally directed upward and serve management control purposes. Daily, weekly, monthly, quarterly, semiannual, and annual time periods are typical for periodic reports. Preprinted forms and computer-generated data contribute to the uniformity of periodic reports.

- **Functional reports.** A **functional report** serves a specified purpose within a company. The functional classification includes accounting reports, marketing reports, financial reports, personnel reports, and a variety of other reports that take their functional designation from their ultimate use. For example, a

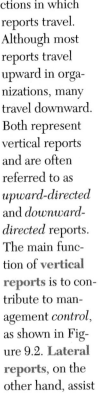

informational report a report that carries objective information from one area of an organization to another

analytical report a report that presents suggested solutions to problems

vertical report a report that can be upward- or downward-directed

lateral report a report that travels between units on the same organizational level

internal report a report that travels within an organization, such as a production or sales report

external report a report prepared for distribution outside an organization

periodic report a report that is issued on regularly scheduled dates

functional report a report that serves a specified purpose within a company

justification of the need for additional personnel or for new equipment is described as a *justification report* in the functional classification.

9-1b Proposals

A **proposal** is a written description of how one organization can meet the needs of another, for example, by providing products or services or solving problems. Businesses issue *calls for bids* that present the specifications for major purchases of goods and certain services. Most governmental and nonprofit agencies issue *requests for proposals*, or RFPs. Potential suppliers prepare proposal reports telling how they can meet that need. Those preparing the proposal create a convincing document that will lead to obtaining a contract.

In our information-intensive society, proposal preparation is a major activity for many firms. In fact, some companies hire consultants or designate employees to specialize in proposal writing. Chapter 11 presents proposal preparation in considerable detail.

As you review these report classifications, you will very likely decide—correctly—that almost all reports could be included in these categories. A report may be formal or informal, short or long, informational or analytical, vertically or laterally directed, internal or external, or periodic or non-periodic, as well as functionally labeled, a proposal, or some other combination of these classifications. These report categories are in common use and provide necessary terminology for the study and production of reports.

9-2 Basis for Reports: The Problem-Solving Process

The upward flow of reports provides management with data that someone might use to make a decision. The purpose is to use the data to solve a problem. Some problems are recurring and call for a steady flow of information; other problems might be unique and call for information on a one-time basis. A problem is the basis for a report. The following steps are used for finding a solution:

1. Recognize and define the problem.
2. Select a method of solution.
3. Collect and organize the data and document the sources.
4. Arrive at an answer.

Only after all four steps have been completed is a report written for presentation. Reports represent an attempt to communicate how a problem was solved. These problem-solving steps are completed *before* the report is written in final form.

9-2a Recognizing and Defining the Problem

Problem-solving research cannot begin until the researchers define the problem. Frequently, those requesting a report will attempt to provide a suitable definition. Nevertheless, researchers should attempt to state the problem clearly and precisely to ensure they are on the right track.

Using Problem Statements, Statements of Purpose, and Hypotheses

The **problem statement** is the particular problem that is to be solved by the research. The **statement of purpose** is the goal of the study and includes the aims or objectives that the researcher hopes to accomplish. Research studies often have both a problem statement and a statement of purpose. For example, a real estate appraiser accepts a client's request to appraise a building to determine its market value. The problem is to arrive at a fair market value for the property. The purpose of the appraisal, however, might be to establish a value for a mortgage loan, to determine the feasibility of adding to the structure, or to assess the financial possibility of demolishing the structure and erecting something else. Thus, the purpose might have much to do with determining what elements to consider in arriving at an answer. In other words, unless you know *why* something is wanted, you might have difficulty knowing *what* is wanted. Once you arrive at the answers to the *what* and *why* questions, you will be on your way to solving the problem.

A **hypothesis** is a statement to be proved or disproved through research. For example, a study of work teams might be made to determine the factors that predict success. An observation might lead one to believe that a key factor in determining success was the quality of communication, as defined by equal participation. For this problem, the hypothesis could be formulated in this way:

Hypothesis: Productivity will increase when skilled manufacturing employees function as members of production teams rather than as single units in a production line.

proposal a written description of how one organization can meet the needs of another

problem statement the particular problem that is to be solved by the research

statement of purpose the goal of the study; includes the aims or objectives the researcher hopes to accomplish

hypothesis a statement to be proved or disproved through research

Because the hypothesis tends to be stated in a way that favors one possibility or is prejudiced toward a particular answer, many researchers prefer to state hypotheses in the null form. The *null hypothesis* states that no relationship or difference will be found in the factors being studied, which tends to remove the element of prejudice toward a certain answer. The null hypothesis for the previous example could be written as follows:

Null hypothesis: No significant difference will be found in productivity between workers organized as teams and workers as individual production line units.

Using the problem/purpose approach, the hypothesis approach, or both, is a choice of the researcher. In many ways, the purpose of a study is determined by the intended use of its results.

Limiting the Scope of the Problem

A major shortcoming that often occurs in research planning is the failure to establish or to recognize desirable limits. The *scope* of the report helps to establish boundaries in which the report will be researched and prepared. Assume, for example, that you want to study the cost of hiring technical support staff. Use the *what, why, when, where,* and *who* questions to reduce such a problem to reasonable proportions.

Note that this process of reducing the problem to a workable size has also established some firm limits to the research. You have limited the problem to cost of technical support personnel, the particular area, and a certain group of users. Note, too, how important the *why* was in helping to establish the limits. Limiting the problem is "zeroing in on the problem."

In some reports, it is desirable to differentiate between the boundaries that were placed on the project outside the control of the researchers and those that were chosen by the researchers. Boundaries imposed outside the control of the researchers are called *limitations*; they might include the assignment of the topic, the allotted budget, and time required to complete the report. These boundaries affect what and how the topic can be researched. Boundaries chosen by the researchers to make the project more manageable are called *delimitations*; they might include the sources and methods chosen for research.

procedures (or methodology) the steps a writer takes in preparing a report; often recorded as a part of the written report

longitudinal studies reports that study the same factors in different time frames

---

Limits You Might Set as the Manager of a Technical Support Department:

What:	A study of salaries of technical support personnel
Why:	To determine whether salaries in our firm are competitive and consistent
When:	Current
Where:	United States
Who:	Technical support personnel at a technology company

Now you can phrase the problem this way:

Statement of purpose: The purpose of this study is to survey salaries of technical support personnel at technology companies working in the United States to determine whether our salaries are competitive and consistent.

Defining Terms Clearly

Words often have more than one meaning, and technical or special-use words might occur in the report that are not widely used or understood. Such terms would require a definition in order for the reader to understand the presented information. In the previously used example concerning the internet product sales a comparison of the internet product sales with those storefront retail outlets would be meaningful only if the information gathered from the latter is similar to that of the former. A list of products sold by an internet-based retail outlet, for example, would help ensure that the same products are sold by storefront outlets.

Documenting Procedures

The procedures or steps a writer takes in preparing a report are often recorded as a part of the written report. This **procedures** section, or **methodology**, adds credibility to the research process and also enables subsequent researchers to repeat, or replicate, the study in another setting or at a later time. Reports that study the same factors in different time frames are called **longitudinal studies**.

The procedures section of a report records the major steps taken in the research, and, possibly, the reasons for their inclusion. It might, for example, tell the types of printed and electronic sources that were consulted, and the groups of people who were interviewed and how they were selected. Steps in the procedures section are typically listed in chronological order so that the reader has an overall understanding of the timetable that existed for the project.

9-3 Selecting a Method of Gathering Information

After defining the problem, the researcher will plan how to arrive at a solution. The research methods you use to collect necessary information can be secondary, primary, or both.

9-3a Secondary Research

Secondary research provides information that has already been created by others. Researchers save time and effort by not duplicating research that has already been undertaken. They can access this information easily through the aid of electronic databases and bibliographic indexes. Suppose that a marketing manager has been asked to investigate the feasibility of implementing a strategic information system. The manager knows other companies are using this technology. By engaging in secondary research, the manager can determine the boundaries of knowledge before proceeding into the unknown.

Certain truths have been established and treated as principles reported in textbooks and other publications. However, because knowledge is constantly expanding, the researcher knows that new information is available. The job, then, is to canvass the literature of the field and attempt to redefine the boundaries of knowledge.

Secondary research can be gathered by means of traditional printed sources or by using electronic tools.

Printed Sources

Major categories of printed sources are books, periodicals, and government documents. Books are typically cataloged in libraries by call number, with larger libraries using the Library of Congress classification system. Traditional card catalogs in libraries have been replaced by online catalogs, which allow the user to locate desired books by author, title, subject, or keyword. A wide assortment of reference books is typically available for use within libraries; these include dictionaries, encyclopedias, yearbooks, and almanacs. Some of these volumes contain general information on a wide array of topics, whereas others are designed for a specific field of study.

Periodicals, referred to as *serials* by librarians, include various types of publications that are released on a periodic basis. Newspapers, magazines, and journals are all types of periodicals. Newspapers, which are usually published daily, are a good initial source for investigation because they give condensed coverage of timely topics. Magazines might be published weekly, monthly, bimonthly, or in some other interval. They are typically written for a general readership, providing expanded coverage in an easy-to-read format. Journals, on the other hand, are written for more specialized audiences, are peer reviewed, and are more research oriented and, thus, more credible. Journal articles share the results of research studies and provide data that support their findings. They also provide bibliographies or citation lists that can be used to locate related materials. Articles on specific topics can be located using both printed and online indexes. A partial list of these sources is shown in Exhibit 9.1.

Electronic Sources

The availability of computer-assisted data searches has simplified the time-consuming task of searching through indexes, card catalogs, and other sources. Weekly and monthly updates keep electronic databases current, and they are easy to use. Databases, such as LexisNexis Academic Universe, have full-text retrieval capability, meaning that you can retrieve the entire article for reviewing and printing. Other databases offer only some articles in full text, with citations or abstracts provided for others. Note the list of electronic databases for business users listed in Exhibit 9.1.

The internet and its subset, the World Wide Web, have made thousands of reference sources available in a matter of seconds. However, the vastness of this resource can be overwhelming to the novice researcher. The following tips will help make your internet search more productive:

- **Choose your search engine or database appropriately.** A *search engine* is a cataloged database of websites that allows you to search specific topics. Several popular search engines exist, including Yahoo!, Ask, and DuckDuckGo. Megasearch engines such as Google and Microsoft Bing, which index billions of web pages, search through a number of other engines to produce "hits."[1] (A *hit* is a located website that contains the word or words specified in the search.) You want to obtain a sufficient number of hits, but not thousands.

> **secondary research** provides information that has already been reported by others

---

Secondary Research Accomplishes the Following Objectives:

- ▸ **Establishes a point of departure for further research**
- ▸ **Avoids needless duplication of costly research efforts**
- ▸ **Reveals areas of needed research**
- ▸ **Makes a real contribution to a body of knowledge**

Exhibit 9.1 | Useful Reference Sources

Printed Indexes

Business Periodicals Index
Education Index
The New York Times Index
Readers' Guide to Periodical Literature
Social Science and Humanities Index
The Wall Street Journal Index

Electronic Databases

ABI/INFORM
Academic Search Elite
Business & Company Resource Center
Business Source Premier
Business Dateline
DIALOG Information Services
ERIC
First Search
General BusinessFile
LexisNexis Academic Universe
FSI Online
Periodical Abstracts
ProQuest
Westlaw

Biography

Who's Who in America
Similar directories for specific geographic areas, industries, and professions

General Facts and Statistics

Statistical Abstract of the United States
Bureau of the Census publications
Dictionaries (general and discipline specific)
Encyclopedia (*Americana* and *Britannica*)
Fortune Directories of U.S. Corporations
World Atlas
LexisNexis Statistics
Almanacs

Report Style and Formation

American Psychological Association. (2020).
   Publication Manual of the American Psychological Association (7th ed.). Washington, DC: Author.
   [www.apastyle.apa.org]
MLA Handbook Ninth Edition (2021).
   New York: Modern
   Language Association of America.

Although the variety of these larger engines is greater, they pose more difficulty in narrowing a search.

Electronic databases provide access to articles from newspapers, magazines, journals, and other types of publications. The database provider might charge a subscription fee or a document delivery fee to access articles. These types of databases are not accessible by a search engine and are often described as the *hidden internet*. Many libraries provide access to these databases. Some databases are suited for topic searches of general interest; others are geared toward specialized fields. A topic search will produce a listing of references and article abstracts, or even full-text articles in some cases. Databases available through your library might include Business Source Premier (an offering of EBSCO), Academic Search Elite, LexisNexis Academic Universe, ABI Inform First Search, Business and Company Resource Center, General BusinessFile, and others.

- **Structure searches from broad to specific.** Use words for your topic that are descriptive and do not have multiple meanings. Once sites have been located for your general topic, you can use *Boolean logic* to narrow the selection. Boolean operands (*and, or,* and *not*) serve to limit the identified sites. The following example shows how these delimiters can assist you in locating precisely what you want:

  ○ Using the key phrase *workplace productivity* will produce all sites that have either of the key words in the title or descriptors.

  ○ Placing "and" between key words will produce hits that have both words.

  ○ Keying *workplace productivity not United States* will eliminate hits that refer to the United States.

- **Use quotation marks when literal topics are desired.** Putting quotation marks around your topic words can drastically affect the number of hits. The quotation marks cause the search engine to look for the designated words as a phrase, thus producing only those sites that have the phrase present. Without the quotation marks, the search engine will treat the words individually and produce many more hits, most of which might not be useful. For example, if you are looking for sites related to "international communication," placing quotation marks around the desired phrase would eliminate the sites that deal with international topics that are not communication oriented.

- **Look for web pages that have collections of links to other related topics.** Clicking on these hyperlinks will allow you to maximize your time investment in the data-gathering phase of your research.

- **Be adaptable to the various access format requirements.** Each search engine and database has its own particular format and instructions for use. The method for specifying and narrowing your search will vary.

9-3b Primary Research

After reviewing the secondary data, you might need to collect primary data to solve your problem. **Primary research** relies on firsthand data, such as responses from pertinent individuals, or observations of people or phenomena related to your study. Recognized methods for obtaining original information are observational studies, experimental research, and normative surveys.

Observational studies are those in which the researcher observes and statistically analyzes certain phenomena to assist in establishing new principles or discoveries. For example, market analysts observe buying habits of certain income groups to determine the most desirable markets. Internal auditors analyze expected patterns in expense reimbursement amounts to identify potential fraud activity. Developing an objective system for quantifying observations is necessary for collecting valid data. For example, to gain insight into the effect of a comprehensive ethics program, a researcher might record the number of incidents of ethical misconduct reported, or the number of calls made to an ethics helpline designed to provide advice about proper conduct. Observational studies typically involve no contact with the human subjects under study.

Experimental research typically involves the study of two or more samples that have exactly the same components before a variable is added to one of the samples. Any differences observed are viewed as due to the variable. Like scientists, businesses use experimental research to solve various problems. For example, a company conducts new employee training with all new hires. Two training methods are presently used: New hires in one regional office receive their training in a traditional classroom setting

Jacob Lund/Shutterstock.com

with other new employees, while employees at the other regional office take an online training class. Management wants to determine whether one method is superior to the other in terms of learning success. During the period of the study, learning differences in the two study groups are noted. Because the training method is assumed to be the only significant variable, any difference is attributed to its influence. Experimental research involves very careful recordkeeping and can require informed consent from the participants who are subjected to experimental methods.

Normative survey research is undertaken to determine the status of something at a specific time. Survey instruments such as questionnaires, opinion surveys, checklists, and interviews are used to obtain information from participants. Election opinion polls represent one type of normative survey research. The term *normative* is used to qualify surveys because surveys reveal "norms" or "standards" existing at the time of the survey. A poll taken two months before an election might have little similarity to one taken the week preceding the election.

Surveys can help verify the accuracy of existing norms. The U.S. Census is conducted every decade to establish an actual population figure, and each person is supposedly counted. In effect, the census tests the accuracy of prediction techniques used to estimate population during the years between censuses. A survey of what employees consider a fair benefits package would be effective only for the date of the survey. People retire, move, and change their minds often. These human traits make survey research of opinions somewhat tentative. Yet surveys remain a valuable tool for gathering information on which to base decisions and policies.

Researchers normally cannot survey everyone, particularly if the population is large and the research budget is limited. **Sampling** is a survey technique that eliminates the need for questioning 100 percent of the population. Sampling is based on the principle that a sufficiently large number drawn at random from a population will be representative of the total population. That is, the sample will possess the same

primary research data collected for the first time, usually for a specific purpose

observational studies studies in which the researcher observes and statistically analyzes certain phenomena to assist in establishing new principles or discoveries

experimental research the study of two samples that have exactly the same components before a variable is added to one of the samples

normative survey research research to determine the status of something at a specific time

sampling a survey technique that eliminates the need for questioning 100 percent of the population

characteristics in the same proportions as the total population. For example, a company collecting market research data before introducing a new low-fat food product would survey a small number of people. The data are considered *representative* if the sample of people surveyed has the same percentage of ages, genders, purchasing power, and so on as the anticipated target market.

As a researcher, you must be cautious about drawing conclusions from a sample and generalizing them to a population that might not be represented by the sample. For example, early-morning shoppers might differ from afternoon or evening shoppers; young adults might differ from senior citizens; male shoppers might differ from female shoppers. A good researcher defines the population as distinctly as possible and uses a sampling technique to ensure that the sample is representative.

Whether a survey involves personal interviewing, or distributing items such as checklists or questionnaires, some principles of procedure and planning are common to both methods. These principles assure the researcher that the data gathered will be both valid (i.e., it will measure what the researcher intended to measure) and reliable (i.e., it will measure data accurately).

- **Validity** refers to the degree to which the data measure what you intend to measure. It generally results from careful planning of the questionnaire or interview questions or items. Cautious wording, preliminary testing of items to detect misunderstandings, and some statistical techniques are helpful in determining whether the responses to the items are valid. A *pilot test* of the instrument is often conducted prior to the full-scale survey so that a smaller number of participants can test the instrument, which can then be revised prior to wide-scale administration.

- **Reliability** refers to the level of consistency or stability over time or over independent samples; that is, reliable data are reasonably accurate or repeatable. Reliability results from asking a large enough sample of people so that the researcher is reasonably confident that the results would be the same even if more people were asked to respond or if a different sample was chosen from the same population. For example, if you were to ask 10 people to react to a questionnaire item, the results might vary considerably. If you were to add 90 more people to the sample, the results might tend to reach a point of stability where more responses would not change

validity the degree to which the data measure what the researcher intends to measure

reliability the level of consistency or stability over time or over independent samples

the results. Reliability would then be reasonably established.

Responses to surveys often represent only a small percentage of the total mailings. In some cases, a return of 3 to 5 percent is considered adequate and is planned for by researchers. In other cases, such as employee surveys or questionnaires, a return of considerably more than half the mailings might be a planned result. Selecting an appropriate data-collection method and developing a sound survey instrument are crucial elements of an effective research study.

9-4 Collecting and Organizing the Data

Collecting the right data and ensuring that they are recorded appropriately is paramount to the success of a business report. Various techniques can assist in this process when collecting both secondary and primary data.

9-4a Collecting Secondary Data

When beginning to collect secondary data, beware of collecting too much information—one of the major deterrents to good report writing. Although you want to be thorough, you do not want to collect and record such a large amount of information that you will hardly know where to begin your analysis.

The availability of computer-assisted data searches has simplified the time-consuming task of searching through indexes, card catalogs, and other sources. For example, suppose you select an online database, such as Business Source Premier or ProQuest, or an internet search engine, such as Google, to research the role of microblogging in the workplace. By inputting the key term *communication* in an online database, you receive the screen output in Figure 9.3. The screen output contains information that will facilitate your research.

First, you can quickly evaluate the relevance of references by reading each article's title and abstract, if available, to determine appropriateness to your topic. Retrieved full-text articles can be read and analyzed for useful information, saved, and printed for later use. Be sure to record a full bibliographic citation for each reference you obtain to avoid the need to relocate the online source or revisit the library to find it again.

After you have located relevant sources, you can take notes using various methods. When your aim is to *learn*, the following technique for taking notes is effective: (1) read an article rapidly and put it aside; (2) *from memory*, list main and supporting points; and (3) review the article to see whether all significant points have been included.

Rapid reading forces concentration, builds a strong understanding of the topic, and reveals relationships

Figure 9.3 | A Sample Computer Data Search Using an Online Database

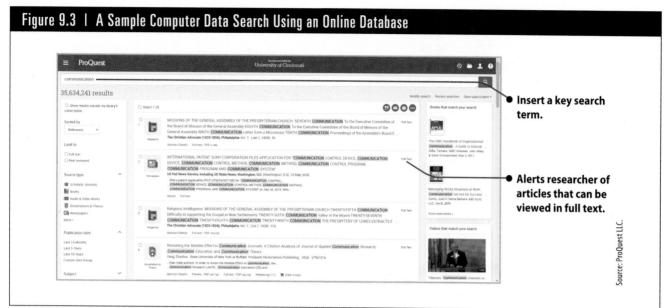

Insert a key search term.

Alerts researcher of articles that can be viewed in full text.

Source: ProQuest LLC.

Source: https://www.proquest.com/

between ideas. In the past, researchers read the article and then, immediately, wrote their notes on cards. Today, researchers typically prefer copying and pasting relevant information into a word-processing file or highlighting important points on a photocopy or printout of an article; then, from the selected passages, they compose their notes by typing them.

You can use two kinds of note-taking: direct quotation or paraphrase. The *direct quotation method* involves citing the exact words from a source. This method is useful when the exact words have specific impact or expert appeal. The *paraphrase method* involves summarizing information in your own words without changing the author's intended meaning. Put direct quotes in quotation marks, and indicate the page numbers, if available.

9-4b Collecting Data Through Surveys

The method of distribution and the makeup of the questionnaire are critical factors in successful survey research.

Selecting a Data-Collection Method

Selecting an appropriate data-collection method is crucial to effective research. Researchers must consider various factors when selecting an appropriate method for collecting data, as illustrated in Exhibit 9.2.

Plagiarism is the presentation of someone else's ideas or words as your own. To safeguard your reputation against plagiarism charges, be certain to give credit where credit is due. Specifically, provide a citation for each (1) direct quotation or (2) passage from someone else's work that you stated in your own words rather than using the author's words—the words are your own, but the idea is not.

To attribute information to another source, develop complete, accurate citations and a reference page according to a recognized referencing method.

fizkes/Shutterstock

Developing an Effective Survey Instrument

No matter which survey technique or combination of techniques is used, the way in which the survey instrument is designed and written has much to do with the validity and reliability of results, the response rate, and the quality of the information received.

The construction of the survey instrument—usually a questionnaire or interview guide—is critical to obtaining reliable and valid data. With the advent of online survey software, much of this process can be automated (refer to Exhibit 9.3). Survey software

plagiarism the presentation of someone else's ideas or words as your own

Exhibit 9.2 | Selecting an Appropriate Data-Collection Method

Method	Advantages	Limitations
Online surveys	• Are relatively inexpensive to administer • Can reach a wide number of people who can complete the survey at their convenience • Allow for anonymity, which may produce more honest responses • Remove difference-in-status barriers	• May yield a low response rate • Are not useful for obtaining detailed information
Telephone surveys	• Provide an inexpensive and rapid data collection • Allow personal contact between the interviewer and the respondent for clarification or follow-up questions	• Must be relatively short to minimize perceived intrusion and to increase typical small return rate • May exclude respondents with unlisted numbers and those without telephones
Personal interviews	• Are useful for obtaining in-depth answers and exploring sensitive topics • Allow personal contact between the interviewer and the respondent for clarification and follow-up questions	• Are time consuming and resource intensive • Require a proper interviewer • Vary in value, depending on the quality and consistency of the interviewer
Email polling	• Is inexpensive • Provides for an easy response • Yields quick results that can be updated electronically as responses are received	• Is limited to respondents with computer access

solutions help you design, send, and analyze surveys, usually via the internet and using drag-and-drop tools and automated functionality. Survey software solutions make the entire process faster, more accurate, and easier to accomplish than manual surveys. Some popular online survey providers include Qualtrics, SurveyHero, SurveyMonkey, and QuestionPro.

Different solutions allow users to set the survey process and dynamics in different ways and may include all or some of these listed features:

• **Survey builder.** Typical survey builders use a drag-and-drop interface and tools for layout and design. The builder creates the front-end look and function of the survey, but it relies on another feature—conditions—to

Exhibit 9.3 | Guidelines for Web-Based Surveys

Scenarios that may be suitable for a web-based survey:
- Respondent features:
  - Respondents are already avid internet users; email addresses known for reminder messages.
  - Respondents are enthusiastic form fillers, will not require monetary incentives.
  - Respondents cover a wide geographic area
- Survey features:
  - Need for complex branching, interactive questionnaire, or multimedia as part of the survey instrument.
  - Survey content will evolve fast (e.g., Delphi surveys).
  - No need for representative results.
- Investigator features:
  - Limited budget for mailing and data processing but good in-house web skills.
  - Precautions can be taken against multiple responses by same individuals.
  - Web survey forms have been piloted with representative participants and demonstrate acceptable validity and reliability with most platform/browser/ISP combinations.
  - Data are required quickly in a readily analyzed form.

Scenarios unsuitable for a web-based survey:
- Respondent features:
  - Target group is under-represented on the internet, e.g., underprivileged or elderly people.
  - Target group is concerned, however unreasonably, about privacy aspects.
  - Target group requires substantial incentives to complete the survey.
  - Need for a representative sample.
- Survey features:
  - Need for accurate timing or observational data on participants.
  - An existing paper instrument has been carefully validated on target group.
  - Need to capture qualitative data or observations about participants.
  - Need to capture accurate timing.
  - Wish to reach the same group of participants in the same way months or years later.
- Investigator features:
  - Limited in-house web or Java expertise, but existing desk top publishing and mailing facility.

Source: Wyatt, J.C. (2000). When to use web-based surveys. *Journal of American Medical Informics Association*, 7(4): 426–429. doi:10.1136/jamia.2000.0070426. Retrieved February 13, 2022 from https://www.ncbi.nlm.nih.gov/pmc/articles/PMC61446/

set how the survey behaves. For conditions, you have two perspectives: questions and answers.

- **Question conditions.** Designing a survey requires conditions for both questions and answers. Question conditions may include tools to format style, randomize questions, or generate x/y choices. A solution may also feature a timer and allow images and videos for interactive questionnaires. A question library may also be available that lets you archive reusable questions.

- **Answer conditions.** On the answer side, survey software solutions may offer options to show/hide questions or randomize choices. Answers can also be preset with conditional triggers that personalize the survey.

- **Survey templates.** Most solutions provide templates to help kickstart your survey process. Templates often accommodate various question formats such as leading questions, dichotomous questions, bipolar questions, and rating scale types.

- **Scoring.** Whatever answer-question conditions are used, survey software has a scoring algorithm set either as default or based on rules. Scoring and tallying are

automated, which speeds up the process of aggregating feedback and generating insights.

- **Email invitation.** A survey solution may include a mailer to send an invite to the questionnaire or may integrate with a third-party app to accomplish this task.

- **Multimedia.** A survey software solution may allow the use of images, videos, and graphics for interactive questionnaires. This functionality can be built-in or may come as an integrated feature with another app.

- **Response management.** Data collection can be set in a variety of ways, for example, applying a quota to manage the number of responses, or automatically categorizing responses and triggering succeeding actions.

- **Data analysis.** This feature varies in sophistication between low-cost and premium plans. Standard analytics show basic summaries, while more advanced solutions may perform cross-tabulation, filtering, weighting, and other multivariate statistical methods.

- **White label.** A survey software solution may let you configure the interface with your brand logo and colors to give your surveys a more professional and appealing look.

- **Multilingual support.** Some solutions host different languages, which is useful for conducting surveys in different global market territories. The feature may include a spell-checker for each language and an auto-detect or opt-in tool that sets the questionnaire to the default language of the respondent.[2]

Some survey software options are free while many provide price plans for small business and enterprise use.

Here are some suggestions for manually developing an effective questionnaire:

- **Provide brief, easy-to-follow directions.** Explain the purpose of the study in a cover letter or in a brief statement at the top of the questionnaire so that the respondents understand your intent. Although a screening question might be needed to determine whether the respondent is qualified to answer a set of questions, minimize confusing "skip-and-jump" instructions such as the following:

  If you answered Yes to item 4, skip directly to item 7; if you answered No, explain your reason in items 5 and 6.

- **Arrange the items in a logical sequence.** If possible, the sequence should proceed from easy to difficult items; simple, nonthreatening items involve the respondents and encourage them to finish. You might group related items, such as demographic questions, or those that use the same response options, such as multiple choice, rating scales, and open-ended questions.

- **Create an appealing, easy-to-comprehend design.** Use different typefaces, bold, underline, and italics to emphasize important ideas. Use text boxes and graphic lines to partition text so that the reader can identify and move through sections quickly.

- **Use short items that ask for a single answer to one idea.** Include only the questions needed to meet the objectives of your study, because long questionnaires affect the return rate negatively.

- **Design questions that are easy to answer and to tabulate.** Participants might not take the time to answer numerous open-ended questions that require essay-style answers. When open-ended questions are included, provide enough space for respondents to answer adequately.

- **Strive to write clear questions that all respondents will interpret in the same way.** Avoid words with imprecise meanings (e.g., *several, usually*), as well as specialized terms and difficult words that respondents might not understand. Use accurate translations for each concept presented if other cultures are involved. Provide examples for items that might be difficult to understand.

- **Ask for information that can be recalled readily.** Asking for "old" information might not result in sound data.

- **Provide all possible answer choices on multiple-choice items.** Add an "undecided" or "other" category so that respondents are not forced to choose a nonapplicable response.

- **Ask for factual information whenever possible.** Opinions might be needed in certain studies, but opinions might change daily. As a general rule, the smaller the sample, the less reliable are any conclusions based on opinions.

- **Decide on an optimal number of choices to place on a ranking scale.** Ranking scales, also called Likert scales, allow participants to indicate their opinion on a numbered continuum. When deciding the numbers to place on the scale, consider the tendency of some groups to choose the noncommittal midpoint in a scale with an odd number of response choices (for example, choosing 3 on a scale from 1 to 5).

- **Avoid questions that might be threatening or awkward to the respondent.** For sensitive issues, such as age and income, allow respondents to select among ranges if possible. Ensure that ranges do not overlap and provide for all possible selections.

- **Consider the advisability of prompting a forced answer.** A forced-answer question can be used to determine which single factor is most critical to a respondent, as shown in the following examples:

  Of the locations listed, which is the most convenient for your use?

  Do you agree to the terms of use provided in the attached document?

  ❑ *Yes*   ❑ *No*

When using forced-choice items, avoid "leading questions" that cause people to answer in a way that is not their true opinion or situation. The following item is an example of such a question:

  Would you participate in unethical acts, such as insider trading, if this potential were provided?

  ❑ *Yes*   ❑ *No*

Various types of items can be used in questionnaire design, depending on your purpose and the characteristics of your participants. Figure 9.4 illustrates the principles of effective questionnaire design.

Figure 9.4 | Example of an Effective Questionnaire

Workplace Stress Survey

Enter a number from the following sliding scale that best describes you.

Strongly Disagree		Somewhat Disagree		Agree		Somewhat Agree		Strongly Agree	
1	2	3	4	5	6	7	8	9	10

I can't honestly say what I really think or get things off my chest at work. _____

My job has a lot of responsibility, but I don't have very much authority. _____

I could usually do a much better job if I were given more time. _____

I seldom receive adequate acknowledgement or appreciation when my work is really good. _____

In general, I am not particularly proud or satisfied with my job. _____

I have the impression that I am repeatedly picked on or discriminated against at work. _____

My workplace environment is not very pleasant or safe. _____

My job often interferes with my family and social obligations, or personal needs. _____

I tend to have frequent arguments with superiors, coworkers or customers. _____

Most of the time I feel I have very little control over my life at work. _____

Add up the replies to each question for your total job stress score. If you scored between 10–30, you handle stress on your job well; between 40–60, moderately well; 70–100 you are encountering problems that need to be resolved.

A final step in questionnaire design is to test the instrument by asking others to complete and critique the questionnaire. For surveys of major importance, researchers typically conduct a pilot study, disseminating the questionnaire to a small group of the population involved. This process allows them to correct problems in clarity and design, and typically leads to a better response and quality of answers. A pilot study might uncover factors affecting your results, which you can address in the final research design, before conducting the actual survey.

Researchers must select, from among the several formats available, the one best suited to the situation. Criteria for selecting one alternative over the others might include the following: Which format leaves the least chance for misinterpretation? Which format provides information in the way it can best be used? Can it be tabulated easily? Can it be cross-referenced to other items in the survey instrument?

9-4c Avoiding Data-Gathering Errors

If acceptable data-gathering techniques have been used, data will measure what they are intended to measure (have validity) and will measure it accurately (have reliability). Hopefully, a carefully designed research process will yield useful data for analysis.

9-4d Documenting Sources of Information

A crucial part of ethical, honest research writing is documenting or referencing sources fairly and accurately. Although time consuming and tedious, careful attention to documentation will mark you as a respected, highly professional researcher.

An important first step is to pledge that you will not, for any reason, present someone else's ideas as your own. Then develop a systematic checklist for avoiding plagiarism. Carelessly forgetting to enclose someone else's words within quotation marks or failing to paraphrase another's words can cause others to question your ethical conduct. When you feel that the tedious work required to document sources fairly and accurately is not worth the time invested, remind yourself of the following reasons for documentation:

- **Citations give credit where it is due—to the one who created the material.** People who document demonstrate high standards of ethical conduct and responsibility in scholarship. Those exhibiting this professional behavior will gain the well-deserved trust and respect of peers and superiors.

- **Documentation protects writers against plagiarism charges.** Plagiarism occurs when

Some Common Errors at the Data-Gathering Stage:

▶ **Using samples that are too small**

▶ **Using samples that are not representative**

▶ **Using poorly constructed data-gathering instruments**

▶ **Using information from biased sources**

▶ **Failing to gather enough information to cover all the important aspects of a problem**

▶ **Gathering too much information**

Follow These General Suggestions for Preparing Accurate Documentation:

▶ **Decide which authoritative style manual to follow** for preparing in-text parenthetical citations or footnotes (endnotes) and the bibliography (references). Some companies and most journals require writers to prepare reports or manuscripts following a particular style manual. Once you are certain you have selected the appropriate manual, follow it precisely as you prepare the documentation and produce the report.

▶ **Be consistent.** If you are carefully following a format, you shouldn't have a problem with consistency. For example, one style manual might require an author's initials in place of the first name in a bibliography; another manual requires the full name. The placement of commas and periods and other information varies among manuals. Consult the manual, apply the rules methodically, and proofread carefully to ensure accuracy and consistency.

someone steals material from another and claims it as their own writing. Besides suffering embarrassment, the plagiarist might be assessed fines, penalties, or professional sanctions.

- **Documentation supports your statements.** If recognized authorities have said the same thing, your work takes on credibility; you have put yourself in good company.

- **Documentation can aid future researchers pursuing similar material.** Documentation must be complete and accurate so that the researcher can locate the source.

Many style guides are available to advise writers on how to organize, document, and produce reports and manuscripts. Exhibit 9.1 includes two of the most popular authoritative style manuals. The *Publication Manual of the American Psychological Association* (APA) has become the most-used guide in the social and "soft" sciences and in many scholarly journals. The *MLA Handbook Ninth Edition* is another authoritative source used in the humanities.

Citations

Two major types of citations are used to document a report: source notes and explanatory notes. Depending on the authoritative style manual used, these notes might be positioned in parentheses within the report, at the bottom of the page, or at the end of the report.

- **Source notes.** These citations acknowledge the contributions of others. They might refer readers to sources of quotations, paraphrased portions of someone else's words or ideas, and quantitative data used in the report. Source notes must include complete and accurate information so that the reader can locate the original source if desired.

- **Explanatory notes.** These citations are used for several purposes: (1) to comment on a source or to provide information that does not fit easily in the text, (2) to support a statistical table, or (3) to refer the reader to another section of the report. The following sample footnote describes the mathematics involved in preparing a table:

*The weighted opinion was derived by assigning responses from high to low as 5, 4, 3, 2, 1; totaling all respondents; and dividing by the number of respondents.

In this case, the asterisk (*) was used, rather than a number, to identify the explanatory footnote both in the text and in the citation. This method is often used when only one or two footnotes are included in the report. If two footnotes appear on the same page, two asterisks (**), or numbers or letters are used to distinguish the second from the first. An explanatory note that supports a graphic, or a source note that provides the reference from which data were taken appears immediately below the graphic.

Referencing Methods

Various reference methods are available for the format and content of source notes: intext parenthetical citations, footnotes, and endnotes. Note the major differences among the methods in the following discussion.

- **In-text parenthetical citations.** The *APA Publication Manual*, *MLA Handbook*, and some other documentation references eliminate the need for separate footnotes or endnotes. Instead, an in-text citation, which contains abbreviated information within parentheses, directs the reader to a list of sources at the end of a report. This list contains all publication information on every source cited. It is arranged alphabetically by the author's last name or, if no author is provided, by the first word of the article title.

- **Footnote citation method.** Placing citations at the bottom of the page on which they are cited is the footnote citation. The reader can conveniently refer to the source if the documentation is positioned at the bottom of the page. Alternatively, a list of footnotes can be included in an endnotes page at the end of the document in the order they appeared. Footnotes and endnotes are not used in APA and MLA referencing, as these styles permit the use of in-text citations only.

- **References (APA) or Works Cited (MLA).** The APA and MLA styles use different terms to distinguish between these types of lists. This document is an alphabetized list of the sources used in preparing a report. Each entry contains the publication information necessary for locating the source. In addition, the bibliographic entries give evidence of the nature of sources the author consulted. The term *bibliography* (literally "description of books") is sometimes used to refer to this list. A researcher often uses sources that provide information but do not result in citations. To acknowledge that you might have consulted these works and to provide the reader with a comprehensive reading list, you might include them in the list of sources.

9-5 Arriving at an Answer

Even the most intelligent person cannot be expected to draw sound conclusions from faulty information. Sound conclusions can be drawn only when information has been properly organized, collected, and interpreted.

9-5a Analyzing the Data

Follow a step-by-step approach to the solution of your research problem. Plan your study and follow the plan. Question every step for its contribution to the objective and keep a record of actions. In a formal research study, the researcher is expected to make a complete report. Another qualified person should be able to make the same study, use the same steps, and arrive at the same conclusion.

If you are using online survey software to conduct your data collection, analysis of the data is likely provided by the program. However, if you have collected your data manually, appropriate statistical analysis must be applied. Statistical analysis is a complex task, involving specialized understanding that is gained through appropriate training, but some of the common terms are identified here. *Tabulation*

techniques should be used to reduce quantitative data, such as numerous answers to questionnaire items. For example, you might want to tabulate the number of males and females participating in the study, along with the appropriate percentages for each gender.

For many kinds of studies, *measures of central tendency* might help in describing distributions of quantitative data. The *range* assists the researcher in understanding the distribution of the scores. The *mean, median,* and *mode* are descriptions of the average value of the distribution.

Other statistical techniques may be used. For example, *correlation analysis* might be used to determine whether a relationship existed between how respondents answered one item and how they answered another. Were males, for example, more likely to have chosen a certain answer to another item on the survey than were females?

The report process is one of reducing the information collected to a size that can be handled conveniently in a written message, as shown in Figure 9.5. Visualize the report process as taking place in a huge funnel. At the top of the funnel, pour in all the original information. Then through a process of compression within the funnel, take the following steps:

1. Evaluate the information for its usefulness.

2. Reduce the useful information through organization of notes and data analysis.

3. Combine like information into understandable forms through the use of tables, charts, graphs, and summaries (refer to Chapter 10).

4. Report in written form the information that remains (refer to Chapter 11).

9-5b Interpreting the Data

Your ethical principles affect the validity of your interpretations. Through all steps in the research process, you must attempt to maintain the integrity of the research. Strive to remain objective, design and conduct an unbiased study, and resist any pressure to slant research to support a particular viewpoint.

Some common errors that seriously hinder the interpretation of data include the following:

- **Trying, consciously or unconsciously, to make results conform to a prediction or desire.** Seeing predictions come true might be pleasing, but objectivity is much more important. Facts should determine conclusions.

- **Hoping for spectacular results.** An attempt to astonish supervisors by preparing a report with revolutionary conclusions can have a negative effect on accuracy.

Figure 9.5 | The Report Process

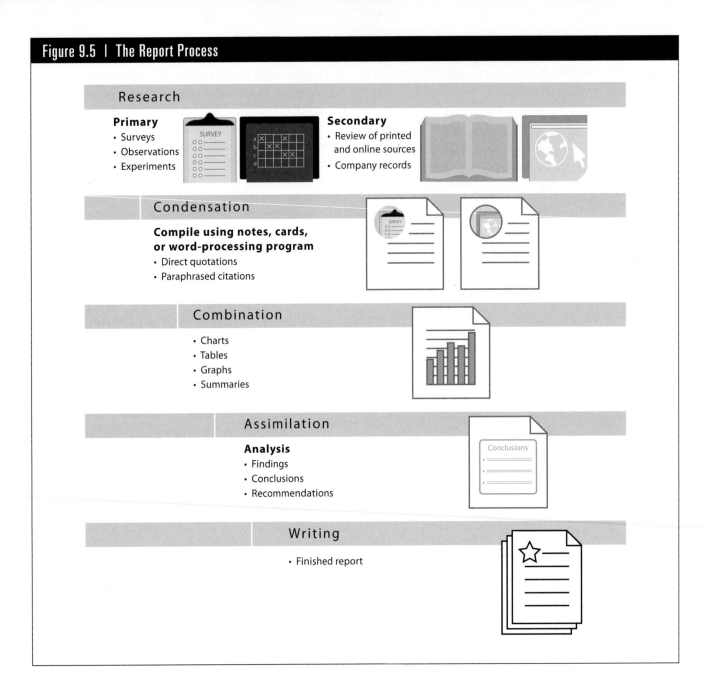

Research

Primary
- Surveys
- Observations
- Experiments

Secondary
- Review of printed and online sources
- Company records

Condensation

Compile using notes, cards, or word-processing program
- Direct quotations
- Paraphrased citations

Combination
- Charts
- Tables
- Graphs
- Summaries

Assimilation

Analysis
- Findings
- Conclusions
- Recommendations

Conclusions

Writing
- Finished report

- **Attempting to compare when commonality is absent.** Results obtained from one study might not always apply to other situations. Similarly, research with a certain population might not be consistent when the same research is conducted with another population.

- **Assuming a cause–effect relationship when one does not exist.** A company president might have been in office one year, and sales might have doubled. However, sales might have doubled in spite of the president rather than because of the president.

- **Failing to consider important factors.** For example, although Eastman Kodak developed the digital camera in 1975, it didn't invest in the technology for fear it would undercut sales of its film business. Only when film's popularity began to wane in the mid-1990s in favor of digital photography did the company push into the digital market. But competitors entered the market faster, and Kodak was never able to fully capitalize on the product it invented.[3]

- **Basing a conclusion on lack of evidence.** "We have had no complaints about our present policy" does not mean that the policy is appropriate. Conversely, lack of evidence that a proposed project will succeed does not necessarily mean that it will fail.

Learn the Terms When Doing Research

Keep in mind the differences in meaning of some common research terms as you analyze your material and attempt to seek meaning from it. Most research reports include all three of the following items or sections:

Finding: A specific, measurable fact from a research study

Conclusion: Summation of major facts and evidence derived from findings

Recommendation: A suggested action based on your research

Consider the following examples of conclusions and recommendations generated by analyzing research findings:

Example 1

Finding: 90 percent of managers responded that poor writing skills are the biggest communication problem in the workplace today.

Conclusion: Greater emphasis on the development of good writing skills is needed at all levels of education.

Recommendation: Schools need to ensure that more time is spent on writing instruction to ensure that employees have the requisite skills for the workplace.

Example 2

Finding: Only 20 percent of online customers rated our system as "Excellent," while nearly 40 percent checked "Needs Improvement."

Conclusion: Our online ordering system needs improvement.

Recommendation: Designers in charge of the online ordering system need to use the findings from our recent customer survey to improve the quality of the system.

- **Assuming constancy of human behavior.** A survey conducted in March indicating 60 percent of the public favors one political party over the other might not have the same results if conducted in November. Because some people paid their bills late last year does not mean a company should refuse to sell to them next year, because reasons for slow payment might have been eliminated.

If you avoid common data-collection errors, you are more likely to collect valid and reliable data and reach sound conclusions. However, if you interpret valid and reliable data incorrectly, your conclusions will still *not* be sound.

10 | Managing Data and Using Graphics

Learning Objectives

After studying this chapter, you will be able to...

10-1 Communicate quantitative information effectively.

10-2 Apply principles of effectiveness and ethical responsibilities in the construction of graphic aids.

10-3 Create appropriate and meaningful graphics.

10-4 Integrate graphics within documents.

10-1 Communicating Quantitative Information

Before you can interpret quantitative data, the elements must be classified, summarized, and condensed into a manageable size. This condensed information is meaningful and can be used to answer your research questions. For example, assume that you have been given 600 completed questionnaires from a study of your current clients' future travel destinations. This large accumulation of data is overwhelming until you tabulate the responses for each questionnaire item by manually inputting or compiling responses received through an online survey, or optically scanning the responses into a computer. Then, you can apply appropriate statistical analysis techniques to the tabulated data.

The computer generates a report of the total responses for each possible answer to each item. For example, the tabulation of responses from each client about their future travel destinations might appear like this:

California	567
New York	423
Alaska	324
Arizona	245
Florida	207

The breakdown reduces 600 responses to a manageable set of information. The tabulation shows only five items, each with a specific number of responses from the total of 600 questionnaires. Because people tend to make comparisons during analysis, the totals are helpful. People generally want to know proportions or ratios, and these are best presented as percentage parts of the total.

Future Travel Destinations	Number	Percentage
California	567	96
New York	423	69.5
Alaska	324	54.5
Arizona	245	46.25
Florida	207	30

Now, analyzing the data becomes relatively easy. Of the survey participants, 96 percent selected California, while only 30 percent selected Florida. Other observations, depending on how exactly you intend to interpret percentages, could be that more than half selected Alaska. Combining data in three categories allows you to summarize that all respondents intend to take a vacation in the South in the future.

When tabulating research results of people's opinions, likes, preferences, and other subjective items, rounding off statistics to fractions helps paint a clear picture for readers. In actuality, if the same group of people were asked this question again a day or two later, a few probably would have changed their minds. For example, a participant who had not indicated a desire to travel to Arizona may have attended a travel show that increased their interest in doing so. The next day, the respondent might indicate a desire to travel to Arizona in the future.

Fractions, ratios, and percentages are examples of **common language**. In effect, common language reduces difficult figures to the "common denominators" of language and ideas. Although "324 of 400 expect to travel to Alaska in the future" is somewhat easy to understand, "54.5 percent prefer …" is even easier, and "one out of two indicate a preference for traveling to Alaska" is even more understandable.

Common language also involves the use of indicators other than actual count or quantity. The Dow Jones Industrial Average provides a measure of stock market performance and is certainly easier to understand than the complete New York Stock Exchange figures. Similarly, oil is counted in barrels rather than in the quart or gallon sizes purchased by consumers. Because of inflation, dollars are not accurate items to use as comparisons from one year to another in certain areas. For example, automobile manufacturers use "automobile units" to represent production changes in the industry. The important thing for the report writer to remember is that reports are communication media, and everything possible should be done to make sure communication occurs effectively.

10-2 Using Graphics

Imagine trying to put in composition style all the information available in a financial statement. Several hundred pages might be necessary to explain material that could otherwise be contained in three or four pages of balance sheets and income statements. Even then, the reader would no doubt be thoroughly confused! To protect readers from being overwhelmed or simply bored with data, report writers can design visually appealing graphics that are appropriate for the data being presented. Data reported in a table, graph, or picture will make your written analysis clearer to the reader.

The term **graphics** is used in this chapter to refer to all types of illustrations used in written

> **common language** reduces difficult figures to the common denominators of language and ideas
>
> **graphics** all types of illustrations used in written and spoken reports

and spoken reports. The most commonly used graphics are tables, bar charts, line charts, pie charts, pictograms, maps, flowcharts, diagrams, and photographs.

10-2a Effective and Ethical Use of Graphics

The use of graphics with a written discussion serves three purposes: to clarify, to simplify, or to reinforce data. As you read this chapter, ask yourself if the discussion would be effective if the accompanying graphic figures were not included. Use the following questions to help you determine whether using a graphic element is appropriate and effective in a written or spoken report.

- **Is a graphic needed to clarify, reinforce, or emphasize a particular idea?** Or can the material be covered adequately in words rather than in visual ways? To maintain a reasonable balance between words and graphics, save graphics for data that are difficult to communicate in words alone.

- **Does the graphic presentation contribute to the overall understanding of the idea under discussion?** Will the written or spoken text add meaning to the graphic display?

- **Is the graphic easily understood?** Does the graphic emphasize the key idea and spur the reader to think intelligently about this information? Follow these important design principles:

  - **Avoid *chartjunk.*** This term, coined by design expert Edward Tufte, describes decorative distractions that bury relevant data.[2] Extreme use of color, complicated symbols and art techniques, and unusual combinations of typefaces reduce the impact of the material presented.

  - **Develop a consistent design for graphics.** Arbitrary changes in the design of graphics (e.g., use of colors, typefaces, three-dimensional, or flat designs) within a written or spoken report can be confusing as the receiver expects consistency in elements within a single report.

  - **Write meaningful titles that reinforce the point that you are making.** For example, a receiver can interpret data faster when graphics use a talking title; that is, a title that interprets the data. Consider the usefulness of the following graphic titles for a manager browsing through survey results in preparation for a meeting with top management:

Descriptive Title:	White Cell Counts During March
Talking Title:	White Cell Counts have Fallen Throughout March

Adapting Your Presentation for YouTube

G-Stock Studio/Shutterstock

YouTube is a great potential resource for a business and can be used to distribute your sales message or training material to a wide audience. The easily accessed website can be a great avenue for sharing business presentations; however, some adaptation is necessary for the best effect.

  - **Keep it short.** The average viewing time for a YouTube clip is 2.5 minutes. If you must stay with a longer presentation format, divide it into several short segments posted as separate videos.

  - **Make it loud and clear.** Use an external microphone rather than relying on one built into the camera. Your audio quality will be much improved.

  - **Avoid bulleted PowerPoint slides.** Bullet points will appear blurry on YouTube and be next to impossible to read. Edit your content and change it to full-screen slides before uploading.

Viewers don't have the time or inclination to struggle through a long, poorly prepared video. Make sure your postings on social media sites are "online compatible."[1]

  - The talking title saves the manager time in understanding the data and also ensures the accuracy of her or his interpretation, recommendations, and the content of her or his presentation. Similarly, poor business decisions can be averted if graphic titles reveal key information. You will learn more about the appropriate use of descriptive and talking headings as you study the preparation of informational and analytical reports in Chapter 11.

- **Is the graphic honest?** Visual data can be distorted easily, leading the reader to form incorrect opinions about the data.

- **Can a graphic used in a presentation be seen by the entire audience?** Electronic presentations, flip charts, whiteboards, and overhead transparencies are the visual means most often used to accompany presentations.

The key to preparing effective graphics is selecting an appropriate graphic for the data and developing a clean, simple design that allows the reader or audience to quickly extract the needed information and meaning.

10-3 Types of Graphic Aids

Using powerful software programs, managers can perform the data management functions discussed in this chapter, producing highly professional graphics. The information can be reproduced in a variety of ways for integrating into reports and supporting highly effective presentations.

Selecting the graphic type that will depict data in the most effective manner is the first decision you must make. After identifying the idea that you want your receiver to understand, you can choose to use a table, bar chart, line chart, pie chart, flowchart, organizational chart, photographs, models, and so on. Use Figure 10.1 to help you choose the graphic type that matches the objective you hope to achieve.

Figures 10.2 through 10.7 illustrate a variety of graphics commonly used in reports. The figures show acceptable variations in graphic design, including placement of the caption (figure number and title), inclusion or exclusion of grid lines, proper labeling of the axes, proper referencing of the source of data, and other features. When designing graphics, adhere to the requirements in your company policy manual or the style manual you are instructed to follow. Then be certain that you design graphics for a particular document or presentation consistently. When preparing a graphic for a slide show or mounted chart, remove the figure number and include the title only.

10-3a Tables

A **table** presents data in columns and rows, which aid in clarifying large quantities of data in a small space. Proper labeling techniques make the content clear. The guidelines for preparing an effective table follow and are illustrated in Figure 10.2.

> **table** a graphic that presents data in columns and rows, which aid in clarifying large quantities of data in a small space

Figure 10.1 | Choosing the Appropriate Graphic to Fit Your Objective

Graphic Type	Objective	Graphic Type	Objective
• Table 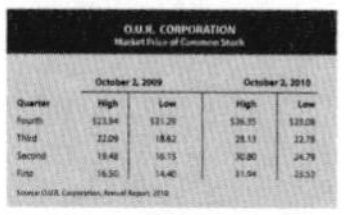	• To show exact figures	• Gantt chart 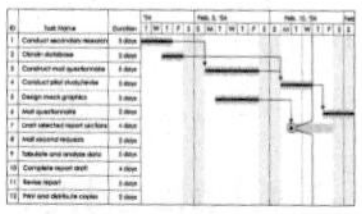	• To track progress toward completing a project
• Bar chart 	• To compare one quantity with another	• Map 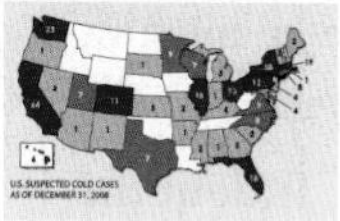	• To show geographic relationships
• Line chart 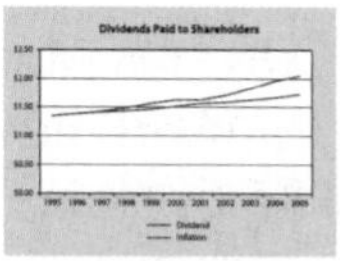	• To illustrate changes in quantities over time	• Flowchart 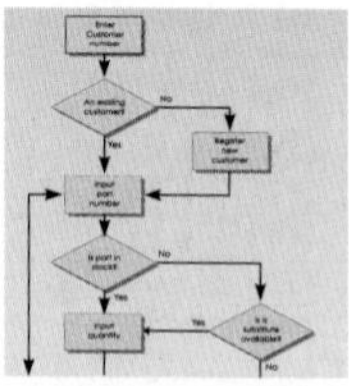	• To illustrate a process or procedure
• Pie chart 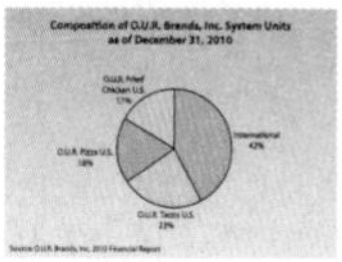	• To show how the parts of a whole are distributed	• Photograph 	• To provide a realistic view of a specific item or place

Rawpixel.com/Shutterstock

Note: Data presented in charts are fictional and for demonstration only.

E4   fx   =VLOOKUP(D4,IF(C4="UK",Table1,Table2),2,TRUE)

	A	B	C	D	E	F	G	H	I	J	K	L
1												
2							Table 1: UK Market			Table 2: USA Market		
3		Last Name	Market	Sales	Bonus		Sales	Bonus		Sales	Bonus	
4		Smith	UK	$5,171	$600		$0	$0		$0	$100	
5		Anderson	UK	$1,381	$0		$2,000	$400		$5,000	$1,000	
6		Clark	USA	$6,272	$1,000		$4,000	$600		$10,000	$1,500	
7		Lewis	UK	$9,168	$900		$6,000	$700				
8		Walker	USA	$10,366	$1,500		$8,000	$900				
9		Reed	UK	$7,375	$700		$10,000	$1,100				
10		Lopez	USA	$4,183	$100							
11												
12												

Source: Microsoft Corporation

Source: https://excelexamples.com/post/how-to-use-vlookup-function-in-excel/

- **Number tables and all other graphics consecutively throughout the report.** This practice enables you to refer to "Figure 1" rather than to "the following table" or "the figure on the following page."

- **Give each table a title that is complete enough to clarify what is included without forcing the reader to review the table.** Table titles can be quite long as they can contain sources of data, numbers included in the table, and the subject, as shown in Figure 10.2. Titles should be written in either all capitals or upper and lowercase letters. Titles that extend beyond one line should be arranged on the page so that they are balanced.

- **Label columns of data clearly enough to identify the items.** Usually, column headings are short and easily arranged. If, however, they happen to be lengthy, use some ingenuity in planning the arrangement.

- **Indent the second line of a label for the rows (horizontal items) two or three spaces.** Labels that are subdivisions of more comprehensive labels should be indented, as should summary labels such as "total."

- **Place a superscript symbol beside an entry that requires additional explanation, and include the explanatory note beneath the visual.**

- **Document the source of the data presented in a visual by adding a source note beneath the visual.** If more than one source was used to prepare a visual, use superscripts beside the various references and provide the sources beneath the figure.

10-3b Bar Charts

A **bar chart** is an effective graphic for comparing quantities (refer to Figure 10.3). The length of the bars, horizontal or vertical, indicates quantity. Vertical bars, as shown Figure 10.3a, are most commonly used. Because of the lengthy labels in Figure 10.3b, horizontal bars are ideal. Variations of the simple bar chart make it useful for a variety of purposes:

- **Grouped bar charts** (also called *clustered bar charts*) are useful for comparing more than one quantity.

- **Segmented bar charts** (also called *subdivided, stacked bar*, or *100 percent bar charts*) show how components contribute to a total figure. The segments in Figure 10.3c illustrate the composition of minerals in three samples.

- **Pictograms** (or pictographs) use pictures or symbols to illustrate objects, concepts, or numerical values. A simple use of a pictogram is a picture of an envelope used to represent an email message. Pictograms are common in everyday life, such as on signs in public places or roads, whereas the term *icon* is specific to interfaces on computers or other electronic devices. An image of a computer is used in Figure 10.3d to show computer sales in a company's first quarter.

bar chart a graphic used to compare quantities

grouped bar chart a graphic used for comparing more than one quantity (set of data) at each point along the *y*-axis (vertical) or *x*-axis (horizontal); also called a clustered bar chart

segmented bar chart a graphic used to show how different facts (components) contribute to a total; also called a subdivided, stacked bar, or 100 percent bar chart

pictogram a graphic that uses pictures or symbols to illustrate objects, concepts, or numerical relationships

Figure 10.3 | Variety of Bar Chart Formats

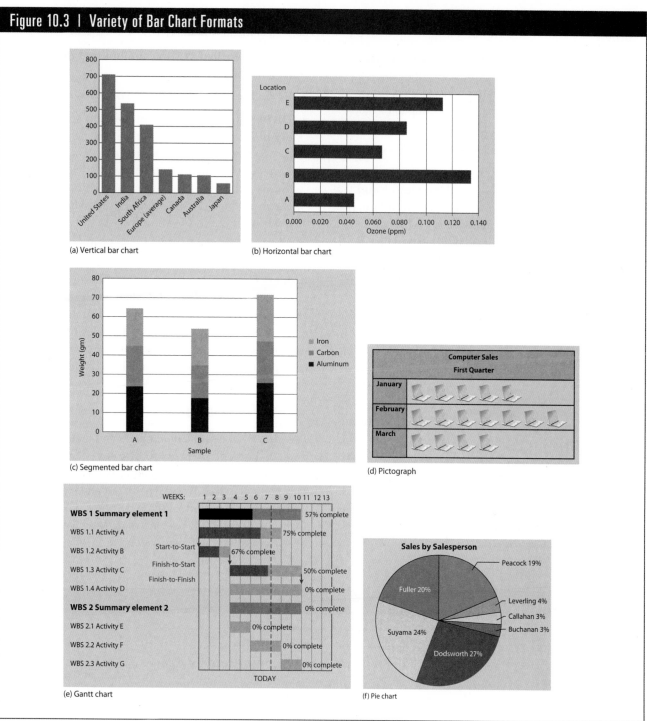

(a) Vertical bar chart

(b) Horizontal bar chart

(c) Segmented bar chart

(d) Pictograph

(e) Gantt chart

(f) Pie chart

Note: Data presented in charts are fictional and for demonstration only.

- The **Gantt chart**, another variation of the bar chart, is useful for tracking progress toward completing a series of events over time. The Gantt chart in Figure 10.3e shows the time spent on various activities necessary to complete a project. This version of the Gantt chart not only schedules the important activities required to complete this research but also plots the *actual* progress of each activity along with the *planned* progress. Simple Gantt charts can be created using a spreadsheet program such as Microsoft Excel.

In addition to the suggestions for developing tables, here are further suggestions related to constructing bar charts:

- **Avoid visual distortion that could exaggerate the data.** Begin the quantitative axis at zero, divide the bars into equal increments, and use bars of equal width.

> **Gantt chart** a specific type of bar chart that is useful for tracking progress toward completing a series of events over time

- **Position chronologically or in some other logical order.**
- **Use color to convey meaning.** For example, use variations in color to distinguish among the bars when the bars represent different data. Avoid large surfaces of bright colors that may be tiring to the audience and detract from the data.
- Avoid fancy formatting such as 3D that makes values more difficult to distinguish.
- **Keep the labeling simple to reduce clutter and increase readability.** Exclude nonessential information such as data labels, gridlines, and explanatory notes if the meaning is understood. To determine labeling needs, consider the audience's use of the data. Omit actual amounts if a visual estimate is adequate for understanding the relationships presented in the chart. Include the data values above the bars or in a data table for an audience who expects specific data.

10-3c Line Charts

> **line chart** a graphic that depicts changes in quantitative data over time and illustrates trends
>
> **area chart** a graphic that shows how different factors contribute to a total; also referred to as a cumulative line chart or surface chart
>
> **pie chart** a graphic that shows how the parts of a whole are distributed

A line chart depicts changes in quantitative data over time and illustrates trends. The line chart shown in Figure 10.4 shows the average income and rent

paid by age. When constructing line charts, keep these general guidelines in mind:

- **Use the vertical axis for amount and the horizontal axis for time.**
- **Begin the vertical axis at zero.**
- **Divide the vertical and horizontal scales into equal increments.** The vertical or quantity increments, however, need not be the same as the horizontal or time increments so that the line or lines drawn will have reasonable slopes. Unrealistic scales might produce startling slopes that could mislead readers.

An **area chart**, also called a *cumulative line chart* or a *surface chart*, is similar to a segmented bar chart because it shows how different factors contribute to a total. An area chart is especially useful when you want to illustrate changes in components over time. For example, the area chart in Figure 10.5 illustrates the sales of three products by month. A reader can easily recognize the sales of each product per month as well as the total profit of the organization.

10-3d Pie Charts

Pie charts, like segmented charts and area charts, show how the parts of a whole are distributed. Pie charts are effective for showing percentages (parts of a whole), but they are ineffective at showing quantitative totals or comparisons. Bars are used for those purposes. The pie chart in Figure 10.3f shows the percentage of total sales contributed by salesperson for an organization.

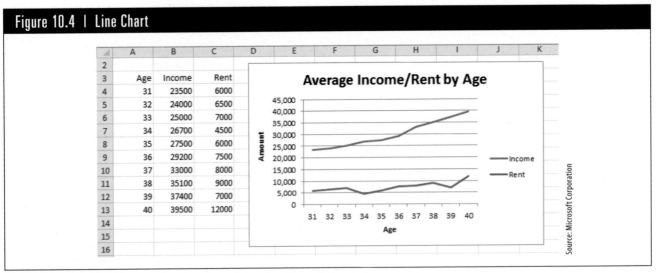

Figure 10.4 | Line Chart

Source: https://www.real-statistics.com/excel-environment/excel-charts/line-charts-multiple-series/

Figure 10.5 | Area Chart

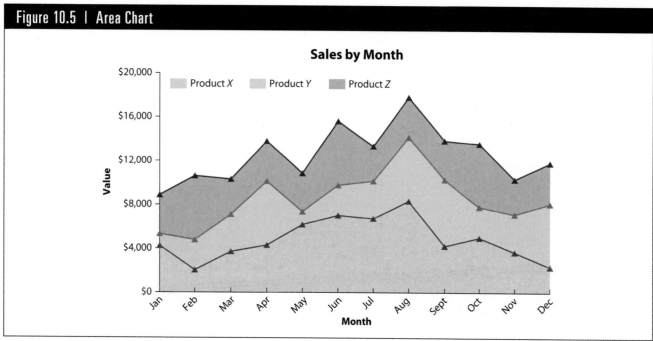

Source: https://jpowered.com/graphs-and-charts/gallery/2d-area-graph.html

Here are some general guidelines for constructing pie charts:

- **Position the largest slice, or the slice to be emphasized, at the 12 o'clock position.** Working clockwise, place the other slices in descending order of size or some other logical order of presentation.

- **Label each slice and include information about the quantitative size** (percentage, dollars, etc.) of each slice. If you are unable to attractively place the appropriate labeling information beside each slice, use a legend to identify each slice.

- **Draw attention to one or more slices for desired emphasis.** Special effects include exploding the slice(s) to be emphasized (i.e., removing it from immediate contact with the pie), or displaying or printing only the slice(s) to be emphasized.

- **Avoid using 3D-type formatting that makes values more difficult to distinguish.**

Your software may limit your ability to follow rules explicitly, and the nature of the data or the presentation may require slight deviations. For example, if you intend to explode the largest pie slice, placing it in the 12 o'clock position may not be desirable because the slice is likely to intrude into the space occupied by a title positioned above the graphic.

10-3e Maps

A **map** shows geographic relationships. This graphic type is especially useful when a receiver may not be familiar with the geography discussed in a report. The map shown in Figure 10.6 shows the net migration by county in the United States. The map gives the information visually and, thus, eliminates the difficulty of explaining the information in words. In addition to being less confusing, a map is more concise and interesting than a written message.

10-3f Flowcharts

A **flowchart** is a step-by-step diagram of a procedure, or a graphic depiction of a system or organization. A variety of problems can be resolved by using flowcharts to support written analyses. For example, most companies have procedure manuals to instruct employees in certain work tasks. Including a flowchart with written instructions minimizes the chance of errors. The flowchart in Figure 10.7 illustrates the steps in the customer service process.

> **map** a graphic that shows geographic relationships
>
> **flowchart** a step-by-step diagram of a procedure, or a graphic depiction of a system or organization

Figure 10.6 | Map Conveying Statistical Data

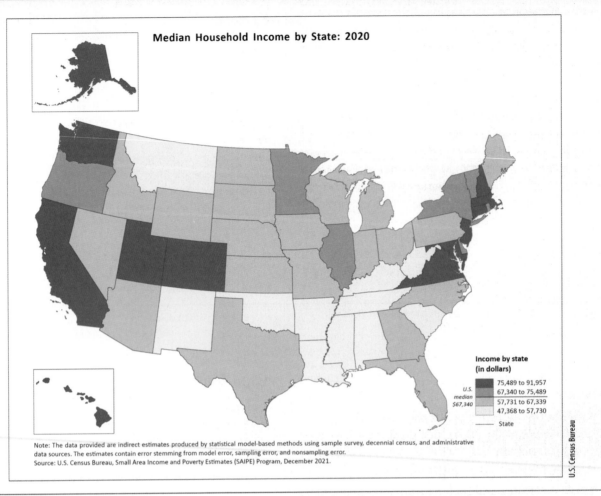

Median Household Income by State: 2020

Income by state
(in dollars)

75,489 to 91,957
67,340 to 75,489
57,731 to 67,339
47,368 to 57,730

U.S.
median
$67,340

State

Note: The data provided are indirect estimates produced by statistical model-based methods using sample survey, decennial census, and administrative data sources. The estimates contain error stemming from model error, sampling error, and nonsampling error.
Source: U.S. Census Bureau, Small Area Income and Poverty Estimates (SAIPE) Program, December 2021.

U.S. Census Bureau

Source: U.S. Census Bureau, 2007–2011 five-year American Community Survey. Retrieved February 17, 2022, from www.census.gov/data.html

Introducing Graphics in Text

The pattern for incorporating graphics in text is (1) introduce, (2) show, and (3) interpret and analyze. The following range of examples, from poor to best, explain how to introduce graphic and tabular material.

		Example	Rationale
✗	Poor:	Figure 1 shows preferences for shopping locations.	Poor because it tells the reader nothing more than would the title of the figure.
✓	Acceptable:	About two-thirds of the consumers preferred to shop in suburban areas rather than in the city (refer to Figure 1).	Acceptable because it interprets the data, but it places the figure reference in parentheses rather than integrating it into the sentence.
✓+	Better:	As shown in Figure 1, about two-thirds of the consumers preferred to shop in suburban areas rather than in the city.	Better than the previous examples but puts the reference to the figure at the beginning, thus detracting from the interpretation of the data.
✓++	Best:	About two-thirds of the consumers preferred to shop in suburban areas rather than in the city, as shown in Figure 1.	Best for introducing figures because it talks about the graphic and also includes introductory phrasing, but only after stressing the main point.

Figure 10.7 | Flowchart of the Customer Service Process

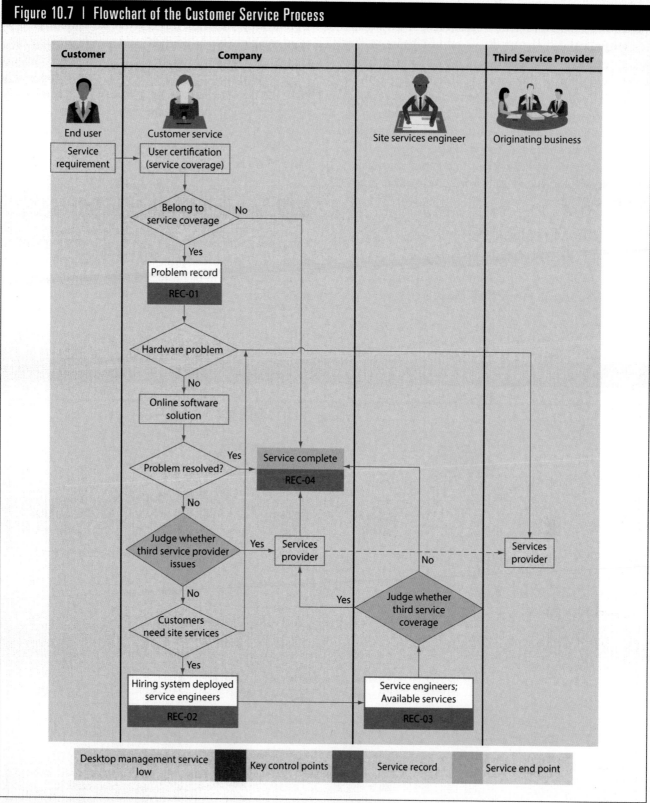

Source: https://www.edrawmax.com/flowchart/examples/

Presenting this information graphically makes it much easier to understand than a written explanation of the process.

Organizational charts, discussed in Chapter 1, are widely used to provide a picture of the authority structure and relationships within an organization. They provide employees with an idea of what their organization looks like in terms of the flow of authority and responsibility. When businesses change (because of new employees or reorganization of units and responsibilities), organizational charts must be revised. Revisions to organizational charts are simple when prepared using word-processing or graphics software.

10-3g Other Graphics

Other graphics, such as architectural plans, photographs, cartoons, blueprints, and lists of various kinds, may be included in reports. Figure 10.8 shows a blueprint of a computer network layout. The availability of graphics and sophisticated drawing software facilitate inclusion of these more complex visuals in reports and spoken presentations. Photographs are used frequently in annual reports to help the general audience understand complex concepts and to make the documents more appealing to read. Frequently, you must include some graphic material in a report; otherwise, the narrative discussion would become unwieldy. In this case, the material might be placed in an appendix and only referred to in the report.

10-4 Including Graphics in Text

Text and graphics are partners in the communication process. If graphics appear before readers have been informed, they will begin to study the graphics and draw their own inferences and conclusions. For this reason,

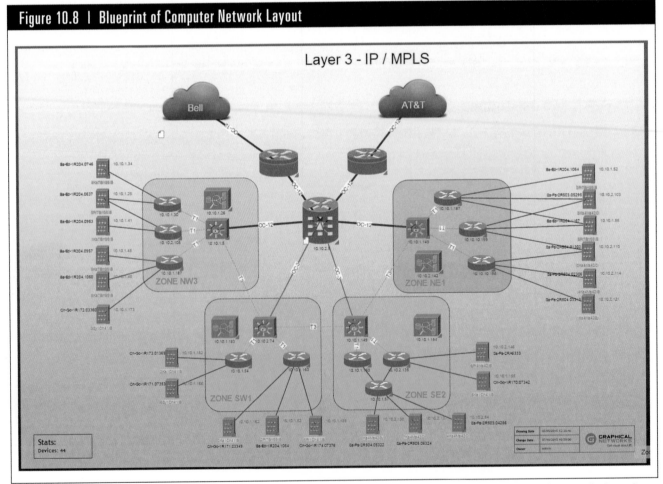

Figure 10.8 | Blueprint of Computer Network Layout

© Sherman, J/Graphical Networks LLC

Source: Sherman, J. (n.d.). The totally biased guide to documenting your network: what can be documented? Retrieved February 17, 2022, from https://graphicalnetworks .com/blog-the-totally-biased-guide-to-documenting-your-network-what-can-be-documented/

Consistency Counts

Throughout the discussion of tables and graphs, the term *graphics* has been used to include all illustrations. Although your report may include tables, graphs, maps, and even photographs, you will find organizing easier and writing about the illustrations more effective if you label each item as a "Figure" followed by a number; then number the items consecutively.

Some report writers prefer to label tables consecutively as "Table 1," and so on, and graphs and charts consecutively in another sequence as "Graph 1," and so on. When this dual numbering system is used, readers of the report may become confused if they come upon a sentence that reads, "Evidence presented in Tables 3 and 4 and Graph 2 supports. ..." Both writers and readers appreciate the single numbering system, which makes the sentence read, "Evidence presented in Figures 3, 4, and 5 supports. ..."

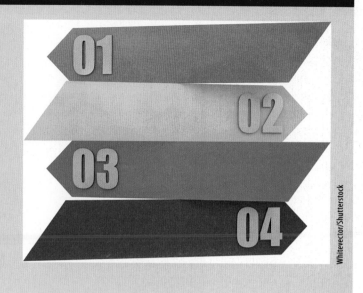

Whitevector/Shutterstock

always introduce a graphic in the text immediately before the graphic appears. A graphic that follows an introduction and brief explanation will supplement what has been said in the report. Additional interpretation and needed analysis should follow the graphic.

10-4a Positioning Graphics in Text

Ideally, a graphic should be integrated within the text material immediately after its introduction. A graphic that will not fit on the page where it is introduced should appear at the top of the following page. In this chapter, figures are placed as closely as possible to their introductions in accordance with these suggestions. However, in some cases, several figures may be introduced on one page, making perfect placement difficult and sometimes impossible.

When interpreting and analyzing the graphic, avoid a mere restatement of what the graphic obviously shows. Instead, emphasize the main point you are making. Contrast the boring style of the following discussion of graphic data with the improved revision:

Obvious Restatement of Data:	When asked to describe their customer service provided at the bookstore, 30 percent said the prices were too high, 21 percent responded lines were too long, and 18 percent wanted a larger variety of merchandise.
Emphasis on Main Point:	The most-cited customer service problem at the bookstore was high prices, while long lines and a need for more merchandise were also concerns. (Improved revision)

Your analysis may include summary statements about the data, compare information in the figure to information obtained from other sources, or extend the shown data into reasonably supported speculative outcomes. Strive to transition naturally from the discussion of the graphic into the next point you wish to make.

fizkes/Shutterstock.com

11 | Organizing and Preparing Reports and Proposals

Learning Objectives

After studying this chapter, you will be able to ...

11-1 Identify the parts of a formal report and the contribution each part makes to the report's overall effectiveness.

11-2 Organize report findings.

11-3 Prepare effective formal reports using an acceptable format and writing style.

11-4 Prepare effective short reports in memorandum, email, and letter formats.

11-5 Create effective proposals for a variety of purposes.

11-1 Parts of a Formal Report

Reports serve a variety of purposes; the type of report you prepare depends on the subject matter, the purpose of the report, and the readers' needs. The differences between a formal report and an informal report lie in the format and, possibly, the writing style. At the short, informal end of the report continuum described in Chapter 9, a report could look exactly like a brief memorandum. At the long, formal extreme of the continuum, the report might include most or all of the parts shown in Figure 11.1.

A business report rarely contains all of the parts shown but may include any combination of them. The preliminary parts and addenda are organizational items that support the body of a report. The body contains the report of the research and covers the four steps in the research process. The organization of the body of a report leads to the construction of the contents page.

Because individuals usually write to affect or influence others favorably, they often add report parts as the number of pages increases. When a report exceeds one or two pages, you might add a cover or title page. When the body of a report exceeds four or five pages, you might even add a finishing touch by placing the report in a binder or binding it in a professional manner. Reports frequently take on the characteristics of the formal end of the continuum simply by reason of length. First, note how the preliminary parts and addenda items shown in Figure 11.1 increase in number as the report increases in length. Second, notice the order in which report parts appear in a complete report and the distribution of reports in print and electronic forms.

Memo and letter reports are often one page in length, but they can be expanded into several pages. Long reports may include some special pages that do not appear in short reports. The format you select—long or short, formal or informal—may help determine the supporting preliminary and addenda items to include.

As discussed previously, automated reports completely eliminate traditional means of communicating data since they rely on business reporting software that uses cutting-edge business intelligence, technology, and smart features such as interactivity, a drag-and-drop interface, and predictive analytics, among others.

Reporting tools are beneficial because they gather data across sources (inventory, sales, conversion, web traffic, social media impressions, time spent, and so on) and then organize it in a visual way for users to read and interpret. Reports can typically be saved into different formats, printed and distributed, visualized, and presented, so it is a great way to convey large amounts of useful information quickly. Also, reporting allows you to ask big-picture questions and then collect the data you need to make the best decisions. Figure 11.3 provides an example of a sales report generate using datapine reporting software.

Figure 11.1 illustrates the parts of a formal report that is manually created. The three basic sections—preliminary parts, report text, and addenda—are combined to prepare a complete formal report.

Figure 11.1 | Parts of a Formal Report: Preliminary Parts, Report Text, and Addenda

Preliminary Parts

Half-title page (Title Fly)	Title page	Authorization	Transmittal	Table of contents	Table of figures	Executive summary
Contains the report title; adds formality.	Includes the title, author, and date; adds formality.	Provides written authorization to complete the report.	Presents the report to the reader and summarizes the main points or analysis.	Provides an overview of the report and order in which information will be presented; contains headings and page numbers.	Includes the number, title, and page number of tables and graphics.	Summarizes the essential elements in the report.

Report Text

Introduction	Body	Analysis
Orients the reader to the topic and previews the major divisions.	Presents the information collected.	Reviews the main points presented in the body and may include conclusions and recommendations.

Addenda

References	Appendix	Index
Includes an alphabetical list of sources used in preparing the report.	Contains supplementary information that supports report, but placing this information in the report would make the report bulky and unmanageable.	Includes an alphabetical guide to subjects in the report.

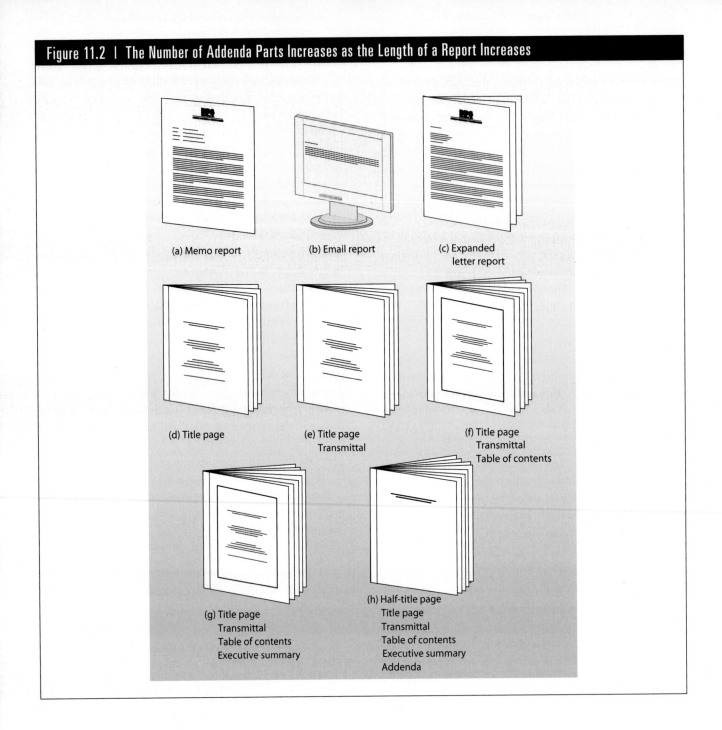

(a) Memo report

(b) Email report

(c) Expanded letter report

(d) Title page

(e) Title page
Transmittal

(f) Title page
Transmittal
Table of contents

(g) Title page
Transmittal
Table of contents
Executive summary

(h) Half-title page
Title page
Transmittal
Table of contents
Executive summary
Addenda

11-1a Preliminary Parts of a Report

Preliminary parts are included to add formality to a report, emphasize report content, and aid the reader in locating information in the report quickly and understanding the report more easily. These parts might include a half-title page, title page, authorization, transmittal, table of contents, table of figures, and executive summary. The most frequently used preliminary parts are described here.

> **preliminary parts** report sections included to add formality to a report, emphasize report content, and aid the reader in locating information in the report quickly and understanding the report more easily

Title Page

The title page includes the title, author, date, and often the name of the person or organization who requested the report. A title page is often added when opting for a formal report format rather than a memorandum or letter arrangement.

The selected title should be descriptive and comprehensive; its words should reflect the content of the report. Avoid short, vague titles or excessively long titles.

Figure 11.3 | Sales Report Generated Using Automated Reporting Software

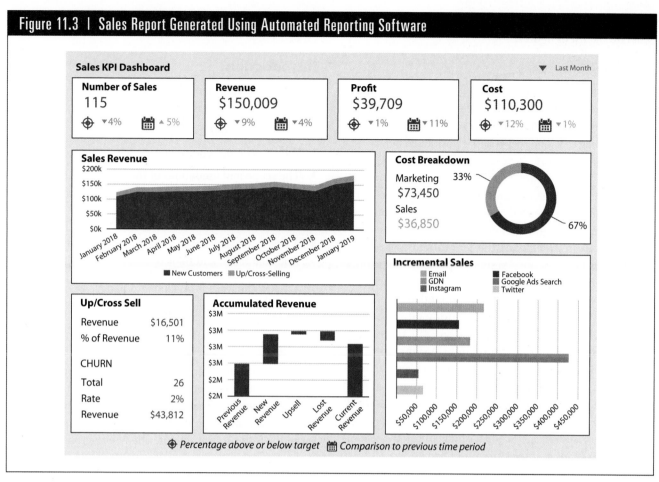

Source: Calzon, B. (2021). 34 sales reports examples you can use for daily, weekly, or monthly reports. Retrieved February 19, 2022 from https://www.datapine.com/blog/sales-report-kpi-examples-for-daily-reports/

Instead, use concise wording to identify the topic adequately. For example, a title such as "Marketing Survey: Internet Providers" leaves the reader confused when the title could have been "Internet Provider Preferences of the Residents of St. Louis." To give some clues on writing a descriptive title, think of the "five W's": *Who, What, When, Where,* and *Why.* Avoid such phrases as "A Study of …," "A Critical Analysis of …," or "A Review of. …"

Follow company procedures or consult a style manual to place the title attractively on the page. Arrange the title consistently on the half-title page, title page, and the first page of a report.

Table of Contents

The table of contents provides the reader with an analytical overview of the report and the order in which information is presented. Thus, this preliminary part aids the reader in understanding the report and in locating a specific section of it. The list includes the name and location (beginning page number) of every report part except those that precede the contents page. Include the list of

figures and the transmittal, executive summary, report headings, references, appendixes, and index. Placing spaced periods (leaders) between the report part and the page numbers helps lead the reader's eyes to the appropriate page number.

Word-processing software simplifies the time-consuming, tedious task of preparing many of the preliminary and addenda report parts, including the table of contents. Because the software can generate these parts automatically, report writers can make last-minute changes to a report with updated preliminary and addenda parts.

Table of Figures

To aid the reader in locating a specific graphic in a report with many graphics, the writer might include a list of figures separate from the contents. The list should include a reference to each figure that appears in the report, identified by both figure number and name, along with the page number on which the figure occurs. The contents and figures can be combined on one page if both lists are brief.

Word-processing software can be used to automatically generate the list of figures.

Executive Summary

The **executive summary** (also called the *abstract*, *overview*, or *précis*) summarizes the essential elements in an entire report. This overview simplifies the reader's understanding of a long report and is positioned before the first page of the report.

Typically, an executive summary is included to assist the reader in understanding a long, complex report. Because of the increased volume of information that managers must review, some of them require an executive summary regardless of the length and complexity of a report. The executive summary presents the report in miniature: the introduction, body, and summary as well as any conclusions and recommendations. Thus, an executive summary should (1) briefly introduce the report and preview the major divisions, (2) summarize the major sections of the report, and (3) summarize the report summary and any conclusions and recommendations. Pay special attention to topic sentences and to concluding sentences in paragraphs or within sections of reports. This technique helps you write concise executive summaries based on major ideas and reduces the use of supporting details and background information.

To assist them in staying up-to-date professionally, busy executives frequently request assistants to prepare executive summaries of articles they do not have time to read, and conferences and meetings they cannot attend. Many practitioner journals include an executive summary (abstract) of each article. The executive summary provides the gist of the article and alerts the executive to articles that should be read in detail. The executive summary is prepared with the needs of specific executive readers in mind. For example, a technically oriented executive may require more detail, whereas a strategist may require more analysis. An executive summary should "boil down" a report to its barest essentials without making the overview meaningless. Top executives should be able to glean enough information and understanding to feel confident about deciding.

Preliminary pages are numbered with small Roman numerals (i, ii, iii, etc.). Figure 11.1 provides more information about the purpose of each preliminary part.

executive summary short summary of the essential elements in an entire report; also called an *abstract*, *overview*, or *précis*

analytical report a type of report designed to solve a specific problem or answer research questions

11-1b Report Text

The report itself contains the introduction, body, summary, and any conclusions and recommendations.

Report pages are numbered with Arabic numerals (1, 2, 3, etc.).

Introduction

The introduction orients the reader to the problem. It may include the following information:

- What the topic is
- Why it is being reported on
- The scope and limitations of the research
- Where the information came from
- An explanation of special terminology
- A preview of the major sections of the report to provide coherence and transitions:
  - How the topic is divided into parts
  - The order in which the parts will be presented

Body

The body, often called the heart of the report, presents the information collected and relates it to the problem. To increase readability and coherence, this section contains numerous headings to denote the various divisions within a report. Refer to the section titled "Organization of Formal Reports" in this chapter for an in-depth discussion of preparing the body.

Analysis

A good report ends with an analysis of what the reported information means or how it should be acted upon. An informational report ends with a brief summary that adds unity to a report by reviewing the main points presented in the body. A summary includes only material that is discussed in a report. Introducing a new idea in the summary may suggest that the study was not completed adequately or that the writer did not plan the report well before beginning to write.

An **analytical report** is designed to solve a specific problem or answer research questions. It will end with an "analysis," which may include a summary of the major research findings, particularly if the report is lengthy. Reviewing the major findings prepares the reader for the conclusions, which are inferences that the writer draws from the findings. If required by the person/organization authorizing the report, recommendations follow the conclusions. Recommendations present the writer's opinion on a possible course of action based on the conclusions.

For a long report, the writer may place the summary, the conclusions, and the recommendations in three separate sections or in one section referred to as *analysis*. For shorter reports, all three sections are often combined.

11-1c Report Addenda

The **addenda** to a report may include materials used in the research that are not appropriate to be included in the report itself. The three basic addenda parts are the references, appendixes, and index. Addenda parts continue with the same page numbering system used in the body of the report.

References

The references (also called *works cited* or *bibliography*) section is an alphabetical listing of the sources used in preparing the report. Because the writer may be influenced by any information consulted, some reference manuals require all sources consulted to be included in the reference list. When the reference list includes sources not cited in the report, it is referred to as a *bibliography* or a list of *works consulted*. If a report includes endnotes rather than in-text parenthetical citations (author and date within the text), the endnotes precede the references. Using word-processing software to create footnotes and endnotes reduces much of the effort of preparing accurate documentation.

Appendix

An appendix contains supplementary information that supports the report but is not appropriate for inclusion in the report itself. This information may include questionnaires and accompanying transmittal letters, summary tabulations, verbatim comments from respondents, complex mathematical computations and formulas, legal documents, and a variety of items the writer presents to support the body of the report and the quality of the research. Placing supplementary material in an appendix helps prevent the report body from becoming excessively long.

If the report contains more than one appendix, label each with a capital letter and a title. For example, the two appendixes (or appendices) in a report could be identified as follows:

Appendix A: Customer Service Survey

Appendix B: Results of Customer Service Survey

Each item included in the appendix must be mentioned in the report. A reference within the report to the two appendixes mentioned in the previous example might appear as follows:

The survey (Appendix A) was distributed to customers on May 4, 2023. The tabulated results (Appendix B) were delivered to management on June 1.

Index

The index is an alphabetical guide to the subject matter in a report. The subject and each page number on which the subject appears are listed. Word-processing software can generate the index automatically. Each time a new draft is prepared, a new index with revised terms and correct page numbers can be generated quickly and easily.

11-2 Organization of Formal Reports

The authors of certain types of publications, known as tabloids, typically have no valid documentation to support their claims, so they make up their own support. Hopefully, absolutely no one believes them. The purpose of such publications is to entertain, not to inform. The writer of a bona fide report, however, must do a much more convincing and thorough job of reporting.

11-2a Writing Convincing and Effective Reports

As discussed in Chapter 9, reports often require you to conduct research to find quotes, statistics, or ideas from others to back up the ideas presented. This support from outside sources serves to bolster the research as well as your credibility. Doing research and taking notes, however, are only parts of the process of putting together a well-documented, acceptable report. Careful organization and formatting ensure that the reader will understand and comprehend the information presented. Although many companies have their own

addenda may include all materials used in the research but not appropriate to be included in the report itself

The Annual Report: Of all the documents corporations publish, none receives as much attention as the annual report. Offering a valuable glimpse into the workings and financial performance of companies, these annual scorecards guide investors' decisions. In addition to projecting profitability, many U.S. firms see the annual reports as a vehicle for illuminating prevailing management philosophy, projecting corporate charisma, and humanizing themselves to the public.

style manuals that give examples of acceptable formats for reports, this section presents some general organization guidelines.

Outlining and Sequencing

The content outline serves as a framework on which to build the report. In the development of the outline, the writer identifies the major and minor points that are to be covered and organizes them into a logical sequence. Outlining is an essential prerequisite to writing the report. The outline is a planning document and is, thus, subject to modification as the writer develops the report.

Developing an outline requires the writer to think about the information to be presented and how it can best be organized for the clear understanding of the reader. Assume, for example, your firm must decide whether to develop their own wellness program or contract with an outside provider. You need to research the steps and costs associated with developing your own program and compare them to the cost and benefits of a packaged service. Your analysis, along with your reasons and recommendations, will be delivered in a **justification report**.

You gather all available information about wellness programs and wellness program providers and compare the two against a list of criteria created by management. Your final selection is to contract with a program provider. Why did you select it? What criteria served as decision guides? When you write the report, you will have to tell the reader—the one who will pay for the provider—how the selection was made so that they are "sold" on your conclusion.

If you organize your report so that you tell the reader everything about the two options—in-house program versus outside provider—each in a separate section, the reader may have trouble making comparisons. Your content outline might look like this:

I. Introduction

    A. The Problem

    B. The Method Used

II. Automated Report Software 1

III. Automated Report Software 2

IV. Conclusion

Note that this outline devotes two Roman numeral sections to the findings, one to the introduction that presents the problem and the method, and one to the conclusion. This division is appropriate because the most space must be devoted to the findings.

> **justification report** a report that outlines comparative information clearly to the reader; used commonly when comparing items for purchase

However, the reader may have difficulty comparing the two options because the information is in two different places. Would discussing the differences in the options in the same section of the report be better? Would costs be compared more easily if they were all in the same section? Most reports should be divided into sections that reflect the criteria used rather than into sections devoted to the alternatives compared.

If you selected your service based on cost, quality, services available, and time to implement, these criteria, rather than the wellness options themselves, might serve as divisions of the findings. Then, your content outline would appear this way:

I. Introduction

    A. The Problem

    B. The Methods Used

II. Product Comparison

    A. Automated Report Software 1 Is Least Expensive

    B. Automated Report Software 1 Provides Greater Functionality

    C. Automated Report Software 1 Is Easier to Use

    D. Automated Report Software 1 Provides Better Technical Support

III. Conclusion: Automated Report Software 1 Is the Best Choice

The outline now has three major sections, with the product comparison consisting of four subsections. When the report is prepared in this way, the features of each wellness approach (the evaluation criteria) are compared in the same section, and the reader is led logically to the conclusion.

Note the headings used in Sections II and III. These are called *talking headings* because they talk about the content of the section and even give a conclusion about the section. Adding page numbers after each outline item will convert the outline into a contents page. Interestingly, the headings justify the selection of an outside provider. As a result, a knowledgeable reader who has confidence in the researcher might be satisfied by reading only the content headings.

In addition to organizing findings for analytical reports by criteria, report writers can also use other organizational plans. When a report is informational and not analytical, you should use the most logical organization. A report on sales might be divided by geographic sales region, by product groups sold, by price range, or by time periods. A report on the development of a product might use chronological order. By visualizing the whole report first, you can then divide it into its major components and, perhaps, divide the major components into their parts.

When developing content outlines, some report writers believe that readers expect the beginning of the body to be an introduction, so they begin the outline with the first heading related to findings. In our example then, Section I would be "Product Comparison." Additionally, when they reach the contents page, writers may eliminate the Roman numeral or other outline symbols.

The research process consists of inductively arranged steps as shown in Figure 11.4: (1) Problem, (2) Method, (3) Findings, and (4) Conclusion. Note how the four steps of research have been developed through headings in the Roman numeral outline and in a contents page for a report. When the report is organized in the same order, its users must read through the body to learn about the conclusions—generally the most important part of the report to users. To make the reader's job easier, report writers may organize the report deductively, with the conclusions at the beginning. This sequence is usually achieved by placing a synopsis or summary at the beginning:

 I. Conclusion Reported in the Synopsis

 II. Body of the Report

  A. Problem

  B. Method

  C. Findings

 III. Conclusion

This arrangement permits the reader to get the primary message early and then to look for support in the body of the report. The deductive arrangement contributes to the repetitious nature of reports, but it also facilitates understanding.

Using Headings Effectively

Headings are signposts informing readers about what text is ahead. Headings take their positions from their relative importance in a complete outline. For example, in a Roman numeral outline, "I" is a first-level heading, "A" is a second-level heading, and "1" is a third-level heading:

 I. First-Level Heading

  A. Second-Level Heading

  B. Second-Level Heading

   1. Third-Level Heading

   2. Third-Level Heading

 II. First-Level Heading

Two important points about the use of headings also relate to outlines:

- **Because second-level headings are subdivisions of first-level headings, you should have at least two subdivisions (A and B).** Otherwise, the first-level heading cannot be divided—something divides into at least two parts, or it is not divisible. Thus, in an outline, you must have a "B" subsection if you have an "A" subsection following a Roman numeral, or you should have no subsections. The same logic applies to the use of third-level headings following second-level headings.

- **All headings of the same level must be treated consistently.** Consistent elements include the physical position on the page, appearance (type style, underline,

Figure 11.4 | The Basic Outline Expands into a Contents Page

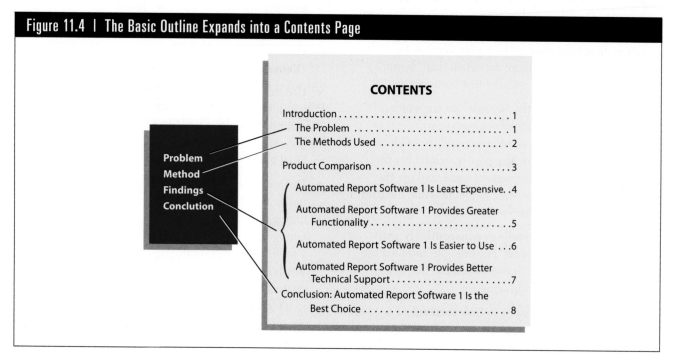

CONTENTS

Introduction 1
 The Problem 1
 The Methods Used 2

Product Comparison 3
 Automated Report Software 1 Is Least Expensive. .4
 Automated Report Software 1 Provides Greater Functionality 5
 Automated Report Software 1 Is Easier to Use . . .6
 Automated Report Software 1 Provides Better Technical Support 7
Conclusion: Automated Report Software 1 Is the Best Choice 8

Problem
Method
Findings
Conclution

etc.), and grammatical construction. For example, if Point A is worded as a noun phrase, Point B should be worded in the same manner. Or if Point I is a complete sentence, Points II and III should also be worded as sentences.

The method illustrated in Figure 11.4 is typical but not universal. Always identify the format specified by the documentation style that you are using and follow it consistently. Develop fourth- and fifth-level headings simply by using boldface, underline, and varying fonts. In short reports, however, organization rarely goes beyond third-level headings; thoughtful organization can limit excessive heading levels in formal reports.

11-3 Choosing a Writing Style for Formal Reports

As stated previously, the writing style of long, formal reports is more formal than that used in many other routine business documents. The following suggestions should be applied when writing a formal report:

- **Avoid first-person pronouns as a rule.** In formal reports, the use of *I* is generally unacceptable. Because of the objective nature of research, the fewer personal references you use, the better. However, in some organizations, the first person is acceptable. Certainly, writing is easier when you can use yourself as the subject of sentences.

- **Use active voice.** "Acceptance was received from the seller" might not be as effective as "The seller accepted the offer." Subjects that can be visualized are advantageous, but you should also attempt to use the things most important to the report as subjects. If "acceptance" were more important than "buyer," the writer should stay with the first version.

- **Use tense consistently.** Because you are writing about past actions, much of your report writing is in the past tense. However, when you call the reader's attention to the content of a graphic, remember that the graphic *shows* in the present tense, and use the future-tense verb if you want to mention that the study *will convince* the reader.

- **Avoid placing two headings consecutively without any intervening text.** For example, always write something following a first-level heading and before the initial second-level heading.

- **Use transition sentences to link sections of a report.** Because you are writing a report in parts, show the connection between those parts by using transition

sentences. "Although some customers may like the new sales program, many will not like the changes" may be a sentence written at the end of a section stressing advantages before transitioning to a section stressing problems.

- **Use a variety of coherence techniques.** Just as transition sentences bind portions of a report together, certain coherence techniques bind sentences together: repeating a word, using a pronoun, or using a conjunction. If such devices are used, each sentence seems to be joined smoothly to the next. The following words and phrases keep you from making abrupt changes in thought:

Time Connectors	Contrast Connectors
• at the same time	• although
• finally	• despite
• further	• however
• initially	• in contrast
• next	• nevertheless
• since	• on the contrary
• then	• on the other hand
• while	• yet

Similarity Connectors	Cause-and-Effect Connectors
• for instance/example	• alternately
• in the same way	• because
• just as	• but
• likewise	• consequently
• similarly	• hence
• thus	• therefore

Other ways to improve transitions include the following:

- **Use tabulations and enumerations.** When you have a series of items, bullet them or give each a number and list them consecutively. This list of writing suggestions is easier to understand because it contains bulleted items.

- **Define terms carefully.** When terms are not widely understood or have specific meanings in the study, define them. Definitions should be written in the term-family-differentiation sequence: "A dictionary (*term*) is a reference book (*family*) that contains a list of all the words in a language (*point of difference*)." "Within the context of this report, a sophomore is a college student in their second year."

- **Check for variety.** In your first-draft stage, most of your attention should be directed toward presenting the right ideas and support. When reviewing the rough draft, you may discover certain portions with a monotonous sameness in sentence length or construction. Changes and improvements in writing style at this stage are easy and well worth the effort.

11-3a Enhancing Credibility

Readers are more likely to accept your research as valid and reliable if you have designed the research effectively and collected, interpreted, and presented the data in an objective, unbiased manner. The following writing suggestions will enhance your credibility as a researcher:

- **Avoid emotional terms.** "The program was fantastic" doesn't convince anyone. However, "The program saw an increase of 18 percent over that of the previous year" does convince.

- **Identify assumptions.** Assumptions are things or conditions that are taken for granted. However, when you assume, state this clearly. Statements such as "Assuming all other factors remain the same …" inform the reader of important assumptions.

- **Label opinions.** Facts are preferred over opinion, but sometimes the opinion of a recognized professional is the closest thing to fact. "In the opinion of legal counsel …" lends conviction to the statement that follows and lends credence to the integrity of the writer.

- **Use documentation.** Citations and references (works cited) are evidence of the writer's scholarship and honesty. These methods acknowledge the use of secondary material in the research.

11-4 Short Reports

Short reports incorporate many of the same organizational strategies as long reports. However, most **short reports** include only the minimum supporting materials to achieve effective communication. Short reports focus on the body—problem, method, findings, and conclusion. In addition, short reports might incorporate any of the following features:

- Personal writing style using first or second person

- Contractions when they contribute to a natural style

- Graphics to reinforce the written text

- Headings and subheadings to partition portions of the body and to reflect organization

- Memorandum, email, and letter formats when appropriate

11-4a Memorandum, Email, and Letter Reports

Short reports are often written in memorandum, email, or letter format. The memorandum report is directed to an organizational insider, as are most email reports. The letter report is directed to a reader outside the organization. Short reports to internal and external readers are illustrated in Model Documents 11.1 and 11.2. The commentary in the right column will help you understand how effective writing principles are applied.

The memo report in Model Document 11.1 communicates a biannual report on computer sales. The periodic report is formatted as a memorandum because it is prepared for personnel within the organization and is a brief, informal report. An outside auditing firm presents an audit in the short report in Model Document 11.2.

The report in Model Document 11.3 is written deductively. Recommendations for the purchase of voice recognition software are described in an expanded letter report written by a consultant to a client (external audience). The consultant briefly describes the requirements of the system, presents the findings in a logical sequence, and provides specific recommendations.

11-4b Form Reports

Form reports meet the demand for numerous, repetitive reports. College registration forms, applications for credit, airline tickets, and bank checks are examples of simple form reports. Form reports have the following benefits:

- When designed properly, form reports increase clerical accuracy by providing designated places for specific items.

- Forms save time by telling the preparer where to put each item and by preprinting common elements to eliminate the need for narrative writing.

- In addition to their advantages of accuracy and saving time, forms make tabulation of data relatively simple. The value of the form is uniformity.

Most form reports, such as a bank teller's cash sheet, are informational. At the end of the teller's work period, cash is counted and totals are entered in designated blanks. Cash reports from all tellers are then totaled to arrive at period totals and, perhaps, to be verified by computer records.

short reports reports that include only the minimum supporting materials to achieve effective communication

form reports reports that meet the demand for numerous, repetitive reports; include college registration forms, applications for credit, airline tickets, and bank checks

To:	Sandy Landers, Jr., President
From:	Jerad Williams, Sales Manager
Date:	August 23, 2023
Subject:	Biannual Sales Report

Sales for the month remained at about the same level as the previous months this year at $221,300. Sales figures for the month by item are as follows:

Model	Quantity Sold	Total Revenue from Sales ($)
Laptops	91	63,700
Desktops	25	15,000
Tablets	162	64,800
Notebooks	103	61,800
Monitors	64	16,000
Total	445	221,300

In terms of our marketing efforts, we sent email alerts to our previous customers notifying them of our monthly specials on computer products. These specials were also highlighted on our web and Facebook pages. As such, we incurred no costs for advertising other than the time incurred by our web page manager to design these messages. We continue to employ two full-time salespeople on the floor and two part-time salespersons to cover the weekend shift. Current staffing levels are sufficient for the current sales volume. Like other "brick-and-mortar" retail outlets, we continue to feel increased competition from online competitors. If company goals include growing the sales of computer products, we need to increase our online presence to more effectively compete head-to-head with these operations and/or strategize ways of drawing more customers to our store who complete sales transactions.

The attached document provides a more detailed breakdown of product sales by model and maker. This data will be used to determine our product promotions for next month. We continue to work with our suppliers on pricing strategies to maintain our competitiveness with online rivals.

Attachment

Includes headings that serve the formal report functions of transmittal and title page.

Uses a deductive approach to present a periodic report requested by management on a weekly basis.

Uses table to highlight standard information; allows for an easy update when preparing subsequent reports.

Attaches an information page that would be an appendix item in a formal report.

Format Pointer:
Uses memorandum format for brief periodic report prepared for personnel within the company.

In addition to their informational purpose, form reports assist in analytical work. A residential appraisal report assists real estate appraisers in analyzing real property. With this information, the appraiser is able to determine the market value of a specific piece of property.

Many form reports are computer-generated. For example, an automated hospital admission process expedites the repetitive patient reports that must be created. The admission clerk inputs the patient information using the carefully designed input screen. If the patient has been admitted previously, the patient's name, address, and telephone number are displayed automatically for the clerk to verify. When the clerk inputs the patient's date of birth, the computer calculates the patient's age, eliminating the need to ask a potentially sensitive question and ensuring accuracy when patients cannot remember their ages.

Swopes Outdoor Center Cash Controls

Parks and Recreation Department

Introduction

The Parks and Recreation Department oversees the activities of the Swopes Outdoor Center located in Swopes Park. The Center and the adjacent grounds can be rented for a variety of services including picnics, parties, weddings, receptions, barbeques, meetings, and sporting events. Rental fees vary depending on the rented area, duration of use, number of people, equipment used, and whether alcohol is served.

The Park consists of 1,400 acres of park land with about 37 miles of trails to run, bike, walk, hike, or ski. Many programs and events are held throughout the year at the park, and fees may be charged for services, such as park use, equipment rental, and instructional programs.

Objective and Scope

The objective of this audit was to determine if the Center had proper cash controls in place and if these controls were in compliance with Municipal Policy and Procedure (P&P) 24-I, Collecting, Securing, Depositing, and Reporting Cash. Our audit included a surprise cash count and a review of cash controls. In addition, we selected a sample of cash receipts and reviewed backup documentation for compliance and accuracy. Finally, we reviewed permit and class documentation to determine if the Center had properly accounted for revenue.

The audit was conducted in accordance with generally accepted government auditing standards, except for the requirement of an external quality control review, and accordingly, included tests of accounting records and other such auditing processes.

Overall Evaluation

Cash control procedures at the Center were generally satisfactory and revenue was properly accounted for. However, the safe key and combination were not properly secured, and a $100 change fund was short $22.

Findings and Recommendations

1. Cash Control Procedures Not Always in Compliance with P&P 24-1.

    a. Finding. Cash control procedures at the Center did not always comply with P&P 24-1. Noncompliance with applicable policies and procedures may weaken the cash control environment and may result in possible irregularities. Specifically, we found the following:

        ◦ Safe key and combination not secured. The safe key and combination were not properly secured. Specifically, the safe key was found in a basket sitting on top of a microwave oven, which was above the safe. The key was attached to a large key ring labeled "Safe Key." In addition, the safe combination was found in an unlocked box mounted on a wall above the safe. According to Center staff, the safe key was left in the basket overnight, and the box was never locked.

        ◦ Change fund not safeguarded. During a follow-up surprise cash count, we found that a $100 change fund, recently placed in the safe, was short $22. Staff were unable to explain why the change fund was short $22.

    b. Recommendation. The Department's Director should ensure that cash controls at the Center comply with P&P 24-1.

    c. Management comments. Management stated, "Management concurs and has taken immediate steps to correct deficiencies, and redefine roles and requirements of staff to meet P&P 24-1."

    d. Evaluation of management comments. Management comments were responsive to the audit finding and recommendation.

Discussion with responsible officials. The results of this audit were discussed with appropriate Municipal officials on June 3, 2023.

Audit Staff:

Laura Linney

June 23, 2023

Dr. Jonathan Franks

1660 Main Street

Kansas City, MO 77539

Dear Dr. Franks:

Recommendations and Comparison for Voice Recognition Software

Administrators have long searched for alternatives to the expense, error rate, and record-completion delays associated with conventional transcription. It is no wonder that, with the recent advances in voice recognition software, medical transcriptionists are looking at this emerging technology as a powerful way of accomplishing essential record-keeping tasks.

This report investigates four of the leading voice recognition applications to determine whether this technology is a practical option for your business and, if so, to determine which application is the best choice.

Requirements for the Purchase of Voice Recognition Software

Based upon stated preferences and system specifications, the following conditions have been established:

- Continuous speech recognition software is preferred, rather than the slower, more unnatural, and lower-priced discrete speech recognition software also on the market.

- The application must run on a Intel-powered PC under Windows 10 and be capable of integration with Microsoft Word 2019.

- The software program must be easily and successfully installed by any intermediate-level computer user in the office.

- The program must be one that can be learned and customized reasonably quickly by nearly anyone in the office.

- The cost limit is $1,500.

Points of Comparison

The different voice recognition software programs compared are Dragon Home, IBM Watson Speech to Text, L&H Voice Xpress Plus, and Philips SpeechLive. Discussion of Dragon Home will also include its Medical One.

Six categories of comparison will be made effectively evaluate these competing programs: (1) accuracy; (2) minimum system requirements; (3) capacity to manage a specialized medical vocabulary and medical records; (4) integration with Microsoft Word; (5) ease and speed of installation, customization, and use; and (6) cost.

Accuracy. Accuracy is the single most significant consideration; without it, the program is useless. Dragon Home 15 scored 99 percent accuracy when it comes to transcribing spoke words.

Average accuracy for Philips SpeechLive was 99 percent, L&H Voice Xpress was 98 percent, and IBM's Watson Speech to Text tested at 95 percent.

Minimum system requirements. All four programs run on Intel-powered PC's utilizing Windows 10 and require 16-bit Sound Blaster-compatible sound cards.

It is important to recall that, as noted earlier, significantly greater system resources are recommended to optimize performance. Given the sufficient system resources, none of these software programs should present a problem for the existing system.

Capacity to manage a customizable, specialized medical vocabulary. Medicine, in general, and each medical specialty, in particular, have their own complex, specialized vocabularies.

- Dragon Home offers a so-called Medical One targeted to medical professionals and is specified as an alternative to transcription. Marketing materials state that an extensive vocabulary of thousands of words, including medical procedures, terms, drugs, diagnoses, and symptoms, are included. The software allows for the creation of multiple vocabularies for specialty customization, if desired.

- IBM and Philips offer medical speech recognition as separate services.

- L&H Voice Xpress Philips does not offer medical vocabularies, either as add-ons or bundled with the software.

Integration with Microsoft Word. All four programs integrate with Word 2019 and can, therefore, be used with existing word-processing software.

Ease and speed of installation, customization, and use. Each of the four programs uses "wizards" to install and configure hardware, and all programs support macros for frequently used phrases.

Installation of all of the programs appears straightforward, and the initial basic "training" is not excessively time-consuming for any of the products. While all provide macros, the medical customization features of Dragon Home's product are considerably greater. Though they will initially require more time and document input, accuracy is increased, and for this reason, Dragon's software is recommended in this comparison.

Cost. Significant price differences exist among these programs. L&H offers the best price by far. IBM and Philips are roughly in the same ballpark. Dragon Home is more expensive at $200 but not significantly so. The only customizable medical software program is Dragon Home Medical One, which is a subscription-based product at about $99 per month.

Recommendation

Dragon Home Medical One is strongly recommended for its superior accuracy, powerful customization features, and industry recognition and awards. No other product comes close, and its strong advantages justify its higher price. Once the program has been customized, and the user has dictated for several weeks and become familiar with the software, acceptably accurate transcription, and instantly available medical records should be possible with Medical One; thereby, solving some of the record-keeping problems faced by your medical practice.

Thank you for the opportunity to provide this information concerning voice recognition software for medical transcription. Please let us know how we can assist you further with this project or with other related matters.

Sincerely,

Francis Williams, Consultant

Format Pointers:

- **Letterhead and letter address function as title page and transmittal.**

- **Uses deductive approach to present main idea to recipient.**

- **Uses heading to denote major division of body.**

- **Uses bulleted list to emphasize important information.**

All data are stored in a computer file and retrieved as needed to generate numerous reports required during a patient's stay, such as the admissions summary sheet, admissions report, pharmacy profile, and even the addressograph used to stamp each page of the patient's record and the identification arm band.

Using the computer to prepare each report in the previous example leads to higher efficiency levels and minimizes errors because recurring data are entered only once. Preparing error-free form reports is a critical public relations tool because even minor clerical errors may cause patients or customers to question the organization's ability to deliver quality service. The "Check Your Communication" section on the Chapter 11 Review Card provides a comprehensive checklist for use in preparing effective reports.

11-5 Proposals

Managers prepare **internal proposals** to justify or recommend purchases or changes in the company; for example, installing a new computer system, introducing telecommuting or other flexible work schedules, or reorganizing the company into work groups. An **external proposal**, as described in Chapter 9, is a written description of how one organization can meet the needs of another by, for example, providing products or services. Written to generate business, external proposals are a critical part of the successful operation of many companies.

Proposals may be solicited or unsolicited. **Solicited proposals** are invited and initiated when a potential customer or client submits exact specifications or needs in a bid request or a request for proposal, commonly referred to as an *RFP*. Governmental agencies, such as the Department of Education, solicit proposals and place orders and contracts based on the most desirable proposal. The bid request or RFP describes a problem to be solved and invites respondents to describe their proposed solutions.

An **unsolicited proposal** is prepared by an individual or firm who sees a problem to be solved and submits a solution. For example, a business consultant is a regular customer at a family-owned retail store. On numerous occasions she has attempted to purchase an item that was out of stock. Recognizing that stock shortages decrease sales and profits, she prepares a proposal to assist the business in designing a computerized perpetual inventory with an automatic reordering system. For the business to accept the proposal, the consultant must convince the business that the resulting increase in sales and profits will more than offset the cost of the computer system and the consulting fee.

> **internal proposals** proposals used by managers to justify or recommend purchases or changes in the company
>
> **external proposal** a proposal written to generate business; one organization describes how it can meet the needs of another by, for example, providing a product or service
>
> **solicited proposals** proposals generated when a potential buyer submits exact specifications or needs in a bid request
>
> **unsolicited proposal** a proposal prepared by an individual or a firm who sees a problem to be solved and proposes a solution

11-5a Proposal Structure

A proposal includes (1) details about the manner in which the problem will be solved and (2) the price to be charged or the costs to be incurred. Often, the proposal is a lengthy report designed to "sell" the prospective buyer on the ability of the bidder to perform. However, a simple price quotation also constitutes a proposal in response to a request for a price quotation.

The format of a proposal depends on the length of the proposal and the intended audience:

Format	Proposal Length and Intended Audience
• Memo or email report	• Short; remains within the organization
• Letter report	• Short; travels outside the organization
• Formal report	• Long; remains within the organization or travels outside the organization

Most work resulting from proposals is covered by a working agreement or contract to avoid discrepancies in the intents of the parties. In some cases, for example, users of outside consultants insist that each consultant be covered by a sizable general personal liability insurance policy that also insures the company. Many large firms and governmental organizations use highly structured procedures to ensure understanding of contract terms.

The following general parts, or variations of them, might appear as headings in a proposal: (1) Problem or Purpose, (2) Scope, (3) Methods or Procedures, (4) Materials and Equipment, (5) Qualifications, (6) Follow-up and/or Evaluation, (7) Budget or Costs, (8) Summary, and (9) Addenda. In addition to these parts, a proposal might include preliminary report parts, such as the title page, transmittal message, and contents, as well as addenda parts, such as references, appendix, and index.

Problem and/or Purpose

Problem and purpose are often used as interchangeable terms in reports. Here is the introductory purpose statement, called "Project Description," in a proposal by a firm to construct a commercial building:

> *Project Description: To redesign company website to improve lead generation by 25 percent. To complete this work, it will be necessary to meet with stakeholders to access project contingencies and risks. As part of the redesign, existing documents will need to be archived and multidepartment training will need to be provided after the redesign is complete.*

Note how the heading "Project Description" has been used in place of "Purpose." In the following opening statement, "Problem" is used as the heading:

> *Problem: Determining how well employees meet organizational goals and identifying appropriate rewards for meeting these goals can be challenging. This report will examine the benefits of using our human resources*

software system to track and measure employees' behaviors and outcomes to ensure your organization is on the path of success.

The purpose of the proposal may be listed as a separate heading (in addition to "Problem") when the proposal intends to include objectives of a measurable nature. When you list objectives, such as "To reduce overall expenses for compensation management by 10 percent," attempt to list measurable and attainable objectives, and list only enough to accomplish the purpose of selling your proposal. Many proposals are rejected simply because writers promise more than they can actually deliver.

Scope

When determining the scope of your proposal, you can place limits on what you propose to do, or on what the material or equipment you sell can accomplish. The term *scope* need not necessarily be the only heading for this section. "Areas Served," "Limitations to the Study," and "Where (*specify topic*) Can Be Used" are examples of headings that describe the scope of a proposal. Here is a "Scope" section from a consulting firm's proposal to conduct a marketing study.

What the Study Will Cover: To assist Ginger Sensations in formulating a marketing strategy, Thomsen Consulting will provide an analysis of all competitors in the natural ingredient body moisturizer business, including their sales, target market, and promotion and distribution methods. In addition, Thomsen will provide an analysis of the market potential for Ginger Sensations' unique product given the competition, product trends, and the target market for the product. Finally, Thomsen will provide recommendations for distribution, promotion, and placement of Ginger Sensations' line of moisturizing products based on its analysis.

Another statement of scope might be as follows:

Scope: This report will examine employment trends for the past five years for the information technology (IT) specialists in the United States and Canada; and will use this data to provide recommendations to Western Data Systems to help it plan future staffing strategies.

Methods and/or Procedures

The method(s) used to solve the problem or to conduct the business of the proposal should be spelled out in detail. In this section, simply think through all the steps necessary to meet the terms of the proposal and write them in sequence. When feasible, you should include a time schedule for implementation of the project.

Materials and Equipment

For large proposals, such as construction or research and development, indicate the nature and quantities of materials and equipment to be used. In some cases, several departments will contribute to this section. When materials and equipment constitute a major portion of the total cost, include prices. Much litigation arises when clients are charged for "cost overruns." When contracts are made on the basis of "cost plus XX percent," the major costs of materials, equipment, and labor/personnel must be thoroughly described and documented.

Qualifications

Assuming your proposal is acceptable in terms of services to be performed or products to be supplied, your proposal must convince the potential buyer that you have the expertise to deliver what you have described and that you are a credible individual or company. Therefore, devote a section to presenting the specific qualifications and special expertise of the personnel involved in the proposal. You may include past records of the bidder and the recommendations of its past customers, and the proposed cost. Note how the brief biography of the principal member in the following excerpt from a proposal contributes to the credibility of the proposer:

Rodney Erickson is a content marketing professional at Marcom, an inbound marketing and sales platform that helps companies attract visitors, convert leads, and close customers. Previously, Rodney worked as a marketing manager for a tech software startup. He graduated with honors from Columbia University with a dual degree in Business Administration and Creative Writing. He had his highly trained team leverage their combined 15 years of experience in social media marketing to design web-based platforms that best meet each client's needs.

In another related section, the proposal might mention other work performed:

Major Clients: Palace Shopping Plaza, Duluth, Minnesota; eLearning Inc., Lansing, Michigan; Surf, Skate, and Ski, Chicago, IL; Minnesota State Teachers' Association, Minneapolis, Minnesota; and CompuTation Software, Corp., Dayton, Ohio. Personal references are available on request.

Follow-Up and/or Evaluation

Although your entire proposal is devoted to convincing the reader of its merit, clients are frequently concerned about what will happen when the proposed work or service is completed. Will you return to make certain your work is satisfactory? Can you adjust your method of research as times change?

If you propose to conduct a study, do not promise more than you can deliver. Not all funded research proves to be successful. If you propose to prepare a study in your firm's area of expertise, you may be more confident. A public accounting firm's proposal to audit a company's records need not be modest. The accountant follows certain audit functions that are prescribed by the profession. However, a proposal that involves providing psychological services probably warrants a thoughtful follow-up program to evaluate the service.

Budget or Costs

The budget or costs of the program should be detailed when materials, equipment, outside help, consultants, salaries, and travel are to be included. A simple proposal for service by one person might consist of a statement such as "15 hours at $200/hour, totaling $3,000, plus mileage and expenses estimated at $550." Present the budget or costs section after the main body of the proposal.

Summary

You might conclude the proposal with a summary. This summary may also be used as the initial section of the proposal if deductive sequence is desired.

Addenda

When supporting material is necessary to the proposal but would make it too bulky or detract from it, include the material as addenda items. A bibliography and an appendix are examples of addenda items. References used should appear in the bibliography or as footnotes. Maps, questionnaires, letters of recommendation, and similar materials are suitable addenda items.

A short, informal proposal that includes several of the parts previously discussed is shown in Model Document 11.4. The proposal consists of two major divisions: "Purpose" and "Scope of Services." The "Scope of Services" section identifies four services to be provided and their costs. Wanting to increase the chances of securing the contract, the writer made sure the proposal was highly professional and had the impact needed to get the reader's attention. To add to the overall effectiveness of the proposal, the writer incorporated appealing, but not distracting, page design features. Printing the proposal with a laser printer using fonts of varying sizes and styles resulted in a professional appearance and an appealing document. The reader's positive impression of the high standards exhibited in this proposal is likely to influence their confidence in the writer's ability to implement the training program.

11-5b Proposal Preparation

Writers have much flexibility when preparing proposals. When they find a particular pattern that seems to be successful, they no doubt will adopt it as their basic plan. The ultimate test of a proposal is its effectiveness in achieving its purpose. The task is to assemble the parts of a proposal in a way that persuades the reader to accept it.

As with most report writing, first prepare the pieces of information that you will assemble later as the "whole" report, and then determine the parts to include, select one part that will be easy to prepare and do so, and then go on to another. When you have completed the parts, you can arrange them in whatever order you like, incorporate the transitional items necessary to create coherence, and then put the proposal in finished form. Allow adequate time after completing the research and writing for proofreading and editing. Figures should be checked carefully for accuracy, because underreporting costs can lead to a financial loss if the proposal is accepted, and over reporting costs may lead to refusal of the proposal. If you fail to allow sufficient time for proposal completion, you may miss the required deadline for proposal submission.

If you become part of a collaborative writing team producing a proposal of major size, you will probably be responsible for writing only a small portion of the total proposal. For example, a proposal team of 16 executives, managers, and engineers might be required to prepare an 87-page proposal presenting a supplier's plan to supply parts to a military aircraft manufacturer. After the group brainstorms and plans the proposal, a project director delegates responsibility for the research and origination of particular sections of the proposal. Finally, one person compiles all the sections, creates many of the preliminary and addenda parts, and then produces and distributes the final product.

Proposal for Promotional Video Creation

For DesignPros, Inc.

By Patricia Lucas, Sales, Multimedia Productions, Inc.

May 14, 2023

Purpose

Multimedia Productions, Inc. proposes to produce, shoot, and edit a promotional video for DesignPros. The purpose of the video will be to showcase new features available on DesignPros's website. The video will be two to three minutes in length and will include live action footage and basic text and graphics. The concept and script will be provided by the client in English.

Scope of Services

Cost estimates for shooting, editing, and creating the video are provided below.

Pre-Production: Provided by the client.

Shooting (1 Camera Operator, 1 Graphic Animator): Up to 10 hours each. $900

This cost includes all necessary equipment for a one-camera shoot, including HD camera and a lav microphone. Shooting will include rehearsing lines, blocking and staging, shooting multiple angles and several takes, close-ups, capturing audio, developing script, and lighting, if needed, as well as demonstrating the website's use. Graphics and animation includes 2D rendering using images sourced by ComputerArts as requested by the client.

Editing (1 Editor, 1 Week) $500

This cost includes digitizing, rough cut, fine edit, transitions, rendering, titling and graphics, color correction, audio syncing, music tracks, and broadcast standards. Two rounds of edits are included.

Exporting/Deliverables $200

This cost includes media conversions, DVD and/or Blu-Ray Disc authoring, and production of a Data Disc with full-resolution video for broadcast and web uploads. A portable "thumb" external hard drive with all final exports in full HD will be delivered to the client upon request. All expenses for video tape, lighting expendables, mileage, and other expenses are included.

Grand Total..$1,600.00

- **Describes the problem and presents the proposed plan as a solution to the problem.**

- **Uses headings to aid the reader in understanding the proposal's organization. Boldface font adds emphasis.**

- **Divides "Scope of Services" into four minor divisions for easier comprehension.**

Format Pointer:

Incorporates page design features to enhance appeal and readability (e.g., headings styles including color; crisp, open fonts and wide line spacing for easy onscreen reading or print copy; bulleted lists; and appealing table).

Ground Picture/Shutterstock

12 | Designing and Delivering Business Presentations

Learning Objectives

After studying this chapter, you will be able to ...

12-1 Plan a business presentation that accomplishes the speaker's goals and meets the audience's needs.

12-2 Organize and develop the three parts of an effective business presentation.

12-3 Select, design, and use presentation visuals effectively.

12-4 Deliver speeches with increasing confidence.

12-5 Discuss strategies for presenting in alternate delivery situations such as culturally diverse audiences, teams, and distance presentations.

12-1 Planning an Effective Business Presentation

The simplicity of writing email and talking on the phone has deterred many workers from learning to communicate in front of people with authority and authenticity.[1] Being a skilled business communicator requires skill in both writing and speaking. A business presentation is an important means of exchanging information for decision making and policy development; relating the benefits of the services offered; and sharing our goals, values, and vision. Because multiple people receive the message at the same time and are able to provide immediate feedback for clarification, presentations can significantly reduce message distortion and misunderstanding.

Many of the presentations you give will be formal, with sufficient time allowed for planning and developing elaborate visual support. You might present information and recommendations to external audiences such as customers and clients whom you've never met or to an internal audience made up of coworkers and managers you know well. You can also expect to present some less formal presentations, often referred to as **oral briefings**. An oral briefing might entail a short update on a current project requested during a meeting without advance notice or a brief explanation in the hallway when your supervisor walks past. Sales representatives give oral briefings daily as they present short, informal pitches for new products and services.

Regardless of the formality of the presentation, the time given to prepare, the nature of the audience (friends or strangers), or the media used (live, distant, web, or on demand), your success depends on your ability to think on your feet and speak confidently as you address the audience's needs. Understanding the purpose you hope to achieve through your presentation and conceptualizing your audience will enable you to organize the content in a way the audience can understand *and* accept.

As with written messages, presentations should be well planned. The steps in the process for planning, preparing, and rehearsing presentations are shown in Figure 12.1.

12-1a Identify Your Purpose and Consider the Channel

Determining what you want to accomplish during a presentation is a fundamental principle of planning an effective presentation. Some speech coaches recommend completing the following vital sentence to lay the foundation for a successful presentation: "At the end of my presentation, the audience will _____." Writer Roger E. Axtell provides two excellent mechanisms for condensing your presentation into a brief, achievable purpose that will direct you in identifying and supporting the major points:[2]

- Ask yourself, "What is my message?" Then, develop a phrase, a single thought, or a conclusion you want the audience to take with them from the presentation. This elementary statement will likely be the final sentence in your presentation—the basic message you want the audience to remember.

- Imagine a member of your audience has been asked to summarize your message. Ideally, you want to hear them describe your central purpose.

If your purpose for presenting is primarily informative and you plan to provide a good deal of information and details, you might wish to select a two-channel approach to message delivery. In other words, you might find it more appropriate to deliver the bulk of the information via email or informal report, and then follow-up with a presentation to answer questions or emphasize key points to ensure the accuracy of the message's reception. Although a presentation is a useful medium for establishing rapport and receiving and providing feedback, it is also one of the most misused communication channels. This is because presentations are often used to deliver large amounts of detailed information, which may only succeed in boring the audience. The challenge of keeping an audience's attention for an extended period of time becomes obvious when we consider that the average attention span in 2021 was 8 seconds,[3] and most educators

oral briefings informal presentations prepared and presented with little time for planning and developing

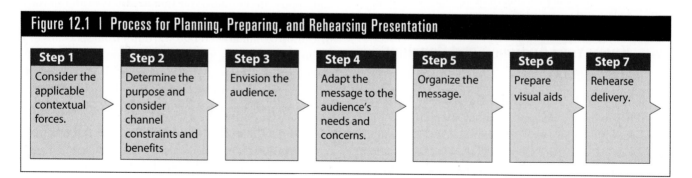

Figure 12.1 | Process for Planning, Preparing, and Rehearsing Presentation

Step 1	Step 2	Step 3	Step 4	Step 5	Step 6	Step 7
Consider the applicable contextual forces.	Determine the purpose and consider channel constraints and benefits	Envision the audience.	Adapt the message to the audience's needs and concerns.	Organize the message.	Prepare visual aids	Rehearse delivery.

and psychologists agree that attention spans have been decreasing over the past decade with the increase in external stimulation. Because of this single challenge, the decision to communicate with a presentation deserves due consideration and, if selected, generally requires substantial planning so as to be effective and enhance, rather than detract from, the presenter's credibility.

For this reason, it is important to emphasize when to choose an oral presentation as the method of message delivery. Presentations are good for the following situations:

- **Inspiring and motivating others.** If the presenter is able to bring enthusiasm and energy and an inspirational message to the situation, then oral message delivery is highly appropriate.

- **Demonstrations of products or for training purposes.** Oral presentations work well when audience members are able to view how a product works and better understand its functions. They are also useful for training purposes, particularly, if the audience is able to apply the presented material through practice or use as part of the presentation.

- **To introduce a complex persuasive written message (generally a report or a proposal).** This helps increase audience interest by emphasizing the key benefits of the proposal in an engaging manner and allows the presenter to answer audience questions.

- **As a follow-up to a complex persuasive written message (generally a report or a proposal).** The personal presence of an advocate can help establish goodwill and credibility and move the persuasive process forward. In these cases, the oral message should generally emphasize the benefits of the proposal and answer audience questions.

- **To deliver bad news to a large audience.** In some circumstances, the personal presence of an organizational representative helps to establish or maintain goodwill and credibility and, by extension, the image and reputation of the firm.

Once the decision has been made that a presentation is the best medium for message delivery, then the preparer needs to do additional planning by analyzing her audience and considering the context of the presentation.

12-1b Know Your Audience and Consider the Context

A common mistake that many presenters make is to presume they know the audience without attempting to find out about it. If you expect to get results, you must commit the time to know your audience and focus your presentation on it—from planning your speech to practicing its delivery.

Bye-Bye, PowerPoint

Lawrence Sumulong/Getty Images

Technology advancements have revolutionized business presentations. Internet-based programming languages, such as Java, make it possible to offer splashy graphics, animation, and real-time data updates on websites, cellphones, and other media players.

As a general rule, audiences *do* want to be in tune with a speaker. Yet people listen to speeches about things of interest to them. "What's in it for me?" is the question most listeners ask. A speech about climate change to a farm group should address the farmers' problems, for example, and not focus on theories of global warming. Additionally, different strategies are needed for audiences who think and make decisions differently. Audiences from different cultures have different expectations regarding public-speaking norms as explained in the box "Cultural Contexts in Public Speaking;" refer to Section 12-5. For example, different strategies are needed for making a successful presentation to sell software to a group of lawyers than to a group of doctors. Lawyers typically think quickly and are argumentative and decisive, whereas doctors are often cautious, skeptical, and don't make quick purchasing decisions.[4]

To deliver a presentation that focuses on the wants and expectations of an audience, you must determine who it is, what motivates it, how members think, and how members make decisions. Helpful information you can obtain about most audiences includes ages, genders, occupations, educational levels, attitudes, values, broad and specific interests, and needs. In addition, you should also consider certain things about the occasion and location. Patriotic speeches to a group of military veterans will differ from speeches to a group of new recruits, just as speeches to university students will differ from speeches to investors. Seek answers to the following questions when you discuss your speaking engagement with someone representing the group or audience:

1. ***Who* is the audience and *who* requested the presentation?** General characteristics of the audience should be considered, as well as the extent of their

knowledge and experience with the topic, attitude toward the topic and you as a credible speaker, the anticipated response to the use of electronic media, and required or volunteer attendance.

2. **Why is this topic important to the audience?** What will the audience do with the information presented? How will the information benefit audience members?

3. **What environmental factors affect the presentation?**

   ○ How many will be in the audience?

   ○ Will I be the only speaker? If not, where does my presentation fit in the program? What time of day?

   ○ How much time will I be permitted? Minimum? Maximum?

   ○ What are the seating arrangements? How far will the audience be from the speaker? Will a microphone or other equipment be available?

   ○ What are my technical requirements, and will they be met at the presentation location?

   ○ Will I have time to test my media before the presentation? If not, how can I ensure that my presentation will go off without any problems or snags?

Answers to these questions reveal whether the speaking environment will be intimate or remote, whether the audience is likely to be receptive and alert or nonreceptive and tired, and whether you will need to use additional motivational or persuasive techniques.

12-2 Organizing the Content

With an understanding of the purpose of your business presentation—why you are giving it and what you hope to achieve—the constraints and benefits of the oral medium, and a conception of the size, interest, and background of the audience, you are prepared to outline your presentation and identify appropriate content.

The biggest mistake that presenters often make is not clearly understanding that oral presentations, as a medium of communication, are quite different from written messages in terms of the kinds of information they are useful for conveying. In other words, the biggest mistake that presenters make is treating a presentation as if it were a written document or formal report. The written channel and the oral channel are generally good for communicating different kinds of information and for achieving quite different goals. Even if a presentation is based on written material, the presenter should start planning as if they were

developing an entirely new message because of this fact. If this isn't understood from the beginning, an oral presentation is likely to fall flat—and the presenter with it. What this means is that rather than writing a script or working from a report, a presenter should begin with an outline of the presentation contents.

First introduced by famous speech trainer Dale Carnegie and still recommended by speech experts today, the simple but effective basic presentation structure includes an introduction, the body, and a closing.

12-2a Introduction

What you say at the beginning sets the stage for your entire presentation and initiates your rapport with the audience. However, inexperienced speakers often settle for unoriginal and overused introductions that reduce the audience's desire to listen, such as "My name is …, and my topic is …" or "It is a pleasure …"; or negative statements, such as apologies for lack of preparation, boring delivery, or late arrival. An effective introduction accomplishes the following goals:

- **Captures the attention of, and involves, the audience.** Choose an attention-getter that is relevant to the subject and appropriate for the situation.

To involve the audience directly, ask for a show of hands in response to a direct question; allow the audience time to think about the answer to a rhetorical question; or explain why the information is important and how it will benefit the listeners. Consider the following examples.

A speech on how to deliver effective presentations might begin with a true story:

"Once I was invited to give a presentation on customer trends. I worked closely with the meeting planner. In fact, she approved every slide I was going to present. This was an executive-level audience, and she wanted the content to be perfect. I researched, I prepped, I practiced, I had great examples.

"Five minutes into my presentation, one executive raised his hand and asked, 'Are these trends based on quantitative research?' My reply was, 'No, they are qualitative cultural trends.' He and half the room tuned out. The presentation flopped. My mistake was basing my whole speech on information from one person. That question killed me, and there was no way to save the presentation in the moment…"

A report presenting a plan for restructuring could introduce the subject and set the stage for the findings (inductive sequence) or the recommendation (deductive sequence).

Inductive: "When the company experienced a dramatic downturn in stock values, a management team immediately began to put together a plan to cut costs and improve productivity."

Attention-Getting Techniques Might Include:

- A shocking statement or startling statistic
- A quotation by an expert or well-known person
- A rhetorical or an open-ended question that generates discussion from the audience
- An appropriate joke or humor
- A demonstration or dramatic presentation aid
- An anecdote or a timely story from a business periodical
- A personal reference, a compliment to the audience, or a reference to the occasion of the presentation

Figure 12.2	Presentation Planner

I. Introduction:
  a. Attention-getting material:
  b. Purpose statement:
    1. Subpoint:
    2. Subpoint:
    3. Subpoint:
  c. Transition to body of presentation:

II. Body
  a. Main Point 1:
  b. Transition to main point 2:
  c. Main Point 2:
  d. Transition to main point 3:
  e. Main Point 3:
  f. Transition to conclusion:

III. Conclusion:
  a. Summary:
  b. Concluding remarks:

Deductive: "By reducing levels of management and cutting red tape, we can decrease costs and improve productivity, ensuring future growth of our company."

Establishes rapport. Initiate rapport with the listeners; convince them that you are concerned that they benefit from the presentation and that you are qualified to speak on the topic. You might share a personal story that relates to the topic but reveals something about yourself or discuss your background or a specific experience with the topic being discussed.

- **Presents the purpose statement and previews the points that will be developed.** To maintain the interest you have captured, present your purpose statement directly so that the audience is certain to hear it. Use original statements and avoid clichés such as "My topic today is …" or "I'd like to talk with you about …"

"The results of our customer service survey indicated that we could improve operations in three ways. Our customer service program includes plans to lower book prices, reduce lines at purchase points, and increase the range of merchandise we offer."

Next, preview the major points you will discuss in the order you will discuss them. For example, you might say, "First, I'll discuss…, then…, and finally.…" Revealing the presentation plan will help the audience understand how the parts of the body are tied together to support the purpose statement, thus increasing their understanding. For a long, complex presentation, you might display a presentation visual that lists the points in the order they will be covered. As you begin each major point, display a slide that contains that point and perhaps a related image. These section slides partition your presentation just as

headings do in a written report, and thus move the listener more easily from one major point to the next. Refer to Figure 12.2 for a template to use when planning your presentations.

12-2b Body

In a typical presentation of 15–20 minutes, limit your presentation to only a few major subpoints (typically three to five) that support or flesh out your primary theme or topic to avoid overwhelming and boring your audience. Making every statement in a presentation into a major point—something to be remembered—is impossible unless the presentation lasts only 2 or 3 minutes.

Once you have selected your major subpoints, locate your supporting material. You can use several techniques to ensure the audience understands your point and to reinforce it:

- **Provide support in a form that is easy to understand.** Three techniques will assist you in accomplishing this goal:

1. **Use simple vocabulary and short sentences that the listener can understand easily and that sound conversational and interesting.** Spoken communication is more difficult to process than written communication; therefore, complex, varied vocabulary and long sentences often

included in written documents are not effective in a presentation.

2. **Avoid jargon or technical terms that the listeners might not understand.** Instead, use plain English that the audience can easily comprehend. Make your speech more interesting and memorable by using word pictures to make your points. Matt Hughes, a speech consultant, provides this example: "If your message is a warning of difficulties ahead, you might say: 'We're climbing a hill that's getting steeper, and there are rocks and potholes in the road.'"[5]

3. **Use a familiar frame of reference.** Drawing analogies between new ideas and familiar ones is another technique for generating understanding. For example, noting that the U.S. blog-reading audience is already one-half the size of the newspaper-reading population helps clarify an abstract or complex concept. Saying that "info dumping" is the verbal equivalent of email spam is a good explanation of the expected consequences of overloading an audience with too many details.[6]

- **Provide relevant statistics.** Provide statistics or other quantitative measures to lend authority and credibility to your points. A word of warning: Do not overwhelm your audience with excessive statistics. Instead, round off numbers and use broad terms or word pictures that the listener can remember. Instead of "68.2 percent" say "more than two-thirds"; instead of "112 percent rise in production" say "our output more than doubled."

- **Use quotes from prominent people.** Comments made by other authorities are helpful in establishing credibility.

- **Use interesting anecdotes.** Audiences like and remember anecdotes or interesting stories that tie into the presentation and make strong emotional connections. In her book *Whoever Tells the Best Story Wins*, Annette Simmons stresses that when telling stories, the storyteller allows the audience to feel their presence and reveals a trace of humanity, which is vital for developing understanding, influence, and strong relationships with the audience. She encourages leaders to craft personal stories into specific, intentional messages that communicate values, vision, and important lessons.[7] By communicating their values, leaders communicate the values they expect from their employees. As with jokes, be sure you can get straight to the point of a story.-

- **Use jokes and humor appropriately.** Jokes or humor can create a special bond between you and the audience, ease your approach to sensitive subjects, disarm a nonreceptive audience, or make your message easier to understand and remember. Plan your joke carefully so that you can (1) get the point across as quickly as possible, (2) deliver it in a conversational manner with interesting inflections and effective body movements, and (3) deliver the punch line effectively. If you cannot tell a joke well, use humor instead—amusing things that happened to you or someone you know, one-liners, or humorous quotations that relate to your presentation. Refrain from any humor that reflects negatively on race, color, religion, gender, age, culture, or other personal areas of sensitivity.

- **Use presentation visuals.** Presentation visuals, such as handouts, presentation software, and demonstrations, enhance the effectiveness of the presentation. Develop presentation visuals that will enable your audience to see, hear, and even experience your presentation.

- **Encourage audience involvement.** Skilled presenters involve their audiences through techniques such as asking reflective questions, role-playing, directing audience-centered activities, and incorporating current events or periodicals that tie directly to the message. One communications coach's advice for getting an audience "to sit up and listen" is to make the presentation contemporary by working Twitter, texting, video, and other technologies into the speech.[8]

12-2c Closing

The closing provides unity to your presentation by "telling the audience what you have already told them." The conclusion should be "your best line, your most dramatic point, your most profound thought, your most memorable bit of information, or your best anecdote."[9] Because listeners tend to remember what they hear last, use these final words strategically. Develop a closing that supports and refocuses the audience's attention on your purpose statement.

- **Commit the time and energy needed to develop a creative, memorable conclusion.** An audience is not impressed with endings such as "That's all I have" or "That's it." Useful concluding techniques include summarizing the main points that have been made in the presentation and using anecdotes, humor, and illustrations. When closing an analytical presentation, state your conclusion and support it with the highlights from your supporting evidence: "In summary, you should select our communication training program because it offers…." In a persuasive presentation, the closing is often an urgent plea for the members of the audience to take some action or to look on the subject from a new point of view.

- **Tie the closing to the introduction to strengthen the unity of the presentation.** For example, you might answer the rhetorical question you asked in the opening, refer to and build on an anecdote included in the introduction, and so on. A unifying close to a speech to motivate women business owners might be, "Life is too short to spend it doing other people's work and paying the price with unhappiness. With appropriate planning, you can spend your days as I do, making a life you love."

- **Use transition words that clearly indicate you are moving from the body to the closing.** Attempt to develop original wordings rather than rely on standard statements such as "In closing" or "In conclusion."

- **Practice your closing until you can deliver it without stumbling.** Use your voice and gestures to communicate this important idea clearly, emphatically, and sincerely rather than fade out at the end as inexperienced speakers often do.

- **Smile and stand back to accept the audience's applause.** A solid closing does not require a "thank you"; instead, wait confidently for the audience's spontaneous applause to thank you for a worthwhile presentation. Appear eager to begin a question-and-answer period or walk with assurance to your seat.

12-3 Designing Compelling Presentation Visuals

Speakers who use presentation visuals are considered better prepared, more interesting, and achieve their goals more often than speakers who do not use visuals. Presentation visuals support and clarify a speaker's ideas and help the audience visualize the message. A speaker using presentation visuals reaches the receiver with double impact—through the eyes and the ears—and achieves the results quoted in an ancient Chinese proverb: "Tell me, I'll forget. Show me, I'll remember. But involve me and I'll understand." Research studies confirm that using visuals enhances a presentation.

The effective use of presentation visuals provides several advantages:[10]

- Clarifies and emphasizes important points

- Increases retention from 14 to 38 percent

- Reduces the time required to present a concept

- Results in a speaker achieving goals 34 percent more often than when presentation visuals are not used

- Increases the occurrence of group consensus by 21 percent when presentation visuals are used in a meeting

12-3a Designing Presentation Visuals

PowerPoint still remains the standard presentation software used in most organizational settings, even though its use has given rise to such sayings as "Death by PowerPoint" and "PowerPoint poisoning." The problem is that too many presenters approach a presentation as if they were reading a document to their audience rather than delivering an interesting and inspiring message. The result is "docu-points," or presentations composed of too many text slides that are overly complex, difficult to understand, and boring. One example is an "electability" PowerPoint slideshow sent by the 2008 Hillary Clinton Campaign to all House Democrats that contained nine slides, 275 words, one table, three bar charts, and two pie charts. Such "docu-points" are usually less effective than a concise, well-designed handout or summary report.[11]

Even though PowerPoint remains a standard in many professional environments, other presentation software packages are available. Prezi is another popular software tool that is available online and provides a very different experience than PowerPoint in that it is nonlinear and more interactive and dynamic. Apple users can use Apple Keynote. Other presentation tools include Google Docs, Canva, ClearSlide, and Beautiful.ai, which uses the power of artificial intelligence to power the design process, making it easier for the user.

Regardless of the software package you choose, your goal is to create an appealing, easy-to-read visual aid that supports and enhances your main points without overwhelming the audience. Presentation visuals should possess the same degree of professionalism as your delivery and personal appearance. You can create dynamic and useful presentation visuals, including slides, handouts, and notes pages, by following these simple guidelines:

- **Limit the number of visual aids used in a single presentation.** Although audiences value being able to "see" your points, they also welcome the variety provided by listening and the break from concentrating on visuals. Design compelling visuals that direct the audience's attention to major points and clarify or illustrate complex information. Use precise, vivid language that will involve the audience and enrich your message and delivery style.

- **Limit slide content to key ideas presented in as few words as possible or, better yet, visually.** Well-organized, crisp slide content enhances the audience's ability to grasp the speaker's meaning and find immediate value in the information. Good content also leads to an extemporaneous delivery rather than a speaker's monotonous reading of scripted slides. Short text lines are also easier for the eye to follow and open up the slide with appealing white space. Whenever possible, present complex information using graphic aids, such as tables, charts, or diagrams.

- **Develop only one major idea using targeted keywords the audience can scan quickly, understand, and remember.** Full sentences can be used for a direct quotation; otherwise, less is more. William Earnest, author of *Save Our Slides*, offers a cure for verbalitis: "PowerPoint is not a word processor"—it is a visual medium in which fewer words are always more.[12]

  - Keep type sizes large enough to read when projected and to discourage crowding slides with text. Strive for these font sizes: slide titles, 44 point; main bullets, 32 point; sub-bullets, 24 point. Do not use text smaller than 18 point, as it is unreadable when projected.

  - Limit slide titles and headings to four words and follow the 7 × 7 rule, which limits text to 7 lines per slide and 7 words per line. Eliminate articles (*a, an, and the*), understood pronouns/possessives (*we, you, and your*), simple verbs and infinitive beginnings (*are and to*), and repetitive phrasing.

  - If you must use text, develop powerful bulleted lists that are easy to follow and remember. For easy recall, limit the list to three to five main bullets, but absolutely no more than seven. To eliminate confusion and rereading, use bulleted lists that are grammatically parallel. One item appearing out of place weakens the emphasis given to each item and can distract audience attention from the message. Be certain each major point relates to the key concept presented in the slide title and each subpoint relates to its major point. Unless sequence is important, use bullets as they add less clutter and are easier to follow than numbers.

- **Choose an effective template and powerful images to reinforce ideas, illustrate complex ideas, and enliven boring content.** Images and shapes are more visually appealing and memorable than words, and they enable audiences to grasp information more easily. Today's audiences expect media-rich, dynamic visuals, not a speaker's dense crutch notes displayed on screen. Although photographs and clip art available in your presentation software gallery are acceptable, avoid images that are overused, outdated, grainy, and convey an unprofessional tone. Instead search for or create high-quality, professional

images that convey the desired message and can project onscreen without distortion.

- **Choose an effective color scheme.** The colors you choose and the way you combine them determine the overall effectiveness of your presentation and add a personal touch to your work. Follow these simple rules to plan a nondistracting, complementary color scheme that has unity with the template graphics.

- **Limit colors to no more than three on a slide, to avoid an overwhelming feel.**

- **Begin by selecting a background color that conveys the appropriate formality and tone.** Choose cool colors (blue and green) in muted shades for formal presentations; choose warm colors (red, orange, and yellow) or brighter shades of cool colors for a less formal and perhaps trendy look. Think carefully about whether your color selection has a natural association with your topic or organization. For example, a presentation on environmentally friendly policies might incorporate colors naturally associated with nature and cleanliness (earth tones, white, and blue); a presentation to Pepsi-Cola would likely be designed around the company colors of red, white, and blue.

- **Choose complementary foreground (text) colors that have high contrast to the background to ensure readability.** To ensure high contrast, choose either dark text on a light background or light text on a dark background. For example, the often-used color scheme with a yellow slide title text and white bulleted list with a blue background is a good choice because the colors are complementary and have high contrast. Choose a slightly brighter color for the slide title that distinguishes it from the color chosen for the bullet list.

Black text against a white background has the greatest contrast. A blue background with yellow text contrasts well, but a light blue background with white text would be difficult to read because of low contrast. Evaluate the readability of the following contrast variations:

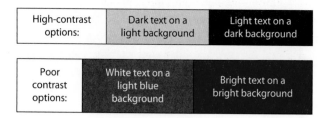

High-contrast options:	Dark text on a light background	Light text on a dark background
Poor contrast options:	White text on a light blue background	Bright text on a bright background

Because the lower resolution of projectors can wash out colors and make them less vibrant than what is seen on a printed page or computer screen, choose options with very high—not minimally high—contrast. Project your presentation ahead of time in the room where you are to present so you can assess the color scheme. You can also double-check for readability and typographical errors at the same time.

- **Choose accent colors that complement the color scheme.** Accent colors are used in small doses to draw attention to key elements: bullet markers; bars/slices in graphs, backgrounds (fills) of shapes and lines, and selected text; or drawings that are color coded for emphasis. Avoid red and green when differentiating important points as almost 10 percent of the population is color impaired and cannot distinguish between red and green. The red and green bars in a graph would be seen as one large area.

- **Choose an appealing font that can be read on-screen easily.** Avoid delicate, decorative, or condensed choices that are difficult to read when projected, and use italics sparingly as they cannot be easily read by people with dyslexia. The clean, simple lines of a sans serif font, such as Calibri, Tahoma, or Verdana, are ideal for projecting on a large screen, newspaper headline, sign, or billboard. A *sans serif* font has no short cross-strokes, known as *serifs*, which provide extra detail that helps to guide the eye on print media. Examples of serif fonts are Cambria, Times New Roman, and Garamond.

- **Follow these keyboarding rules for easy reading.** Use capital letters sparingly as they are difficult to read from a distance. Capitalize the first letter of important words in slide titles (initial caps) and the first letter of the first word and proper nouns in a bulleted list (sentence case). Omit hard-to-see punctuation at the end of bulleted lists and elsewhere, and avoid abbreviations and hyphenations that might cause confusion.

- **Reflect legal and ethical responsibility in the design of presentation visuals.** Like the graphics you developed in Chapter 10, presentation visuals should be uncluttered, easily understood, and should depict information honestly.

- **Proofread the visual carefully following the same systematic procedures used for printed letters and reports and electronic communication.** Misspellings in visuals are embarrassing and diminish your credibility. Double-check to be certain that names of people, companies, and products are spelled correctly.

Figure 12.3 offers a review of slide design guidelines. The poor example (left) relies on text to convey the message and a beautiful but unrelated image, whereas the good example (right) illustrates the point.

12-3b Adding Multimedia to PowerPoint Presentations

Multimedia uses a combination of different forms such as text, audio, images, animation, video, and interactive content. Multimedia contrasts with other media that only use rudimentary computer displays, such as text-only, diagrams, or pictures, and other traditional forms of printed or hand-produced material.

Multimedia use in presentations provides several advantages, including the following:

- Increases learning effectiveness

- Is more appealing than traditional presentation methods

- Offers significant potential for improving personal communications, education, and training efforts

Figure 12.3 | Designing Compelling Slides

1. Gather
2. Organize
3. Present

Amnaj Khetsamtip/Shutterstock

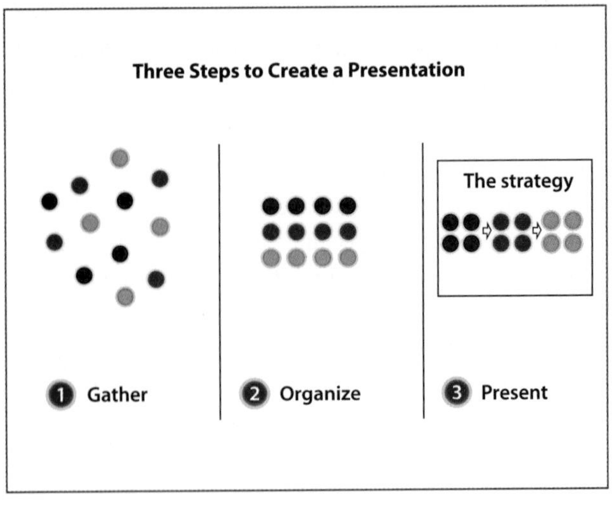

Original slide on the left, revised slide on the right

The revised slide:
- Uses graphics to better illustrate the emphasized points.
- Proofreads carefully to avoid misspellings that damage credibility.
- Uses a high contrast background to assure legibility.
- Uses a simple but appealing template.

Three Steps to Create a Presentation

The strategy

1 Gather   2 Organize   3 Present

When you make a recording of a presentation, all its elements (narration, animation, pointer movements, timings, and so on) are saved in the presentation itself. In essence, the presentation becomes a video that your audience can watch in PowerPoint.

You have two options for turning your presentation into a video that's ready to view:

1. Save/export your presentation to a video file format (.mp4 or .wmv).

2. Save your presentation as a PowerPoint Show (.ppsx) file. (A PowerPoint Show appears full screen in Slide Show, ready to view immediately.)

Save as a Video File

After you've created your slides and recorded any timing and narrations and laser pointer gestures that you want to include, you're ready to create a video file.

1. On the **File** menu, select **Save** to ensure all your recent work has been saved in PowerPoint presentation format (.pptx).

2. Click **File** > **Export** > **Create a Video**. (Or, on the **Recording** tab of the ribbon, click **Export to Video**.)

3. In the first drop-down box under the **Create a Video** heading, select the video quality you want, which pertains to the resolution of the finished video. The higher the video quality, the larger the file size. (You may want to test them to determine which one meets your needs.)

Option	Resolution	For displaying on
Ultra HD (4K)*	3840 × 2160, largest file size	Large monitors
Full HD (1080p)	1920 × 1080, large file size	Computer and HD screens
HD (720p)	1280 × 720, medium file size	Internet and optical discs
Standard (480p)	852 × 480, smallest file size	Portable devices

*The **Ultra HD (4K)** option is only available if you're using Windows 10.

4. The second drop-down box under the **Create a Video** heading tells whether your presentation includes narration and timings. (You may switch this setting if you like.)

   ▶ If you haven't recorded timed narration, by default the value is **Don't Use Recorded Timings and Narrations**.

   ▶ The default time spent on each slide is 5 seconds. You can change that timing in the **Seconds to spend on each slide** box. To the right of the box, click the up arrow to increase the duration, or click the down arrow to decrease the duration.

   ▶ If you have recorded a timed narration, by default the value is **Use Recorded Timings and Narrations**.

5. Click **Create Video**.

6. In the **File name** box, enter a file name for the video, browse for the folder that will contain this file, and then click **Save**.

7. In the **Save as type** box, choose either **MPEG-4 Video** or **Windows Media Video**.

   You can track the progress of the video creation by looking at the status bar at the bottom of your screen. The video creation process can take up to several hours depending on the length of the video and the complexity of the presentation.

   Tip: For a long video, you can set it up to be created overnight. That way, it'll be ready for you the following morning.

8. To play your newly created video, go to the designated folder location and double-click the file.

Save as a PowerPoint Show

When someone opens a PowerPoint Show file, it appears full-screen in Slide Show, rather than in edit mode. The viewer begins watching the presentation immediately.

1. On the **File** menu, select **Save** to ensure all your recent work has been saved in PowerPoint presentation format (.pptx).

2. On the **File** menu, select **Save As.**

3. Choose the folder location where you want to store your PowerPoint Show file.

4. In the **Save as type** box, choose **PowerPoint Show (*.ppsx).**

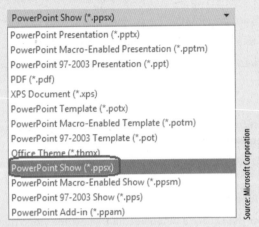

Source: Microsoft Corporation

5. Select **Save.**

After you create a video, you can share it with others by using the following methods:

▸ **Email your presentation to others**

▸ **Save to a file share or other location**

▸ **Upload it to your organization's Microsoft Stream video-sharing site, as described in the next section, "Save to a video-sharing site."**

For more information on turning PowerPoint presentations into videos, visit https://support.office.com/en-us/article/ Save-your-presentation-as-a-video-fafb9713-14cd-4013-bcc7-0879e6b7e6ce

Source: Microsoft Office Support.

- Reduces training costs
- Is easy to use
- Tailors information to the individual
- Provides high-quality video images and audio
- Offers system portability[13]
- Can contain closed captions and transcripts

Multimedia use in presentations also presents some potential disadvantages, such as:

- being more expensive
- being more difficult to configure
- requiring special hardware
- introducing potential problems of compatibility with other software or hardware[14]

Multimedia can be incorporated into PowerPoint simply by copying images from the web or from personal cameras and merging them with text and graphic design elements to create engaging presentations that can be used in-house, with clients, or as presentations that are downloadable from the internet. Links to audio and video files can also be embedded in PowerPoint and played during presentations. Possibilities include playing sounds and movies continuously throughout the slide show, across several sequential slides, or only when clicking on a sound or movie image.

12-3c Design Tips for Audience Handouts and Notes Pages

Audience handouts should add value for individual audience members; otherwise, the information can better be conveyed in a projected format for group benefit. An effective handout can help audience members remember your message, serve as a reference for later consideration or action, and encourage involvement when space is provided for note taking or response. Handouts, transcripts, and notes are helpful for audiences with visual impairments who rely on screen readers and other accessibility technologies. You can prepare useful presenter notes on small index cards or on pages generated by electronic presentation software.

12-4 Refining Your Delivery

After you have organized your message, you must identify the appropriate delivery method, refine your vocal qualities, and practice your delivery.

12-4a Delivery Method

Four presentation methods can be used: memorized, scripted, impromptu, and extemporaneous. Impromptu and extemporaneous styles are generally more useful for business presentations.

Memorized presentations are written out ahead of time, memorized, and recited verbatim. Memorization has the greatest limitations among the speech styles. Speakers are almost totally unable to react to feedback, and the speaker who forgets a point and develops a mental block might lose the entire speech. Memorized speeches tend to sound monotonous, restrict natural body gestures and motions, and lack conviction. For short religious or fraternal rites, however, the memorized presentation is often impressive.

Manuscript, or *scripted*, **presentations** involve writing the speech word for word and reading it to the audience. For complex material and technical conference presentations, manuscript presentations ensure content coverage. Additionally, this style protects speakers against being misquoted (when accuracy is absolutely critical) and fits into exact time constraints, as in television or radio presentations. Speeches are sometimes read when time does not permit adequate preparation or when several different presentations are given in one day (e.g., the speaking demands of the president of the United States and other top-level executives). Manuscript presentations limit speaker–audience rapport, particularly when speakers keep their eyes and heads buried in their manuscripts. Teleprompters that project the manuscript out of view of the audience allow the speaker to appear to be speaking extemporaneously.

Impromptu presentations are frightening to many people because the speaker is called on without prior notice. Experienced speakers can easily analyze the request, organize supporting points from memory, and present a simple, logical response. In many cases, businesspeople can anticipate a request and be prepared to discuss a particular idea when requested (e.g., a status report on an area of control at a team meeting). Because professionals are expected to present ideas and data spontaneously on demand, businesspeople must develop the ability to deliver impromptu presentations.

Extemporaneous presentations are planned, prepared, and rehearsed, but not written in detail. Brief notes prompt the speaker on the next point, but the words are chosen spontaneously as the speaker interacts with the audience and identifies its specific needs. Extemporaneous presentations include natural body gestures, sound conversational, and can be delivered with conviction because the speaker is speaking "with" the listeners and not "to" them. The audience appreciates a warm, genuine communicator and will forgive an occasional stumble or groping for a word that occurs with an extemporaneous presentation.

12-4b Vocal Qualities

The sound of your voice is a powerful instrument used to deliver your message and to project your professional image. To maximize your vocal strengths, focus on three important qualities of speech: phonation, articulation, and pronunciation.

Phonation involves both the production and the variation of the speaker's vocal tone. You project your voice and convey feelings—even thoughts—by varying your vocal tones. Important factors of phonation are pitch, volume, and rate. These factors permit us to recognize other people's voices over the phone.

- **Pitch.** The highness or lowness of the voice is called pitch. Pleasant voices have medium or low pitch; however, a varied pitch pattern is desirable. The pitch of the voice rises and falls to reflect emotions; for example, fear and anger are reflected in a higher pitch; sadness, in a lower pitch. Lower pitches for both men and women are perceived as sounding more authoritative; higher pitches indicate less confidence and suggest pleading or whining. Techniques discussed later in this section can help you lower the pitch of your voice.

- **Volume.** The loudness of tones is referred to as volume. Generally, good voices are easily heard by everyone in the audience but are not too loud. Use variety to hold the audience's attention, emphasize words or ideas, and create a desired atmosphere (energetic, excited tone versus a dull, and boring one).

memorized presentations a presentation in which a speaker writes out a speech, commits it to memory, and recites it verbatim

manuscript presentation a presentation in which a speaker writes out the entire speech and reads it to the audience; also called a scripted presentation

impromptu presentations a presentation in which a speaker is called on without prior notice

extemporaneous presentations a presentation in which a speaker plans, prepares, and rehearses but does not write everything down; brief notes prompt the speaker, but the exact words are chosen spontaneously as the speaker interacts with the audience and identifies its specific needs

phonation the production and variation of a speaker's vocal tone

- **Rate.** The speed at which words are spoken is called rate. Never speak so quickly that the audience cannot understand your message or so slowly that they are distracted or irritated. Vary the rate with the demands of the situation. For example, speak at a slower rate when presenting a complex concept or emphasizing an important idea. Pause to add emphasis to a key point or to transition to another major section of the presentation. Speak at a faster rate when presenting less important information or when reviewing.

An inherent problem related to speaking rate is verbal fillers—also called non-words. Verbal fillers, such as *uhhh*, *ahhh*, *ummm*, and *errr*, are irritating to the audience and destroy your effectiveness. Many speakers fill space with their own verbal fillers; these include *you know, I mean, basically, like I said, okay*, and *as a matter of fact*. Because of the conversational style of impromptu and extemporaneous presentations, a speaker will naturally struggle for a word or idea from time to time. Become aware of verbal fillers you frequently use by critiquing a recording of yourself and then focus on replacing fillers with a 3- to 5-second pause. This brief gap between thoughts gives you an opportunity to think about what you want to say next and time for your audience to absorb your idea. Presenting an idea (sound bite) and then pausing briefly is an effective way to influence your audience positively. The listener will not notice the slight delay, and the absence of meaningless words will make you appear more confident and polished. Also avoid annoying speech habits, such as clearing your throat or coughing, that shift the audience's attention from the speech to the speaker.

The following activities will help you achieve good vocal qualities:

- **Breathe properly and relax.** Nervousness affects normal breathing patterns and is reflected in vocal tone and pitch. The better prepared you are, the better your phonation will be. Although relaxing might seem difficult to practice before a speech, a few deep breaths, just as swimmers take before diving, can help.

- **Listen to yourself.** A recording of your voice reveals much about pitch, intensity, and duration. Most people are amazed to find their voices are not quite what they had expected. "I never dreamed I sounded that bad" is a common reaction. Nasal twangs usually result from a failure to speak from the diaphragm, which involves taking in and letting out air through the larynx, where the

---

articulation smooth, fluent, and pleasant speech

---

vocal cords operate. High pitch can occur from the same cause, or it can be a product of speaking too fast or experiencing stage fright.

- **Develop flexibility.** A good speaking voice is somewhat musical, with words and sounds similar to notes in a musical scale. Read each of the following sentences aloud and emphasize the *italicized* word in each. Even though the sentences are identical, emphasizing different words changes the meaning.

- *I* am happy you are here.
- I *am* happy you are here.
- I am *happy* you are here.
- I am happy *you* are here.
- I am happy you *are* here.
- I am happy you are *here.*

- *Maybe I'm the only happy one.*
- *I really am.*
- *Happy best describes my feeling.*
- *Yes, you especially.*
- *You may not be happy, but I am.*
- *Here and not somewhere else.*

Articulation involves smooth, fluent, and pleasant speech. It results from the way in which a speaker produces and joins sounds. Faulty articulation is often caused by not carefully forming individual sounds. Common examples include:

- Dropping word endings—saying *workin'* for working

- Running words together—saying *kinda* for *kind of* and *gonna* for *going to*

- Imprecise enunciation—saying *dis* for *this, wid* for *with, dem* for *them, pin* for *pen*, or *pitcher* for *picture*

These examples should not be confused with *dialect*, which people informally call an *accent*. A dialect is a variation in pronunciation, usually of vowels, from one part of the country to another. Actually, everyone speaks a dialect; speech experts can often identify, even pinpoint, the section of the country from where a speaker comes. In the United States, common dialects are New England, New York, Southern, Texan, Midwestern, and so forth. Within each of these, minor dialects often arise regionally or from immigrant influence. The simple fact is that when people interact, they influence one another even down to their speech sounds. Many prominent speakers have developed a rather universal dialect, known as Standard American Speech or American Broadcast English that seems to be effective no matter who the audience is. This model for professional language is widely used by newscasters and announcers and is easily understood by those who speak English as a second language because they likely listened to this speech pattern on television as they learned the language.

You can improve the clarity of your voice, reduce strain and voice distortion, and increase your expressiveness by following these guidelines:

- **Stand up straight with your shoulders back and breathe from your diaphragm rather than your chest.** If you are breathing correctly, you can then use your mouth and teeth to form sounds precisely. For example, vowels are always sounded with the mouth open and the tongue clear of the palate. Consonants are responsible primarily for the distinctness of speech and are formed by an interference with or stoppage of outgoing breath.

- **Focus on completing the endings of all words, not running words together, and enunciating words correctly.** To identify recurring enunciation errors, listen to a recording and seek feedback from others.

- **Obtain formal training to improve your speech.** Pursue a self-study program by purchasing recordings that help you reduce your dialect and move more closely to a universal dialect. You can also enroll in a diction course to improve your speech patterns or arrange for private lessons from a voice coach.

Pronunciation involves using the principles of phonetics to create accurate sounds, rhythm, stress, and intonation. People might articulate perfectly but still mispronounce words. A dictionary provides the best source to review pronunciation. Two pronunciations are often given for a word, the first one being the desired pronunciation and the second an acceptable variation. An American adopting a pronunciation commonly used in England, such as *shedule* for *schedule* or *a-gane* for *again*, could be seen negatively. In some cases, leeway exists in pronunciation. The first choice for pronouncing *data* is to pronounce the first *a* long, as in *date*; but common usage is fast making pronunciation of the short *a* sound, as in *cat*, acceptable. Likewise, the preferred pronunciation of *often* is with a silent *t*. Good speakers use proper pronunciation and refer to the dictionary frequently in both pronunciation and vocabulary development.

When your voice qualities combine to make your messages pleasingly receptive, your primary concerns revolve around developing an effective delivery style.

12-4c Delivery Style

Speaking effectively is both an art and a skill. Careful planning and practice are essential for increasing speaking effectiveness.

Before the Presentation

Follow these guidelines when preparing for your presentation:

- **Prepare thoroughly.** You can expect a degree of nervousness as you anticipate speaking before a group.

This natural tension is constructive because it increases your concentration and your energy and enhances your performance. However, even those seasoned to the spotlight can experience a debilitating case of the jitters. In spring 2013, New Kids on the Block singer Jonathan Knight walked offstage in the middle of a concert in New York, prompting him to tweet apologies about his anxiety.[15] Being well prepared is the surest way to control speech anxiety. Develop an outline for your presentation that supports your purpose and addresses the needs of your audience, and take advantage of every opportunity to gain speaking experience.

- **Prepare effective presentation support tools.** Follow the guidelines presented in the preceding section to select and design visuals, handouts, and notes pages appropriate for your audience and purpose. Additionally, develop a contingency plan in the event of technical difficulties with computer equipment, such as hard copies of the slides or a backup computer preloaded and ready. Arrive early so you can troubleshoot unexpected technological glitches. Despite your degree of planning, however, technical problems might occur during your presentation. Remain calm and correct them as quickly and professionally as you can. Take heart in the fact that Bill Gates's computer once crashed when he introduced a new version of Windows!

- **Practice, but do not rehearse.** Your goal is to become familiar with the key phrases on your note cards so that you can deliver the presentation naturally as if you are talking with the audience—not reciting the presentation or acting out a role. Avoid over practicing, which can make your presentation sound mechanical and limit your ability to respond to the audience.

- **Practice the entire presentation.** This practice will allow you to identify (1) flaws in organization or unity; (2) long, complex sentences or ineffective expressions; and (3) "verbal potholes." Verbal potholes include word combinations that could cause you to stumble, words you have trouble pronouncing ("irrelevant" or "statistics"), and words that accentuate your dialect ("get" can sound like "git" regardless of the intention of a Southern speaker).

- **Spend additional time practicing the introduction and conclusion.** You will want to deliver these important parts with finesse while making a confident connection

pronunciation using principles of phonetics to create accurate sounds, rhythm, stress, and intonation

with the audience. A good closing leaves the audience in a good mood and can help overcome some possible weaknesses during the speech. Depending on the techniques used, consider memorizing significant brief statements to ensure their accuracy and impact (e.g., a direct quotation or an exact statistic).

- **Practice displaying presentation visuals so that your delivery appears effortless and seamless.** Your goal is to make the technology virtually transparent—positioned in the background to support you as the primary focus of the presentation. First, be sure you know the basic commands for advancing through your presentation without displaying distracting menus. Develop the skill to return to a specific slide in the event of a computer glitch or an audience question.

- **Seek feedback on your performance to help you to polish your delivery and improve organization.** Critique your own performance by practicing in front of a mirror and evaluating a recording of your presentation. If possible, present your presentation to a small audience ahead of time for feedback and to minimize anxiety when presenting to the real audience.

- **Request a lectern to hold your notes and to steady a shaky hand, at least until you gain some confidence and experience.** Keep in mind, though, that weaning yourself from the lectern will eliminate a physical barrier between you and the audience. Without the lectern, you will speak more naturally. If you are using a microphone, ask for a portable microphone so that you can move freely.

- **Request a proper introduction if the audience knows little about you.** An effective introduction will establish your credibility as a speaker on the subject and will make the audience eager to hear you. You can prepare your own introduction as professional speakers do, or you can provide concise, targeted information that answers the following three questions: (1) Why is the subject relevant? (2) Who is the speaker? and (3) What credentials qualify the speaker to talk about the subject? Talk with the person introducing you to verify any information, especially the pronunciation of your name, and to review the format of the presentation (time limit, question-and-answer period, and so on). Be certain to thank the person who made the introduction as you begin your presentation. "Thank you for your kind introduction, Ms. Garcia" is adequate. Then follow with your own introduction to your presentation topic.

- **Dress appropriately to create a strong professional image and to bolster your self-confidence.** An audience's initial impression of your personal appearance, your clothing and grooming, affects their ability to accept you as a credible speaker. Because first impressions are difficult to overcome, take time to groom yourself immaculately and to select clothing that is appropriate for the speaking occasion and consistent with the audience's expectations.

- **Arrive early to become familiar with the setup of the room and to check the equipment.** Check the location of your chair, the lectern, the projection screen, light switches, and electrical outlets. Check the microphone and internet connection and ensure that all equipment is in the appropriate place and working properly. Project your electronic presentation so you can adjust the color scheme to ensure maximum readability. Finally, identify the technician who will be responsible for resolving any technical problems that might occur during the presentation.

During the Presentation

The following are things you can do during your presentation to increase your effectiveness as a speaker:

- **Communicate confidence, warmth, and enthusiasm for the presentation and the time spent with the audience.** "Your listeners won't care how much you know until they know how much you care" is pertinent advice.[16]

  - **Exhibit a confident appearance with an alert posture.** Stand tall with your shoulders back and your stomach tucked in. Stand in the "ready position"—no slouching, hunching over the lectern, or rocking. Keep weight forward with knees slightly flexed so that you are ready to move easily, rather than being rooted rigidly in one spot, hiding behind the lectern.

  - **Smile genuinely throughout the presentation.** Pause as you take your place behind the lectern, and smile before you speak the first word. Smile as you finish your presentation and wait for the applause.

  - **Maintain steady eye contact with the audience in random places throughout the room.** Stay with one person approximately 3 to 5 seconds—long enough to finish a complete thought or sentence to convince the listener you are communicating individually with them. If the audience is large, select a few friendly faces and concentrate on speaking to them rather than to a sea of nondescript faces.

  - **Refine gestures to portray a relaxed, approachable appearance.** Vary hand motions to emphasize important points; otherwise, let hands fall naturally to your side. Practice using only one hand to make points unless you specifically need two hands, such as when drawing a figure or showing dimensions or location. Eliminate any nervous gestures that can distract the audience (e.g., clenching your hands in front of or behind your body, steepling your hands, placing your hands in your pockets, jingling keys or change, or playing with a ring or pen).

- **Move from behind the lectern and toward the audience to reduce the barrier created between you and the audience.** You can stand to one side and casually present a relaxed pose beside the lectern. However, avoid methodically walking without a purpose.

- **Exercise strong vocal qualities.** Review the guidelines provided for using your voice to project confidence and credibility.

- **Watch your audience.** They will tell you how you are doing and whether you should shorten your speech. Be attentive to negative feedback in the form of talking, coughing, moving chairs, and other signs of discomfort.

- **Use your visuals effectively.** Many speakers will go to a great deal of effort to prepare good presentation visuals—and then not use them effectively. Inexperienced speakers often ignore the visual altogether or fall into the habit of simply nodding their heads toward the visual. Neither of these techniques is adequate for involving the audience with the visual. In fact, if the material is complex, the speaker is likely to lose the audience completely.

  - **Step to one side of the visual so the audience can see it.** Use a pointer if necessary. Direct your remarks to the audience, so that you can maintain eye contact and resist the temptation to look over your shoulder or turn your back to read the information from the screen behind you.

  - **Paraphrase the visual rather than reading it line for line.** To increase the quality of your delivery, develop a workable method of recording what you plan to say about each graphic.

- **Handle questions from the audience during the presentation.** Questions often disrupt carefully laid plans. At the same time, questions provide feedback, clarify points, and ensure understanding. When people ask questions that will be answered later in the presentation, say, "I believe the next slide will clarify that point; if not, we will come back to it." If the question can be answered quickly, you should do so while indicating that it will also be covered more later. Anticipate and prepare for questions that might be raised. You can generate presentation visuals pertaining to certain anticipated questions and display them only if the question is posed.

An audience will appreciate your thorough and complete explanation and your ability to adjust your presentation to their needs—this strategy is much more professional than stumbling through an explanation or delaying the answer until the information is available. Speakers giving electronic presentations have ready access to enormous amounts of information that can be displayed instantly for audience discussion. Hyperlinks created within a presentation file will move a speaker instantaneously to a specific slide, another file, or an embedded music or video file.

- **Keep within the time limit.** Be prepared to complete the presentation within the allotted time. In many organizations, speakers have one or more rehearsals before delivering reports to a group, such as a board of directors. These rehearsals, or dry runs, are made before other executives, and are critiqued, timed, revised, and rehearsed again. Presentation software makes rehearsing your timing as simple as clicking a button and advancing through the slides as you practice. By evaluating the total presentation time and the time spent on each slide, you can modify the presentation and rehearse it again until the presentation fits the time slot.

After the Presentation

How you handle the time following a presentation is as important as preparing for the presentation itself:

- **Be prepared for a question-and-answer period.** Encourage the audience to ask questions, recognizing an opportunity to ensure that your presentation meets audience needs. Paraphrasing the question allows you time to reflect on what was asked, ensures that everyone heard the question, and assures the questioner that they were understood. You can ask the questioner if your answer was adequate. Be courteous even to hostile questioners so you will maintain the respect of your audience. Stay in control of the time by announcing that you have time for one or two more questions, and then invite individual questions when the presentation is over.

- **Distribute handouts.** Distribute the handout when it is needed rather than at the beginning of the presentation. Otherwise, the audience might read the handout while you are explaining background information needed to understand the written ideas. If you expect the audience to take notes directly on the handout, or if the audience will need to refer to the handout immediately, distribute the handout at the beginning of the presentation or before it begins. To keep control of the audience's attention, be sure listeners know when they should be looking at the handout or listening to you. If the handout is intended as resource material only, post the handout to a web page or place it on a table at the back of the room and at the front for those who come by to talk with you after the presentation.

12-5 Adapting to Alternate Delivery Situations

As you've learned, presenting a dynamic presentation that focuses on the audience's needs and expectations is the fundamental principle in presenting effectively. Along with the solid foundation you've set for spoken communication, you'll also need to adapt your presentation style to the ever-changing business environment and the special needs of culturally diverse audiences. Delivering team presentations and presenting in distance formats are other common situations you'll need to master.

12-5a Culturally Diverse Audiences

When speaking to a culturally diverse audience, you will want to be as natural as possible while adjusting your message for important cultural variations. Using empathy, you can effectively focus on the listener as an individual rather than a stereotype of a specific culture. Be open and willing to learn, and you will reap the benefits by communicating effectively with people who possess a variety of strengths and creative abilities. Additionally, follow these suggestions for presenting to people from outside your own culture:

- **Speak simply.** Use simple English and short sentences. Avoid acronyms and expressions that can be confusing to non-native English speakers—namely slang, jargon, figurative expressions, and sports analogies.

- **Avoid words that trigger negative emotional responses such as anger, fear, or suspicion.** Such "red flag" words vary among cultures; thus, try to anticipate audience reaction and choose your words carefully.

- **Enunciate each word precisely and speak somewhat slowly.** Clear, articulate speech is especially important when the audience is not familiar with various dialects and vocabulary. Avoid the temptation to speak in a loud voice, a habit considered rude in any culture, and especially annoying to Japanese listeners, who perceive the normal tone of North Americans as too loud.

- **Be extremely cautious in the use of humor and jokes.** Cultures that prefer more formality might think

you are not serious about your purpose or find your humor and jokes inappropriate. Many cultures from Asian countries, for example, do not appreciate jokes about family members and the elderly.

- **Learn the culture's preferences for a direct or indirect presentation.** Although North Americans tend to prefer directness, with the main idea presented first, people from many cultures, such as Japanese, Latin American, and Arabic, consider a straightforward approach tactless and rude.

- **Adapt to subtle differences in nonverbal communication.** The direct eye contact expected by most North Americans is not typical of many cultures from Asian countries where listeners often keep their eyes lowered and avoid eye contact to show respect. Arab audiences might stare into your eyes in an attempt to "see into the window of the soul." Cultures also vary on personal space and degree of physical contact (such as a slap on the back or an arm around the other as signs of friendship).

- **Adapt your dress and presentation style to fit the formality of the culture.** Some cultures prefer a higher degree of formality than the casual style of North Americans. To accommodate, dress conservatively; strive to connect with the audience in a formal, reserved manner; and use highly professional visuals rather than jotting ideas on a flip chart.

- **Seek feedback to determine whether the audience is understanding your message.** Observe listeners carefully for signs of misunderstanding, restating ideas as necessary. Consider allowing time for questions after short segments of your presentation. Avoid asking "Is that clear?" or "Do you understand?" as these statements might elicit a "Yes" answer if the person perceives saying "No" to be a sign of incompetence.

Potential frustrations can also occur when presentations or meetings bring together North Americans, who see "time as money," with people of cultures who are not time conscious and believe that personal relationships are the basis of business dealings (e.g., Asian and Latin American cultures). When communicating with cultures that are not time driven, be patient with what you might consider time-consuming formalities and courtesies, and lengthy decision-making styles when you would rather get right down to business or move to the next point. Recognize that the presentation might not begin on time or stay on a precise schedule. Allow additional time at the beginning of the presentation to establish rapport and credibility with the audience, and perhaps provide brief discussion periods devoted to building relationships during the presentation.

Even though the western approach to business presentations has spread as a type of ideal throughout much of the globe, it is important to recognize that public speaking is not a universal, but rather, a culturally variable communication practice, one that is often patterned, context-bound, and locally meaningful. Many non-western speakers appear to be guided by norms of eloquence, tradition, authority, and community, rather than beliefs that everyone in the community is on equal footing and, thus, has the opportunity to speak and should do so by delivering fact-filled information in a conversational way.[17]

Although little research has been done on public speaking in other countries, some information exists. For example, Kenyan and Ugandan students found doing research during the preparation process odd and somewhat pedantic. Speaker credibility in Kenya is often determined by factors such as wealth, social status, age, education, ethnicity, and marital status. Some African speeches are circular. They resemble a bicycle wheel with spokes wandering out repeatedly to the rim to make a point or tell a story, and then returning back to the center, the thesis. They are one-point speeches with a great deal of supporting material. Americans listening to such a speech might feel bewildered and even bored because they are unable to follow the logic that ties all the points together, whereas Kenyan listeners would be absorbed in the stories and delighted with their subtle convergence back into the central theme.[18]

Even those from cultures within the western world may have other public-speaking ideals. In the United States, the Blackfeet, an indigenous people who reside in Montana and Canada, hold that the typical public speaker is the elder male whose experience and wisdom give him the right to speak in public. The most valuable form of communication, according to the Blackfeet, is attentive listening to others (especially the elders) and to one's natural surroundings. Because public speakers hold a high position in society, they deserve community members' respect. Young, inexperienced Blackfeet should feel too embarrassed to speak in public, and elders who are expected to speak should appreciate that the community depends on their guidance. Finally, the Blackfeet hold that the world around them should be listened to rather than talked about.[19]

While the western ideal highlights the role of two types of participants, speakers and audiences, who are on relatively equal footing in terms of social status, and public-speaking practices, non-western speech communities may involve a more stratified set of participants with differently defined social roles and privileges. Western Desert Aboriginal communities in central Australia offer a context in which multiple participants work to build speech sequences.[20] Here, collective decision making is achieved through public discourse in which multiple speakers offer continual, repeating, and overlapping summary accounts, this rapid and "vociferous vocal participation of all present parties" signifies the value of the communal voice over the voice of the individual.[21]

While institutional and personal successes are desired outcomes within the western cultural ideal, these ends are not prominent in many non-western speech communities. Though some non-western speakers valued being perceived as competent or skilled, the public speaking aims of "upward mobility" and "self-improvement" seem uncommon in non-western public-speaking contexts.[22] This may be linked to the fact that many of these contexts exist in stratified social hierarchies in which upward mobility is less attainable or is culturally less desirable.[23] This difference may also be connected to the focus on public speaking as a collective, rather than individual, endeavor in many non-western contexts.

Speaking appropriately in many non-western contexts establishes social authority for the speaker and often works to maintain social hierarchies within speech communities. While western contexts place a large emphasis on the role of the speaker as an individual, many non-western ways of public speaking emphasize community over individuality by placing value on speakers' abilities to speak on behalf of the group as a whole, or to represent subgroups within the larger community.[24]

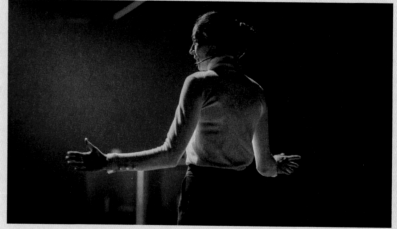

Gorodenkoff/Shutterstock

Be patient and attentive during long periods of silence; in many cultures people are inclined to stay silent unless they have something significant to say or if they are considering (not necessarily rejecting) an idea. In fact, some Japanese people have asked how North Americans can think and talk at the same time. Understanding patterns of silence can help you feel more comfortable during these seemingly endless moments, and less compelled to fill the gaps with unnecessary words or to make concessions before the other side has a chance to reply.

Other significant points of difference between cultures are the varying rules of business etiquette. Should you use the traditional American handshake or some other symbol of greeting? Is using the person's given name acceptable? What formal titles should be used with a surname? Can you introduce yourself, or must you have someone else who knows the other person introduce you? Are business cards critical, and what rules should you follow when presenting a business card? Should you have business cards that are printed in two languages?

Gift giving can be another confusing issue. When you believe a gift should be presented to your event host, investigate the appropriateness of gift giving, the types of gifts considered appropriate or absolutely inappropriate, and the colors of wrapping to be avoided in the speaker's culture. Liquor, for example, is an inappropriate gift in Arab countries.

Gaining competence in matters of etiquette will enable you to make a positive initial impression and concentrate on the presentation rather than agonizing over an awkward, embarrassing slip in protocol. Your audience will appreciate your willingness to learn and value their customs. Being sensitive to cultural issues and persistent in learning specific differences in customs and practices can minimize confusion and unnecessary embarrassment.

12-5b Team Presentations

Because much of the work in business today is done in teams, many presentations are planned and delivered by teams of presenters. Well-conducted team presentations give an organization an opportunity to showcase its brightest talent while capitalizing on each person's unique presentation skills. Email, collaborative software, and other technologies make it easy to develop, edit, review, and deliver impressive team presentations.

The potential payoff of many team presentations is quite high—perhaps a $200,000 contract or a million-dollar account. Yet, according to experts, team presentations fail primarily because presenters don't devote enough time and resources to develop and rehearse them.[25] Resist the sure-to-fail strategy of "winging" a team presentation rather than taking the time to do it correctly. Instead, adapt the skills you already possess in planning and delivering an individual presentation to ensure a successful team presentation. Follow these guidelines as you plan and prepare your team presentation:

- **Select a winning team.** Begin by choosing a leader who is well liked and respected by the team, is knowledgeable of the project, is well organized, and will follow through. Likewise, the leader should be committed to leading the team in the development of a cohesive strategy for the presentation as well as the delegation of specific responsibilities to individual members. Frank Carillo, president of Executive Communications Group, warns team presenters that a frequent problem with "divvying up" work into pieces is that the "pieces don't fit together well when they come back."[26] The core team members, along with management, should choose a balanced mix of individuals who each have something important to contribute to the team. Use these questions to guide team selection: What are this member's complementary strengths and style (e.g., technical expertise, personality traits, and presentation skills)? Can this member meet the expectations of the audience (e.g., a numbers person, technical person, person with an existing relationship with the audience)? Is this member willing to support the team strategy and commit to the schedule?[27]

- **Agree on the purpose and schedule.** The team as a whole should plan the presentation using the same process used for an individual presentation. Agreeing on the purpose to be achieved and selecting content that focuses on a specific audience will prevent the challenges caused by an individual's submitting off-target material. The quality of the presentation deteriorates when material must be redone hurriedly in the final days before the deadline or when unacceptable material is included just because the team worked so hard on it. Mapping out a complete presentation strategy can also minimize bickering among team members because of uneven workloads or unfavorable work assignments.

- **Practice ahead of time.** The team must be well prepared, which will require several rehearsals. Each member must know what others will say to avoid repetition and to fit the time slot. The team must also work out logistical details such as where people will stand, who will run the slides, and when handouts will be distributed. A great deal of the rehearsal time for a team presentation should be spent planning and rehearsing appropriate verbal and physical transitions between team members. The transitions serve to introduce each part of the presentation and make the whole presentation cohesive. This continuity makes the team look polished and conveys team commitment.

The team will also need to agree on a standard design for presentation visuals to ensure consistency in the visuals prepared by individual presenters. Assign a person to merge the various files, to edit for consistency in design elements and the use of jargon and specialized terminology, and to proofread carefully for grammatical accuracy.

Developing a rehearsal schedule ensures adequate time for preparation and practice. Many experts recommend five practice sessions to produce team presentations that are delivered with a unified look. Planning time in the schedule to present before a review team is especially useful for obtaining feedback on team continuity and adjustments needed to balance major discrepancies in the delivery styles of individual presenters.

Follow these suggestions for delivering seamless, impressive team presentations:

- **Decide who will open and conclude the presentation.** The team member who knows the audience and has established rapport is a logical choice for these two critical sections of a presentation. If no one knows the audience, select the member with the strongest presentation skills and personality traits for connecting well with strangers. This person will introduce all team members and give a brief description of the roles they will play in the presentation.

- **Build natural bridges between segments of the presentation and presenters.** A lead presenter must build a bridge from the points that have been made that will launch the following presenter smoothly into what they will discuss. If a lead presenter forgets to make the connection to the next section clear, the next person must summarize what's been said and then preview their section. These transitions might seem repetitive to a team that has been working extensively with the material; however, audiences require clear guideposts through longer team presentations. Also, courtesies, such as maintaining eye contact, thanking the previous speaker, and clearing the presentation area for the next speaker, communicate an important message that the presenters are in sync and work well together.

- **Deliver as a team.** You must present a unified look and communicate to the audience that you care about the team. Spend your time on the "sideline" paying close attention to the current presenter, monitoring the audience for feedback, and being ready to assist the presenter with equipment malfunctions, handouts, and so on. Avoid side conversations and reading notes, yawning, or coughing. To keep an audience engaged in a team presentation, Frank Carillo recommends that team members not presenting should focus on the presenter at least two-thirds of the time. "It may be the 27th time you've heard it, but for that audience it's the first time. Keep it fresh for the listeners."[28]

- **Field questions as a team.** Decide in advance who will field questions to avoid awkward stares and silence that erode the audience's confidence in your team. Normally, the person presenting a section is the logical person to field questions about that section. You can refer questions to team members who are more knowledgeable, but avoid casting pleading looks for someone else to rescue you. Rather, check visually to see if the person wants to respond, and ask if they would like to add information. Tactfully contradict other presenters *only* when the presenter makes a mistake that will cause misunderstanding or confusion. Although you should be ready to help presenters having difficulty, resist the urge to tack on your response to a presenter's response when the question has already been answered adequately.

12-5c Distance Presentations

The COVID-19 pandemic changed business worldwide. Suddenly, we were forced to conduct business online far more than we used to. And that meant a lot more video meetings and conferences.

Videoconferencing has been used for some time for large, high-exposure activities, such as quarterly executive staff presentations, company-wide addresses, new product launches, and crisis management. The technology's lower cost, improved quality, and increased ease of use have opened videoconferencing to many settings.

Substantial cost savings from reduced travel is a compelling reason for companies to use videoconferencing. Threats of terrorism and contagious disease provide more reasons for companies to restrict business travel and look for alternative delivery methods. In addition, important communication benefits, such as the following, can be achieved with videoconferencing:[29]

- Improving employee productivity by calling impromptu videoconferences to clear up issues

- Involving more people in key decisions rather than limiting important discussions to those who are allowed to travel

- Involving expertise critical to the mission, regardless of geographic boundaries

- Creating a consistent corporate culture rather than depending on memos to describe company policy

- Improving employees' quality of life by reducing travel time that often cuts into personal time (e.g., Saturday night layovers for a reasonable airfare)

Prostock-studio/Shutterstock.com

Internet conferencing, or *webcasting,* allows a company to conduct a presentation in real time over the internet simultaneously with a conference telephone call. Because it runs on each participant's internet browser, a presentation can reach hundreds of locations at once. While listening to the call, participants can go to a designated website and view slides or a PowerPoint presentation that is displayed in sync with the speaker's statements being heard on the phone. Participants key comments and questions in chat boxes or press a keypad system to respond to an audience poll, thus giving valuable feedback without interrupting the speaker.

Companies deliver live web presentations on issues ranging from internal briefings on new developments and organizational and procedural changes to product strategy and training presentations. Ernst & Young uses web presentations to announce organizational changes and has found it to be an effective alternative to memos and emails that weren't always remembered or understood. People most affected by an organizational change are able to interact with leaders announcing the change.

Follow these guidelines for adapting your presentation skills to videoconferences and web presentations:

- **Determine whether a distance delivery method is appropriate for the presentation.** Is the presentation purpose suited to the technology? Can costs in time, money, and human energy be justified? Are key people willing and able to participate? For example, a videoconference for a formal presentation, such as an important speech by the CEO to a number of locations, justifies the major expense and brings attention to the importance of the message. Distance delivery formats

---

internet conferencing a method of real-time conferencing that allows a company to conduct a presentation in real time over the internet simultaneously with a conference telephone call; also called webcasting

---

are inappropriate for presentations that cover highly sensitive or confidential issues, for persuasive or problem-solving meetings where no relationship has been established among the participants, and whenever participants are unfamiliar with and, perhaps, unsupportive of the technology.

- **Establish rapport with the participants prior to the distance presentation.** If possible, meet with or phone participants beforehand to get to know them and gain insights about their attitudes. This rapport will enhance your ability to interpret subtle nonverbal cues and to cultivate the relationship further through the distance format. Emailing or faxing a short questionnaire or posting presentation slides with a request for questions is an excellent way to establish a connection with participants and to ensure that the presentation is tailored to audience needs. Some enterprising distance presenters engage participants in email discussions before the presentation and then use this dialogue to develop positive interaction during the presentation.

- **Become proficient in delivering and participating through distance technology.** Begin by becoming familiar with the equipment and the surroundings. Although technical support staff might be available to manage equipment and transmission tasks, your goal is to concentrate on the contribution you are to make, and not your intimidation with the delivery method.

- **Concentrate on projecting positive nonverbal messages.** Keep a natural, friendly expression; relax and smile. Avoid the tendency to stare into the camera. Instead, look naturally at the entire audience as you would in a live presentation. Speak clearly with as much energy as you can. If a lag occurs between the video and audio transmission, adjust your timing to avoid interrupting other speakers. Use gestures to reinforce points, but avoid fast or excessive motion that will appear blurry. Avoid side conversations, coughing, and clearing your throat, which could trigger voice-activated microphones. Pay close attention to other presenters to guard against easy distraction in a distance environment, as well as to capture subtle nonverbal cues. You will need to judge the vocal tone of the person asking a question, because you might not see faces.

- **Adjust camera settings to enhance communication.** Generally, adjust the camera so that all participants can be seen, but zoom in more closely on participants when you wish to clearly observe nonverbal language. Project a wide-angle shot of yourself during rapport-building comments at the presentation's beginning and zoom in to signal the start of the agenda or to emphasize an important point during the presentation. Some systems accommodate a split screen, but others allow participants to view either you or your presentation visuals only. You will want to switch the camera between a view of you and your visuals, depending on what is needed at the time.

- **Develop high-quality graphics appropriate for the particular distance format.** Even more than in a live presentation, you will need graphics to engage and maintain participants' attention. Graphics are a welcome variation to the "talking head"—you—displayed on the screen for long periods. Some companies provide assistance from a webmaster or graphics support staff in preparing slide shows specifically for distance presentations. Also, e-conferencing companies will develop and post presentation slides and host live web presentations, including managing email messages and audience polling. Regardless of the support you receive, you should understand basic guidelines for preparing effective visuals for videoconferencing and web presentations.

- **Videoconferences.** Readability of text will be a critical issue when displaying visuals during a videoconference because text becomes fuzzy when transmitted through compressed video. Select large, sturdy fonts, and choose a color scheme that provides high contrast between the background and the text. Stay with a tested color scheme such as dark blue background, yellow title text, and white bulleted list text to ensure readability. Avoid shades of red and green, as these colors are difficult for those who have color vision deficiencies. Projecting your visuals ahead of time so you can adjust the color scheme, font selections, and other design elements is an especially good idea.

- **Web presentations.** In addition to considering overall appeal, clarity, and readability, web presentations must be designed for minimal load time and compatibility with various computers. For your first presentation, consider using a web template in your electronic presentations software, and experiment with the appropriateness of other designs as you gain experience.

Stand-alone presentations designed specifically for web delivery require unique design strategies to compensate for the absence of a speaker.[30]

- Consider posting text-based explanations in the notes view area or adding vocal narration.

- Develop interactive slide formats that allow viewers to navigate to the most useful information in your presentation. For example, design an agenda slide that includes hyperlinks to the first slide in each section of the presentation.

- Select simple, high-quality graphics that convey ideas effectively.

- Plan limited animation that focuses audience attention on specific ideas on the slide.

- Consider adding video if bandwidth is not an issue.

12-5d Crisis Communication

Crisis communication requires management in situations that affect an organization's relationships with its stakeholders, particularly those that draw media attention. Discussions of crisis management typically focus on three issues: (1) planning and preparing for crisis events, (2) behavior of the organization during a crisis, and (3) communicating with important publics during the crisis.

The types of disasters that an organization might face can be divided into three categories: natural disasters, normal accidents, and abnormal or intentional accidents. Natural disasters include fires, earthquakes, or hurricanes. Normal accident is a term to describe industrial disasters such as those that occurred at Three Mile Island, Chernobyl, Bhopal, and Alaska due to the Exxon Valdez spill, and Louisiana because of the BP oil spill. Abnormal accidents occur because of deliberate action, such as bombings, kidnappings, cyberattacks, and other types of sabotage.

The communication objective in any crisis management strategy should depend upon the stage of the crisis. In cases when communication programs can begin before a crisis occurs, messages should provide internalizing information to build a positive public opinion toward the organization. When it appears a crisis is imminent, the strategy should shift from internalizing messages to instructing messages that tell the public how to respond to the crisis. During the breakout stage of the crisis, instructing communication should intensify so that the affected publics know what to do. As the crisis subsides, communication may shift to adjusting messages intended to help people cope with the effects of the crisis. When the crisis is over, the organization can shift back to an internalizing message strategy.

Any crisis communication plan should provide training for dealing with the media regarding crisis management; identify communication lines with local communities and intervening agencies, such as the police; and provide a strategy for communicating with employees.

During a crisis, an organization should follow these steps:

1. **Get control of the situation.** This involves defining the problem and setting measurable

communication objectives. In addition, it is important to communicate to employees how and where to get information.

2. **Gather information about the situation.** It is important that an organization has a means to stay up to date with the situation as it is happening so that it can respond quickly and appropriately. One way to accomplish this task is to create a crisis center that creates crisis response plans, monitors potential crises, and develops crisis response capabilities.

3. **Communicate early and often.** It will benefit the organization's credibility to be prepared, to explain what is happening and what the company is doing about it, and to provide information about what resources are available to affected parties to deal with the situation.

4. **Communicate directly with affected parties.** It is important to be prepared to communicate with the media and to do so promptly. It is also important to communicate directly with others who are affected, such as employees, customers, shareholders, and communities.

An organization should not wait for a crisis to develop relationships with members of the media if it wants to take advantage of the media's image-building capabilities. It is important that someone in the organization takes time to cultivate these relationships. Building relationships with the media is generally considered a better method than sending out mass-produced public releases that may average a response rate of only 2 percent.[31]

Preparing to deliver a crisis briefing requires special attention to maintaining credibility, particularly composure. At the time of the briefing, make sure that you arrive on time and look professional. It might be helpful to take a page from presidential candidates and consider whether loosening your tie or taking off your jacket will help you to better establish common ground with an audience of people who don't wear a suit to work. During the briefing, practice the following points:

- **Anticipate questions and determine who will answer them.** Ideally, question-and-answer sheets should be prepared for management personnel who may be asked questions by the news media. During a briefing, anticipate which questions might be asked and who should best respond.

- **Prepare and deliver a brief statement.** After introducing yourself and others representing your company, deliver a brief statement (less than 2 minutes in length) that focuses only on the facts that can be confirmed at that time.

- **Outline your organization's current response effort and action plan.**

- **Express your key points from the public's point of view.** Telling the audience how the company's actions will contribute to better health or preserve jobs in the community may help your audience to better appreciate your points.

- **Use plain language.** Avoid language with which only those in your industry, company, or professional specialization are familiar.

- **Maintain control.** Focus on your goals for the interview, and offer responses aimed at achieving those goals.

- **Be honest.** Unless the corporate attorney has advised you against it, tell the truth. If there is a problem, then focus the bulk of your discussion on the steps you are taking to avoid the problem in the future. Don't guess at the answer. If you don't know something, say so.

- **Take responsibility.** Again, unless the corporate attorney has advised otherwise, take responsibility for problems rather than blaming others.

- **Remain calm and avoid arguments.** Becoming emotional can undermine your credibility and make you look as if you have lost control and composure.

- **Rephrase the question.** You don't need to accept a questioner's premise. If a reporter uses words that you wouldn't use, don't repeat them. Correct them if necessary.

- **Try to be friendly, helpful, and patient.** Shake hands with attendees, and call them by name. Be enthusiastic about your company and your job, if appropriate for the occasion. Avoid becoming impatient with attendees or acting as if they or their questions are stupid.

- **Limit the question-and-answer session to no more than 10 minutes.**

- **Don't speculate or make predictions.**

- **Don't make any remarks "off the record."** Such comments might lead reporters to believe there is more to the story that they can pursue.

As with many other types of professional communication situations, adequate preparation is often the key to a successful crisis briefing.[32]

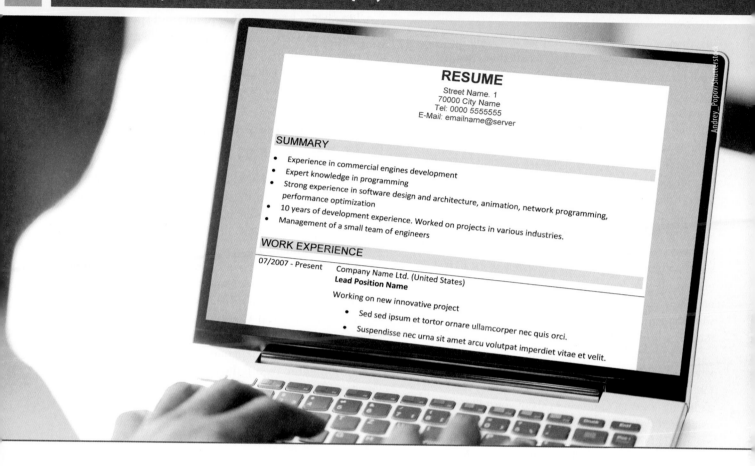

13 | Preparing Résumés and Application Messages

Learning Objectives

After studying this chapter, you will be able to ...

13-1 Prepare for employment by considering relevant information about yourself as it relates to job requirements.

13-2 Identify career opportunities using traditional and electronic methods.

13-3 Prepare an organized, persuasive résumé suitable for print and electronic postings.

13-4 Use employment tools other than the résumé that can enhance employability.

13-5 Write an application message that effectively introduces an accompanying print (designed) or electronic résumé.

13-1 Preparing for the Job Search

Managing your career begins with recognizing that securing a new job is less important than assessing the impact of that job on your life. Work isn't something that happens from 8 a.m. to 5 p.m., with life happening after 5 p.m. Life and work are interconnected, and true satisfaction comes from being able to fully express yourself in what you do. This means merging who you are—your values, emotions, capabilities, and desires—with the activities you perform on the job.[1]

An ideal job provides satisfaction at all of Maslow's need levels, from basic economic to self-actualizing needs. The right job for you will not be drudgery; the work itself will be satisfying and give you a sense of well-being. Synchronizing your work with your core beliefs and talents leads to enthusiasm and fulfillment. You will probably work 10,000 days of your life, not including the time spent commuting and on other related activities. Why spend all this time doing something unfulfilling when you could just as easily spend it doing what you enjoy?

Your **résumé** is a vital communication tool that provides a basis for judgment about your capabilities on the job. In preparing this document, your major tasks will be gathering essential information about yourself and the job, using traditional and electronic resources, planning and organizing the résumé to showcase your key qualifications, and adapting the résumé for various types of delivery. You will need to supplement your résumé with examples of your accomplishments and abilities. Finally, you'll prepare persuasive application messages appropriate for the delivery of your résumé.

13-1a Gathering Essential Information

The job search begins with research—collecting, compiling, and analyzing information—to assess your marketability. The research phase of the job search involves Step 1 of Figure 13.1 and is broken down into more detail as follows:

1. **Gather relevant information for decision making.** Complete a self-assessment to identify your own job-related qualifications and an analysis of the career field that interests you as well as a specific job in that field. Follow up in an interview with a career person in your field to acquire additional information.

2. **Prepare a company/job profile.** Compile the information you gathered into a format that allows you to compare your qualifications with the company and job requirements.

> **résumé** a vital communication tool that provides a basis for judgment about a person's capabilities on the job

This organized information will help you determine a possible match between you and the potential job.

3. **Identify unique selling points and specific support.** Determine several key qualifications and accomplishments that enhance your marketability. These are the key selling points you'll target in your résumé and later in a job interview.

13-1b Identifying Potential Career Opportunities

Plan to begin your job search for prospective employers months in advance. Waiting too long to begin and then hurrying through the job search process could affect your ability to land a satisfying job.

Before you begin, take the time to develop an organized strategy for your search efforts. You might download a template such as Microsoft's job application log (https://templates.office.com/) or create a spreadsheet using Excel of Google Sheets to help you track your contacts. You'll need a record of the name, address, email address, and telephone number of each potential employer. Later, record the date of each job contact you make and receive (along with what you learned from the contact), the name of the contact person, the date you sent a résumé, and so on. Your search for potential career opportunities likely will involve traditional and electronic job search sources.

Using Traditional Sources

Traditional means of locating a job include printed sources, networks, career services centers, employers' offices, employment agencies and contractors, and professional organizations.

Printed Sources

Numerous printed sources are useful in identifying firms in need of employees. Responses to advertised positions in the employment sections of newspapers should be made as quickly as possible after the ad is circulated. If your résumé is received early and is impressive, you could get a favorable response before other applications are received. If an ad requests that responses be sent to a box number without giving a name, be cautious. The employer could be legitimate but does not want present employees to know about the ad or does not want applicants to phone or drop by. However, you have a right to be suspicious of someone who wants to remain obscure while learning everything you reveal in your résumé. Print job listings can also be found in company newsletters, industry directories, and trade and professional publications, which are often available on the internet.

Figure 13.1 | Process of Applying for a Job

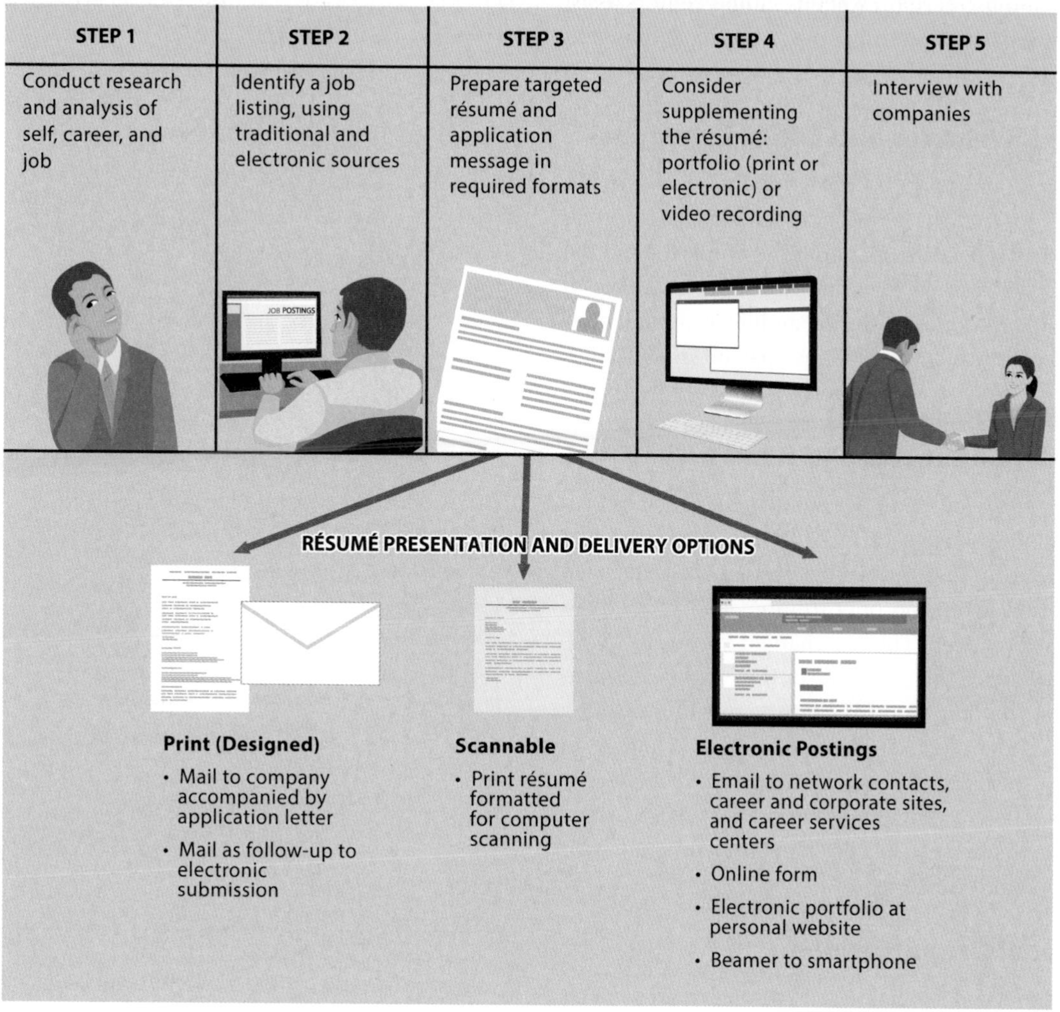

STEP 1	STEP 2	STEP 3	STEP 4	STEP 5
Conduct research and analysis of self, career, and job	Identify a job listing, using traditional and electronic sources	Prepare targeted résumé and application message in required formats	Consider supplementing the résumé: portfolio (print or electronic) or video recording	Interview with companies

RÉSUMÉ PRESENTATION AND DELIVERY OPTIONS

Print (Designed)
- Mail to company accompanied by application letter
- Mail as follow-up to electronic submission

Scannable
- Print résumé formatted for computer scanning

Electronic Postings
- Email to network contacts, career and corporate sites, and career services centers
- Online form
- Electronic portfolio at personal website
- Beamer to smartphone

Many job openings are never advertised. Therefore, developing a network of contacts is often the most valuable source of information about jobs. A number of professional networking sites exist online. Today, LinkedIn is the most popular networking website for business professionals. Facebook and Instagram play the dual role of enabling personal as well as professional networking. Many entrepreneurs actively exploit social media, such as Facebook and Twitter, to promote their businesses and services. These are just a few of the social networking opportunities available.

Your network could include current and past employers, guest speakers in your classes or at student organization meetings, business contacts you met while interning or participating in shadowing or over-the-shoulder experiences, professors, and so on. Let these individuals know the type of job you are seeking and ask their advice for finding employment in today's competitive market.

Career Services Centers

You will want to register with your college's career services center at least three semesters before you graduate. Typically, the center has a website and a browsing room loaded with career information and job announcement bulletins. Career counseling is available at most career services centers, including workshops on résumé writing, interviewing, etiquette, mock interviews, "mocktail" parties for learning to mingle at pre-interview social events, and more. Through the center, you can learn about job fairs at which you can meet prospective employers and schedule on-campus, phone, and video interviews with company recruiters.

Most career services centers use electronic tracking systems. Rather than submitting printed résumés, students upload their résumés into a computer file, following the specific requirements of the tracking system used by the college or university. A search of the résumé database generates an interview roster of the top applicants for a campus recruiter's needs. Some centers assist students in preparing electronic portfolios to supplement their résumés.

Employers' Websites and Office Locations

Most organizations post job openings on their website. For local businesses, it might be useful to schedule an informational interview to learn more about the employer and the type of skills that it looks for in new employees. Although you should not ask for a job during an informational interview, the contact you have made may pay off in the future as part of your professional network.

Employment Agencies and Contractors

City, county, state, and federal employment agencies provide free or inexpensive services. Some agencies offer online listings or phone recordings so that applicants can get information about job opportunities and procedures for using their services. The fee charged by private agencies is paid by either the employee or the employer, is usually based on the first month's salary, and is due within a few months. Some agencies specialize in finding high-level executives or specialists for major firms. Employment contractors specialize in providing temporary employees and might be able to place you in a position on a temporary basis until you find a full-time job.

Professional Organizations

Officers of professional organizations, through their contacts with members, can be good sources of information about job opportunities. A lot of job information is exchanged at meetings of professional associations. In addition to job listings in journals or on organization's websites, interviews are sometimes conducted at conference locations.

In addition to the professional growth that comes from membership in professional organizations, active participation is a good way to learn about jobs. Guest speakers share valuable information about the industry and its career and job opportunities. Employers are often favorably impressed when membership and experiences gained are included on the résumé and discussed during an interview. They are even more impressed if the applicant has been an officer in the organization, as it indicates leadership, community commitment, and willingness to serve without tangible reward, social acceptance, or high level of aspiration. By joining and actively participating in professional, social, and honorary organizations, you increase your opportunities to develop rapport with peers and professors and gain an edge over less-involved applicants.

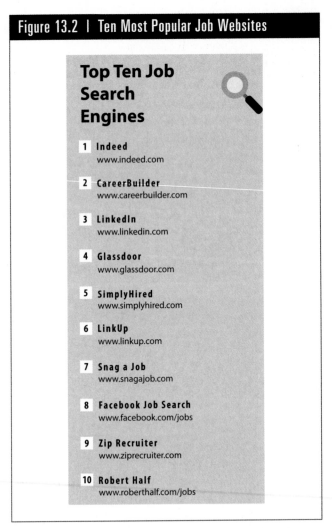

Figure 13.2 | Ten Most Popular Job Websites

Top Ten Job Search Engines

1 **Indeed**
   www.indeed.com

2 **CareerBuilder**
   www.careerbuilder.com

3 **LinkedIn**
   www.linkedin.com

4 **Glassdoor**
   www.glassdoor.com

5 **SimplyHired**
   www.simplyhired.com

6 **LinkUp**
   www.linkup.com

7 **Snag a Job**
   www.snagajob.com

8 **Facebook Job Search**
   www.facebook.com/jobs

9 **Zip Recruiter**
   www.ziprecruiter.com

10 **Robert Half**
   www.roberthalf.com/jobs

Source: The Top 12 Job Search Engines For 2022. (2022). Retrieved March 1, 2022 from https://careersidekick.com/tools/job-search-websites/

Using Electronic Employment Resources

Companies and job hunters are using the internet to assist in various stages of the job search process. Job boards, such as CareerBuilder, Monster, and Indeed, provide a variety of services to both job applicants and employers. Figure 13.2 provides a list of the top ten job websites as calculated by Career Sidekick.[2]

The job boards include jobs of all levels, occupations, and locations. Others specialize in certain kinds of jobs. Most job sites provide the following features and information:

- **Search and apply for job openings.** There are thousands of online job banks. Most work in the same basic way: employers pay to post job openings; job seekers search the openings and apply for those that interest them. Most sites allow you to search by occupation, location, industry, and other characteristics.

- **Post your résumé.** Sometimes you can post your résumé without applying for a specific job. On some job sites, employers can then review your résumé for positions they haven't even posted.

- **Get a feel for job requirements and pay.** Job boards can be a good research tool. They can help you learn what kinds of workers employers want, the skills they expect, and the pay and benefits they offer.

When using job sites, as with other online resources, be aware of possible fraudulent activities. For example, you should not have to pay to post your résumé or search job openings. However, you may have to register to use all of the features of a job website. Likewise, some job postings are scams. Be wary of any that ask you for an "up-front" investment of money for products or instructions. Also, be wary of those that offer commissions or pay thousands of dollars for job duties, such as processing checks on behalf of foreign nationals or reshipping goods from your home. Finally, never give out personal information. A legitimate company won't ask you for your social security number, credit card numbers, bank account information, or any other personal details.

Locating Career Guidance Information

According to one career consultant, "Most people in the old days could go into an organization [during a job interview] and not really know about it and hope for the best. Now, people can understand the organization before they even apply."[3] The internet places a wealth of information at your fingertips that will prepare you for the job interview if you use it as a research tool. Suggestions for effectively using career guidance information on the internet follow:

- **Visit career sites for information related to various phases of the job search.** You'll find a wide range of timely discussions on career sites: planning a job search, finding a job you love, researching employers, working a career fair, crafting winning résumés and cover messages or letters, negotiating a salary, and so on.

- **Visit corporate websites to learn about companies.** You can locate information online for targeting your résumé appropriately and to prepare for the job interview. Read mission statements or descriptions of services to see how the organization describes itself and review the annual report and strategic plan to learn about their financial condition and predicted growth rates. Search for "What's New" or "News" sections promoting new developments, as well as career opportunities and job postings. Evaluating the development and professional nature of the website will give you an impression of the organization. Supplement this information with independent sources to confirm the company's stability and status, as negative news likely will not be posted on the website.

- **Identify the specific skills that companies are seeking.** Study the job descriptions provided on corporate home pages and job sites to identify the skills required for the job and the latest industry buzzwords. Use this information to target your résumé to a specific job listing and to generate keywords for an electronic résumé.

- **Network with prospective employers.** It's easy to network online by attending electronic job fairs, chatting with career counselors, participating in news groups and LISTSERVs applicable to your field, and corresponding by email with contacts in companies. The value of these electronic networking experiences is to learn about an industry and career, seek valued opinions, and uncover potential job opportunities. By applying effective communication strategies for an online community, you can make a good impression, create rapport with employment contacts online, and polish your interviewing skills.

Using the Internet to Identify Job Listings

When using the internet or online databases to search for specific job openings, follow these general suggestions to get started:

- Input words and phrases that describe your skills rather than job titles because job titles vary by company.

- Use specific phrases such as "entry-level job" or "job in advertising" rather than "job search."

- Start with a wider job description term, such as "pharmaceutical sales jobs," then narrow down to the specific subject, geographic region, state, and so forth.

- Don't limit yourself to one search engine or online job site; try several, and bookmark interesting sites.

- Stay focused on your goal, and don't get distracted as you go.

13-2 Planning a Targeted Résumé

To match your interests and qualifications with available jobs, you'll need an effective résumé. To win a job interview in today's tight market where job seekers outnumber positions, you need more than a general résumé that documents your education and work history. The powerful wording of a **targeted résumé** reflects the requirements of a specific job listing that you

> **targeted résumé** a résumé that reflects the requirements of a specific job listing

have identified through traditional and electronic job search methods.

An employer typically scans résumés quickly, looking for reasons to reject the applicant, schedule an interview, or place it in a stack for rereading. This initial scan and a second brief look for those who make the cut give little time to explain why you are the best person for the job. To grab an employer's attention, you must selectively choose *what to say, how to say it,* and *how to arrange it* on the page so that it can be read quickly but thoroughly. A concise, informative, easy-to-read summary of your relevant qualifications will demonstrate that you possess the straightforward communication skills demanded in today's information-intensive society.

The goal of the résumé is to get an interview, so your résumé must show that you are, at least on the surface, qualified for the job for which you are applying. The best way to do this is to match your skills to those the employer is seeking. Hopefully, you have already done your homework and familiarized yourself with the type of skills, experience, and qualifications that employers in your field are looking for by finding and analyzing job advertisements for the position you desire. If you have performed this task well, you should have a solid understanding of the skills and qualifications you will need. You should have also spent some time reviewing your own life history to identify situations in which you have demonstrated those skills and abilities.

If you have done both of these tasks effectively, you should be well prepared to write a résumé that matches your skills with those an employer is seeking. These are the skills and qualifications that should be easily gleaned from a quick scan of your completed résumé. Other skills and experiences should be omitted so that your résumé is well targeted to the specific position that you are seeking. This fact should be almost immediately obvious to the employer reviewing your materials.

It is also important to remember that your résumé is not being reviewed in a vacuum. It is likely that the employer also is reviewing dozens of other résumés at the same time they are reading yours. For this reason, you should also have a solid knowledge of what your competitors bring to the table and how well you compare. A strategic job seeker will have a clear idea of their strongest selling points as compared with others and will have considered how to best showcase these favorably.

13-2a Standard Parts of a Résumé

A winning résumé contains standard parts that are adapted to highlight key qualifications for a specific job. The sample résumés and in-depth explanation of each standard part

Another name for résumé is *"curriculum vitae"* or *"CV,"* which is Latin for *"course of one's life."*

Rawpixel.com/Shutterstock

provided in Model Documents 13.1 through 13.4 will prepare you for creating a résumé that describes your qualifications best.

Identification

Your objective is to provide information that will allow the interviewer to reach you. Include your name, current address, phone number, and email address. Provide a clear, benign email address that reflects a positive impression, such as one that includes your proper name and the email provider (e.g., no "mustangsally@gmail.com"). You should also include your website address or professional networking link to provide access to more detailed information.

To ensure that the interviewer can quickly locate the identification information, center it on the page or use graphic design elements to call attention to your name. You should include a permanent address (parent's or other relative's address) if you are interviewing when classes are not in session. In addition, leave a clear, straightforward greeting on your phone that portrays you as a person serious about securing a job. Eliminate music, clever sayings, or background noise.

Job and/or Career Objective

Following the "Identification" section, state your job/career objective—the job you want. Interviewers can see quickly whether the job you seek matches the one they have to offer. A good job/career objective must be specific enough to be meaningful yet general enough to apply to a variety of jobs. The following example illustrates a general objective that has been revised to describe a specific job:

General Objective	Specific Objective
• A challenging position that enables me to contribute to an organization's success.	• Position where my creative web design skills and ability to work under pressure will enable me to contribute to organizational success.

- A position with a stable organization that provides an opportunity for development and career advancement.

- Position where my accounting knowledge, attention to detail, and strong work ethic will enable me to contribute to a firm's financial success.

In addition to addressing your skills, values, and goals, a useful objective statement is positioned so as to show how these abilities will contribute to an organization. Some employment specialists have criticized objective statements as being generally too self-centered and, thus, not particularly useful. Other experts argue that a statement of your job or career objective can limit your job opportunities; your objective should be obvious from your qualifications. A strategic job applicant will consider the usefulness of including an objective statement when taken into consideration with other aspects of their résumé and how well they can best compete for a position.

Career Summary

To survive the interviewer's 40-second scan, you must provide a compelling reason for a more thorough review of your résumé. To accomplish this goal, another strategy is to craft a persuasive introductory statement that quickly synthesizes your most transferable skills, accomplishments, and attributes, and place it in a section labeled "Summary" or "Professional Profile." As stated earlier, be aware that you are competing with others, so you want to position yourself favorably in comparison by highlighting your personal strengths as they relate to the desired skills or abilities.

In other words, the synopsis of your key qualifications should communicate why you should be hired. Your answer should evolve naturally from the career objective and focus on your ability to meet the needs of the company you have identified from your extensive research.

A high-impact career summary should be developed for your profile on job websites or professional networking sites. A version of this summary can be provided on your résumé as well. Compose a career summary that will interest any interviewer so that they will instantly see you as an applicant with exactly the skills needed for the job, as in the following example:

> Hardworking banking professional with two years of experience processing residential and commercial real-estate loans. Very active in professional organizations locally, resulting in a large network of potential clients. Named "Most Promising Young Banker" by the Iowa Banking Association in 2022.

This example combines the applicant's career objective—loan officer at a bank—with her unique selling points: her involvement in the local business community

and acknowledgment of her promise by a recognized and relevant professional organization.

Separate Objective and Career Summary

Objective: Position where my proven customer service skills and strong work habits will enable me to contribute to a growing company.
Career Summary: Six years of experience in a telephone service center; promoted to team leader after two years and supervisor after four.

Combined Objective With Career Summary

Professional Profile: Entry-level position in investment banking or finance. Internship experience with two investment banking firms, where I prepared and delivered multiple sales presentations to potential high-volume clients.

Linked Objective and Career Summary

Profile: Position as sales representative in which demonstrated commission selling and hard work bring rewards.
Accomplishments:

▸ Three years' straight commission sales.

▸ Average of \$35,000–\$55,000 a year in commissioned earnings.

▸ Consistent success in development and growth of territories.

Qualifications

The "Qualifications" section varies depending on the information identified in the analysis of self, career, and job. This information is used to divide your qualifications into appropriate parts, label them appropriately, and arrange them in the best sequence. Usually, qualifications stem from your education and work experience (words that appear as headings in the résumé). Order these categories according to which you perceive as more impressive to the employer, with the more impressive category appearing first. For example, education is usually the chief qualification of a recent college graduate. However, a sales representative with related work experience might list experience first, particularly if the educational background is inadequate for the job sought.

Education

Beginning with the most recent, list the degree, major, school, and graduation date. Include a blank line between schools for easy reading. The interviewer will probably want to know first whether you have the appropriate degree, then the institution, and then other details. Recent or near college graduates should omit high school activities because that information is "old news." However, include high school activities if they provide a pertinent dimension to your qualifications. For example, having attended high school abroad is a definite advantage to an applicant seeking employment in an international firm. In addition, high school accomplishments could be relevant for freshmen or sophomores seeking cooperative education assignments, scholarships, or part-time jobs. Of course, this information will be replaced with college activities when the résumé is revised for subsequent jobs or other uses.

Include overall and major grade point averages if they are B or better—but be prepared to discuss any omissions during an interview. Some recruiters recommend that every candidate include their grade point average because an omission might lead the reader to assume the worst. Honors and achievements that relate directly to education can be incorporated in this section or included in a separate section. Listing scholarships, appearances on academic lists, and initiations into honor societies is common; but consider also including business-relevant skills you've developed, including client projects, team building, and field experiences. If honors and achievements are included in the "Education" section, be sure to include plenty of white space or use bullets to highlight these points (refer to Model Documents 13.1 and 13.3).

The "Education" section could also include a list of special skills and abilities such as foreign language and computer competency. A list of courses typically required in your field is unnecessary and occupies valuable space. However, you should include any courses, workshops, or educational experiences that are not usual requirements, such as internships, cooperative education semesters, "shadowing," and study abroad.

Work Experience

The "Work Experience" section provides information about your employment history. For each job held, list the job title, company name, dates of employment, primary responsibilities, and key accomplishments. The jobs can be listed in reverse chronological order (beginning with the most recent) or in order of job relatedness. Begin with the job that most obviously relates to the job being sought if you have gaps in your work history, if the job you are seeking is very different from the job you currently hold, or if you are just entering the job market and have little, if any, related work experience.

Arrange the order and format of information about each job (dates, job title, company, description, and accomplishments) so that the most important information is emphasized—but format all job information consistently. If you have held numerous jobs in a short time, embed dates of employment within the text rather than surround them with white space. Give related job experience added emphasis by listing it first or surrounding it with white space.

Employers are interested in how you can contribute to their bottom line, so a winning strategy involves concentrating on accomplishments and achievements. Begin with the job title and company name that provides basic information about your duties, and then craft powerful descriptions of the quality and scope of your performance. These bullet points will provide deeper insight into your capability, ambition, and personality and set you apart from other applicants who take the easy route of providing only a work history.

Return to the in-depth analysis you completed at the beginning of the job search process to recall insights as to how you can add immediate value to this company. Consider the following questions to spur your recognition of marketable skills from your education, work, and community experiences.[4]

My Marketable Skills

- How does my potential employer define success in the job for which I'm applying? How do I measure up?

- What is my potential employer's bottom line (money, attendance, sales, etc.)? When have I shown that I know how to address that bottom line?

- What project am I proud of that demonstrates I have the skill for my job objective?

- What technical or management skills do I have that indicate the level at which I perform?

- What problem did I solve, how did I solve it, and what were the results?

Because interviewers spend such a short time reading résumés, the style must be direct and simple. Therefore, a résumé should use crisp phrases to help employers see the value of the applicant's education and experiences. To save space and to emphasize what you have accomplished, use these stylistic techniques:

1. Omit pronouns referring to yourself (*I, me, and my*).

2. Use subject-understood sentences.

3. Begin sentences with action verbs as shown in the following examples:

Instead of	Use
• I had responsibility for developing sales materials.	• Developed sales materials, including brochures and website promotions.
• My duties included meeting with potential clients to review financial products.	• Met with potential clients and used interpersonal communication skills to sell a wide range of financial products.
• I was the treasurer of my fraternity and managed a charitable fund-raising event.	• Managed a $200,000-plus budget and organized a charitable fund-raising event that garnered $15,000, a 25 percent increase over previous year.
• I worked in retail sales, selling fashions and accessories.	• Named salesperson of the year for sales of more than $50,000.
• I was the president of the Student Marketing Association and a member of a winning case-competition team.	• Demonstrated excellent leadership skills as president of Student Marketing Association and collaborative teamwork skills as member of winning case-competition group.

Action verbs are especially appropriate for résumés because employers are looking for people who will work. Note the subject-understood sentences in the right column of the previous example: action words used as first words provide emphasis. One of the best places to find action words is in the advertisements for the jobs for which you are applying. Using key phrases from the job advertisement can help the applicant in two ways: (1) you look like a good fit with the company because you use the same language, and (2) your résumé will more likely be identified by the search software used to select the best qualified applicants for interviews. The following list provides examples of action verbs that are useful in résumés:

achieved	drafted	participated
analyzed	increased	planned
assigned	initiated	recruited
assisted	interpreted	researched
boosted	managed	streamlined
compiled	monitored	supervised
developed	organized	wrote

A quick web search will result in additional action verbs from which to select.

To avoid a tone of egotism, do not use too many adjectives or adverbs that seem overly strong. Plan to do some careful editing after writing your first draft.

Honors and Activities

Make a trial list of any other information that qualifies you for the job. Divide the list into appropriate divisions and then select an appropriate label. Your heading might be "Honors and Activities." You might include a section for "Activities," "Leadership Activities," or "Memberships," depending on the items listed. You might also include a separate section on "Military Service," "Civic Activities," "Volunteer Work," or "Interests." If you have only a few items under each category, use a more general term and combine the lists. If your list is lengthy, divide it into more than one category as interviewers prefer "bite-size" pieces that are easy to read and remember.

Resist the urge to include everything you have ever done; keep in mind that every item you add distracts from other information. Consider summarizing information that is relevant but does not merit several separate lines—for example, "Involved in art, drama, and choral groups." To decide whether to include certain information, ask these questions: How closely related is it to the job being sought? Does it provide job-related information that has not been presented elsewhere?

Personal Information

Because a résumé should primarily contain information that is relevant to an applicant's experience and qualifications, you must be selective when including personal information that is not related to the job you are seeking. The space could be used more effectively to include more about your qualifications or to add more white space. Personal information is commonly placed at the end of the résumé just above the "References" section because it is less important than qualifications (education, experience, and activities).

Under the 1964 Civil Rights Act (and subsequent amendments) and the Americans with Disabilities Act (ADA), employers cannot make hiring decisions based on gender, age, marital status, religion, national origin, or disability. Employers prefer not to receive information about these protected areas because questions could be raised about whether the information was used in the hiring decision.

Follow these guidelines related to personal information:

- **Do not include personal information that could lead to discriminatory hiring.** Exclude height, weight, color of hair and eyes, and a personal photograph on the résumé.

- **Reveal ethnic background (and other personal information) only if it is job related.** For example, certain businesses might be actively seeking employees in certain ethnic groups because the cultural knowledge and foreign language skills associated with

Living Online?

Your social media profiles, photos, and "innermost" thoughts create a "shadow" résumé that may hurt your employment opportunities far into the future.

A recent employer survey indicated that almost all (98 percent) do background research about employees online.[5] Seventy-eight percent of employers believe that current employees should maintain a work-appropriate social media profile.[6]

dolphfyn/Shutterstock.com

an ethnic background is a legitimate part of the job description. For such a business, ethnic information is useful and appreciated.

- **Include personal information (other than information covered by employment legislation) that will strengthen your résumé.** Select information that is related to the job you are seeking or that portrays you as a well-rounded, happy individual off the job. Include interests, hobbies, favorite sports, and willingness to relocate. You can also include the following topics if you have not covered them elsewhere in the résumé: spoken and written communication skills, computer competency, foreign language or computer skills, military service, community service, scholastic honors, job-related hobbies, and professional association memberships.

- **Consider whether personal information might be controversial.** For example, listing a sport that an interviewer might perceive to be overly time consuming or dangerous would be questionable. An applicant seeking a position with a religious or political organization could benefit from revealing a related affiliation.

References

Providing potential employers a list of references (people who have agreed to supply information about you when requested) complements your employment credentials. Listing names, addresses, phone numbers, and email addresses of people who can provide information about you adds credibility to the résumé. Employers, former employers, and college instructors are good possibilities. Friends, relatives, and neighbors are not (because of their perceived bias in your favor). Some career experts recommend

including a peer to document your ability to work as a member of a team, an important job skill in today's team-oriented environment.[7] According to Bob Daugherty, former head of U.S. recruiting for PricewaterhouseCoopers, the best references are people who work for the organization you are looking to join.[8] You'll gain these employee referrals by developing strong relationships through proactive and professional networking via traditional and electronic means. Update your reference list often to be certain that your choices remain relevant and credible (e.g., none are deceased or dismissed for embezzlement).

References can be handled on the résumé in several ways. As the closing section of your résumé, you can provide a list of references; include a brief statement that references are available on request or from a career services center; or omit any statement regarding references, assuming that references are not needed until after an interview. You can list references directly on the résumé if you have limited qualifications to include, if you know that a company interviews applicants *after* references are contacted, or when you believe the names of your references will be recognizable in your career field. You could include a statement such as "For references …," or "For additional information …," and give the address of the career services center of your college or university, the job bank posting your credentials, or the URL of your electronic portfolio.

Withholding the names of references until they are requested prevents unnecessary or untimely requests going to your present employer. This action also conveys genuine courtesy to the references. Even the most enthusiastic references could become apathetic if required to provide recommendations to endless interviewers. For this same reason, be sure to communicate with your references regularly if your job search continues longer than expected. Suggestions for communicating with references are discussed in Chapter 14.

When preparing a separate list of references to be given after a successful interview, place the word *References* and your name in a visible position as shown in Model Document 13.2. Balance the list (name, address, phone number, and relationship of reference to applicant) attractively on the page, and use the same paper used for printing the résumé. Whether it is handed to the interviewer personally or mailed, the references page professionally complements your résumé. Confident that you have a good message, you are now ready to put it in writing—to construct a résumé that will impress an employer favorably.

13-2b Types of Résumés

The general organization of all résumés is fairly standard: identification (name, address, phone number, and email address), job objective, qualifications, personal information, and references. The primary organizational challenge is in dividing the qualifications section into parts, choosing labels for them, and arranging them in the best sequence. When you review your self-, career, and job analyses data and your career/job profile, you will recognize that your qualifications stem mainly from your education and your experience. Your task is to decide how to present these two categories of qualifications. Résumés usually are organized in one of three ways: reverse chronological order (most recent activity listed first), functional order (most important activity listed first), or a chrono-functional order, which combines the chronological and functional orders, as the name implies. To determine which organizational plan to use, draft your résumé in each.

Chronological Résumé

The **chronological résumé** is the traditional organizational format for résumés. Two headings normally appear in the portion that presents qualifications: "Education" and "Experience." Which one should appear first? Decide which one you think is more impressive to the employer and put that one first. Within each section, the most recent information is presented first. Reverse chronological order is easier to use and is more common than functional order; however, it is not always more effective.

The chronological résumé is an especially effective format for applicants who have progressed up a clearly defined career ladder and want to move up another rung. Because the format emphasizes dates and job titles, the chronological résumé is less effective for applicants who have gaps in their work histories, are seeking jobs different from the job currently held, or are just entering the job market with little or no experience.[9]

If you choose the chronological format, look at the two headings from the employer's point of view, and reverse their positions if doing so is to your advantage. In the "Experience" section, jobs are listed in reverse-chronological order. Assuming you have progressed typically, your latest job is likely to be more closely related to the job being sought than the first job held. Placing the latest or current job first will give it the emphasis it deserves. Include beginning and ending dates for each job.

Functional Résumé

In a **functional résumé**, points of primary interest to employers—transferable skills—appear in major headings. These headings highlight what an applicant can *do* for the employer—functions that the applicant can perform well. Under each heading, an applicant could draw from educational and/or work-related experience to provide supporting evidence.

A functional résumé requires a complete analysis of self, career, and the job sought. Suppose, for example, that a person seeking a job as an assistant hospital administrator wants to emphasize qualifications by placing them in major headings. From the hospital's advertisement of the job and from accumulated job appraisal information, an applicant sees this job as both an administrative and a public-relations job. The job requires skill in communicating and knowledge of accounting and finance. Thus, headings in the "Qualifications" section of the résumé could be "Administration," "Public Relations," "Communication," and "Budgeting." Under "Public Relations," for example, an applicant could reveal that a public relations course was taken at a state university, from which a degree is to be conferred in May, and that a sales job at ABC Store provided abundant opportunity to apply the principles learned. With other headings receiving similar treatment, the qualifications portion reveals the significant aspects of education and experience.

Order of importance is the best sequence for functional headings. If you have prepared an accurate self-and job analysis, the selected headings will highlight points of special interest to the employer. Glancing at headings only, an employer can see that you understand the job's requirements and have the qualities needed for success.

Having done the thinking required for preparing a functional résumé, you are well prepared for a question that is commonly asked in interviews: "What can you do for us?" The answer is revealed in your

> **chronological résumé** the traditional organizational format for résumés, with headings that spotlight an applicant's education and experience
>
> **functional résumé** the organizational format for résumés that highlights an applicant's transferable skills

major headings. They emphasize the functions you can perform and the special qualifications you have to offer.

If you consider yourself well qualified, a functional résumé is worth considering. If your education or experience is scant, a functional résumé could be best for you. Using "Education" and "Experience" as headings (as in a chronological résumé) works against your purpose if you have little to report under the headings; the format would emphasize the absence of education or experience.

Chrono-Functional Résumé

The **chrono-functional résumé** combines features of chronological and functional résumés. This format can give quick assurance that educational and experience requirements are met and still use other headings that emphasize qualifications.

13-3 Preparing Résumés for Electronic and Print Delivery

Most employers prefer to receive résumés in standard format through electronic media. Whether presented on paper or electronically, the arrangement of a résumé is just as important as the content. If the arrangement is unattractive, unappealing, or in poor taste, the message might never be read. Errors in keyboarding, spelling, and punctuation could be taken as evidence of a poor academic background, lack of respect for the employer, or carelessness. Recognize that résumés serve as your introduction to employers and indicate the quality of work you'll produce.

As in preparing other difficult documents, prepare a rough draft as quickly as you can and then revise as many times as needed to prepare an effective résumé that sells you. After you are confident with the résumé, ask at least two other people to check it for you. Carefully select people who are knowledgeable about résumé preparation and the job you are seeking, and who can suggest ways to present your qualifications more effectively. After you have incorporated those changes, ask a skillful proofreader to review the document.

To accommodate employers' preferences for the presentation and delivery of résumés, you should be aware of three versions of résumés, as shown in Model Documents 13.1, 13.3, and 13.4:

chrono-functional résumé a résumé that combines features of chronological and functional résumés

beamer a quick version of a résumé designed in a format suitable for broadcasting on smartphones; also called a *beamable résumé*

a chronological résumé printed on paper, a functional résumé, and a scannable résumé to be read by a computer.

13-3a Preparing Electronic Résumé Submissions

In the digital age of instant information, you'll use various online methods to apply for a job and present your qualifications to prospective employers.

The easiest and most common method of putting your résumé online is through emailing a résumé to a job bank for posting or to a networking contact who asked you to send a résumé. Many job banks, corporate sites, and career services centers require you to respond to specific openings by completing an online form or pasting your résumé into a designated section of the form. Frequently, you can input information directly on the website or download the form to be submitted by email or mail. You might also choose to post your résumé on your personal website as part of an electronic portfolio that showcases evidence of your qualifications. You could also develop a **beamer**, or *beamable résumé*, a quick version of your résumé designed in a format suitable for reading on smartphones. Recruiting professionals predict that millions of these electronic résumés will be exchanged silently at conferences, business meetings, and power lunches, similar to exchanging business cards.[10]

Electronic submissions are quick and easy but present new challenges and many opportunities to jeopardize your employment chances and compromise your privacy.

Just consider recent struggles you might have faced in dealing with viruses and unwelcomed emails, attempting to access nonworking links, and more. Before uploading your résumé, follow these suggestions to ensure that your electronic submission is both professional and technically effective:

- **Choose postings for your résumé with purpose.** Online résumé postings are not confidential. Once your résumé is online, anyone can read it, including your current employer. You might also begin to receive junk mail and cold calls from companies who see your résumé online; even more seriously, you could become a victim of identity theft. To protect your privacy online, limit personal information disclosed in the résumé and post only to sites with password protection allowing you to approve the release of your résumé to specific employers. Dating your electronic résumé will also prevent embarrassment should your employer find an old version of your résumé, which could occur as a result of the exchange of résumés between career sites, and delays in updating postings.

Ned Avers

45 Chester Street

Watertown, IA 62205

(530) 555-1565

na@gmail.com

→ **Includes email address that reflects professional image.**

Mortgage Loan Processor

- Mortgage industry professional with loan-processing experience and a comprehensive knowledge of conventional and government loan programs.

- Thorough in gathering borrower information, verifying loan documents, and reviewing file documentation to guide each loan from preapproval to closing.

- Computer savvy in MS Office Suite and proprietary mortgage-processing software.

Loan Processing Expertise

Conforming & Nonconforming Loans, FRMs, ARMs, GPMs, Jumbo Loans, Fannie Mae & Freddie Mac Guidelines, FHA, VA, USDA Rural Development Loans

Professional Experience

Watertown First Federal Bank—Watertown, IA

Loan Processor, 2019 to Present

- Regarded as one of the bank's most productive loan processors, handling an average of 22 files monthly.

- Outperformed company average in achieving loan-processing turn-around time of 12 days or less (compared to typical 15 to 20 days).

- Provided expedient service cited as key to consistently high customer satisfaction and a 10 percent increase in referrals in 2013.

- Ensured all files were complete prior to underwriting hand-off and coordinated effectively with title companies to ensure smooth closings.

- Successfully processed some of the most challenging loan applications (e.g., first-time borrowers, self-employed applicants, and borrowers with problematic credit histories).

Bank of Iowa—Watertown, IA

Teller, 2016 to 2019

- Provided friendly service to individual and commercial bank customers within regional financial institution.

Education

Watertown Community College—Watertown, IA

Associate of Science in Business, 2016

Overall GPA: 3.95

Format Pointers:
- Places name at top center for easy viewing (top right is also acceptable).

- Uses bold font to distinguish identification section and headings from remaining text.

- Creates visual appeal through custom format rather than commonly used template, short readable sections focusing on targeted qualifications, and streamlined bulleted lists.

Diversity Consideration: Follows standard format and rules for résumés for application with a U.S. company. Specific formats vary for specific countries and federal governments.

Ned Avers

45 Chester Street

Watertown, IA 62205

(530) 555-1565

na@gmail.com

References

Leona Harden

Manager of Teller Services

Bank of Iowa

345 Main Street

Watertown, IA 65009

530-555-3209

lharden@bankofiowa.com

Relationship: Immediate supervisor, 2016 to 2019

Fred Murray, Instructor

Accounting Department

Watertown Community College

Postal Drop ACC 201

Watertown, IA 65009

530-555-8956

fmurray@wcc.edu

Relationship: Academic advisor and instructor for accounting courses

Linda Larsen, Manager

Watertown Boys and Girls Club

437 Oak Street

Watertown, IA 65009

530-555-3232

llarsen@wbgc.org

Relationship: Supervisor for volunteer activities

Includes professor and immediate supervisors as references, but excludes friends, relatives, or clergy to avoid potential bias.

Includes for each reference full contact information, including email address, if available, and relationship to job applicant.

Format Pointers:
- **Prepares reference page at same time as résumé and makes available immediately after successful interview. Paper (color, texture, and size) and print type match résumé.**

- **Balances references attractively.**

Jerad Barker

134 Caswell Avenue.

Middleton, CT 03055

821-555-1212 (home)

821-555-3434 (cell)

JBarker@hotmail.com

Dedicated civil engineer with experience in structural and transportation design and proven leadership abilities.

Core Competencies

- Structural Investigation & Design
- Computer Aided Design (CAD)
- Conceptual Design & Development
- Traffic Engineering
- Land Development
- Construction Drawings
- Project Management
- Hydraulics & Hydrology

- Soils & Earthwork
- Budgeting and Scheduling
- Impact Studies & Specifications
- Groundwater Monitoring
- Floodplain Management
- Construction Drawings
- Standard Specifications

Education

Bachelor of Science: Civil Engineering, emphasis in Structures
May 2019

Northern State University, Uptown, NY

Relevant Projects

Urban Lake and Park Development for City of Hartford, CT

Scope of design included storm water runoff, earthwork, structural analysis of retaining wall, and parking/sidewalk design.

- Designated Project Manager of four-member team.

- Retained quality control over project scope to preserve manageable size and avoid State violations.

- Initiated communication with city engineers and Fish & Game personnel on project-related issues and guidance.

- Maintained project schedule and completed on time. Received an 'A' grade on project.

Highway Design for State of Connecticut

The project scope included design of one-mile stretch of highway through private and public lands. Design challenges included steep terrain, storm water runoff, super-elevation for curves, and negotiating homes, businesses, and cemetery.

- Design included horizontal and vertical design based on minimal earthwork and minimal disturbance to local businesses and public land.

(continued on next page)

Callouts:

Includes clear objective and descriptive summary statements to grab attention and invite close reading.

Arranges qualifications into sections that emphasize applicant's relevant skills and accomplishments.

- Maintained project schedule and completed on time. Received an 'A' grade on project.

Selected Achievements

- Earned status of Engine Boss and Incident Commander Type 4 and oversaw wildfire control, including methods of attack, personnel and equipment requirements, and strategic planning; maintained personnel and public safety.

- Supervised up to 150 personnel and all equipment needs including air tankers, engines, helicopters, and water tenders.

- Used sound judgment and decision-making skills to preserve safety of crew and implement strategic plans of attack against wildfires.

- Developed strong leadership and communication skills as demonstrated by high-level of performance by crewmembers.

- Implemented training regimens for crew; many members promoted as a result.

Employment History

Delivery/Yard Crew: Big Tree Lumber Co., Hartford, CT, 2019–Present

Forestry Technician: Danbury City Park, Danbury, CT FT Seasonal, 2016–2019

Type 2, 3, and 6 Crewmember: Metro Fire Dept., Newport, CT FT Seasonal, 2012–2019

Technical and Related Skills

MS Word, Excel, PowerPoint, and Project/AutoCAD/ HEC-HMS/Haestad Methods: WaterCAD, SewerCAD, and Flowmaster

Familiar Codes and Methods: NEPA, UBC, ASD, NDS, and LRFD

Connecticut Commercial Driver's License

Format Pointers:
- Places name at top center, where it can be easily seen.
- Uses bold font to distinguish identification section and headings from remaining text.
- Creates visual appeal with easy-to-read columnar format and balanced page arrangement.

Protect your references' privacy by omitting their names when posting online. Withholding this information will prevent unwelcomed calls by recruiters and other inappropriate contacts and threats to privacy. Because technology allows you to broadcast your résumé to all available positions on a career site, read postings carefully, and apply only to those that match your qualifications. This action improves the efficiency of the job selection process for the company and the applicant, and depicts fair, ethical behavior.

- **Don't hurry.** The speed, convenience, and informality of filling in online boxes or composing an email cover letter for an attached résumé can lead to sloppiness that reflects negatively on your abilities and attitude. Make sure every aspect of your electronic submission is top-notch just as you would for a print résumé. Provide all information exactly as requested; write concise, clear statements relevant to the job sought, and proofread carefully for grammatical and spelling errors. If you direct an employer to an electronic portfolio, devote necessary time to make it attractive, informative, and technically sound. Double-check your files to ensure they can be opened and retain an appealing format. Finally, read the posting carefully to learn how long your résumé will remain active, how to update it, and how to delete it from the site.

- **Include your résumé in the format requested by the employer or job bank.** You could be instructed to send the résumé as an attachment to the message or include it in the body of an email message, known as an **inline résumé**. The inline résumé is becoming the preferred choice as fear of computer viruses and daily email overload prevent employers from opening attachments. Unless instructed to send your attachment in a specific format such as Word, save your résumé and cover letter in one file, beginning with the cover letter. A plain text version, referred to as a **text résumé**, removes formatting and lacks the appeal of your designed résumé; however, you can be confident that an employer can open the file and won't have to spend time "cleaning up" your résumé if it doesn't transmit correctly. For this reason, you'll also paste the text version of your résumé below your email message when sending an inline résumé.

As an added safeguard, send yourself and a couple of friends a copy of the résumé and see how it looks on different computers before sending it out to an employer. If you wish, follow-up with a print résumé and cover letter on high-quality paper.

- **Include a keyword summary after the identification section.** You'll want to grab the employer's attention by placing the keywords on the first screen (within the first 24 lines of text). Providing this relevant information will motivate the employer to keep scrolling down to see how the keywords are supported rather than click to the next résumé.

- **Email a cover message to accompany an online résumé.** Some companies consider this cover email message to be prescreening for a job interview. Write a formal, grammatically correct message just as you would if you were sending an application letter in the mail.

Some print résumés become electronic files when they are scanned by the employer into an electronic database where they can be read and sorted by a computer. Companies of all sizes are using **electronic applicant-tracking systems** to increase efficiency of processing the volume of résumés received in a competitive market. Such systems store scanned résumés in an electronic database where they can be sorted by keywords, with a resulting ranking of applicants. The system can also automatically prepare letters of rejection and interview offers and store the résumés of hired applicants for future promotion consideration.

When seeking a job with a company that scans résumés into an electronic database, you will need to submit a **scannable résumé** as well as a print résumé that will be read by a person. If you are unsure whether a company scans résumés, call and ask. If still in doubt, take the safe route and submit your résumé in both formats.

Formatting a Scannable Résumé

To ensure that the scanner can read your résumé accurately and clearly, you must prepare a plain résumé with no special formatting. Follow these guidelines to prepare an electronic résumé that can be scanned accurately:

- **Use popular, nondecorative typefaces.** Typefaces such as Cambria and Times New Roman are clear and distinct and will not lose clarity in scanning.

- **Use 10- to 14-point font.** Computers cannot read small, tight print well. With a larger font, your résumé may extend to two pages, but page length is not an issue because a computer is reading the résumé.

  - **Do not include italics, underlining, open bullets, or graphic lines and boxes.** Use boldface or all capitals for emphasis. Italicized letters that touch and underlining that runs into the text result in a garbled scanned image. Design elements such as graphic lines, shading, and shadowing effects can confuse equipment. Use solid bullets (•) because an open bullet (•) could be read as an "o."

- **Use ample white space.** Use at least one-inch margins. Leave plenty of white space between the sections of a résumé so that the computer recognizes the partitions.

- **Print on one side of white, standard-size paper with sharp laser print.** Colored and textured paper scans poorly, and the scanner can pick up dirty specks on a photocopy.

- **Use a traditional résumé format.** Complex layouts that simulate catalogs or newspaper columns can confuse scanners.

- **Do not fold or staple your résumé.** If you must fold it, do not do so on a line of text.

> **inline résumé** a résumé included in the body of an email message
>
> **text résumé** a plain text (unformatted) version of a résumé
>
> **electronic applicant-tracking systems** systems that increase the efficiency of processing résumés by storing scanned résumés in an electronic database where they can be sorted by keywords, with a resulting ranking of applicants
>
> **scannable résumé** a résumé formatted to ensure a scanner can accurately read and convert it into a digital format

Making a Scannable Résumé Searchable

You have two concerns in preparing a scannable résumé. You want to (1) be certain information is presented in a manner the computer can read and (2) maximize the number of "hits" your résumé receives in a computerized résumé search. Follow these guidelines for making your print résumé searchable:

- **Position your name as the first readable item on the page.** Follow with your address, phone number and email below your name on separate lines.

- **Add powerful keywords in a separate section called "Keywords" or "Keyword Summary" that follows the identification.** To identify keywords, ask yourself what words best describe your qualifications. Make maximum use of industry jargon and standard, easily recognizable abbreviations (e.g., B.A., M.S.) in the keyword summary and the body of the résumé, as these buzzwords will likely be matches with the computer's keywords.

- **Format the keyword summary to maximize hits.** Capitalize the first letter of each word and separate each keyword with a period. Position keywords describing your most important qualifications first, and then move to the least important ones. Order is important because some systems stop scanning after the first 80 keywords. The usual order is (a) job title, occupation, or career field; (b) education; and (c) essential skills for a specific position. Be certain to include keywords that describe interpersonal traits, such as *adaptable, flexible, sensitive, team player, willing to travel, ethical, industrious, innovative, open minded,* and *detail oriented.*

- **Support your keywords with specific facts in the body of the résumé.** Use synonyms of your keywords in the body in the event the computer does not recognize the keyword (e.g., use *M.B.A.* in the keyword summary and *Master of Business Administration* in the body; use *presentation graphics software* in the keyword summary and a specific program in the body). One unfortunate applicant reported using "computer-assisted design" consistently throughout his résumé when the computer was searching for "CAD." Also, use a specific date of graduation in the education section. Some computer programs read two dates beside an institution to mean the applicant did not earn the degree (e.g., 2007–2011).

The scannable résumé replace with the following: Kerri Sears prepared when seeking a position in management information systems appears in Model Document 13.4. The scannable résumé is formatted for scanning into an electronic database to be matched with employer requirements.

13-3b Preparing a Print (Designed) Résumé

For print (designed) résumés, appearance is critical. A print résumé must look professional and reflect current formatting and production standards while maintaining a distinctive conservative tone. Graphic design sites, such as Canva, provide templates and guidance on creating a visually appealing résumé. Follow these guidelines for designing and producing a highly professional print résumé:

- **Develop an appealing résumé format that highlights your key qualifications and distinguishes your résumé.** Use the power of your word-processing software for style enhancements rather than settle for overused, inflexible templates. Study the example résumés in this chapter and models from other sources for ideas for enhancing the style, readability, and overall impact of the document. Then, create a custom design that best highlights your key qualifications.

- **Format information for quick, easy reading.** To format your résumé so that it can be read at a glance, follow these guidelines:

  ○ Use attention-getting headings to partition major divisions and add graphic lines and borders to separate sections of text.

  ○ Use an outline format when possible to list activities and events on separate lines, and include bullets to emphasize multiple points.

  ○ Use 10-point fonts or larger to avoid reader eye strain.

  ○ Use type styles and print attributes to emphasize key points. For example, to draw attention to the identification and headings, select a bold sans serif font (e.g., Calibri or Arial) slightly larger than the serif font (e.g., Cambria or Times New Roman) used for the remaining text. Capitalization, indention, and print enhancements (underline, italics, and bold) are useful for adding emphasis. Limit the number of type styles and enhancements, however, so the page is clean and simple to read.

  ○ Include identification on each page of a multiple-page résumé. Place your name and a page number at the top of the second and successive pages, with "Continued" at the bottom of the first page. The interviewer is re-exposed to your name, and pages can be reassembled if separated.

Kerri Sears

ksears@purdue.edu

Current Address	Permanent Address
420 Jaker Ave., Apt. 22	2800 N. Creekside St.
West Lafayette, IN 47906	Fort Wayne, IN 46825
(765) 555-2424	(260) 555-1234420

Skill Keywords

A full-time position developing management information systems in the banking industry, which will allow me to apply my database development and financial analysis skills.

Education

Purdue University, West Lafayette IN, expected May 2017 GPA: 3.6/4.0

(Major GPA: 3.8/4.0)

Bachelor of Science in Management

Minor: Management Information Systems

Significant Courses

Database Management Systems, Applied Systems Analysis and Design, Decision Support and Expert Systems, Computer Communications Systems

Computer Skills

Proficient with Windows, Mac, Linux and with MS Office (Word, Excel, PowerPoint, and Access), Sass, Tableau, PowerBuilder, Oracle, and MySQL

Work Experience

Assistant Coordinator/Tutor

Purdue University Writing Lab, West Lafayette, IN January 2019 to Present

- Hire, train, and supervise tutors while creating a motivational climate

- Coordinate promotions through the production of marketing materials and promotional events

- Tutor students with business writing needs

Financial Analyst Intern

Merrill Lynch, Chicago, IL Summer 2019

- Prepared balance sheet and income statement analyses

- Evaluated various tax statements and other financial publications

- Joined a project team for establishing databases of pertinent information for use in analyzing future plans, forecasts, and acquisitions

(continued on next page)

Positions name as first readable item.

Includes position sought and reason to hire in separate section.

Omits references to use space for additional qualifications; references furnished when requested.

Edges out competition by expanding on related experience and work achievements.

Business Analyst Intern

State Farm, Bloomington, IL Summer 2018

- Assisted in developing and maintaining computer-based systems and analyzed financial systems and provided systems analysts with documentation of business requirements for proposed systems

- Developed written procedures for new system applications

Activities/Honors

AIESEC International Exchange Organization Vice President, fall 2019 to present

Alpha Sigma Phi Fraternity Treasurer, fall 2017 to 2019

Lions Club Fundraising Assistant, fall 2016 to spring 2017

National City Bank Scholarship Award, June 2016

Dean's list: fall 2016 to fall 2019

Format Pointer:
Keeps résumé simple and readable by computer: easy-to-read font of 10 to 14 points; solid bullets; and no italics, underlining, or graphic lines or borders.

- **Create an appealing output to produce top professional quality.**

  ○ Check for consistency throughout the résumé. Consistency in spacing, end punctuation, capitalization, appearance of headings, and sequencing of details within sections will communicate your eye for detail and commitment to high standards.

  ○ Balance the résumé attractively on the page, with approximately equal margins. Allow generous white space so that the résumé looks uncluttered and easy to read.

- **Consider adding a statement of your creativity and originality.** Be certain that your creativity will not be construed as gimmickry and distract from the content of the résumé. Demonstrating creativity is particularly useful for fields such as advertising, public relations, graphic design, and those requiring computer proficiency.

- Select paper of a standard size (8-1/2" by 11"), neutral color (white, buff, or gray), and high quality (preferably 24-pound, 100 percent cotton fiber). Consider using a mailing envelope large enough to accommodate the résumé without folding. The unfolded documents on the reader's desk will get favorable attention and will scan correctly if posted to an electronic database.

- Print with a laser printer that produces high-quality output. Position paper so the watermark is read across the sheet in the same direction as the printing.

Some employers insist that the "best" length for a résumé is one page, stating that long résumés are often ignored. However, general rules about length are more flexible. Most students and recent graduates can present all relevant résumé information on one page. However, as you gain experience, you might need two or more pages to format an informative, easy-to-read résumé. A résumé forced on one page will likely have narrow margins and large blocks of run-on text (multiple lines with no space to break them). This dense format is unappealing and complicates the interviewer's task of skimming quickly for key information.

The rule about length is simple: Be certain your résumé contains only relevant information presented as concisely as possible. A one-page résumé that includes irrelevant information is too long. A two-page résumé that omits relevant information is too short.

The résumés illustrated in Model Documents 13.1 and 13.3 demonstrate the organizational principles for chronological and functional résumés. A references page is illustrated in Model Document 13.2. Study the various layouts to decide on one that will highlight your key qualifications most effectively.

13-4 Supplementing a Résumé

Some candidates feel their career accomplishments are not appropriately captured in a standard résumé. Two additional tools for communicating your qualifications and abilities are the portfolio and the employment video.

13-4a Professional Portfolios

The **professional portfolio** (also called the *electronic portfolio* or *e-portfolio* when presented in a digital format) can be used to illustrate past activities, projects, and accomplishments. It is a collection of artifacts that demonstrate your communication, people, and technical skills. Although portfolios were once thought of as only for writers, artists, or photographers, they are now seen as appropriate for other fields of work when the applicant wants to showcase abilities, such as user experience design (UXD).

Many portfolios are now presented in digital format, making the portfolio easier to organize and distribute to prospective employers via a personal website, blogs, digital portfolio tools, or other media. With the availability of user-friendly software, college campuses are offering e-portfolio tools that aid students in reflecting on their experiences and producing e-portfolios. Sites like Cargo Collective, Squarespace, and Wix are widely accessible and commonly used tools that students can use to build their own online portfolios, even if their college does not offer an e-portfolio system and they can continue to host their site even after graduation. Students are now expected to have personal and school email accounts. Personal accounts or "student portals" containing a student's course history, schedule, and financial concerns are assigned by the school (especially those with a learning management system [LMS], such as Blackboard or Canvas), and some schools also require the use of digital portfolios like Pathbrite, Book Creator, etc.

A clear understanding of your audience's needs and your qualifications will allow you to develop a logical organizational structure for your portfolio. Some possible items to include are:

- Sample speeches with digitized audio or video clips of the delivery
- Performance appraisals
- Awards
- Certificates of completion
- Reports, proposals, or written documents prepared for classes or on the job
- Brochures or programs describing workshops attended
- Commendation messages, records, or surveys showing client or customer satisfaction with service

After selecting the items for inclusion in your portfolio, select the appropriate software or binder you will use to showcase your accomplishments. Once you're organized, you can add items that demonstrate you have the characteristics the employer is seeking. Maintain your portfolio even after you are hired because it can demonstrate your eligibility for promotion, salary increase, or advanced training, or even justify why you should not be laid off.

Many examples of e-portfolios can be found on online; many universities provide examples and information on how to create effective student e-portfolios.

13-4b Employment Videos

A video recording can be used to extend visually the impact of the printed résumé. A video can capture your stage presence and ability to speak effectively and add a human dimension to the written process. Current technology enables applicants to embed video segments into **multimedia résumés** created with presentation software, such as Camtasia, and sent to prospective employers on an applicant's personal website.

Video résumés, which job seekers post on sites such as YouTube, are the latest trend in developing creative job qualifications. You can learn some important lessons for your video project by taking a look at the abundance of good and bad examples already posted. If possible, solicit the help of someone with film experience and follow these simple suggestions for creating a visually enhanced résumé that is brief, showcases your key qualifications, and reflects your personality:[11]

- Keep your video simple with one stationary shot using a good camera and tripod. Avoid gimmicky effects and excessive panning that distract from the message.
- Use proper lighting, making sure that the employer can see your face. Avoid light behind you that casts shadows.
- Invest in a good-quality microphone and speak clearly and at an appropriate pace for easy listening.
- Choose clothing appropriate for the job you are seeking. Video yourself wearing different clothing and watch the video to select the ideal choice. Avoid clothing that gaps and bunches when you sit, as well as bright colors and clothing patterns that tend to vibrate when filmed.
- Edit your video to eliminate dead air and other imperfections that detract from a professional image.

Employment videos are more commonly used to obtain employment in career fields for which

> **professional portfolio** a digital portfolio distributed to prospective employers via a personal website blog, digital portfolio tool, or other media; also called an electronic portfolio or e-portfolio
>
> **multimedia résumés** a résumé created with presentation software, such as Camtasia, and sent to prospective employers on an applicant's personal website
>
> **video résumés** a résumé created as a video for posting on sites such as YouTube

verbal delivery or visual performance is a key element. These fields include broadcasting and the visual and performing arts. The following guidelines apply when preparing an employment video:

- Be sure the video makes a professional appearance and is complimentary to you. A "home movie" quality recording will be a liability instead of an asset to your application.

- Avoid long "talking head" segments. Include segments that reflect you in a variety of activities; shots that include samples of your work are also desirable.

- Remember that visual media (such as photographs and videos) encourage the potential employer to focus on your physical characteristics and attributes, which might lead to undesired stereotyping and discrimination.

Be sure to advertise the availability of your portfolio and employment video to maximize its exposure. List your URL address in the identification section of your résumé. In your application letter, provide a link to your portfolio to motivate the prospective employer to view it. Talk enthusiastically about the detailed supplementary information available during your job interview and encourage the interviewer to view it when convenient. Note Karen Cunningham's promotion of her work as a marketing assistant when you read her application letter later in this chapter (refer to Model Document 13.5).

13-5 Composing Application Messages

When employers invite you to send either a print or electronic résumé, they may expect you to include an **application message** (also known as a *cover message or cover letter*). Because most applications are now made online, fewer employers ask for application letters. However, you should be knowledgeable about composing an application message for those situations in which they are expected.

As you have learned, a résumé summarizes information related to the job's requirements and the applicant's qualifications. An application message complements a résumé by speaking more directly to a specific job posting by (1) introducing the applicant, (2) attracting interest to the résumé, and (3) interpreting the résumé in terms of employer benefits.

> **application message** a message placed on top of the résumé so it can be read first by the employer; also called a cover message
>
> **unsolicited application messages** an unrequested message sent to many prospective employers that contains the same basic message

Because it creates interest and points out employer benefits, the application message is persuasive and, thus, written inductively. It is designed to convince an employer that qualifications are adequate just as a sales message is designed to convince a buyer that a product will satisfy a need. Like sales messages, application messages can be either solicited or unsolicited. Job advertisements *solicit* applications. Unsolicited application messages have greater need for attention-getters; otherwise, solicited and unsolicited application messages are based on the same principles.

Unsolicited application messages are the same basic message (perhaps with slight modifications) sent to many prospective employers. By sending unsolicited messages, you increase your chances of locating potential openings and possibly alert employers to needs they had not previously identified for someone of your abilities. However, sending unsolicited messages has some disadvantages. Because the employer's specific needs are not known, the opening paragraph will likely be more general (less targeted to a specific position) than the opening paragraph in solicited messages. The process could also be time consuming.

Karen Cunningham wrote the letter in Model Document 13.5 to accompany a chronological résumé she prepared after completing the company/job profile for a marketing assistant. The time Karen devoted to analyzing the job, the company, and her qualifications was well spent.

13-5a Persuasive Organization

A persuasive message is designed to convince the reader to take action, which, in this case is to read the résumé and invite you to an interview. Because an application message is persuasive, organize it as you would a sales message:

Sales Message	Application Message
Gets attention	Gets attention
Introduces product	Introduces qualifications
Presents evidence	Presents evidence
Encourages action	Encourages action
=	=
(sells a product, service, or idea)	(results in an interview)

Like a well-written sales message, a well-written application message uses a central selling feature as a theme. The central selling feature is introduced in the first or second paragraph and is stressed in the paragraphs that follow. Two to four paragraphs are normally sufficient for supporting evidence. Consider the order of importance as a basis for their sequence, with the most significant aspects of your preparation coming first.

Karen Cunningham

455 Ash Lane, Apt. 3

Birmingham, AL 67003

(504) 555-9876

kcunningham@gmail.com

November 21, 2023

Larry Canton, Hiring Manager

Dayton Ltd.

120 Main Street

Birmingham, AL 67012

Dear Larry Canton:

I am interested in your position of Marketing Assistant, which was posted on your corporate website. The combination of my natural ability, technical expertise, and work experience all make me an ideal candidate for this role.

As a recent graduate of Alabama State University with an emphasis in Marketing, I am intimately familiar with developments in social media promotion and data mining applications. I would also bring value to a company like yours through my experience in the private sector in various internship positions and my positive "can do" attitude.

For the past six months, I have interned in the Marketing Department of Ajax Corp., where I participated in the development of a marketing program for a new computer-networking product. As part of that team, I also wrote promotional materials for the company website and sent a weekly email newsletter to current customers.

I consider myself to be a productive worker with a solid work ethic who exerts optimal effort to ensure that all tasks given to me are completed on time and to the highest standards. My personal strengths include, but are not limited to the following:

- Being a motivated self-starter who takes the initiative and can work with minimal supervision.

- Being committed to providing a superior service to any company for which I work.

- Being computer literate with extensive software knowledge and proficiency covering a wide variety of applications.

Greater details of my accomplishments and achievements can be found in my attached résumé. I am available for interview at any time and can start work at short notice. Thank you for the time you have taken to consider my application, and I eagerly look forward to hearing from you.

Sincerely,

Karen Cunningham

Addresses letter to specific person, using correct name and job title.

Identifies how applicant learned of the position, the specific position sought, and background.

Discusses how education relates to job requirements.

Introduces résumé for additional information.

Encourages employer to act without sounding pushy or apologetic.

Format Pointers:
- **Formats as formal business letter because the message is accompanying a print résumé.**

- **An abbreviated email message including an online résumé in ASCII or RTF format would be appropriate for electronic submission.**

- **Uses the same high-quality, standard size and neutral colored paper as was used for the résumé.**

- **Includes the writer's address and contact information.**

Gain the Receiver's Attention

To gain attention, begin the message by identifying the job sought and describing how your qualifications fit the job requirements. This information will provide instant confirmation that you are a qualified applicant for an open position. An employer who reads hundreds of application letters and résumés will appreciate this direct, concise approach.

For an announced job, you should indicate in the first paragraph how you learned of the position—for example, employee referral, customer referral, executive referral, newspaper advertising, or job fair. Your disclosure will confirm that you are seeking an open job; and it will also facilitate an evaluation of the company's recruiting practices. Note that the opening of the letter in Model Document 13.5 indicates that the applicant learned of the position through a posting on the company's corporate website.

An opening for an unsolicited message must be more persuasive: you must convince the interviewer to continue to read your qualifications even though a job might not exist. As in the opening of a solicited message, indicate the type of position sought and your qualifications, but be more creative in gaining attention. The following paragraph uses the applicant's knowledge of recent company developments and an intense interest in the company's future to gain receiver attention.

> In the past three years, OfficeWorx has experienced phenomenal growth through various acquisitions, mergers, and market expansion. With this growth comes new opportunities, new customers, and the need for new team players to work in store management. While following the growth of OfficeWorx, I have become determined to join this exciting team and am eager to show you that my educational background, leadership abilities, and internship experience qualify me for the job.

Provide Evidence of Qualifications

For graduates entering the world of full-time work for the first time, educational backgrounds are usually more impressive than work histories. They can benefit from interpreting their educational experiences as meaningful, job-related experiences. An applicant for a human resources position should do more than merely report having taken courses in organizational behavior.

> In my business communication class, I could see the specific application of principles encountered in my organizational behavior and marketing classes. Questions about leadership and motivation seemed to recur throughout the course: What really motivates people? Why do people fear change? How can those fears be overcome? What communication practices can be used to motivate people and help them accept change? The importance of communication was a focus of many courses and my research report, "How to Get the Most from Others."

Your application message will not necessarily refer to information learned in a class. Recognizing that managers must be tactful (a point on which the person reading the message will surely agree), the applicant included some details of a class. This technique is basic in persuasion: Do not just say a product or idea is good; say what makes it good. Do not just say that an educational or work experience was beneficial; say what made it so.

By making paragraphs long enough to include interpretation of experiences on a present or previous job, you show an employer that you are well prepared for your next job. For example, the following excerpt from an applicant for a human resources position is short and general:

> I have worked in human resources for the past five years and have received high performance evaluations from my supervisor.

Added details and interpretation could make the value of the work experience more convincing:

> I have a strong passion for helping others, which is why I have found such fulfillment in human resources, providing support to my fellow employees and assisting them in ways that benefit them both personally and professionally. I also enjoy looking for solutions to common HR problems, which I feel would be a great asset in the position with your company. Since this consultant position works directly with multiple clients, assisting them in their human resources needs, I believe my innovative nature and strong skill set will help me succeed.

The applicant has called attention to qualities that managers like to see in employees: willingness to listen, problem-solving skills, concern for clients or customers, a positive attitude, innovation, fairness, and tact. As a learning experience, the human resources job has taught or reinforced principles that the employer sees as transferrable to the job being sought.

In this section, you can discuss qualifications you have developed by participating in student organizations, student government, athletics, or community organizations. Be specific in describing gained skills that can be applied directly on the job—for example, organization, leadership, spoken and written communication skills, and budgeting and financial management. You can also use your involvement as a channel for discussing important personal traits vital to the success of a business, such as interpersonal skills, motivation, imagination, responsibility, and team orientation.

> For the past year, I have served as treasurer for Alpha Chi Epsilon. In that duty, I have managed a $200,000 annual budget. By coordinating our yearly charitable fundraising event, I have exercised leadership, organizational, and communication skills.

Finally, end this section with an indirect reference to the résumé. If you refer to it in the first or second paragraph, readers might turn from the message at that point and look at the résumé. Avoid the obvious statement "Enclosed please find my résumé" or "A résumé is enclosed." Instead, refer indirectly to the résumé while restating your qualifications. The following sentence emphasizes that references can confirm the applicant's qualifications:

> References listed on the enclosed résumé would be glad to comment on my marketing education and experience.

Encourage Action

Once you have presented your qualifications and referred to your enclosed résumé, the next move is to encourage the receiver to extend an invitation for an interview. The goal is to introduce the idea of action without apologizing for doing so and without being demanding or "pushy." If the final paragraph (action closing) of your message is preceded by impressive paragraphs, you need not press hard for a response. Just mentioning the idea of a future discussion is probably sufficient. If you have significant related experience that you have developed as a central selling feature, mentioning this experience in the action closing adds unity and stresses your strongest qualification one last time. Forceful statements about *when* and *how* to respond are unnecessary and irritating. Avoid these frequently made errors:

- **Setting a date.** "May I have an appointment with you on January 15?" The date you name could be inconvenient; or even if it is convenient for the employer, your forwardness in setting it could be resented.

- **Expressing doubt.** "If you agree," "I hope you will," and "Should you decide" use subjunctive words that indicate a lack of confidence.

- **Sounding apologetic.** "May I take some of your time?" or "I know how busy you are" might seem considerate, but an apology is inappropriate when discussing ways you can contribute to a company.

- **Sounding overconfident.** "I will call you next week to set an appointment time that works for both of us." This statement is presumptuous and egotistical.

- **Giving permission to call.** "You may call me at (857) 555-6543." By making the call sound like a privilege ("may call") you could alienate the reader. Implied meaning: You are very selective about the calls you take, but the employer does qualify.

The following sentences are possible closing sentences that refer to an invitation to interview. They are not intended as model sentences that should appear in your message. Because finding the right job is so important, you will be well rewarded for the time and thought you invest in original wording.

- **"When a date and time can be arranged, I would like to talk with you."** The statement does not indicate who will do the arranging, and the meeting place and the subject of the conversation are understood.

- **"I would appreciate an opportunity to discuss the marketing assistant's job with you."** The indirect reference to action is not forceful. However, if the applicant has impressive qualifications, the reader will want an interview and will not need to be pushed.

- **"I look forward to talking with you about how my skills and experiences can benefit Beck Restaurant Group."** The statement asks for the interview and re-emphasizes the applicant's strong qualifications.

13-5b General Writing Guidelines

An excellent application message might be the most difficult message you ever attempt to write. It's natural to feel uncomfortable writing about yourself; however, your confidence will increase as you study the wealth of model documents available through your career services center and other sources. The writing principles you've been introduced to in this chapter should help you write a thoughtful, original message that impresses the interviewer. Instead of standard verbiage included in dozens of models, your self-marketing connects *your* experiences to your future with a specific company and reflects *your* personality and values. The following writing techniques will help distinguish your application message from the competition:

- **Substitute fresh, original expressions that reflect contemporary language.** Overly casual expressions and overused statements will give your message a dull, unimaginative tone. Obvious ideas such as "This is an application," "I read your ad," and "I am writing to apply for" are sufficiently understood without making direct statements. With the application message *and* résumé in hand, a reader learns nothing from "I am enclosing my résumé for your review." Observe caution in choosing overused words such as *applicant, application, opening, position, vacancy,* and *interview*.

- **Avoid overuse of I and writer-focused statements.** Because the message is designed to sell your services, some use of *I* is natural and expected; but restrict the number of times *I* is used, especially as the first word in a paragraph. Focus on providing specific evidence that you can meet the company's needs. The employer is not interested in reading about your need to earn more income, to be closer to your work, to have more pleasant surroundings, or to gain greater advancement opportunities.

- **Avoid unconvincing generalizations that could sound boastful.** Self-confidence is commendable, but overconfidence (or worse still, just plain bragging) is objectionable. Overly strong adjectives, self-judgmental terms, and unsupported generalizations damage your credibility. Instead of labeling your performance as "superior" or "excellent," or describing yourself as "an efficient, technically skilled team player," give supporting facts that show the interviewer you can deliver on what you're selling.

- **Tailor the message to the employer's need.** To impress the interviewer that your message is not a generic one sent to everyone, provide requested information, and communicate an understanding of the particular company, job requirements, and field.

- **Provide requested information.** Job listings often request certain information: "Must provide own transportation and willing to travel. Give educational background, work experience, and salary expected." Discuss these points in your application message. Preferably, the question of salary is left until the interview, allowing you to focus your message on your contributions to the company—not what you want from the company (money). Discussion of salary isn't meaningful until after a mutually successful interview; however, if an ad requests a statement about it, the message should address it. You may give a minimum figure or range, indicate willingness to accept a figure that is customary for work of that type, or indicate a preference for discussing salary at the interview.

- **Communicate knowledge of the company, job requirements, and language of the field.** Your statements about a company's rapid expansion or competitive advantage show you really are interested in the company, read widely, do more than you are required to do, and gather information before making decisions. However, phrase these statements carefully to avoid the perception of insincere flattery. For example, referring to the employer as "*the* leader in the field," "*the* best in the business," or "a great company" could appear as an attempt to get a favorable decision as a reward for making a complimentary statement. To reflect your understanding of the job requirements, use indirect statements that are informative and tactful. Direct statements such as "The requirements of this job are ..." presents information the employer presumes you already know; "An auditor should be able to

..." and "Sales personnel should avoid ..." sound like a lecture and could be perceived as condescending. Discussing experiences related to a specific job requirement or your preference for work that requires this skill reveals your understanding without a direct statement. Including terminology commonly used by the profession allows you to communicate clearly in terms the reader understands; it also saves space and implies your background in the field.

- **Focus on strengths and portray a positive attitude.** Concentrate on the positive aspects of your education or experience that have prepared you for the particular job. Apologizing for a shortcoming or admitting failure only weakens your case and raises questions about your self-esteem. Do not discuss your current employer's shortcomings. Regardless of how negatively you perceive your present employer, that perception has little to do with your prospective employer's needs. Also, if you speak negatively of your present employer, you could be perceived as someone who would do the same to the next employer.

13-5c Finishing Touches

The importance of professional formatting and careful proofreading of job application messages is generally understood. Still, employers frequently voice concern with the sloppiness and unprofessional appearance and content of electronic submissions. To survive the skeptical eye of an interviewer scanning for ways to reject an applicant, allow yourself time to produce a professional-looking document regardless of the presentation or delivery option you've chosen.

In regard to preparing an application message for email submission, career experts recommend formatting it as a business letter with the complete address of the company exactly as presented in a letter sent by mail and a formal closing such as "Sincerely." To help people reach you, include a full signature block with your mailing and email addresses, and phone number(s). The recipient can easily contact you without opening your attachments. Although seemingly unnecessary, the email address is useful when a recipient forwards your email to someone else who might want to reply to you but cannot see your email address. Exclude quotes from your signature block that could be misunderstood or offensive. Add an enclosure notation drawing attention to your résumé attachment provided as requested by the employer, such as "Résumé attached as Word document."

To compete with the high volumes of junk mail, daily messages, and fear of computer viruses, you must provide a motive for an interviewer to open an unexpected message from an unknown person. Messages with missing or vague

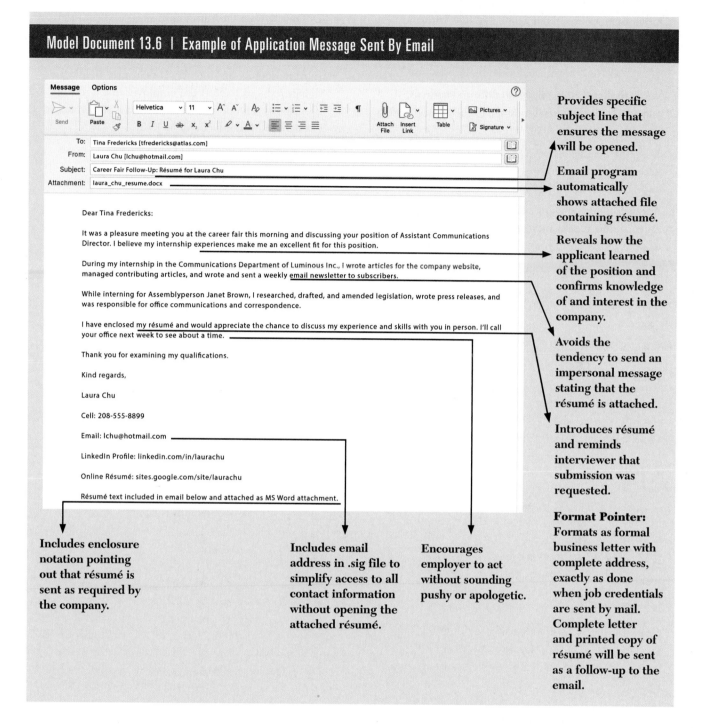

Message | Options

To: Tina Fredericks [tfredericks@atlas.com]
From: Laura Chu [lchu@hotmail.com]
Subject: Career Fair Follow-Up: Résumé for Laura Chu
Attachment: laura_chu_resume.docx

Dear Tina Fredericks:

It was a pleasure meeting you at the career fair this morning and discussing your position of Assistant Communications Director. I believe my internship experiences make me an excellent fit for this position.

During my internship in the Communications Department of Luminous Inc., I wrote articles for the company website, managed contributing articles, and wrote and sent a weekly email newsletter to subscribers.

While interning for Assemblyperson Janet Brown, I researched, drafted, and amended legislation, wrote press releases, and was responsible for office communications and correspondence.

I have enclosed my résumé and would appreciate the chance to discuss my experience and skills with you in person. I'll call your office next week to see about a time.

Thank you for examining my qualifications.

Kind regards,

Laura Chu

Cell: 208-555-8899

Email: lchu@hotmail.com

LinkedIn Profile: linkedin.com/in/laurachu

Online Résumé: sites.google.com/site/laurachu

Résumé text included in email below and attached as MS Word attachment.

Provides specific subject line that ensures the message will be opened.

Email program automatically shows attached file containing résumé.

Reveals how the applicant learned of the position and confirms knowledge of and interest in the company.

Avoids the tendency to send an impersonal message stating that the résumé is attached.

Introduces résumé and reminds interviewer that submission was requested.

Format Pointer: Formats as formal business letter with complete address, exactly as done when job credentials are sent by mail. Complete letter and printed copy of résumé will be sent as a follow-up to the email.

Includes enclosure notation pointing out that résumé is sent as required by the company.

Includes email address in .sig file to simplify access to all contact information without opening the attached résumé.

Encourages employer to act without sounding pushy or apologetic.

---

subject lines might be ignored or deleted immediately. To bring attention to your message, include the name of the person referring you to the position directly in the subject line or mention your email is a follow-up to a conversation, for example, "RE: Follow-Up: Résumé for…." If the message is unsolicited, describe the specific value you can add to the company, for example, "Résumé for Forensics Accountant with Extensive ACL Skills." Stay away from tricks such as marking an email "urgent" or adding "re" to pass your message off as a reply to an earlier message.

Check any instructions provided by the prospective employer and follow them precisely. Typically, however, you will want to send a complete letter and copy of your résumé by regular mail as a follow-up to the email submission. Model Document 13.6 shows a sample application email an applicant sent after talking with a current employee.

Include these steps in your finishing phase:

- Regardless of your delivery option, address your application letter or email message to the specific individual who is responsible for hiring for the position you are seeking, rather than sending the document to the "Human Resources Department" or "To Whom It May Concern." If necessary, consult the company's annual report or website, or call the company to locate this information.

- Verify the correct spelling, job title, and address, and send a personalized message to the appropriate individual.

- Keep the message short and easy to read. A one-page letter is sufficient for most applications from students and graduates entering the job market.

- Apply visual enhancements—learned previously—to enhance the appeal and readability of the message and to draw attention to your strengths.

- Definitely keep the paragraphs short and consider listing your top four or five achievements or other important ideas in a bulleted list.

- In print documents, include "Enclosure" below the signature block to alert the employer that a résumé is enclosed. The proper letter format is shown in the example in Model Document 13.5.

- Get opinions from qualified individuals and make revisions where necessary.

14 | Interviewing for a Job and Preparing Employment Messages

Learning Objectives

After studying this chapter, you will be able to ...

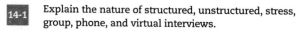 **14-1** Explain the nature of structured, unstructured, stress, group, phone, and virtual interviews.

14-2 Explain the steps in the interview process.

14-3 Prepare effective answers to questions often asked in job interviews, including illegal interview questions.

 14-4 Compose effective messages related to employment (including application, follow-up, thank-you, job-acceptance, job-refusal, resignation, and recommendation request messages).

14-1 Understanding Types of Employment Interviews

Most companies conduct various types of interviews before hiring a new employee. Although the number and type of interviews vary among companies, applicants typically begin with a screening interview often completed by phone or videoconferencing, an in-depth interview, an on-site interview with multiple interviewers, and, sometimes, a stress interview. Depending on the goals of the interviewer, interviews follow a structured or an unstructured approach.

14-1a Structured Interviews

In a **structured interview**, the interviewer follows a predetermined agenda, including a checklist of questions and statements designed to elicit necessary information and reactions from the interviewee. Because each applicant answers the same questions, the interviewer has comparable data to evaluate. A particular type of structured interview is the behavior-based interview, in which you are asked to give specific examples of occasions in which you demonstrated particular behaviors or skills. The interviewer already knows what skills, knowledge, and qualities successful candidates must possess. The examples you provide will indicate whether you possess them.[1]

Many companies are finding computer-assisted interviews to be a reliable and effective way to conduct screening interviews. Applicants use a computer to provide answers to a list of carefully selected questions. A computer-generated report provides standard, reliable information about each applicant that enables an interviewer to decide whether to invite the applicant for a second interview. The report flags any contradictory responses (e.g., John indicated he was terminated for absenteeism but later indicated that he thought his former employer would give him an outstanding recommendation), highlights any potential problem areas (e.g., Susan responded that she would remain on the job less than a year), and generates a list of structured interview questions for the interviewer to ask (e.g., "Todd, you said you feel your former employer would rate you average. Why don't you feel it would be higher?").

Research has shown that applicants prefer computer-assisted interviews to human interviews and that they respond more honestly to a computer, feeling less need to give polite, socially acceptable responses. Because expert computer systems can overcome some of the inherent problems with traditional face-to-face interviews, the overall quality of the selection process improves. Typical interviewer errors include talking too much, forgetting to ask important questions, being reluctant to ask sensitive or tough questions, forming unjustified negative first impressions, obtaining unreliable and illegal information that makes an applicant feel judged, and using interview data ineffectively.[2] Regardless of whether the interview is face to face or computer assisted, you will need to provide objective, truthful evidence of your qualifications as they relate to specific job requirements.

14-1b Unstructured Interviews

An **unstructured interview** is a freewheeling exchange and can shift from one subject to another, depending on the interests of the participants. Some experienced interviewers are able to make a structured interview seem unstructured. The goal of many unstructured interviews is to explore unknown areas to determine the applicant's ability to speak comfortably about a wide range of topics.

14-1c Stress Interviews

A **stress interview** is designed to place the interviewee in an anxiety-producing situation so that an evaluation can be made of the interviewee's performance under stress. In all cases, interviewees should attempt to assess the nature of the interview quickly and adjust behavior accordingly. Understanding that interviewers sometimes deliberately create anxiety to assess your ability to perform under stress should help you handle such interviews more effectively. As the following discussion of different interviewer styles reveals, you can perform much better when you understand the interviewer's purpose.

14-1d Series Interviews

As organizations have increased emphasis on the team approach to management and problem solving, selecting employees who best fit their cultures and styles has become especially important. Involving key people in the organization in the candidate selection process has led to new interview styles. In a series interview, the candidate meets individually with a number of different interviewers. Each interviewer will likely ask questions from a differing

structured interview an interview format generally used in the screening process, in which the interviewer follows a predetermined agenda, including a checklist of items or a series of questions and statements designed to elicit the necessary information or interviewee reaction

unstructured interview a freewheeling exchange that may shift from one subject to another, depending on the interests of the participants

stress interview an interview format designed to place the interviewee in an anxiety-producing situation so that an evaluation of the interviewee's performance under stress may be made

perspective; for instance, a line manager might ask questions related to the applicant's knowledge of specific job tasks, while the vice president of operations might ask questions related to the applicant's career goals. Some questions will likely be asked more than once in the process. A popular trend in organizations that desire a broad range of input in the hiring decision but want to avoid the drawn-out nature of series interviews is to conduct group interviews.

14-1e Phone Interviews

Employers use telephone interviews as a way of identifying and recruiting candidates for employment. Phone interviews are often used to screen candidates to narrow the pool of applicants who will be invited for in-person interviews. They are also used as a way to minimize the expenses involved in interviewing out-of-town candidates.

While you're actively job searching, it's important to be prepared for a phone interview on a moment's notice. You never know when a recruiter or a networking contact might call and ask if you have a few minutes to talk.

Prepare for a phone interview just as you would for a regular interview. Compile a list of your strengths and weaknesses, as well as a list of answers to typical phone interview questions. In addition, plan on being prepared for a phone conversation about your background and skills. Other considerations to make when preparing for a phone interview include:

- Keeping your résumé in clear view, on the top of your desk, or taping it to the wall near the phone, so it's at your fingertips when you need to answer questions

- Having a short list of your accomplishments available to review

- Having a pen and paper handy for note taking

- Turning call-waiting off so your call isn't interrupted

Unless you're sure your cellphone service is going to be perfect, you might consider using a landline rather than your cellphone to avoid a dropped call or static on the line.

14-1f Virtual Interviews

Virtual recruitment is on the rise, with most interviews being conducted over a video call. Studies indicate that video technology is being used by at least 60 percent of hiring managers and recruiters. A survey of 506 companies revealed that 47 percent use video interviewing to shorten the hiring timeframe, and 22 percent would consider it for interviewing candidates that aren't local.[3]

Companies save money and time by screening candidates through video interviews from remote locations. **Virtual interviews** help widen the applicant pool, decrease the cost of travel because they can be conducted regardless

of geography, and fill the position more quickly. The consensus is that the video interview is excellent for screening applicants, but a face-to-face interview is appropriate whenever possible for the important final interview.

Various companies have direct hookups with the career services centers of colleges and universities to interview students. These virtual interviews allow students to meet large companies whose representatives typically would not visit colleges with small applicant pools, and to interview with companies whose representatives could not travel because of financial constraints or other reasons. Students simply sit in front of a camera, dial in, and interview with multiple interviewers; in some cases, several applicants are interviewed simultaneously. As you would imagine, some candidates who interview well in person can fail on camera or in a group conference call. Virtual interviewing is an excellent method for screening out candidates who are unable to communicate their competence, enthusiasm, and conviction in a technology-rich environment.

You should prepare for a virtual interview differently than you would for a traditional interview. First, suggest a preliminary telephone conversation with the interviewer to establish rapport. Arrive early and acquaint yourself with the equipment; know how to adjust the volume and other camera functions for optimal performance after the interview begins. Second, concentrate on projecting strong nonverbal skills: speak clearly, but do not slow down; be certain you are centered in the frame; sit straight; look up, not down; and use gestures and an enthusiastic voice to communicate energy and reinforce points while avoiding excessive motion that will appear blurry. Third, realize voices can be out of step with the pictures if there is a lag between the video and audio transmissions. You will need to adjust to the timing (e.g., slow down your voice) to avoid interrupting the interviewer.

14-2 Preparing for an Interview

College students frequently schedule on-campus interviews with representatives from various business organizations. Following the on-campus interviews, successful candidates often are invited for further interviews at the company location. The purpose of the second interview is to give executives and administrators, other than the human resources interviewer, an opportunity to appraise the candidate. Whether on campus or at the company location, interview methods and practices vary with the situation.

Pre-interview planning involves learning something about the company or organization, studying yourself, and making sure your

> **virtual interviews** interview conducted using videoconferencing technology

appearance and mannerisms will not detract from the impression you hope to make.

14-2a Research the Company

Nothing can hurt a job candidate more than knowing little about the organization. Preparation will also arm candidates with information needed to develop pertinent qualifications and point their stories to solve an employer's specific problems.

Companies that have publicly traded stock are required to publish annual reports that are available in school libraries or online. Be sure to read news items and blog posts, and sign up to receive news alerts from the prospective company for current company information up until the day of the interview. Use social networking utilities, such as LinkedIn and Hoovers.com, to find profiles of company leaders and gain insights into the types of managers this company employs.

Employees of the company or other applicants who have interviewed might be of help to the interviewee. Employee reviews of selected companies, salaries, and sample interview questions are available online on such web sites as Glassdoor, and some universities share taped interviews with various company recruiters. Information about the company and the job seen as pertinent in an interview includes the following:

Company Information

Be sure to research the following on the companies with which you interview:

▸ **Name.** Know, for example, that the publishing company, Cengage Learning, was named to reflect the company's mission to be a "center of engagement" for its global customers.[4]

▸ **Status in the industry.** Know the company's share of the market, its *Fortune* 500 standing (if any), its sales, and its number of employees.

▸ **Latest stock market quote.** Be familiar with current market deviations and trends.

▸ **Recent news and developments.** Read current business periodicals, news, and blogs for special feature articles on the company, its new products, and its corporate leadership.

▸ **Scope of the company.** Is it local, national, or international?

▸ **Corporate officers.** Know the names of the chairperson, president, and chief executive officer.

▸ **Products and services.** Study the company's offerings, target markets, and innovative strategies.

Job Information

Be sure to know the following about the job you are seeking:

▸ **Job title.** Know the job titles of typical entry-level positions.

▸ **Job qualifications.** Understand the specific knowledge and skills desired.

▸ **Probable salary range.** Study salaries in comparable firms, as well as regional averages.

▸ **Career path of the job.** What opportunities for advancement are available?

14-2b Study Yourself

When you know something about the company, you will also know something about the kinds of jobs or training programs the company has to offer. Next, compare your qualifications to the company/job profile. This systematic comparison of your qualifications and job requirements helps you identify pertinent information (strengths or special abilities) to be included in your résumé. If you cannot see a relationship between you and the job or company, you might have difficulty demonstrating the interest or sincerity needed to sell yourself.

14-2c Plan Your Appearance

An employment interviewer once said she would not hire a job applicant who did not meet her *extremities* test: fingernails, shoes, and hair must be clean and well kept. This interviewer felt that if the candidate did not take care of those details, the candidate could not really be serious about, or fit into, her organization. Other important guidelines include avoiding heavy makeup and large, excessive jewelry. Select conservative clothes, and be certain clothing is clean, unwrinkled, and properly fitted. Additionally, avoid smoking, drinking, or wearing heavy fragrance.

You can locate a wealth of information on appropriate interview dress from numerous electronic and printed sources. Also, talk with professors in your field, professors of business etiquette and professional protocol, personnel at your career services center, and graduates who have recently acquired jobs in your field. Research the company dress code—real or implied—ahead of time. If you *look* and *dress* like the people who already work for the company, the interviewer will be able to visualize you working there.

14-2d Plan Your Time and Materials

One of the worst things you can do is be late for an interview. If something should happen to prevent your arriving on time, phone an apology. Another mistake is to miss the interview entirely. Plan your time so that you will arrive early and can unwind and mentally review the things you plan to accomplish. Be sure to bring a professional briefcase or notebook that contains everything you will need during the interview. These items might include copies of your résumé, a list of references and/or recommendations, a professional-looking pen, paper for taking notes, highlights of what you know about the company, a list of questions you plan to ask, and previous correspondence with the company.

14-2e Practice

The job interview could be the most important face-to-face interaction you ever have. You will be selling yourself in competition with others. How you listen and how you talk are characteristics the interviewer will be able to measure. Your actions, your mannerisms, and your appearance will combine to give the total picture of how you are perceived. Added to the marketable skills you have acquired from your education, experience, and activities, your interview performance can give a skilled interviewer an excellent picture of you. Practicing for an interview will prepare you to handle the nervousness that is natural when interviewing. However, do not memorize answers, as it will sound rehearsed and insincere. Instead, think carefully about how your accomplishments match the job requirements and practice communicating these ideas smoothly, confidently, and professionally.

Prepare for standard interview questions and other interview issues by following suggestions provided later in this chapter. Once you are satisfied you have identified your key selling points, have a friend ask you interview questions you have developed and surprise you with others. Participate in mock interviews with someone in your career services center or with a friend, alternating roles as interviewer and interviewee. Then, follow each practice interview with a constructive critique of your performance.

14-3 Conducting a Successful Interview

The way you handle an interview will vary somewhat depending on your stage in the hiring process. Regardless of whether you are being screened by a campus recruiter in person, by phone, or by videoconference, or have progressed to an on-site visit, an interview will have three parts: the opening formalities, an information exchange, and the closing.

14-3a The Opening Formalities

According to management consultant Dan Burns, most candidates don't realize that in the first 60 seconds, interviewers typically decide whether the candidate will be moved to the top of the list or dropped from consideration. Burns emphasizes that skills missing during the interview are important because he assumes these same deficiencies will carry over during employment.[5] Clearly, because the impression created during the first few seconds of an interview often determines the outcome, you cannot afford to take time to warm up in an interview. You must enter the door selling yourself!

Common courtesies and confident body language can contribute to a favorable first impression in the early moments when you have not yet had an opportunity to talk about your qualifications:

- **Use the interviewer's name and pronounce it correctly.** Even if the interviewer calls you by your first name, always use the interviewer's surname unless specifically invited to do otherwise.

- **Be aware of changing practices about handshakes.** Handshakes are rapidly falling out of favor as an acceptable form of greeting because of the COVID-19 pandemic. Bringing up concerns at the beginning of an interaction might come across as paranoid or rude, but it may be the only way to actually avoid the now-dreaded handshake. Expressing something like, "Nice to meet you, but I'm trying not to shake hands to help keep everyone safe" is straightforward. The odds of that person appreciating your candor and cleanliness will likely be in your favor. At best, they'll be grateful and agree. At worst, they'll be offended, though, honesty remains the best policy.[6]

- **Wait for the interviewer to ask you to be seated.** If you aren't invited to sit, choose a chair across from or beside the interviewer's desk.

- **Maintain appropriate eye contact and use your body language to convey confidence.** Sit erect and lean forward slightly to express interest. For a professional image, avoid slouching, chewing gum, and fidgeting.

- **Be conscious of nonverbal messages.** If the interviewer's eyes are glazing over, end your answer, but expand it if eyes are bright and the head is nodding vigorously. If the interviewer is from a different culture, be conscious of subtle differences in nonverbal communication that could affect the interviewer's perception of you. For example, a North American interviewer who sees eye contact as a sign of trust might perceive an Asian female who keeps her eyes lowered as a sign of respect to be uninterested or not listening.[7] Women should also be aware of typical "feminine behavior" during the interview. For instance, women nod more often than men when an interviewer speaks. Women are also likely to smile more and have a rising intonation at the end of sentences; such behaviors can convey a subservient attitude.[8]

Following the introductions, many interviewers will begin the conversation with nonbusiness talk to help you relax and to set the stage for the information exchange portion of the interview. Other interviewers bypass these casual remarks and move directly into the interview.

14-3b The Information Exchange

Much of the information about you will appear on your résumé or application form and is already available to the interviewer. Thus, the interviewer most likely will seek to go beyond such facts as your education, work experience, and extracurricular activities. They will attempt to assess your general attitude toward work and the probability of your fitting successfully into the organization.

Presenting Your Qualifications

Your preparation pays off during the interview. Like a prosecutor ready to win a case, you are ready to present evidence that you should be hired. According to Joyce Kennedy and Thomas Morrow, leading career consultants, your case will have three major points: you must convince the interviewer that you (1) can do the job, (2) will do the job, and (3) will not stress out everyone else while doing the job.[9] That's an overwhelming task. Where do you begin? You learned during your study of persuasive writing that saying you're the best at what you do is not convincing. To convince an interviewer to allow you to continue to the next interview or to extend you a job offer, you must provide specific, concrete evidence that your qualifications match the job description and equip you to add immediate value to the company. Use the following guidelines to help you relate your skills and knowledge to the job:

- **List five or six key points that you want to emphasize.** You will probably want to present your education as a major asset. You should point out its relationship to the job sought. Even more important, the fact that you have succeeded in academics indicates that you have the ability and self-discipline to learn. Because most companies expect you to learn something on the job, your ability to learn and, thus, quickly become productive will be your greatest asset. Even lack of work experience can be an asset: you have acquired no bad work habits that you will have to unlearn.

- **Additionally, be sure to provide evidence of your interpersonal skills.** Communicate that you can get along with others and are sensitive to diversity.

  - What did you do in college that helped you get along with others?

  - Were you a member, an officer, or president of an organization? What did you accomplish? How did others perceive you? Were you a leader? How did your followers respond to your leadership style? To your commitment to ethical standards?

  - Can you organize projects, motivate people to complete important goals, and deal with difficult people?

The extracurricular activities listed on your résumé give an indication of these traits, but how you talk about them in your interview helps demonstrate them. "I started as the public relations vice president and was subsequently elected to a higher office for four semesters, eventually becoming president" is a statement that proves your leadership qualities. If you can show that your organization moved to greater heights, you will appear successful as well. You can also use questions about your extracurricular activities to show that you have broad, balanced interests rather than a single, time-consuming avocation that could lead to burnout and stress if carried to the job.

What are other skills that graduating students need to succeed in a cross-cultural, interdependent workforce? While academic performance is weighted more heavily for some types of jobs than others, the ability to juggle a complicated schedule is weighed heavily by many employers as an important job-success factor. Additionally, a UNESCO report of employer views revealed certain skills to be essential for workers in today's business climate, as shown in Figure 14.1.[10]

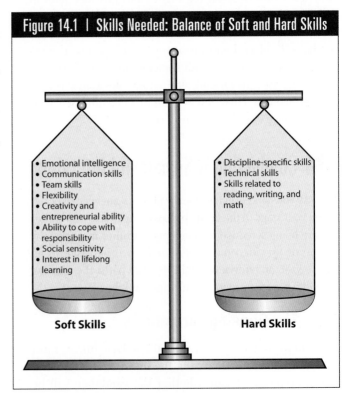

Figure 14.1 | Skills Needed: Balance of Soft and Hard Skills

Soft Skills
- Emotional intelligence
- Communication skills
- Team skills
- Flexibility
- Creativity and entrepreneurial ability
- Ability to cope with responsibility
- Social sensitivity
- Interest in lifelong learning

Hard Skills
- Discipline-specific skills
- Technical skills
- Skills related to reading, writing, and math

Consider these general job-success traits, and then use your knowledge of the job requirements and your own strengths to develop your "central selling features." These key points, when targeted toward your audience, are the central elements of a winning argument: You are able and willing to become a contributing part of a high-performance team that will enhance the company's performance.

- **Be prepared to answer standard interview questions.** These questions are designed to show (a) why you want the job, (b) why you want to work for this organization, and (c) why the company should want you. Practice concise but fully developed answers that reflect your personality and your communication power. Although one-word answers aren't adequate, long-winded answers can prevent interviewers from asking you other planned questions critical to making an informed decision.

- **Be prepared to answer behavioral questions.** These questions are designed to challenge you to provide evidence of your skills or the behaviors required to perform the job. Rather than asking applicants how they feel about certain things, interviewers are finding that asking potential employees for specific examples to illustrate their answers is a more objective way to evaluate applicants' skills. A sample list of behavioral interviewing questions by skill can be found in Exhibit 14.1.

Other behavioral questions include the following:

- Describe a time when you worked well under pressure, worked effectively with others, organized a major project, motivated and led others, solved a difficult problem, or used persuasion to convince someone to accept your idea.

- What was the most difficult problem you had to overcome in your last job (or for an academic or extracurricular activity)? How did you cope with it? What

lesson did you learn from the situation? Share a time you applied the lesson learned.

- Tell me about a time you had difficulty working with a supervisor or coworker (or professor or peer in a team in a class setting). How did you handle the situation?

- Describe something you have done that shows initiative and willingness to work or required you to think on your feet to solve a problem.

- How have your extracurricular activities, part-time work experience, or volunteer work prepared you for work in our company?

- Tell me about a time you hit a wall trying to push forward a great idea.

To prepare for answering behavioral questions, brainstorm to identify stories that illustrate how your qualifications fit the job requirements. These stories should show you applying the skills needed on the job. Career counselors recommend using the STAR method (Situation or Task/Action/Result) as a consistent format to help you present a complete answer to these open-ended questions. You first describe a situation or task you were involved in, the action you took, and finally the result of your effort.[11]

- **Be prepared to demonstrate logical thinking and creativity.** Many interviewers ask applicants to solve brain teasers and riddles, create art out of paper bags, and solve complex business problems. Some are asked to "do the job before we give it to you," for example, write a press release on the spot or field a tech-support call.[12] These techniques are used to gauge an applicant's ability to think quickly and creatively and observe an emotional response to an awkward situation. You cannot anticipate this type of interview question, but you can familiarize yourself with mind teasers that have been used. Most importantly, however, recognize the

Exhibit 14.1 | Behavioral Interview Questions By Skill

Skills	Behavioral Questions
Adaptability	• Tell me about a situation when you had to be tolerant of an opinion that was different from your own. • Tell me about a time when you had to adjust to changes over which you had no control.
Communication	• Tell me about a time when you were able to use persuasion to convince someone to see things your way. • Tell me about a time when you dealt with an irate customer.
Goal Setting	• Describe a goal you set for yourself and how you reached it. • Tell me about a goal that you set and did not reach.
Problem Solving	• Tell me about a situation where you had to solve a difficult problem. • Tell me about a time when you had to analyze information and provide a recommendation.
Teamwork	• Tell me about a time when you worked on a team and a member was not doing their share. • Tell me about a time when you were working in a team in which the members did not get along.
Time Management	• Describe a situation in which you had to do a number of things at the same time. • Tell me about a time when you were unable to complete a project on time.

interviewer's purpose; relax, and do your best to show-case your logical reasoning, creativity, or your courage to even try.

- **Display a professional attitude.** First, communicate your sincere interest in the company; show that you are strongly interested in the company and not just taking an interview for practice. Reveal your knowledge of the company gained through reading published information and refer to the people you have talked with about the working conditions, company achievements, and career paths.

Second, focus on the satisfaction gained from contributing to a company rather than the benefits you will receive. What's important in a job goes beyond financial reward. All applicants are interested in a paycheck; any job satisfies that need—some will pay more, some less. Recognize that the paycheck is a part of the job and should not be your primary concern. Intrinsic rewards such as personal job satisfaction, the feeling of accomplishment, and contributing to society are ideas to discuss in the interview. You should like what you are doing and find a challenging job that will satisfy these needs.

- **Be prepared to discuss salary and benefits.** For most entry-level positions, the beginning salary is fixed. However, if you have work experience, excellent scholarship records, or added maturity, you might be able to obtain a higher salary. The interviewer should initiate the salary topic. What you should know is the general range for candidates with your qualifications so that your response to a question about how much you would expect is reasonable.

If you have other job offers, you are in a position to compare salaries, jobs, and companies. In this case, you might suggest to the interviewer that you would expect a competitive salary and that you have been offered X dollars by another firm. If salary has not been mentioned, and you really want to know about it, simply ask courteously how much the salary would be for someone with your qualifications. In any case, if you really believe the job offers the non-monetary benefits you seek, do not attempt to make salary a major issue.

- **Typically, an interviewer will introduce the subject of benefits without your asking about them.** In some cases, a discussion of total salary and "perks" is reserved for a follow-up interview. If nothing has been said about certain benefits, you should take the liberty of asking, particularly when an item is especially important to you.

- **Be knowledgeable of interview questions and information on your social networking sites that might lead to discriminatory hiring practices.**

The Equal Employment Opportunity Commission (EEOC) and Fair Employment Practices Guidelines make it clear that an employer cannot legally discriminate against a job applicant on the basis of race, color, gender, age, religion, national origin, or disability. Interviewers must restrict questions to an applicant's ability to perform specific job-related functions essential to the job sought. Generally, the following topics should not be introduced:

- *National origin and religion.* "You have an unusual accent; where were you born?" "What religious holidays will require you to miss work?"

- *Age.* "I see you attended Central High School; what year did you graduate?" "Could you provide a copy of your birth certificate?"

- *Disabilities, health conditions, and physical characteristics not reasonably related to the job.* "Do you have a disability that would interfere with your ability to perform the job?" "Have you ever been injured on the job?" "Have you ever been treated by a psychiatrist?" "How much alcohol do you consume each week?" "What prescription drugs are you currently taking?"

- *Marital status, spouse's employment, or dependents.* "Are you married?" "Who is going to care for your children if you work for us?" "Do you plan to have children?" "Is your spouse employed?" Additionally, employers may not ask the names or relationships of people with whom you live.

- *Arrests or criminal convictions that are not related to the job.* "Have you ever been arrested other than for traffic violations? If so, explain." Keep in mind that the arrest/conviction record of a person applying for a job as a law enforcement officer or a teacher could be highly relevant to the job, but the same information could be illegal for a person applying for a job as an engineer.

As interviewers may ask illegal questions because of lack of training or an accidental slip, you must decide how to respond. You can refuse to answer and state that the question is improper, though you risk offending the interviewer. A second option is to answer the inappropriate question, knowing it is illegal and unrelated to job requirements. A third approach is to provide a low-key response such as "How does this question relate to how I will do my job?" or to answer the legitimate concern that likely prompted the question. For example, an interviewer who asks, "Do you plan to have children?" is probably concerned about how long you might remain on the job. An answer to this concern would be, "I plan to pursue a career regardless of whether I decide to raise a family." If you

Personality tests can be used to enhance multiple aspects of human resources (HR), but they are commonly associated with the recruiting and hiring processes—also known as "pre-hire." These assessments are completed by potential candidates and reviewed by recruiters, hiring managers, and HR administrators to provide value in a number of ways.

magic pictures/Shutterstock

1. Finding a Culture Fit

Personality tests are often used to gain insight into a candidate's compatibility with their team and the company at large. Hiring isn't an exact science, and mapping out personality traits helps businesses avoid unnecessary turnover by gauging if a candidate aligns with company values.

"Hiring the right person for a job often consists of factors that go way beyond skills, knowledge, experience, and professional expertise. [Personality tests] help us realize if the professional, personal, and cultural visions of our company and future employee will align, at least to a reasonable extent," said Ihor Shcherbinin, director of recruitment at Distant Job.

2. Satisfying Role Requirements

The recruitment process can be costly and time-consuming, so when a company decides to open up a new role, it means that there is a significant need for employees who can deliver on certain requirements. This puts a lot of pressure on recruiting teams and hiring managers to make accurate assessments of candidates' potential in real-life situations.

"Certain positions require someone who is more detail-oriented or more analytical," said Charlotte Kackley, HR manager at Merchant Maverick. "By having candidates complete the assessment, we can get a better understanding of which of those qualities the candidate possesses."

Personality tests can provide granular insight into candidates' thought processes and working styles. If a company is looking to hire someone with strong leadership abilities, for example, a personality test can be a valuable tool for understanding their approach to conflict management and problem solving. The best part is that hiring managers can rely on tangible data instead of making long-term decisions based on limited interactions during the interview process.

3. Improving HR Efficiency

There's a lot that happens behind-the-scenes during the recruitment process. Vetting candidates requires time and coordination, which can be a major bottleneck for companies during hiring sprees. According to Brad Touesnard, founder and CEO of SpinupWP, "Personality tests can speed the recruitment process by filtering out unsuitable applicants before the interview stage."

Personality tests have proven to be especially helpful for remote hiring efforts where accessing and engaging with candidates can be logistically challenging. The process of scouting employees looks completely different than it did a year ago, and personality tests play an important role in ushering in a new, streamlined era of recruitment.

"Web-based test interface and evaluation significantly reduces recruitment time while increasing our chances of making a quality hire. It also extends the reach of talent scouting as it lets HRs go beyond physical boundaries to assess skills and make a hire from anywhere in the world," said Matthew Paxton, founder of Hypernia.[13]

---

can see no legitimate concern in a question, such as "Do you own your home, rent, or live with parents?" answer, "I'm not sure how that question relates to the job. Can you explain?"[14]

Asking Questions of the Interviewer

Both the interviewer and interviewee want to know as much as possible about each other before making a commitment to hire. A good way to determine whether the job is right for you is to ask pertinent questions.

Good questions show the interviewer that you have initiative and are interested in making a well-informed decision. Responses can provide insight to job requirements that you can then show you possess. Therefore, be sure not to say, "I don't have any questions." Focus on questions that help you gain information about the company and the job that you could not learn from published sources or persons other than the interviewer. Respect the interviewer's time by avoiding questions that indicate you are unprepared (e.g., questions about the company's scope, products or services,

▶ How would you describe the ideal employee, or what's the best background for this job?

▶ What is a typical day like in this job?

▶ What type of people would I be working with (peers) and for (supervisors)?

▶ Why do you need someone for this job (why can this job not be done by a current employee)?

▶ What circumstances led to the departure of the person I would be replacing? What is the turnover rate of people in this job? (Or how many people have held this job in the past five years?)

▶ Why do you continue to work for this company (to an interviewer with several years' tenure with the company)?

▶ Would you describe the initial training program for people in this position?

▶ What types of ongoing employee in-service training programs are provided?

▶ How much value does your firm place on a master's degree?

▶ How do you feel this field has changed in the past 10 years? How do you feel it will change in the next 10 years?

▶ What advice do you wish you had been given when you were starting out?

▶ When do you expect to make your decision about the position?

job requirements, or new developments). Avoid questions about salary, required overtime, and benefits that imply you are interested more in money and the effort required than in the contribution you can make.

14-3c The Closing

The interviewer will provide cues indicating that the interview is completed by rising or making a comment about the next step to be taken. At that point, do not prolong the interview needlessly. Simply rise, thank the interviewer for the opportunity to meet and close by saying you look forward to hearing from the company. The tact with which you close the interview can be almost as important as the first impression you made. Be enthusiastic. If you really want the job, you must ask for it.

Your ability to speak confidently and intelligently about your abilities will help you secure a desirable job. Effective interviewing skills will be just as valuable once you begin work. You will be involved in interviews with your supervisor for various reasons: to seek advice or information about your work and working conditions, to receive informal feedback about your progress, to receive a deserved promotion, and to discuss other personnel matters. In addition, your supervisor will likely conduct a performance appraisal interview to evaluate your performance. This formal interview typically occurs annually on the anniversary of your start of employment.

14-3d Additional Considerations for Phone and Virtual Interviews

Although many of the guidelines for interviewing also apply to phone and virtual interviews, some additional considerations are useful. For example, you will need to make sure that you are located in a quiet place, so that no distracting noises can be heard in the background. Other persons should be asked to leave, and pets should be put in another room or outside.

If you receive an unexpected call from an interviewer and the time isn't convenient, ask if you could talk at another time, and suggest some alternatives.

During the interview, you should:

- avoid smoking, chewing gum, eating, or drinking;

- keep a glass of water handy, in case you need to wet your mouth;

- smile—smiling will add enthusiasm to your voice and help to project a positive image to the listener;

- speak slowly and enunciate clearly;

- use the person's title (Dr., Reverend, or Professor and their last name) and only use a first name if the interviewer asks you to;

- avoid interrupting the interviewer;

- pause if you need to collect your thoughts; and

- give short answers.

Remember, your goal is to set up a face-to-face interview. After you thank the interviewer, ask if it would be possible to meet in person.

14-4 Preparing Other Employment Messages

Preparing a winning résumé and application letter is an important first step in a job search. To expedite your job search, you will need to prepare other employment messages. For example, you might complete an application form, send a follow-up message to a company that does not respond to your résumé, send a thank-you message after an interview, accept a job offer, reject other job offers, and communicate with references. A career change will require a carefully written resignation letter.

14-4a Application Forms

Before beginning a new job, you will almost certainly complete the employer's application and employment forms. Some application forms, especially for applicants who apply for jobs with a high level of responsibility, are very long. They can actually appear to be tests in which applicants give their answers to hypothetical questions and write defenses for their answers. Application forms also ensure consistency in the information received from each candidate and can prevent decisions based on illegal topics which might be presented in a résumé.

14-4b Follow-Up Messages

When an application message and résumé do not elicit a response, a follow-up message might bring results. Sent a few weeks after the original message, it includes a reminder that an application for a certain job is on file, presents additional education or experience accumulated and its relationship to the job, and closes with a reference to a desired action. In addition to conveying new information, follow-up messages indicate persistence (a quality that impresses some employers). Model Document 14.1 shows a good example of a follow-up message.

14-4c Thank-You Messages

What purposes are served in sending a thank-you message, even though you expressed thanks in person after the interview or after a discussion with a special employer at a career fair? After a job interview, a written message of appreciation is a professional courtesy and enhances your image within the organization. To be effective, it must be sent promptly. For maximum impact, send a thank-you message the day of the interview or the following day. Even if during the interview you decided you do not want the job, or you and the interviewer mutually agreed that the job is not for you, a thank-you message is appropriate. As a matter of fact, if you've made a positive impression, interviewers might forward your résumé to others who are seeking qualified applicants.

The medium you choose for sending this message depends on the intended audience. If the company you've interviewed with prefers a traditional style, send a letter in complete business format on high-quality paper that matches your résumé and application letter. If the company has communicated with you extensively by email, follow the pattern and send a professional email that can be read in a timely manner. Choosing to send an email rather than

---

Model Document 14.1 | Example of a Follow-Up Message

Dear Janet Nelson:

I recently applied for the position of marketing assistant. I understand you're probably busy reviewing applicants, but I wanted to reach out to see if you had any updates on your decision timeline.

I'm very excited about the opportunity to work at Fairfield, Inc., and I believe that my skills, specifically, my experience updating social media sites, would make me an ideal match for the position.

For your convenience, I've attached my application materials. Please let me know if you need any additional information. I can be reached at 310-555-8973 or jchen@gmail.com. I look forward to hearing from you.

- **States main idea and clearly identifies position being sought.**
- **Summarizes additional qualifications.**

- **Refers to enclosed résumé; assures employer that applicant is still interested in job.**

Format Pointers:
- **Format as formal business letter but could be sent as an electronic message if previous communication with the employer had been by email.**

- **Print letter and envelope with laser printer on paper that matches résumé and application letter.**

using slower mail delivery can give you a competitive edge over other candidates whose mailed letters arrive several days later than yours.

After an interview has gone well and you think a job offer is a possibility, include these ideas in the message of appreciation: express gratitude, identify the specific job applied for, refer to some point discussed in the interview (the strength of the interview), and close by making some reference to the expected call or message that conveys the employer's decision. The tone of this business message should remain professional regardless of the personal relationship you might have developed with the interviewer and the informality encouraged by email. The message could be read by many others once it is placed in your personnel file as you complete annual appraisals and compete for promotions. Specific points to cover are illustrated in Model Document 14.2.

The résumé, application letter, and thank-you message should be stored in a computer file and adapted for submission to other firms when needed. Develop a database for keeping a record of the dates on which documents and résumés were sent to certain firms and answers were received, names of people talked with, facts conveyed, and so on. When an interviewer calls, you can retrieve and view that company's record while you are talking with the interviewer.

14-4d Job-Acceptance Messages

A job offer may be extended either by phone or in writing. If a job offer is extended over the phone, request that the company send a written confirmation of the job offer. The confirmation should include the job title, salary, benefits, starting date, and anything else negotiated.

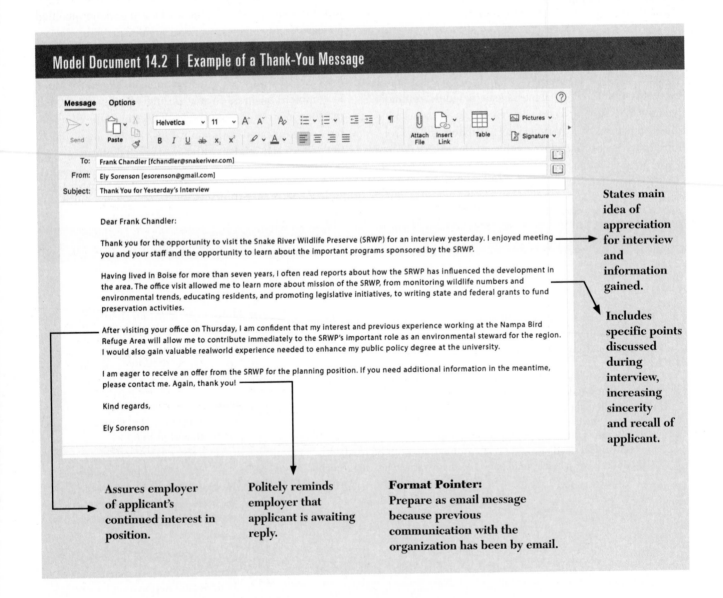

Model Document 14.2 | Example of a Thank-You Message

To: Frank Chandler [fchandler@snakeriver.com]
From: Ely Sorenson [esorenson@gmail.com]
Subject: Thank You for Yesterday's Interview

Dear Frank Chandler:

Thank you for the opportunity to visit the Snake River Wildlife Preserve (SRWP) for an interview yesterday. I enjoyed meeting you and your staff and the opportunity to learn about the important programs sponsored by the SRWP.

Having lived in Boise for more than seven years, I often read reports about how the SRWP has influenced the development in the area. The office visit allowed me to learn more about mission of the SRWP, from monitoring wildlife numbers and environmental trends, educating residents, and promoting legislative initiatives, to writing state and federal grants to fund preservation activities.

After visiting your office on Thursday, I am confident that my interest and previous experience working at the Nampa Bird Refuge Area will allow me to contribute immediately to the SRWP's important role as an environmental steward for the region. I would also gain valuable realworld experience needed to enhance my public policy degree at the university.

I am eager to receive an offer from the SRWP for the planning position. If you need additional information in the meantime, please contact me. Again, thank you!

Kind regards,

Ely Sorenson

States main idea of appreciation for interview and information gained.

Includes specific points discussed during interview, increasing sincerity and recall of applicant.

Assures employer of applicant's continued interest in position.

Politely reminds employer that applicant is awaiting reply.

Format Pointer:
Prepare as email message because previous communication with the organization has been by email.

Often, companies require a written acceptance of a job offer. Note the deductive sequence of the message shown in Model Document 14.3: acceptance, details, and closing (confirms the report-for-work date).

14-4e Job-Refusal Messages

Like other messages that convey unpleasant news, job-refusal messages are written inductively—with a beginning that reveals the nature of the subject, explanations that lead to a refusal, the refusal, and a pleasant ending. Of course, certain reasons (even though valid in your mind) are better left unsaid, such as questionable company goals or methods of operation, negative attitude of present employees, possible bankruptcy, unsatisfactory working conditions, and so on. The applicant who prefers not to be specific about the reason for turning down a job might write this explanation: *After thoughtfully considering job offers received this week, I have decided to accept a job in the finance department of a commercial bank.*

You might want to be more specific about your reasons for refusal when you have a positive attitude toward the company or believe you will want to reapply at some later date. The letter excerpt in Model Document 14.4 includes the reasons for refusal.

14-4f Resignation Messages

Resigning from a job requires effective communication skills. You might be allowed to give your notice in person or be required to write a formal resignation. Your supervisor will inform you of the company's policy. Regardless of whether the resignation is given orally or in writing, show empathy for your employer by giving enough time to allow the employer to find a replacement. Because your employer has had confidence in you, has benefited from your services, and will have to seek a replacement, your impending departure is bad news. As such, the message may be written inductively or deductively, as shown in Model Document 14.5. It calls attention to your job, gives your reasons for leaving it, conveys the resignation, and closes on a positive note.

A resignation is not an appropriate instrument for telling managers how a business should be operated. Harshly worded statements could result in immediate termination or cause human relations problems during your remaining working days. If you can do so sincerely, recall positive experiences you had with the company. Doing so will leave a lasting record of your goodwill, making it likely that your supervisor will give you a good recommendation in the future.

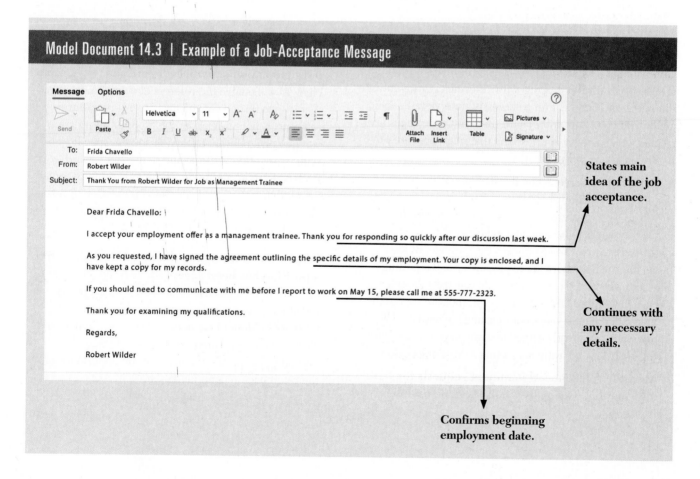

Model Document 14.3 | Example of a Job-Acceptance Message

To: Frida Chavello
From: Robert Wilder
Subject: Thank You from Robert Wilder for Job as Management Trainee

Dear Frida Chavello:

I accept your employment offer as a management trainee. Thank you for responding so quickly after our discussion last week.

As you requested, I have signed the agreement outlining the specific details of my employment. Your copy is enclosed, and I have kept a copy for my records.

If you should need to communicate with me before I report to work on May 15, please call me at 555-777-2323.

Thank you for examining my qualifications.

Regards,

Robert Wilder

States main idea of the job acceptance.

Continues with any necessary details.

Confirms beginning employment date.

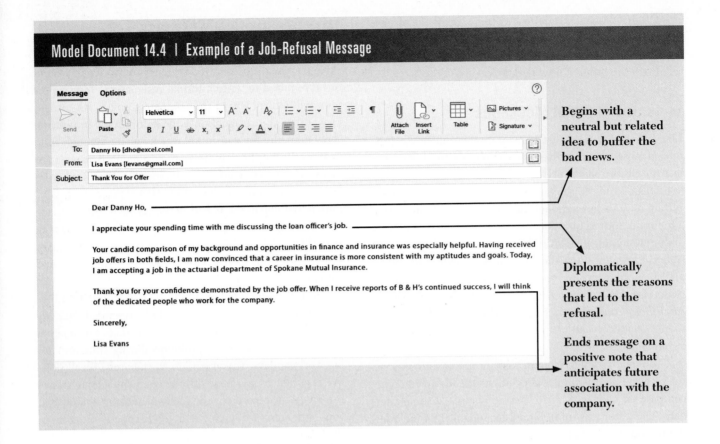

Begins with a neutral but related idea to buffer the bad news.

To: Danny Ho [dho@excel.com]
From: Lisa Evans [levans@gmail.com]
Subject: Thank You for Offer

Dear Danny Ho,

I appreciate your spending time with me discussing the loan officer's job.

Your candid comparison of my background and opportunities in finance and insurance was especially helpful. Having received job offers in both fields, I am now convinced that a career in insurance is more consistent with my aptitudes and goals. Today, I am accepting a job in the actuarial department of Spokane Mutual Insurance.

Thank you for your confidence demonstrated by the job offer. When I receive reports of B & H's continued success, I will think of the dedicated people who work for the company.

Sincerely,

Lisa Evans

Diplomatically presents the reasons that led to the refusal.

Ends message on a positive note that anticipates future association with the company.

14-4g Recommendation Requests

Companies seek information from references at various stages. Some prefer talking with references prior to an interview, and others, after a successful interview. Specific actions on your part will ensure that your references are treated with common courtesy and that references are prepared for the employer's call.

- Remind the reference that they had previously agreed to supply information about you. Identify the job for which you are applying, give a complete address to which the message is to be sent, and indicate a date by which the prospective employer needs the message. By sharing information about job requirements and reporting recent job-related experiences, you can assist the reference in writing an effective message. Indicate your gratitude, but do not apologize for making the request. The reference has already agreed to write on your behalf and will likely take pleasure in assisting a deserving person.

- **Alert the reference of imminent requests for information, especially if considerable time has elapsed since the applicant and reference have last seen each other.** Enclosing a recent résumé and providing any other pertinent information (e.g., name change) will enable the reference to write a message that is specific and convincing. To ensure on-target job references, politely explain the types of information you perceive relevant to the job sought: specific job skills, work ethic, attitude and demeanor toward work, leadership style, and so on. If the job search becomes longer than anticipated, a follow-up message to references explaining the delay and expressing gratitude for their efforts is appropriate.

- **Send a sincere, original thank-you message after a position has been accepted.** This thoughtful gesture will build a positive relationship with a person who might continue to be important to your career. The message in Model Document 14.6 is brief and avoids clichés and exaggerated expressions of praise, but instead gives specific examples of the importance of the reference's recommendation.

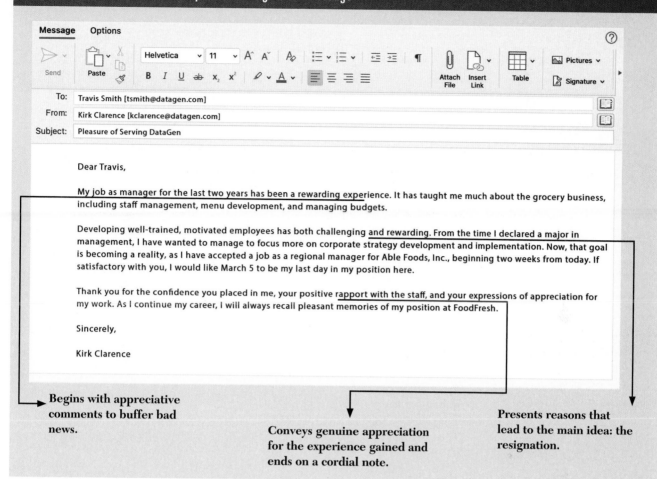

Model Document 14.5 | Example of a Resignation Message

Message **Options**

To: Travis Smith [tsmith@datagen.com]
From: Kirk Clarence [kclarence@datagen.com]
Subject: Pleasure of Serving DataGen

Dear Travis,

My job as manager for the last two years has been a rewarding experience. It has taught me much about the grocery business, including staff management, menu development, and managing budgets.

Developing well-trained, motivated employees has both challenging and rewarding. From the time I declared a major in management, I have wanted to manage to focus more on corporate strategy development and implementation. Now, that goal is becoming a reality, as I have accepted a job as a regional manager for Able Foods, Inc., beginning two weeks from today. If satisfactory with you, I would like March 5 to be my last day in my position here.

Thank you for the confidence you placed in me, your positive rapport with the staff, and your expressions of appreciation for my work. As I continue my career, I will always recall pleasant memories of my position at FoodFresh.

Sincerely,

Kirk Clarence

Begins with appreciative comments to buffer bad news.

Conveys genuine appreciation for the experience gained and ends on a cordial note.

Presents reasons that lead to the main idea: the resignation.

Model Document 14.6 | Example of a Thank-You Message to a Reference

Thank you so much for the letter of recommendation you prepared for my application to ComNet Associates. I learned today that I have been hired and will begin work in June.

Because the position is in public relations, I believe your comments about my performance in your communication classes carried a great deal of weight. Jason Miller commented he was impressed with the wealth of evidence and examples you provided to support your statements unlike the general recommendations he frequently receives.

Dr. Watson, I appreciate your helping me secure an excellent position in a highly competitive job market. Thanks for the recommendation and your outstanding instruction. I look forward to talking with you about how I am faring in the real world when I return to campus for fall homecoming.

States main idea of appreciation for recommendation. Informs reference of success in locating a job.

Communicates sincere appreciation for assistance; uses specific examples and avoids exaggeration.

Restates main idea and anticipates continued relationship; is original and sincere.

Grammar and Usage Appendix

Polishing your language skills will aid you in preparing error-free documents that reflect positively on you and your company. This appendix is an abbreviated review that focuses on common problems frequently encountered by business writers and offers a quick refresh of key skills.

Grammar

Sentence Structure

1. Rely mainly on sentences that follow the normal subject-verb-complement sequence for clarity and easy reading.

<u>Jennifer</u> and **I** <u>withdrew</u> for two <u>reasons</u>.
(subject)   (verb)   (complement)

Original	**Better**
There are two <u>reasons</u> for our withdrawal.	Two <u>reasons</u> for our withdrawal are….
	<u>Jennifer and</u> I withdrew for two reasons.
<u>It</u> is necessary that we withdraw.	<u>We</u> must withdraw.
<u>Here</u> is a copy of my résumé.	The enclosed <u>résumé</u> outlines….

There, *it*, and *here* are *expletives*—filler words that have no real meaning in the sentence.

2. Put pronouns, adverbs, phrases, and clauses near the words they modify.

Incorrect	**Correct**
Deepti put a new type of gel in her hair, <u>which</u> she had just purchased.	Deepti put a new type of gel, <u>which</u> she had just purchased, in her hair.
He works <u>only</u> in the call center during peak periods.	He works in the call center <u>only</u> during peak periods.
The clerk stood near the fax machine <u>wearing a denim jacket</u>.	The clerk <u>wearing a denim jacket</u> stood near the fax machine.

3. Do not separate subject and predicate unnecessarily.

Incorrect	**Correct**
<u>She</u>, hoping to receive a bonus, <u>worked</u> rapidly.	Hoping to receive a bonus, <u>she worked</u> rapidly.

4. Place an introductory phrase near the subject of the independent clause it modifies.

Otherwise, the phrase dangles. To correct the dangling phrase, change the subject of the independent clause, or make the phrase into a dependent clause by assigning it a subject.

Incorrect

<u>When</u> a young boy, <u>my mother</u> insisted I learn a second language.

[Implies that the mother was once a young boy]

<u>Working</u> at full speed every morning, <u>fatigue</u> overtakes me in the afternoon.

[Implies that "fatigue" was working at full speed]

<u>To function</u> properly, <u>you</u> must oil the machine every hour.

[Implies that if "you" are "to function properly," the machine must be oiled hourly]

Correct

<u>When I was a young boy</u>, my mother insisted I learn a second language.

<u>Working</u> at full speed every morning, I become tired in the afternoon.

<u>Because I work</u> at full speed every morning, <u>fatigue</u> overtakes me in the afternoon.

<u>If the equipment</u> is to function properly, you must oil it every hour.

<u>To function properly</u>, the <u>equipment</u> must be oiled every hour.

5. Express related ideas in similar grammatical form (use parallel construction).

Incorrect

The machine operator made three resolutions:

(1) <u>to be punctual,</u>
(2) <u>following instructions carefully</u>, and third, <u>the reduction of waste</u>.

The human resources manager is concerned with the <u>selection</u> of the right worker, <u>providing</u> appropriate orientation and the <u>worker's progress</u>.

Correct

The machine operator made three resolutions: <u>to be punctual, to follow instructions carefully</u>, and <u>to reduce waste</u>.

The human resources manager is concerned with <u>selecting</u> the right worker, <u>providing</u> appropriate orientation, and <u>evaluating</u> the worker's progress.

6. Do not end a sentence with a needless preposition.

Where is the new sushi bar to be <u>located</u> (not *located at*)?

The applicant did not tell us where he was <u>going</u> (not *going to*).

End a sentence with a preposition if for some reason the preposition needs emphasis.

I am not concerned about what he is paying <u>for</u>. I am concerned about what he is paying <u>with</u>.

The prospect has everything—a goal to work <u>toward</u>, a house to live <u>in</u>, and an income to live <u>on</u>.

7. Avoid split infinitives. Two words are required to express an infinitive: *to* plus a *verb*. The two words belong together. An infinitive is split when another word is placed between the two.

Incorrect

The superintendent used <u>to</u> occasionally <u>visit</u> the offices.

I plan <u>to</u> briefly <u>summarize</u> the report.

Correct

The superintendent used <u>to visit</u> the offices occasionally.

I plan <u>to summarize</u> the report briefly.

Identify the weakness in each sentence and write an improved version.

1. It is essential that you learn to design spreadsheets that make financial information meaningful to users.

2. There are many online tools available that build relationships with customers.

3. I am submitting an employee testimonial to the company website, which I first posted to a presentation blog.

4. More companies are videoconferencing because of the need to significantly reduce travel costs.

5. To operate efficiently, you must perform periodic maintenance on your computer.

6. Planned store improvements include widening the aisles, improved lighting, and lower shelves for a sophisticated feel.

Pronoun Reference

1. Make a pronoun agree in number with its antecedent (the specific noun for which a pronoun stands).

   (a) Use a plural pronoun when it represents two or more singular antecedents connected by *and*.

   The secretary <u>and</u> the treasurer will take <u>their</u> vacations.

   ["The" before "treasurer" indicates that the sentence is about two people.]

   The <u>secretary</u> and <u>treasurer</u> will take <u>his</u> vacation.

   [Omitting "the" before "treasurer" indicates that the sentence is about one person who has two sets of responsibilities. Using "their" instead of "his" would also be appropriate if you are unaware of the person's preferred pronouns.]

   (b) Parenthetical remarks (remarks that can be omitted without destroying the basic meaning of the sentence) that appear between the pronoun and its antecedent have no effect on the form of the pronoun.

   President Rivera, <u>not the managers</u>, is responsible for his strategic goals.

   [Because "his" refers to President Rivera and not to "managers," "his" is used instead of "their."]

   (c) Use the singular pronoun "they/their" with *each, everyone, no*, and their variations

   <u>Each</u> student and team member will perform <u>their</u> own data collection.

   <u>Each</u> member has paid <u>their</u> annual dues.

   <u>Everyone</u> is responsible for <u>their</u> work.

   (d) Use a singular pronoun when two or more singular antecedents are connected by *or* or *nor*.

   <u>Neither</u> Brandon <u>nor</u> Will can complete <u>his</u> work.

   Ask <u>either</u> Maria <u>or</u> Suzanne about <u>her</u> in-service training.

   (e) Use pronouns that agree in number with the intended meaning of collective nouns.

   The <u>team</u> has been asked for <u>its</u> contributions. ["Team" is thought of as a unit; the singular "its" is appropriate.]

   The <u>team</u> have been asked for <u>their</u> contributions. ["Team" is thought of as more than one individual; the plural "their" is appropriate.]

(f) Avoid using pronouns if you are not sure about the gender of the person who needs to be referenced.

Ask Pat about in-service training.

I am not sure if Chris's full name is Christopher or Christine.

The administrative assistant will take minutes during the meeting. [It is assumed that this employee will take minutes for them, or the group at this business event.]

2. **Place relative pronouns as near their antecedents as possible for clear understanding.**

A relative pronoun joins a dependent clause to its antecedent.

Ambiguous	**Clear**
The <u>members</u> were given receipts <u>who</u> have paid.	The <u>members who</u> have paid were given receipts.
The agreement will enable you to pay <u>whichever</u> is lower, <u>6 percent</u> or $50.	The agreement will enable you to pay <u>6 percent or $50</u>, <u>whichever</u> is lower.

Restate a noun instead of risking a *vague* pronoun reference.

Vague	**Clear**
The officer captured the suspect even though <u>he</u> was unarmed.	The officer captured the suspect even though <u>the officer</u> was unarmed.

3. **Do not use a pronoun by itself to refer to a phrase, clause, sentence, or paragraph.**

A pronoun should stand for a noun, and that noun should appear in the writing.

Incorrect	**Correct**
He expects to take all available accounting courses and obtain a position in a public accounting firm. <u>This</u> appeals to him.	He expects to take all available accounting courses and obtain a position in a public accounting firm. <u>This plan</u> appeals to him.

Exercise 2

In each of the following sentences, choose the correct word in parentheses.

1. Conversation skills and good listening (affect, affects) a leader's effectiveness.
2. Each sales rep (was, were) trained to encourage customers to buy more than one size or color since shipping was free.
3. The production manager, not the controller, presented (her, their) strongly opposing views.
4. Neither Stephen nor Chris (was, were) recognized for their contribution.
5. The company restructured (its, their) recreation event to avoid being perceived as frivolous.
6. The committee will present (its, their) recommendation at the next staff meeting.
7. Jenna forgot to retain her receipts; (this, this oversight) caused a delay in reimbursement.

Pronoun Case

1. **Use the correct case of pronouns.** *Case* tells whether a pronoun is used as the subject of a sentence or as an object in it.

   (a) Use nominative-case pronouns (also known as subjective-case pronouns) (*I, he, she, they, we, you, it, who*) as subjects of a sentence or clause.

   You and I must collaborate. ["You" and "I" are subjects of the verb "collaborate."]

   Those <u>who</u> work will be paid. ["Who" is the subject of the dependent clause "who work."]

(b) Use objective-case pronouns (*me, him, her, them, us, you, it, whom*) as objects of verbs and prepositions.

His mother texted <u>him</u> about the family emergency. ["Him" is the object of the verb "texted."]

The customer feedback survey was sent to the project manager and <u>them</u>. ["Them" is the object of the preposition "to."]

To <u>whom</u> should we send the analysis? ["Whom" is the object of the preposition "to."]

Tip: Restate a subordinate clause introduced by *who* or *whom* to determine the appropriate pronoun.

She is the type of manager <u>whom</u> we can promote. [Restating "whom we can promote" as "We can promote her (whom)" clarifies that "whom" is the object.]

She is the type of manager <u>who</u> can be promoted. [Restating "who can be promoted" as "She (who) can be promoted" clarifies that "who" is the subject.]

Tip: Change a question to a statement to determine the correct form of a pronoun.

<u>Whom</u> did you call? [You did call *whom*.]

<u>Whom</u> did you select for the position? [You did select *whom* for the position.]

(c) Use the nominative case when forms of the linking verb *be* require a pronoun to complete the meaning.

It was <u>he</u> who received credit for the sale.

It is <u>she</u> who deserves the award.

["It was he" may to some people sound just as distracting as the incorrect "It was him." Express the ideas in a different way to avoid the error and an expletive beginning.]

He was the one who received credit for the sale.

She deserves the award.

(d) Use the possessive form of a pronoun before a gerund (a verb used as a noun).

We were delighted at <u>his</u> (not *him*) assuming a leadership role.

["Assuming a leadership role" is used here as a noun. "His" in this sentence serves the same purpose it serves in "We were delighted with his initiative."]

Exercise 3

In each of the following sentences, choose the correct pronoun in parentheses.

1. The professor agreed to award (we, us) partial credit for the confusing question.
2. Pilar requested that tasks be divided equally between Addison and (her, she).
3. It was Sun-Young (who, whom) recommended revising the company's technology policy to include social networking sites.
4. The manager seemed unaware of (his, their) inability to relate to younger employees.
5. Emma is a leader in (who, whom) we have great confidence.

Verb Agreement

1. Make subjects agree with verbs.

(a) Ignore intervening phrases that have no effect on the verb used.

Good material <u>and</u> fast delivery <u>are</u> (not <i>is</i>) essential.

<u>You</u>, not the carrier, <u>are</u> (not <i>is</i>) responsible for the damage. [Intervening phrase, "not the carrier," does not affect the verb used.]

The <u>attitude</u> of these investors <u>is</u> (not <i>are</i>) a deep concern. [The subject is "attitude;" "of these investors" is a phrase coming between the subject and the verb.]

(b) Use a verb that agrees with the noun closer to the verb when <i>or</i> or <i>nor</i> connects two subjects.

Only one or two <u>questions are</u> (not <i>is</i>) necessary.

Several paint brushes or one paint <u>roller is</u> (not <i>are</i>) necessary.

(c) Use singular verbs with plural nouns that have a singular meaning or are thought of as singular units.

The <u>news is</u> good.   **<u>Economics is</u> a required course.**

Twenty <u>dollars is</u> too much.   **Ten <u>minutes is</u> sufficient time.**

(d) Use a singular verb for titles of articles, firm names, and slogans.

"Etiquette in the Age of Social Media" <u>is</u> an interesting article.

Forestieri and Chaudrue <u>is</u> the oldest firm in the city.

"Eat Smart for Hearts" <u>is</u> a campaign slogan directed at better nutrition for senior adults.

2. Choose verbs that agree in person with their subjects. *Person* indicates whether the subject is (1) speaking, (2) being spoken to, or (3) being spoken about.

First person:	I am, we are.
	[Writer or speaker]
Second person:	You are.
	[Receiver of message]
Third person:	He is, she is, they are.
	[Person being discussed]

<u>She doesn't</u> (not *don't*) eat well or exercise regularly.

<u>They don't</u> recognize the value of strong networking skills.

Verb Tense and Mood

1. Use the appropriate verb tense. *Tense* indicates time. Tense can be either simple or compound.

Simple tenses:

Present:	I <u>see</u> you. [Tells what is happening now]
Past:	I <u>saw</u> you. [Tells what has already happened]
Future:	I <u>will see</u> you. [Tells what is yet to happen]

Compound tenses:

Present perfect:	I <u>have seen</u> you. [Tells of past action that extends to the present]
Past perfect:	I <u>had seen</u> you. [Tells of past action that was finished before another past action]
Future perfect:	I <u>will have seen</u> you. [Tells of action that will be finished before a future time]

(a) Use present tense when something was and still is true.

The speaker reminded us that Rhode Island <u>is</u> (not *was*) smaller than Wisconsin.

The consultant's name <u>is</u> (not *was*) Jayden Abrams.

(b) Avoid unnecessary shifts in tense.

The carrier <u>brought</u> (not *brings*) my package but <u>left</u> without asking me to sign for it.

Verbs that appear in the same sentence are not required to be in the same tense.

The contract that <u>was prepared</u> yesterday <u>will be signed</u> tomorrow.

2. Use subjunctive mood to express situations that are untrue or highly unlikely. Be sure to use *were* for the present tense of *to be* to indicate the subjunctive mood. Use *was* when the statement could be true.

I wish the story <u>were</u> (not *was*) true.

If I <u>were</u> (not *was*) you, I would try again.

Exercise 4

In each of the following sentences, choose the correct verb in parentheses.

1. Only one of the free smartphone applications (has, have) value to me.
2. Taxpayers, not the government, (are, is) held accountable for paying the national debt.
3. Neither the manager nor the employees (was, were) aware of the policy change.
4. Both Josh and McKenzie (was, were) notified of the impending layoffs.
5. The news from the rescue mission (is, are) encouraging.
6. *Good to Great* (has, have) been placed in the company library.
7. The sales manager announced that Portsmouth, South Carolina, (is, was) the site for the annual sales meeting.
8. Tyler (don't, doesn't) expect preferential treatment.
9. The client studied the financial analysis for a minute and (starts, started) asking questions.
10. If the applicant (was, were) experienced with databases, they would have been hired.

Adjectives and Adverbs

1. **Use an adjective to modify a noun or pronoun and an adverb to modify a verb, an adjective, or another adverb.**

   Adjective: Bryan gave an **impressive** sales pitch.

   Adverb: The new employee looked **enthusiastically** at the sales prospect. [The adverb "enthusiastically" modifies the verb "looked."]

   The team leader was **really** visionary. [The adverb "really" modifies the adjective "visionary."]

   Worker A progressed **relatively faster** than did Worker B. [The adverb "relatively" modifies the adverb "faster."]

2. **Use an adjective after a linking verb when the modifier refers to the subject instead of the verb.**
   [A linking verb connects a subject to the rest of the sentence. "He is old." "She seems sincere."]

   The man entering the building looked <u>suspicious</u>. [The adjective "suspicious" refers to "man," not to "looked."]

3. **Use comparatives (to compare two) and superlatives (to compare three or more) carefully.**

   She is the <u>faster</u> (not *fastest*) of the two workers.

   Edwin is the <u>better</u> (not *best*) writer of the two team members.

   Exclude a person or thing from a group with which that person or thing is being compared.

   He is more observant than <u>anyone else</u> (not *anyone*) in his department. [As a member of his department, he cannot be more observant than himself.]

   "The X-60 is newer than <u>any other machine</u> (not *any machine*) in the plant." [The X-60 cannot be newer than itself.]

Exercise 5

In each of the following sentences, choose the correct adjective or adverb in parentheses.

1. Despite the dangers, employees change their computer passwords (infrequent, infrequently).
2. Daniel looked (impatient, impatiently) at the new production assistant.
3. The server moved (quick, quickly) from table to table.
4. Of the several people I met during the recent speed networking event, Eva made the (better, best) impression.
5. The Chicago plant has a higher safety record than (any, any other) plant.

Punctuation

Commas

1. **Use a comma**

   (a) Between coordinate clauses joined by *and, but, for, or,* and *nor.*

   He wanted to pay his bills on time, <u>but</u> he did not have the money.

   (b) To separate introductory clauses and certain phrases from independent clauses. Sentences that begin with dependent clauses (often with words such as *if, as, since, because, although,* and *when*) almost always need a comma.

Prepositional phrases and verbal phrases with five or more words require commas.

Dependent clause:	**If you can postpone your departure**, the research team will be able to finalize its proposal submission. [The comma separates the introductory dependent clause from the independent clause.]
Infinitive:	**To get the full benefit of our insurance plan**, complete and return the enclosed card. [A verb preceded by "to" ("to get")]
Participial:	**Believing that her earnings would continue to increase**, she requested a higher credit card limit. [A verb form used as an adjective: "believing" modifies the independent clause "she requested a higher credit card limit."]
Prepositional phrase:	**Within the next few days**, you will receive written confirmation of this transaction. [Comma needed because the phrase contains five words]
	Under the circumstances we think you are justified. [Comma omitted because the phrase contains fewer than five words and the sentence is clear without the comma]

(c) To separate three or more words in a series.

You must choose between <u>gray, green, purple</u>, and <u>white</u>. [Without the comma after "purple," no one can tell for sure whether four choices are available, the last of which is "white," or whether three choices are available, the last of which is "purple and white."]

You must choose between <u>purple</u> and <u>white</u>, <u>gray</u>, and <u>green</u>. [Choice is restricted to three, the first of which is "purple and white."]

(d) Between two or more independent adjectives that modify the same noun.

New employees are given a <u>long</u>, <u>difficult</u> examination. [Both "long" and "difficult" modify "examination."]

We want <u>quick</u>, <u>factual</u> news. [Both "quick" and "factual" modify "news."]

Do not place a comma between two adjectives when the second adjective modifies the adjective and noun as a unit.

The supervisor is an <u>excellent team player</u>. ["Excellent" modifies the noun phrase "team player."]

(e) To separate a nonrestrictive clause (a clause that is not essential to the basic meaning of the sentence) from the rest of the sentence.

Kent Murray, <u>who is head of customer resource management</u>, has selected Century Consulting to oversee the product launch. [The parenthetical remark is not essential to the meaning of the sentence.]

The man <u>who is head of customer resource management</u> has selected Century Consulting to oversee the product launch. [Commas are not needed, because "who is head of customer resource management" is essential to the meaning of the sentence.]

(f) To set off or separate dates, addresses, geographical names, degrees, and long numbers:

On <u>July 2, 2023,</u> Jason Kennedy made the final payment. [Before and after the year in month-day-year format]

I saw him in <u>Tahoe City, California,</u> on the 12th of October. [Before and after the name of a state when the name of a city precedes it]

<u>Jesse Marler,</u> president [Between the printed name and the title on the same line beneath a signature or in a letter address]

Tristan A. Highfield President of Academic Affairs [No comma is used if the title is on a separate line.]

(g) To separate parenthetical expressions or other elements interrupting the flow from the rest of the sentence.

Ms. Watson, <u>speaking on behalf of the entire department,</u> accepted the proposal. [To set off a parenthetical expression]

<u>Cole,</u> I believe you have earned a vacation. [After a direct address]

<u>Yes,</u> you can count on me. [After the words No and Yes when they introduce a statement]

Arun Ramage, <u>former president of the Jackson Institute,</u> spoke to the group. [To set off appositives when neutral emphasis is desired]

The job requires experience, <u>not formal education.</u> [Between contrasted elements]

Exercise 6

Insert needed commas. Write "correct" if you find no errors.

1. The employee who is featured in our latest infomercial is active in the community theatre.
2. Emojis which are pictographs of facial expressions symbols, and objects communicate emotion in electronic messages.
3. Sean Cohen a new member of the board remained silent during the long bitter debate.
4. Top social networking sites include Facebook Instagram and TikTok.
5. The entire population was surveyed but three responses were unusable.
6. If you tag websites in a social bookmarking site you can locate them easily for later use.
7. To qualify for the position applicants must have technology certification.
8. We should be spending less money not more.
9. On May 9 2023 the company's Twitter site was launched.
10. Yes the president approved a team-building event to replace our annual golf outing.

Semicolons and Colons

1. Use a semicolon

(a) To join the independent clauses in a compound sentence when a conjunction is omitted.

Your voice counts; email us with your ideas and concerns.

(b) To join the independent clauses in a compound–complex sentence.

> **As indicated earlier, we prefer delivery on Saturday morning at four o'clock; but Friday night at ten o'clock will be satisfactory.**

> **We prefer delivery on Saturday morning at four o'clock; but, if the arrangement is more convenient for you, Friday night at ten o'clock will be satisfactory.**

(c) Before an adverbial conjunction. Use a comma after the adverbial conjunction.

Adverbial conjunction:	The shipment arrived too late for our weekend sale; <u>therefore</u>, we are returning the shipment to you.

Other frequently used adverbial conjunctions are *however, otherwise, consequently,* and *nevertheless*.

(d) Before words used to introduce enumerations or explanations that follow an independent clause.

Enumeration with commas:	Many factors affect the direction of the stock market; <u>namely</u>, interest rates, economic growth, and employment rates.
Explanation forming a complete thought:	We have plans for improvement; <u>for example</u>, we intend…. The engine has been "knocking"; <u>that is</u>, the gas in the cylinders explodes before the pistons complete their upward strokes.

Note: The following exceptions require a comma to introduce the enumeration or explanation:

Enumeration without commas:	Several Web 2.0 tools are available, <u>for example</u>, blogs and wikis. [A comma, not a semicolon, is used because the enumeration contains no commas.]
Explanation forming an incomplete thought:	A trend is to replace expensive employee networking events with purposeful recreation, <u>for instance</u>, community service events. [A comma, not a semicolon, is used because the explanation is not a complete thought.]

(e) In a series that contains commas.

> **Some of our workers have worked overtime this week: Smith, 6 hours; Hardin, 3; Cantrell, 10; and McGowan, 11.**

2. Use a colon

(a) After a complete thought that introduces a list of items. Use a colon following both direct and indirect introductions of lists.

Direct introduction:	The following three factors influenced our decision: an expanded market, an inexpensive source of raw materials, and a ready source of labor. [The word "following" clearly introduces a list.]
Indirect introduction:	The carpet is available in three colors: green, burgundy, and blue.

Do not use a colon after an introductory statement that ends with a preposition or a verb (*are, is, were, include*). The list that follows the preposition or verb finishes the sentence.

Incomplete sentence:	We need to (1) expand our market, (2) locate an inexpensive source of materials, and (3) find a ready source of labor. [A colon does not follow "to", because the words preceding the list are not a complete sentence.]

(b) To stress an appositive (a noun that renames the preceding noun) at the end of a sentence.

> **A majority of white-collar criminals report that a single factor led to their crimes: pressure to achieve revenue targets. Our progress is due to the efforts of one person: Brooke Keating.**

Exercise 7

Insert semicolons, colons, and commas where needed, and delete them where they are unnecessary. Write "correct" if you find no errors.

1. Some privacy concerns have become less important in recent years, however, most people feel extremely vulnerable to privacy invasion.

2. The following agents received bonuses Barnes, $750, Shelley, $800, and Jackson, $950.

3. Employees were notified today of the plant closing they received two weeks' severance pay.

4. This paint does have some disadvantages for example a lengthy drying time.

5. Soon after the applications are received, a team of judges will evaluate them, but the award recipients will not be announced until January 15.

6. The program has one shortcoming: flexibility.

7. The new bakery will offer: frozen yogurt, candies, and baked goods.

8. We are enthusiastic about the plan because: (1) it is least expensive, (2) its legality is unquestioned, and (3) it can be implemented quickly.

Apostrophes

1. Use an apostrophe to form possessives.

(a) Add an apostrophe and *s* ('*s*) to form the possessive case of a singular noun or a plural noun that does not end with a pronounced *s*.

Singular noun:	<u>Jenna's</u> position
	<u>firm's</u> assets
	<u>employee's</u> benefits
Plural noun without a pronounced *s*:	<u>men's</u> clothing
	<u>children's</u> games
	<u>deer's</u> antlers

(b) Add only an apostrophe to form the possessive of a singular or plural noun that ends with a pronounced *s*.

Singular noun with pronounced *s*:	<u>Niagara Falls'</u> site
	<u>Ms. Jenkins'</u> interview
Plural noun with pronounced *s*:	two <u>managers'</u> decision
	six <u>months'</u> wages

Exception: An apostrophe and *s* (*'s*) can be added to singular nouns ending in a pronounced *s* if an additional *s* sound is pronounced easily.

Singular noun with additional *s* sound: <u>boss's</u> decision

        <u>class's</u> party

        <u>Jones's</u> invitation

(c) Use an apostrophe with the possessives of nouns that refer to time (minutes, hours, days, weeks, months, and years) or distance in a possessive manner.

eight <u>hours'</u> pay	two <u>weeks'</u> notice
<u>today's</u> global economy	ten <u>years'</u> experience
a <u>stone's</u> throw	a <u>yard's</u> length

Exercise 8

Correct the possessives.

1. The new hires confidence was crushed by the managers harsh tone.
2. This companies mission statement has been revised since it's recent merger.
3. Employees who are retained may be asked to accept a reduction of one weeks pay.
4. Vendors' have submitted sealed bids for the construction contract that will be opened in two week's.
5. Younger workers must appreciate older employees extensive company knowledge.

Hyphens

1. Use a hyphen

(a) Between the words in a compound adjective. (A *compound adjective* is a group of adjectives appearing together and used as a single word to describe a noun.)

An <u>eye-catching</u> device   A <u>two-thirds</u> interest

Do not hyphenate a compound adjective in the following cases:

1. When the compound adjective follows a noun.

   A design that is <u>eye catching</u>.

   Today's consumers are <u>convenience driven</u>.

   Note: Some compound adjectives that are familiar hyphenated words or phrases remain hyphenated when they follow a noun.

   The news release was <u>up-to-date</u>.

   For jobs that are <u>part-time</u>, ...

2. An expression made up of an adverb that ends in *ly*, or an adjective that is not a compound adjective does not require a hyphen.

   <u>commonly accepted</u> principle

   <u>widely quoted</u> authority

3. A simple fraction or a percentage.

Simple fraction:	<u>Two thirds</u> of the respondents
Percentage:	<u>15 percent</u> sales increase

(b) To prevent misinterpretation.

<u>Recover</u> a chair [To obtain possession of a chair once more]

<u>Re-cover</u> a chair [To cover a chair again]

<u>Eight inch</u> blades [Eight blades, each of which is an inch long]

<u>Eight-inch</u> blades [Blades eight inches long]

Exercise 9

Add necessary hyphens and delete those that are unnecessary. Write "correct" if you find no errors.

1. The web based application was unavailable because of a denial of service attack.

2. State of the art computers provide quick access to timely-business information.

3. A large portion of holiday orders are time sensitive.

4. A two thirds majority is needed to pass the 5-percent increase in employee wages.

5. Nearly one-half of the respondents were highly-educated professionals.

Quotation Marks and Italics

1. Use quotation marks

(a) To enclose direct quotations.

Single-sentence quotation:	The supervisor said, "We will make progress."
Interrupted quotation:	"We will make progress," the supervisor said, "even though we have to work overtime."
Multiple-sentence quotation:	The manager said, "Have a seat, Seth. Please wait a moment while I complete this email."
	[Place quotation marks before the first word and after the last word of a multiple-sentence quotation.]
Quotation within a quotation:	The budget director said, "Believe me when I say 'A penny saved is a penny earned' is the best advice I ever had."
	[Use single quotation marks to enclose a quotation that appears within a double quotation.]

(b) To enclose titles of songs, magazine and newspaper articles, lecture titles, and themes within text.

"Candle in the Wind" "Making an Impact"

The chapter, "Online Presence," ...

(c) To enclose a definition of a defined term. Italicize the defined word.

The term *downsizing* is used to refer to "the planned reduction in the number of employees."

(d) To enclose words used in humor, a word used when a different word would be more appropriate, slang expressions that need to be emphasized or clarified for the reader, or nicknames. These words can also be shown in italics.

Humor/different word:	Our "football" team …
	[Hints that the team appears to be playing something other than football]
	Our football "team" …
	[Hints that "collection of individual players" would be more descriptive than "team"]
	… out for "lunch."
	[Hints that the reason for being out is something other than lunch]
Slang:	The "tipping point" for the planned reorganization is securing support of union management.
Nicknames:	And now for some comments by Robert "Bob" Johnson.

2. Use italics

(a) To mention words, letters, numbers, and phrases within a sentence.

He had difficulty learning to spell *recommendation*.

(b) To emphasize a word that is not sufficiently emphasized by other means.

Our goal is to hire the *right* person, not necessarily the most experienced candidate.

(c) To indicate the titles of books, magazines, and newspapers.

Creating a *Culture of Excellence*

The New York Times

Reader's Digest

Exercise 10

Add necessary quotation marks and italics.

1. Cynthia Cooper's Extraordinary Circumstances is required reading in some forensic accounting classes.

2. The article How to Persuade People to Say Yes appeared in the May 2023 issue of Training Journal.

3. The consultant's accomplishments are summarized on her opening blog page. [Indicate that a word other than *accomplishments* may be a more appropriate word.]

4. Connie said I want to participate in a volunteer program that serves such a worthy cause. [Direct quotation]

5. The term flame is online jargon for a heated, sarcastic, sometimes abusive message or posting to a discussion group.

6. Limit random tweets, but focus on ideas and issues that are interesting and relevant.

Dashes, Parentheses, and Periods

1. Use a dash

   (a) To place emphasis on appositives.

        His answer—the correct answer—was based on years of experience.

        Compare the price—$125—with the cost of a single repair job.

   (b) When appositives contain commas.

        Their scores—Chloe, 21; Tairus, 20; and Drew, 19—were the highest in a group of 300.

   (c) When a parenthetical remark consists of an abrupt change in thought.

        The committee decided—you may think it's a joke, but it isn't—that the resolution should be adopted.

        Note: Use an em dash (not two hyphens) to form a dash in computer-generated copy.

2. Use parentheses for explanatory material that could be left out.

   Three of our employees (Kristen Hubbard, Alex Russo, and Mark Coughlan) took their vacations in August.

   All our employees (believe it or not) have perfect attendance records.

3. Use a period after declarative and imperative sentences, and courteous requests.

   We will attend. [Declarative sentence]

   Complete this report. [Imperative sentence]

   Will you please complete the report today.

   [Courteous request is a question but does not require a verbal answer with requested action.]

Exercise 11

Add necessary dashes, parentheses, or periods.

1. Additional consultants, programmers and analysts, were hired to complete the computer conversion. [Emphasize the appositive.]
2. The dividend will be raised to 15 cents a share approved by the Board of Directors on December 1, 2023. [De-emphasize the approval.]
3. Would you please link this YouTube video to my slide show?

Number Usage

1. Use figures

   (a) In most business writing, because figures provide deserved emphasis and are easy for readers to locate if they need to reread for critical points. Regardless of whether a number has one digit or many, use figures to express dates, sums of money, mixed numbers and decimals, distance, dimension, cubic capacity, percentage, weights, temperatures, and chapter and page numbers.

        May 10, 2023   165 pounds

        $9 million   Chapter 3, page 29

        5 percent (use % in a table)

        more than 200 applicants (or two hundred) [An approximation]

(b) With ordinals (*th, st, rd, nd*) only when the number precedes the month.

The meeting is to be held on June 21.

The meeting is to be held on the 21st of June.

(c) With ciphers but without decimals when presenting even-dollar figures, even if the figure appears in a sentence with another figure that includes dollars and cents.

Miranda paid $70 for the cabinet.

Miranda paid $99.95 for the table and $70 for the cabinet.

(d) Numbers that represent time when a.m. or p.m. is used. Words or figures may be used with o'clock.

Please meet me at 10:15 p.m.

Please be there at ten o'clock (or 10 o'clock).

Omit the colon when expressing times of day that include hours but not minutes, even if the time appears in a sentence with another time that includes minutes.

The award program began at 6:30 p.m. with a reception at 7 p.m.

2. **Spell out**

(a) Numbers if they are used as the first word of a sentence.

Thirty-two people attended.

(b) Numbers one through nine if no larger number appears in the same sentence.

Only three auditors worked at the client's office.

Send 5 officers and 37 members.

(c) The first number in two consecutive numbers that act as adjectives modifying the same noun; write the second number in figures. If the first number cannot be expressed in one or two words, place it in figures also.

The package required four, 44-cent stamps. [A hyphen joins the second number with the word that follows it, thus forming a compound adjective that describes the noun "stamps."]

We shipped 250, 180-horsepower engines today. [Figures are used because neither number can be expressed in one or two words.]

Exercise 12

Correct the number usage in the following sentences taken from a letter or a report.

1. The question was answered by sixty-one percent of the respondents.
2. The meeting is scheduled for 10:00 a.m. on February 3rd.
3. These 3 figures appeared on the expense account: $21.95, $30.00, and $35.14.
4. The purchasing manager ordered 50, 2-TB hard drives.
5. 21 members voted in favor of the $2,000,000 proposal.
6. Approximately one hundred respondents requested a copy of the results.
7. Mix two quarts of white with 13 quarts of brown.
8. Examine the cost projections on page eight.

Capitalization

1. **Proper nouns (words that name a particular person, place, or thing) and adjectives derived from proper nouns.** Capitalize the names of persons, places, geographic areas, days of the week, months of the year, holidays, deities, specific events, and other specific names.

Proper nouns	Common nouns
Kendra Moore	An applicant for the management position
Bonita Lakes	A land development
Centre Park Mall	A new shopping center
Veteran's Day	A federal holiday
Information Age	A period of time
Proper adjectives:	Irish potatoes, Roman shades, Swiss army knife, Chinese executives, British accent, Southern dialect

   Do not capitalize the name of the seasons unless they are personified.

   Old Man Winter

2. **The principal words in the titles of books, magazines, newspapers, articles, discography, albums, movies, plays, television series, songs, and poems.**

   The Carrot Principle [Book]

   "Smart Moves for New Leaders" [Article]

   Time [Magazine]

   The White Album [Discography or albums]

3. **The names of academic courses that are numbered, are specific course titles, or contain proper nouns.** Capitalize degrees used after a person's name and specific academic sessions.

   Addison Malone is enrolled in classes in <u>French</u>, <u>mathematics</u>, <u>science</u>, and <u>English</u>.

   Students entering the MBA program must complete <u>Accounting 6093</u> and <u>Finance 5133</u>.

   Allison Ward, <u>M.S.</u>, will teach <u>International Marketing</u> during <u>Spring Semester</u> 2023.

   Professor O'Donnell earned a <u>master's</u> degree in business from Harvard.

4. **Titles that precede a name.**

Mr. Ronald Moxley	Editor Deeden
Dr. Lauren Zolna	President Lopez
Uncle Iain	Professor Copley

   Do not capitalize titles appearing alone or following a name unless they appear in addresses.

   The <u>manager</u> approved the proposal submitted by the <u>editorial assistant</u>.

   Jon Sharma, <u>executive vice president</u>, is responsible for that account.

   Clint has taken the position formerly held by his <u>father</u>.

   Address all correspondence to Colonel Michael Anderson, <u>Department Head</u>, 109 Crescent Avenue, Baltimore, MD 21208.

5. The main words in a division or department name if the official or specific name is known or the name is used in a return address, a letter address, or a signature block.

Official or specific name known:	Return the completed questionnaire to the <u>Public Relations Department</u> by March 15.
Official or specific name unknown:	Employees in your <u>information systems division</u> are invited …
Return or letter address, signature block:	Mr. Blake Cain, <u>Manager</u>, <u>Public Relations Department</u>

6. Most nouns followed by numbers (except in page, paragraph, line, size, and verse references).

Policy No. 8746826	Exhibit A	Chapter 7
page 97, paragraph 2	Figure 3-5	Model L-379
Flight 340, Gate 22	size 8, Style B	319 jacket

7. The first word of a direct quotation.

The placement officer warned, "Those with offensive email habits may be the first to lose their jobs during layoffs."

Do not capitalize the first word in the last part of an interrupted quotation or the first word in an indirect quotation.

"We will proceed," he said, "with the utmost caution." [Interrupted quotation]

He said that the report must be submitted by the end of the week. [Indirect quotation]

8. The first word following a colon when a formal statement or question follows.

Here is an important rule for report writers: Plan your work and work your plan.

Each sales staff should ask this question: Do I really look like a representative of my firm?

Exercise 13

Copy each of the following sentences, making essential changes in capitalization.

1. The first question professor Burney asked me during interviewing 101 was "why do you want to work for us?"
2. The remodeling will give the store a more sophisticated feel according to the Public Relations Director.
3. As the Summer Season arrives, gas prices are expected to rise.
4. We recently purchased digital juice, an excellent source for copyright-free animated images.
5. Thomas Frieden, Director of the Centers for Disease Control, is the agency's key communicator.

Words Frequently Misused

The following words are frequently misused. If you're not certain of their meaning or usage, check a dictionary or style guide.

1. Accept, except
2. Advice, advise
3. Affect, effect
4. Among, between
5. Amount, number
6. Capital, capitol
7. Cite, sight, site
8. Complement, compliment
9. Continual, continuous
10. Credible, creditable
11. Council, counsel
12. Different from, different than
13. Each other, one another
14. Eminent, imminent
15. Envelop, envelope
16. Farther, further
17. Fewer, less
18. Formally, formerly
19. Infer, imply
20. Its, it's
21. Lead, led
22. Lose, loose
23. Media, medium
24. Personal, personnel
25. Principal, principle
26. Reason is, because
27. Stationary, stationery
28. That, which
29. Their, there, they're
30. To, too, two

Exercise 14

Select the correct word or phrase in parentheses.

1. What (affect, effect) will the change have on us?
2. The consultant plans to (advice, advise) the company to eliminate the fourth shift for at least three months.
3. The (amount, number) of complaints from customers declined with the addition of online chat.
4. The (cite, sight, site) of the new 24/7 fitness center is being debated.
5. I consider your remark a (compliment, complement); I agree that the granite countertops (compliment, complement) the deep, earthy tones in the room.
6. The three panelists were constantly interrupting (each other, one another).
7. Generally, staple merchandise is placed (farther, further) from the cashier than impulse items.
8. Limit your discussion to five or (fewer, less) points.
9. I (infer, imply) from Avanti's comments to the press that the merger will occur.

10. The hurricane seems to be (losing loosing) (its, it's) force, which is (different from, different than) predictions.

11. The chemical engineer (lead, led) the research team's investigation to eliminate (lead, led) from gas emissions.

12. Employees may handle (personal, personnel) business during e-breaks beginning next week.

13. Customer perception is the (principal, principle) reason for the change.

14. (Their, There, They're) planning to complete (their, there, they're) strategic plan this week.

15. The (to, too, two) external auditors expect us (to, too, two) complete (to, too, two) many unnecessary reports.

Solutions to Exercises

Exercise 1—Sentence Structure

1. You must learn to design spreadsheets that make financial information meaningful to users.

2. Many online tools are available that build relationships with customers.

3. I am submitting an employee testimonial, which I first posted to a presentations blog, to the company website.

4. More companies are videoconferencing because of the need to reduce travel costs significantly.

5. You must perform periodic maintenance on your computer to keep it operating efficiently. [The introductory phrase dangles.]

6. Option 1: Planned store improvements include widening the aisles, improving lighting, and lowering shelves for a sophisticated feel.

    Option 2: Planned store improvements include widened aisles, improved lighting, and lowered shelves for a sophisticated feel.

Exercise 2—Pronoun Reference

1. affect	**5.** its
2. was	**6.** its
3. their	**7.** this oversight
4. was	

Exercise 3—Pronoun Case

1. us	**4.** their
2. her	**5.** whom
3. who	

Exercise 4—Verb Agreement, Tense, and Mood

1. has
2. are
3. were
4. were
5. is
6. has
7. is
8. doesn't
9. started
10. were

Exercise 5—Adjectives and Adverbs

1. infrequently
2. impatiently
3. quickly
4. best
5. any other

Exercise 6—Commas

1. Correct

2. Emojis, which are pictographs of facial expressions, symbols, and objects, communicate emotion in electronic messages.

3. Sean Cohen, a new member of the board, remained silent during the long, bitter debate.

4. Top social networking sites include Facebook, Instagram, and TikTok.

5. The entire population was surveyed, but three responses were unusable.

6. If you tag websites in a social bookmarking site, you can locate them easily for later use.

7. To qualify for the position, applicants must have technology certification.

8. We should be spending less money, not more.

9. On May 9, 2023, the company's Twitter site was launched.

10. Yes, the president approved a team-building event to replace our annual golf outing.

Exercise 7—Semicolons and Colons

1. Some privacy concerns have become less important in recent years; however, most people feel extremely vulnerable to privacy invasion.

2. The following agents received bonuses: Barnes, $750; Shelley, $800; and Jackson, $950.

3. Employees were notified today of the plant closing; they received two weeks' severance pay.

4. This paint does have some disadvantages, for example, a lengthy drying time.

5. Soon after the applications are received, a team of judges will evaluate them; but the award recipients will not be announced until January 15.

6. Correct

7. The new bakery will offer frozen yogurt, candies, and baked goods.

8. We are enthusiastic about the plan because (1) it is least expensive, (2) its legality is unquestioned, and (3) it can be implemented quickly.

Exercise 8—Apostrophes

1. hire's; manager's

2. company's; its

3. week's

4. Vendors; weeks

5. employees'

Exercise 9—Hyphens

1. web-based; denial-of-service attack

2. State-of-the-art; timely business

3. Correct

4. two-thirds; 5 percent

5. one half; highly educated

Exercise 10—Quotation Marks and Italics

1. Cynthia Cooper's *Extraordinary Circumstances* is required reading in some forensic accounting classes. [Italicizes a book title]

2. The article "How to Persuade People to Say Yes" appeared in the May 2023 issue of *Training Journal*. [Encloses the name of an article in quotation marks and italicizes the title of a journal]

3. The consultant's "accomplishments" are summarized on her opening blog page. [Uses quotation marks to introduce doubt about whether accomplishments is the right label; her undertakings may have been of little significance]

4. Connie said, "I want to participate in a volunteer program that serves such a worthy cause." [Uses quotations marks in a direct quotation]

5. The term *flame* is online jargon for "a heated, sarcastic, sometimes abusive message or posting to a discussion group." [Italicizes a defined term and encloses the definition in quotes]

6. Limit random "tweets," but focus on ideas and issues that are interesting and relevant. [Uses quotation marks to emphasize or clarify a word for the reader]

Exercise 11—Dashes, Parentheses, and Periods

1. Additional consultants—programmers and analysts—were hired to complete the computer conversion.

2. The dividend will be raised to 15 cents a share (approved by the Board of Directors on December 1, 2023).

3. Would you please link this YouTube video to my slide show. [Uses a period to follow a courteous request that requires no verbal response]

Exercise 12—Number Usage

1. The question was answered by 61 percent of the respondents.

2. The meeting is scheduled for 10 a.m. on February 3.

3. These three figures appeared on the expense account: $21.95, $30, and $35.14.

4. The purchasing manager ordered fifty, 2-TB Flash drives.

5. Twenty-one members voted in favor of the $2 million proposal.

6. Approximately 100 respondents requested a copy of the results. [Approximations above nine that can be expressed in one or two words may be written in either figures or words, but figures are more emphatic.]

7. Mix 2 quarts of white with 13 quarts of brown.

8. Examine the cost projections on page 8.

Exercise 13—Capitalization

1. The first question Professor Burney asked me during Interviewing 101 was "Why do you want to work for us?"

2. The remodeling will give the store a more sophisticated feel according to the public relations director.

3. As the summer season arrives, gas prices are expected to rise.

4. We recently purchased Digital Juice, an excellent source for copyright-free animated images.

5. Thomas Frieden, director of the Centers for Disease Control, is the agency's key communicator.

Exercise 14—Words Frequently Misused

1. effect

2. advise

3. number

4. site

5. compliment; complement

6. one another

7. farther

8. fewer

9. infer

10. losing; its; different from

11. led; lead

12. personal

13. principal

14. they're; their

15. two; to; too

Style Appendix

Letter and Punctuation Styles

Decisions about page format impact the effectiveness of the message. Many companies have policies that dictate the page layout, letter and punctuation style, and other formatting issues. In the absence of company policy, make your format choices from among standard acceptable options illustrated in this appendix.

Page Layout, Punctuation, and Letter Style

The default margins set by word-processing software typically reflect the standard line length to increase the efficiency of producing business correspondence. Letters are balanced on the page with approximately equal margins on all sides of the letter, a placement often referred to as fitting the letter into a picture frame. Short letters (one or two paragraphs) are centered on the page; all other letters begin 1 inch from the top of the page. Side margins may be adjusted to improve the appearance of extremely short letters.

Current word-processing software has increased the default line spacing and space between paragraphs for easier on-screen reading. If you prefer the tighter, traditional spacing, simply adjust the line spacing to 1.0. Also, to conserve space but keep the fresh, open look, try reducing the line spacing in the letter address but retaining the wider line and paragraph spacing in the body of the letter. Another new default is a crisp, open font such as Calibri (replacing the common Times New Roman) designed for easy reading on monitors.

New Document Look

July 27, 2023   **Tap Enter 2 times**

Abbie S. Jackson

1938 South Welch Avenue

Northwood, NE 65432-1938   **Tap Enter 1 time**

Dear Abbie Jackson,   **Tap Enter 1 time**

Your recent article, "Are Appraisers Talking to Themselves?" has drawn many favorable comments from local real estate appraisers.
　　　　　Tap Enter 1 time

The Southeast Chapter of the Society of Real Estate Appraisers …

Traditional Spacing

July 24, 2023   **Tap Enter 4 times**

Abbie S. Jackson

1938 South Welch Avenue

Northwood, NE 65432-1938   **Tap Enter 2 times**

Dear Abbie Jackson,   **Tap Enter 2 times**

Your recent article, "Are Appraisers Talking to Themselves?" has drawn many favorable comments from local real estate appraisers.

Tap Enter 2 times

The Southeast Chapter of the Society of Real Estate Appraisers …

Punctuation Styles. Two punctuation styles are customarily used in business letters: mixed and open. Letters using mixed punctuation style have a colon after the salutation and a comma after the complimentary close. Letters using open punctuation style omit a colon after the salutation and a comma after the complimentary close. Mixed punctuation is the traditional style; however, efficiency-conscious companies are increasingly adopting the open style (and other similar format changes), which is easier to remember.

Letter Styles. Business letters are typically formatted in either block or modified block letter styles. The Sample Letters section has examples of these two styles:

- **Block.** Companies striving to reduce the cost of producing business documents adopt the easy-to-learn, efficient block format. All lines (including paragraphs) begin at the left margin.
- **Modified Block.** Modified block is the traditional letter format still used in many companies. The dateline, complimentary close, and signature block begin at the horizontal center of the page. Paragraphs may be indented ½ inch if the writer prefers or the company policy requires it. However, the indention creates unnecessary keystrokes that increase the production cost. All other lines begin at the left margin.

Standard Letter Parts

Professional business letters include seven standard parts. Other parts are optional and may be included when necessary.

1. Dateline. When the letterhead shows the company name, address, telephone and/or fax number, and logo, the letter begins with the *dateline.* Use the month-day-year format (September 2, 2016) for most documents prepared for U.S. audiences. When preparing government documents or writing to an international audience, use the day-month-year format (2 September 2016). Company policy may require another format.

2. Letter Address. The ***letter address*** includes a personal or professional title (e.g., Mr., Ms., or Dr.) or the receiver's first and last name, the name of the person and company receiving the letter, and the complete address.

3. Salutation. The ***salutation*** is the greeting that opens a letter. To show courtesy for the receiver, include a personal or professional title (e.g., Mr., Ms., Dr., or Senator) or the receiver's first and last name. Refer to the first line of the letter address to determine an appropriate salutation. "Dear Dr. Henson" is an appropriate salutation for a letter addressed to Dr. Donna Henson (first line of letter address). "Ladies and Gentlemen" is an appropriate salutation for a letter addressed to "Wyatt Enterprises," where the company name is keyed as the first line of the letter address.

4. Body. The ***body*** contains the message of the letter. Because extra space separates the paragraphs, paragraph indention, which requires extra setup time, is not necessary. However, for organizations that require paragraph indention as company policy, the modified block format with indented paragraphs is the appropriate choice.

Letter and Punctuation Styles

5. Complimentary Close. The ***complimentary close*** is a phrase used to close a letter in the same way that you say goodbye at the end of a conversation. To create goodwill, choose a complimentary close that reflects the formality of your relationship with the receiver. Typical examples are "Sincerely," "Regards," "Cordially," and "Respectfully." Using "yours" in the close has fallen out of popularity (as in "Sincerely yours" and "Very truly yours"). "Sincerely" is considered neutral and is thus appropriate in a majority of business situations. "Cordially" can be used for friendly messages, and "Respectfully" is appropriate when you are submitting information for the approval of another.

6. Signature Block. The *signature block* consists of the writer's name keyed below the complimentary close, allowing space for the writer to sign legibly. A woman may include a courtesy title to indicate her preference (e.g., Miss, Ms., or Mrs.), and a woman or man may use a title to distinguish a name used by both men and women (e.g., Shane, Leslie, or Stacy) or initials (E. M. Goodman). A business or professional title may be placed on the same line with the writer's name or directly below it as appropriate to achieve balance.

Title on the Same Line	Title on the Next Line
Ms. Leslie Tatum, President	Ms. E. M. Goodman
Perry Watson, Manager	Assistant Manager
Quality Control Division Head	Richard S. Templeton
	Human Resources Director

7. Reference Initials. The *reference initials* consist of the keyboard operator's initials keyed in lowercase below the signature block. The reference initials and the signature block identify the persons involved in preparing a letter in the event of later questions. Reference initials are frequently omitted when a letter is keyed by the writer. However, company policy may require that the initials of all people involved in preparing a letter be placed in the reference initials line to identify accountability in the case of litigation. For example, the following reference initials show the indicated level of responsibility. The reference line might also include department identification or other information as required by the organization.

SF:lm:cd

Person who signed	Person who wrote document	Person who keyed
document		document

Optional Letter Parts

Delivery and Addressee Notations. A *delivery notation* provides a record of how a letter was sent. Examples include air mail, certified mail, Federal Express, registered mail, and fax transmission. Addressee notations such as "Confidential" or "Personal" give instructions on how a letter should be handled.

Attention Line. An *attention line* is used for directing correspondence to an individual or department within an organization while still officially addressing the letter to the organization. The attention line directs a letter to a specific person (Attention Laura Ritter), position within a company (Attention Human Resources Director), or department (Attention Purchasing Department). Current practice is to place the attention line in the letter address on the line directly below the company name and use the same format for the envelope address.

Reference Line. A *reference line* (Re: Contract No. 983–9873) directs the receiver to source documents or to files.

Subject Line. A *subject line* tells the receiver what a letter is about and sets the stage for the receiver to understand the message. For added emphasis, use initial capitals or all capitals, or center the subject line if modified block style is used. Omit the word subject because its position above the body clearly identifies its function.

Second-Page Heading. The second and succeeding pages of multiple-page letters and memo-randums are keyed on plain paper of the same quality as the letterhead. Identify the second and succeeding pages with a ***second-page heading*** including the name of the addressee, page number, and the date. Place the heading 1 inch from the top edge of the paper, using either a vertical or horizontal format as illustrated. The horizontal format is more time consuming to format but looks attractive with the modified block format and may prevent the document from requiring additional pages.

Vertical Format

Communication Systems, Inc.

Page 2

January 19, 2023

Horizontal Format

Communication Systems, Inc. 2 January 19, 2023

Company Name in Signature Block. Some companies prefer to include the ***company name*** in the signature block, but often it is excluded because it appears in the letterhead. The company name is beneficial when the letter is prepared on plain paper or is more than one page (the second page of the letter is printed on plain paper). Including the company name also may be useful to the writer wishing to emphasize that the document is written on behalf of the company (e.g., a letter establishing an initial customer contact).

Enclosure Notation. An ***enclosure notation*** indicates that additional items (brochure, price list, and résumé) are included in the same envelope. Key the plural form (Enclosures) if more than one item is enclosed. You may identify the number of enclosures (Enclosures: 3) or the specific item enclosed (Enclosure: Bid Proposal). Avoid abbreviations (Enc.) that may give the impression that your work is hurried and careless and may show disrespect for the recipient. Some companies use the word *Attachment* on memorandums when the accompanying items may be stapled or clipped and not placed in an envelope.

Copy Notation. A ***copy notation*** indicates that a courtesy copy of the document was sent to the person(s) listed. Include the person's personal or professional title and full name after keying "c" for *copy* or "cc" for *courtesy copy*. Key the copy notation below the enclosure notation, reference initials, or signature block (depending on the optional letter parts used).

Postscript. A ***postscript***, appearing as the last item in a letter, is commonly used to emphasize information. A postscript in a sales letter, for example, is often used to restate the central selling point; for added emphasis, it may be handwritten or printed in a different color. Often handwrit-ten postscripts of a personal nature are added to personalize the printed document. Postscripts should not be used to add information inadvertently omitted from the letter. Because its position clearly labels this paragraph as a postscript, do not begin with "PS."

Computer File Notation. A ***computer file notation*** provides the path and file name of the letter. Some companies require this documentation on the file copy to facilitate revision. Place the computer file notation a single space below the last keyed line of the letter.

Sample Letters

Block Letter Style with Open Punctuation

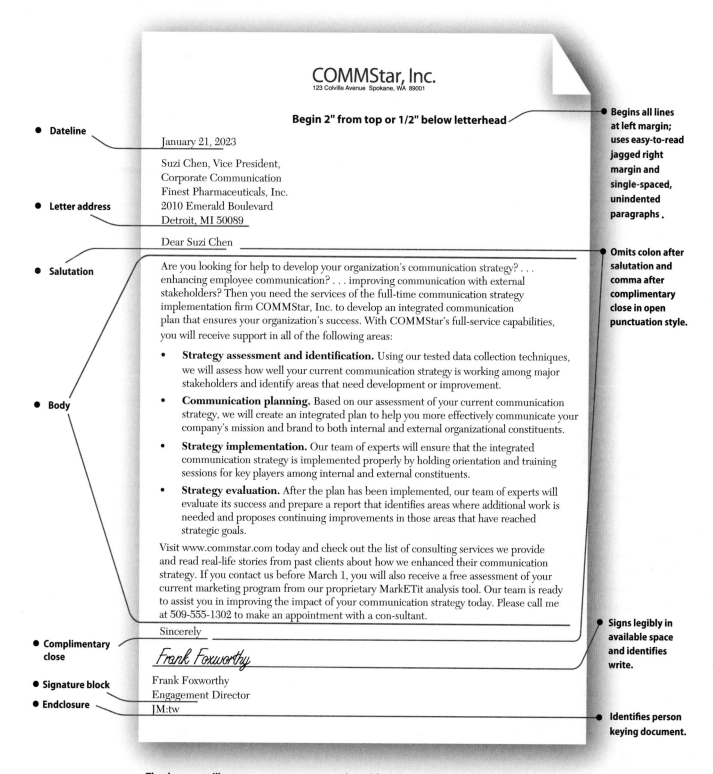

Dateline

Letter address

Salutation

Body

Complimentary close

Signature block

Enclosure

COMMStar, Inc.
123 Colville Avenue Spokane, WA 89001

Begin 2" from top or 1/2" below letterhead

January 21, 2023

Suzi Chen, Vice President,
Corporate Communication
Finest Pharmaceuticals, Inc.
2010 Emerald Boulevard
Detroit, MI 50089

Dear Suzi Chen

Are you looking for help to develop your organization's communication strategy? . . . enhancing employee communication? . . . improving communication with external stakeholders? Then you need the services of the full-time communication strategy implementation firm COMMStar, Inc. to develop an integrated communication plan that ensures your organization's success. With COMMStar's full-service capabilities, you will receive support in all of the following areas:

- **Strategy assessment and identification.** Using our tested data collection techniques, we will assess how well your current communication strategy is working among major stakeholders and identify areas that need development or improvement.

- **Communication planning.** Based on our assessment of your current communication strategy, we will create an integrated plan to help you more effectively communicate your company's mission and brand to both internal and external organizational constituents.

- **Strategy implementation.** Our team of experts will ensure that the integrated communication strategy is implemented properly by holding orientation and training sessions for key players among internal and external constituents.

- **Strategy evaluation.** After the plan has been implemented, our team of experts will evaluate its success and prepare a report that identifies areas where additional work is needed and proposes continuing improvements in those areas that have reached strategic goals.

Visit www.commstar.com today and check out the list of consulting services we provide and read real-life stories from past clients about how we enhanced their communication strategy. If you contact us before March 1, you will also receive a free assessment of your current marketing program from our proprietary MarkETit analysis tool. Our team is ready to assist you in improving the impact of your communication strategy today. Please call me at 509-555-1302 to make an appointment with a con-sultant.

Sincerely

Frank Foxworthy

Frank Foxworthy
Engagement Director
JM:tw

Begins all lines at left margin; uses easy-to-read jagged right margin and single-spaced, unindented paragraphs .

Omits colon after salutation and comma after complimentary close in open punctuation style.

Signs legibly in available space and identifies write.

Identifies person keying document.

The document illustrates contemporary spacing with 1.15 spaces between lines. If using traditional single spacing (1.0), tap Enter 2 times to double-space between paragraphs and 4 times to quadruple space after the dateline and the complimentary close.

Modified Block Letter Style with Mixed Punctuation

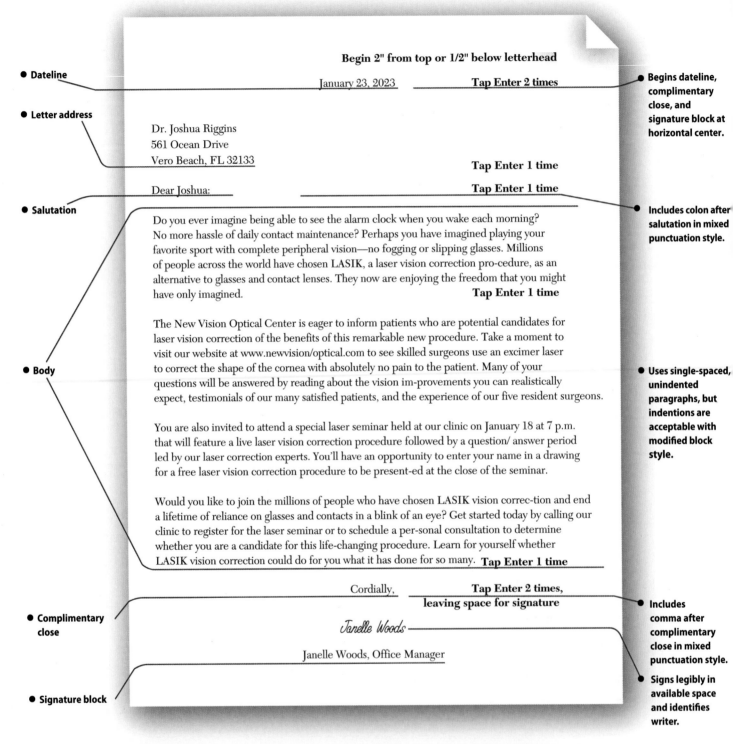

Dateline

Letter address

Salutation

Body

Complimentary close

Signature block

Begin 2" from top or 1/2" below letterhead

January 23, 2023   **Tap Enter 2 times**

Dr. Joshua Riggins
561 Ocean Drive
Vero Beach, FL 32133

Tap Enter 1 time

Dear Joshua: **Tap Enter 1 time**

Do you ever imagine being able to see the alarm clock when you wake each morning? No more hassle of daily contact maintenance? Perhaps you have imagined playing your favorite sport with complete peripheral vision—no fogging or slipping glasses. Millions of people across the world have chosen LASIK, a laser vision correction pro-cedure, as an alternative to glasses and contact lenses. They now are enjoying the freedom that you might have only imagined.   **Tap Enter 1 time**

The New Vision Optical Center is eager to inform patients who are potential candidates for laser vision correction of the benefits of this remarkable new procedure. Take a moment to visit our website at www.newvision/optical.com to see skilled surgeons use an excimer laser to correct the shape of the cornea with absolutely no pain to the patient. Many of your questions will be answered by reading about the vision im-provements you can realistically expect, testimonials of our many satisfied patients, and the experience of our five resident surgeons.

You are also invited to attend a special laser seminar held at our clinic on January 18 at 7 p.m. that will feature a live laser vision correction procedure followed by a question/ answer period led by our laser correction experts. You'll have an opportunity to enter your name in a drawing for a free laser vision correction procedure to be present-ed at the close of the seminar.

Would you like to join the millions of people who have chosen LASIK vision correc-tion and end a lifetime of reliance on glasses and contacts in a blink of an eye? Get started today by calling our clinic to register for the laser seminar or to schedule a per-sonal consultation to determine whether you are a candidate for this life-changing procedure. Learn for yourself whether LASIK vision correction could do for you what it has done for so many.   **Tap Enter 1 time**

Cordially,   **Tap Enter 2 times, leaving space for signature**

Janelle Woods

Janelle Woods, Office Manager

Begins dateline, complimentary close, and signature block at horizontal center.

Includes colon after salutation in mixed punctuation style.

Uses single-spaced, unindented paragraphs, but indentions are acceptable with modified block style.

Includes comma after complimentary close in mixed punctuation style.

Signs legibly in available space and identifies writer.

Document illustrates contemporary spacing. If using traditional spacing (1.0) between lines, tap Enter 2 times to double-space between paragraphs and 4 times to quadruple space after the dateline and the complimentary close.

Envelope and Memo Styles

Envelopes

An envelope should be printed on the same quality and color of paper as the letter and generated using the convenient envelope feature of your word-processing program. Adjust defaults as needed to adhere to the recommendations of the United States Postal Service (USPS). To increase the efficiency of mail handling, use the two-letter abbreviations for states, territories, and Canadian provinces. USPS official state abbreviations are available at www.USPS.com.

Most companies today do not follow the traditional USPS recommendation to key the letter address in all capital letters with no punctuation. The mixed case format matches the format used in the letter address, looks more professional, and allows the writer to generate the envelope automatically without rekeying text. No mail-handling efficiency is lost as today's optical character readers that sort mail can read both uppercase- and lowercase letters easily. Proper placement of the address on a large envelope and a small envelope generated using an envelope template available with word-processing software is shown here:

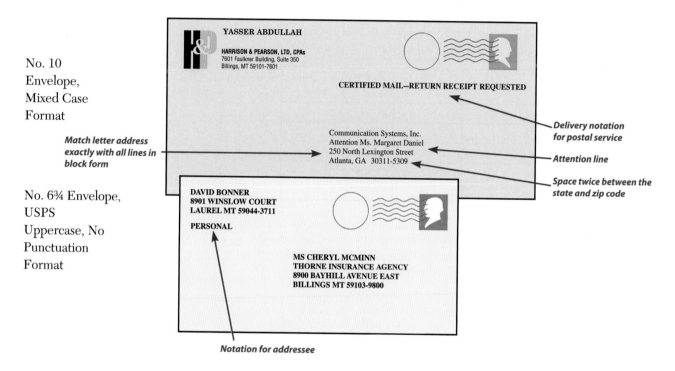

No. 10 Envelope, Mixed Case Format

Match letter address exactly with all lines in block form

No. 6¾ Envelope, USPS Uppercase, No Punctuation Format

YASSER ABDULLAH

HARRISON & PEARSON, LTD, CPAs
7601 Faulkner Building, Suite 350
Billings, MT 59101-7601

CERTIFIED MAIL—RETURN RECEIPT REQUESTED

Communication Systems, Inc.
Attention Ms. Margaret Daniel
250 North Lexington Street
Atlanta, GA   30311-5309

Delivery notation for postal service

Attention line

Space twice between the state and zip code

DAVID BONNER
8901 WINSLOW COURT
LAUREL MT 59044-3711

PERSONAL

MS CHERYL MCMINN
THORNE INSURANCE AGENCY
8900 BAYHILL AVENUE EAST
BILLINGS MT 59103-9800

Notation for addressee

Additionally, to create a highly professional image, business communicators should fold letters to produce the fewest number of creases. Here are the proper procedures for folding letters for large (No. 10) and small (No. 6¾) envelopes:

Folding and Inserting Procedures for Large Envelopes

Step 1
With letter face up, fold slightly less than 1/3 of sheet up toward top.

Step 2
Fold down top of sheet to within 1/2 inch of bottom fold.

Step 3
Insert letter into envelope with last crease toward bottom of envelope.

Folding and Inserting Procedures for Small Envelopes

Step 1
With letter face up, fold bottom up to 1/2 inch from top.

Step 2
Fold right third to left.

Step 3
Fold left third to 1/2 inch from last crease.

Step 4
Insert last creased edge first.

Memorandum Formats

To increase productivity of memorandums (memos), which are internal messages, companies use formats that are easy to input and that save time. Most companies use customized or standard memo templates found in most word-processing software that include the basic headings (To, From, Date, and Subject) to guide the writer in providing the needed transmittal information. Memos may be printed on memo forms, plain paper, or letterhead, depending on the preference of the company. Follow the guidelines for formatting a memo illustrated here.

Begin 2" from top of page or 1/2" below letterhead

To: Samuel Ledbetter, President

From: Darlene Wang, Sales Manager

Date: April 1, 2023

Subject: Monthly Sales Report, Computer Department

Sales for the month remained at about the same level as previous months this year, at $212,100. Sales figures for the month by item are as follows:

Item	Quantity Sold	Total Revenue from Sales ($)
Laptops	91	63,700
Desktops	25	15,000
Tablets	162	64,800
Notebooks	103	61,800
Monitors	34	6,800

In terms of our marketing efforts, we sent email alerts to our previous customers, notifying them of our monthly specials on computer products. These specials were also highlighted on our web and Facebook pages. As such, we incurred no costs for advertising other than the time incurred by our web page manager to design these messages.

We continue to employ two full-time salespeople on the floor and two part-time salespersons to cover the weekend shift. Current staffing levels are sufficient for the current sales volume.

Like other "brick-and-mortar" retail outlets, we continue to feel increased competition from online competitors. If company goals include growing the sales of computer products, we need to:

- increase our online presence to more effectively compete head-to-head with these operations and/or,
- strategize ways of drawing more customers to our store who complete sales transactions.

The attached document provides a more detailed breakdown of product sales by model and maker. This data will be used to determine our product promotions for next month. We continue to work with our suppliers on pricing strategies to maintain our competitiveness with online rivals.

Attachment

Formal Report

Formal Report Format

Page arrangement for reports varies somewhat, depending on the documentation style guide followed or individual company preferences. Take advantage of your software's automatic formatting features for efficient formatting and generating report parts. Portions of a sample report are shown below.

Margins. For formal reports, use 1-inch side margins. If the report is to be bound, increase the left margin by ½ inch. Use a 2-inch top margin for the first page of each report part (table of contents and executive summary) and a 1-inch top margin for all other pages. Leave at least a 1-inch bottom margin on all pages.

Spacing. Although documentation style guides typically specify double-spacing of text, company practice is often to single-space reports. Double-spacing accommodates editorial comments and changes but results in a higher page count. Even if you choose to double-space the body of a report, you may opt to single-space some elements, such as the entries in your references page and information in tables or other graphic components.

Headings. Several levels of headings can be used throughout the report and are typed in different ways to indicate the level of importance. Suggested formatting guidelines for a report divided into three levels are illustrated in the document on the next page. Develop fourth- and fifth-level headings simply by using boldface, underline, and varying fonts.

Formal Report Parts

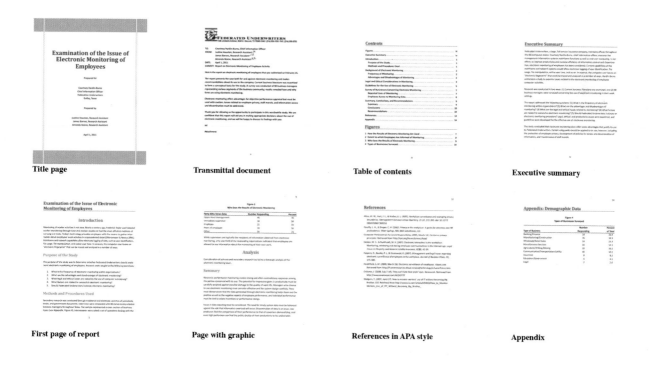

Title page Transmittal document Table of contents Executive summary

First page of report Page with graphic References in APA style Appendix

- **Capitalizes all letters in report title.**

- **Places first-and second-level headings at left margin and capitalizes initial letters. Larger font size makes the first level stand out.**

- **Includes intervening text between first-and second-level headings.**

- **Uses default indentation and decreased spacing between enumerated and bulleted items.**

- **Places third-level subheadings at left margin and capitalizes the first letter.**

Format Pointers:
- **This report document illustrates Word 2019 Style Set with style formats applied for the report title, the three heading levels, and the enumerated list. Creating a custom style set allows businesses to create a report style that is consistent with their company image and brand.**

- **The increased spacing after each paragraph eliminates the need for indented paragraphs.**

2" top margin

REPORT TITLE Title style (26-point font)

Tap Enter 1 time

xxx xxxxxx xxxxxxx xxxxx xxxxxxxxx xxxx xxxxxx xxxxxx xxxxxxx xxxxx xx xxxxxx xxxx x xxxxx xxxxx xxxxxxxxx xxx xxxx xxxxx xxxxx.

Tap Enter 1 time

First-Level Heading Heading 1 (14-point font)

Tap Enter 1 time

xxx xxxxxx xxxxxxx xxxxx xxxxxxxxx xxxx xxxxxx xxxxxx xxxxxxx xxxxx xx xxxxxx xxxx x xxxxx xxxxx xxxxxxxxx xxx xxxx xxxxx xxxxx.

Tap Enter 1 time

Second-Level Subheading Heading 2 (13-point font)

Tap Enter 1 time

xxx xxxxxx xxxxxxx xxxxx xxxxxxxxx xxxx xxxxxx xxxxxx xxxxxxx xxxxx xx xxxxxx xxxx x xxxxx xxxxx xxxxxxxxx xxx xxxx xxxxx xxxxx.

Tap Enter 1 time

1. xxxx x xxxxxx xx xxxxxx xxxx xxx xxxxxxxxx xx xxxxx xxxxx xx. xx xxxx xxx.

Space automatically reduced between enumerated items.

2. xxxx x xxxxxx xx xxxxxx xxxx xxx xxxxxxxxx xx xxxxx xxxxx xx. xx xxxx xxx xxxxx xxxx xx x xxxxxxxxxx.

Tap Enter 1 time

Second-Level Subheading

Tap Enter 1 time

xxx xxxxxx xxxxxxx xxxxx xxxxxxxxx xxxx xxxxxx xxxxxx xxxxxxx xxxxx xx xxxxxx xxxx x xxxxx xxxxx xxxxxxxxx xxx xxxx xxxxx xxxxx.

Tap Enter 1 time

Heading 3 (11-point font)

Third-Level Subheading. xxx xxxxxx xxxxxxx xxxxx xxxxxxxxx xxxx xxxxxx xxxxx xxxxxxx xxxxx xx xxxxxx xxxx x xxxxx xxxxx xxxxxxxxx xxx xxxx xxxx xxxxx.

Tap Enter 1 time

Third-Level Subheading. xxx xxxxxx xxxxxxx xxxxx xxxxxxxxx xxxx xxxxxx xxxxx xxxxxxx xxxxx xx xxxxxx xxxx x xxxxx xxxxx xxxxxxxxx xxx xxxx xxxx xxxxx.

MLA Referencing

A number of widely used reference styles are available for documenting the sources of information used in report writing. Two of the more popular style manuals for business writing are as follows:

Publication Manual of the American Psychological Association, 7th ed., Washington, DC: American Psychological Association, 2020.

MLA Handbook, 9th ed., New York: Modern Languages Association of America, 2021. The *MLA Handbook* is designed for high school and undergraduate college students; the *MLA Style Manual and Guide to Scholarly Publishing,* 3rd ed. (2008) is designed for graduate students, scholars, and professional writers.

These sources, commonly referred to as the APA and MLA styles, provide general rules for referencing and give examples of the citation formats for various types of source materials. This section reflects the rules along with examples for the MLA style. Whenever you are not required to use a particular documentation style, choose a recognized one and follow it consistently. Occasionally, you may need to reference something for which no general example applies. Choose the example that is most like your source and follow that format. When in doubt, provide more information, not less. Remember that a major purpose for listing references is to enable readers to retrieve and use the sources. This section illustrates citation formats for some common types of information sources and refers you to various electronic sites that provide further detailed guidelines for preparing electronic citations.

In-Text Parenthetical Citations

The *MLA Handbook* supports the use of **in-text citations**. Abbreviated information within parentheses in the text directs the reader to a list of sources at the end of a report. The list of sources at the end contains all bibliographic information on each source cited in a report. This list is arranged alphabetically by the author's last name or, if no author is provided, by the first word of the title.

The in-text citations contain minimal information needed to locate the source in the complete list. The *MLA* style includes the author's last name and the page number for both quotes and paraphrases, but not the date of publication. Note the format of the in-text parenthetical citations shown below.

One author not named in the text, direct quotation

"A recent survey … shows that more and more companies plan to publish their annual reports on the internet" (Prinn 13).

Direct quotation, no page number on source

According to James, "traditional college students have a perspective that is quite different from adult consumers" (par. 2).

Use par. 2 *in place of missing page number only if paragraphs are numbered in original text.*

Multiple authors for sources not named in the text wording

Globalization is becoming a continuous challenge for managers … (Tang and Crofford 29).

"For all its difficulty, teamwork is still essential … " (Nunamaker et al. 163).

For sources by more than three authors, use et al. *after the last name of the first author or include all last names. Do not underline or italicize* et al.

More than one source documenting the same idea

… companies are turning to micromarketing (Heath 48; Roach 54).

More than one source by the same author documenting the same idea

Past research (Taylor, "Performance Appraisal" 6, "Frequent Absenteeism" 89) shows …

Reference to author(s) or date in the text wording

Kent Spalding and Brian Price documented the results …

In 2006, West concluded … (E2).

Omit a page number when citing a one-page article or nonprint source.

No author provided

… virtues of teamwork look obvious ("Teams Triumph in Creative Solutions" 61).

Include full title or shortened version of it.

Works Cited

The **works cited** page located at the end of your document contains an alphabetized list of the sources used in preparing a report, with each entry containing publication information necessary for locating the source. A researcher often uses sources that provide information but do not result in citations. If you want to acknowledge that you have consulted these works and provide the reader with a comprehensive reading list, include these sources in the list of works cited and refer to list as Works Consulted. Your company guidelines may specify whether to list works cited only or works consulted. If you receive no definitive guidelines, use your own judgment. If in doubt, include all literature cited and read, and label the page with the appropriate title so that the reader clearly understands the nature of the list.

To aid the reader in locating sources in lengthy bibliographies, you may include several subheadings denoting the types of publications documented, for example, books, articles, unpublished documents and papers, government publications, and nonprint media. Check your reference manual to determine if subheadings are allowed.

Formats for Print and Recorded References

Note that the following rules apply for MLA works cited.

Indention and spacing	Begin first line of each entry at left margin and indent subsequent lines ½ inch. Although the MLA style manual specifies double-spacing within and between entries, common practice in preparing reports is to single-space each entry and double-space between entries.
Author names	List last name first for first author only. Use "and" before final author's name.
Date	Place date at the end of citation for books and after periodical title and volume for articles. Months are abbreviated.
Capitalization	In titles of books, periodicals, and article titles, capitalize all main words.
Italicizing and quotation marks	Italicize titles of books, journals, and periodicals (or underline if directed). Place titles of articles within quotation marks.
Page notations	Omit the use of *p.* or *pp.* on all citations.

MLA (9th Edition Style)

Works Cited

Centento, Antonio. "The Appropriate Men's Attire for Every Occasion." *businessinsider.com.* Business Insider, 12 September 2014. Web. 23 October 2014.

Freeburg, Beth Winfrey, & Arnett, Sally E. "The Impact of Appearance Management Training, Work Status, and Plans After High School on Opinions Regarding Appearance at Work and School." *Journal of Career and Technical Education* 25.2 (2010).

"Proper Business Attire and Etiquette." *tcbsolutions.net.* The Country's Best Solutions, n.d. Web. 23 October 2014.

"Dress Speak for Men." *ECG.* Executive Communications Group, n.d. Web. 23 October 2014.

"Dress Speak for Women." *ECG.* Executive Communications Group, n.d. Web. 23 October 2014.

Goman, Carol Kinsey. "What It Really Means to Dress for Success." *Forbes.com.* Forbes, 20 March 2012. Web. 23 October 2014.

Smith, Jacquelyn. "Here's What 'Business Casual' Really Means." *businessinsider.com.* Business Insider, 19 August 2014. Web. 23 October 2014.

Heathfield, Susan M. "Dress for Work Success: A Business Casual Dress Code." *About.com.* About, n.d. Web. 23 October 2014.

Jensen, Andrew. "How Does Workplace Attire Affect Productivity?" *Andrew Jensen.* Andrew Jensen, 27 June 2014. Web. 23 October 2014.

LeTrent, Sarah. "Decoding the workplace dress code." *CNN.com.* Cable News Network, 15 August 2012. Web. 23 October 2014.

APA Referencing

Crediting Sources

According to the APA Style, references in the article follow the author-date citation system and are placed at the end of the article in alphabetical order. This helps the reader determine the source from the text with the reference list. All references that are cited throughout the text must be listed in the reference section at the end of the article. Likewise, all the sources mentioned in the reference section need to be present in the text. Care needs to be taken while citing the two sources as they need to be indistinguishable. The authors' name and the year should be spelled correctly.

One Work by One Author

To cite one work by one author, the author-date method is used wherein the last name of the author (without any suffixes such as Jr.) and the year of publication should be added in the content.

Brown's (2006) recent report on the use of experiments shows a correlation between results and participants.

The most recent report on the use of experiments shows a correlation between results and participants (Brown, 2006).

In the first example, the name of the author is present as a part of the sentence. In such cases, only the year of publication should be cited in parentheses. In other cases (as in the second example), the name and the year can be placed at the end in parentheses and separated by a comma. The month of publication need not be included. In rare cases where the name and the year come along with discussion in the article, they need not be in parentheses.

In 2006, Brown's report on the use of experiments shows ....

One Work by Multiple Authors

If the source consists of only two authors, use both the names throughout the text when they are cited. If the source consists of more than two authors, cite only the last name of first the author followed by "et al." along with the year if it is the first cited reference in a paragraph. The "et al." should be followed by a period and should not be italicized.

Thanavaro & Moore (2017) found

Kernis et al. (1993) found

Groups as Authors

Authors in the name of groups such as universities, medical institutes, agencies, or study groups are usually spelled out every time they are referenced. In most cases, they are spelled out in the first instance and then abbreviated in the following instances. If the name of the group is better spelled out, for example the University of Arizona, then it doesn't need be abbreviated. If the name is lengthy and the abbreviation can be easily recalled, then it can be used as an abbreviation thereafter.

Authors with the Same Surname

If the source contains two (or more) authors with the same surname, include the initials of the authors to avoid confusion.

J. Dawson (1986) and T. Dawson (1986) accept the ….

Works with No Identified Author or with an Anonymous Author

If the source has an author that cannot be identified, cite the title and the year of the work. The title should be in double quotation marks and italicized if it is a report, a book, a brochure, or a periodical.

("Relativity," 2005)

College Bound Seniors (2008)

Two or More Works within the Same Parentheses

Cite references of two or more works within parentheses in alphabetical order (as they would appear in the reference list). Also, for two or more works by the same author, arrange them in the same manner but by year of publication.

Training materials are available (Department of Veterans Affairs, 2001, 2003)

Secondary Sources

Secondary sources need to be used in moderation, for instance, when the original source cannot be availed. The secondary source is listed in the reference section, but while citing it in the text it should have the name of the original source followed by the citation of the secondary one.

Allport's diary (as cited in Nicholson, 2003)

Personal Communications

Interviews, lectures, email, phone conversations, messages, and the like that cannot be recovered are classified under personal communications. They should only be cited in the text/article and not in the reference list. Provide the initials and surname of the communicator and also the date if possible.

A. M. Raulson (personal communication, January 28, 2007) says …

Reference List

The sources cited at the end of the article classified under the reference list guides readers to recover and pinpoint each of them. Only sources that have been used for the exploration and basis for the article should be included. Journals using the APA Style broadly make use of reference lists and not bibliographies. The reference section should begin on a fresh page apart from the article, and the sources should be in a double-spaced format.

Reference List Format

The reference list is formatted using the following APA Style guidelines.

- The lines succeeding the first line of each source must be indented to ½ inch from the left margin.

- The authors' last name should be used first. Provide the last name and the initials for all authors of the same work. If there are more than 20 authors cited, use ellipses after the 19th author's name, and then provide the last author's name.

- The list should be in alphabetical order by the surname of the first author of each source.

- If there are several works by one author, cite the sources in a sequential order starting from the oldest to the most recent.

- Sustain the capitalization and punctuation that is used in the original source.

- All major words in the titles of journals should be capitalized.

- Only the first letter of the first word in a title, subtitle, proper nouns, and the first word after a colon or a dash should be capitalized. This is done when you are referring to chapters, books, web pages, or articles. The second word in a hyphenated compound word should not be capitalized.

- Book and journal titles with longer works need to be italicized.

- Journal articles or essay titles with shorter works need not be italicized, underlined, or in quotes.

Glossary

A

acknowledgment message a document that indicates that an order has been received and is being processed

active listening requires that the listener fully concentrates, understands, responds, and then remembers what is being said

active voice when the subject of a sentence is the doer of an action

addenda may include all materials used in the research but not appropriate to be included in the report itself

adjourning now widely accepted as stage five of team development, involves the conclusion of the project and team members going their separate ways, though they may continue to keep in touch

adjustment messages messages that are fair responses by businesses to legitimate requests in claim messages by customers

agenda a meeting outline that includes important information (e.g., date, beginning and ending times, place, topics to be discussed, and responsibilities of those involved)

AIDA the four basic steps of the persuasive process, including gaining attention, generating interest, creating desire, and motivating action

analytical report a report that presents suggested solutions to problems

analytical report a type of report designed to solve a specific problem or answer research questions

application message a message placed on top of the résumé so it can be read first by the employer; also called a cover message

area chart a graphic that shows how different factors contribute to a total; also referred to as a cumulative line chart or surface chart

articulation smooth, fluent, and pleasant speech

attribution the assignment of meaning to other people's behavior

B

bar chart a graphic used to compare quantities

beamer a quick version of a résumé designed in a format suitable for broadcasting on smartphones; also called a *beamable résumé*

brainstorming the generation of many ideas by team members

C

casual listening listening for pleasure, recreation, amusement, and relaxation

central selling point the primary appeal on which a persuasive message focuses

chronemics the study of how a culture perceives time and its use

chrono-functional résumé a résumé that combines features of chronological and functional résumés

chronological résumé the traditional organizational format for résumés, with headings that spotlight an applicant's education and experience

claim a request for an adjustment

clichés overused expressions that can cause their users to be perceived as unoriginal, unimaginative, lazy, and perhaps even disrespectful

coherence cohesion, so that each sentence is linked to the preceding sentences in some way

common language reduces difficult figures to the common denominators of language and ideas

connotative meaning the literal meaning of a word plus an extra message that reveals the speaker's or writer's qualitative judgment

consensus represents the collective opinion of the group, or the informal rule that all team members can live with at least 70 percent of what is agreed upon

context a situation or setting in which communication occurs

D

counterproposal in a bad-news message, an alternative to the action requested that follows the negative news and can assist in preserving future relationships with the audience

cross-functional team a team that brings together employees from various departments to solve a variety of problems

D

deductive (or direct) sequence when the message begins with the main idea followed by supporting details

deductive a message in which the major idea precedes the details

deductive paragraph a paragraph in which the topic sentence precedes the details

denotative meaning the literal meaning of a word that most people assign to it

diversity skills the ability to communicate effectively with people of all genders, ages, cultures, and underrepresented groups

doublespeak also called doubletalk or corporate speak; euphemisms that deliberately mislead, hide, or evade the truth

downward communication a type of communication that flows from supervisor to employee, from policy makers to operating personnel, or from top to bottom on the organizational chart

E

electronic applicant-tracking systems systems that increase the efficiency of processing résumés by storing scanned résumés in an electronic database where they can be sorted by keywords, with a resulting ranking of applicants

emoji any of various small images, symbols, or icons used in text fields in electronic communication (as in text messages, email, and social media) to express the emotional attitude of the writer, convey information succinctly, or communicate a message playfully without using words

empathetic listening listening to others in an attempt to share their feelings or emotions

ethics the principles of right and wrong that guide one in making decisions that consider the impact of one's actions on others as well as on the decision maker

ethnocentrism the assumption that one's own cultural norms are the right way to do things

euphemism a kind word substituted for one that may offend or suggest something unpleasant

executive summary short summary of the essential elements in an entire report; also called an *abstract*, *overview*, or *précis*

experimental research the study of two samples that have exactly the same components before a variable is added to one of the samples

extemporaneous presentations a presentation in which a speaker plans, prepares, and rehearses but does not write everything down; brief notes prompt the speaker, but the exact words are chosen spontaneously as the speaker interacts with the audience and identifies its specific needs

external messages messages directed to recipients outside the organization

external proposal a proposal written to generate business; one organization describes how it can meet the needs of another by, for example, providing a product or service

external report a report prepared for distribution outside an organization

F

Fair Credit Reporting Act a federal law that provides consumers the right to know the nature of the information in their credit file and gives them other protections when they apply for and are denied credit

flowchart a step-by-step diagram of a procedure, or a graphic depiction of a system or organization

formal communication network a network of communication flow typified by the formal organizational chart; dictated by the technical, political, and economic environment of the organization

formal report a carefully structured report that is logically organized and objective, contains a lot of detail, and is written in a style that tends to eliminate such elements as personal pronouns

forming stage one of team development, in which team members become acquainted with each other and the assigned task

form reports reports that meet the demand for numerous, repetitive reports; include college registration forms, applications for credit, airline tickets, and bank checks

functional report a report that serves a specified purpose within a company

functional résumé the organizational format for résumés that highlights an applicant's transferable skills

G

Gantt chart a specific type of bar chart that is useful for tracking progress toward completing a series of events over time

good-news messages messages that convey pleasant information

goodwill an attitude of kindness or friendliness that results in a good relationship

graphics all types of illustrations used in written and spoken reports

grouped bar chart a graphic used for comparing more than one quantity (set of data) at each point along the *y*-axis (vertical) or *x*-axis (horizontal); also called a clustered bar chart

H

haptics the use of the sense of touch

horizontal (or lateral) communication interactions between organizational units on the same hierarchical level

hypothesis a statement to be proved or disproved through research

I

impression formation the process of integrating a variety of observations about a person into a coherent impression of that person

impromptu presentation a presentation in which a speaker is called on without prior notice

inductive a message in which the major idea follows the details

inductive paragraph a paragraph in which the topic sentence follows the details

informal communication network a network of communication flow that continuously develops as people interact within the formal system to accommodate their social and psychological needs

informal report usually a short message written in natural or personal language

informational report a report that carries objective information from one area of an organization to another

inline résumé a résumé included in the body of an email message

instant messaging (IM) a real-time email technology that blends email with conversation; sender and receiver who are online at the same time can type messages that both see immediately

intensive listening listening to obtain information, solve problems, or persuade or dissuade

interferences also called barriers; numerous factors that hinder the communication process

internal messages messages intended for recipients within the organization

internal proposals proposals used by managers to justify or recommend purchases or changes in the company

internal report a report that travels within an organization, such as a production or sales report

internet conferencing a method of real-time conferencing that allows a company to conduct a presentation in real time over the internet simultaneously with a conference telephone call; also called webcasting

interpersonal intelligence the ability to read, empathize, and understand others

intrapersonal communication one's perceptions, memories, experiences, feelings, interpretations, inferences, evaluations, attitudes, opinions, ideas, strategies, images, and states of consciousness

intrapersonal intelligence one's communication with oneself, including memories, experiences, feelings, ideas, and attitudes

J

jargon specialized terminology that professionals in some fields use when communicating with colleagues in the same field

justification report a report that outlines comparative information clearly to the reader; used commonly when comparing items for purchase

L

lateral report a report that travels between units on the same organizational level

libel written defamatory remarks

line chart a graphic that depicts changes in quantitative data over time and illustrates trends

listening for information listening that involves the search for data or material

longitudinal studies reports that study the same factors in different time frames

M

manuscript presentation a presentation in which a speaker writes out the entire speech and reads it to the audience; also called a scripted presentation

map a graphic that shows geographic relationships

meme an amusing or interesting item (such as a captioned picture or video) or genre of items that is spread widely online, especially through social media

memorized presentations a presentation in which a speaker writes out a speech, commits it to memory, and recites it verbatim

metacommunication a nonverbal message that, although not expressed in words, accompanies a message that is expressed in words

monochronic time (M-time) a time orientation associated with monochronic cultures, which value schedules

multimedia résumé a résumé created with presentation software, such as Camtasia, and sent to prospective employers on an applicant's personal website

N

netiquette the buzzword for proper behavior on the internet

neutral-news messages messages that are of interest to the reader but are not likely to generate an emotional reaction

norm a standard or average behavior

normative survey research research to determine the status of something at a specific time

norming stage three of team development, in which team members develop strategies and activities that promote goal achievement

O

observational studies studies in which the researcher observes and statistically analyzes certain phenomena to assist in establishing new principles or discoveries

oral briefings informal presentations prepared and presented with little time for planning and developing

organizational communication the movement of information within the company structure

organizational culture a pattern of shared basic assumptions that the group has learned as it solved its problems with external adaptation and internal integration, and which has worked well enough to be taught to new members as the correct way to perceive, think, and feel in relation to these problems

outgroup homogeneity effect the tendency to think members of other groups are all the same

outlining the process of identifying central ideas and details, and arranging them in the right sequence; this should be completed prior to writing

P

passive voice when the subject of a sentence is the receiver of an action

performing stage four of team development, in which team members reach the optimal performance level

periodic report a report that is issued on regularly scheduled dates

personal space the physical space immediately surrounding someone, into which any encroachment feels threatening to or uncomfortable for them

persuasion the ability of a sender to influence others to accept their point of view

persuasive claims messages that assume that a claim will be granted only after explanations and persuasive arguments have been presented

persuasive requests messages that assume that a requested action will be taken after persuasive arguments are presented

phonation the production and variation of a speaker's vocal tone

pictogram a graphic that uses pictures or symbols to illustrate objects, concepts, or numerical relationships

pie chart a graphic that shows how the parts of a whole are distributed

plagiarism the presentation of someone else's ideas or words as your own

polychronic time (P-time) a time orientation associated with polychronic cultures, which tend to value interpersonal relationships

preliminary parts report sections included to add formality to a report, emphasize report content, and aid the reader in locating information in the report quickly and understanding the report more easily

primary research data collected for the first time, usually for a specific purpose

problem statement the particular problem that is to be solved by the research

procedures (or methodology) the steps a writer takes in preparing a report; often recorded as a part of the written report

product development team usually cross-functional in nature; a group of employees who concentrate on innovation and the development cycle of new products

professional portfolio a digital portfolio distributed to prospective employers via a personal website blog, digital portfolio tool, or other media; also called an electronic portfolio or e-portfolio

projected cognitive similarity the tendency to assume others have the same norms and values as your own cultural group

pronunciation using principles of phonetics to create accurate sounds, rhythm, stress, and intonation

proposal a written description of how one organization can meet the needs of another

proxemics the branch of knowledge that deals with the amount of space that people feel it necessary to set between themselves and others

proxemics the study of cultural space requirements

Q

quality assurance team a team that focuses on product or service quality; projects can be either short or long term

R

redundancy a phrase in which one word unnecessarily repeats an idea contained in an accompanying word (e.g., "exactly identical")

reflexivity the capacity for reflection

reliability the level of consistency or stability over time or over independent samples

resale a discussion of goods or services already bought

role tasks employees assume that can involve power and authority that surpass their formal position in the organizational chart

routine claims messages that assume that a claim will be granted quickly and willingly without persuasion

routine requests messages that assume that a request will be granted quickly and willingly without persuasion

résumé a vital communication tool that provides a basis for judgment about a person's capabilities on the job

S

sales promotional material statements made about related merchandise or service

sampling a survey technique that eliminates the need for questioning 100 percent of the population

scannable résumé a résumé formatted to ensure a scanner can accurately read and convert it into a digital format

secondary research provides information that has already been reported by others

segmented bar chart a graphic used to show how different facts (components) contribute to a total; also called a subdivided, stacked bar, or 100 percent bar chart

self-awareness an understanding of the self, including one's attitudes, values, beliefs, strengths, and weaknesses

self-concept how we think about ourselves and describe ourselves to others

self-esteem how we like and value ourselves and how we feel about ourselves

self-fulfilling prophecy the idea that we see ourselves in ways that are consistent with how others see us

short reports reports that include only the minimum supporting materials to achieve effective communication

slander spoken defamatory remarks

social networking sites websites that provide virtual communities in which people with shared interests can communicate

solicited proposals proposals generated when a potential buyer submits exact specifications or needs in a bid request

stakeholders people inside and outside the organization who are affected by decisions

statement of purpose the goal of the study; includes the aims or objectives the researcher hopes to accomplish

status one's formal position in the organizational chart

stereotypes mental pictures that one group forms of the main characteristics of another group, creating preformed ideas of what people in this group are like

stereotyping a standardized mental picture that is held in common by members of a group and that represents an oversimplified opinion, prejudiced attitude, or uncritical judgment

storming stage two of team development, in which team members deal with conflicting personalities, goals, and ideas

stress interview an interview format designed to place the interviewee in an anxiety-producing situation so that an evaluation of the interviewee's performance under stress may be made

structured interview an interview format generally used in the screening process, in which the interviewer follows a predetermined agenda, including a checklist of items or a series of questions and statements designed to elicit the necessary information or interviewee reaction

subjunctive sentences sentences that speak of a wish, necessity, doubt, or condition contrary to fact, and employ such conditional expressions as *I wish, as if, could, would,* and *might*

synergy a situation in which the whole is greater than the sum of the parts

T

table a graphic that presents data in columns and rows, which aid in clarifying large quantities of data in a small space

targeted résumé a résumé that reflects the requirements of a specific job listing

task force a team of workers that is generally given a single goal and a limited time to achieve it

team a small number of people with complementary skills who work together for a common purpose

telecommuting also called teleworking; working at home or other remote locations and sending and receiving work from the company office electronically

territoriality a term associated with nonverbal communication that refers to how people use space (territory) to communicate ownership or occupancy of areas and possessions

text messaging messages that can be sent from one cellphone to another, a cellphone to a computer, or computer to computer; a refinement of computer instant messaging

text résumé a plain text (unformatted) version of a résumé

tone the way a statement sounds; it conveys the writer's or speaker's attitude toward the message and the receiver

topic sentence a sentence that identifies the portion of the topic being discussed and presents the central idea of the paragraph

U

unsolicited application message an unrequested message sent to many prospective employers that contains the same basic message

unsolicited proposal a proposal prepared by an individual or a firm who sees a problem to be solved and proposes a solution

unstructured interview a freewheeling exchange that may shift from one subject to another, depending on the interests of the participants

upward communication a type of communication that is generally a response to requests from supervisors

V

validity the degree to which the data measure what the researcher intends to measure

vertical report a report that can be upward- or downward-directed

video résumé a résumé created as a video for posting on sites such as YouTube

virtual interview interview conducted using videoconferencing technology

virtual team three or more people who collaborate from different physical locations, perform interdependent tasks, have shared responsibility for the outcome of the work, and rely on some form of technology to communicate with one another

visual kinesic communication gestures, winks, smiles, frowns, sighs, attire, grooming, and all kinds of body movements

vocal kinesic communication intonation, projection, and resonance of the voice

W

webinars seminars that are held using the internet for transmission

weblog (or blog) a type of online journal, typically authored by an individual, that does not allow visitors to change the original material posted but only to add comments

References

Chapter 1

1. Koncz, A. (2007, March 15). Employers cite communication skills, honesty/integrity as key for job candidates. *National Association of Colleges and Employers*. Retrieved from www.naceweb.org/press/display.asp?year=2007&prid+254.

2. *Huffington Post* (2013). What big businesses can teach you about building company culture. Retrieved May 13, 2014 from https://www.huffingtonpost.com/2013/12/10/what-big-business-can-tea_n_4194514.html.

3. Tapscott, D. (2008, December 8). Supervising Net Gen. *Business Week* Online, 5. Retrieved from Business Source Complete Database.

4. Slayton, M. (1980). *Common sense and everyday ethics*. Washington, D.C.: Ethics Resource Center.

5. Brzezinski, N. (2014). Diversity and ethics, keys to corporate success: Interview with Global CEO Skanska. *Huffington Post*. Retrieved May 13, 2014 from https://www.huffingtonpost.com/natalia-lopatniuk-brzezinski/diversity-ethics-keys-to-_b_4901755.html.

6. A gift or a bribe? (2002, September). *State Legislatures*, 2 (8), 9.

7. Mathison, D. L. (1988). Business ethics cases and decision models: A call for relevancy in the classroom. *Journal of Business Ethics*, 10, 781.

8. Wile, R. (2014). France didn't actually ban work email after 6 PM-But what did happen is still really funny. *Business Insider*. Retrieved May 13, 2014 from https://www.businessinsider.com/the-truth-about-frances-work-email-ban-2014-4#ixzz31dgeCZqP.

9. Siu, A. (2022). Black News Channel accused of gender discrimination, "sexist" workplace by 13 women in lawsuit. Retrieved January 13, 2022 from https://www.thewrap.com/black-news-channel-accused-of-gender-discrimination-sexist-workplace-by-13-women-in-lawsuit/.

10. Indeed Editorial Team. (2021). Five diversity skills to develop. Retrieved January 14, 2022 from https://www.indeed.com/career-advice/career-development/diversity-skills.

11. Earley, P. C., & Ang, S. (2003). *Cultural Intelligence: Individual Interactions Across Cultures*. Stanford: Stanford Business Books.

12. Cross TL, Bazron BJ, Dennis KW, Isaacs MR (1989) *Towards a Culturally Competent System of Care* Vol. 1. Georgetown University Child Development Centre, Washington DC.

13. Lund, S., Madgavkar, A., Manyika, J., Smit, S., Ellingrud, K., Meaney, M., & Robinson, O., (2021). The future of work after COVID-19. Retrieved January 14, 2022 from https://www.mckinsey.com/featured-insights/future-of-work/the-future-of-work-after-covid-19

14. Semuels, Alana. (2020). Machines and Ai Are Taking over Jobs Lost to Coronavirus. Retrieved January 14, 2022 from https://time.com/5876604/machines-jobs-coronavirus/

15. Dua, A., Chenge, W., Lund, S., DeSmet, A., Robinson, O., & Sanghvi, S. (2020). What 800 executives envision for the postpandemic workforce. Retrieved January 14, 2022 from https://www.mckinsey.com/featured-insights/future-of-work/what-800-executives-envision-for-the-postpandemic-workforce.

16. Miller, B. K., & Butler, J. B. (1996, November/December). Teams in the workplace. *New Accountant*, 18–24.

17. Kaplan A. M. & Haenlein M. (2010). Users of the world, unite! The challenges and opportunities of social media. *Business Horizons*, 53 (1), 61.

18. Felts, C. (1995). Taking the mystery out of self-directed work teams. *Industrial Management*, 37 (2), 21–26.

19. Ray, D., & Bronstein, H. (1995). *Teaming Up*. New York: McGraw-Hill.

20. The trouble with teams. (1995, January 4). *Economist*, 61.

21. Frohman, M. A. (1995, April 3). Do teams … but do them right. *Industry Week*, 21–24.

22. Zuidema, K. R., & Kleiner, B. H. (1994). New developments in developing self-directed work groups. *Management Decision*, 32 (8), 57–63.

23. Barry, D. (1991). Managing the baseless team: Lessons in distributed leadership. *Organizational Dynamics*, 20 (1), 31–47.

24. Powell, A., Piccoli, G., & Ives, B. (2004). Virtual teams: A review of current literature and directions for future research. *The DATABASE for Advances in Information Systems*, 35 (1).

Chapter 2

1. McKinsey Global Institute (2020). What 800 Executives Envision for the Postpandemic Workforce. Retrieved January 14, 2022 from https://www.mckinsey.com/featured-insights/future-of-work/what-800-executives-envision-for-the-postpandemic-workforce

2. Alexander, Andrea, et al (2021). Reimagining the Postpandemic Workforce. Retrieved January 14, 2022 from https://www.mckinsey.com/business-functions/people-and-organizational-performance/our-insights/reimagining-the-postpandemic-workforce.

3. Lund, s., Madgavkar, a., Manyika, J., & Smit, S. (2020). What's next for remote work: An analysis of 2,000 tasks, 800 jobs, and nine countries. Retrieved January 14, 2022 from https://www.mckinsey.com/featured-insights/future-of-work/whats-next-for-remote-work-an-analysis-of-2000-jobs-and-nine-countries

4. Varner, I. & Beamer, L. (2009). *Intercultural communication in the global workplace*. Thousand Oaks, CA: Sage.

5. Aritz, J. & Walker, R. (2012). The effects of leadership style on intercultural group communication in decision-making meetings. The Language Factor in International Business: New Perspectives on Research, Teaching and Practice. In P. Heynderickx, S. Dieltjens, G. Jacobs, P. Gillaerts, & E. D. Groot (Eds). *The language factor in international business: New perspectives on research, teaching and practice*. Bern: Peter Lang.

6. Varner, I. & Beamer, 2009.

7. Wood, J.T. (1997). *Communication theories in action*. Belmont, CA: Wadsworth.

8. Shedletsky, L. J. (1989). The mind at work. In L. J. Shedletsky (Ed.), *Meaning and mind: An intrapersonal approach to human communication*. Bloomington, IN: ERIC and the Speech Communication Association.

9. Gardner, H., & Krechevsky, M. (1993). *Multiple intelligences: The theory in practice*. New York: Basic Books.

10. Evered, R., & Tannebaum, R. (1992). A dialog on dialog. *Journal of Management Inquiry*, 1, 43–55, p. 45.

11. Mehrabian, A. (1971). *Silent Messages*. Belmont, CA: Wadsworth.

12. Wolvin, A.D., & Coakley, C.G. (1996). *Listening*, 5th Ed. Madison, WI: Brown and Benchmark, p. 15.

13. Purdy, M. The listener wins, https://featuredreports.monster.com/listen/overview.

14. Senge, Peter M, Kleiner, Art, Roberts, Charlotte, Ross Richard B, & Smith, Bryan J. (1994). *The Fifth Discipline Fieldbook*. New York: Currency Doubleday.

15. Drucker, Peter. (1990). *The Fifth Discipline. The art and practice of the learning organization*. London: Random House.

16. Murphy, J.J. (2016). *Pulling together: 10 rules for high-performance teamwork*. Napierville, IL: Sourcebooks.

17. Johansson, F. (2004). *The Medici effect*. Boston, MA: Harvard Business School Press.

18. Hunt, V. Layton, D., & Prince, S. (2015). Diversity Matters. Retrieved March 1, 2022 from https://www.mckinsey.com/~/media/mckinsey/business%20functions/organization/our%20insights/why%20diversity%20matters/diversity%20matters.ashx

19. Sommers, S. R. (2006). On racial diversity and group decision making: Identifying multiple effects of racial composition on jury deliberations. *Journal of Personality and Social Psychology*, 90 (4), 597–612. DOI: 10.1037/0022-3514.90.4.597

20. Openness predicts a team's strength. (n.d.). Retrieved March 1, 2022 from https://www.atlassian.com/practices/open/research

21. Sgroi, D. (2015). Happiness and productivity: Understanding the happy-productive worker. Global Perspectives Series: Paper 4. Retrieved March 1, 2022 from https://www.smf.co.uk/wp-content/uploads/2015/10/Social-Market-Foundation-Publication-Briefing-CAGE-4-Are-happy-workers-more-productive-281015.pdf#page=9

22. McDaniel, S. H., & Salas, E. (2018). The science of teamwork: Introduction to the special issue. *American Psychologist*, 73(4), 305–307. Retrieved March 1, 2022 from https://dx.doi.org/10.1037/amp0000337

23. Wigert, B. & Agrawal, S. (2018). Employee burnout, Part 1: The 5 main causes. Retrieved March 1, 2022 from https://www.gallup.com/workplace/237059/employee-burnout-part-main-causes.aspx

24. The seven key trends impacting today's workplace: Results from the 2014 TINYpulse Employee Engagement and Organizational Culture Report. (2014). Retrieved March 1, 2022 from https://www.tinypulse.com/2014-employee-engagement-organizational-culture-report

25. Wu, L., Wang, D. & Evans, J.A. (2019). Large teams develop and small teams disrupt science and technology. *Nature* 566, 378–382 (2019). Retrieved March 1, 2022 from https://doi.org/10.1038/s41586-019-0941-9

26. Staats, B., Milkman, K. & Fox, C. (2012). The team scaling fallacy: Underestimating the declining efficiency of larger teams. For *Organizational Behavior and Human Decision Processes* 118, 132–142. Retrieved March 1, 2022 from https://isiarticles.com/bundles/Article/pre/pdf/4578.pdf

27. Cain, A. & Lebowitz, S. (2020) The "2 pizza rule" is a secret to productive meetings that helped Amazon CEO Jeff Bezos become one of the world's richest men. Here's why it's smart. Retrieved March 1, 2022 from https://www.businessinsider.com/amazon-jeff-bezos-two-pizza-rule-productive-meetings-2017-7

28. Gratton, L. (2007, June 6). Working together … When apart. *Wall Street Journal*. Retrieved from https://online.wsj.com/news/articles/SB118165895540732559.

29. Baldrige, L. (2003). *Letitia Baldrige's New Complete Guide to Executive Manners*. New York: Simon and Schuster.

30. Hunt, V. D. (1993). *Managing for quality: Integrating quality and business strategy* (121). Homewood, IL: Business One Irwin.

31. Munter, M. (1998, June). Meeting technology: From low-tech to high-tech. *Business Communication Quarterly*, 61 (2), 80–87.

32. Gillespie, Iain (2015). Multitasking Makes You Stupid, Studies Find. Retrieved March 1, 2022 from https://www.smh.com.au/technology/multitasking-makes-you-stupid-studies-find-20150520-gh5ouq.html

33. Zoom etiquette for meeting attendees (n.d.). Retrieved January 14, 2022 from https://emilypost.com/advice/zoom-etiquette-tips-for-better-video-conferences

34. Setera, K (2020). FBI warns of teleconferencing and online classroom hijacking during COVID-19 pandemic. Retrieved March 1, 2022 from https://www.fbi.gov/contact-us/field-offices/boston/news/press-releases/fbi-warns-of-teleconferencing-and-online-classroom-hijacking-during-covid-19-pandemic

35. Waiting Room. (2022). Retrieved March 1, 2022 from https://support.zoom.us/hc/en-us/articles/115000332726-Waiting-Room

36. FBI: Watch out for 'Zoom-Bombings' on online video meeting apps. (n.d.). Retrieved January 14, 2022 from https://www.entrepreneur.com/article/348502

Chapter 3

1. Canavor, N., & Meirowitz, C. (2005). Good corporate writing: Why it matters, and what to do; Poor corporate writing—in press releases, ads, brochures, web sites and more—is costing companies credibility and reviews. Here's how to put the focus back on clear communication. *Communication World*, 22 (4), 30–34.

2. Schein, E. H. (1992). *Educational Culture and Leadership* (p.12). New York: Jossey-Bass.

3. Tilt, M. (n.d.). Insights into Adobe's award winning company culture. Retrieved January 21, 2022 from https://inside.6q.io/adobes-award-winning-company-culture/

4. Cameron, K. S., & Quinn, R. E. (2011). *Diagnosing and Changing Organizational Culture: Based on the Competing Values Framework*. New York: John Wiley & Sons.

5. Godiva Chocolates $15M false advertising class action settlement (2022). Retrieved January 21, 2022 from https://topclassactions.com/lawsuit-settlements/open-lawsuit-settlements/godiva-chocolates-15m-false-advertising-class-action-settlement/

6. Wall Street Staff (2020). Misleading marketing: Cheerios, 5-Hour Energy drink among products tagged with outrageous claims. Retrieved January 21, 2022 from https://www.usatoday.com/story/money/2020/12/16/39-most-outrageous-product-claims-of-all-time/115127274/

7. Consider the Consumer (2020). Settlement alert: Prevagen class action settlement finally agreed upon. Retrieved January 21, 2022 from https://considertheconsumer.com/class-action-settlements/prevagen-class-action-settlement

8. Papandrea, D. (n.d.) The biggest resume lies to avoid. Retrieved January 21, 2022 from https://www.monster.com/career-advice/article/the-truth-about-resume-lies-hot-jobs#

9. Kika, T. (2019). Who is Mina Chang? Meet the Trump staffer caught in a web Of resume lies. Retrieved January 21, 2022 from https://www.ibtimes.com/who-mina-chang-meet-trump-staffer-caught-web-resume-lies-2865666

10. Telushkin, J. (1997). Avoid words that hurt. *USA Today*, 74.

11. Bump, Pamela (2019). What Video Marketers Can Learn from 7 Emmy Nominated Commercials. Retrieved January 21, 2022 from https://blog.hubspot.com/marketing/emmy-nominated-commercials-2019?_ga=2.157404472.322383123.1572228834-1582690004.1559596502

Chapter 4

1. Charlton, J. (Ed.). (1995). *The Writer's Quotation Book*. Stamford, CT: Ray Freeman.

2. Is email making bosses ruder? (2005). *European Business Forum*, 21, 72.

3. Rindegard, J. (1999). Use clear writing to show you mean business. *InfoWorld*, 21 (47), 78.

4. Dyrud, M. A. (1996). Teaching by example: Suggestions for assignment design. *Business Communication Quarterly*, 59 (3), 67–70.

5. Redish, J. C. (1993). Understanding readers. In C. M. Barnum & S. Carliner (Eds.), *Techniques for Technical Communicators*. New York: Prentice-Hall.

6. Ibid.

7. Reia, M. (2021). Trump's 'Chinese Virus' tweet helped lead to rise in racist anti-Asian Twitter content. Retrieved January 25, 2022 from https://abcnews.go.com/Health/trumps-chinese-virus-tweet-helped-lead-rise-racist/story?id=76530148

8. Sverdlik, Y. (2017). AWS outage that broke the Internet caused by mistyped Command. Amazon says Tuesday's mayhem resulted from mistake during a routine debugging exercise. Retrieved January 2022 from https://www.datacenterknowledge.com/archives/2017/03/02/aws-outage-that-broke-the-internet-caused-by-mistyped-command

9. Australia's A$50 note misspells responsibility. (2019) Retrieved January 25, 2022 from https://www.bbc.com/news/world-australia-48210733

Chapter 5

1. Murray, A. (2022). We're losing control of our data' as breaches reach an all-time high. Data compromises- -especially in the form of cyberattacks- -are increasing. Retrieved January 29,2022 from https://www.zdnet.com/article/data-breaches-reached-an-all-time-high-in-2021/

2. Ibid.

3. Greig, J. (2021). Losses from BitMart breach reach $200 million. The security breach was caused by a stolen private key that had two of BitMart's hot wallets compromised. Retrieved January 29, 2022 from https://www.zdnet.com/article/bitmart-breach-losses-reach-200-million/

4. Travelers Risk Control (n.d.). Cyber security training for employees. Retrieved January 29, 2022 from https://www.travelers.com/resources/business-topics/cyber-security/cyber-security-training-for-employees

5. Hear no evil, see no evil: Business e-mail overtakes the telephone. (2007, August 20). *Network*. Retrieved from www.networkworld.com/community/node/18555.

6. Silverman, D. (2009, April 14). Words at work: How to revise an email so that people will read it. Retrieved from https://blogs.harvardbusiness.org/silverman/2009/04/how-to-revise-an-email-so-that.html.

7. Silverman, D. (2009, April 14). Words at work: Is your email businesslike-or brusque? Retrieved from https://blogs.harvardbusiness.org/silverman/2009/04/is-your-email-businesslike-or.html.

8. New technology makes work harder. (1999, June 1). *BBC News*. Retrieved from https://news.bbc.co.uk/2/hi/science/nature/357993.stm.

9. What Is the Difference Between Instant Messaging and Texting? (2021). Retrieved March 19, 2022 from https://blog.textedly.com/difference-between-texting-and-instant-messaging

10. Saddleton, L. (2022). Use of memes, gifs and emojis has changed the landscape for eDiscovery. Retrieved March 19, 2022 from https://www.canadianlawyermag.com/inhouse/news/general/use-of-memes-gifs-and-emojis-has-changed-the-landscape-for-ediscovery/363599

11. Ibid.

12. McGrath, C. (2006, January 22). The pleasures of the text. *The New York Times*, 15.

13. Knapp, L. (2007, January 20). Switching to texting has pluses, minuses: Getting started. *Seattle Times*, E6. Retrieved from General Business File database.

14. Electronic Privacy Information Center. (2008, September 15). Public opinion on privacy. Retrieved from www.epic.org/privacy/survey.

15. 9th circuit court rules on text-messaging privacy. (2008, July 15). *Law.com*. Retrieved from www.law.com/jsp/legaltechnology/pubArticleLT-jsp?id=1202422970200.

16. Chantel, J. (2021). Text messaging laws every business has to know about SMS compliance. Retrieved January 29, 2022 from https://blog.textedly.com/text-messaging-laws-every-business-has-to-know-about

17. Brown, P. B. (2005, December 31). Resolved: I will take good advice. *The New York Times*. Retrieved from https://www.nytimes.com/2005/12/31/business/31offline.html.

18. Wetsman, N. (2021). Making Elizabeth Holmes' cringey texts public is the ultimate crime deterrent. This is maybe my worst nightmare. Retrieved January 29, 2022 from https://www.theverge.com/22691464/elizabeth-holmes-trial-text-messages-crime

19. Fortin, J. (2021). Minnesota troopers deleted texts and emails After Floyd protests, major testifies. Retrieved January 29, 2022 from https://www.nytimes.com/2021/09/06/us/mn-state-patrol-texts-emails-lawsuit.html

20. Varchaver, N. (2003). The perils of e-mail. *Fortune*, 147 (3), 96+.

21. Ibid.

22. Downer, K. (2008). A great website in five steps. *Third Sector*, 9.

23. Alcantara, A, (2021). Lawsuits over digital accessibility for people with disabilities are rising. Maximize compatibility with current and future user tools. Retrieved January 29, 2022 from https://www.wsj.com/articles/lawsuits-over-digital-accessibility-for-people-with-disabilities-are-rising-11626369056

24. What does the ADA say about websites? (n.d.) Retrieved January 29, 2022 from https://siteimprove.com/en-us/accessibility/ada-compliance-website/

25. Seventy-nine percent of large international companies are using. (2010, February 23). *Bloomberg*. Retrieved from https://www.bloomberg.com/apps/news?pid=newsarchive&sid=a_M.jlgajlbw.

26. Fichter, D. (2001, November/December). Zooming in: Writing content for intranets. *Online*, 25(6), 80+.

27. Porteous, C. (2021). Ninety seven percent of Fortune 500 companies rely on social media. Here's how you should use it for maximum impact. Retrieved January 29, 2022 from https://www.entrepreneur.com/article/366240

28. Quible, Z. K. (2005). Blogs and written business communication courses: A perfect union. *Journal of Education for Business*, 80 (6), 327–332.

29. Jones, D. (2005, May 10). CEOs refuse to get tangled up in messy blogs. *USA Today*. Retrieved from Academic Search Premier database.

30. DeBare, I. (2005, May 5). Tips for effective use of blogs in business. *San Francisco Chronicle*, C6.

31. How to write for the web. (2008, March 26). *The Online Journalism Review*. Retrieved from www.ojr.org/ojr/wiki/writing.

32. Siu. E. (2022). Beginner's guide to business blogging in 2022. Retrieved January 29, 2022 from https://www.singlegrain.com/blog-posts/beginners-guide-to-business-blogging/

33. Hutchins, J. P. (2005, November 14). Beyond the water cooler. *ComputerWorld*, 39 (46), 45–46.

34. Goodnoe, E. (2005, August 8). How to use wikis for business. *Information Week*. Retrieved from www.informationweek.com/news/management/showArticle.jhtml?articleID=16760331&pgno=3&queryText=&isPrev=.

35. Johnson, C. Y. (2008, July 7). Hurry up, the customer has a complaint: As blogs expand the reach of a single voice, firms monitor the Internet looking for the dissatisfied. *The Boston Globe*. Retrieved from www.Boston.com.

36. Gilliland, N. (2020). Thirty brands with excellent social media strategies. Retrieved January 29, 2022 from https://econsultancy.com/30-brands-with-excellent-social-media-strategies/

37. Leland, K., & Bailey, K. (1999). *Customer Service for Dummies* (2nd Ed.). New York: Wiley.

38. Berkley, S. (2003, July). Help stamp out bad voicemail! *The Voice Coach Newsletter*. Retrieved from www.greatvoice.com/archive_vc/archiveindex_vc.html.

39. McCarthy, M. L. (1999, October). Email, voicemail and the Internet: How employers can avoid getting cut by the double-edged sword of technology. *Business Credit*, 100 (9), 44+.

40. Norris, D. (2007). Sales communications in a mobile world: Using the latest technology and retaining the personal touch. *Business Communication Quarterly*, 70, 492–498.

41. Cell phone etiquette. (2001, March). *Office Solutions*, 18 (3), 13.

42. Krotz, J. L. (2008). Cell phone etiquette: 10 dos and don'ts. *Microsoft Business*. Retrieved from www.microsoft.com/smallbusiness/resources/technology/communications/cell-phone-etiquette-10-dos-and-donts.aspx#Cellphoneetiquettedosanddonts.

43. Cell phone etiquette. (2001, March). *Office Solutions*, 18 (3), 13.

44. Seventy virtual team statistics you can't ignore: 2021/2022 data analysis, benefits & challenges, (2022). Retrieved January 2022 from https://financesonline.com/virtual-team-statistics/

45. Ibid.

46. Ibid.

47. Ibid.

48. Ibid.

Chapter 6

1. Bourn, C. (n.d.). When did we stop getting the memo? From indispensable office communication to relic of a bygone age, let's remember the memorandum. Retrieved February 2, 2022 from https://melmagazine.com/en-us/story/when-did-we-stop-getting-the-memo

2. Ibid.

3. Kelcher, L. (n.d.) Why should you use a business memo? Retrieved February 2, 2022 from https://smallbusiness.chron.com/should-use-business-memo-10374.html

4. Williamson, M. (2008, June 11). Twittering the Internet. *TechnologyStory.com*. Retrieved from http://www.technologystory.com/2008/06/11/twittering-the-internet.

Chapter 7

1. Sonnemaker, T. (2020). Airbnb just laid off 25% of its employees, but it's also paying their health insurance costs for a year, on top of three months' salary. Retrieved March 30, 2022 from https://www.businessinsider.com/airbnb-layoffs-generous-severance-package-2020-5

2. Ethical workforce reflects honest management. (2008, June). *Internal Auditor*, 18–19.

3. Advice from the pros on the best way to deliver bad news. (2003, February). *IOMA's Report on Customer Relationship Management*, 5–6.

4. Purina on pet food recall 4-26-07. (2007). *American Kennel Club*. Retrieved from https://clubs.akc.org/brit/NEWS/07.PurinaPetFoodRecall.htm.

5. Workers get better at bearing bad news. (2005, October 11). *Personnel Today*, 46.

6. Expert offers advice about how to lay off employees. (2008, October 9). *Immediate Care Business*. Retrieved from https://www.immediatecarebusiness.com/hotnews/layingoff-employees.html.

7. Kitterman, T. (2021). Five top crises from 2021-and the warnings they offer for the year ahead. Retrieved February 4, 2022 from https://www.prdaily.com/5-top-crises-from-2021-and-the-warnings-they-offer-for-the-year-ahead/

8. Coombs, W. T. (2007). Protecting organization reputations during a crisis: The development and application of situational crisis communication theory. *Corporate Reputation Review* 10 (3), 163–176; Coombs, W. T. (2004). Impact of past crisis on current crisis communications: Insights from situational crisis communication theory. *Journal of Business Communication* 41 (3), 265–289; Coombs, W. T., & Holladay, S. J. (2002). Helping crisis managers protect reputational assets: Initial tests of the situational crisis communication theory. *Management Communication Quarterly* 16 (2), 165–186.

9. Coombs, W. T. (2007). Protecting organization reputations during a crisis: The development and application of situational crisis communication theory. *Corporate Reputation Review* 10 (3), 163–176; Coombs, W. T. (2004). Impact of past crisis on current crisis communications: Insights from situational crisis communication theory. *Journal of Business Communication* 41 (3), 265–289; Coombs, W. T. & Holladay, S. J. (2002). Helping crisis managers protect reputational assets: Initial tests of the situational crisis communication theory. *Management Communication Quarterly* 16 (2), 165–186.

Chapter 8

1. Cody, S. (1906). *Success in letter writing: Business and social* (pp. 122–126). Chicago: A. C. McClurg.

2. Lotus Cars. Retrieved July 28, 2013 from www.lotuscars.com/gb/our-cars/current-range/elise-range.

3. http://home.mcafee.com/Store/PackageDetail.aspx?pkgid=275.

4. Sinclair, B. (2003, July 20). Handle client complaints. *The Web design business kit*. Retrieved from http://www.sitepoint.com/article/handle-client-complaints/.

Chapter 9

1. Grimes, B. (2003, May 6). Fooling Google. *PC Magazine*, 22(8), 74.

2. Robinson, C. (n.d.). What is survey software? A comprehensive guide to benefits, features, types, pricing and more. Retrieved February 13, 2022 from https://financesonline.com/survey-software-comprehensive-guide-benefits-features-types-pricing/

3. McIntyre, Douglas A., Ashley C. Allen, Samuel Weigley, & Michael B. Sauter. (October 17, 2012). The worst business decisions of all time. *24/7 Wall St.* Retrieved from http://247wallst.com/specialreport/2012/10/17/the-worst-businessdecisions-of-all-time/3/.

Chapter 10

1. Gallo, C. (2008, December 10). Making YouTube work for your business. *Business Week Online*. Retrieved from www.businessweek.com/stories/2008-12-09/making-youtube-work-for-yourbusinessbusinessweek-business-news-stockmarket-and-financial-advice.

2. Martin, M. H. (1997, November 27). The man who makes sense of numbers. *Fortune*, 273–275.

Chapter 12

1. Kalytiak, T. (2008, October). Overcoming speaking anxiety: Toastmasters sculpt shy speakers into outstanding orators. *Alaska Business Monthly*. Retrieved from http://www.akbizmag.com.

2. Axtell, R. E. (1992). *Do's and Taboos of Public Speaking: How to Get Those Butterflies Flying in Formation*. New York: John Wiley.

3. Ranieri & Co. (2021).Changing attention span and what it means for content in 2021. Retrieved April 21, 2021 from https://www.ranieriandco.com/post/changing-attention-span-and-what-it-means-for-content-in-2021#:~:text=A%20recent%20study%20by%20Microsoft,to%20stop%2C%20collaborate%20and%20listen%3F

4. Britz, J. D. (1999, October). You can't catch a marlin with a meatball. *Presentations*, 13 (10), A1–22.

5. Hughes, M. (1990). Tricks of the speechwriter's trade. *Management Review*, 9 (11), 56–58.

6. Somerville, J. (2003). Presentation tip: Stop the verbal spam. About.com: Entrepreneurs. Retrieved from http://entrepreneurs.about.com/cs/marketing/a/infodumping.htm.

7. Simmons, A. (2007). *Whoever Tells the Best Story Wins: How to Use Your Own Stories to Communicate with Power and Impact*. New York: Amacon.

8. Gallo, C. (2009, April 8). Making your presentations relevant. *Business Week Online*, 15.

9. Axtell, R. E. (1992). *Do's and Taboos of Public Speaking: How to Get Those Butterflies Flying in Formation*. New York: John Wiley.

10. Decker, B. (1992). *You've Got to Be Believed to Be Heard*. New York: St. Martin's Press.

11. Hillary Clinton's campaign sends "docu-points" to House Dems. (2008, May 10). *Presentation Zen*. Retrieved from http://www.presentationzen.com/presentationzen/2008/05/hillary-campaig.html.

12. Earnest, W. (2007). *Save Our Slides: PowerPoint Design That Works*. Dubuque, IA: Kendall/Hunt.

13. Mukherjee, R. (2014, May 7). Multimedia Presentations: The Pros and the Cons. Retrieved from https://blog.udemy.com/multimedia-presentation/

14. Mukherjee, R. (2014, May 7). Multimedia Presentations: The Pros and the Cons. Retrieved from https://blog.udemy.com/multimedia-presentation/

15. CNN Staff (2008, April 5). Jonathan Knight exists New Kids on the Block show mid-concert. *CNN Entertainment*.

16. Decker, B. (1992). *You've Got to Be Believed to Be Heard*. New York: St. Martin's Press.

17. Boromisza-Habashia, D., Hughesa, J. M.F., & Malkowski, J. A. (2015, December.). Public speaking as cultural

ideal: Internationalizing the public speaking curriculum. *Journal of International and Intercultural Communication*, 1–15.

18. Miller, A.N. (2002). An exploration of Kenyan public speaking patterns with implications for the American introductory public speaking course. *Communication Education*, 51, 168–182. doi:10.1080/03634520216505, p. 180.

19. Carbaugh, D. (2005). *Cultures in Conversation*. Mahwah, NJ: Lawrence Erlbaum Associates.

20. Liberman, K. (1990). Intercultural communication in Central Australia. In D. Carbaugh (Ed.), *Cultural Communication and Intercultural Contact* (pp. 177–183). Hillsdale, NJ: Lawrence Erlbaum Associates.

21. Ibid., p. 177.

22. Albert, E. (1964). "Rhetoric," "logic," and "poetics" in Burundi: Culture patterning of speech behavior. *American Anthropologist*, 66 (6), 35–54; Bauman, R. (1975). Verbal art as performance. *American Anthropologist*, 77 (2), 290–311; and Habashi et al.

23. Kulick, D., & Schieffelin, B.B. (2004). Language socialization. In A. Duranti (Ed.), *A Companion to Linguistic Anthropology* (pp. 349–368). Malden, MA: Blackwell.

24. Carbaugh; Liberman.

25. Hanke, J. (1998, January). Presenting as a team. *Presentations*, 12 (1), 74–82.

26. Ibid.

27. Ibid

28. Ibid

29. Davids, M. (1999). Smiling for the camera. *Journal of Business Strategy*, 20 (3), 20–24.

30. Turner, C. (1998, February). Become a web presenter? (Really it's not that hard). *Presentations*, 12 (2), 26–27.

31. Sturges, D. L. (1994). Communicating through crisis: A strategy for organizational survival. *Management Communication Quarterly*, 7, 297–316.

32. Mitroff, I.I., & Alpasian, M. C. (2004, Spring). A toolkit for managing crises and preparing for the unthinkable. *The Mitroff Report*, 1, 81–88.

Chapter 13

1. Jackson, T. (2003). Find a job you love and success will follow. *Career Journal* (The Wall Street Journal). Retrieved from http://www.careerjournal.com/jobhunting/strategies/20030415-jackson.html

2. The Top 12 Job Search Engines For 2022. (2022). Retrieved March 1, 2022 from https://careersidekick.com/tools/job-search-websites/

3. Riley, M. F. (2009). The Riley guide: Employment opportunities and job resources on the internet. Retrieved from http://www.rileyguide.com.

4. Ireland, S. (2002, July–August). A resume that works. *Searcher*, 10 (7), 98–110.

5. McKeon, K. (2020). Five personal branding tips for your job search. Retrieved April 3, 2022 from https://themanifest.com/digital-marketing/5-personal-branding-tips-job-search

6. Cotriss, D. (2022). Keep it clean: social media screenings gain in popularity. Retrieved April 3, 2022 from https://www.businessnewsdaily.com/2377-social-media-hiring.html

7. Harshbarger, C. (2003). You're out! *Strategic Finance*, 84 (11), 46–50.

8. Garone, E. (2009, March 18). Do references really matter? WSJ.com: Careers Q&A. Retrieved from http://online.wsj.com/article/SB123672074032087901.html.

9. Are you using the wrong resume? (2009). Careerbuilder.com. Retrieved from http://www.careerbuilder.com/Article/CB-998-Cover-Letters-and-Resumes-Are-You-Using-the-Wrong-R%C3%A9sum5C3%A9/.

10. Resumes you don't see everyday. (2006). Retrieved from http://www.dummies.com/WileyCDA/DummiesArticle/id-1610.html.

11. Sipper, R. A. (2007, October 15). Tips for creating a YouTube video resume. Retrieved from http://www.associatedcontent.com/article/414702/tips_for_creating_a_youtube_video_resume.html?cat=3.

Chapter 14

1. Vogt, P. (2006). Acing behavioral interviews. *Career Journal.com*. Retrieved from www.careerjournaleurope.com/jobhunting/interviewing/19980129-vogt.html

2. Marion, L. C. (1997, January 11). Companies tap keyboards to interview applicants. *The News and Observer*, p. B5.

3. Castrillon, C. (2020.) Here's how to ace your next video interview. Retrieved March 4, 2022 from https://www.forbes.com/sites/carolinecastrillon/2020/04/14/heres-how-to-ace-your-next-video-interview/?sh=46e998eb275c

4. Thomson Learning announces name change to Cengage Learning. (2007, October). High Beam Research. Retrieved from www.highbeam.com/doc/1G1-168632242.html (pay to view).

5. Burns, D. (2009). *The first 60 seconds: Win the job interview before it begins*. Naperville, IL: Sourcebooks.

6. Jernigan, J. (2020). Should you stop shaking hands at job interviews or with clients? Retrieved April 3, 2022 from https://theamericangenius.com/business-news/should-you-stop-shaking-hands-at-job-interviews-or-with-clients/

7. Lai, P., & Wong, I. (2000). The clash of cultures in the job interview. *Journal of Language for International Business*, 11 (1), 31–40.

8. Austin, N. K. (1996, March). The new job interview. *Working Woman*, 23–24.

9. Kennedy, J. L., & Morrow, T. J. (1994). *Electronic résumé revolution: Create a winning résumé for the new world of job seeking*. New York: John Wiley.

10. Kleiman, P. (2003, May). Armed for a multitude of tasks. *The Times Higher Education Supplement*, p. 4.

11. MIT Career Development Center (2008, September 16). *STAR method: Behavioral interviewing*. Retrieved from www.lpnet.org/site/programs/docs/STAR%20MethodHandout.pdf.

12. Stern, L. (2005, January 17). The tough new job hunt. *Newsweek*, 73–74.

13. Dattner, B. (2008). The use and misuse of personality tests for coaching and development: Why many companies use some personality assessments and not others. Retrieved March 4, 2022 from https://www.psychologytoday.com/us/blog/credit-and-blame-work/200806/the-use-and-misuse-personality-tests-coaching-and-development#:~:text=Around%2080%20percent%20of%20the,reliability%20or%20validity%20than%20horoscopes.

14. Interviews: Handling illegal interview questions. *JobWeb*. Retrieved from http://www.jobweb.org/interviews.aspx?id=1343.

Index

A

ABI Inform First Search, 156
abstract, 184
academic and business writing, 60
Academic Search Elite, 156
accents, 210
accident crisis, 133
acknowledgment messages, 112–114
active voice, 63–64
    formal reports, 188
    readability, 71
addenda
    formal reports, 184
    proposals, 196
adhocracy culture, 45
adjourning, 36
adjustment messages, 105
Adobe, 45
age bias, 76
agenda, 40
aggressive interpersonal communication, 32
AIDA (attention, interest, desire, action), 137
Allen, Sharon, 130
Alpha Chi Epsilon, 244
Amazon Web Services (AWS), 77
American Broadcast English, 210
Americans with Disabilities Act (ADA), 91
analogies, 68
analysis, 184
analytical reports, 152, 184
analytics, 257
antivirus software program, 86
APA Publication, 164
apology letter, 55
appendix, 185
Apple Keynote, 204
application forms, 259
application messages, 242
    encouraging action, 245
    evidence of qualifications, 244–245
    formatting, 246
    gaining receiver's attention, 244
    persuasive organization, 242, 244–245
    proofreading, 246
    unsolicited, 242
    writing, 245–246
appreciation messages, 57, 103–105
area charts, 174
Arthur Andersen, 90
articulation, 210–211
Ask, 155
assertive interpersonal communication, 32
attribution, 23
audience
    adapting message to needs and concerns
        of, 51–53
    age of, 49
    compliments, 52
    culturally diverse, 214–216
    culture, 49–50
    economic level, 49
    education/occupational background, 49
    envisioning, 49–51
    expectations, 50
    mental picture of, 50
    outlining message benefits to, 53–54
    persuasive messages, 136
    presentations, 200–201
    rapport, 50
    reaction to message, 54
    relationship with product, service, or idea,
        138
    revising messages to grab attention, 65–67
    viewpoint of, 51–52
audience handouts, 208
awareness, 14
Axtell, Roger E., 199

B

bad-news messages
    channels of communication, 118
    closing positively, 122–123
    constructive criticism, 128
    counterproposal, 122
    denying claim, 126
    denying credit, 126–128
    developing, 120–123
    exceptions to inductive approach, 119
    facts, analysis, and reasons, 120–121
    inductive approach, 118–119
    introductory paragraph, 120
    negative organizational news, 128–134
    passive voice, 121
    refusing request, 123–125
    refuting supporting details, 118
    silver lining idea, 122
    writing, 121–122
Balwani, Sunny, 90
bar charts, 172–174
Barnlund, Dean, 24
barriers to effective communication, 4
    cultures, 13
    perception, 49
beamable résumés, 232
beamer, 232
Beautiful.ai, 204
behavioral adaptability, 14
behavior-based interviews, 250
Bernal, Jesus, 91
bias, confronting, 12
bias-free language, 75–76
bibliography, 185
Bilstein, 139
BitMart, 81
blogs, 93
body
    formal reports, 181, 184
    presentations, 202–203
body language, 27, 29, 253
borders, 67
brainstorming, 40
breaking bad news message, 130–131

C

Canva, 204
career guidance information, 225
career services centers, 223–224
career summary, 227
Carillo, Frank, 216, 217
casual listening, 28, 29
cellphones
    communication, 96
    text messaging, 88
Cellular Telecommunications Industry
    Association (CTIA), 89
central selling point, 137–138
Chang, Mina, 52–53
channel and medium, 46–48
channels of communication, 46–48
    choosing, 118
    presentations, 199–200
chartjunk, 170
Chipotle, 94
chronemics, 13, 26
chrono-functional résumés, 232
chronological context, 46
chronological résumés, 231
chunking, 66
Cisco Systems, 98
claim messages, 145
    persuasive claims, 105
    routine claims, 105
claims, 105
clan culture, 45
ClearSlide, 204
clichés, 68
clip art, 67
clustered bar charts, 172
code of ethics, 11
cognitive knowledge, 14
coherence, 61
common language, 169
communicating
    persuasively, 53
    quantitative data, 169
    within organizations, 4–8
communication, 3
    barriers to effective, 4
    cellphones, 96

bulleted lists, 66–67
bureaucracy, 4
Burns, Dan, 253
business activities and laws, 8
Business and Company Resource Center, 156
business communication
    contextual forces influencing, 8–20
    effective, 3
Business English as Lingua Franca (BELF), 59
Business Source Premier, 156
business writing, 59–60
    academic and, 60
    EP and BELF, 59
    style and tone, 59

intercultural communication barriers, 13
interferences, 4
internal messages, 7
internal proposals, 194
internal reports, 152
internet
    career guidance information, 225
    identifying job listings, 225
    job search, 225
    netiquette, 84
internet conferencing, 218
interpersonal communication, 8, 32
interpersonal intelligence, 25
interpersonal skills, 253–254
interviews
    appearance, 252
    asking questions of interviewer, 257–258
    behavioral questions, 255
    closing, 258
    computer-assisted interviews, 250
    conducting successful, 253–258
    discriminatory hiring practices, 256
    extracurricular activities, 254
    first impressions, 253
    information exchange, 254
    interpersonal skills, 254–255
    key points to emphasize, 254
    logical thinking and creativity, 255–256
    nonverbal messages, 253–254
    opening formalities, 253–254
    personality testing, 257
    phone interviews, 251
    practicing for, 253
    preparing for, 251–253
    professional attitude, 256
    researching company, 252
    salary and benefits, 256
    series interviews, 250–251
    standard questions, 255
    STAR method (Situation or Task/Action/
        Result), 255
    stress interviews, 250
    structured interviews, 250
    time and materials, 252–253
    virtual interviews, 251
in-text parenthetical citations, 164–165, 185
intranets, 15
intrapersonal communication, 25
intrapersonal intelligence, 25
introduction
    formal reports, 184
    presentations, 201–202
iPad, 138

J

jargon, 70
    email, 84
    presentations, 203
job-acceptance messages, 260–261
job and/or career objective, 226–227
job-refusal messages, 261, 262
job search
    career services centers, 223–224
    electronic employment resources, 224–225
    employers' websites and office
        locations, 224
    employment agencies and contractors, 224

gathering essential information, 222, 223
    identifying potential career opportunities,
        222–225
    internet, 224, 225
    locating career guidance information, 225
    networks, 223
    printed sources, 222–223
    professional organizations, 224
    social media, 223
    traditional sources, 222
Jones' Parliamentary Procedure at a Glance, 40
Jourard, Sidney, 27
JPMorgan, 22
justification reports, 153

K

Karlstrom, Johan, 9
Kennedy, Joyce, 254
kinesic messages, 25–27
kinesics, 25–27
Knight, Jonathan, 211
Kraft Foods, Inc., 17

L

laptops, 15
lateral communication, 7
lateral reports, 152
law and electronic messaging, 88–90
leadership, groups, 33
legal behavior, 9
legal constraints, 8–11
letters, 102
    apology, 55
    rough draft of, 78
    short reports, 189
    unified, 62
LexisNexis Academic Universe, 155, 156
libel, 53
Library of Congress classification system, 155
Likert scales, 162
Lincoln, Abraham, 70
Lincoln Business Data, Inc., 141
line charts, 174
lines, 62
LinkedIn, 47, 94, 223, 252
listening, 29
Living Essentials, 52
Lombardi, Vince, 138
longitudinal studies, 154
long reports, 151–152
Lotus Dynamic Performance Management
    (DPM), 139

M

management
    explaining and clarifying procedures and
        work assignments, 3
    unethical tone set by, 9
managers, communication, 3
manuscript presentations, 209
maps, 175, 176
market culture, 45
Max Verstappen, 139
McAfee Total Protection technology, 140
measures of central tendency, 165

me attitude, 51
meetings, 38–42
    consensus, 41
    distributing agenda in advance, 40
    effective, 39–41
    electronic meetings, 39
    encouraging participation, 40–41
    face-to-face meetings, 39
    generic agenda, 40
    identifying purpose of, 39
    maintaining order, 40–41
    managing conflict, 41
    minutes, 41
    negative attitudes of workers, 38–39
    purpose, 82
    satisfactory arrangements for, 40
    toward, 38
meme, 88
memorized presentations, 209
memos, 101, 102, 114, 189
    unified, 62
messages
    adapting to audience needs and concerns,
        51–53
    adjustment messages, 105
    appreciation, 56
    central idea, 54–55
    chunking, 66
    claim messages, 105
    clear and understandable ideas, 53
    clichés, 68
    communicating ethically and responsibly,
        52–53
    concise communication, 70–72
    contextual forces, 44–46
    deductive sequence, 102
    direct sequence, 102
    evaluating effectiveness, 66
    good-news messages, 101–105
    grabbing audience's attention, 65–67
    headings, 67
    honor, honesty, and credibility, 52
    informing and persuading others, 3
    misunderstanding, 3
    negative tone, 72–73
    neutral-news messages, 101
    organizational culture, 44–45
    organizing, 53–57
    outdated expressions, 68
    passive voice, 71–73
    persuasive requests, 107
    planning and preparing, 44
    positive tone, 72–73
    procedural messages, 114–116
    profanity, 70
    proofreading, 66
    readability and appeal of text, 63
    receiver-centered statements, 51
    redundancies, 71
    routine messages, 112
    routine requests, 107
    sender-centered statements, 51
    style and tone, 68–76
    topics, 61
    viewpoint supported with objective
        facts, 53
    visual enhancements, 66–67
    white space, 67

visual kinesic communication, 26
vocal kinesic communication, 26
vocal qualities, 209–211
voice mail, 95

W

Warby Parker, 5
Web 2.0, 93
webcasting, 218
Web Content Accessibility Guidelines, 91, 92
webinars, 98
weblogs, 93
websites, 92
websites communication, 91–95
   hits, 155
   writing, 92
white space, 67
wikis, 93–94
win/lose philosophy, 31

win/win philosophy, 32
word processors
   addenda, 183
   improving sentence readability, 68
work experience, 228–229
workplace, 3
   diversity challenges, 11
   employees, 5
works cited, 185
works consulted, 185
work teams, 17–18, 35
World Wide Web Consortium (W3C), 92
writer's pride of ownership, 66
writing, 44
   application messages, 245–246
   bad-news messages, 121–122
   blogs, 93
   business, 59–60
   electronic communication, 66
   email, 82–90

   formal reports, 188–189
   planning persuasive messages before, 136
   revising, 65–66
   wikis, 93–94
"Writing: A Ticket to Work...or a Ticket Out"
   report, 44
written communication, 46

Y

Yahoo!, 155
you attitude, 51
YouTube, 94, 241
   presentations, 170

Z

Zapier, 94
Zoom, 47